Fodor's 2011
COSTA RICA

Fodor's Travel Publications   New York, Toronto, London, Sydney, Auckland
www.fodors.com

Be a Fodor's Correspondent

Share your trip with Fodor's.

Our latest guidebook to Costa Rica—now in full color—owes its success to travelers like you. Throughout, you'll find photographs submitted by members of Fodors.com to our "Show Us Your . . . Costa Rica" photo contest. Facing this page is our grand prize–winning photograph of tree frogs, taken by Monica Richards. Stumbling upon hundreds of these little guys near a watering hole in one of Bosque del Cabo's gardens was one of the highlights of her trip to the Osa Peninsula.

We are especially proud of this color edition. No other guide to Costa Rica is as up to date or has as much practical planning information, along with hundreds of color photographs and illustrated maps. We've also included "Word of Mouth" quotes from travelers who shared their experiences with others on our forums. If you're inspired and can plan a better trip because of this guide, we've done our job.

We invite you to join the travel conversation: Your opinion matters to us and to your fellow travelers. Come to Fodors.com to plan your trip, share an experience, ask a question, submit a photograph, post a review, or write a trip report. Tell our editors about your trip. They want to know what went well and how we can make this guide even better. Share your opinions at our feedback center at fodors. com/feedback, or email us at editors@fodors.com with the subject line "Costa Rica Editor." You might find your comments published in a future Fodor's guide. We look forward to hearing from you.

Happy traveling!

Tim Jarrell, Publisher

FODOR'S COSTA RICA 2011

Editor: Margaret Kelly

Writers: Leland Baxter-Neal, David Dudenhoefer, Gillian Gillers, Liz Goodwin, Heidi Johanson, Dorothy MacKinnon, Holly Sonneland, Mark Sullivan, Jeffrey Van Fleet

Production Editor: Evangelos Vasilakis

Maps & Illustrations: David Lindroth, Mark Stroud, *cartographers;* Bob Blake, Rebecca Baer, *map editors;* William Wu, *information graphics*

Design: Fabrizio La Rocca, *creative director;* Guido Caroti, Siobhan O'Hare, *art directors;* Tina Malaney, Nora Rosansky, Chie Ushio, Jessica Walsh, Ann McBride, *designers;* Melanie Marin, *senior picture editor*

Cover Photo: (Man Rappelling): Randy Faris/Corbis

Production Manager: Amanda Bullock

ISBN 978-1-4000-0476-8

ISSN 1522-6131

SPECIAL SALES

This book is available at special discounts for bulk purchases for sales promotions or premiums. Special editions, including personalized covers, excerpts of existing books, and corporate imprints, can be created in large quantities for special needs. For more information, write to Special Markets/Premium Sales, 1745 Broadway, MD 6-2, New York, New York 10019, or e-mail specialmarkets@randomhouse.com.

AN IMPORTANT TIP & AN INVITATION

Although all prices, opening times, and other details in this book are based on information supplied to us at press time, changes occur all the time in the travel world, and Fodor's cannot accept responsibility for facts that become outdated or for inadvertent errors or omissions. So **always confirm information when it matters,** especially if you're making a detour to visit a specific place. Your experiences—positive and negative—matter to us. If we have missed or misstated something, **please write to us.** We follow up on all suggestions. Contact the Costa Rica editor at editors@fodors.com or c/o Fodor's at 1745 Broadway, New York, NY 10019.

PRINTED IN CHINA

10 9 8 7 6 5 4 3 2 1

CONTENTS

ABOUT
THIS BOOK

Our Ratings

Sometimes you find terrific travel experiences and sometimes they just find you. But usually the burden is on you to select the right combination of experiences. That's where our ratings come in.

As travelers we've all discovered a place so wonderful that its worthiness is obvious. And sometimes that place is so experiential that superlatives don't do it justice: you just have to be there to know. These sights, properties, and experiences get our highest rating, **Fodor's Choice**, indicated by orange stars throughout this book.

Black stars highlight sights and properties we deem **Highly Recommended**, places that our writers, editors, and readers praise again and again for consistency and excellence.

By default, there's another category: any place we include in this book is by definition worth your time, unless we say otherwise. And we will.

Disagree with any of our choices? Care to nominate a place or suggest that we rate one more highly? Visit our feedback center at www.fodors.com/feedback.

Budget Well

Hotel and restaurant price categories from ¢ to $$$$ are defined in the opening pages of each chapter. For attractions, we always give standard adult admission fees; reductions are usually available for children, students, and senior citizens. Want to pay with plastic? **AE, D, DC, MC, V** following restaurant and hotel listings indicate whether American Express, Discover, Diners Club, MasterCard, and Visa are accepted.

Restaurants

Unless we state otherwise, restaurants are open for lunch and dinner daily. We mention dress only when there's a specific requirement and reservations only when they're essential or not accepted—it's always best to book ahead.

Hotels

Hotels have private bath, phone, TV, and air-conditioning and operate on the European Plan (aka EP, meaning without meals), unless we specify that they use the Continental Plan (CP, with a Continental breakfast), Breakfast Plan (BP, with a full breakfast), or Modified American Plan (MAP, with breakfast and dinner), or are all-inclusive (AI, including all meals and most activities). We

always list facilities but not whether you'll be charged an extra fee to use them, so when pricing accommodations, find out what's included.

Listings	
★	Fodor's Choice
★	Highly recommended
✉	Physical address
✛	Directions or Map coordinates
⌖	Mailing address
☎	Telephone
🖷	Fax
⊕	On the Web
✉	E-mail
🎟	Admission fee
☉	Open/closed times
Ⓜ	Metro stations
☰	Credit cards
Hotels & Restaurants	
🏨	Hotel
🛏	Number of rooms
⚘	Facilities
❢❢	Meal plans
✗	Restaurant
⚐	Reservations
🏛	Dress code
⌇	Smoking
🍷	BYOB
Outdoors	
⚐	Golf
⚠	Camping
Other	
⚑	Family-friendly
⇨	See also
✉	Branch address
☞	Take note

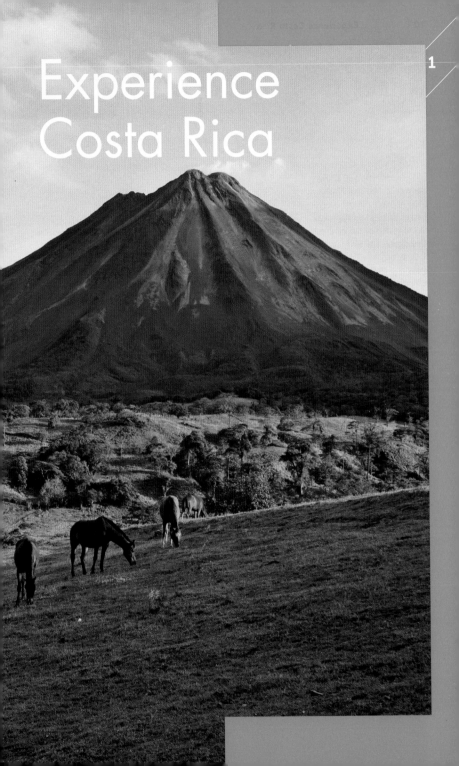

Experience
Costa Rica

WHAT'S WHERE

Numbers correspond to chapters.

3 San José. Do you know the way to San José? You will soon enough. Almost everyone passes through on their way to the beach or the mountains. This capital city isn't much to look at, but it has great restaurants and nightlife, and fascinating museums dedicated to gold and jade.

4 The Central Valley. You won't want to linger long in the Central Valley, as it lacks any of the country's big-name attractions. But there are quite a few day-trip possibilities, including exploring mountain villages, rafting through white-water rapids, and gaping into the mouths of some of the country's most accessible active volcanoes.

5 The Northern Plains. The Northern Plains attract those who don't like sitting still. After zipping along cables through the misty jungle of Monteverde Cloud Forest, windsurfing on glittering Lake Arenal, or watching the nightly fireworks of Arenal Volcano, you can reward yourself with a dip in the bubbly waters of Tabacón Hot Springs.

6 The North Pacific. If you came for beaches, the Northern Pacific is for you. Each has a unique personality: Flamingo's endless stretch of sand draws

Elevation	
12,500	3,810
10,000	3,048
7,500	2,286
5,000	1,525
4,000	1,220
3,000	915
2,500	762
2,000	610
1,500	457
1,000	305
750	230
500	152
250	75
100	30
feet	meters

sun worshippers; Tamarindo's nightlife is legendary; Avellanas's strong swells challenge surfers; Ostional's nesting sea turtles bring nature lovers; and the Papagayo Peninsula's all-inclusive resorts provide every creature comfort.

7 The Central Pacific.
The area's not just for spring-breakers (although it helps in funky surf towns like Jacó). Drive down the coast to the cluster of small hotels and restaurants at Manuel Antonio. The national park, on a peninsula jutting into the ocean, has the easiest wildlife-viewing on the planet.

8 The South Pacific. Also known as "the Amazon of Costa Rica," rustic lodges in the Osa Peninsula sit on the edge of the country's wildest region. Hikes reveal toucans and scarlet macaws in the treetops, and boating trips often include swimming with whales and dolphins.

9 The Caribbean. Despite its name, Costa Rica's Caribbean isn't known for white-sand beaches or crystal-blue waters. Come here for the spirited music, tasty food, and the chance to mix with the Afro-Caribbean population. The coast also attracts turtle-watchers, as four different kinds nest at Tortuguero National Park.

COSTA RICA PLANNER

When to Go

The sunniest, driest season in most of the country occurs from roughly mid-December through April, which is the busiest tourist season. Afternoon showers kick in by May and last through November most everywhere, with a brief dry season in June and July. Costa Rica promotes the rainy season as the "green season," touting lush vegetation, smaller crowds, and lower prices. Showers interrupt your afternoon beach time, and remote roads can be washed out during the worst of the rains.

Temperatures generally range between 20°C (70°F) and 30°C (85°F). It's the humidity, not the heat, that causes you discomfort, especially in the dense forest of the Caribbean coast, the northern lowlands, and the Osa Peninsula. The arid North Pacific is Costa Rica's hottest region, with temperatures frequently exceeding 33°C (90°F) in the dry season.

One final point: we typically hear, "I didn't realize the rain forest would be so…*rainy*." Well, you heard it here: it rains often and heartily in the rain forest. The dense foliage and elaborate root systems rely on there being frequent showers year-round.

Getting Here

San José's Aeropuerto Internacional Juan Santamaría is in the center of the country, so it's especially convenient for destinations in the Central Valley and along the Central Pacific. The closest destinations are less than an hour away. The only other international gateway is Liberia's Aeropuerto Internacional Daniel Oduber Quirós in the western part of the country. Flying here makes sense if you're planning to spend most of your time in Guanacaste or on the Nicoya Peninsula.

A relatively small number of travelers arrive in Costa Rica by road, especially with the difficulties taking rental cars between countries. Long-distance buses travel directly to San José from the larger cities in Nicaragua and Panama, but these are arduous journeys. The Managua–to–San José route takes between 8 and 10 hours.

Getting Around

To save time, many people take domestic flights to their ultimate destination. SANSA flies to various destinations from its hubs in San José's Aeropuerto Internacional Juan Santamaría and Liberia's Aeropuerto Internacional Daniel Oduber Quirós. Nature Air flies out of San José's domestic airport, tiny Aeropuerto Tobias Bolaños. Both offer flights to resort areas, especially those near the beaches. Regional airports are very small, often with a one-room terminal and a staff that arrives at about the same time as the plane.

Costa Rican towns are connected by regular bus service. Buses between major destinations have comfortable seats and air-conditioning. If you have to transfer along the way, you may get a converted school bus cooled only by the tropical breezes. If you're traveling a long distance, make sure to request a *directo* (express) bus. Otherwise you may stop in every small town along the way.

The country's recently improved highway system means renting a car is a great way to get around. You can travel on your own schedule, stopping where you like. Larger airports have rental desks; at smaller airports a representative will meet you and drive you to the nearby office.

Festivals and Celebrations

Every day is a patron saint's day somewhere in Costa Rica, and unless you spend all your time ensconced in a resort, you'll probably see a sign for some community's annual *festejo patronal* (patron-saint festival), in homage to its namesake and protector. A loud firecracker explosion rouses participants at dawn to kick off the festivities.

The festivals mirror Costa Rica: devoutly Catholic but increasingly secularized, with bingo games, rickety carnival rides— a certain amount of luck and prayer is in order here—horse parades, and amateurish bullfights (the bull is not killed in Costa Rica). The Imperial—Costa Rica's most popular brand of beer—flows copiously. But it is still a religious tradition, and an important part of the day is a Mass and parade where the saint's figure is carried through the streets.

New Year's Day *(Año Nuevo)* is a time that most Costa Ricans spend with family and friends. Mid-January brings the **Santa Cruz Fiestas** *(Fiestas de Santa Cruz),* with bullfights, rodeo, folk dancing and marimba music. **Día de la Candelaria**, to honor the famed virgin, is celebrated on February 2.

Holy Week, or Semana Santa, lasting from Palm Sunday through Easter Sunday, is a huge celebration in Costa Rica, especially on Good Friday, when there are religious processions all over the country. Not a thing is open Thursday and Friday. Good luck making reservations during this time. **Día de Juan Santamaría** on April 11 is a public holiday commemorating Costa Rica's national hero. **Día del Trabajo**, on May 1, is Costa Rica's Labor Day.

Day of the Virgin of the Angels *(Día de la Virgen de los Angeles),* on August 2, celebrates Costa Rica's patron saint with religious processions from San José to the Basilica de Nuestra Señora de Los Angeles in Cartago. **Independence Day** *(Día de la Independencia)* is celebrated on September 15 with lantern-lighted parades the night before and marching bands throughout the country.

Immaculate Conception *(Inmaculada Concepción de la Virgen María),* on December 8, is observed with Masses to honor the Virgin Mary. The celebration of **Christmas** *(Navidad)* goes on throughout December, and extends into the last week of the month, with year-end festivals including bullfights around San José.

Money Matters

The local currency is known as the *colón*. You may want to get a small amount of *colónes* before your trip to pay for meals or taxi rides once you arrive. However, there are currency exchange booths in the international arrivals terminal of San José's Aeropuerto Internacional Juan Santamaría. The airport also has an automatic teller machine that dispenses both dollars and colónes, but it's hidden away in the stairway of the parking garage. Any employee can point you in the right direction.

Most ATMs (Cajero automático) are linked to both the Cirrus and the Plus networks, so they can be used by holders of most U.S.-issued debit and credit cards. Make sure before you leave that your PIN has four numbers, as most machines don't accept longer ones.

Credit cards are accepted by almost all businesses catering to tourists. Because businesses are charged a hefty fee for credit-card purchases, some will add a small surcharge or impose a minimum purchase amount if you use plastic. It's always a good idea to ask beforehand.

COSTA RICA
TOP ATTRACTIONS

Arenal Volcano

(A) Costa Rica has half a dozen active volcanoes, but none put on a show like the Arenal Volcano. During the day you're likely to see smoke billowing from the crater. This doesn't compare with what you'll see at night, when orangey red lava oozes down the perfectly shaped cone. If you're very lucky, the clouds will part long enough for you to spot glowing rocks shooting into the air.

Selvatura Park

(B) Soaring over the treetops on a zip line is a thrilling experience. But canopy tours aren't just for adrenaline junkies. Many rain forests have hanging bridges and elevated platforms to give you a bird's-eye view of the rain forest. Many of the best, like Selvetura, are around Monteverde Cloud Forest Biological Reserve and the Santa Elena Reserve, but others are clustered around Lake Arenal and Manuel Antonio.

Manuel Antonio National Park

(C) Some of the country's most thrilling views can be seen from the trails through Manuel Antonio National Park. As you emerge from the rain forest, don't be surprised to find yourself alone on a palm-shaded beach. Make sure to look up—three types of monkey make their home in the canopy, and on a good day you might see them all.

Corcovado National Park

(D) Bird-watchers come to this vast and pristine rain forest with hopes of catching a glimpse of the endangered harpy eagle. It's notoriously difficult to see, but other feathered friends—like the scarlet macaw, the orange-bellied trogon, and the golden-hooded tanager—practically pose for pictures. No need to head off into the rain forest with your binoculars; dozens of hummingbirds are likely to dart around you as you relax by the pool.

Playa Carrillo

(E) This long, picturesque beach, backed by a line of swaying palms and protective cliffs, is certainly one of the most beautiful stretches of sand in the country. Perfect for swimming, snorkeling, or just walking, the beach isn't marred by a single building. Visit on a weekday and it's possible that you may have the entire shore to yourself.

Turrialba

(G) Heavy rainfall, steep mountains, and rocky terrain make this region a magnet for white-water rafting enthusiasts, and there's a river to match anyone's level of expertise. Not far from San José, the Central Valley has outfitters who offer everything from easy day trips to challenging multiday excursions. Many of these companies congregate around the community of Turrialba, the country's white-water capital and close to the Rio Pacuare and Rio Reventazón.

Nicoya Peninsula

(F) Popular with the sun-and-fun crowd, the peninsula still has a yet-to-be-discovered feel. Maybe that's because its sandy shores are never covered with a checkerboard of beach blankets. Drive a few miles in any direction and you can find one all to yourself. But civilization isn't far away, some of the country's best restaurants are within reach.

Monteverde Cloud Forest Biological Reserve

(H) The roads leading here are terrible, but you won't mind a bit once you see the mist-covered reserve. Because of the constant moisture, this private park is unbelievably lush. It's gorgeous during the day, but many prefer to take a night hike, when you can see colorful birds asleep in the branches, hairy tarantulas in search of prey, and nocturnal mammals like the wide-eyed kinkajoo.

FAQS

Do I need any special documents to get into the country?

Aside from a passport that's valid for at least one month after date of entry, you don't need anything else to enter the country. You'll be given a 90-day tourist visa as you pass through immigration. You're no longer required to have your passport with you at all times during your trip, but make sure to carry a photocopy.

How difficult is it to travel around the country?

It's extremely easy. Thanks to the domestic airlines, getting to your ultimate destination takes far less time than just a few years ago; almost every worthwhile spot is within an hour of San José. Long-distance buses and vans are usually very comfortable, so don't overlook these as a way to get to far-flung destinations. Renting a car is a great way to get around, because you're not tied to somebody else's schedule. The roads are well marked, the signs are easy to read, and the traffic is pretty light outside urban areas. It's good to have a detailed map if you're driving in rural areas, as it's easy to miss a turn.

Are the roads as bad as they say?

Yes and no. You'll still find potholes the size of bathtubs on the road leading to Monteverde Cloud Forest Biological Reserve, and the gravel roads on the Nicoya Peninsula are often so grooved by the rain that they feel like an endless series of speed bumps. But many of the roads, including the Pan-American Highway that runs the length of the country, have been markedly improved. The most dramatic improvements have been made near the resort area of Lake Arenal. Repairs to the road between Nuevo Arenal and La Fortuna have cut your travel time almost in half. During and immediately after the summer rainy season is the worst time for driving. The constant deluge takes its toll on the pavement.

Should I rent a four-wheel-drive vehicle?

Probably so. If your trip will take you mostly to the beaches, you won't necessarily need a 4WD vehicle. If you're headed to more mountainous areas, such as any destination in the Northern Plains, you'll definitely want one. But even on the most badly maintained roads through the mountains, you'll see locals getting around just fine in their beat-up sedans. There's usually only a minor difference in the cost, so there's no reason not to go for the 4WD.

Should I get insurance on the rental car?

Even if your own insurance covers rental cars, go ahead and take full insurance. The cost is often less than $10 a day. For that you get the peace of mind of knowing that you're not going to be hassled for a scratch on the fender or a crack in the windshield. One traveler reported returning a rental car with a front bumper completely detached, and because he had full insurance the clerk just smiled and wished him a good trip home.

Should I consider a package tour?

If you're terrified of traveling on your own, sign up for a tour. But Costa Rica is such an easy place to get around that there's really no need. Part of the fun is the exploring—finding a secluded beach, hiking down to a hidden waterfall, discovering a great craft shop—and that's just not going to happen on a tour. If you're more comfortable with a package tour, pick one with a specific focus, like bird-watching or boating, so that you're less likely to get a generic tour.

Do I need a local guide?

Guides are a great idea for the first-time visitor in search of wildlife. A good guide will know where to find the animals, and will bring along a telescope so that you can get an up-close look at that sloth high in the trees or the howler monkeys across the clearing. After the first day, however, you'll probably grab your binoculars and head out on your own. It's much more gratifying to tell the folks back home that you discovered that banded anteater all by yourself.

Will I have trouble if I don't speak Spanish?

No problema. Most people in businesses catering to tourists speak at least a little English. If you encounter someone who doesn't speak English, they'll probably point you to a coworker who does. Even if you're in a far-flung destination, locals will go out of their way to find somebody who speaks your language.

Can I drink the water?

Costa Rica is the only Central American country where you don't have to get stressed out about drinking the water. The water is potable in all but the most remote regions. That said, many people don't like the taste of the tap water and prefer bottled water.

Are there any worries about the food?

None whatsoever. Even the humblest roadside establishment is likely to be scrupulously clean. If you have any doubts about a place, just move on to the next one. There's no problem enjoying fruit, cheese, bread, or other local products sold from the stands set up along the roads.

Do I need to get any shots?

You probably don't have to get any vaccinations or take any special medications. The U.S. Centers for Disease Control and Prevention warn that there is some concern about malaria, especially in remote areas along the Caribbean coast. If you

plan to spend any amount of time there, you may want to talk with your doctors about antimalarial medications well before your trip.

Should I bring any medications?

The only thing we recommend is using an insect repellent containing the active ingredient DEET. Ordinary repellents, even those labeled "extra strength," aren't going to do the trick against the mosquitoes of the tropics. To find a repellent with DEET, your best bet is a sporting goods store rather than your local drugstore. A formulation with 10% to 25% DEET will be fine; those with more are likely to irritate your skin.

Can I use my ATM card?

Most ATMs are on both the Cirrus and Plus networks, so they accept debit and credit cards issued by U.S. banks. Some might accept cards with just the MasterCard or just the Visa logo; if that's the case, try a machine at a different bank. Know the exchange rate before you use an ATM for the first time so that you know about how much local currency you want to withdraw.

Do most places take credit cards?

Almost all tourist-oriented businesses accept credit cards. You may encounter smaller restaurants and hotels that don't accept them at all, but these are pretty rare. Some businesses don't like to accept credit cards because their banks charge them exorbitant fees for credit-card transactions. They will usually relent and charge you a small fee for the privilege.

COSTA RICA TODAY

Government

Costa Rica is a democratic republic whose structure will be very familiar to any citizen of the United States. The 1949 constitution divides the government into independent executive, legislative, and judicial branches. All citizens are guaranteed equality before the law, the right to own property, freedom of speech, and freedom of religion.

Costa Rica elected its first female president in 2010, the fifth Latin American country to take such a step. Centrist candidate Laura Chinchilla, veteran of several posts in previous administrations, won election handily and became the first person here to hold the title La Presidenta. All indications are that she plans to continue the probusiness platform and infrastructure development of her predecessor, Oscar Arias.

The country is famous for lacking an army, which was abolished when the constitution was ratified in 1949. The country's stable government and economy have made this possible, even as its neighbors were embroiled in civil war. The country does maintain a small national guard.

Economy

By the mid-1980s, Costa Rica had diversified its economy beyond agriculture and tourism was bringing in more money than its three major cash crops: coffee, bananas, and pineapples. High-tech companies such as Intel and Motorola and pharmaceutical companies like Proctor and Gamble and GlaxoSmithKline opened plants and service centers in Costa Rica, providing well-paid jobs for educated professionals.

In 2007, there were huge demonstrations in the streets of San José before a vote on the proposed Central American Free Trade Agreement. Opponents of the plan, which would liberalize trade between Costa Rica, its neighbors, and the United States, said it would spell disaster for the country's agricultural industry. Voters narrowly approved the plan in November.

The economy continues to bedevil Costa Rica. Although economic growth continues to rise, it still has a 5% trade deficit and annual inflation of about 9%. But unemployment has dropped in recent years to just over 5%, comparable to that of the United States.

Tourism

Today Costa Rica faces the challenge of conserving its natural resources while still permitting modern development. The government has been unable or unwilling to control illegal logging, an industry that threatens to destroy the country's old-growth forests. Urban sprawl in the communities surrounding San José and the development of megaresorts along the Pacific coast threaten forests, wildlife, and the slow pace of life that makes Costa Rica so desirable.

Although tourism injects much-needed foreign cash into the economy, the government has not fully decided the best way to promote its natural wonders. The buzzwords now are not just ecotourism and sustainable development, but also adventure tourism and extreme sports. The two sides do not always see eye to eye.

Religion

Because it was a Spanish colony, Costa Rica continues to have a close relationship to the Catholic Church. Catholicism was made the country's official religion in the country's constitution. Because of this, priests are the only type of religious leader authorized to perform civil marriages. (Others require the assistance of a legal official.)

More than 90% of Costa Ricans consider themselves Catholics. But even among this group, most people do not have a strong identification with the church or with its teachings. The live-and-let-live attitude of most Costa Ricans does not mesh well with religious doctrine. That's also probably why the evangelical churches that have made inroads in neighboring countries have not succeeded here.

Although every village has a church on its main square, it's usually hopping once a year—when the town's patron saint is honored. These are times for food, music, and dancing in the streets. If the celebrations lack much religious fervor—well, that's Costa Rica for you.

Sports

Like everyone else on this soccer-mad isthmus, Costa Ricans take their game seriously and can get nasty when it comes to their national team; U.S. players reported being pelted with batteries and bags of urine during one game. When the national team returned after humiliating losses in the 2006 World Cup, an angry crowd met them at the airport chanting "dog" at the coach.

On the national level, the big local rivalry ("derby" in soccer parlance) is between LD Alajuelense and Deportivo Saprissa (La Monstruo Morado, or "The Purple Monster"). Each has won the Costa Rican championship 24 times, which makes the rivalry particularly intense. You can tell how important the sport is when you fly into the country. As your plane flies across the Central Valley, you'll notice that every village, no matter how small, has a soccer field. When not being used for sports, they often double as pastures for horses.

Cash Crops

If nearby Honduras was the original "Banana Republic," 19th-century Costa Rica was a "Coffee Republic." Coffee remains inexorably entwined with the country, with economists paying close attention to world prices and kids in rural areas still taking class time off to help with the harvest.

The irony is that it's hard to get a decent cup of the stuff here. True to economic realities of developing countries, the high-quality product gets exported, with the inferior coffee staying behind for the local market. (The same is true of bananas, Costa Rica's other signature agricultural product.) The best places to get a cup of high-quality Costa Rican coffee are upscale restaurants and hotels. Owners understand foreign tastes and have export-quality coffee on hand. Gift shops sell the superior product as well.

The Central Valley is where you'll find many of the coffee plantations. You'll recognize them immediately by the rows of brilliant green plants covered in red berries. Because many of these plants are sensitive to light, they are often shaded by tall trees or even by canopies of fabric. Tours of the plantations are a great way to get to know the local cash crop.

In recent years, the producers of coffee have focused on quality rather than quantity. That's why bananas are now the top agricultural export, followed by pineapples. Both grow in sunny lowland areas, which are abundant on both the Atlantic and Pacific coasts. These crops are treated with just as much care as coffee. You're likely to see bunches of bananas wrapped in plastic bags—while still on the tree. This prevents blemishes that make them less appealing to foreign consumers.

ECOTOURISM, COSTA RICA STYLE

Perhaps more than anyone else, two men who wrote a field guide about tropical birds were responsible for the ecotourism movement in Costa Rica.

According to Carlos Manuel Rodríguez, the country's former minister for environment and energy, "When *A Guide to the Birds of Costa Rica* by F. Gary Stiles and Alexander Skutch was published in the late 1980s, the government noticed that it was bringing bird-watchers here," he told a reporter for *The Guardian*, a London newspaper. "From then on, a national tourism plan was developed."

The country's leaders, seeing so many of its primary growth forests being felled at an alarming rate by loggers and farmers, established its national park system in 1970. But it wasn't until nearly two decades later, when *A Guide to the Birds of Costa Rica* was published, that they realized that the land they had set aside could help transform the tiny country's economy.

Of the 1.5 million people who travel each year to Costa Rica, many are bird-watchers who come in search of the keel-billed toucan, the scarlet-rumped tanager, or any of the 850 other species of birds. Other travelers are in search of animals, such as two types of sloths, three types of anteater, and four species of monkey, all of them surprisingly easy to spot in the country's national parks and private reserves.

But other people come to Costa Rica to go white-water rafting on the rivers, soar through the treetops attached to zip lines, or take a spin in a motorboat. And many people combine a little bit of everything into their itineraries.

Which raises a couple of questions: Is the person coming to see the wildlife practicing ecotourism? Is the adventure traveler? And exactly what is the definition of ecotourism, anyway?

Defining Ecotourism

The word ecotourism is believed to have been coined by Mexican environmentalist Héctor Ceballos-Lascuráin in 1983. According to Ceballos-Lascuráin, ecotourism "involves traveling to relatively undisturbed natural areas with the specific object of studying, admiring, and enjoying the scenery and its wild plants and animals."

His original definition seemed a bit too general, so in 1993 he amended it with a line that stressed that "ecotourism is environmentally responsible travel."

Ceballos-Lascuráin said he is pleased that ecotourism has gained such acceptance around the world. But he is also concerned that the term has been "variously abused and misused in many places."

The trouble, he said, is a misunderstanding about what is meant by the term ecotourism. In Costa Rica, for example, it has been used to describe everything from hiking through the rain forest to rumbling over the hillsides in all-terrain vehicles, and from paddling in a kayak to dancing to disco music on a diesel-powered yacht.

"I am sad to see," Ceballos-Lascuráin told a reporter for EcoClub, "that 'ecotourism' is seen mainly as adventure tourism and carrying out extreme sports in a more or less natural environment, with little concern for conservation or sustainable development issues."

That is not to say that adventure sports can't be part of a green vacation. It all depends what impact they have on the environment and the local community.

Going Green

Over the past decade, the concept of ecotourism has made a strong impression on the average traveler. Many people now realize that mass tourism can be damaging to environmentally sensitive places like Costa Rica but that much can be done to alleviate the negative effects. At the same time, *ecotourism* has become a marketing term used to attract customers who have the best intentions. But is there really such a thing as an eco-friendly car-rental company or a green airline?

In addition to giving travelers the chance to observe and learn about wildlife, ecotourism should accomplish three things: refrain from damaging the environment, strengthen conservation efforts, and improve the lives of local people.

The last part might seem a bit beside the point, but environmentalists point out that much of the deforestation in Costa Rica and other countries is by poor people trying to eke out a living through sustenance farming. Providing them with other ways to make a living is the best way to prevent this.

What can you do? Make sure the hotel you choose is eco-friendly. A great place to start is the Costa Rican Tourism Board (⊕ *www.turismo-sostenible.co.cr*). It has a rating system for hotels and lodges called the Certification for Sustainable Tourism. The Costa Rica–based Rainforest Alliance (⊕ *www.rainforest-alliance.org*) has a convenient searchable database of sustainable lodges. The International Ecotourism Society (⊕ *www.ecotourism.org*) has a database of tour companies, hotels, and other travel services that are committed to sustainable practices.

Other Things You Can Do

What else can help? Make sure your tour company follows sustainable policies, including contributing to conservation efforts, hiring and training locals for most jobs, educating visitors about the local ecology and culture, and taking steps to mitigate negative impacts on the environment.

Here are a few other things you can do:

Use locally owned lodges, car-rental agencies, or tour companies. Eat in local restaurants, shop in local markets, and attend local events. Enrich your experience and support the community by hiring local guides.

Stray from the beaten path—by visiting areas where few tourists go, you can avoid adding to the stress on hot spots and enjoy a more authentic Costa Rican experience.

Support conservation by paying entrance fees to parks and protected sites and contributing to local environmental groups.

Don't be overly aggressive if you bargain for souvenirs, and don't shortchange local people on payments or tips for services.

The point here is that you can't assume that companies have environmentally friendly practices, even if they have pictures of animals on their Web site or terms like eco-lodge in their name. Do business only with companies that promote sustainable tourism, and you'll be helping to preserve this country's natural wonders for future generations.

WEDDINGS AND HONEYMOONS

Ever dreamed of getting married on a sandy beach shaded by palm trees? Many people who envision such a scene immediately think of the Caribbean. But Costa Rica is fast becoming a favored destination for tropical nuptials.

One reason is that compared with the complicated procedures in many other destinations, getting married in Costa Rica is fairly easy. There are no residency restrictions or blood-test requirements. At least a month in advance, couples of the opposite sex who are over 18 should provide their local wedding planner with a copy of their birth certificates and passports so they can be submitted to the local authorities.

Things are a bit more complicated if there was a previous marriage. The couple needs to provide documentation that the marriage was terminated. Divorce papers must be translated into Spanish and notarized.

The Big Day

Judges, attorneys, and Catholic priests have legal authority to certify a marriage in Costa Rica. (Most foreign couples avoid the latter because a Catholic wedding requires months of preparation.) The official ceremony is very simple, but couples are free to add their own vows or anything else they would like. The officiant will register the marriage with the civil registry and the couple's embassy.

At the wedding, the couple needs to have at least two witnesses who are not family members. Many couples choose their best man and maid of honor. If necessary, the wedding planner can provide witnesses.

The license itself takes three months to issue and is sent to the couple's home address. For an extra fee couples can ask for the process to be expedited. Virtually all Western countries recognize the legality of a Costa Rican marriage.

Beautiful Backdrops

Although Costa Rica offers no shortage of impressive backdrops for a ceremony, the Central Pacific coast sees the most tourist weddings and honeymoons. May and June are the most popular months, but many people choose January or February because you are virtually guaranteed sunny skies. Manuel Antonio's Makanda by the Sea, La Mariposa, Si Como No, and Punta Leona's Villa Caletas are among the many lodgings here with events staffs well versed in planning ceremonies and tending to the legalities.

There are many details to attend to: flowers, music, and photography. Most large hotels have on-staff wedding planners to walk you through the process. Couples can also hire their own wedding planner, which is often less expensive. Either way, wedding planners will likely have a wide range of services available, and couples can pick and choose.

Honeymoons

As far as honeymoons go, there's no place in Costa Rica that is inappropriate. Although honeymoons on the beach, especially along the Northern Pacific and Central Pacific coasts, are popular, many couples opt for treks to the mountains or the rain forests. Dozens of newlyweds choose offbeat adventures, such as spotting sea turtles along the Caribbean coast or swimming with pilot whales off the Osa Peninsula.

KIDS AND FAMILIES

With so much to keep them interested and occupied, Costa Rica is a blast with kids. What makes it so much fun is that the activities here are things the whole family can do together: discovering a waterfall in a rain forest, snorkeling with sea turtles, or white-water rafting down a roaring river. There are also activities for kids that will allow parents time to stroll hand-in-hand down a deserted beach.

Choosing a Destination

Basing yourself in one place for several days is a great idea. Climbing into the car every day or two not only makes the kids miserable but means that the best part of the day is spent traveling. The good news is that there are many destinations where you could stay for a week and still not do and see everything.

Headed to the beach? Remember that for families, not all beaches are created equal. Choose a destination with a range of activities. Manuel Antonio, on the Central Pacific coast, is your best bet. The proximity to the national park is the main selling point, but you're also close to other nature preserves. As for activities, there's everything from snorkeling and surfing lessons to kayaking excursions to zip-line adventures. And the range of kid-friendly restaurants is unmatched anywhere in the country. On the Nicoya Peninsula, Playas del Coco and Playa Tamarindo have a decent amount of activities for the small fry.

Santa Elena, the closest town to Monteverde Cloud Forest Biological Reserve, is another great base. There are several nature preserves in the area, and they offer both day and night hikes. If skies are cloudy—as they often are—there are indoor attractions like the display of slithering snakes. The town is compact and walkable, and has many eateries with children's menus. La Fortuna, the gateway to the Lake Arenal area, has activities from waterfall hikes to canopy tours. The town itself isn't very attractive, so you'll want to choose a place nearby.

Believe it or not, the San José area is not a bad base. Activities like white-water rafting are nearby, and on rainy days you can visit the city's excellent museums dedicated to gold and jade. The hotels in the surrounding countryside are often a long drive from good restaurants. We prefer the hotels in the city, as dozens of restaurants line the pedestrian-only streets.

Kid-Friendly Activities

You can't beat the beach in Costa Rica. Avoid those without lifeguards, and take warning signs about rip currents very seriously. Snorkeling and surfing lessons are great for older kids, but stick with a licensed company rather than that enthusiastic young person who approaches you on the beach.

Canopy tours are good for kids of all ages. Ask the staff about how long a tour will take, because once you set out on a hike over a series of hanging bridges, you often have no choice but to continue on to the end. Zip lines are appropriate for older teens, but they should always be accompanied by an adult.

For the smallest of the small fry, the butterfly enclosures and hummingbird gardens that you find near most resort areas are wonderful diversions. Indoor activities, like the display of frogs at Santa Elena, fascinate youngsters. And don't avoid the easier hikes in the national parks. Seeing animals in the wild is likely to start a lifelong love of animals.

GREAT ITINERARIES

BEACHES, RAIN FORESTS, AND VOLCANOES

Day 1: Arrival

Arrive in San José (most arrivals are in the evening) and head straight to one of the small luxury hotels north of the city in the Central Valley. A favorite of ours is Finca Rosa Blanca, a fairy-tale retreat overlooking miles of coffee farms.

Logistics: Brace yourself for long lines at immigration if you arrive in the evening along with all the other large flights from North America. Try to get a seat near the front of the plane, and don't dawdle when disembarking.

Day 2: Poás Volcano and Tabacón Hot Springs

Volcán Poás, where you can peer over the edge of a crater, lies nearby. Fortify yourself with the fruits, jellies, and chocolates sold by vendors on the road up to the summit. A scenic drive takes you to the La Fortuna area. Drop your luggage at one of many fantastic hotels (Montaña de Fuego is our pick for fabulous volcano views), and go directly to Tabacón Hot Springs & Resort. Take a zip-line or hanging-bridges tour through the forest canopy and then pamper yourself with a spa treatment. Finish the day by sinking into a volcanically heated mineral bath with a cocktail at your side as the sun sets behind fiery Volcán Arenal.

Logistics: Get an early start to get the best views of Poás. Shuttle vans can get you to Arenal and have hotel-to-hotel service.

Day 3: Caño Negro Wildlife Refuge

Spend your entire day in the Caño Negro Wildlife Refuge, a lowland forest reserve replete with waterfowl near the Nicaraguan border.

Logistics: Book your trip the night before; tour operators in La Fortuna keep evening hours for exactly that reason. All transport will be included.

Day 4: Scenic Drive to the Central Pacific

Today's a traveling day—a chance to really see the country's famous landscape and infamous roads. (Believe us, they get a lot worse than this route.) A few hours' drive from Arenal takes you to fabled Manuel Antonio on the Central Pacific coast. Beyond-beautiful hotels are the norm here, and you have your choice of seaside villas or tree-shrouded jungle lodges. We like the hillside La Mariposa, which has commanding views.

Logistics: Hotel-to-hotel shuttle-van services can get you to Manuel Antonio. If you drive instead, start out as early as possible. You'll pass through two mountainous stretches (between La Fortuna and San Ramón, and between Atenas and the coast) that fog over by midafternoon.

Day 5: Manuel Antonio National Park

Manuel Antonio is Costa Rica's most famous national park for a reason: it has beaches, lush rain forest, mangrove swamps, and rocky coves with abundant marine life. You can—and should—spend an entire day exploring the park, home to capuchin monkeys, sloths, agoutis, and 200 species of birds. It's also one of two locales in the country where you'll see squirrel monkeys.

Logistics: Almost all Manuel Antonio hotels have transport to the park. If yours doesn't, taxis are plentiful and cheap.

Day 6: Beach Yourself

Days 1 through 5 were "on the go" days. Reward yourself today with lots of relaxation. Manuel Antonio means beaches, and there are several to choose from. Manuel Antonio and neighboring Quepos mean restaurants, too, the best selection of any beach community in the country.

Logistics: Most everything you need here is strung along the 5-km (3-mi) road between Quepos and Manuel Antonio National Park. It's practically impossible to get lost.

Day 7: San José

A morning drive back to San José gives you time to spend the afternoon in the city. We like the cozy, classy Hotel Le Bergerac. Visit the Teatro Nacional, the capital's must-see sight, and save time for late-afternoon shopping. An evening dinner caps off your trip before you turn in early to get ready for tomorrow morning's departure.

Logistics: As the number of visitors to Costa Rica grows, so does the number of passengers using Aeropuerto Internacional Juan Santamaría. We recommend that you check in three hours before your flight. Better safe than sorry.

TIPS

■ Aside from Day 2, it's entirely possible to do this route without a car.

■ Hotels in the Central Valley and San José are used to booking visitors for their first and last nights in the country, and may allow you to leave items so you don't have to lug them around.

■ Arenal lies equidistant between Liberia and San José, but we suggest flying into San José for this itinerary because road access to Arenal and from Manuel Antonio is better.

■ Cloud cover makes volcano viewing the luck of the draw, and no one can negotiate with Mother Nature. Early mornings and dry season give you the best chances for seeing Arenal and Poás in action.

■ Get as early a start as possible if you're driving. The mountain roads between San José and La Fortuna and between Manuel Antonio and San José can fog over by midafternoon.

GREAT ITINERARIES

MORE BEACHES, RAIN FORESTS, AND VOLCANOES

Day 1: Arrival

Most arrivals to Liberia, Costa Rica's second international airport, are in early afternoon. You can't go wrong with any North Pacific beach, but we like Playa Hermosa for its pivotal location, one that lets you use it as a base for visiting area attractions. Check out small, personal, breezy Hotel Playa Hermosa/Bosque del Mar, the perfect antidote to the mega-resorts that lie not too far away.

Logistics: The big all-inclusives up here have their own minivans to whisk you in air-conditioned comfort from airport to resort. Smaller lodgings such as Hotel Playa Hermosa/Bosque del Mar can arrange to have transport waiting, with advance notice.

Day 2: Playa Hermosa

Morning is a great time to laze on the beach in this part of Costa Rica. The breezes are refreshingly cool and the sun hasn't started to beat down. After lunch, explore Playa Hermosa's metropolis, the small town of Playas del Coco. Quite frankly Coco is our least favorite beach up here. But we like the town for its little souvenir shops, restaurants, and local color.

Logistics: Taxis are the easiest way to travel between Playa Hermosa and Coco, about 10 minutes away. Have your hotel call one, and flag one down on the street in town when it's time to return.

Day 3: Rincón de la Vieja Volcano

The top of Rincón de la Vieja Volcano with its steaming, bubbling, oozing fumaroles lies about 90 minutes from Hermosa. Lather on the sunscreen and head for the Hacienda Guachipelín and its volcano-viewing hikes, canopy tours, rappelling, horseback riding, mountain biking, and river tubing. Cap off the day with a spa treatment, complete with thermal mud bath.

Logistics: If you don't have a rental car, book a private driver for the day, which can usually be arranged through your hotel.

Day 4: Golf or Diving

Golf is big up here. The 18-hole Garra de León course at the Paradisus Playa Conchal resort is about 45 minutes from Hermosa. The other popular, slightly pricey, sport here is scuba diving. Dive operators are based in nearby Playas del Coco or Playa Panamá. A daylong course gives you a taste of the deep.

Logistics: The resort will arrange transport to and from the golf course, and dive operators will pick you up from and return you to your hotel.

Day 5: Palo Verde National Park

We like the morning guided tours at Palo Verde National Park, one of the last remaining dry tropical forests in Central America. The Organization for Tropical Studies, which operates the biological station here, has terrific guides. Spend the afternoon observing nature in a more relaxed fashion with a float down the nearby Río Corobicí. (These are not the screaming rapids so famed in white-water circles.)

Logistics: This excursion is a bit roundabout, so this is the day your own vehicle would come in handiest. But you can also hire a private driver (arranged through your hotel). Bring water to drink: it gets hot here.

Day 6: Sailing

Make your final day a relaxing one with a few hours on the waves. Many sailboats operate from this section of coast. Our choice is the 52-foot *Samonique III*, which sails out of Playa Flamingo most afternoons at 2. A four-hour excursion includes sandwiches, appetizers, and an open bar. Legendary Pacific sunsets are tossed in at no extra charge.

Logistics: The *Samonique III* folks can arrange transport from hotel to boat and back again.

Day 7: Departure

Grab a last dip in the ocean this morning, because your flight departs from Liberia in the early afternoon.

Logistics: The advent of international flights to Liberia has fueled this region's meteoric rise to fame, but the airport's size has not kept pace with the number of passengers. Expansion is eventually on the way, but presently, lines can be long. Allow yourself plenty of time for check-in.

TIPS

■ Fly into Liberia. Although it's logical to think "San José" when planning flights to Costa Rica, it makes no sense if you plan to spend your entire time in the North Pacific.

■ A car is ideal for this itinerary, yet many area attractions and tour operators provide transport to and from area lodging if you aren't too far afield (one of the reasons we like Playa Hermosa).

■ All-inclusive resorts do a good job of organizing local excursions with local operators, so if you're staying at one, take advantage of them.

■ Getting from beach to beach often requires travel back inland. There is no real (i.e., navigable) coastal road.

■ If ever there were a case for an off-season vacation, this is it. This driest, hottest part of the country gets very dry and hot from January through April. The rains green everything up, and frankly, we prefer the region during the low season after April.

THE PEOPLE OF COSTA RICA

Unlike many of its neighbors, Costa Rica never had a dominant indigenous population. When Christopher Columbus arrived in the early 16th century, he didn't encounter empires like those in present-day Mexico and Peru. Instead, a small contingent of Carib Indians rowed out in canoes to meet his ship. The heavy gold bands the indigenous peoples wore led to the land being called Costa Rica, or "Rich Coast."

On the mainland, the Spanish encountered disparate tribes like the Chorotega, Bribri, Cabecar, and Boruca peoples. Archeological evidence shows that they had lived in the region for thousands of years. But that would change with breathtaking speed. European diseases felled many of their members, and the brutality of slavery imposed by the colonial power drove most of those remaining into the mountains.

Some of these peoples still exist, although in relatively small communities. Several thousand Bribri, Kekoldi, and other peoples live in villages scattered around Talamanca, a mountainous region close to the border of Panama. Although many traditions have been lost over the years, some have managed to retain their own languages and religions. If you're interested in seeing the local culture, tour companies in the coastal communities of Limón and Puerto Viejo de Talamanca can arrange visits to these villages.

That isn't to say that there's no local culture. More than 90% of the country's residents are *mestizos*, or mixed-race descendants of the Spanish. But few people express any pride in their Spanish heritage. Perhaps that is because Spain had little interest in Costa Rica, the smallest and poorest of its Central American colonies. Instead, the people here created a unique culture that mixes parts of Europe, Latin America, and the Caribbean. There's a strong emphasis on education, and the 95% literacy rate is by far the highest in the region. There's a laid-back attitude toward life, typified by the common greeting of *pura vida*, which translates literally as "pure life" but means something between "no worries" and "don't sweat the small stuff."

It sounds like a cliché, but Costa Ricans are an incredibly welcoming people. Anyone who has visited other Central American cultures will be surprised at how Ticos seem genuinely happy to greet newcomers. If you ever find yourself lost in a town or village, you may find locals more than willing to not only point you in the right direction but walk you all the way to your destination.

Others cultures have added their own spice to Costa Rica. On the Caribbean coast you'll find Afro-Caribbean peoples, descendants of Jamaicans who arrived in the late 19th century to build the railroad and remained to work on banana and cacao plantations. In the seaside town of Limón, cruise ships frequently call, and the passengers who hurry down the gangplank encounter steel-drum music, braided hair, and rickety houses painted every color of the rainbow. They may think that they have discovered the "real" Costa Rica, and they have, in a way. But they also have barely scratched the surface.

Biodiversity

WORD OF MOUTH

"I spotted this huge iguana measuring approx. 4 feet sunning along Playa Uvita; he allowed me to get within inches to take several pictures."

—Photo by Justin Hubbell, Fodors.com member

Costa Rica's forests hold an array of flora and fauna so vast and diverse that scientists haven't even named thousands of the species found here. The country covers less than 0.03% of the Earth's surface, yet it contains nearly 5% of the planet's plant and animal species. Costa Rica has at least 9,000 plant species, including more than 1,200 types of orchids, some 2,000 kinds of butterflies, and 876 bird species.

Costa Rica acts as a natural land bridge between North and South America, so there is a lot of intercontinental exchange. But the country's flora and fauna add up to more than what has passed between the continents. Costa Rica's biological diversity is the result of its tropical location, its varied topography, and the many microclimates resulting from the combination of mountains, valleys, and lowlands. The isthmus also acts as a hospitable haven to many species that couldn't complete the journey from one hemisphere to the other. The rain forests of Costa Rica's Caribbean and southwestern lowlands are the most northerly home of such southern species as the crab-eating raccoon. The tropical dry forests of the northern Pacific slope are the southern limit for such North American species as the Virginia opossum. And then there are the dozens of northern bird species that spend their winter holidays here.

Research and planning go a long way in a place like Costa Rica. A short trip around the country can put you in one landscape after another, each with its own array of plants and animals. The country's renowned national park system holds examples of all of its major ecosystems, and some of its most impressive sights. In terms of activities, there's more interesting stuff to do here than could possibly ever fit into one vacation. But keep in mind that somewhere around three-fourths of the country has been urbanized or converted to agriculture, so if you want to see the spectacular nature that we describe in this book, you need to know where to go. *In addition to this section on biodiversity, you'll find regional planning information, national park highlights, and a list of our favorite ecolodges at the front of each chapter.*

Largo de Nicaragua

NICARAGUA

Bahía Salinas

Guanacaste National Park

○ San José

Caño Negro National Wildlife Refuge

Golfo de Santa Elena

Orosi
• Cacao

SANTA ELENA PENINSULA

CORDILLERA DE GUANACASTE

Rincón de la Vieja National Park

• Rincón de la Vieja

• Miracalles

Santa Rosa National Park

• Tenorio

Lake Arenal

Arenal Volcano National Park

Golfo de Papagayo

Liberia ○

Arenal
Chato

Juan Castro Blanco National Park

Quesada ○

Congo

CORDILLERA DE TILARÁN

Platanar •

Palo Verde National Park

Porvenir •

Poás

Tamarindo ○

Barra Honda National Park

Monteverde Cloud Forest Biological Reserve

Poás Volcano National Park

Alajuela ○

NICOYA PENINSULA

Puntarenas ○

CORDILLERA

0 ——— 30 mi
0 ——— 30 km

Tammbor ○

Gulf of Nicoya

Carara Biological Reserve

PACIFIC OCEAN

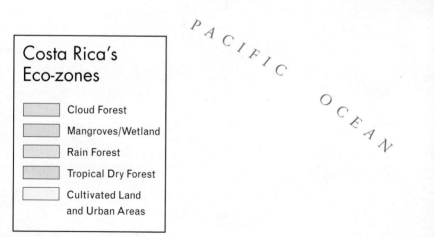

Costa Rica's Eco-zones

Cloud Forest

Mangroves/Wetland

Rain Forest

Tropical Dry Forest

Cultivated Land and Urban Areas

Costa Rica's Eco-zones

Barra del Colorado
Wildlife Refuge

Caribbean Sea

La Virgen

Braulio Carillo
National Park

Cacho
Negro

Tortuguero
National Park

Brava

Limón

Turrialba Volcano
National Park

Hereas   Irazú   Turrialba

SAN JOSÉ   Irazú Volcano
National Park

CENTRAL   Cartago

Cahuita
National Park

Cerro Chirripó
National Park

La Amistad
National Park

Chirripó
(Highest point in
Costa Rica 3,810m)

CORDILLERA   Eli

Quepos   San Isidro   Ena   Utyum

DE   Nai   PANAMA

TALAMANCA

Manuel Antonio
National Park   San Rafael

Bine

VALLE DE EL GENERAL

Río Terraba

Drake   Golfito   Piedras Blancas
National Park

Drake Bay   OSA PENINSULA   Dulce
Gulf

Corcovado
National Park

KEY	
▲	Mountain
●	Volcano
⬛	National Parks, Wildlife Refuges and Biological Reserves

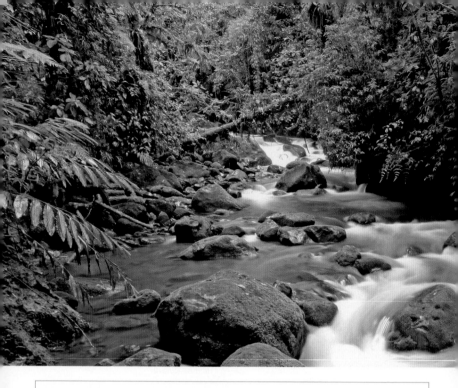

RAIN FOREST

Warm and wet, Costa Rica's rain forest is the quintessential dripping, squawking, chirping, buzzing jungle. In this sultry landscape of green on green, birds flap and screech overhead and twigs snap under the steps of unseen creatures. All of the ingredients for life—water, sunlight, and more water—drench these areas.

The amount of rain in a rain forest is stunning. The enormous swath of forest in the Caribbean lowlands averages more than 4 meters (13 feet) of rain a year. Corcovado National Park, on the Osa Peninsula, can get 5.5 meters (18 feet).

The soaring canopy soaks up the lion's share of sunlight, seriously depriving the plants below. Underneath the highest trees are several distinct layers of growth. The understory is made up of smaller and younger trees, shaded, but also protected from harsh winds and rainfall. Shrubby species and even younger trees stand farther below, and small plants, fungus, dead trees, and fallen leaves cover the constantly decomposing forest floor.

Light rarely passes through these layers and layers of growth. At the forest floor, plants lie poised, in a stasis of sorts, waiting for one of the giants above to fall and open a patch of sky. When this does happen, an incredible spectacle occurs as the waiting plants unveil an arsenal of evolutionary tricks. Vines twist out, looking for other trees to pull themselves up along, shoots explode from hidden bulbs, and ferns and lianas battle for height and access to the sun.

But as competitive as the jungle sounds, it is essentially a series of ecosystems based on interdependence and cooperation. Trees depend on the animals that eat their fruit to disperse their seeds. Fungi feed off the nutrients produced by the decomposing forest floor. From death comes life—an abundance of life.

Costa Rica's rain forests have suffered from agriculture and cattle farming, but they're still home to the majority of the nation's biodiversity, with more species per square mile than anywhere else.

ADVENTURE HIGHLIGHTS

■ Novice bird-watchers can enroll in La Selva's Saturday morning bird-watching 101 class. It's taught by some of the finest naturalists in the country.

■ Join the folks at Brisas del Nara, 20 mi outside of Manual Antonio, for an all-day horseback riding excursion through the protected Cerra Nara mountain zone. It ends with a swim in a natural pool with a 350-foot waterfall.

■ Stray way off the beaten path on a multiday hike through Corcovado National Park with tropical biologist Mike Boston from Osa Aventura.

FLORA

To enter into a Costa Rican rainforest is to be overwhelmed by the diversity and intensity of life. A single hectare contains almost 100 species of trees, and many of the more than 1,000 species of orchids are nested into their branches.

The Silk Cotton Tree

GUARIA MORADA

Almost every tree here plays host to lichens, woody vines called lianas, and rootless epiphytes, including the national flower, *guaria morada* (*Guarianthe skinneri*). Because this is an orchid species, you'll find it in several different shapes and colors: the flowers can be from pure white to deep magenta, and the base of its lip can range from yellow to white. There can be anywhere from 4 to 14 flowers per stem.

THE SILK COTTON TREE

The silk cotton tree (*Ceiba pentandra*), known locally as ceiba, is one of the most easily recognizable of the rain forest giants. Growing nearly 60 meters (200 feet) tall, it can be identified close to the ground by its tall, winding, and narrow roots, which act as buttresses to support the enormous trunk.

Guaria morada

STRANGLER FIG

Aptly called *matapalo* in Spanish, meaning "tree killer," the strangler fig begins its life as an epiphyte, living high in the branches of another tree. Over several years, it slowly grows dangling roots to the forest floor that capture nutrients from the soil, thicken, and eventually meld onto the host tree. Eventually—it might take as long as 100 years—the strangler completely engulfs its host. In time the "strangled" tree decomposes and disintegrates, leaving the strangler fig—replete with branches, leaves, flowers, and fruit—standing hollow but victorious.

Strangler Fig

FALSE BIRD OF PARADISE

No avid photographer will return from Costa Rica without snapping a few shots of a heliconia, one of the most vibrant families of plants in the rain forest. This genus of flowering plant, containing between 100 and 200 species, includes the false bird of paradise (*Heliconia rostrata*), a dangling, impossibly colorful flower of alternating bulbous protrusions, colored red and tipped with green and yellow. Its vibrant colors and nectar make it a favorite for hummingbirds.

False Bird of Paradise

2

FAUNA

Keep an eye out for three-wattled bellbirds, chestnut-mandibled toucans, or the Baird's tapir. A host of wild-cats, include the jaguar, ocelot, jaguarundi, puma, and margay.

Scarlet Macaw

SCARLET MACAWS
Every bit the pirate's crimson parrot, these large and noisy birds mate for life, travel in pairs or large groups, and can often be found gathered in almond trees in low-elevation forests of the central and southern Pacific coast. Their cousin, the critically endangered great green macaw, travels across the Caribbean lowlands, following the ripening of the mountain almond.

Harpy Eagle

HARPY EAGLE
The endangered harpy eagle, nearly extinct from Costa Rica, is the country's largest and most powerful raptor. It's named for the Greek spirits that carried the dead to the underworld of Hades, who are said to have the faces of humans but the bodies of eagles. Harpy eagles are huge—females are more than 0.6 meters (2 feet) in length and have a 1.8-meter (6-foot) wingspan. They hunt above the canopy, searching for large mammals or, occasionally, large birds like the macaw.

Three-toed-sloth

THREE-TOED OR TWO-TOED SLOTH
Through difficult for us to spot, the barely moving three-toed sloth and two-toed sloth are principal meals for the harpy eagle. This animal fur is a small self-sustaining ecosystem unto itself: because the forest is so wet and the sloth so inert, two species of blue-green algae thrive on its fur and provide it with needed camouflage. Non-parasitic insects also live here, feeding off the algae and keeping the growth under control.

Blue Morpho

MORPHO BUTTERFLY
The bright blue morpho butterfly bounces through the jungle like a small piece of sky on a string. The entire life cycle, from egg to death, is approximately 137 days, and the adult butterflies live for only about a month. Once they emerge from the cocoon, morphos have few predators, thanks to the poisonous compounds that they retain from feeding habits back in their caterpillar days. In fact, the hairy brown tufts on the morpho caterpillar have been known to irritate human skin.

■ TIP→The vibrantly colored red-eyed tree frog, like the white tent bat, sometimes rests on the underside of large jungle leaves; gently turn a few leaves over as you're hiking and take a peek. You might get lucky.

EXPERIENCING A RAIN FOREST

Photographing a spiderweb

For an ecosystem as diverse as the rain forest, it is fitting that there are a variety of ways to explore and experience it.

HIKING

Hiking or walking through any one of Costa Rica's numerous national parks is an easy way to fully experience the vibrancy of the life found there. And we can't say this too many times: guided hikes are the way to go for anyone who hopes to catch a glimpse of the more exotic and hard-to-find species or better understand the complexity of the surrounding ecosystems.

MOUNTAIN BIKING

During the dry season, some parks open up trails for mountain bikers. But once the rains begin, a bike trip can turn into a long slog through the mud. Before you rent a bike, ask about the conditions of the trails.

RAFTING

Gentle, slow-moving rivers beg to be explored by canoe or kayak. It's a wonderful way to experience the deep calm of the jungle, and stealthy enough to increase your chances of seeing wildlife. If you're more of a thrill seeker, choose from any of the white-water rafting tours that pass through rain forests.

CANOPY TOURS

Canopy tours are a wonderful way to get a bird's—or sloth's—view of the rain forest. Suspension bridges and zip lines, originally used for canopy research, offer a fantastic glimpse into the upper reaches of the forest. If you're not very mobile or don't feel like walking, go on a rain forest tram; it's like a small, slow-moving gondola that carries passengers gently through the jungle canopy.

TOP DESTINATIONS

Most of Costa Rica's rain forest can be found across the Caribbean lowlands and on the southern Pacific Coast.

LA SELVA

If anybody knows anything about the rain forest, it is the researchers at the La Selva biological station, situated in the midst of 3,900 acres of protected forest in the Caribbean lowlands. The station, run by the Organization for Tropical Studies, was founded by famed biologist Leslie Holdridge in 1954 and is one of the most important sites worldwide for research on tropical rain forest. The research station can sleep up to 80 people in dormitory-style rooms, and feed as many as 100 in the dining hall. More than 50 km (31 mi) of trails provide access to a variety of ecosystems. *(See Chapter 5.)*

MANUEL ANTONIO NATIONAL PARK

For a tame, up-close glimpse of the rain forest and some of its more photogenic inhabitants, Manuel Antonio National Park is a favorite. Located on the central Pacific coast, Manuel Antonio is one of Costa Rica's most visited—and smallest—national parks. Capuchin monkeys are used to humans to the point of practically ignoring them, unless a snack is poking out from an unattended backpack. The highly endangered squirrel monkeys are less bold, but can be seen

A green and black poison frog, La Selva

at the park or from nearby hotels. Sloths are a common sight along the trail, as are a host of exotic birds and other creatures. But despite the apparent vibrancy of life found here, Manuel Antonio is isolated, with no biological bridges to other forests, and threatened by encroaching development. *(See Chapter 7.)*

CORCOVADO NATIONAL PARK

At the other end of the spectrum is Corcovado National Park, the remote, untamed jewel of Costa Rica's biodiversity crown. Covering one-third of the Osa Peninsula, Corcovado National Park holds about one-quarter of all tree species in Costa Rica and at least 140 identified species of mammals. Covering 172 square mi (445 square km), the park includes Central America's largest tract of lowland Pacific rain forest, including some old-growth areas. Corcovado is home to the largest concentration of jaguars left in the country, and the biggest population of scarlet macaw. There are at least 117 species of amphibians and reptiles, and more than 360 bird species. Ranger stations and campsites are available for the more adventurous, and luxurious eco-lodges surround the park for those who don't like to rough it. *(See Chapter 8.)*

Squirrel Monkey; danmike, Fodors.com member

VOLCANOES

As part of the Pacific Ring of Fire, the country has three volcanic mountain ranges: Guanacaste, Central, and Tilarán. There are around 300 volcanic points in Costa Rica, but only five have formed volcanoes that have erupted in recent memory: Turrialba, Irazu, Poás, Rincón de la Vieja, and Arenal.

Costa Rica's volcanoes are the result of friction between two enormous tectonic plates—the Cocos plate and the Caribbean plate. As these plates rub against each other, the friction partially melts rock, creating magma or lava. Magma is forced toward the surface, leaking through cracks or weak spots in the crust along with volcanic gas. In Rincón de la Vieja, lava and gas escapes through craters high on the volcano, as well as seeping up through the surrounding ground, creating bubbling mud pits, hot springs, and fumaroles.

The volcanic mountain ranges divide the country's Pacific and Caribbean slopes and are responsible for the differences in climate between each side. Rain-laden trade winds blowing westward can't pass over these ranges without shedding their precipitation and rising. This creates Guanacaste's rain shadow: the dry plains and tropical dry forest that lie leeward, or west of the mountains. The mountains block the rain-producing weather system and cast a "shadow" of dryness.

Costa Rica's volcanic lakes occur when there is no natural drainage from a crater. The chemicals, minerals, and gasses from below the Earth's crust infuse the water and vibrantly color it. Irazú's lake is neon green; the baby-blue lagoon in Poás is extremely acidic and gives off toxic sulfur clouds and massive amounts of carbon dioxide.

The surface ecology of a volcano varies. Rincón de la Vieja is skirted by Guanacaste's signature grasslands and tropical dry forest. Poás Volcano is blanketed with rain forest and tipped with cloud forest. Some of the country's best coffee is grown on the slopes of Poás.

ADVENTURE HIGHLIGHTS

■ A hike through lush cloud forest will take you to the five magnificent waterfalls at La Paz Waterfall Gardens in Poás Volcano National Park.

■ Anglers love the guapote, tilapia, and machaca pulled from Lake Arenal.

■ The Arenal area is the jumping-off point for Class II–IV white-water rafting trips on the Blancas, Arenal, Toro, and San Carlos rivers.

■ Take the tough hike to La Fortuna Waterfall, near Arenal. Swimming under the waterfall is a slice of paradise.

FLORA

The habitat and ecology of these geologic giants is influenced mostly by their surrounding ecology zones and elevation. Conditions around the crater of an active volcano are intensely harsh but some tougher species do manage to survive.

Ferns

FERN

Contrary to popular stereotypes, ferns don't necessarily grow in shady, moist environments. The tongue fern (*Elaphoglossum lingua*) extends long, rubbery, tongue-shaped leaves and has evolved to grow around the lava rock and hardened ash. You'll find it around the top of the Poás Volcano. Farther down, you'll find other types of ferns adapted to friendlier conditions.

OAK

Forests in Costa Rica's higher mountain areas share some plant species with cloud forests. However, the plants here have adapted to live in cold temperatures and, if the volcano is active, in compacted ash. Surrounding the Botos Lagoon, on the south side of the principal Poás crater, is high-elevation cloud forest of oak (*Quercus costaricensis and Q. copeyensis*), small cedar (*Brunellia costaricensis*), and the flowering cyprus (*Escallonia poasana*)—trees that are typically crowded with epiphytes, bromeliads, and mosses.

Great Roble Oak

MYRTLE

Myrtle (*Myrtaceae*), and other low-lying shrubs survive this environment thanks to their slow growth rate. Myrtle, poor man's umbrella (*Gunnera insignis*), papelillo (*Senecio oerstedianus*), and other shrubs and ferns cover the higher bluffs around Irazu's crater. Mistletoe (*Psittacanthus*) can be found near the major volcanoes in the Central Valley. These flowering plants are interesting because they attach to trees by haustoria, a special structure that penetrates the host plant and absorbs its water and nutrients. When the mistletoe dies, it leaves a mark on the tree, a woodrose or *rosa de palo*.

Wild Balsam aka Touch-me-not Balsam

WILD BALSAM

Wild balsam, oak, and poor man's umbrella carpet the inactive cones around Rincón de la Vieja. Tropical dry forest species grow further down. Look for the guanacaste tree (*Enterolobium cyclocarpum*), Spanish cedar (*Cedrela odorata*), oak (*Q. oocarpa*), and the country's largest wild population of the guardia morada orchid, Costa Rica's national flower.

Myrtle

FAUNA

Like the flora around a volcano, the wildlife diversity of this region is dictated by the ecology around the mountain. Also, the more humans there are, the fewer animals you'll see.

PUMA

In the Barva region, pumas (also called mountain lions and cougars) and even jaguars still stalk the more remote forests, searching for the tapir or an unlucky spider monkey. The puma is an excellent climber and can jump to branches 5 meters (16 feet) off the ground, essentially giving monkeys nowhere to hide. Pumas have never been hunted for their pelts, but are suffering from habitat destruction. In Costa Rica, they are rarely found outside protected areas.

Puma

FIERY-THROATED HUMMINGBIRD

Birds are one of the most populous types of creature to live on the flanks of Poás and many more of Costa Rica's volcanoes. The fiery-throated hummingbird, the summer tanager, the sooty robin, and the emerald toucanet are among the 79 bird species that have been recorded at Poás. The fiery-throated hummingbird is recognizable by its forecrown, throat, and breast colors, as well as its bluish hump and blue-black tail.

North American Porcupine

NORTH AMERICAN PORCUPINE

The much drier region of Rincón de la Vieja has a distinctly different—and broader—set of animal inhabitants, including the North American porcupine and the agouti (a large, short-legged relative of the guinea pig). Pumas, ocelots, raccoons, and three species of monkeys (the howler, the white-faced capuchin, and the Central American spider monkey) are among the larger mammals. More than 300 bird species have been recorded there, including the collared aracari, the bare-necked umbrella bird, and the three-wattled bellbird.

Fiery-Throated Hummingbird

NINE-BANDED ARMADILLO

Irazú is home to smaller creatures such as the nine-banded armadillo, the eastern cottontail, and the little spotted cat. The nine-banded armadillo has a long snout and fantastic sense of smell. It can hold its breath for up to six minutes. This helps it keep dirt out of its nostrils while digging. Under stressful conditions, a female armadillo can prolong her pregnancy for up to three years by delaying the implantation of the fertilized egg into the uterus wall.

Nine-banded armadillo

EXPERIENCING THE VOLCANOES

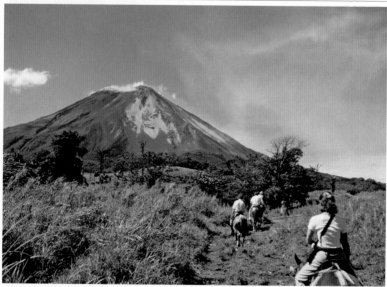

Horseback riding in Arenal

The Guatuso people believed that the fire god lived inside the Arenal Volcano . . . and in 1968, the gods were not happy. After 500 years of dormancy, Arenal erupted savagely, burying three small villages and killing 87 people. Today, thousands live at its base in the thriving town of La Fortuna, which is literally in Arenal's shadow.

HIKING

Volcano tourism is a major draw for international visitors, but given the dangers at the active sites, activities at the top are limited. There are no zip lines across open craters, and there's no snorkeling in acidic volcano lakes. At the peak, activities are limited to viewing, hiking, and photography. But the otherworldly look and feel of these sights is reason enough to visit. On rare clear nights at Arenal, you can see lava spewing and flowing down the side of the mountain.

STANDING IN AWE

Volcanic activity is not, however, limited to a volcano's peak. The underground heat that fuels these giants also results in hot springs, bubbling mud pits, and geysers, among other geological wonders. Minerals from the dormant Tenorio Volcano create a fascinating effect in one of the rivers running down its side, the Rio Celeste, giving it a baby-blue tint. Arenal's reflection can be seen in pools of water heated by the same underground lava spewing from its peak.

HORSEBACK RIDING

Many of Costa Rica's volcanoes are the centerpieces to broad national parks. Depending on the park, the infrastructure can be outstanding or nonexistent. Arenal and Poás have good horseback-riding trails and outfitters.

TOP DESTINATIONS

Costa Rica's volcanoes are often the centerpieces of large national parks.

ARENAL VOLCANO

At 1,680 meters (5,512 feet), Arenal Volcano, rising on the northwestern plains of San Carlos, is every bit an awesome sight. Tall and perfectly conical, its sides are scarred by a history of violent eruptions and textured by decades of flowing lava. Located at the northern end of the Tilarán Mountain Range, northwest of the capital, it is Costa Rica's best-known volcano, its most active, and one of the 10 most active volcanoes in the world. Unfortunately, Arenal's peak is often shrouded from sight because of the gasses and steam that escape from the crater. One scary bit of research concluded that Arenal has a 400-year cycle of major eruptions, and the activity since the 1968 explosion is small in comparison with what it's capable of. *(See Chapter 5.)*

RINCÓN DE LA VIEJA

A mass of slopes, craters, and biodiversity that bridges the continental divide, Rincón de la Vieja is in Costa Rica's arid northwest. It's not the classic conical volcano, but rather a ridge made of a series of craters that include bare, rocky bowls with brilliantly colored lakes, and velvety cones covered in rain forest. Scientists believe Rincón de la Vieja was

On the Road to Arenal; piper35w, Fodors.com member

born of simultaneous volcanic activity at nine different eruption points. The Rincón de la Vieja National Park covers nearly 35,000 acres and is a wonderland of volcanic activity that includes bubbling mud pits, hot springs, and geysers, as well as refreshing lagoons and spectacular waterfalls. *(See Chapter 6.)*

POÁS VOLCANO

Poás Volcano is Costa Rica's most visited national park, in part because it is the closest active volcano to the capital of San José and the Aeropuerto Internacional Juan Santamaría. Located in the Cordillera Volcánica Central Mountain Range, Poás is topped by three craters, the tallest reaching 2,708 meters (8,885 feet) above sea level. Only the main cone has shown any volcanic eruptions in the last 200 years. You can get a good look at the crater from the viewing deck. *(See Chapter 5.)*

Note: A 6.2 earthquake struck only 10 km (6 mi) from Poás in January 2009, destroying two nearby villages and killing 23 people (at this writing, 7 people had still not been found). However, seismologists and geologists assured the public that it was not related to any volcanic activity at Poás.

Gaudy Leaf Frog; Marco13, Fodors.com member.

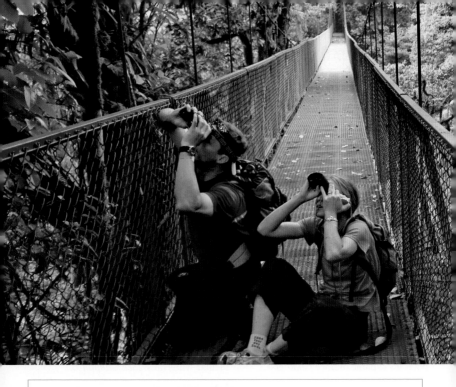

CLOUD FOREST

The four mountain ranges that make up Costa Rica's own piece of the continental divide split the country into its Caribbean and Pacific regions. At these higher altitudes, temperatures cool, clouds settle, and rainfall increases. The forests found here are shrouded in mist and rich in biodiversity. Welcome to Costa Rica's famed cloud forests.

Like its lowland rain forest cousins, cloud forests are packed with plant and animal species, thanks largely to their water-drenched conditions. There's an average of 5 meters (16 feet) of rainfall a year, but that number doubles when you factor in the amount of moisture gleaned from the clouds and fog that drift through every day. Like rain forests, giant hardwoods reaching as high as almost 60 meters (200 feet) set the ceiling for this ecology zone, while a variety of smaller trees, ferns, shrubs, and other plants fill the understories. Epiphytes flourish here, as do mosses, lichens, and liverwort. These plants cling to passing moisture and capture it like sponges. As a result, cloud forests are constantly soaking wet even when there is no rain.

Because conditions in a cloud forest can be harsh, many of the tougher and more adaptable rain forest species make their home here. The relentless, heavy cloud cover can block sunlight even from the highest reaches of the forest, and deeper inside, light is rare. Photosynthesis and growth is slower, so the plants tend to be smaller with thicker trunks and stems. These unique conditions also produce an unusually high number of endemic and rare species.

The Monteverde Cloud Forest Preserve, one of the world's most famous protected cloud forests, shelters innumerable life-forms. There are more than 100 mammal species; 400 bird species, including at least 30 species of hummingbird; 500 plus species of butterfly; and more than 2,500 plant species, including 420 types of orchids. There are only a handful of protected cloud forests here and worldwide and this type of ecozone is increasingly threatened by human encroachment.

ADVENTURE HIGHLIGHTS

■ Leave the car at home and travel on horseback to or from the Arenal Volcano area and Monteverde Cloud Forest. Contact Desafío Adventures, the only guides we recommend for this journey.

■ Expert birder Marino Chacón of the Savage Hotel will give you an education on one of his daylong natural history hikes around San Gerardo de Dota cloud forest.

■ Selvatura, right next to Monteverde, is the only canopy tour in the area with a zip line built entirely inside the cloud forest.

FLORA

A typical hectare (2½ acres) of rain forest might be home to nearly 100 species of trees. Contrast that with a mere 30 in the richest forests of North America.

ROBLE TREE

Majestic roble, or oak—principally the white oak (Quercus copeyensis) and black oak (*Quercus costarricensis*)—is the dominant tree of Costa Rica's cloud forests and grows to 60 meters (200 feet). The deciduous hardwood *cedro dulce*, or Spanish cedar (*Cedrela tonduzii*), is also a giant at 40 meters (147 feet). These two are joined by evergreens like the *jaúl*, or alder, and the *aguacatillo*, a name meaning "little avocado" that's given to a variety of trees from the *lauracea* family.

White Oak Tree

POOR MAN'S UMBRELLA

If you're caught in the rain, take cover under a poor man's umbrella (*Gunnera insignis* and *Gunnera talamancana*), whose broad and sturdy leaves sometimes grow large enough to shelter an entire family. These shrubby plants love the dark, moist interior of the cloud forest.

Poor Man's Umbrella

EPIPHYTES

Epiphytes thrive in cloud and rain forests, thanks to all the moisture and nutrients in the air. The *stanhopea* orchid is interesting because of its clever pollination tricks. The blossoms' sweet smell attracts bees, but the flower's waxy surface is slippery so they slide down inside. As they slowly work their way out, they brush up against the flower's column and collect pollen. This pollen is then transferred to the sticky stigma of other flowers.

Bromeliads, another family of flowering plants, competes with epiphytes for space on the branches and trunks of the forest's trees. The spiraling leaves form catches for water, falling plant material, and insect excretion. These are mineral-rich little ponds for insects and amphibians, and drinking and bathing water for birds and other animals.

Epiphyte Stanhopea

STAR ORCHID

The star orchid (*Epidendrum radicans*) is one of the few orchids that is not an epiphyte. It mimics in color and shape other nectar-filled flowers in order to attract butterflies who unwittingly become pollinators.

Star Orchid

FAUNA

The resplendent quetzal, the blue-crowned motmot, the orange-bellied trogon, and the emerald toucanet are just some of the hundreds of species that can be logged in a cloud forest.

GLASS FROGS

One of the more bizarre amphibians is the transparent glass frog of the *Centrolenellu* genus, whose internal organs can be seen through its skin. It lives in trees and bushes and can often be heard at night near the rivers and streams. Cloud forests have fewer amphibian species than rain forests, but amphibian populations worldwide have plummeted in recent decades. No one knows the cause yet. Some blame acid rain and pesticides; others believe it is yet another sign of coming ecological disaster.

Glass Frogs

RESPLENDENT QUETZAL

Perhaps the most famed resident of Costa Rica's cloud forests is the illustrious resplendent quetzal. Every year, bird-watchers come to Costa Rica hoping to spot the green, red, and turquoise plumage of this elusive trogon. Considered a sacred creature by the Maya and the namesake of Guatemala's currency, the quetzal spends much of its time perched in its favorite tree, the *aguacatillo*.

Resplendent Quetzal

COLLARED TROGON

The collared trogon and the orange-bellied trogon are in the same family as the quetzel. They all share square black-and-white tail plumage and bright orange or yellow chest feathers. The collared trogon perches very quietly and is easy to miss. Luckily, it doesn't fly far, so its flight is easy to follow.

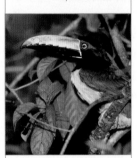
Collared Aracari

HOWLER MONKEYS

One of the largest New World monkeys, howlers are named for their loud, barking roar that can be heard for miles. If you want to spot a howler, be sure to scan the treetops; their diet consists mainly of canopy leaves, and they rarely leave the protection of the trees. Other cloud forest mammals include the white-faced capuchin monkey, white-nosed coatis, porcupines, red brocket deer, and Alston's singing mouse.

Collared Trogon

EXPERIENCING A CLOUD FOREST

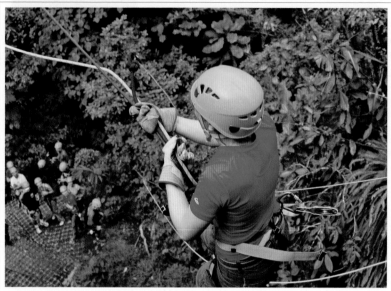

Zipline tour in Selvature just outside of Monteverde Cloud Forest

You may need to get down and dirty—well, more like wet and muddy—to experience a cloud forest's natural wonders, but then, that's half the fun.

HIKING

Well-guided hikes through this eerie landscape make it easier to spot the less obvious features of this complex ecosystem. Compared with the barren tropical dry forest, and colorful rain forest, cloud forests don't easily offer up their secrets. Binoculars and a good guide will go a long way toward making your hike and wildlife-spotting richer experiences.

BIRD-WATCHING

Bird-watching is rewarding in the cloud forest, where some of the most vibrant and peculiar of nature's winged creatures can be found. Rise early, enjoy some locally grown coffee, and check the aguacatillo trees for quetzals. If you opt to go without a guide, bring along waterproof binoculars and a good guidebook (we recommend *The Birds of Costa Rica*, by Richard Garrigues and Robert Dean) for spotting and identifying birds.

CANOPY TOURS

Canopy tours and suspended bridges run right through the upper reaches of the cloud forest—an ecosystem in its own right. Spot birds, monkeys, and exotic orchids from a viewpoint that was once nearly impossible to reach. Get even closer to butterflies, amphibians, snakes, and insects at various exhibits in the parks' research centers.

FISHING

If freshwater fishing in spectacular surroundings is right up your alley, check out the Savegre River, in the San Gerardo de Dota Valley. It's been stocked with wild rainbow trout since the 1950s.

TOP DESTINATIONS

Regardless of which cloud forest you visit, bring a raincoat and go with a guide if you want to see wildlife. You'll marvel at their ability to spot a sloth at a hundred paces.

MONTEVERDE CLOUD FOREST BIOLOGICAL RESERVE

Costa Rica's most famous cloud forest reserve is packed with an astonishing variety of life: 2,500 plant species, 400 species of birds, 500 types of butterflies, and more than 100 different mammals have been catalogued so far. The reserve reaches 1,535 meters (5,032 feet) above sea level, spans the Tilarán Mountain Range, and encompasses 9,885 acres of cloud forest and rain forest. There are 13 km (8 mi) of well-marked trails, zip-line tours, and suspended bridges for canopy viewing, bird tours, guided night walks, and a field research station with an amphibian aquarium. Allow a generous slice of time for leisurely hiking; longer hikes are made possible by some strategically placed overnight refuges along the way. *(See Chapter 5.)*

SAN GERARDO DE DOTA

One of Costa Rica's premier nature destinations, San Gerardo de Dota is a damp, epiphyte-laden forest of giant oak trees and an astonishing number of resplendent quetzals. Outdoor enthusiasts may

Banded Anteater; maddytem, Fodors.com member

never want to leave these parts—some of the country's best hiking is in this valley, and it's popular with bird-watchers. It's also great for horseback riding and trout fly-fishing. *(See Chapter 8.)*

BRAULIO CARRILLO NATIONAL PARK

Descending from the Cordillera Volcánica Central Mountain Range, the Braulio Carrillo National Park is an awesome, intimidating, and rugged landscape of dense cloud forest that stretches toward the rain forests of the Caribbean lowlands. The enormous park encompasses 117,580 acres of untamed jungle and is less than an hour's drive from San José. The country's principal east-bound highway cuts a path straight through it. Elusive (and endangered) jaguars and pumas are among the many animal species here, and scenic viewpoints are plentiful along the highway. A handful of trails, including the Los Niños Circular Trail and the Los Guarumos Trail, can be taken into the park's interior. *(See Chapter 5.)*

Braulio Carrillo National Park

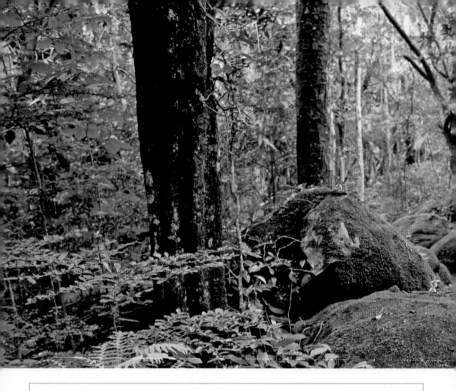

TROPICAL DRY FOREST

The most endangered biome in the world, these seasonal forests swing between two climate extremes—from drenching wet to bone dry. To survive, plants undergo a drastic physical transformation: forests burst into life during the rainy months, and are brown, leafless, and seemingly dead during the dry season.

WORD OF MOUTH

"I wouldn't be too concerned about that heat BECAUSE it is so dry…no humidity to speak of which can make things comfortable when you're in the shade. I've always visited Guanacaste in or around February and prefer it for that reason."

—joeschmo

For about half the year, northwestern Costa Rica is as wet as the rest of the country. The weather blows in from the Pacific and it can rain every day. During the dry season, from January to April, weather patterns change, winds shift, and the land becomes parched.

Tall deciduous hardwoods are the giants in this ecology zone, with spindly branches creating a seasonal canopy as high as 30 meters (100 feet). A thorny and rambling understory of smaller trees and bushes thrives thanks to the plentiful light permitted once the canopy falls to the forest floor. The challenges of the dry months have forced plants to specialize. The hardwoods are solitary and diffuse, their seeds spread far and wide by animals and insects. Some even flower progressively through the dry season, depending on the plant species and the particular bees and birds that have evolved to pollinate them.

Dry season is perfect for bird- and animal-watching since the lack of foliage makes wildlife-spotting easy. Keep your eyes peeled for monkeys, parrots, lizards, coyotes, rabbits, snakes, and even jaguars.

There was once one great uninterrupted swath of dry forest that began in southern Mexico, rolled across Mesoamerica, and ended in northwest Costa Rica. Today, less than 2% of the Central American tropical dry forest remains, the majority of it in Costa Rica. But even here, the forest is fractured into biologically isolated islands, thanks to decades of logging and agriculture. The Guanacaste parks system has managed to corral off large chunks of land for preservation, and private and government efforts are under way to create biological corridors between isolated dry forests so that animals and plants can roam farther and deepen their gene pools, so critical to their survival.

ADVENTURE HIGHLIGHTS

■ Adrenalin-spiked tours with Hacienda Guachipelín (just outside of Rincón de la Vieja National Park) include river tubing, rappelling, zip lines, and a tarzan swing. Let the knowledgeable folks from the Organization for Tropical Studies (OTS) take you on a guided bird-watching tour through Palo Verde National Park. Boat rides float you past hundreds of waterfowl.

■ Take the kids on a bird- and monkey-watching journey down the Río Corobicí, in Palo Verde National Park.

FLORA

Among other types of flora, tropical forests are filled with deciduous hardwoods, such as mahogany (*Swietenia macrophylla*), black laurel (*Cordia gerascanthus*), ronrón (*Astronium graveolens*), and cocobolo (*Dalbergia retusa*). Much of the wood is highly prized, so many of these trees are facing extinction outside national parks and protected areas.

Guanacaste

GUANACASTE

Perhaps the most striking and easy-to-spot resident of Costa Rica's tropical dry forest is the guanacaste (*Enterolobium cyclocarpum*), an imposing tree with an enormous, spherical canopy that seems straight out of the African savanna. The guanacaste is the northwest province's namesake and Costa Rica's national tree. It's most easily identified standing alone in pastures. Without the competition of the forest, a pasture guanacaste sends massive branches out low from its trunk, creating an arching crown of foliage close to the ground. The ear-shaped seedpods are also a distinct marker; the hard seeds inside are popular with local artisan jewelers.

Frangipani; plumboy, Fodors.com member

FRANGIPANI TREE

The frangipani tree (*Plumeria rubra*) can grow up to 8 meters (26 feet) and has meaty pink, white, or yellow blossoms. The flowers are most fragrant at night to lure sphinx moths. Unfortunately for the moth, the blooms don't produce nectar. The plant simply dupes their pollinators into hopping from bloom to bloom and tree to tree in a fruitless search for food.

GUMBO-LIMBO

Costa Ricans call the gumbo-limbo tree (*Bursera simaruba*) *indio desnudo* (naked Indian) because of its red, peeling bark. This tree is also found in Florida, and the wood has historically been used for making carousel horses in the United States.

Gumbo-limbo

CORNIZUELO

The spiky, cornizuelo (*Acacia collinsii*) is an intriguing resident of the lower levels because of its symbiotic relationship with ants. This small evergreen tree puts out large thorns that serve as a home for a certain ant species. In exchange for food and shelter, the ants provide the tree protection from other leaf-munching insects or vines. Sometimes the ants will even cut down encroaching vegetation on the forest floor, allowing the tree to thrive.

Cornizuelo

FAUNA

Tropical forests are literally crawling with life. Bark scorpions, giant cockroaches, and tarantulas scuttle along the forest floor, and the buzz from wasps and cicadas gives the air an almost electric feel. A careful eye may be able to pick out walking sticks frozen still among the twigs. The jaguar, and one if its favorite prey, the endangered tapir, also stalk these forests.

White-faced capuchin

WHITE-FACED CAPUCHIN
Monkeys are common all over Costa Rica, and the dry forests are home to three species: the howler monkeys, with their leathery black faces and deep barking call, are the loudest of the forest's mammals; the white-faced capuchin travel in playful packs; and the endangered spider monkey require large, undisturbed tracts of forest for a healthy population to survive. This last group is in steep decline—another indicator of the overall health of this ecoregion.

COYOTE
Nearly unique to the dry tropical forest is the coyote, which feeds on rodents, lizards, and an assortment of small mammals, as well as sea turtle eggs (when near the beach) and other improvised meals. Like the Virginia opossum and the white-tailed deer, the coyote is believed to have traveled south from North America through the once-interconnected tropical dry forest of Mesoamerica.

Coyote

NEOTROPICAL RATTLESNAKE
The venomous neotropical rattlesnake and the exquisite painted wood turtle are among the reptiles that exclusively call this region home. Salvin's spiny pocket mouse, the eastern cottontail rabbit, and both the spotted and hooded skunk are also unique to Costa Rica's dry forests.

BLACK-HEADED TROGON
With an open canopy for much of the year, and plentiful ground rodents and reptiles, these forests are great hunting grounds for birds of prey like the roadside hawk and the spectacled owl. The white-throated magpie jay travels in noisy mobs, while the scissor-tailed flycatcher migrates from as far north as the southern United States. The rufous-naped wren builds its nest in the spiky acacia trees. The black-headed trogon, with its bright yellow breast, and the elegant trogon both nest exclusively in Costa Rica's tropical dry forest.

Black-headed Trogon

Neotropical Rattlesnake

EXPERIENCING A DRY TROPICAL FOREST

Rincón de la Vieja National Park

Many of Costa Rica's roads are rough at best, and tropical forests are often remote. We recommend hiring a 4WD for getting around.

HIKING

The absolute best way to experience these endangered woods is to strap on your hiking boots, grab a hat and lots of water, and get out and walk. Most of the dry forests are protected lands and found in Guanacaste's national parks. Some have road access, making it possible to drive through the park, but most are accessible only by hiking trails. During the rainy season, roads become mud pits and hiking trails are almost impassable, so it's best to visit during the dry season.

BIRD- AND WILDLIFEWATCHING

Most people come to these areas for bird-watching and wildlifespotting, but it's best done during the dry season, when all the foliage drops from the trees.

Bring a good bird or wildlife guide, binoculars, lots of water (we can't stress this enough), and plenty of patience. It's a good idea to find a watering hole and just hunker down and let the animals come to you. If you don't want to explore the forest alone, tours can be arranged through hotels, ranger stations, and private research centers inside the parks. In terms of bird and wildlife guides, we recommend *The Birds of Costa Rica* by Richard Garrigues and Robert Dean and *The Mammals of Costa Rica* by Mark Wainwright. If you'd like to know more about plants, pick up *Tropical Plants of Costa Rica* by Willow Zuchowski.

BIKING

Some parks allow biking, but again, this is certainly something you don't want to do during the rains. Contact the park that you'll be visiting ahead of time for trail and rental information.

TOP DESTINATIONS

Most of Costa Rica's remaining tropical dry forests are located in the northwest of the country, not too far from the Nicaragua border.

SANTA ROSA NATIONAL PARK

The largest piece of tropical dry forest under government protection in Central America spreads out over Santa Rosa National Park, about 35 km (22 mi) north of Guanacaste's capital, Liberia. The park, which covers 380 square km (146 square mi), also includes two beaches and coastal mangrove forest. Thanks to trails and equipped campsites, you can venture deep into the park. During the dry season, visibility is excellent and chances are good in terms of spotting some of the hundreds of bird and animal species there. Playa Nancite, Santa Rosa's northern beach, is also one of the world's most important and most protected beaches for the nesting of olive ridley sea turtles. They come ashore by the hundreds of thousands between May and October (during the rainy season when access to the beaches are difficult) in a phenomenon called the *arribada. (See Chapter 6.)*

GUANACASTE NATIONAL PARK

Santa Rosa bumps up against Guanacaste National Park, which is composed of some tropical dry forest and former farmland that's being regenerated to its

Hummingbird Nesting; reedjoella, Fodors.com member

natural state. The park is intended to serve as a much-needed biological corridor from Santa Rosa up to the cloud forests of the Orosi and Cacao volcanoes, to the east. Park infrastructure is generally lacking, though three biological stations offer some accommodations. *(See Chapter 6.)*

RINCÓN DE LA VIEJA NATIONAL PARK

More tropical dry forest can be found inside the Rincón de la Vieja National Park, ringing the base of the two volcanoes of this protected area—Santa María and Rincón de la Vieja. *(See Chapter 6.)*

PALO VERDE NATIONAL PARK

Farther south, Palo Verde National Park skirts the northeastern side of the Río Tempisque, straddling some of the country's most spectacular wetlands and tropical dry forest. Thanks to these two very different ecology zones, Palo Verde is packed with very diverse bird, plant, and animal species—bird-watchers love this park. The Organization for Tropical Studies has a biological station at Palo Verde and offers tours and accommodations. Park guards also maintain a ranger station with rustic overnight accommodations. *(See Chapter 6.)*

Canopy Tour at Rincón de la Vieja National Park

WETLANDS & MANGROVES

Wetlands are any low-lying areas that are perpetually saturated with water. Their complex ecosystems support a variety of living things—both endemic species unique to the area and visitors who travel half-way around the hemisphere to get here. Here, land species have evolved to live much of their lives in water.

One of the more common types of wetlands in Costa Rica is a floodplain, created when a river or stream regularly overflows its banks, either because of heavy rains or incoming ocean tides. Thanks to huge deposits of sediment that are left as the floodwaters recede, the ground is extremely fertile and plants thrive, as do the animals that feed here.

Mangroves are a particularly unique type of wetland and cover 1% of the country. They are found at the edges of tidal areas, such as ocean inlets, estuaries, and canals where saltwater mixes with fresh. Mangrove forests are made up of a small variety of plants, principally mangrove trees, but attract a huge variety of animals.

Mangrove trees are able to survive in this stressful habitat because they have developed the ability to cope with constant flooding, tolerate a lack of oxygen, and thrive in a mix of salt and freshwater thanks to uniquely adapted roots and leaves. The nutrient-rich sediment and mud that build up around these trees and between their prop roots create habitat for plankton, algae, crabs, oysters, and shrimp. These, in turn, attract larger and larger animals that come to feed, giving mangrove forests a remarkable level of biodiversity.

These thick coastal forests are protective barriers for inland ecosystems; they dissipate the force of storm winds and sudden surges in tides or floods triggered by coastal storms or tsunamis.

Sadly, coastal development is a big threat to mangroves. It is illegal to clear mangrove forests, but enforcement is weak, and builders of marinas, docks, and beachfront developments have been caught doing it. Wetlands are also threatened by the human encroachment and the diversion of water for agricultural use.

ADVENTURE HIGHLIGHTS

■ Witness the awesome spectacle of nesting turtles at Tortuguero National Park. Turtle-watching excursions require a certified guide and only take place between the February and November nesting season.

■ Anglers can hook mackerel, tarpoon, snook, calba, and snapper in the canals and along the coast of Tortuguero and Barra Colorado.

■ Take a mellow kayaking tour through the mangrove estuary of Isla Damas, near Manuel Antonio. You'll probably see monkeys, crocodiles, and any number of birds.

FLORA

Wetland and mangrove plants share an ability to live in soggy conditions. However, not all wetland plants are able to survive brackish water in the way coastal mangrove flora can.

Water Hyacinth

WATER HYACINTH

The succulent, floating water hyacinth (*Eichornia crassipes*) is recognizable by its lavender-pink flowers that are sometimes bundled at 8 to 15 per single stalk. The stems rise from a bed of thick, floating green leaves, whereas the plant's feathery roots hang free in the still freshwater. The water hyacinth is prolific and invasive; they've even been known to clog the canals of Tortuguero.

THORNY SENSITIVE PLANT

Aquatic grasses and herbs grow along the shallower edges of swamps and marshlands where they can take root underwater and still reach the air above. The curious dormilona, or thorny sensitive plant (*Mimosa pigra*) is another invasive wetland shrub and can be identified by the way its fernlike leaves wilt shyly to the touch, only to straighten out a little later.

Thorny sensitive plant

RED MANGROVE

Costa Rica has seven species of mangrove trees, including red mangrove (*Rhizophora mangle*), black mangrove (*Avicennia germinans*), the white mangrove (*Laguncularia racemosa*), and the more rare tea mangrove (*Pelliciera rhizophorae*). Red mangrove is easily identified by its tall arching prop roots that give it a firm foothold against wind and waves. The tidal land is also unstable, so all mangroves need a lot of root just to keep upright. As a result, many have more living matter underwater than above ground. They also depend on their prop roots for extra nutrients and oxygen; the red mangrove filters salt at its roots.

Red Mangrove

BLACK MANGROVE

The black mangrove can grow as tall as 12 meters (40 feet) and has adapted to survive in its habitat by excreting salt through special glands in its leaves. It grows on the banks above the high-tide line and has evolved to breathe through small roots it sends up vertically in case of flooding.

Black Mangrove

FAUNA

Though the diversity of plant life in mangrove swamps and wetlands is small compared with other ecozones, this habitat attracts an extremely wide variety of fauna.

RAINBOW PARROTFISH

Rainbow parrotfish, in addition to many other fish species, spend time as juveniles in mangrove areas, feeding in the relative safety of the roots until they're big enough to venture out into more open water. Parrotfish have a few unusual abilities: they are hermaphroditic and can change sex in response to population density; at night they wrap themselves in a protective mucus cocoon; and they eat coral and excrete a fine white sand. One parrotfish can create a ton of sand per year, which ultimately washes ashore. Think about it the next time you're lying on the beach.

Rainbow Parrotfish

CRAB-EATING RACCOON

Bigger creatures are attracted to these mangroves precisely because of the veritable buffet of sea snacks. The crab-eating raccoon will prowl the canopy of the mangrove forests as well as the floor, feeding on crabs and mollusks. The endangered American crocodile and the spectacled caiman can be found listing through waters or sunning themselves on the banks of mangrove habitat.

Crab-eating Raccoon

BLACK-CROWNED NIGHT HERON

Mangroves are critical nesting habitats for a number of birds, including the endangered mangrove hummingbird, the yellow-billed continga, the Amazon kingfisher, and the black-crowned night heron. Interestingly, black-crowned night herons don't distinguish between their own young and those from other nests, so they willingly brood strange chicks.

BLACK-BELLIED WHISTLING DUCK

Bird-watchers love the wide-open wetlands and marshes, with flocks of thousands of migrating and resident species. In these tropical floodplains pink-tinged roseate spoonbills will be found stalking the shallow water alongside the majestic great egret and the bizarre and endangered jabiru stork. Keep an eye out for the black-bellied whistling duck, which actually perches and nests in trees. These migrant ducks can also be found in some southern U.S. states.

Black Crowned Night Heron

Black-Bellied Whistling Duck

EXPERIENCING THE WETLANDS & MANGROVES

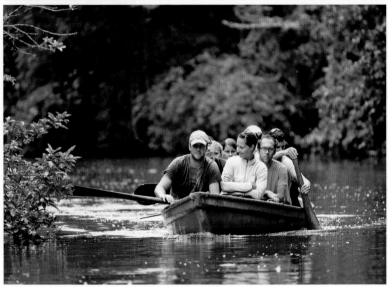

Paddling through Tortuguero at dawn; Thornton Cohen, Fodors.com member

Wildlife viewing in general can be very rewarding in these areas, because a wide variety of creatures come together and share the habitat.

BIRD-WATCHING

The most populous and diverse of the creatures that live in and depend on wetlands and mangroves are birds, so bring some binoculars and your field guide and prepare to check off some species. For good photos, take a long lens and tripod, and get an early start—midday sun reflecting off the ubiquitous water can make your photos washed out or create some challenging reflections.

VIEWING PLATFORMS

Hiking can be more difficult in these areas because wetlands are by definition largely underwater. But some areas have elevated platforms that make for great up-close viewing of the interior parts of marshes and shallow lagoons.

BOATING

The best way to see Costa Rica's remaining mangrove forests is by boat—we recommend using a kayak or canoe. These vessels allow you to slip along canals and protected coastlines in near silence, increasing your chance of creeping up on many of the more impressive creatures that call this habitat home. A guided boat tour is also recommended—a good naturalist or biologist, or even a knowledgeable local, will know where creatures habitually hang out and will be able to distinguish between thick branches and a knotted boa at the top of a shore-side tree.

FISHING

Canals that are not part of protected areas can be ripe for fishing—another, tastier way to get a close-up look at some of the local fauna. Make sure to ask about what's biting, as well as local fishing regulations.

TOP DESTINATIONS

The Ramsar Convention on Wetlands is an intergovernmental treaty to provide a framework for the conservation of the world's wetlands. There are 11 Ramsar wetlands in Costa Rica: all are impressive but we've listed only our top three.

PALO VERDE NATIONAL PARK

Within the Palo Verde National Park is perhaps Costa Rica's best-known wetland—a system that includes shallow, permanent freshwater lagoons, marshes, mangroves, and woodlands that are seasonally flooded by the Tempisque River. A good portion of this 45,511-acre park is covered by tropical dry forest, as mentioned earlier. In fact, this park has 12 different habitats, creating one of the most diverse collections of life in the country. At least 55 aquatic plants and 150 tree species have been identified here, and the largest number of aquatic and wading birds in all of Mesoamerica can be found at Palo Verde wetlands. A total of 279 bird species have been recorded within the Palo Verde, so little surprise that it's listed by the Ramsar Convention as a wetland of international importance. The Organization of Tropical Studies maintains a research station at the park with limited accommodations but great views of the marshes, as well as extremely knowledgeable guides. *(See Chapter 6.)*

Alpha Howler Monkey; Liz Stuart, Fodors.com member

TORTUGUERO NATIONAL PARK

Ninety-nine percent of mangrove forests are found on Costa Rica's Pacific coast. But the best place to see some of the remaining 1% on the Caribbean side is Tortuguero National Park. Like Palo Verde, Tortuguero is home to a wide variety of life—11 distinct habitats in total, including extensive wetlands and mangrove forests. Beach-nesting turtles (*tortugas*) are the main attraction here, but the park is included in the Ramsar list of internationally important wetlands. Many of the species listed above can be spotted along the banks of Tortuguero's famous canals. *(See Chapter 6.)*

CAÑO NEGRO NATIONAL WILDLIFE REFUGE

A third Ramsar wetland is found in the Caño Negro National Wildlife Refuge, in the more remote northern plains close to the border with Nicaragua. Caño Negro has a seasonal lake that can cover as many as 1,975 acres and grow as deep as 3 meters (10 feet). The lake is actually a pool created by the Frio River that dries up to nearly nothing between February and May. The park also has marshes, semipermanently flooded old-growth forest, and other wetland habitats. *(See Chapter 5.)*

Tortuguero; StupFD, Fodors.com member

SHORELINE

Costa Rica has a whopping 1,290-km-long (799-mi-long) coastline that varies from expansive beaches, tranquil bays, muddy estuaries, and rocky outcroppings. They're backed by mangrove, rain, transitional, and tropical dry forests.

WORD OF MOUTH

"If you only have time for a quick, affordable little beach getaway, Flamingo Beach could be just what you are looking for. The sunsets in this area really are fantastic."

—Linda137

Each of Costa Rica's costal environments, as well as the currents and the wind, has it's own distinct impact on the ecology of the beach.

Costa Rica's sand beaches come in different shades and textures: pulverized black volcanic rock (Playa Negra), crushed white shells (Playa Conchal), finely ground white coral and quartz (Playa Carrillo), and gray rock sediment (many stretches along both coasts). These strips of sand may seem devoid of life, they're actually ecological hotbeds, where mammals, birds, and amphibians, live, feed, or reproduce. The hardiest of creatures can be found in the tidal pools that form on rockier beaches; keep an eye out for colorful fish, starfish, and sea urchins, all of which endure pounding waves, powerful tides, broiling sun, and predator attacks from the air, land, or sea.

By law, all of Costa Rica's beaches are public, but beaches near population centers get strewn with trash quite quickly. It's one of the great ironies of Costa Rica that a country renowned for its environmental achievements litters with such laissez-faire. Limited access tends to make for more scenic beaches. If you're worried about pollution, keep an eye out for Blue Flag beaches (marked on our maps with blue flags), an ecological rating system that evaluates water quality—both ocean and drinking water—trash cleanup, waste management, security, signage, and environmental education. Blue flags are awarded to communities, rather than to individual hotels, which feeds a sense of cooperation. In 2002, the competition was opened to inland communities. Out of 120 that applied, 88 communities—58 beaches and 30 inland towns—won flags at the 2009 ceremonies.

ADVENTURE HIGHLIGHTS

■ From October 15 to February 15, Playa Grande sees throngs of leatherback turtles come ashore to nest. Sixty days later, the hatchlings will scramble toward the water.

■ Gentle, consistent waves and lots of good surfing schools makes Samara, on the northern Pacific coast, a good choice for first-timers hoping to catch a wave.

■ Snorkeling is phenomenal near Cahuita's coral reef on the Caribbean coast. Watch out for colorful blue parrot fish, angelfish, sponges, and seaweeds.

FLORA

The plants along the coast play an important role in maintaining the dunes and preventing erosion in the face of heavy winds and other forces.

COCONUT PALMS

Coconut palm trees are the most distinctive plants in any tropical setting. No postcard photo of a white-sand beach would be complete without at least one palm tilting precariously over the shore. Palm trees (from the Arecaceae family) require a lot of sunlight and will, thanks to their strong root system, often grow at nearly horizontal angles to escape the shade of beachside forests. The coconut palm is also the proud parent of the world's largest seed—the delicious coconut—which can float long distances across the ocean, washing up on a foreign shore and sprouting a new tree from the sand.

Coconut Palms

MANZANILLO DE PLAYA

Steer clear of the poisonous manchineel, or *manzanillo de playa* (*Hippomane mancinella*), the most toxic tree in Costa Rica. Its fruit and bark secrete a white latex that's highly irritable to the touch and poisonous—even fatal—if ingested. Don't burn it either because the smoke can also cause allergic reactions. The tree can be identified by its small, yellowish apples and bright green leaves. It's found along the northern Pacific coast, stretches of the Nicoya Peninsula, the Central Pacific's Manuel Antonio National Park, and on the Osa Peninsula.

Manzaniillo de playa

SEAGRAPE

Seagrape (*Coccoloba uvifera*) and similar types of shrubby, ground-hugging vegetation grow closer to the water, around the edges of the beach. These plants play a part in keeping the beach stable and preventing erosion.

Seagrape

MANGROVE

Mangrove swamps are rich, murky forests that thrive in brackish waters up and down Costa Rica's coasts. They grow in what's known as the intertidal zone, the part of the coast that's above sea level at low tide and submerged at high tide. Mangrove trees (*rhizophora*) are just one of the species that live in these coastal swamps—you can recognize them by their stilt-roots, the long tendril-like roots that allow the tree to breathe even when it's partially submerged. These forests are vibrant and complex ecosystems in their own right *and were explained earlier in this chapter*.

Mangrove tree

FAUNA

Beaches are tough environments where few animals actually make their home. But as we all know, you don't have to live on the beach to enjoy it.

OLIVE RIDLEY TURTLE

At 34 to 45 kilos (75 to 100 lbs) the olive ridley (*Lepidochelys olivacea*) is the smallest of the five marine turtles that nest in Costa Rica. During mass nesting times (*arribada*), anywhere from tens to hundreds of thousands of females drag themselves ashore, gasping audibly, to lay their eggs. Between dusk and dawn, the prehistoric creatures crawl over the beach, sometimes even over one another, on their way between the ocean and their nests. People who are lucky enough to witness the event never forget it. Costa Rica's shores are also visited by the green turtle, the hawksbill, the loggerhead, and the leatherback turtle.

Olive Ridley Turtle

IGUANAS

A common sight on Costa Rica's sandy shores are iguanas. The green iguana (*Iguana iguana*) and the black spiny-tailed iguana, or black iguana (*Ctenosaura simi*), are often found sunning themselves on rocks or a few feet from the shade (and protection) of trees. Interestingly, green iguana has been known to lay eggs and share nests with American crocodiles and spectacled caimans.

Iguanas

PAINTED GHOST CRAB

These intriguingly named crabs are called "ghosts" because they move so quickly that they seem to disappear. They're also one of the few creatures that actually live full-time on the beach. Sun beats down, wind is strong, danger lurks everywhere, and there's little to no cover, but painted ghost crabs (*Ocypode cuadrata*) survive all this by burrowing deep under the sand where the temperature and humidity is more constant and there's safe protection from surface threats, like the black iguana.

Painted Ghost Crab

BROWN PELICAN

Brown pelicans fly in tight formation, dropping low over the sea and running parallel with the swells in search of shoals of fish. Browns are unique in that they're the only pelican species that plunge from the air to catch their food. After a successful dive, they have to guard against gulls, who will actually try to pluck the freshly caught fish from their pouch.

Brown Pelican

EXPERIENCING THE SHORELINE

Nesting Olive Ridley Turtles at Ostional Wildlife Refuge

Costa Rica's beaches have tons of activities. If you like getting wet, the ocean is bathwater warm and there are watersports outfitters just about everywhere. There are also plenty of hammocks and cafés.

HORSEBACK RIDING

Horseback riding on the beach is great fun, but you can't do it everywhere. Many of the most popular beaches have outlawed it for health reasons, especially if it's where a lot of people swim.

SURFING

Costa Rica is a world-class surfing destination, and the Pacific coast in particular has enough surf spots to satisfy both pros and novices. You can arrange lessons in most beach towns. Surfing is an activity that involves a lot of floating, so it allows for plenty of wildlife-watching: keep a weather eye for jumping fish, sting rays, dolphins, and squads of brown pelicans.

TURTLE TOURS

Witnessing the nesting ritual of Costa Rica's visiting sea turtles is a truly unforgettable experience. Various organizations oversee the nesting beaches and arrange tours. The onslaught of mother turtles is most intense throughout the night, so setting out just before dawn is the best way to see and take pictures of the phenomenon in progress at first light.

⚠Take great care at beaches that drop off steeply as you enter the water. This is an indicator not only of large waves that crash straight onto the shore but also of strong currents.

TOP DESTINATIONS

Differences in the look of the sand, the quality of the waves, and the beauty of the backdrop all affect your beach experience. Costa Rica's beach scenes are wildly diverse, so a little planning can go a long way.

BALLENA NATIONAL MARINE PARK

This unique park is along one of the more remote stretches of coastline, on the southern end of the Central Pacific region, and encompasses several beaches. *Ballena*, which is Spanish for "whale," gets its name for a peculiar sandbar formation at Playa Uvita beach that goes straight out toward the ocean before splitting and curving in two directions, much like a whale's tale. *(See Chapter 8.)*

MANUEL ANTONIO NATIONAL PARK

On the northern end of the Pacific, Manuel Antonio National Park shelters some of the country's more precious beaches. A series of half-moon bays with sparkling sands are fronted by transitional forest—a combination of flora and fauna from the tropical dry forests farther north and the tropical rain forests that stretch south. Wildlife is abundant at Manuel Antonio, and the towering jungle at the beach's edge can give the area a wild and paradisiacal feel. *(See Chapter 7.)*

Uvita Beach; Toronto Jeff, Fodors.com member

THE NICOYA PENINSULA

A succession of incredible beaches are scattered along this region of the Pacific coast, from Montezuma to Mal País, Sámara to Punta Guiones. Ostional, just north of Guiones, offers something none of the others can: the *arribada*. The beach is part of the Ostional Wildlife Refuge, granting an extra level of protection to the area. *(See Chapter 6.)*

THE CARIBBEAN

This coast has an entirely different feel from the Pacific. North of Limon, there are miles of undeveloped, protected beaches where green sea turtles come from July to October to lay eggs. There have also been sightings of the loggerhead, hawksbill, and leatherback turtles. The currents here are strong, so don't plan on swimming.

To the south of Limon, beaches are bordered by dense green vegetation all year long, and the quality of the sand can change dramatically as you wander from cove to cove. Some of the country's healthiest living coral reefs are offshore, so snorkeling is worthwhile. Beaches of note are Playa Negra, Playa Blanca, Playa Negro, and Punta Uva. *(See Chapter 9.)*

Montezuma; Justin Hubbell, Fodors.com member

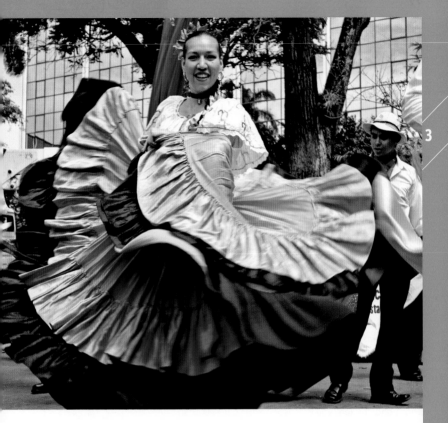

San José

WORD OF MOUTH

"The Pre-Columbian Gold Museum is excellent and always has a special exhibit going as well. It is fun just to walk along the Avenue Central (pedestrian) where you find the Gold Museum. The Central Market is interesting but keep in mind that some surrounding areas are "sketchy" so pay attention to your instincts."

—peggionthego

WELCOME TO SAN JOSÉ

TOP REASONS TO GO

★ **Historic Barrios Amón and Otoya:** These northern neighborhoods abutting and sometimes overlapping downtown have quiet tree-lined streets and century-old houses turned trendy hotels and restaurants.

★ **Gold and Jade museums:** For a sense of indigenous Costa Rica, frequently forgotten during the nation's march to modernity, the country's two best museums are must-sees.

★ **Eating out:** After traveling around Costa Rica eating mostly rice and beans and chicken, you'll appreciate San José's varied restaurants.

★ **Shopping:** San José is the best place to stock up on both essentials and souvenirs. Look for folkloric crafts, ceramics, textiles, leather-and-wood rocking chairs, and, of course, coffee.

★ **Location, location, location:** From the capital's pivotal position, you can be on a coffee tour, at the base of a giant volcano, or riding river rapids in just 30 minutes.

1 Downtown. This area holds San José's historic and commercial districts and many top attractions: the Museo del Jade (Jade Museum), Museo del Oro (Gold Museum), Mercado Central (Central Market), and Teatro Nacional (National Theater).

2 West of Downtown. The mostly residential neighborhoods here are anchored by large Parque Metropolitano La Sabana (La Sabana Park) and the Museo de Arte Costarricense (Museum of Costa Rican Art).

GETTING ORIENTED

The metropolitan area holds more than 1 million residents, but the city proper is small, with some 300,000 people living in its 44 square km (17 square mi). Most sights are concentrated in three downtown neighborhoods, La Soledad, La Merced, and El Carmen, named for their anchor churches. Borders are fuzzy: one barrio (neighborhood) flows into the next, districts overlap, and the city itself melts into its suburbs with nary a sign to denote where one community ends and another begins.

3 North of Downtown.
Historic barrios Amón and Otoya and the Museo de los Niños (Children's Museum) are a few of the attractions to the north.

4 East of Downtown.
Several good restaurants and hotels and the Universidad de Costa Rica (University of Costa Rica) are ensconced in the San Pedro suburb.

SAN JOSÉ PLANNER

When to Go

Although it sits just 9 degrees north of the equator, San José's altitude keeps the temperatures pleasant year-round, with highs of 26°C to 28°C (79°F to 83°F) and lows of 17°C to 19°C (65°F to 68°F). Early settlers put down roots here, attracted by moderate temperatures, rich volcanic soil, and long distance from pirates. The result is a capital that really does live up to its billing as "the city of eternal spring." December and January are the coolest, windiest months. In March and April the heat and dust pick up noticeably.

The first rains arrive in May and provide a welcome break in the temperatures. May through August the pattern is usually sunny mornings, brief afternoon showers, and clear, brisk evenings. September and October become waterlogged; it can rain nonstop for days at a time. Rains finally dissipate by mid- to late November as the transition to another dry season begins.

San José in a Day

If you have only a day to spend in San José, the must-see stops are the Teatro Nacional (National Theater)—we recommend the guided tour—and the Museo del Oro Precolombino (Precolumbian Gold Museum). That's easy to accomplish since they sit on the same block.

With more time, take in the Museo del Jade (Jade Museum) and Museo Nacional (National Museum). Or visit to the Museo para la Paz (Peace Museum). The Museo de los Niños (Children's Museum), north of downtown, is a kid pleaser. (It's in a dicey part of the barrio El Carmen, more north of downtown than actually in downtown; take a taxi.) Our Good Walk (⇨ *below*) gives you a taste of the city in just an hour.

Bypass San José?

OK. So San José isn't necessarily the Costa Rica you came to see. Those beaches and rain forests beckon, after all. If that is, indeed, the case, you can avoid the city altogether.

The international airport actually lies just outside the city of Alajuela, about 30 minutes northwest of the capital. Look for lodgings in Alajuela, San Antonio de Belén, Escazú, or Santa Ana—all within striking distance of the airport. Or head west. *For information about lodgings near Aeropuerto Internacional Juan Santamaría, see Chapter 3.*

Few international flights arrive in the morning, but they do exist, especially via Miami. Get here early, and you can head out of town immediately.

A third option is to join the growing number of visitors flying into Daniel Oduber International Airport in Liberia, where Costa Rica's northern and western reaches (including the north Pacific) are at your fingertips.

Day Trips from the Capital

The capital sits smack-dab in the middle of the country and in the middle of the fertile Central Valley. Although a day trip to either coast would be grueling—despite Costa Rica's small size, it takes longer than you think to get from place to place—you can easily pop out to the Central Valley's major sights and be back in the city in time for dinner. Several of these attractions provide pickup service in San José, some for a nominal additional cost. Alternatively, tour operators include many of these attractions on their itineraries.

DESTINATION	FROM SAN JOSÉ (BY CAR)	
Basílica de los Ángeles	30 mins southeast	⇨ p. 161
Butterfly Farm	45 mins west	⇨ p. 145
Café Britt	30 mins north	⇨ p. 160
Carara National Park	2 hrs southwest	⇨ p. 360
Doka Coffee Estate	1 hr west	⇨ p. 145
Guayabo National Monument	2 hrs southeast, 4WD necessary	⇨ p. 171
INBioparque	10 mins north	⇨ p. 152
Irazú Volcano	60 mins east	⇨ p. 163
La Paz Waterfall Gardens	2 hrs north	⇨ p. 238
Orosi Valley	60 mins southeast	⇨ p. 164
Poás Volcano	60 mins northwest	⇨ p. 186
Rain Forest Aerial Tram	45 mins north	⇨ p. 528
River Rafting	2–2½ hrs southeast or north	⇨ p. 169
Sarchí	60 mins northwest	⇨ p. 193
Tortuga Island	3 hrs west	⇨ p. 374
Tropical Bungee	60 mins west	⇨ p. 192
World of Snakes	60 mins west	⇨ p. 192
Zoo Ave	45 mins west	⇨ p. 145

Play It Safe

San José is safer than other Latin American capitals. Violent crime is rare; the greatest threat you're likely to face is petty theft. Standard big-city precautions apply:

3

■ Exchange money only at banks. Street money changers slip counterfeit bills into their stash, or doctor their calculators to compute unfavorable rates. In the extreme, they might grab your cash and run off.

■ Select ATMs in well-lighted areas. Better still, use a bank's ATM during opening hours, when a guard will likely be present. Go with a buddy, and conceal cash immediately.

■ Use only licensed red taxis with yellow triangles on the front doors. The license plate of an official taxi begins with TSJ ("Taxi San José").

■ Park in guarded, well-lighted lots (about $1 an hour). If you must park on the street, make sure informal *guachimen* (watchmen) are present. Usually this is someone with a big stick who will expect payment of about $1 per hour. Do not leave anything valuable in your parked vehicle.

SAN JOSÉ PLANNER

Essentials

Currency Exchange
BAC San José (✉ *Avda. 2, Cs. Central–1, Barrio El Carmen* ☎ *2295–9797*). **Banco Nacional** (✉ *Avda. 1, Cs. 2–4, Barrio La Merced* ☎ *2212–2000*). **Scotiabank** (✉ *Behind Teatro Nacional, Barrio La Soledad* ☎ *2521–5680*).

Medical Assistance
Clínica Bíblica (✉ *Avda. 14, Cs. Central–1, Barrio El Pacífico* ☎ *2522–1000* ⊕ *www.clinicabiblica.com*). **Hospital La Católica** (✉ *Attached to San Antonio Church on C. Esquivel Bonilla, Guadalupe* ☎ *2246–3000* ⊕ *www.hospitallacatolica.com*).

Shuttle Companies
Grayline (☎ *2232–3681* ⊕ *www.graylinecostarica.com*). **Interbus** (☎ *2283–5573* ⊕ *www.interbusonline.com*).

Taxis **Alfaro** (☎ *2221–8466*). **Coopetaxi** (☎ *2235–9966*). **San Jorge** (☎ *2221–3434*). **Taxis Unidos Aeropuerto** (☎ *2222–6865* ⊕ *www.taxiaeropuerto.com*).

Visitor Info
Instituto Costarricense de Turismo (*ICT* ✉ *C. 5, Avdas. Central–2, Barrio La Soledad* ☎ *2222–1090* ⊕ *www.visitcostarica.com* ✉ *Aeropuerto Juan Santamaría Alajuela* ☎ *2443–1535*).

Getting Here and Around

By Air: Aeropuerto Internacional Juan Santamaría (16 km/ 10 mi northwest of downtown) receives international flights and those of domestic airline SANSA. Domestic Nature Air flights use tiny, informal Aeropuerto Internacional Tobías Bolaños (3 km/2 mi west of downtown).

By Bus: San José's bus stations are all in sketchy neighborhoods. Always take a taxi to and from them. Better: Use air-conditioned minivan shuttles instead of buses to travel into and out of the capital.

City buses are cheap (30¢–50¢) and easy to use. For Paseo Colón and La Sabana, take buses marked SABANA-CEMENTERIO from stops at Avenida 2 between Calles 5 and 7 or Avenida 3 next to the post office. For Los Yoses and San Pedro, take the SAN PEDRO bus from Avenida Central between Calles 9 and 11.

By Car: Paved roads fan out from Paseo Colón west to Escazú and northwest to the airport and Heredia. For the Pacific coast, Guanacaste, and Nicaragua, take the Carretera Interamericana (Pan-American Highway; PAH) north (CA1). Calle 3 runs north into the highway to Guápiles, Limón, and the Atlantic coast through Braulio Carrillo National Park, with a turnoff to Sarapiquí. Follow Avenida Central or 2 east through San Pedro to enter the PAH south (CA2), which has a turnoff for Cartago, Volcán Irazú, and Turrialba before it heads toward Panama.

Avoid driving in the city. Streets are narrow, rush hour (7–9 AM and 5–7 PM) traffic is horrible, and drivers can be reckless. What's more, San José and neighboring San Pedro enforce rigid weekday driving restrictions (6 AM– 7 PM) for all private vehicles, including your rental car. The last digit of your license plate determines your no-driving day: Monday (1 and 2), Tuesday (3 and 4), Wednesday (5 and 6), Thursday (7 and 8), and Friday (9 and 0).

By Taxi: You can hail cabs on the street or call for one. All licensed cabs are red with a gold triangle on the front doors (though Taxis Unidos Aeropuerto—which goes to the airport—are orange). A 3-km (2-mi) ride costs around $3; tipping isn't customary. By law cabbies must use *marías* (meters) within the metropolitan area.

DID YOU KNOW?

In addition to the world's largest collection of American jade, San José's Museo del Jade has a risqué display of pre-Columbian ceramic fertility symbols—indicative of humankind's eternal preoccupation with sex.

ECO-LODGES IN SAN JOSÉ

Clean? Green? Pristine? San José is none of these, but even in Costa Rica's congested capital, you can count on a handful of pioneers who keep the environmental spirit alive.

The capital's few pockets of greenery are its parks, and, in this regard, the city does itself proud. The grandiose monuments so common in other Latin America countries are not very prominent. Small is the watchword in Costa Rica, so parks are places to enjoy mini eco-refuges rather than shrines to past heroes and glories. A trio of parks—Morazán, España, and Nacional—graces the area just northeast of downtown and provides a mostly contiguous several blocks of peace and quiet. The vast La Sabana park on San José's west side once served as the country's international airport. Its lush greenery and ample space for recreation get our vote as being one of the most pleasing uses of urban space. The capital's parks have one big downside: after dark, a small cast of unsavory characters replaces the throngs of day-trippers. Make a point to vacate city parks when the sun goes down.

GOOD PRACTICES

Use public transportation whenever possible. Buses travel everywhere in San José and suburbs, and taxis are relatively easy to find. In addition to reducing your carbon footprint, it also saves you the hassle of driving and parking in an already congested city.

Ask if your hotel recycles glass, plastic and aluminum. A few lodgings—and, unfortunately, "few" is the operative term here—do. Take advantage if you can.

Don't litter—the city has a burdensome trash problem—although you'll swear no one else here follows this advice. Dispose of your trash properly.

TOP ECO-LODGES IN SAN JOSÉ

To ensure that your hotel really is eco-friendly, do a bit of research or ask a few questions. Check on the property's lighting—does it use compact florescent bulbs? What about sensors or timers? Is any form of alternative energy, like solar or wind power, employed? Are there low-flow faucets, showers, and toilets? What sort of recycling programs are in place for guests *and* staff? Answers to such questions give you a sense of whether a property is green or not. Below are a of couple San José properties that do more than pay lip service to the environmental movement.

CLARION HOTEL AMÓN PLAZA

From its active in-hotel recycling program and its eco-friendly store that sells no products made from endangered woods, to its small garden that acquaints you with rainforest plant species and its liaison program with the community, the Amón Plaza is greener than most countryside hotels.

HOTEL RINCÓN DE SAN JOSÉ

Your hot water in this small Barrio Otoya hotel will be solar heated, and the place makes maximum use of natural lighting during the day in its public areas. The Rincón de San José uses only biodegradable products whenever possible, it also engages in an active recycling program. Even captured rainwater finds its way into your room's toilet basin.

HOTEL PRESIDENTE

Costa Rica's first "carbon neutral" hotel has taken major steps to reduce its carbon footprint. What is left over is offset by a tree-planting project the lodging supports. The Presidente has organized a small but growing consortium of San José hotels to take up recycling. All in all, not bad for a place located smack-dab in the center of the city.

PEDESTRIANS ONLY

3

The government is forever announcing some grandiose plan to make San José more livable and a bit less of an urban hell. Few, however, make it off the ground, mostly due to a chronic lack of funds. Two have come to fruition, though, and you will notice the benefit.

For years, the city government has been turning downtown streets into pedestrian-only malls. Some 34 blocks in the center city—sections of Avenidas Central and 4, and Calles 2, 3, and 17—now have *bulevar* (boulevard) status, with more on the drawing board. Thank the European Union for much of the funding.

Rigid weekday driving restrictions cover all of San José and parts of neighboring San Pedro. The last digit of your license plate dictates the day of the week when you may not bring a car into the large restricted zone. The city still hosts far too many cars, but the 20% reduction in vehicles each weekday has made a noticeable difference.

By Jeffrey Van Fleet

The center of all that is Costa Rica probably won't be the center of your trip to Costa Rica. If you're like many visitors, you'll spend two nights in San José—tops. Most international flights arrive in the evening and leave in the morning, so you'll probably head out of town early on the first day, only to return the night before heading home. But consider giving the capital a chance.

Amid the noise and traffic, shady parks, well-maintained museums, lively plazas, terrific restaurants, and great hotels do exist. Further, the city makes a great base for day trips: from downtown it's a mere 30- to 40-minute drive to the tranquil countryside and myriad outdoor activities of the surrounding Central Valley.

You'd never know San José is as old as it is—given the complete absence of colonial architecture—but settlers migrating from then provincial capital Cartago founded the city in 1737. After independence in 1821, San José cemented its position as the new nation's capital after struggles and a brief civil war with fellow Central Valley cities Cartago, Alajuela, and Heredia. Revenues from the coffee and banana industries financed the construction of stately homes, theaters, and a trolley system (later abandoned and now visible only in old sepia photographs).

As recently as the mid-1900s, San José was no larger than the present-day downtown area; old-timers remember the vast coffee and cane plantations that extended beyond its borders. The city began to mushroom only after World War II, when old buildings were razed to make room for concrete monstrosities. The sprawl eventually connected the capital with nearby cities.

New York or London it is not, but for the Tico living out in Tilarán, today's San José glitters every bit as much. It has attracted people from all over Costa Rica, yet it remains, in many ways, a collection of distinct neighborhoods where residents maintain friendly small-town ways. For you, this might mean the driver you're following will decide to abruptly stop his vehicle to buy a lottery ticket or chat with a friend on the street.

Or it might mean you have to navigate a maze of fruit-vendor stands on a crowded sidewalk. But this is part of what keeps San José a big small town.

No, you shouldn't sacrifice precious beach or rain forest time for a stay in San José. But the city is worth a day or two—as a way to ease into Costa Rica at the start of a visit or as a way of wrapping things up with a well-deserved dose of civilization.

EXPLORING

The Irish group U-2 could have written its song "Where the Streets Have No Name" about San José. Admittedly, some of its streets have names, but no one seems to know or use them. Streets in the center of the capital are laid out in a grid, with *avenidas* (avenues) running east and west, and *calles* (streets), north and south. Odd-number avenues increase in number north of Avenida Central; even-number avenues, south. Streets east of Calle Central have odd numbers; those to the west are even.

The farther you get from downtown, the scarcer street signs become. Costa Ricans rely instead on a charming and exasperating system of designating addresses by the distance from landmarks, as in "100 meters north and 50 meters west of the school." Another quirk: "100 meters" always refers to one city block, regardless of how long it actually is. Likewise, "200 meters" is two blocks, and so on. (As you can imagine, getting a pizza delivered here is quite a challenge.)

Historically, the reference point was the church, but these days it might be a bar, Burger King, or even a long-gone landmark: the eastern suburb of San Pedro uses the *higuerón*, a fig tree that was felled long ago but lives on in the hearts of Costa Ricans. Your best bet is to follow the time-honored practice of *ir y preguntar* (keep walking and keep asking).

DOWNTOWN

It's a trend seen the world over: businesses and residents flee city centers for the space, blissful quiet, and lower-priced real estate of the 'burbs. Although Costa Rica's capital is experiencing this phenomenon, downtown still remains the city's historic and vibrant (if noisy and congested) heart. Government offices have largely stayed put here, as have the most attractions. It's impossible to sightsee here without finding yourself downtown.

Boundaries are fuzzy. For example, the neighborhoods of El Carmen, La Merced, and La Soledad are anchored in downtown but sprawl outward from the center city. And, in an effort to seem trendier, several establishments in downtown's northern fringes prefer to say that they're in the more fashionable barrios of Amón or Otoya.

TOP ATTRACTIONS

6 Museo del Jade. The Jade Museum has the world's largest collection of

★ American jade—that's "American" in the hemispheric sense. Nearly all the items on display were produced in pre-Columbian times, and most of the jade (pronounced *hah*-day in Spanish) dates from 300 BC to AD 700. In the spectacular Jade Room, pieces are illuminated from behind so you can appreciate their translucency. A series of drawings explains how this extremely hard stone was cut using string saws with quartz-and-sand abrasive. Jade was sometimes used in jewelry designs, but it was most often carved into oblong pendants. The museum also has other pre-Columbian artifacts, such as polychrome vases and three-legged *metates* (small stone tables for grinding corn), and a gallery of modern art. The final room on the tour has a startling display of ceramic fertility symbols. A photo-filled, glossy, English-language guide to the museum sells for $15; the Spanish version is only $3. The museum is looking for a new home at this writing, with tentative plans to transfer the collection to an as-yet-unconstructed facility somewhere near the Plaza de la Democracia. Opening of such a facility is slated for 2011 or 2012, but the idea hasn't moved much past the drawing-board phase. A larger facility would allow all 5,000-plus pieces in the collection to be displayed. At present, you can see only about a quarter of them. The museum's location on the first floor of a tall office building gives it a downtown feel, even if it's at the northern edge of the city center. ✉ *INS building, Avda. 7, Cs. 9–11, Barrio Amón* ☎ *2287–6034* 🖃 *$7* ⊗ *Weekdays 8:30–3:30, Sat. 9–1.*

3 Museo del Oro Precolombino. The dazzling, modern Pre-Columbian

★ Gold Museum, in a three-story underground structure beneath the Plaza de la Cultura, contains Central America's largest collection of pre-Columbian gold jewelry—20,000 troy ounces in more than 1,600 individual pieces—all owned by the Banco Central and displayed attractively in low-lit, bilingual exhibits. Many pieces are in the form of frogs and eagles, two animals perceived by the region's early cultures to have great spiritual significance. All that glitters here is not gold: most spectacular are the varied shaman figurines, which represent the human connection to animal deities. One of the halls houses the Museo Numismática (Coin Museum; admission included with Gold Museum), a repository of historic coins and bills and other objects used as legal tender throughout the country's history. Rotating art exhibitions happen on another level of the complex. ✉ *Eastern end of Plaza de la Cultura, C. 5, Avdas. Central–2, Barrio La Soledad* ☎ *2243–4202* ⊕ *www.museosdelbancocentral.org* 🖃 *$9, $5 students* ⊗ *Daily 9:30–5.*

2 Teatro Nacional. The National Theatre is enchanting. Chagrined that

★ touring prima donna Adelina Patti bypassed San José in 1890 for lack of a suitable venue, wealthy coffee merchants raised import taxes and hired Belgian architects to design this building, lavish with cast iron and Italian marble. The theater was inaugurated in 1897 with a performance of Gounod's *Faust,* featuring an international cast. The sandstone exterior is marked by Italianate arched windows, marble columns with bronze capitals, and statues of strange bedfellows Ludwig van Beethoven (1770–1827) and 17th-century Spanish golden-age playwright Pedro Calderón de la Barca (1600–81). The Muses of Dance, Music, and Fame are silhouetted in front of an iron cupola.

The sumptuous neo-baroque interior sparkles, too. Given the provenance of the building funds, it's not surprising that frescoes on the stairway inside depict coffee and banana production. Note Italian painter Aleardo Villa's famous ceiling mural *Alegoría del Café y Banano* (*Allegory of Coffee and Bananas*), a joyful harvest scene that appeared on Costa Rica's old five-colón note. (The now-defunct bill is prized by collectors and by visitors as a souvenir, and is often sold by vendors in the plaza between the theater and the Gran Hotel Costa Rica next door.) French designer Alain Guilhot created the building's nighttime external illumination system. (He did the same for the Eiffel Tower.) The soft coppers, golds, and whites highlight the theater's exterior nightly from 6 PM to 5 AM.

You can see the theater's interior by attending one of the performances that take place several nights a week (tickets are reasonable); intermission gives you a chance to nose around. The theater prizes punctuality, one of the few institutions in this country to do so. Performances start on time. Stop at the *boletería* (box office) in the lobby and see what strikes your fancy. (Don't worry if you left your tuxedo or evening gown back home; as long as you don't show up for a performance wearing shorts, jeans, or a T-shirt, no one will care.)

For a nominal admission fee you can also move beyond the lobby on an informative guided daytime visit. Thirty-minute tours in English or Spanish are given at 9, 10, and 11 AM and 1, 2, and 3 PM. If you're downtown on a Tuesday between February and Christmas, take in one of the Teatro al Mediodía (Theater at Midday) performances that begin at 12:10 PM. It might be a chamber-music recital or a one-act play (in Spanish). Admission is $2. A similar program with similar admission called Música al Atardecer (Music at Dusk) takes place each Thursday at 5:10 PM. The theater is sometimes closed for rehearsals, so call before you go. ⊠ *Plaza de la Cultura, Barrio La Soledad* ☎ *2221–1329* ⊕ *www.teatronacional.go.cr* ⊡ *$7* ⊗ *Mon.–Sat. 9–4.*

NEED A BREAK?

Duck into the Café del Teatro Nacional, off the theater lobby, to sit at a marble table and sip a hazelnut mocha beneath frescoed ceilings. The frescoes are part of an allegory of seminude figures celebrating the 1897 opening of the theater. Coffee runs from $2 to $5, depending on how much alcohol or ice cream is added. Sandwiches and cakes are $3 to $6. The café keeps the same hours as the theater but is open only until curtain time on performance nights and during intermission.

WORTH NOTING

⑬ Catedral Metropolitana. Built in 1871 and completely refurbished in the late 1990s to repair earthquake damage, the neoclassical Metropolitan Cathedral, topped by a corrugated tin dome, isn't terribly interesting outside. But inside are patterned floor tiles, stained-glass windows depicting various saints and apostles, and framed polychrome bas-reliefs illustrating the 14 Stations of the Cross. This renovation did away with one small time-honored tradition: rather than purchase and

San José
Exploring

TO
GUADALUPE

SAN FRANCISCO

108

21

MIRAFLORES

6

TO
SAN PEDRO,
UNIVERSIDAD DE
COSTA RICA 202

OTOYA

Calle 9
Calle 11
Calle 15

Casa
Amarilla

6

7

5

8

Avda. 7

ARANJUEZ

Avenida 9
Avenida 11
Calle 17

C. 19
Avenida 11
Avenida 15
Avenida 13
Calle 21
Calle 23
Calle 25

Avenida 11
Avenida 9

Calle 37

ESCALANTE

Avenida 5

CUESTA DE
MORAS

9

Avenida 1

LA CALIFORNIA

Calle 15
Calle 17
Calle 19
Calle 25

12   11   10

Avenida Central

Avenida 6

Avenida 8

Avenida 10

MILFLOR

Calle 11
Calle 173

Calle José Martí
Calle 21
Calle 23
Calle 23bis

204

LOS YOSES

Avenida 8
Avenida 10
Avenida 12
Calle 35

Avenida 16bis

CERRITO

KEY
┼┼┼ Rail Lines
Pedestrian Zone

light a votive candle, the faithful now deposit a 50-colón coin illuminating a bulb in a row of tiny electric candles.

The interior of the small Capilla del Santísimo (Chapel of the Host) on the cathedral's north side evokes ornate old Catholicism, much more so than the main sanctuary itself, and is a place for reflection and prayer. A marble statue of Pope John Paul II graces the garden on the building's north side. Masses are held throughout the day on Sunday starting at 7 AM, with one in English each Saturday at 4 PM, except the first Saturday of the month, when it starts at 3 PM. Thanks to a late-2008 restoration, the magnificent 1891 Belgian pipe organ fills the church with music once again. Although not technically part of the cathedral complex, a small statue of Holocaust victim Anne Frank graces the pedestrian mall on the building's south side. It was donated by the Embassy of the Netherlands. ⊠ *C. Central, Avdas. 2–4, Barrio La Merced* ☎ *2221–3820* ⊘ *Weekdays 6–6, Sun. 6AM–9PM.*

❼ Centro Nacional de la Cultura. Costa Rica cherishes its state enterprises. Here the government is your light and water utility, your phone company, your Internet service provider, your bank, your insurance agent, and your hospital. It is also your distillery, and this complex served as the headquarters of the Fábrica Nacional de Licores (FANAL, or National Liquor Factory) until 1981, when it moved to a modern facility west of Alajuela. In a heartwarming exception to the usual "tear it down" mentality so prevalent in San José, the Ministry of Culture converted the sloped-surface, double-block 1853 factory into the 14,000-square-meter National Cultural Center, with ministry offices, two theaters, and a museum. The metal **Teatro FANAL** (☎ *2222–2974*), once the fermentation area, now hosts frequent theater and music performances. The clay-brick **Teatro 1887** (☎ *2222–2974*) served as the factory's personnel office, and today dedicates itself to performances by the National Dance Company. What is now the theater's lobby was once the chemical testing lab. The stone-block storage depot next to the water towers at the southeast side of the complex became the Museo de Arte y Diseño Contemporáneo *(⇨ below).* A stone gate and sundial grace the entrance nearest the museum. The complex sits amid government offices, at the point where downtown's northern reaches fade into the more residential neighborhood of Barrio Otoya. ⊠ *C. 13, Avdas. 3–5, Barrio Otoya* ☎ *2257–5524* ⊘ *Weekdays 8–5, Sat. 10–5.*

⑯ Correos de Costa Rica *(Central Post Office).* The handsome, carved orange exterior of the post office, dating from 1917, is hard to miss among the bland buildings surrounding it. Collectors should stop at the second-floor **Museo Filatélico** *(Philatelic Museum* ☎ *2223–9766)* for its display of historic stamps. Early-20th-century telegraphs and telephones are also on display. The museum is open weekdays 8–5; admission is the purchase of a prepaid postcard sufficient for mailing

A GOOD WALK

This walk takes about an hour at a stroll. If you take a more leisurely approach, lingering at the parks or museums, it could take hours.

Everyone finds their way to the **Plaza de la Cultura**, a favorite meeting spot in the heart of the city, and it makes a good kick-off point for a walk. The ornate **Teatro Nacional** sits on the south side of the plaza. Pop in and buy a ticket for an evening performance, and/or grab a cup of coffee at the lobby café. The **Museo del Oro Precolombino** lies under the plaza. The gold collection could easily captivate you for an hour or two. From here, head two blocks north on Calle 5 to **Parque Morazán**, whose centerpiece Templo de Música is the symbol of the city. Traffic is particularly dangerous here, so take heed. The **Edificio Metálico**, a metal building that serves as a school, fronts the park's north side.

Continue just east of the park on Avenida 3 to the small **Parque España**, one of the city's most pleasant green spaces. The ornate building on the park's north side is the Andrew Carnegie–funded Casa Amarilla. At Avenida 7 is the modern Instituto Nacional Segoros (INS) building, whose ground-floor **Museo del Jade** has an extensive American jade collection. The Ministry of Culture complex, the **Centro Nacional de la Cultura**, fronts the park's east side. From Parque España, walk one long block east to the **Parque Nacional**. Two blocks south on Calle 17 is a pleasant pedestrian mall.

Pass the Asamblea Legislativa, where Costa Rica's congress meets, and come to the **Museo Nacional**. Loop around to the museum's west side to one of the higher levels on the Plaza de la Democracia, a great vantage point for sunsets. Avenida Central fronts the plaza's north side. Head back downhill, into the city center. The avenue becomes a lively pedestrian mall at Calle 9, and two blocks later you return to the Plaza de la Cultura.

to North America. Also of interest to philatelists is the office to the left as you face the stamp windows; it sells first-day issues. From the balcony you can see the loading of *apartados* (post-office boxes) going on below: Costa Ricans covet these hard-to-get boxes, as the city's lack of street addresses makes mail delivery a challenge. ☒ C. 2, *Avdas. 1–3, Barrio La Merced* ☎ 2202–2900 ⊕ *www.correos.go.cr* ☉ *Weekdays 7:30–5, Sat. 7:30–1.*

🄆 **Mercado Central** *(Central Market).* This block-long melting pot is a warren of dark, narrow passages flanked by stalls packed with spices (some purported to have medicinal value), fish, fruit, flowers, pets, and wood and leather crafts. But the 1880 structure is a kinder, gentler introduction to a Central American market; there are no pigs or chickens or their accompanying smells to be found here. A few stands selling tourist souvenirs congregate near the entrances, but this is primarily a place where the average Costa Rican comes to shop. There are also dozens of cheap restaurants and snack stalls, including the country's first ice-cream vendor. Be warned: the concentration of shoppers makes this a hot spot for pickpockets, purse snatchers, and backpack slitters.

Enter and exit at the southeast corner of the building (Avda. Central at C. 6). The green-and-white SALIDA signs direct you to other exits, but they spill onto slightly less–safe streets. Use the image of the Sacred Heart of Jesus, the market's patron and protector, near the center of the building, as your guide; it faces that safer corner by which you should exit. (Things probably weren't planned that way.) ⊠ *Bordered by Avdas. Central–1 and Cs. 6–8, Barrio La Merced* ⊘ *Mon.–Sat. 6–6.*

CITY TOURS

Grayline Tours (☎ 2220–2106 ⊕ www.graylinecostarica.com) operates sightseeing and shopping tours. Tico Walks (☎ 2283–8281) gives two-and-a-half-hour guided walks of downtown. Show up in front of the Teatro Nacional at 10 AM, Tuesday, Thursday, Saturday, or Sunday.

⑱ Monumento al Zaguate. An estimated one million street dogs roam Costa Rica's cities and towns. In this newest addition to the growing selection of outdoor public art in central San José, sculptor Francisco Munguía calls attention to their plight. His steel sculpture on the pedestrian boulevard next to the Central Market is a monument to San José's zaguates ("mutts" in Costa Rican Spanish), and the models for the painted caricatures were six of the 23 dogs Munguía and his wife Deborah have rescued over the years. The artist's goal is for Bobi, Ewok, Oso, Pauleta, Shampú, and Tábata—those are the animals' names—to encourage residents to adopt a dog, too. ⊠ *Avda.Central and Cs.6–8, Barrio La Merced.*

NEED A BREAK?

A slew of unnamed *sodas*—that's the Costa Rican term for a mom-and-pop eatery—populate the heart of the Mercado Central. Grab a quick bite while you shop. It's all very informal.

To sample the crème de la crème of locally made ice cream, head to Pop's. Mango is a favorite flavor. After a long walk on crowded sidewalks, it may be just what the doctor ordered. This chain is everywhere, and you'll find several outlets downtown. ⊠ *C. 3, Avdas. Central–2 Barrio La Soledad.*

⑧ Museo de Arte y Diseño Contemporáneo. This wonderfully minimalist space is perfect as the country's premier modern-art venue. The Museum of Contemporary Art and Design, or MADC as it's known around town, hosts changing exhibits by artists and designers from all over Latin America. You can arrange for a guided visit with a couple of days' notice. The museum occupies part of a government-office complex in that gray area where downtown San José transitions into residential neighborhoods. ⊠ *C. 15, Avdas. 3–5, Barrio Otoya* ☎ *2257–7202* ⊕ *www.madc.ac.cr* ⊡ *$3* ⊘ *Mon.–Sat. 9:30–4:45.*

⑩ Museo Nacional. In the mango-colored Bellavista Fortress, which dates from 1870, the National Museum gives you a quick and insightful lesson in English and Spanish on Costa Rican culture from pre-Columbian times to the present. Cases display pre-Columbian artifacts, period dress, colonial furniture, religious art, and photographs. Some of the country's foremost ethnographers and anthropologists are on the

museum's staff. Outside are a veranda and a pleasant, manicured courtyard garden. A former army headquarters, this now-tranquil building
saw fierce fighting during a 1931 army mutiny and the 1948 revolution,
as the bullet holes pocking its turrets attest. But it was also here that
three-time president José "Don Pepe" Figueres abolished the country's
military in 1949. ⊠ *C. 17, between Avdas. Central and 2, Barrio La
Soledad* ☎ *2257–1433* ⊕ *www.museocostarica.go.cr* ⊡ *$7, $2 students*
⊙ *Tues.–Sat. 8:30–4:30, Sun. 9–4:30.*

⑫ Museo para la Paz. Former president Oscar Arias won the 1987 Nobel
Peace Prize for his tireless efforts to bring reconciliation to a war-torn
Central America, and today he remains a vocal force for international
peace and social justice. His Arias Foundation operates the Peace
Museum, with bilingual exhibits documenting the isthmus's turbu-
lent history and promoting the cause for peace. Messages from other
Nobel laureates—the Dalai Lama, Lech Walesa, Rigoberta Menchú,
Jimmy Carter, Al Gore, and Henry Kissinger among them—adorn one
room. Begin your visit in the auditorium watching a 12-minute video in
English, *The Dividends of Peace.* There's also an hour-long video that
delves into the topic. The museum usually doesn't appear to be open
when you walk by. Call and let the attendant know you're coming.
⊠ *Avda. 2 and C. 13, Barrio La Soledad* ☎ *2223–4664* ⊕ *www.arias.
or.cr* ⊡ *Free* ⊙ *Weekdays 8–noon and 1:30–4:30.*

⑭ Parque Central. At the city's nucleus, tree-planted Central Park is more
plaza than park. A life-size bronze statue of a street sweeper (*El Barren-
dero*) cleans up some bronze litter; look also for *Armonía* (*Harmony*),
a sculpture of three street musicians. In the center of the park is a spi-
derlike, ochre-color gazebo donated by former Nicaraguan dictator
Anastasio Somoza. Several years ago a referendum was held to decide
whether to demolish the despot's gift, but Ticos voted to preserve the
bandstand for posterity. ⊠ *Bordered by Avdas. 2–4 and Cs. 2–Central,
Barrio La Merced.*

⑤ Parque España. One of our favorite spots is this shady little park. A
bronze statue of Costa Rica's Spanish founder, Juan Vásquez de Cor-
onado, overlooks an elevated fountain on its southwest corner; the
opposite corner has a lovely tiled guardhouse. A bust of Queen Isabella
of Castile stares at the yellow compound to the east of the park, the
Centro Nacional de la Cultura. Just west of the park is a two-story,
metal-sided school made in Belgium and shipped to Costa Rica in pieces
more than a century ago. Local lore holds that the intended destination
for the appropriately named Edificio Metálico (Metal Building) was
really Chile, but that Costa Rica decided to keep the mistakenly shipped
building components. The yellow colonial-style building to the east of
the modern INS building is the 1912 Casa Amarilla, home of Costa
Rica's Foreign Ministry (closed to the public.) The massive ceiba tree in
front, planted by John F. Kennedy and the presidents of all the Central
American nations in 1963, gives you an idea of how quickly things
grow in the tropics. A garden around the corner on Calle 13 contains
a 2-meter-wide section of the Berlin Wall donated by Germany's foreign
ministry after reunification. Ask the guard to let you into the garden

3

if you want a closer look. ✉ *Bordered by Avdas. 7–3 and Cs. 11–17, Barrio El Carmen* ☏ *2257-7202.*

❹ **Parque Morazán.** Anchored by the 1920 Templo de Música (Temple of Music), a neoclassic bandstand that has become the symbol of the city, downtown's largest park is somewhat barren, though the pink and golden trumpet trees on its northwest corner brighten things up when they bloom in the dry

months. The park is named for Honduran general Francisco Morazán, whose dream for a united Central America failed in the 1830s. Avoid the park late at night, when a rough crowd and occasional muggers appear. ✉ *Avda. 3, Cs. 5–9, Barrio El Carmen.*

❾ **Parque Nacional.** A bronze monument commemorating Central America's battles against American invader William Walker in 1856 forms the centerpiece of the large, leafy National Park. Five Amazons, representing the five nations of the isthmus, attack Walker, who shields his face from the onslaught. Costa Rica maintains the lead and shelters a veiled Nicaragua, the country most devastated by the war. Guatemala, Honduras, and El Salvador might dispute this version of events, but this is how Costa Rica chose to commission the work by French sculptor Louis Carrier Belleuse, a student of Rodin, in 1895. Bas-relief murals on the monument's pedestal depict key battles in the war against the Americans. ✉ *Bordered by Avdas. 1–3 and Cs. 15–19, Barrio La Soledad.*

❶ **Plaza de la Cultura.** The crowds of people, vendors, and street entertainers at the Plaza de la Cultura—it's a favored spot for marimba bands, clowns, jugglers, and colorfully dressed South Americans playing Andean music—hide the fact that the expanse is really just a mass of concrete. The ornate Teatro Nacional dominates the plaza's southern half. Pop in and buy a ticket for an evening performance. The Museo del Oro Precolombino, with its highly visited exhibits of gold, lies under the plaza. The plaza's western edge is defined by the Gran Hotel Costa Rica, with its 24-hour Café 1930. ✉ *Bordered by Avdas. Central–2 and Cs. 3–5, Barrio La Soledad.*

⓫ **Plaza de la Democracia.** President Oscar Arias built this terraced open space west of the Museo Nacional to mark 100 years of democracy and to receive dignitaries during the 1989 hemispheric summit. The view west toward the dark-green Cerros de Escazú is nice in the morning and fabulous at sunset. Swarms of graffiti artists, who protested a free-trade agreement with the United States, trashed the plaza throughout 2007. After a 2008 remodeling and sprucing up, it sparkles once again. Jewelry, T-shirts, and crafts from Costa Rica, Guatemala, and South America are sold in a string of stalls along the western edge. They are worth a stop. The city is looking to move the vendors to another location at this writing. ✉ *Bordered by Avdas. Central–2 and Cs. 13–15, Barrio La Soledad.*

Museo del Oro Precolumbino has the largest collection of pre-Columbian gold jewelry in Central America.

🔟 Plaza del Banco Central. An extension of Avenida Central, this plaza is popular with hawkers, money changers, and retired men, and can be a good place to get a shoe shine and listen to street musicians. Outside the western end of Costa Rica's modern federal-reserve bank building, don't miss *Presentes*, 10 sculpted, smaller-than-life figures of bedraggled *campesinos* (peasants). *La Chola*, a bronze 500-kg (1,100-lb) statue of a buxom rural woman, resides at sidewalk level on the small, shady plaza south of the bank. It's public art at its best. Beware: the money changers here are notorious for circulating counterfeit bills and using doctored calculators to shortchange unwitting tourists. Instead, change money at banks or through cash machines, where you get the best rate. ✉ *Bordered by Avdas. Central–1 and Cs. 2–4, Barrio La Merced.*

🔟 Teatro Popular Melico Salazar. Across Avenida 2 on the north side of Parque Central stands San José's second major performance hall (after the Teatro Nacional). The 1928 building is on the site of a 19th-century military barracks felled by an earthquake. The venue was later named for Costa Rican operatic tenor Manuel "Melico" Salazar (1887–1950). It was constructed specifically to provide a less highbrow alternative to the Teatro Nacional. But these days the Melico is plenty cultured and provides the capital with a steady diet of music and dance performances. ✉ *Avda. 2 and C. 2, Barrio La Merced* ☎ *2233–5424* ⊕ *www. teatromelico.go.cr.*

NORTH AND EAST OF DOWNTOWN

Immediately northeast of downtown lie Barrio Amón and Barrio Otoya. Both neighborhoods are repositories of historic houses that have escaped the wrecking ball; many now serve as hotels, restaurants, galleries, and offices. (A few are even private residences.) Where these barrios begin and end depends on who's doing the talking. Locales on the fringes of the city center prefer to be associated with these "good neighborhoods" rather than with downtown. Barrio Escalante, to the east, isn't quite as gentrified but is fast becoming fashionable.

RAINY DAY TIPS

■ Do outdoor sightseeing in the morning, before the afternoon rains arrive.

■ Duck into museums—our top choices are the Gold and Jade museums.

■ Do as Costa Ricans do and *tomar café* (take a coffee break).

■ Don't wait until the evening rush hour (5–7 PM) to get a cab— empty ones are nearly nonexistent when it rains.

The sprawling suburb of San Pedro begins several blocks east of downtown San José. The town is home to the University of Costa Rica and all the intellect and cheap eats and nightlife that a student or student-wannabe could desire. But away from the heart of the university, San Pedro is awash in the consumerism of malls, fast-food restaurants, and car dealerships—although it manages to mix in stately districts such as the stylish Los Yoses for good measure. To get to San Pedro, take a $2 taxi ride from downtown and get off in front of Banco Nacional, just beyond the rotunda with the fountain at its center.

㉑ Jardín de Mariposas Spyrogyra. Spending an hour or two at this magical Spyrogyra Butterfly Garden is entertaining and educational for nature lovers of all ages. Self-guided tours enlighten you on butterfly ecology and let you see the winged creatures close up. After an 18-minute video introduction, you're free to wander screened-in gardens along a numbered trail. Some 30 species of colorful butterflies flutter about, accompanied by six types of hummingbirds. Try to come when it's sunny, as butterflies are most active then. A small, moderately priced café borders the garden and serves sandwiches and Tico fare. ⊠ *50 m east and 150 m south of main entrance to El Pueblo shopping center, Barrio Tournón* ☎ *2222–2937* ⊕ *www.butterflygardencr.com* ✉ *$6, $3 children under 12* ☉ *Daily 8–4.*

㉑ Museo de los Niños. San José's Children's Museum is in a former prison, and big kids may want to check it out just to marvel at the castlelike architecture and the old cells that have been preserved in an exhibit about life behind bars. Three halls in the complex are filled with eye-catching seasonal exhibits for kids, ranging in subject from local ecology to outer space. The exhibits are annotated in Spanish, but most are interactive, so language shouldn't be much of a problem. The museum's most popular resident is the Egyptian exhibit's sarcophagus; the mummy draws the "oohs" and "aahs." Officially, the complex is called the Centro Costarricense de Ciencia y Cultura (Costa Rican Center of

CLOSE UP

Missing History

Blame it on the earthquakes. Costa Ricans are quick to attribute the scarcity of historic architecture in San José and around the country to a history of earth tremors. Indeed, major earthquakes have struck various locales around Costa Rica 10 times since the mid-18th century (6 times in the 20th century), felling untold numbers of historical structures.

But blame it on the wrecking ball, too, says architect Gabriela Sáenz, who works with the Ministry of Culture's Center for Research and Conservation of Cultural Patrimony. The tear-it-down approach really began to take its toll in the 1970s, an era when boxy, concrete buildings were in vogue around the world, Sáenz says. Costa Rica didn't establish its first school of architecture until 1972, staffed by faculty from Mexico, England, and Brazil. "It was hard for a real Costa Rican tradition to take hold," she explains. Mix that with a lack of government regulation and

what Sáenz calls a typical Tico do-your-own-thing penchant, and the result is a city full of squat buildings.

The tide began to turn in 1995 with the passage of the Law of Historic and Architectural Patrimony. More than 300 historic structures in the country are currently protected under the legislation, and new buildings are added to the registry each year. But legal protection is no guarantee of funding necessary to actually restore a historic landmark.

You need to look hard, but San José really does have several diamonds in the rough. The National Theater and Central Post Office remain the two most visited examples of historic architecture in the capital. But the National Museum, the National Center of Culture, and several small hostelries and restaurants around town—especially in Barrios Amón and Otoya—are all modern transformations and restorations of structures with histories.

Science and Culture), and that will be the sign that greets you on the front of the building. The Galería Nacional, adjoining the main building, is more popular with adults; it usually shows fine art by Costa Rican artists free of charge. Also adjoining the museum is the classical music venue Auditorio Nacional. Though just a short distance from downtown, the walk here takes you through a dodgy neighborhood. You'll definitely feel as though you've stepped out of the hustle and bustle of the center city. Take a taxi to and from. ✉ *North end of C. 4, Barrio El Carmen* ☎ *2258–4929* ⊕ *www.museocr.com* ✉ *$2* ☉ *Tues.– Fri. 8–4:30, weekends 9:30–5.*

NEED A BREAK?

We have to admit that Costa Rican baked goods tend toward the dry-as-dust end of the spectrum. But Italian-style bakery **Giacomín**, near the University of Costa Rica, is an exception—it seems that a touch of liqueur added to the batter makes all the difference. Stand, European-style, at the downstairs espresso bar, or take your goodies to the tables and chairs on the upstairs balcony. Both branches close from noon to 2. You'll also find outlets in Escazú, Heredia, and Santa Ana out in the Central Valley.

Are You Ready for Some Fútbol?

Sports mean one thing in San José: soccer. Very young boys (and a slowly increasing number of girls) kick around a ball—or some other object if no ball is available—in street pickup games, and they grow into fans passionate about their local team. But everyone puts aside regional differences when the reputation of Costa Rica's national team is on the line, as it is during the World Cup.

Consult the Spanish-language daily *La Nación* or ask at your hotel for details

on upcoming games—you simply show up at the stadium box office. Prices range from $2 to $12. *Sombra numerado* (shaded seats) are the most expensive.

Professional soccer matches are usually played on Sunday morning or Wednesday night in either of two San José stadiums. The Estadio Ricardo Saprissa (next to the Clínica Integrada de Tibás) is home to Saprissa, the capital's beloved hometown team, and is in the northern suburb of Tibás.

WEST OF DOWNTOWN

Paseo Colón, one of San José's major boulevards, heads due west from downtown and leads to the vast La Sabana park, the city's largest parcel of green space. La Sabana anchors the even vaster west side of the city. A block or two off its exhaust-ridden avenues are quiet residential streets, and you'll find the U.S., Canadian, and British embassies here.

㉒ Museo de Arte Costarricense. A splendid collection of 19th- and 20th-century Costa Rican art, labeled in Spanish and English, is housed in 12 exhibition halls here. Be sure to visit the top-floor Salón Dorado to see the stucco, bronze-plate bas-relief mural depicting Costa Rican history, created by French sculptor Louis Feron. Guided tours are offered Tuesday–Friday 10–3. Wander into the sculpture garden in back and take in Jorge Jiménez's 7-meter-tall *Imagen Cósmica,* which depicts pre-Columbian traditions. The museum sparkles following a two-year restoration and a 2010 reopening. ⊠ *C. 42 and Paseo Colón, Paseo Colón* ☎ *2222–7155* ⊕ *www.musarco.go.cr* ☒ *$5, free Sun.* ⊙ *Tues.– Fri. 10–6, weekends 10–4.*

㉓ Parque Metropolitano La Sabana. Though it isn't centrally located, La Sabana (The Savannah) comes the closest of San José's green spaces to achieving the same function and spirit as New York's Central Park. A statue of 1930s president León Cortes greets you at the principal entrance at the west end of Paseo Colón. Behind the statue a 5-meter-tall menorah serves as a gathering place for San José's small Jewish community during Hanukkah. La Sabana was once San José's airport, and the whitewashed Museo de Arte Costarricense, just south of the Cortes statue, served as terminal and control tower.

The round Gimnasio Nacional (National Gymnasium) sits at the park's southeast corner and hosts sporting events and the occasional concert. At this writing a 40,000-seat stadium is under construction—a controversial gift from the government of China, which has decided to use its own construction workers rather than employ local people—near the park's northwest corner. Opening is scheduled for mid-2011. In between are acres of space for soccer, basketball, tennis, swimming, jogging, picnicking, and kite flying. The park hums with activity on weekend days. You're welcome to join in the early-morning outdoor aerobics classes on Saturday and Sunday. A project is under way to replace many of the park's eucalyptus trees with more bird-friendly species native to Costa Rica.

A small building boom is taking place these days, with condos and office buildings going up around the perimeter of the park, another resemblance to New York's Central Park. (Because of building codes, "skyscraper" means a maximum of about 10 floors in earthquake-prone Costa Rica.) Like most of San José's green spaces, La Sabana should be avoided at night. ⊠ *Bordered by C. 42, Avda. de las Américas, and Autopista Próspero Fernández, Paseo Colón.*

NEED A BREAK?

Costa Rica gave the world the so-called canopy tour, and you used to have to go pretty far afield to zip via cables through the treetops Tarzan-style. The metro area now counts two outlets of the Urban Canopy (⊠ *Parque Metropolitano La Sabana, La Sabana* ☎ *2215–2544* ⊠ *Parque del Este, near the Christ statue on the Sabanilla Highway, Sabanilla* ⊡ *$25* ⊗ *9–5*) The west-side branch in La Sabana park takes you over a series of eight cables, four bridges, and a rappel climb. On the far east side, the outlet in the Parque del Este contains a series of seven cables, with hiking trails for before or after offering ample birding opportunities.

WHERE TO EAT

Wherever you eat in San José, be it a small *soda* (informal eatery) or a sophisticated restaurant, dress is casual. Meals tend to be taken earlier than in other Latin American countries; few restaurants serve past 9 or 10 PM. Local cafés usually open for breakfast at 7 AM and remain open until 7 or 8 in the evening. Restaurants serving international cuisine are usually open from 11 AM to 9 PM. Some cafés that serve mainly San José office workers limit evening hours and close entirely on Sunday. Restaurants that do open on Sunday do a brisk business: it's the traditional family day out (and the maid's day off). △ **Watch your things, no matter where you dine. Prowlers have been known to sneak into even the best restaurants, targeting purses slung over chair arms or placed under chairs.**

WHAT IT COSTS IN DOLLARS				
¢	$	$$	$$$	$$$$
Restaurants	under $5	$5–$10	$10–$15	$15–$25	over $25

Restaurant prices are per person for a main course at dinner.

San José's ubiquitous red taxicabs.

DOWNTOWN

$$
ECLECTIC
✕ **Balcón de Europa.** With old sepia photos and a strolling guitarist who seems to have been working the room forever, Balcón de Europa transports you to the year of its inception, 1909. Pasta specialties such as the *plato mixto* (mixed plate with lasagna, tortellini, and ravioli) are so popular that they haven't changed much either. (Why tamper with success?) A new owner has, however, added French and Mediterranean dishes to the menu—try the blanquette of veal or the couscous. Among the lighter fare are a scrumptious hearts-of-palm salad or a sautéed corvina. Grab a table away from the door (i.e., from the noise of the bus stop across the street). FYI: old-timers refer to the place as Balcón de Franco; the late, legendary chef Franco Piatti was the restaurant's guiding light for years. ⊠ *Avda. Central and C. 9, Barrio La Soledad* ☎ *2221–4841* ▤ *AE, D, DC, MC, V* ⊗ *Closed Mon.* ✛ *F3.*

$
CAFÉ
✕ **Café de la Posada.** The lack of alfresco dining in this tropical city is disappointing, but this café's covered terrace with tables fronting the Calle 17 pedestrian mall is a pleasant exception. The owners come from Argentina, and they know how to make a great cappuccino. Salads, quiches, and empanadas are specialties. The best bargains are the four rotating *platos del día* (daily specials), with entrée, salad, beverage, and dessert for $4. If you opt for dinner, make it an early one: the place closes at 7 on weeknights. ⊠ *C. 17, Avdas. 2–4, Barrio La Soledad* ☎ *2258– 1027* ▤ *AE, D, DC, MC, V* ⊗ *Closed Sun. No dinner Sat.* ✛ *H4.*

$$
CHINESE
✕ **Don Wang.** In a country where "Chinese cuisine" often means rice and vegetables bearing a suspicious resemblance to *gallo pinto* ("spotted rooster," a typical Costa Rican dish of black beans and rice), Don Wang's authenticity is a treat. Cantonese cuisine is the mainstay—the

owner comes from that region of China—but these folks will Szechuan it up a bit if you ask. Mornings give way to the immensely popular dim sum, called *desayuno chino*, literally "Chinese breakfast." You can order dim sum all day, but the $5 specials last only until 11 AM. The dining area is built around a stone garden and small waterfall. There's no television blaring here, a refreshing change from many Costa Rican restaurants. ⊠ *C. 11, Avdas. 6–8, Barrio La Soledad* ☎ *2233–6484* ⊕ *www.donwangrestaurant.com* ⊟ *AE, D, DC, MC, V* ✣ *G4.*

HAVE SOME SAUCE

Any self-respecting Tico home or restaurant keeps a bottle of **Salsa Lizano**, one of the country's signature food products, on hand. Its tang brightens up meat, vegetable, and rice dishes. Bottles of the stuff make great souvenirs, and you can buy them at **Más x Menos** (pronounced Más *por* Menos) supermarkets throughout the country. The main San José branch is at Avenida Central, between Calles 11 and 13.

3

$ ✕ **La Criollita.** Kick off your day with
COSTA RICAN   breakfast at this emerald-green restaurant. Mornings are the perfect time to snag one of the precious tables in the back garden, an unexpected refuge from noise and traffic. Breakfast platters come with eggs on the side: the *americano* has pancakes and toast; the *tico* comes with bread, fried bananas, and *natilla* (sour cream); and the huge *criollita* has ham or pork chops. Government workers from nearby offices start arriving late in the morning, and the lunchtime decibel level increases appreciably. (This is the one time of day we recommend avoiding the place.) Everyone filters out about 2 PM, and once again, you have a quiet place for coffee and dessert. ⊠ *Avda. 7, Cs. 7–9, Barrio Amón* ☎ *2256–6511* ⊟ *AE, D, DC, MC, V* ☾ *Closed Sun. No dinner Sat.* ✣ *G3.*

$ ✕ **Mama's Place.** Mama's is a Costa Rican restaurant with a difference:
COSTA RICAN   the owners are Italian, so in addition to *corvina al ajillo* (sea bass sautéed with garlic) and other staple Tico fare, they serve homemade seafood chowder, traditional Italian pastas, and meat dishes with delicate wine sauces. The brightly decorated coffee shop opens onto busy Avenida 1; the more subdued dining room upstairs accommodates the overflow crowd. (You'll see former Chicago Bears football coach Mike Ditka's autographed picture up there.) At lunchtime it's usually packed with business types drawn to the delicious and inexpensive daily specials—choose from the rotating *platos del día* (daily specials) with pasta, meat, fish, or poultry—all to the accompaniment of ample focaccia. Mama's closes at 7 PM on weeknights. ⊠ *Avda. 1, Cs. Central–2, Barrio El Carmen* ☎ *2223–2270 or 2256–5601* ⊟ *AE, D, DC, MC, V* ☾ *Closed Sun. No dinner Sat.* ✣ *E3.*

$ ✕ **Manolo's.** For any San José dweller, a mention of Manolo's brings
COSTA RICAN   their signature menu item *churros con chocolate* (fried dough with hot fudge sauce) to mind. But this 24-hour eatery is also known for its great sandwiches and espressos. Its location on the Avenida Central pedestrian thoroughfare and its outdoor tables allow for some of the city's best people-watching. Inside, however, the place feels more like a diner than a café, down to its plastic-coated menu and its promise of breakfast food at any hour. The owner always prepares a few Spanish

favorites in addition to the typical Tico fare, such as *tortilla española* (a thick potato-and-onion omelet). ⊠ *Avda. Central, Cs. Central–2, Barrio La Merced* ☎ *2221–2041* ▭ *AE, D, DC, MC, V* ✦ *E4.*

$ ✕ **News Café.** Pounce on one of the street-side tables if they're free.

AMERICAN   (They probably won't be available: a regular expat crowd holds court here.) The passing parade on Avenida Central is yours for the price of a cup of coffee. Breakfast and dinner fare is hearty, but the café is most popular at lunchtime and cocktail hour. You can get a Caesar salad and other American dishes here, including good burgers, sandwiches, and salads. The café is on the first floor of the 1960s landmark Hotel Presidente. ⊠ *Avda. Central and C. 7, Barrio La Soledad* ☎ *2222–3022* ▭ *AE, D, DC, MC, V* ✦ *F4.*

$ ✕ **Nuestra Tierra.** But for the traffic zipping by on one of San José's busi-

COSTA RICAN   est thoroughfares—and on that note, opt for a table on the side facing less busy Calle 15—you might think you're out in the rural Central Valley. Bunches of onions and peppers dangle from the ceiling, recalling a provincial Tico ranch. The generous homemade meals are delicious, and the incredibly friendly waitstaff, who epitomize Costa Rican hospitality and dress in folkloric clothing, prepare your coffee filtered through the traditional cloth *chorreador.* The place is open 24 hours, just in case *gallo pinto* (Costa Rican–style rice and beans) pangs hit at 3 AM. Some disparage the place as "too touristy." Perhaps it is, but it's also fun. ⊠ *Avda. 2 and C. 15, Barrio La Soledad* ☎ *2258–6500* ▭ *No credit cards* ✦ *G4.*

¢   ✕ **Shakti.** The baskets of fruit and vegetables at the entrance and the

VEGETARIAN   wall of herbal teas, health-food books, and fresh herbs for sale by the register tell you you're in a vegetarian-friendly joint. The bright and airy macrobiotic restaurant—much homier than Vishnu, its major vegetarian competition—serves breakfast, lunch, and an early dinner, closing at 7 PM weekdays and 6 PM Saturday. Homemade bread, soy burgers, pita sandwiches (veggie or, for carnivorous dining companions, chicken), macrobiotic fruit shakes, and a hearty plato del día that comes with soup, green salad, and a fruit beverage fill out the menu. The *ensalada mixta* is a meal in itself, packed with root vegetables native to Costa Rica. ⊠ *Avda. 8 and C. 13, Barrio La Soledad* ☎ *2222–4475* ▱ *Reservations not accepted* ▭ *MC, V* ☉ *Closed Sun.* ✦ *G5.*

$$$ ✕ **Tin Jo.** The colorful dining rooms of this converted house just south-

ASIAN   east of downtown evoke Japan, India, China, Indonesia, or Thailand.

Fodor'sChoice   In the Thai Room a 39-foot mural depicts a Buddhist temple. You can

★   select from all of the above cuisines, with menus to match the varied dining areas. Start with a powerful Singapore sling (brandy and fruit juices) before trying such treats as *kaeng* (Thai shrimp and pineapple curry in coconut milk), *mu shu* (a beef, chicken, or vegetable stir-fry with crepes), samosas (stuffed Indian pastries), and sushi rolls. The vegetarian menu is extensive, too. Tin Jo stands out with always exceptional food, attention to detail, and attentive service that make it, hands down, the country's top Asian restaurant. ⊠ *C. 11, Avdas. 6–8, Barrio La Soledad* ☎ *2257–3622 or 2221–7605* ▭ *AE, D, DC, MC, V* ✦ *G4.*

¢ ✕ **Vishnu.** HACIENDO UN NUEVO MUNDO, proudly proclaims the sign at the
VEGETARIAN door. "Making a new world" might be a bit ambitious for a restaurant
goal, but Vishnu takes its vegetarian offerings seriously. The dining
area looks institutional—you'll sit at a sterile booth with Formica
tables and gaze at posters of fruit on the walls—but the attraction is
the inexpensive macrobiotic food. A yummy, good-value bet is usually the plato del día (soup, beverage, and dessert), but the menu also
includes soy burgers, salads, fresh fruit juices, and a yogurt smoothie
called *morir soñando* (literally, "to die dreaming"). ✉ *Avda. 1, west
of C. 3, Barrio El Carmen* ☎ *2233–9976* ⌣ *Reservations not accepted*
▭ *AE, D, DC, MC, V* ✛ *F3.*

NORTH AND EAST OF DOWNTOWN

$$ ✕ **Café Mundo.** You could easily walk by this corner restaurant without
CAFÉ noticing its tiny sign behind the foliage. The upstairs café serves meals
Fodor's Choice on a porch, on a garden patio, or in two dining rooms. The soup of the
★ day and fresh-baked bread start you out; main courses include shrimp
in a vegetable cream sauce or *lomito en salsa de vino tinto* (tenderloin
in a red-wine sauce). Save room for the best chocolate cake in town,
drizzled with homemade blackberry sauce. Café Mundo is a popular,
low-key gay hangout that draws a mixed gay-straight clientele. This is
one of the few center-city restaurants with its own parking lot. ✉ *C.
15 and Avda. 9, Barrio Otoya* ☎ *2222–6190* ▭ *AE, D, DC, MC, V*
☾ *Closed Sun. No lunch Sat.* ✛ *G2.*

$ ✕ **Crokante.** Don't be surprised to see a lot of white coats here. The
ECLECTIC place is a lunch favorite of physicians from the large hospital down the
street who come here for the filling, $6 *plato ejecutivo* lunch special.
(Two of the three owners are doctors, too.) If you prefer to order off
the menu, you'll find a good selection of steaks, pastas, and seafood.
There's something reassuringly American about the main courses, but
the appetizers (spicy hummus, breaded calamari, and mussels in moz-
zarella cheese) tread into a more experimental realm. The outdoor
terrace overlooks a railroad track and busy street; you'll find inside
dining to be quieter during the day. Evenings give way to more leisurely
dining, with soft, live music on Friday and Saturday nights. ✉ *C. 15,
Avda. 11, Barrio Otoya* ☎ *2258–1017* ▭ *AE, D, DC, MC, V* ☾ *Closed
Sun. No lunch Sat.* ✛ *H2.*

$$$ ✕ **Jürgen's.** Jürgen's is a common haunt for *politicos*, and San José's elites
ECLECTIC meet to eat here. Decorated in gold and terra-cotta with leather and
wood accents, the dining room of this contemporary restaurant feels
more like a lounge than a fine restaurant. In fact, the classy bar, with
a large selection of good wine and good cigars, is a prominent feature.
The inventive menu, with such delicacies as medallions of roast duck
and tuna fillet encrusted with sesame seeds, sets this place apart from
the city's more traditional venues. ✉ *250 m north of the Subaru dealer-
ship, on Blvd. Barrio Dent, Barrio Dent* ☎ *2283–2239* ▭ *AE, D, DC,
MC, V* ☾ *Closed Sun. No lunch Sat.* ✛ *B5.*

$ ✕ **La Trattoria.** The green and gold here might make a Green Bay Packers
ITALIAN fan feel right at home, but it's the excellent, reasonably priced home-
made pasta dishes that make this popular lunch spot worth the stop.
Begin your meal with fresh bread and any number of excellent antipasti,

continuing on with your favorite pasta dish. And for dessert, who can resist tiramisu? ⊠ *Behind Automercado, Barrio Dent, San Pedro* ☎ *2224–7065* ▭ *AE, D, DC, MC, V* ⊘ *No dinner Sun.* ✛ *B5.*

$$$$
FRENCH

✕ **Le Chandelier.** San José doesn't get classier than this restaurant, where formal service and traditional sauce-heavy French dishes are part of the experience. The dining room is elegant, with wicker chairs, a tile floor, and original paintings. The Swiss chef, Claude Dubuis, might start you off with saffron ravioli stuffed with ricotta cheese and walnuts. His main courses include such unique dishes as corvina in a *pejibaye* (peach palm) sauce, hearts of palm and veal chops glazed in a sweet port-wine sauce, and the more familiar *pato a la naranja* (duck à l'orange), or, for a tropical twist on that classic dish, *pato a la maracuyá* (duck in passion fruit). ⊠ *50 m west and 100 m south of ICE building, San Pedro* ☎ *2225–3980* ⊕ *www.lechandeliercr.com* ▭ *AE, D, DC, MC, V* ⊘ *Closed Sun. No lunch Sat.* ✛ *C5.*

$
JAPANESE

✕ **Matsuri.** It's a bit off the beaten tourist path and it's in a shopping center, but this is one of the capital's best sushi joints. The chefs here have created 48 recipes for original rolls, sushi, and sashimi, using high-quality imported ingredients. Bento boxes serve as the weekday lunch specials. The oohing and aahing you hear upstairs is for the chefs performing at the teppanyaki grills to the delight and applause of patrons. ⊠ *Plaza Cristal, 600 m south of Pop's ice-cream shop, Curridabat* ☎ *2280–5522* ▭ *AE, D, DC, MC, V* ✛ *H5.*

$
ITALIAN

✕ **Pane e Vino.** Look closely at the extensive menu here: there are 40 varieties of the capital's best thin-crust pizza, and no one will rush you if you spend too much time pondering what you want. This lively two-level restaurant—it's a small chain, but this was the first location—rounds out its offerings with a complete selection of pastas. You can dine until midnight daily, except on Sunday, when you'll have to finish dinner by 10 PM. The Pizza Allessandre, topped with prosciutto, mozzarella, and olives, is the most popular dish, and for good reason. ⊠ *50 m west and 15 m south of Más X Menos, San Pedro* ☎ *2280–2869* ▭ *AE, MC, V* ✛ *H5.*

$
MEDITERRANEAN

✕ **Pub Olio.** Although this combination pub and restaurant serves the full contingent of Mediterranean cuisine, we like to visit the place for drinks and Spanish-style *tapas* (appetizers). The century-old redbrick house with stained-glass windows draws everybody from tie-clad businessmen to university students who have money to spend on something more upscale than run-of-the-mill campus-area bars. Groups liven up the large front room—the quieter, smaller back rooms maintain a bit more romance. The staff hauls umbrella-covered tables out to the sidewalk on warm evenings. Olio is extremely proud that it offers a copy of its menu in Braille. ⊠ *200 m north of Bagelmen's, Barrio Escalante* ☎ *2281–0541* ▭ *AE, D, DC, MC, V* ⊘ *Closed Sun. No lunch Sat.* ✛ *H5.*

WEST OF DOWNTOWN

$$$
SPANISH
Fodor's Choice
★

✕ **Casa Luisa.** A big open window looking into the kitchen—where chef María Luisa Esparducer and her staff proudly show off their trade—is the first thing you encounter as you're shown to your table in this homey, upscale Catalan restaurant. The place is eclectic, with wood floors, arresting artwork, soft lighting, and flamenco music in the background. Start the meal with gazpacho or eggplant pâté, accompanied by a glass of top Spanish wine. The excellent main dishes include rosemary lamb chops, suckling pig, and rabbit in white wine sauce with truffles. Finish with a platter of nuts, dates, and figs drizzled with a wine sauce or the decadent *crema catalana* with a *brûlée* glaze. We give Casa Luisa the nod as the city's best Spanish restaurant for its combination of style and coziness. ⊠ *400 m south and 40 m east of the Contraloría, Sabana Sur* ☎ *2296–1917* ▭ *AE, D, DC, MC, V* ☺ *Closed weekends* ✛ *A4.*

$$
MIDDLE EASTERN
✕ **Lubnan.** Negotiate the quirky wrought-iron-and-burlap revolving door at the entrance, and you've made it into one of San José's few Middle Eastern restaurants. The Lebanese owners serve a wide variety of dishes from their native region, so if you can't decide, the *mezza* serves two people and gives you a little bit of everything. For your own individual dish, try the juicy shish kebab *de cordero* (of lamb), or, if you're feeling especially adventurous, the raw ground-meat *kebbe naye* (with wheat meal) and *kafta naye* (without wheat meal). A hip bar in the back serves the same menu, but definitely eat out in the front restaurant Thursday night for the 9 PM belly-dancing show. ⊠ *Paseo Colón, Cs. 22–24, Paseo Colón* ☎ *2257–6071* ▭ *AE, D, DC, MC, V* ☺ *Closed Mon. No dinner Sun.* ✛ *B3.*

$$
★
PERUVIAN
✕ **Machu Picchu.** A few travel posters and a fishnet holding crab and lobster shells are the only props used to evoke Peru, but no matter: the food is anything but plain, and the seafood is excellent at both the east- and west-side branches of this mainstay. The *pique especial de mariscos* (special seafood platter), big enough for two, presents you with shrimp, conch, and squid cooked four ways. The ceviche here is quite different from and better than that served in the rest of the country. A blazing Peruvian hot sauce served on the side adds zip to any dish, but be careful—apply it by the drop. Oh, and one more warning: the pisco sours go down very easily. ⊠ *C. 32, 130 m north of KFC, Paseo Colón* ☎ *2222–7384* ⊠ *150 m south of Ferretería El Mar, San Pedro* ☎ *2283–3679* ▭ *AE, D, DC, MC, V* ☺ *Paseo Colón location closed Sun.* ✛ *A3.*

$$
ECLECTIC
✕ **Park Café.** Don't let appearances deceive you: the colonial-style house is only a decade old, but attention to architectural detail and antique furnishings make you think the building was transplanted from Antigua or Granada. An all-tapas menu makes up the fare here, with such tasty dishes as Thai-style tuna salad or red-snapper couscous. The menu varies from year to year, depending on what the owner has uncovered during his two-month European autumn buying trip. On that topic, owner Richard Neat is onetime proprietor of a two-star Michelin restaurant in London, and one of the few British chefs to achieve that distinction. Space is limited, making reservations a must. The January–April dry season takes the pressure off a bit, allowing seating to spill over from the covered veranda to the open courtyard. ⊠ *100 m north of Rosti Pollos, Sabana Norte* ☎ *2290–6324* ⊕ *parkcafecostarica.blogspot.com* ⬗ *Reservations essential* ▭ *AE, MC, V* ☺ *Closed Sun. and Mon.* ✛ *A4.*

¢   × **Soda Tapia.** One of San José's most popular restaurants fronts the
COSTA RICAN   east side of La Sabana park. You can dine outdoors, but you'll have to
contend with the traffic noise and the sight of the guard flagging cars
in and out of the tiny parking lot. The place stays open until 2 AM and
around the clock on weekends. ⊠ *Sabana Este* ☎ *2222–6734* ⊟ *AE,
D, DC, MC, V* ⊕ *A4.*

WHERE TO STAY

San José has plenty of chains, including Best Western, Holiday Inn,
Radisson, Quality Inn, Clarion, Meliá, and Barceló (the last two are
Spanish chains). But it also has historic houses with traditional archi-
tecture that have been converted into small lodgings.

The historic houses are usually without concierge or pool and are
found mainly in Barrios Amón and Otoya, and in the eastern suburb
of San Pedro. The city also has a lower tier of lodgings with the simplicity (and prices) beloved of backpackers. Most smaller hotels don't
have air-conditioning, but it rarely gets warm enough at this altitude
to warrant it.

Many lodgings operate at near-full occupancy in high season (December through April). Reconfirm all reservations 24 hours in advance. If
you're flying out early in the morning and prefer to stay near the airport, consider booking a hotel near Alajuela or San Antonio de Belén
(⇨ *See Chapter 4*).

WHAT IT COSTS IN DOLLARS				
	¢	$	$$	$$$	$$$$
Hotels	under $50	$50–$75	$75–$150	$150–$250	over $250

Hotel prices are for two people in a standard double room in high season,
excluding service and tax (16.4%).

DOWNTOWN

Staying in the downtown area allows you to travel around the city as most
Ticos do: on foot. Stroll the parks, museums, and shops, and then retire
to one of the many small or historic hotels with plenty of character.

$$–$$$ ▦ **Aurola Holiday Inn.** The upper floors of this veritable skyscraper in
a city of low-lying buildings give you commanding vistas of the surrounding mountains—day views are the best, since San José doesn't
glitter quite like New York at night. The good restaurant and casino
are also on the top floor, making full use of their vantage points. Inside,
however, you could just as well be in Ohio, as the interior decora-
tion betrays no local influence. The high-ceiling lobby is modern and
airy, with lots of shiny marble, and the place has all the facilities a
business traveler's heart could desire. The entire hotel—rooms and
public areas—is non-smoking. ■ TIP➔ **You'll get the hotel's best rates
by reserving in advance via the local Costa Rican number or the hotel's
own Web site, rather than the international Holiday Inn site.** Pros: business facilities; central location. **Cons:** sameness of chain hotel; park
across street dicey at night. ⊠ *Avda. 5 and C. 5, Barrio El Carmen*

✉ *Apdo. 7802–1000* ☎ *2523–1260; 866/465–4329 in North America* 🖷 *2255–1171* ⊕ *www.aurolahotels.com* ⬐ *188 rooms, 12 suites* ⌂ *In-room: safe, refrigerator, Wi-Fi. In-hotel: 2 restaurants, room service, bar, pool, gym, spa, laundry service, Internet terminal, parking (free), no-smoking rooms* ▭ *AE, D, DC, MC, V* ⦿ *BP* ✛ *F3.*

$$ 🏨 **Gran Hotel Costa Rica.** You cannot get more centrally located than the longtime grande dame of San José lodgings. It's a good deal for the money and the first choice of travelers who want to be where the action is (or want an in-house casino). A formal dining room and grand piano just off the lobby evoke the hotel's 1930s heyday. Rooms are large and bright, with small windows and tubs in the tiled baths. Even if you don't stay here, the arcaded Café 1930 that fronts the hotel is a pleasant stop for a bite any time of the day or night—it's open 24 hours. ■ TIP➜ Check the hotel's Internet site for frequent Web-only special rates. **Pros:** central location; great people-watching from ground-floor café. **Cons:** some street noise; some rooms have thin walls. ✉ *Avda. 2 and C. 3, Barrio La Soledad* ✉ *Apdo. 527–1000* ☎ *2221–4000; 800/949–0592 in U.S.* ⊕ *www.grandhotelcostarica.com* ⬐ *104 rooms, 5 suites* ⌂ *In-room: no a/c (some), safe, refrigerator, Wi-Fi. In-hotel: 3 restaurants, room service, bar, gym, laundry service, Internet terminal, parking (free), no-smoking rooms* ▭ *AE, D, DC, MC, V* ⦿ *BP* ✛ *F3.*

$–$$ 🏨 **Hotel Balmoral.** You're just as likely to hear Japanese spoken in the Balmoral's lobby as you are Spanish and English; the place is quite popular with Asian visitors. As with the Presidente across the street, you'll find all the standard amenities of a medium-price business-class hotel here, and, like the Presidente, the Balmoral draws a huge number of leisure travelers, too. But we prefer the Balmoral's dark wood and plush, older feel, as well as the bright, airy restaurant El Patio, which dishes up Costa Rican specialties amid two floors of greenery. **Pros:** central location; good restaurant. **Cons:** some street noise; some rooms showing their age. ✉ *Avda. Central and C. 7, Barrio La Soledad* ☎ *2222–5022; 800/691–4865 in North America* ⊕ *www.balmoral.co.cr* ⬐ *112 rooms, 8 suites* ⌂ *In-room: safe, Wi-Fi. In-hotel: restaurant, bar, gym, laundry service, Internet terminal, parking (free)* ▭ *AE, D, DC, MC, V* ⦿ *BP* ✛ *F4.*

$$ 🏨 **Hotel Fleur de Lys.** Can a three-floor Victorian house with a brassy hot-pink-and-lavender exterior offer anything of interest beyond its front doors? Peek inside. The answer is a resounding yes. A quiet elegance that you'd never imagine lies inside this 80-year-old home, with garden restaurant and art gallery, on a block-long street that gets little traffic. Unsurprisingly, given the name of the place, rooms are tagged with names of flowers rather than numbers. We like the suites, which have raised bathtubs—two of them have whirlpool tubs as well—and dramatic glassed-in balcony entrances. Smoking is permitted in the hotel's common areas only. **Pros:** cozy rooms; close to sights. **Cons:** some noise from downstairs bar. ✉ *C. 13 and Avdas. 2–6, Barrio La Soledad* ✉ *Apdo. 10736–1000* ☎ *2223–1206* ⊕ *www.hotelfleurdelys.com* ⬐ *31 rooms, 6 suites* ⌂ *In-room: no a/c, safe, Wi-Fi. In-hotel: restaurant, bar, laundry service, Internet terminal, parking (free), no-smoking rooms* ▭ *AE, MC, V* ⦿ *BP* ✛ *G4.*

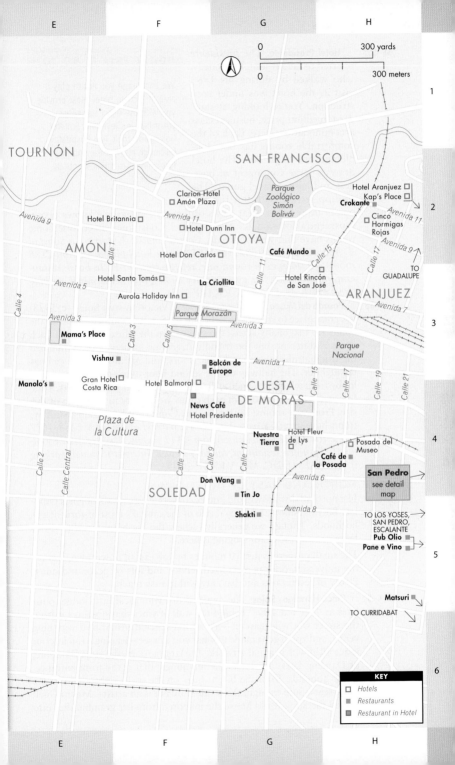

$$–$$$ 🖼 **Hotel Presidente.** The *presidente* referred to here is John F. Kennedy, who walked by during his 1963 visit as the hotel was under construction. You're looking at standard, medium-price, business-class accommodations here. Each of the comfortable rooms has one double and one single bed. The hotel draws a large contingent of business and leisure-travel guests. The rooftop terrace with hot tub has one of those secret great views of the city that no one knows about. **Pros:** central location; eco-friendly hotel. **Cons:** some street noise; some rooms have thin walls. ⊠ *Avda. Central and C. 7, Barrio La Soledad* ⬧ *Apdo. 2922–1000* ☎ *2256–1165* ⊕ *www.hotel-presidente.com* ⟿ *88 rooms, 12 suites* ⚘ *In-room: safe, refrigerator, Wi-Fi. In-hotel: restaurant, room service, bar, gym, laundry service, Internet terminal, parking (free)* ▭ *AE, D, DC, MC, V* |❍| *BP* ⊕ *F4.*

> **DONDE ESTA EL HO-JO?**
>
> We encourage you not to play it safe at a chain hotel. Most provide you with the exact sameness you'd find in Cleveland. Smaller hotels and their Tico hospitality (although many are owned by foreigners) are quintessentially Costa Rica.

$–$$ 🖼 **Posada del Museo.** This green, wooden, Victorian-style house (c. 1928) is a great place to stay if you're bound for San José's museums; hence the name. It's diagonally across the street from the Museo Nacional. Each room is different, but the friendly Argentine owners have maintained the original tiles, wooden double doors, and artfully painted ceilings throughout. The hallway on the second floor overlooks the two-story lobby from what the owners call their "Romeo and Juliet balcony." The Internet-ready data ports in each room are a rarity in a lodging of this size. **Pros:** cozy rooms; near museums. **Cons:** rush-hour train passes by; fronts busy street. ⊠ *Avda. 2 and C. 17, Barrio La Soledad* ☎ *2258–1027* ⊕ *www.hotelposadadelmuseo.com* ⟿ *11 rooms, 3 suites* ⚘ *In-room: no a/c. In-hotel: restaurant, laundry service, Internet terminal, parking (free)* ▭ *AE, D, DC, MC, V* |❍| *BP* ⊕ *H4.*

NORTH AND EAST OF DOWNTOWN

Just north of downtown, old homes converted into small lodgings populate Barrios Amón and Otoya, two of the capital's most historic neighborhoods. Though we generally eschew the big hotel franchises, our favorite San José chain lodging is here.

The small properties just 10 minutes by cab east of downtown, toward the university, offer personalized service and lots of peace and quiet. Plenty of restaurants and bars are within easy reach.

¢–$ 🖼 **Cinco Hormigas Rojas.** The name of this whimsical little lodge trans-
★ lates as "five red ants." Behind the wall of vines that obscures it from the street is a wild garden—it's an unexpected urban bird-watching venue, and you'll get a guide to what you can see—leading to an interior space filled with original artwork. The largest room (the Hoja Dansante, or Dancing Leaf) overlooks the minijungle that is the front entrance. Color abounds, from the bright hues on the walls right down to the toilet seats. Sure enough, the resident owner is an artist—Mayra Güell turned the 80-year-old house she inherited from her grandmother into

Eco- or Sustainable Tourism

Ecotourism, a relatively recent addition to the English language, has been defined as travel to natural areas to observe and learn about wildlife, tourism that refrains from damaging the environment, or tourism that strengthens conservation and improves the lives of local people. The latter two definitions could also apply to sustainable tourism, which has a wider scope than ecotourism and pushes for improvements in everything from city hotels to cruise ships. Whereas proponents of ecotourism believe it has the potential to conserve nature by providing economic opportunities for the rural poor, who are responsible for much of the deforestation in the tropics, sustainable tourism advocates note that all tourism has the potential for negative impacts, and they push

for improvement across the entire industry.

If you define ecotourism as tourism that contributes to conservation and community development, then ecotourism is always sustainable tourism. However, not all sustainable tourism is ecotourism, since tourism businesses located far from natural areas can and should implement sustainable practices. The list of hotels certified by the Costa Rican Tourism Board's Sustainable Tourism Certification program, for example, ranges from award-winning eco-lodges to city hotels that have made improvements such as installing sewage treatment systems and switching to energy-saving lightbulbs. For conscientious travelers who are looking for close contact with nature, sustainable may not be enough.

San José's most original bed-and-breakfast–cum–art gallery. She tosses in thoughtful touches such as a healthful boxed breakfast if you're heading out on an early-morning excursion, and coffee and tea 24/7. If you need everything just so and cherish the sameness and predictability of a chain hotel, look elsewhere, but if there's an artistic, bohemian bent to your personality, this is your place. **Pros:** friendly owner; artistic decor; bird-filled patio. **Cons:** small, dark rooms. ⊠ *C. 15, between Avdas. 9–11, Barrio Otoya* ☎ *2257–8581* ⊕ *www.cincohormigasrojas. com* ⇨ *4 rooms, 2 with bath* ♿ *In-room: no a/c (some), no phone, no TV (some), Wi-Fi. In-hotel: laundry service, Internet terminal, parking (paid)* ⊟ *AE, MC, V* ⎟○⎟ *BP* ✛ *H2.*

$$–$$$
Fodor's Choice
★
🏨 **Clarion Hotel Amón Plaza.** The mango-colored Amón Plaza achieves everything we like in a business-class hotel. It provides all the services and amenities you could need while transcending its chain status. Though large for a Barrio Amón lodging, the low-rise hotel doesn't overpower the surrounding neighborhood, and takes pride in the fact that each of its 80-plus rooms is slightly different. (One common feature: there's nothing mini about the minibars.) The price of the suites (but not the double rooms) includes all international calls and shuttle transport to anywhere in the metro area. Friday night sees cocktails and a buffet dinner at the hotel's open-air Cafetal de la Luz to the accompaniment of light music, but the café makes for a pleasant stop any time, any day, whether you stay here or not. **Pros:** business facilities;

friendly staff; eco-friendly hotel. **Cons:** lacks intimate hospitality of a smaller hotel; some rooms showing their age; sits on steep street. ⊠ *Avda. 11 and C. 3 Bis, Barrio Amón* ☎ *2523–4600; 877/424–6423 in North America* ⊕ *www.hotelamonplaza.com* ⇌ *81 rooms, 28 suites* ⚲ *In-room: safe, refrigerator, Wi-Fi. In-hotel: 2 restaurants, room service, bar, gym, spa, laundry service, Internet terminal, parking (free), no-smoking rooms* ⊟ *AE, D, DC, MC, V* ⏿ *BP* ✛ *F2.*

¢–$ ⊞ **Hotel Aranjuez.** Several 1940s-era houses with extensive gardens and lively common areas—where visitors swap travel advice—constitute this family-run bed-and-breakfast. Each room is different; some have private gardens or small sitting rooms. The Aranjuez is a short walk from most San José attractions and has discount tour services. The complimentary breakfast buffet is an amazing spread of eggs, pastries, tropical fruit, good Costa Rican coffee, and more, served on a marvelous, palm-shaded garden patio. And, a rarity in the heart of the city, this place walks the ecowalk, too, with solar-heating panels for hot water, composted gardens, and recycling. Luxurious it is not, but this is deservedly one of San José's most popular budget lodgings; reserve well in advance during the high season. Smoking isn't permitted in the hotel. ■TIP→ **Be sure to confirm your reservation 48 hours before you arrive and, if possible, on the day of your arrival, giving an estimated arrival time. If you don't, you might find yourself without a room when you arrive, despite your reservation.** You'll get a small discount if you pay in cash. **Pros:** good budget value; good place to meet other budget travelers. **Cons:** cumbersome reservations system; far from sights; very popular so difficult to procure space. ⊠ *C. 19, Avdas. 11–13, Barrio Aranjuez* ☎ *2256–1825; 877/898–8663 in U.S.* 🖷 *2223–3528* ⊕ *www. hotelaranjuez.com* ⇌ *36 rooms, 31 with bath* ⚲ *In-room: no a/c, safe, Wi-Fi (some). In-hotel: restaurant, laundry service, Internet terminal, parking (free), no-smoking rooms* ⊟ *MC, V* ⏿ *BP* ✛ *H2.*

$$ ⊞ **Hotel Britannia.** This mango-color home is the largest and most luxurious of the old Barrio Amón houses that now serve as lodgings. Technically, the Britannia is two houses in one: a stately old building with tile porch that has changed little since its construction in 1910 (except for the conversion of the old wine cellar into an intimate international restaurant) and a newer addition with slightly smaller, carpeted rooms. We like the deluxe rooms and junior suites in the original house: they're spacious—with high ceilings and windows on the street side—and worth the extra money, though street noise might be a problem if you're a light sleeper. All rooms are nonsmoking. **Pros:** good value; cozy rooms. **Cons:** borders on sketchy neighborhood; some dark rooms. ⊠ *C. 3 and Avda. 11, Barrio Amón* ⊡ *Apdo. 3742–1000, San José* ☎ *2223–6667; 800/263–2618 in North America* ⊕ *www.hotelbritanniacostarica.com* ⇌ *19 rooms, 5 suites* ⚲ *In-room: no a/c (some), safe, Wi-Fi. In-hotel: restaurant, room service, bar, laundry service, Internet terminal, no-smoking rooms* ⊟ *AE, MC, V* ⏿ *BP* ✛ *F2.*

$$ ⊞ **Hotel Don Carlos.** One of the city's first guesthouses (technically it's three
★   houses), the Don Carlos has been in the same family for four generations. But the spirit of Carlos Bálser, the hotel's Liechtenstein-born founder—painter, geologist, archaeologist, and general jack-of-all-trades—lives

on. Most rooms in the rambling old coffee-baron house have ceiling fans and big windows. Those in the Colonial Wing have a bit more personality, and several newer rooms on the third floor have views of the Irazú and Barva volcanoes. Orchids and pre-Columbian statues adorn the abundant public areas, and the 272-tile mural in the lobby depicts the history of San José. Even if you don't stay here—and this is an old favorite among Fodors.com forums users—the Don Carlos has arguably the best hotel gift shop in the country, well worth a stop. **Pros:** good value; good place to meet fellow travelers. **Cons:** some noise in interior rooms; some reports of long waits in restaurant. ⊠ *C. 9 and Avda. 9, Barrio Amón* ☎ *Box 025216, Dept. 1686, Miami, FL 33102-5216* ☏ *2221–6707; 866/675–9259 in North America* ⊕ *www.doncarloshotel. com* ⟿ *33 rooms, 31 with bath* ⚷ *In-room: no a/c (some), safe, Wi-Fi. In-hotel: restaurant, room service, laundry service, Internet terminal, parking (free)* ☰ *AE, D, DC, MC, V* ⦿*CP* ⊹ *G2.*

$$
Fodor's Choice
★

Hôtel Le Bergerac. Any other lodging of this caliber would be content to live off its reputation, and we'd never begrudge Le Bergerac if it did rest on its well-established laurels. But management is always tweaking and remodeling, and each time you return, you'll likely discover something new. (What *doesn't* change much is the rates.) The hotel occupies two former private homes and is furnished with antiques. All rooms have custom-made wood-and-stone dressers and writing tables; deluxe rooms have two beds, private garden terraces or balconies, and large bathrooms. The location on a steep hill might disorient you; you could walk upstairs to your room, fling open the terrace doors, expecting to walk out onto a balcony, and find instead a ground-level patio and mountain view. The in-hotel restaurant, L'Ile de France *(⇨ Where to Eat)*, is one of the city's best, so dinner reservations are essential, even for guests. Breakfast is served on a garden patio adjoining the hotel restaurant. As befits the name, on parle français. There are many small, upscale hotels in San José, but great service, attention to detail, and ample gardens set this place apart. Hands down, this is our favorite lodging in the city. **Pros:** top-notch service; cozy rooms; terrific restaurant. **Cons:** rooms on the small side; not near sights. ⊠ *C. 35, Avdas. Central–2, 1st entrance to Los Yoses, San Pedro* ☎ *Apdo. 1107–1002, San José* ☏ *2234–7850* ⊕ *www.bergerachotel.com* ⟿ *26 rooms* ⚷ *In-room: no a/c, safe, Internet. In-hotel: restaurant, bar, laundry service, Internet terminal, parking (free), no-smoking rooms* ☰ *AE, D, DC, MC, V* ⦿*BP* ⊹ *B6.*

$

Hotel Milvia. Apply the principles of feng shui to an old militia arms depository, and you get a charming bed-and-breakfast on a San Pedro backstreet. Manager Florencia Urbina belongs to a local art consortium called Bocaracá, whose motto is "Art in Society." She takes that maxim seriously: the group's lush tropical paintings adorn the lobby, breakfast salon, small bar, and common areas. Your room will be decorated with lovely hand-painted tiles and classic Tico furniture, and you pass through a Zen meditation garden each time you enter and exit the building. The Milvia is a great value, and makes for a charming, artsy retreat. Julia Roberts and Susan Sarandon are a couple of celebrities who've stayed here. **Pros:** good value; artistic decor. **Cons:** far from sights;

even farther from airport. ✉ *100 m north and 100 m east of Centro Comercial Muñoz y Nanne, San Pedro* ⌖ *Apdo. 1660–2050, San Pedro* ☎ *2225–4543* ⊕ *www.hotelmilvia.com* ⊠ *9 rooms* ♿ *In-room: no a/c, safe, Wi-Fi. In-hotel: bar, laundry service, Internet terminal, parking (free), no-smoking rooms* ⊟ *AE, MC, V* ⋔ *CP* ⊕ *D5.*

$ ⌗ **Hotel Rincón de San José.** Never mind that the interior looks more European than Latin American. (It was once called the Hotel Edelweiss, and everyone still refers to it by its old name.) This elegant little inn has comfortable guest quarters in a charming area near the Parque España. Rooms have carved doors, custom-made furniture, and small bathrooms. Most have hardwood window frames and floors; several have bathtubs. A 2008 expansion doubled the hotel's size, and though newer rooms echo the style of the older ones, they lack some of the hardwood accents. Complimentary breakfast is served in the garden courtyard, which doubles as a bar. The owners speak German and Dutch, in addition to the requisite English and Spanish. **Pros:** good value; friendly management; eco-friendly hotel. **Cons:** small rooms; rooms fronting street get some noise. ✉ *Avda. 9 and C. 15, Barrio Otoya* ☎ *2221–9702* ⊕ *www.hotelrincondesanjose.com* ⊠ *42 rooms* ♿ *In-room: no a/c, safe, Wi-Fi (some). In-hotel: bar, laundry service, public Wi-Fi, Internet terminal, parking (paid)* ⊟ *AE, MC, V* ⋔ *BP* ⊕ *H3.*

$$ ⌗ **Hotel Santo Tomás.** Don't be put off by the fact that the front of this century-old former coffee-plantation house butts up against the sidewalk on a busy street; close the front door behind you, and you'll find the lobby and rooms are set back away from the traffic noise. On the fringe of Barrio Amón, the hotel has spacious rooms with wood or tile floors and lots of deep, varnished-wood furnishings. Some of the tiled bathrooms have skylights. A bright breakfast room adjoins an interior patio, and if you keep traveling back into the interior of the building, you'll find a small outdoor pool, a rarity in a hotel of this size in the capital. The especially friendly, helpful staff makes this a real find. All rooms here are nonsmoking. **Pros:** good value; friendly staff; central location. **Cons:** difficult parking; borders on sketchy neighborhood; small rooms. ✉ *Avda. 7, Cs. 3–5, Barrio Amón* ☎ *2255–0448; 877/446—0658 in North America* ⊕ *www.hotelsantotomas.com* ⊠ *19 rooms* ♿ *In-room: no a/c, safe, Wi-Fi. In-hotel: restaurant, bar, pool, gym, public Wi-Fi, Internet terminal, parking (paid), no-smoking rooms* ⊟ *MC, V* ⋔ *BP* ⊕ *F3.*

¢–$ ⌗ **Kap's Place.** This lodging literally sprawls: one of the three annexes is almost two blocks away from the main building. (And if you drive by too quickly, you'll likely miss that main building with its unassuming sign and white metal door.) Inside are bright, tropical rooms with lots of tile and wood; coffee and tea are brewing all the time in the reception area, and you can use the shared kitchen. You'll be asked to sign a two-page agreement when you register, attesting that you'll keep the noise down and won't bring unregistered guests to your room. The owners are committed to maintaining a family atmosphere here. **Pros:** you can pay with a credit card if you stay in the main building, but not in one of the annexes; good budget value; quiet. **Cons:** far from sights; small rooms; reception could be in another building. ✉ *C. 19 and*

Avdas. 11–13, 200 m west, 50 m north of Shell station, Barrio Aranjuez 🕿 *2221–1169* ⊕ *www.kapsplace.com* ⤵ *23 rooms, 20 with bath* ☼ *In-room: no a/c, safe (some), no TV (some), Wi-Fi (some). In-hotel: public Wi-Fi, Internet terminal, parking (paid), no-smoking rooms* ⊟ *AE, D, DC, MC, V* ⦿ *BP* ⊹ *H2.*

WEST OF DOWNTOWN

San José's vast west side contains only a smattering of lodgings, but among them is one of the city's best.

$$–$$$$

Fodor's Choice

★

☷ **Hotel Grano de Oro.** Two wooden houses—one dates from the turn of the 20th century, and the other from the 1950s—have been converted into one of the city's most charming inns, decorated throughout with old photos of the capital and paintings by local artists. Public areas have a glitzy elegance; head up to your room for the old coffee-plantation feel for which the hotel is known. Each room is different, and although you can't go wrong with any of them, the older house's rooms are the nicest, especially the Garden Suite, with hardwood floors, high ceilings, and a private garden. The sumptuous restaurant, run by a French-trained chef, wraps around a lovely indoor patio and bromeliad-filled gardens, and has become one of the capital's premier dining venues. The hotel's sundeck has a view of both the city and the far-off volcanoes. The Grano de Oro is a consistent favorite with posters to Fodors.com forums. **Pros:** friendly management; top-notch service; superb restaurant. **Cons:** remodeling took away country feel in some areas; far from sights; need taxi to get here. ⊠ *C. 30, Avdas. 2–4, Paseo Colón* ⌖ *1701 N.W. 97th Ave., SJO 36, Box 025216, Miami FL 33102-5216* 🕿 *2255–3322* ⊕ *www.hotelgranodeoro.com* ⤵ *40 rooms, 3 suites* ☼ *In-room: no a/c, safe, refrigerator, Wi-Fi. In-hotel: restaurant, room service, bar, spa, laundry service, Internet terminal, Wi-Fi hotspot, parking (free), no-smoking rooms* ⊟ *AE, D, DC, MC, V* ⦿ *EP* ⊹ *A4.*

$–$$$

☷ **Hotel Parque del Lago.** The management that brought you the South Pacific's Lapa Ríos (⇨ *See Cabo Matapalo in Chapter 7*), also runs things at this eco-conscious, west-side lodging. The business travelers who make up the bulk of the clientele are well served as much by the business services as by the recycling protocols and environmentally friendly soap. Rooms are a mix of sizes, but all have big windows, polished furniture, and armoires, in addition to ample closet space. **Pros:** good business facilities; friendly staff; eco-friendly hotel. **Cons:** far from sights; smallish rooms. ⊠ *C. 40, Avda. 2, Paseo Colón* 🕿 *2547–2000* ⊕ *www.parquedellago.com* ⤵ *33 rooms, 7 suites* ☼ *In-room: safe, refrigerator, Wi-Fi. In-hotel: restaurant, bar, gym, laundry service, Internet terminal, parking (free)* ⊟ *AE, D, DC, MC, V* ⦿ *BP* ⊹ *A3.*

NIGHTLIFE AND THE ARTS

THE ARTS

The best source for theater, dance, film, and arts information is the "Viva" entertainment section of the Spanish-language daily *La Nación*. The paper also publishes the "Tiempo Libre" section each Friday, highlighting what's going on over the weekend. *San José Volando* is a free monthly magazine found in many upscale hotels and restaurants, and publishes features about what's going on around town. Listings in both publications are in Spanish but are easy to decipher.

The "Weekend" section of the English-language weekly, the *Tico Times*, lists information about arts and culture, much of it events of interest to the expatriate community. The paper comes out each Friday.

ART GALLERIES

San José's art galleries, public or private, museum or bohemian, keep daytime hours only, but all kick off a new show with an evening opening. They're free and open to the public, and they offer a chance to rub elbows with Costa Rica's art community (and to sip wine and munch on appetizers). Listings appear in *La Nación*'s "Viva" section. Your time in the capital might coincide with one of these by happenstance. (They're rarely announced in the paper more than a day or two in advance.) Look for the term *inauguración* (opening).

FILM

Dubbing of movies is rare; films are screened in their original language, usually English, and subtitled in Spanish. (Children's movies, however, *are* dubbed, although a multiplex cinema may offer some *hablada en inglés*, or screenings in English.) Plan to pay $5 for a ticket. Don't expect anything too avant-garde in most theaters; month-old Hollywood releases are the norm. Following trends seen elsewhere, theaters are fleeing downtown for the suburban malls.

Cine San Pedro (⊠ *Mall San Pedro, San Pedro* ☎ 2283–5716) is a 10-theater multiplex a short taxi ride from downtown. One of the few downtown theaters left, **Cine Variedades** (⊠ *C. 5, between Avdas. Central and 1, Barrio El Carmen* ☎ 2222–6108) shows mainstream Hollywood movies but has kept that old movie-palace feel. The **Sala Garbo** (⊠ *Avda. 2 and C. 28, Paseo Colón* ☎ 2222–1034) theater shows arty films, often in languages other than English with Spanish subtitles.

THEATER AND MUSIC

More than a dozen theater groups (many of which perform slapstick comedies) hold forth in smaller theaters around town. If your Spanish is up to it, call for a reservation. The curtain rises at 8 PM, Friday through Sunday, with some companies staging performances on Thursday night, too. If your Spanish isn't up to theater, there are plenty of dance and musical performances.

There are frequent dance performances and concerts in the **Teatro FANAL** and **Teatro 1887**, both in the **Centro Nacional de la Cultura** (⊠ *C. 13, Avdas. 3–5, Barrio Otoya* ☎ 2257–5524). The **Eugene O'Neill Theater**

"Our first full day in San José was full of wandering through the streets and markets. We happened upon this friendly artist who shared his paintings with us." —Photo by Liz Stuart, Fodors.com member

(⌧ *Centro Cultural Costarricense–Norteamericano, Avda. 1 and C. 37, Barrio Dent, San Pedro* ☎ *2207–7554*) has chamber concerts and plays most weekend evenings. The cultural center is a great place to meet expatriate North Americans.

For six decades, the **Little Theatre Group** (☎ *8858–1446* ⊕ *www. littletheatregroup.org*) has presented English-language community-theater productions several times a year at various venues around town. The "Weekend" section of the English-language *Tico Times* has listings. The **Teatro La Aduana** (⌧ *C. 25, Avda. 3, Barrio La California* ☎ *2257–8305*) holds frequent dance and stage performances, and is home to the Compañía Nacional de Teatro (National Theater Company).

The baroque **Teatro Nacional** (⌧ *Plaza de la Cultura, Barrio La Soledad* ☎ *2221–1329*) is the home of the excellent National Symphony Orchestra, which performs on Friday evening and Sunday morning between April and November. The theater also hosts visiting musical groups and dance companies. Tickets are $4–$40. San José's second-most popular theater, the **Teatro Popular Melico Salazar** (⌧ *Avda. 2, Cs. Central–2, Barrio La Merced* ☎ *2233–5424*) has a full calendar of music and dance shows, as well as a few offbeat productions. Something goes on nearly every night of the week; tickets are $2–$20.

NIGHTLIFE

The metro area's hottest nightlife has migrated to the Central Valley suburbs of Escazú and Heredia these days. (⇨ *See Chapter 4.*) Both are about 20-minute taxi rides from downtown San José. The capital isn't devoid of places to go in the evening, however. It still contains plenty of bars, dance places, and restaurants and cafés where you can spend the evening. Take taxis to and from when you go. Most places will be happy to call you a cab—or, if there's a guard, he can hail you one—when it's time to call it a night.

AREAS

No one could accuse San José of having too few watering holes, but aside from the hotels there aren't many places to have a quiet drink, especially downtown. Barrios Amón and Otoya have little in the way of nightlife outside the occasional hotel bar.

The young and the restless hang out in the student-oriented places around the University of Costa Rica in the eastern suburb of San Pedro. The Calle de la Amargura (Street of Bitterness), named for the route Jesus took to the crucifixion, is much more secular than its name suggests and rocks loudly each night. (Nighttime robberies have occurred on "The Calle," so be wary.)

Don't write off every place around the university as rowdy. There are a few quiet bars and cafés where you can carry on a real conversation. Barrios La California and Escalante, an area anchored by the Santa Teresita church, amorphously connect central San José with San Pedro, and house some of the city's trendiest nightspots.

BARS

Intensely and proudly bohemian **Café Expresivo** (✉ *350 m east of church of Santa Teresita, Barrio Escalante* ☎ *2224–1202*) hosts poetry readings and acoustic guitar concerts and serves light pastas and sandwiches. **El Observatorio** (✉ *C. 23, across from Cine Magaly, Barrio La California* ☎ *2223–0725*) strikes an unusual balance between casual and formal: it's the kind of place where folks over 30 go to watch a soccer game but wear ties.

★ **Jazz Café San Pedro** (✉ *Avda. Central next to Banco Popular, San Pedro* ☎ *2253–8933* ⊕ *www.jazzcafecostarica.com*) draws big crowds, especially for live jazz on Tuesday and Wednesday nights. (Beware: the place gets very smoky.) The moniker "Jazz Café" used to suffice, but with the 2008 opening of a branch in the Central Valley suburb of Escazú, the location was added to the name. An older expat crowd hangs out at

Mac's American Bar (✉ *South side of La Sabana Park, next to the Tennis Club, Sabana Sur* ☎ *2234–3145*), which usually has the TV tuned to a sporting event. It gets our nod for serving the city's best burgers.

A refreshing change from the ubiquitous Imperial beer is what you'll find at **Stan's Irish Pub** (✉ *125 m west of Casa Presidencial, Zapote* ☎ *2253–4360* ⊕ *www.irishpubcostarica.com*), which has Guinness on tap as well as an around-the-world selection of brews. Videos from the '60s, '70s, and '80s provide the backdrop at **Vyrus** (✉ *100 m west of Spoon, San Pedro* ☎ *2280–5890*). Inside is dark, coupley, and kissy; the outdoor balcony is much more conducive to singing along with that Duran Duran song you haven't heard in ages.

CAFÉS AND RESTAURANTS

For a country so economically dependent on coffee, there's little evidence of a café culture here. Costa Ricans do observe coffee breaks religiously at home and at work, but outside a few places we list below, making a special trip somewhere to converse with friends over coffee isn't too common.

Café 1930 (✉ *Avda. 2 and C. 3, Barrio La Soledad* ☎ *2221–4011*), under the arcades at the entrance to the Gran Hotel Costa Rica, pulls 24-hour duty as a pleasant place for a drink or coffee. The highly recommended restaurant **Café Mundo** (✉ *C. 15 and Avda. 9, Barrio Otoya* ☎ *2222–6190*) is a quiet spot for a drink frequented by gay and bohemian crowds.

Near the university, **Fezcafé** (✉ *C. de la Amargura, San Pedro* ☎ *2280– 6982*) is a quiet alternative to the rowdy nightlife nearby, at least until 8 PM on weeknights.

Walk by **Manolo's** (✉ *Avda. Central between Cs. Central and 2, Barrio La Merced* ☎ *2280–6982*) any hour of the night and a lively crowd is sure to be chatting over coffee and *churros con chocolate*. Smack-dab in the center of the campus nightlife, **Omar Khayyam** (✉ *C. de la Amargura, San Pedro* ☎ *2253–8455*) is a blissfully quiet refuge. Share a jug of wine and falafel or hummus with fried yuca on the covered patio.

Fill up on Spanish-style tapas at Mediterranean bar and restaurant **Pub Olio** (✉ *200 m north of Bagelmen's, Barrio Escalante* ☎ *2281–0541*). It draws a mix of professionals and older college students.

CASINOS

Ask about casino rules before you dive in and play: there are a few Costa Rican variations—for example, you don't get a bonus for blackjack, but you do for three of a kind or straights under local rules. (And yet some places boast that they play exactly as they do in Las Vegas.)

The term casino gets tossed around loosely in Costa Rica: a hotel can put a couple of video poker machines in its lobby and claim it operates a casino. The casino at the pink Hotel del Rey in Barrio El Carmen— arguably the city's most famous and definitely its most notorious gambling establishment—swarms with prostitutes. Avoid it.

A few of the city's larger hotels have casinos we do recommend, including the Clarion Amón Plaza, the Aurola Holiday Inn (the view from the casino is breathtaking), and the Gran Hotel Costa Rica. By law, casinos may open only from 6 PM to 2 AM.

DANCE CLUBS

San José's discos attract a *very* young crowd. Quite frankly, you'll feel ancient if you've passed 21. Live-music halls draw dancers of all ages, but most of these populate rougher neighborhoods on the city's south side and are best avoided.

For a dance-hall experience in a good neighborhood, we recommend the enormous **El Tobogán** (⊠ *200 m north and 100 m east of La República, Barrio Tournón* ☎ *2223–8920*), an alternative to the postage stamp–size floors of most discos. Live Latin bands get everyone on their feet Friday and Saturday nights, and Sunday afternoon.

FOLKLORE

Noches Costarricenses (Costa Rican Nights) performances take place at **Pueblo Antiguo** (⊠ *3 km [2 mi] west*

of Hospital México, La Uruca ☎ *2257–4171*), a Tico version of Colonial Williamsburg (it depicts Costa Rica between 1880 and 1930) west of the city. The spectacle gets under way on Friday and Saturday nights from 6:30 to 9:30, with dinner and music and dance performances. The $55 price includes transportation to and from San José hotels and English-speaking guides. Arrange this through your hotel's front desk.

GAY AND LESBIAN

San José is reasonably open to gay and lesbian visitors, but given pronouncements of disapproval by city officials, you might want to temper your openness. Be discreet, and you'll be fine. The capital has a few bars, restaurants, and dance places patronized primarily by a gay and lesbian clientele, although all are welcome. Another tier of businesses, exemplified by the venerable Café Mundo, draws a mixed gay-straight clientele. The places we list have drawn crowds for years.

Al Despiste (⊠ *Across from Mudanzas Mundiales, Zapote* ☎ *2234–5956*) is a gay bar that serves light bocas (appetizers) and has dance nights Wednesday–Sunday. **Club Oh!** (⊠ *C. 2, Avdas. 14–16A, Barrio El Pacífico* ☎ *2248–1500* ⊕ *www.clubohcr.com*) is a mostly gay, techno-heavy disco with two dance floors and weekly drag shows. Take a taxi to and from here; the neighborhood's sketchy.

El Bochinche (⊠ *C. 11, Avdas. 10–12, Barrio La Soledad* ☎ *2221–0500* ⊕ *www.bochinchesanjose.com*) is a gay bar and dance club that doubles as a Mexican restaurant. A gay and lesbian crowd frequents **La Avispa** (⊠ *C. 1, Avdas. 8–10, Barrio La Soledad* ☎ *2223–5343* ⊕ *www.laavispa.co.cr*), which has two dance floors with videos and karaoke as well as a quieter upstairs bar with pool tables. The last Friday of each month is ladies' night.

GREAT VIEWS

Several miradores (lookout points) dot the mountains north and south of the city. **Ram Luna** (⊠ *10 km [6 mi] south of San José, near Church of San Luis Tolosa, Aserrí* ☎ *2230–3060*), in the far southern suburbs, is the most famous of these. You come here for the view—the lights of the Central Valley sparkle at your feet—and the music, more than the food. (Costa Rican fare is the staple here.) Make reservations if you plan to be here for Wednesday evening's folklore show.

SHOPPING

Although it might seem more "authentic" to buy your souvenirs at their out-country source, you can find everything in the city, a real bonus if you're pressed for time. If the capital has any real tourist shopping district, it's found loosely in the cluster of streets around Parque Morazán, just north of downtown, an area bounded roughly by avenidas 1 and 7 and calles 5 and 9. Stroll and search, because many other businesses congregate in the area as well.

The northeastern suburb of Moravia has a cluster of high-quality crafts and artisan shops—for good reason very popular with tour groups—in the three blocks heading north from the Colegio María Inmaculada. The street is two blocks behind the city's church.

MALLS

Old-timers lament the malling over of San José. Several huge enclosed centers anchor the metro area. These are complemented by dozens of smaller malls. Expect all the comforts of home—food courts and movie theaters included. **Mall San Pedro** (⊠ *Rotonda de la Hispanidad, San Pedro* ☎ *2283–7540*) sits in its namesake suburb, a short 10-minute taxi ride from downtown San José. The mammoth **Terramall** (⊠ *Autopista Florencio del Castillo, Tres Ríos* ☎ *2278–6970*) is the far eastern suburbs' prime shopping destination.

SPECIALTY STORES

BOOKS AND MAGAZINES

The *New York Times*, the *Wall Street Journal*, the *Miami Herald*, and *USA Today* arrive in San José the morning of publication, printed here and bound on bond paper. Find them at a select few outlets and shops in large hotels or at the airport.

With several locations around the metro area, **Casa de las Revistas** (⊠ *C. 5, Avdas. 3–5, Barrio El Carmen* ☎ *2256–5092*) has San José's best selection of magazines in English.

Librería Internacional (⊠ *300 m west of Taco Bell, Barrio Dent* ☎ *2253–9553*) is the city's largest bookstore. It evokes Borders or Barnes & Noble, though on a much smaller scale, and stocks English translations of Latin American literature as well as myriad coffee-table books on Costa Rica. The affable owners of **7th Street Books** (⊠ *C. 7, Avdas. Central–1, Barrio La Soledad* ☎ *2256–8251*) make this store *the* place to stop in and see what's going on in the expat community. It has the city's best selection of books in English and is also strong on Latin America and tropical ecology. You can pick up the *Tico Times* here.

CRAFTS

The arts-and-crafts tradition in Costa Rica isn't as strong as in, say, Guatemala or Peru. At first glance you might be disenchanted with what you see in the run-of-the-mill souvenir shops. Keep your disappointment in check until you visit two of San José's outstanding purveyors of fine artisan work.

Fodor'sChoice Downtown San José's must-stop shop is **Galería Namu** (⌖ *Avda. 7, Cs.*
★ *5–7, behind Aurola Holiday Inn, Barrio Amón* ☎ *2256-3412* ⊕ *www. galerianamu.com*), which sells Costa Rican folkloric art and the best indigenous crafts in town. Its inventory brims with colorful creations by the Guaymí, Boruca, Bribri, Chorotega, Huetar, and Maleku peoples— all Costa Rican indigenous groups. You can also find exquisitely carved ivory-nut Tagua figurines and baskets made by Wounan Indians from Panama's Darién region and Tuno textiles from Honduras' Miskito coast. Take note of carved balsa masks, woven cotton blankets, and hand-painted ceramics.

The store looks expensive—and indeed, the sky's the limit in terms of prices—but if your budget is not so flush, say so: the good folks here can help you find something in the $10–$20 range that will make a more cherished souvenir of your trip than a *Pura Vida* T-shirt. As a bonus you'll get an information sheet describing your work's creator and art style. Namu has a reputation for fair prices for customers, and for fair pay to artists or artisans.

★ The staff and selection at **Kaltak Artesanías** (⌖ *50 m north of Colegio María Inmaculada, Moravia* ☎ *2297-2736*) make it a real standout from all the Moravia shops. Walk in with some unformulated "I'm not sure what I want" notions, and the staff will help you find that perfect souvenir from among the selection of ceramics (Pefi and Osenbach designs, trademarks of two well-known artisans in the capital, are well represented), wood-and-leather rocking chairs, oxcarts of all sizes, orchids, and carvings from native *cocobolo* and *guápinol* woods and ash wood.

MUSIC

San José's music stores stock the Latin sounds of every artist from Chayanne to Shakira, but Costa Ricans take special pride in their hometown Latin-fusion group, the Grammy Award–winning Editus.

In addition to selling everything else imaginable, downtown department store **Universal** (⌖ *Avda. Central, between Cs. Central and 1, Barrio El Carmen* ☎ *2222-2222*) stocks a good selection of Latin CDs in its first-floor music department.

SOUVENIRS

Hotel gift shop **Boutique Annemarie** (⌖ *Hotel Don Carlos, C. 9 and Avda. 9, Barrio Amón* ☎ *2233-5343*) has a huge selection of popular souvenirs and CDs of Costa Rican musicians.

Continued on page 126

LAST-MINUTE SOUVENIR SHOPPING

by Holly K. Sonneland

 San José's markets can be crowded, but they're great fun for the savvy shopper. There are plenty of Costa Rican souvenirs for every pocketbook, and the city's bustling downtown is compact enough to make it easy to visit a few markets in a day . . . or even an afternoon. It's a great way to explore the city and take care of last-minute gift shopping.

Some markets have a mishmash of items, whereas others are more specialized. Pick up cigars or peruse antiques in the back of the sleepy La Casona building downtown, or head over to the strip of covered traveler-friendly souvenir stands by Plaza de la Democracia to browse the artsy wares. Festive fake flora in glittery, tropical blue, green, and orange hues can be found at the permanent artisan bazaars.

For a lively experience, head to the gritty and labyrinthine Mercado Central edifice right on Avenida Central where you can jostle among working-class Ticos as you pick up an Imperial beer logo–emblazoned muscle T-shirt or a homemade herbal love potion. Keep a tight hold on your bag, and have fun practicing your spanish with the vendors.

GREAT GIFT IDEAS

Costa Rica's souvenirs pop with bright color and have that distinct, *"pura vida"* (pure life) flair.

COFFEE: The authentic modern-day Costa Rica souvenir, not to mention most appreciated back home. Load up on whole bean (*grano entero*), or, if you must get ground (*molido*), buy the *"puro,"* otherwise it might have pre-added sugar. Café Britt is the country's most famous brand (¢2,500/lb).

MAYAN OCARINAS

(¢2,500–¢7,000) Calling the ocarina two-faced would be an insult, but only because you wouldn't be giving it nearly enough credit. The Mayan resonant vessel flutes depict over a half-dozen animal faces when flipped around and were often given as gifts to travelers by the Chorotega indigenous group in northwestern Guanacaste.

HAMMOCKS: Swinging in one of these is the official posture of *pura vida.* Structured hammocks with wooden dowels on the ends (¢12,000 and up) are optimal, but dowel-less, cocoon-like hammocks (¢10,000 and up) are infinitely more compactable. Get a chair hammock (¢6,000) if you have limited hanging space back home.

OXCARTS: From the Sarchí region, the oxcart has become Costa Rica's most iconic craftsman artifact. Full-size ones can run a few hundred dollars, and many dealers can arrange to have them shipped for you. There's also a coffee table-size version (¢7,000) or, better yet, an oxcart napkin holder (¢1,500).

COFFEE BREWERS: The original Costa Rican coffeemaker is called *el chorreador.* It's a simple wooden stand that's fitted with cloth sock-like filters. Finely ground coffee is dumped in the sock, and hot water is filtered into the mug beneath. Unadorned ones to sleek cherry wood cost around ¢1,700 and up. Don't forget to buy extra sock filters (¢250).

LOCAL LIBATIONS: If you don't have room for a six-pack, be sure to take home what is probably the world's best beer label, Imperial, on a stein or T-shirt (both ¢2,500). Or, snag a bottle of Costa Rica's signature sugarcane liquor, *guaro,* most commonly sold under the Cacique brand.

JEWELRY: Go for oversized wooden hoop earrings (₡3,000), wire-wrought gold and silver baubles (₡3,500), or plaster-molded earrings adorned with toucans, frogs, and pineapples (₡1,500). Jewelry made from carved-out coco shells are popular, too.

TROPICAL WOODS AND PAPERS: Sleek mango-wood vases (₡8,250), inlaid rosewood cutting boards (₡8,000), and hand-painted rum rum wood mugs (₡3,850) are among the many elegant woodworks here. There's also scratch-and-sniff writing materials that would make Willy Wonka proud, with banana, mango, lemon, and coffee-scented (sorry, no schnozberry) stationery sets (₡3,700).

BRIBRÍ CEREMONIAL MASKS: The Bribrí people, from the central Caribbean and one of Costa Rica's last active indigenous groups, don these masks in their annual end-of-the-year festival, Dansa de los Diablitos (Dance of the Devils). It's an animistic production that depicts the avenging of the tribe for the decimation wrought by the conquistadors. Cheaper imitations abound, but Galería NAMU has the best—and most authentic—selection (₡65,000 to ₡100,000).

FOLKLORIC DRESSES AND SHIRTS: While they're often only pulled out on national holidays like Independence Day, a flounced dress (₡8,000 and up) or pinafore (₡5,000) might be just the kitschy gift you're looking for. Ranchero-style shirts (₡8,000) and straw hats (₡2,000) are also an option.

MACHETES: Knives and machetes are commonly used in the country's rural jungle areas and happily sold in leather slings to travelers (₡7,000). Also, knives (₡2,000–3,000) and other items, like frogs and butterflies made out of colored resin, might not be considered traditional but represent the Rastafarian side of the country. Be aware, weapons are not welcome in carry-on luggage on planes.

* All prices listed in colons

SAN JOSÉ MARKETS

San José's navigable city center, and its proximity to the airport, make it the perfect last-minute shopping spot.

MERCADO CENTRAL

This market is geared towards locals and has some of the lowest prices anywhere. Here you can visit flower and medicinal herb (of dubious medicinal properties) shops not found in other markets. ⊠ Avenidas Central and 1, Calles 6 and 8 ⊙ Mon.–Sat. 8–6; Dec., open Sun.

LA CASONA

Souvenirs and tobacco products abound in this rambling, two-story building. At the far eastern end, go up the back stairs to the discount room, where regular items are discounted 25%–30%. Also upstairs is José "Chavo" Navarro's antique shop. ⊠ Calle Central, between Avenidas Central and 1 ☎ 2222–7999 ⊙ 9:30–6.

GALERÍA NAMU

Almost inarguably the best—and, importantly, the only free-trade—store selling indigenous artwork and handcrafts. Owner Aisling French and her staff have developed extensive ties with the Costa Rica's few remaining

Shopping for coffee at Mercado Central.

tribal peoples, bringing their top-notch artisanship to the city. In particular, NAMU sells the highest quality Bribrí ceremonial masks in the country, and has recently developed ties with the Wounan tribe in Panama, who produce museum-quality chunga palm baskets. ⊠ Avenida 7, between Calles 5 and 7 (across from Alliance Française) ☎ 2256–3412 ⊙ Mon.–Sat. 9-6:30.

PLAZA DE LA DEMOCRACIA

This strip of stands across the plaza from the National Museum is the most traveler-oriented market. Vendors also don't pay taxes here, so while some items (bulk coffee) are more expensive, others (choreadores) are actually cheaper than they are in Mercado Central. Hammocks are at the far north end, and Stand 82 has some of the best woodworks, along with Stands 25 and 66. Custom-made earrings are at Stand 40. ⊠ Calle 13, between Avenidas Central and 2 ⊙ Daily, 8 until dusk.

ARTESANÍAS DEL SOL

This is a good place to get souvenirs, especially the popular piggy banks, basic pottery, and baskets, without the crowds. Christmas decorations are sold from September through December. ⊠ 100 meters west of Plaza del Sol, Curridabat, eastern San José ☎ 2225–6800 ⊙ Daily, 8–6; Dec., daily, 8–8.

SHOPPING KNOW-HOW

Colorful clay piggy banks

MAKING A DEAL

Bargaining isn't the sport it is in other countries, and if Tico vendors do bargain, it's often only with travelers who expect it. Before you try to strike a deal, know that Ticos are not confrontational, and haggling, even if not ill-intended, will come off as rude.

Your best bet for getting a deal is to buy in bulk, or simply suggest you'll come back later and walk away. If the vendors really want to lower the price, they'll call you back. If you're buying a single item, you can ask a vendor to offer you a lower price once, at most twice, but don't push it further.

Costa Ricans are painfully polite and are particularly fond of terms of endearment, and it's worth it to indulge in the gentility when talking with market vendors. If you're comfortable enough with your Tico Spanish, or *pachuco*, use the terms in return. For example, Ticos employ a whole arsenal of royal-themed lingo: *rey* and *reina*, or king and queen, are ubiquitous forms of address, especially with middle-aged Ticos, although *reina* is more common than *rey*. You can easily use a "*Gracias, mi reina*," to the (female) vendor who's just given you a good price, but "*¿Cómo está mi rey?*" to a 20-something male vendor sounds a little strange. That being said, if you're a 20-something female shopper, be prepared to hear "*¿En cómo puedo servirle mi reina?*" literally, "How can I serve you my queen?" (said endearingly, not lecherously) from every other 50-year-old vendor whose stand you pass. *Regalar*, a verb that literally means "to gift," can be used to ask a vendor to hand you the item that you want to buy (*Puede regalarme esa bolsa verde, porfa?* I'll take that green bag, please?) or to cut you a deal (*Me la regala en tres mil?* Can you sell it to me for three thousand [colones]?)

Of course, if your Spanish is rusty, smiling always helps.

■ TIP→ While most of the shops in these markets take credit cards, vendors will be more likely to cut you a deal if you pay in cash.

PLAYING IT SAFE

Petty crime is on the rise in Costa Rica, but that shouldn't keep you from exploring the markets. It's important to note that what were once recommended precautions are now strongly advised. Keep cash in breast pockets and leave credit cards and important documents in the hotel. Also leave behind jewelry and fancy gear, especially cameras, that will make you stand out. (The lighting in the markets—all of them indoor—is very poor, and photos inevitably don't turn out anyway.) Most of the markets, like the rest of the city, are generally safe during the day but best avoided in the evening.

Ceremonial mask from Namu Gallery

Some 100 souvenir vendors congregate in the block-long covered walkway known as the **Calle Nacional de Artesanía y Pintura** (⊠ *C. 13, Avdas. Central–2, western side of Plaza de la Democracia*), and offer some real bargains in hammocks, wood carvings, and clothing. The city is looking to move the vendors to another location at this writing. Dozens of souvenir vendors set up shop on the two floors of **La Casona** (⊠ *C. 2, Avdas. Central–1, Barrio El Carmen* ☎ *2222–7999*), in a rickety old downtown mansion. It's much like a flea market, and it's a fun place to browse.

La Ranita Dorada (⊠ *Avda. 1, between Cs. 9 and 11, Barrio El Carmen* ☎ *2256–6808*) sells pretty standard souvenir fare—although it has quite a large selection of wood products— but the friendly staff, who happily take the time to give personalized service, make this place worth a stop.

LAST, LAST MINUTE BUYS

If you really didn't have time to shop, never fear. Aeropuerto Internacional Juan Santamaría has two noteworthy souvenir shops—**Britt Shop Costa Rica, Green Trails,** and **Terra Verde**—for those last-minute purchases. Choose from various blends of coffee ($5 per pound) and such merchandise as hand-carved bowls and jewelry, aromatherapy candles, banana-paper stationery, and Costa Rica travel books—Fodor's included. (Merchandise selection is slightly different in each.) There's nary another store in the country carrying such a variety all in one place. The catch is that the airport shops charge U.S. prices.

Mercado Central (⊠ *Bordered by Avdas. Central–1 and Cs. 6–8, Barrio La Merced*) doesn't bill itself for souvenir shopping—the maze of passageways is where the average Costa Rican comes to stock up on day-to-day necessities—but a few stalls of interest to tourists congregate near the entrances. If you can't find it at **Mundo de Recuerdos** (⊠ *Across from Colegio María Inmaculada, Moravia* ☎ *2240–8990*), it probably doesn't exist. Here's the largest of the Moravia shops with simply everything—at least of standard souvenir fare—you could ask for under one roof.

The museum-shop concept barely exists here, but the shop at the entrance of the **Museo del Oro Precolombino** (⊠ *C. 5, Avdas. Central–2, Barrio La Soledad* ☎ *2243–4217*) is the exception. Look for a terrific selection of pre-Columbian-theme jewelry, art, exclusively designed T-shirts, coin- and bill-theme key chains, notebooks, and mouse pads.

The Central Valley

WORD OF MOUTH

"We happened upon this workshop (Taller Eloy Alfaro e Hijos) by accident. It was one of the neatest experiences I've had in my visits to Costa Rica. They were constructing the world's largest oxcart for an exhibition. The family workshop runs completely on water, not electricity."

—Photo by jvcostarica, Fodors.com member

WELCOME TO THE CENTRAL VALLEY

TOP REASONS TO GO

★ **Coffee:** Get up close and personal with harvesting and processing on coffee tours at two of the valley's many plantations: Café Britt and Doka Estate.

★ **The Orosi Valley:** Spectacular views and quiet, bucolic towns make this area a great day trip or overnight from San José.

★ **Rafting the Pacuare River:** Brave the rapids as you descend through tropical forest on one of the best rivers in Central America.

★ **The views:** Ascend the volcanic slopes that border the valley, meeting superb views almost anywhere you go.

★ **Avian adventures:** Flock to Tapantí National Park to see emerald toucanets, resplendent quetzals (if you're lucky), and nearly every species of Costa Rican hummingbird. Rancho Naturalista is the bird lovers' hotel of choice.

1 Areas north and west of San José. The areas north and west of San José are dominated by coffee farms and small valley towns whose beautiful hotels attract lots of tourists on their first and last nights in the country. Café Britt and Doka Estate are both here, as is the international airport, near Alajuela.

2 Cartago and Irazú Volcano. In the eastern Central Valley are Cartago and Irazú Volcano. Cartago is an older city than San José, with a couple of historic attractions. Irazú is Costa Rica's tallest volcano. On a clear day you can see both the Atlantic and Pacific oceans from its peak.

GETTING ORIENTED

The Central Valley is something of a misnomer, and its Spanish name, the *meseta central* (central plateau) isn't entirely accurate either. The two contiguous mountain ranges that run the length of the country—the Cordillera Central range (which includes Poás, Barva, Irazú, and Turrialba volcanoes) to the north and the Cordillera de Talamanca to the south—don't quite line up in the middle, leaving a trough between them. The "valley" floor is 914 to 1,524 meters (3,000 to 5,000 feet) above sea level. In the valley, your view toward the coasts is obstructed by the two mountain ranges. But from a hillside hotel, your view of San José and the valley can be spectacular.

3 Turrialba. Rafting trips on the Pacuare and Reventazón are based in Turrialba, a bustling little town. The nearby Guayabo Ruins, of a city deserted in AD 1400, is Costa Rica's only significant archaeological site.

4 Orosi Valley. An often overlooked beauty is the Orosi Valley. The drive into the valley is simply gorgeous, and a tranquil way to spend a day. Birding destination Tapantí National Park is at the southern edge of the valley.

THE CENTRAL VALLEY PLANNER

How Much Time?

Central Valley is the Costa Rica of history and tradition, and many visitors overlook it. You could spend an entire week here without getting bored, but if you have only a week or two in Costa Rica, we recommend a maximum of two days before heading to rain forests and beaches in other parts of the country. Spending a day after you arrive, then another day or two before you fly out gives you a taste of the region, breaks up the travel time, and makes your last day interesting, rather than spent in transit back to San José. The drive between just about any two points in the Central Valley is two hours or less, so it's ideal for short trips. In a day you can explore the Orosi Valley and Cartago, raft the Pacuare River, or hop from the Butterfly Farm to a coffee plantation.

Word of Mouth

"Irazu does resemble a 'moonscape.' It is also very cold and breezy. The crater has emerald-green water. Pretty, but we were pretty much out of the car to see the crater, then back in to warm up!"

—MarciaM

Choosing a Place to Stay

Most international flights fly into Costa Rica in the evening and head out again early the next morning, meaning you likely have to stay your first and last nights in San José or nearby. Think of the Central Valley as "the nearby." For getting away from it all and still being close to the country's main airport, the lodgings around San José make splendid alternatives to staying in the city itself. It may pain you to tear yourself away from that beach villa or rain forest lodge, but you can still come back to something distinctive here on your last night in Costa Rica. Rustic *cabinas* (cottages), sprawling coffee plantations, nature lodges, and hilltop villas with expansive views are some of your options. The large chains are here as well, but the real gems are the so-called boutique hotels, many of which are family-run places and have unique designs that take advantage of exceptional countryside locations. Subtropical gardens are the norm, rather than the exception, and air-conditioning is usually not necessary.

Getting Around

The Central Valley has an extensive network of paved roads in relatively good shape, though this being Costa Rica, you can stumble upon gravel or dirt stretches when you least expect it. The Pan-American Highway runs roughly east–west through the valley and the center of San José. (It's numbered CA1 north and west and CA2 south and east of the capital.) Mountains ring the valley, so most trips to or from the lowlands require a drive up in elevation then back down. The bus network is good, but because sights tend to be spread out, it's less time-consuming to travel by car. The country's major airport is in Alajuela, so it's a perfect place to rent a vehicle. Consider taking taxis, too, if you'd rather leave the driving to someone else. They're plentiful, drivers know the roads (most of the time), and the prices are reasonable. Even several $10 taxi rides per day—and $10 gets you a reasonable distance—are cheaper than a rental car.

Faith and Folklore

The Central Valley wears its tradition, both religious and secular, on its collective sleeve. Costa Rica's biggest annual religious festival takes place in Cartago each August 2 and commemorates what tradition holds was a 1635 apparition of the Virgin Mary. It never captured the worldwide attention of Mexico's Guadalupe, France's Lourdes, or Portugal's Fatima, but no matter. The 1 million pilgrims who visit the site on that day alone are testament to its popularity here.

Nearby, at Ujarrás in the Orosi Valley, sit the ruins of the country's first church. Prayers to the Virgin Mary said here are reputed to have staved off pirate attacks—we have no other explanation—and numerous earthquakes. That second one is tougher to explain: This part of the valley has suffered its share of earth tremors throughout history.

Costa Ricans flee to the beach for Semana Santa, or Holy Week, in March or April, but the small community of San Joaquín, halfway between Alajuela and Heredia, makes a nice antidote to the beach crowds. The town holds some of the country's most impressive processions reenacting Jesus' trial and crucifixion.

Turning more pagan, Escazú holds the title of Costa Rica's spirit capital. Witches, mostly benevolent, but a few malevolent ones, too, are reputed to populate the community. You'd never know it from all the fast-food restaurants, car dealerships, and shopping malls you see as you pull into town. But old-timers high in the hills have hair-raising stories to tell about those proverbial things that go bump in the night.

Those hills above Escazú also host the annual Día del Boyero, or Oxcart Drivers' Day, the second Sunday in March. Oxen and carts parade to the church to be blessed by the priest. Those blessings must stick; oxcarts continue to be a favored mode of work transport throughout the Central Valley.

Dining and Lodging Prices

WHAT IT COSTS IN DOLLARS

	¢	$	$$	$$$	$$$$
Restaurants	under $5	$5–$10	$10–$15	$15–$25	over $25
Hotels	under $50	$50–$75	$75–$150	$150–$250	over $250

Restaurant prices are per person for a main course at dinner. Hotel prices are for two people in a standard double room in high season, excluding service and tax (16.4%).

When to Go

Known for its "eternal spring," the Central Valley lacks the oppressive seasonal heat and rain of other parts of the country. Average highs are 24°C to 27°C (75°F to 80°F). Microclimates here are dictated by elevation: Cartago and the Irazú volcano perch at a higher elevation and are frequently more overcast and chillier than San José, especially at night. Heredia sits at about the same elevation as the capital, and enjoys a similar climate. The western valley slopes downward in elevation from San José, and you'll notice a slight warming by the time you get to Santa Ana, Alajuela, or San Antonio de Belén. The same goes for the Orosi Valley with its lower altitude. Turrialba sits lower still and represents a transition zone between the temperate Central Valley and balmy Caribbean coast. Afternoon downpours are common for an hour or two from mid-May to December (with a slight drop-off around July, but more prolonged rains in September and October), but the amount of rain is modest compared with the Caribbean coast and the southern Pacific. Don't rule out the rainy season—fewer travelers mean you won't need reservations, rain is usually during afternoon siesta hours, and the valley is swathed in green after a few months of moisture. Holy Week (the week before Easter) and the last two weeks of the year are prime vacation times for Ticos, so reserve cars and hotel rooms in advance.

VOLCÁN IRAZÚ

The word *Irazú* is likely a corruption of Iztaru, a long-ago indigenous community whose name translated as "hill of thunder." The name is apt.

The volcano is considered active, but the gases and steam that billow from fumaroles on the northwestern slope are rarely visible from the peak above the crater lookouts. The mountain's first recorded eruption took place in 1723; the most recent was a series of eruptions that lasted from 1963 to 1965. Boulders and mud rained down on the countryside, damming rivers and causing serious floods, and the volcano dumped up to 20 inches of ash on sections of the Central Valley.

When conditions are clear, you can see the chartreuse lake inside the Cráter Principal. The stark moonscape of the summit contrasts markedly with the lush vegetation of Irazú's lower slopes, home to porcupines, armadillos, coyotes, and mountain hares. Listen for the low-pitched, throaty song of the *yigüirro*, or clay-colored thrush, Costa Rica's national bird. Its call is most pronounced just before the start of the rainy season.

BEST TIME TO GO

Early morning, especially in the January–April dry season, affords the best views, both of the craters and the surrounding countryside. Clouds move in by late morning. Wear warm, waterproof clothing if you get here that early; although rare, temperatures have dropped down close to freezing around dawn.

FUN FACT

Irazú has dumped a lot of ash over the centuries. The most recent eruptive period began on the day that John F. Kennedy arrived in Costa Rica in March 1963. The "ash storm" that ensued lasted on and off for two years.

BEST WAYS TO EXPLORE

VOLCANIC TIPS

A paved road leads all the way to the summit, where a small coffee shop sells hot beverages, and a persistent pair of coatis cruise the picnic tables for handouts. (Please resist the urge to feed them!) The road to the top climbs past vegetable fields, pastures, and native oak forests. You pass through the villages of Potrero Cerrado and San Juan de Chicuá before reaching the summit's bleak but beautiful main crater.

HIKING

Even before you get to the main entrance, check out the park's Prusia Sector, which has hiking trails that pass through majestic oak and pine forests and picnic areas. They're very popular with Tico families on weekends, so if you want the woods to yourself, come on a weekday. Trails in the park are well marked; avoid heading down any paths marked with PASO RESTRINGIDO ("passage restricted") signs.

BIRD-WATCHING

The road to Irazú provides some of the best roadside birding opportunities in the country, especially on a weekday when there isn't a constant parade of cars and buses heading up to the crater. Some of the most fruitful areas are on either side of the bridges you'll pass over. Reliable bird species that inhabit these roadsides are: acorn and hairy woodpeckers, the brilliant flame-throated warbler, and, buzzing around blossoms, the fiery-throated, green violet-ear, and (aptly named) volcano hummingbirds. Once past the main entrance, there are also plenty of opportunities to stop and bird roadside. Look for volcano juncos on the ground and slaty flowerpiercers visiting flowering shrubs.

TOP REASONS TO GO

THE VIEW

How many places in the world let you peer directly into the crater of an active volcano? Costa Rica offers you two: here at Irazú, and the Northern Plains' Volcán Poás. Poás's steaming cauldron is spookier, but Irazú's crater lake with colors that change according to the light is nonetheless impressive.

MORE VIEWS

"On a clear day, you can see forever," goes the old song from the musical of the same name. Irazú is one of the few places in Costa Rica that lets you glimpse both the Pacific and Atlantic (Caribbean) oceans at once. Clear is the key term here: clouds frequently obscure the view. Early morning gives you your best shot.

EASY TO GET TO

Irazú's proximity to San José and the entire eastern Central Valley makes it an easy half-day or day trip. Public transportation from the capital, frequently a cumbersome option to most of the country's national parks, is straightforward.

ECO-LODGES IN THE CENTRAL VALLEY

Suburbia oozes out with each passing year eating up once-idyllic Central Valley land, but it's still surprisingly easy to find vast undeveloped stretches, even in the metro area.

You'd never know it driving the highway west from San José through the valley of shopping malls and car dealerships, but Costa Rica's Central Valley is home to an ample amount of greenery. Two of the country's five active volcanoes (Irazú and Turrialba) loom here. Suburbia gives way to farmland in the hills far above Escazú and Santa Ana and makes for tranquil day hikes. A terrific selection of country lodges populates the hills north of Alajuela and Heredia, and a stay in one of them is certain to give you that "so close (to the international airport) and yet so far" convenience. Tapantí National Park, in the far eastern sector of the valley, contains a real live cloud forest—it's not quite Monteverde, but it is far easier to get to—and Guayabo National Monument nearby is home to Costa Rica's only true archaeological ruins. The medium-size city of Turrialba has fast become the country's white-water center. And the Orosi Valley defines pastoral tranquility.

GOOD PRACTICES

Make a point of getting out and meeting the local people here in the Central Valley. We'd argue that the tidy towns in this region are Costa Rica at its most "authentic," its most "Tico." Folks here still greet you with a hearty "Buenos días" each day. Respond in kind.

Consider taking public transportation in the Central Valley. Communities here are bunched close enough together to be well served by public buses, and taxis can fill in the gaps. Plus, as development increases in the valley, managing your own vehicle here begins to resemble city driving.

TOP ECO-LODGES IN THE CENTRAL VALLEY

FINCA ROSA BLANCA COUNTRY INN, HEREDIA

The hotel on this eight-acre working coffee plantation just outside Heredia is one of just four properties in the country to have achieved the coveted "Five Leaves" status in the Certification for Sustainable Tourism. (⇨ *Certificate of Sustainable Tourism in Chapter 5*). In 2008, it also became Costa Rica's only lodging to receive a perfect score in this regard. In addition to all the amenities you'd expect from one of the Central Valley's most sumptuous accommodations, you can also take Finca Rosa Blanca's unique Sustainability Tour for a behind-the-scenes look at what a hotel can do to be more eco- and community-friendly. What other tour in Costa Rica lets you take in the workings of the laundry room, the solar panels, and the compost pile?

RANCHO NATURALISTA, TURRIALBA

Some 450 species of birds live on the property—few lodgings can make such a claim, let alone one so close to the metropolitan area. But the fittingly named Rancho Naturalista near Turrialba has fast become the birding center of the Central Valley. From the bird checklist in the welcome packet in your room, to the resident professional birding guide, to the delightful deck where you can continue to bird-watch even after trekking around the grounds for the day, this is one of Costa Rica's premier locales for bird-watchers of all experience levels.

XANDARI RESORT HOTEL & SPA, ALAJUELA

Xandari is a favorite of honeymooners who might not be aware of its environmental stewardship. The 40-acre property in the hills above Alajuela maintains an active program of recycling and uses on-site, organically grown fruits and vegetables. The hotel is also turning back a portion of its coffee plantation to tree cover, which has been set aside as a nature reserve. Coffee is still cultivated on the remainder of the plantation and ends up in your morning cup or as part of the coffee-scrub spa treatment.

COMMUNITY OUTREACH

A glance at high schools around the Central Valley reveals a growing number of outdoor eco-themed wall paintings, all part of an ever-growing annual Environmental Mural Contest. The name says it all: students from area schools compete each year to design and create original murals conveying environmental messages.

The works represent combined efforts of schools' art and biology departments, with students devoting an average of four months from the project's start to finish. Many of the murals measure 50 square meters, or around 540 square feet. The competition is designed to foster artistic skills, teamwork, and, of course, environmental awareness among students and faculty who take part.

The contest is directed by the nonprofit FUNDECOR foundation, a local non-governmental organization whose objective is to put the brakes on deforestation and promote environmental consciousness. Local businesses support the effort.

4

THE CENTRAL VALLEY

Updated by
Jeffrey Van
Fleet

San José sits in a mile-high-ish mountain valley ringed by volcanoes whose ash has fertilized the soil and turned the region into Costa Rica's breadbasket. This is the land that coffee built, and the small cities of the Central Valley exhibit a tidiness and prosperity you don't see in the rest of the country.

For you, the visitor, the valley is chock-full of activities that will keep you occupied for a couple of days. There's no shortage of terrific lodgings out here—everything from family-run boutique hotels to the big international chains are yours for the night.

GETTING HERE

Although Aeropuerto Internacional Juan Santamaría is billed as San José's airport, it sits just outside the city of Alajuela. You can get taxis from the airport to any point in the Central Valley for $8 to $80. On your left, just before exiting the terminal, you'll see a counter where you can hire a taxi. Some hotels arrange pickup.

All points in the western Central Valley can be reached by car. For San Antonio de Belén, Heredia, Alajuela, and points north of San José, turn right at the west end of Paseo Colón onto the Pan-American Highway (Autopista General Cañas). All the attractions in the eastern Central Valley are accessible from San José by driving east on Avenidas 2, then Central, through San Pedro, then following signs from the intersection to Cartago. To get to the Orosi Valley, head straight through Cartago, turn right at the Basílica de Los Angeles, and follow the signs to Paraíso. The road through Cartago and Paraíso continues east to Turrialba.

Buses leave the international airport for Alajuela several times an hour; from Alajuela you can catch buses to Grecia, Sarchí, and San Ramón. Less frequent buses (one to three per hour) serve Heredia. For travel between the airports and Escazú, Cartago, or Turrialba, you have to change buses in San José, which usually means taking a taxi between bus terminals. All buses heading toward San José from Alajuela can drop you off at the airport, but you need to ask the driver when you board, and then remind him again as you draw near to the stop, *"Aeropuerto, por favor"* ("Airport, please").

GETTING AROUND

The best way to get around the Central Valley is by car. Most of the car-rental agencies in San José have offices at or near the airport in Alajuela. They will deliver vehicles to many of the hotels listed in this chapter, except those in Turrialba and the Orosi Valley.

Many visitors never consider taking a local bus to get around, but doing so puts you in close contact with locals—an experience you miss out on if you travel by taxi or tour bus. It's also cheap. If your Spanish and sense of direction are up to snuff and you have the time, give it a shot. Your hotel can help you get to the correct bus stop and a current schedule. Always opt for a taxi at night or when you're in a hurry.

All Central Valley towns have taxis, which usually wait for fares along the central parks. Taxis in Alajuela, Cartago, and Heredia can take you up to Poás, Irazú, and Barva volcanoes, but the trips are quite expensive (about $50). If you don't have a car, the only way to get to Tapantí National Park is to take a cab from Orosi (about $15 each way).

WEST OF SAN JOSÉ

As you drive north or west out of San José, the city's suburbs and industrial zones quickly give way to arable land, much of which is occupied by coffee farms. Within Costa Rica's coffee heartland are plenty of tranquil agricultural towns and two provincial capitals, Alajuela and Heredia. Both cities owe their relative prosperity to the coffee beans cultivated on the fertile lower slopes of the Poás and Barva volcanoes. The upper slopes, too cold for coffee crops, are dedicated to dairy cattle, strawberries, ferns, and flowers, making for markedly different and thoroughly enchanting landscapes along the periphery of the national parks. Because the hills above these small valley towns have some excellent restaurants and lodgings, rural overnights are a good alternative to staying in San José.

ESCAZÚ

5 km/3 mi southwest of San José.

Costa Rica's wealthiest community and the Central Valley's most prestigious address, Escazú nevertheless mixes glamour with tradition, BMWs with oxcarts, Louis Vuitton with burlap produce sacks. As you exit the highway and crest the first gentle hill, you might think you made a wrong turn and ended up in Southern California, but farther up you return to small-town Central America. Narrow roads wind their way up the steep slopes, past postage-stamp coffee fields and lengths of shoulder-to-shoulder, modest houses with tidy gardens and the occasional oxcart parked in the yard. Unfortunately, the area's stream of new developments and high-rises has steadily chipped away at the rural landscape—each year you have to climb higher to find the kind of scene that captured the attention of many a Costa Rican painter in the early 20th century. In their place are plenty of fancy homes and condos, especially in the San Antonio and San Rafael neighborhoods. Escazú's historic church faces a small plaza, surrounded in part by weathered adobe buildings. The town center is several blocks north of the busy road to Santa Ana, which is lined with a growing selection of restaurants, bars, and shops.

GETTING HERE AND AROUND

To drive to Escazú from San José, turn left at the western end of Paseo Colón, which ends at the Parque La Sabana. Take the first right, and get off the highway at the second exit. The off-ramp curves sharply left; follow it about 1 km (½ mi), sticking to the main road, to El Cruce at the bottom of the hill (marked by a large Scotiabank). Continue through the traffic light for San Rafael addresses; turn right for the old road to Santa Ana. The trip takes about 15 minutes. A steady stream of buses for Escazú runs from several stops around Terminal Coca-Cola in San José (⊠ Avdas. 1–3, Cs. 14–16), with service from 5 AM to 11 PM.

ESSENTIALS

Bank/ATM Banco Nacional (✉ *Southwest side of Parque Central* ☎ *2228–0009*). **Banco de Costa Rica ATM** (✉ *North side of church*).

Internet Bagelmen's (✉ *San Rafael de Escazú, 500 m southwest of the Trejos Montealegre shopping center* ☎ *2228–4460*). **Internet CF** (✉ *Northwest corner of Parque Central, upstairs in Plaza Escazú mall* ☎ *2289–5706*).

Medical Assistance Farmacia San Miguel (✉ *North side of Parque Central* ☎ *2228–2339*). **Hospital CIMA** (✉ *Next to PriceSmart, just off the highway to Santa Ana 12 km/7½ mi west of downtown San José* ☎ *2208–1000*).

Post Office Correos (✉ *100 m north of church*).

Taxis Coopetico (☎ *2224–7979*).

HOCUS POCUS

During colonial days, Escazú was dubbed the City of Witches because many native healers lived in the area. Locals say that Escazú is still Costa Rica's most haunted community, home to witches who will tell your fortune or concoct a love potion for a small fee, but you'd be hard-pressed to spot them in the town's busy commercial district. Try a soccer field instead; the city's team is christened Las Brujas ("the witches"). You'll see a huge number of witch-on-a-broomstick decals affixed to vehicles here, too.

EXPLORING

High in the hills above Escazú is the tiny community of **San Antonio de Escazú**, famous for its annual oxcart festival held the second Sunday of March. The view from here—of nearby San José and distant volcanoes—is impressive by both day and night. If you head higher than San Antonio de Escazú, brace yourself for seemingly vertical roads that wind up into the mountains toward **Pico Blanco**, the highest point in the Escazú Cordillera, which is a half-day hike to ascend. Our preference is **San Miguel**, one peak east. Although you can hike these hills on your own, it is far safer to go with an outfitter. **Aventuras Pico Tours** (☎ *2289–6135* ⊕ *www.picotours.com*) is based up here. Its Tico owner has scaled some of the world's highest summits, and can lead you on a variety of hikes.

WHERE TO EAT

$$
SOUTHERN
✕ **Barbecue Los Anonos.** For four decades, Costa Ricans have flocked to Los Anonos to enjoy its family-friendly grill fest. The original dining room, a rustic collection of deep booths with wooden benches, has been expanded upon to add a more elegant space decorated with historic photos. The crowd tends toward families on weekend nights, whereas weekdays are busier during lunch, when business executives come for the economical meals. The best bet is the grilled meat, and there is plenty to choose from, including imported U.S. beef and less expensive Tico cuts. Fresh fish, shrimp, and half a dozen salads round out the choices. ✉ *400 m west of Los Anonos Bridge* ☎ *2228–0180* ⊟ *AE, D, DC, MC, V* ⊙ *Closed Mon.*

$
ITALIAN
✕ **Cerros.** This San Antonio hills favorite combines smoky thin-crust pizza with the essence of the Central Valley—simple and sincere. Pull up a chair to one of the gingham-covered tables on the semi-enclosed patio, and you have the perfect view of a Costa Rican microcosm. The valley

drops down just behind the soccer field and the green-trimmed church across the street, revealing the shimmering panorama of Escazú, Alajuela, and Heredia. The pizza is the main draw, but pastas, meat dishes, and Costa Rican standbys are well represented. ⊠ *South side of soccer field, San Antonio de Escazú* ☎ *2228–1831* ⊟ *AE, D, DC, MC, V* ⊗ *No lunch weekdays.*

$$
\$\$
$$

SPANISH

✕ **El Gaitero.** Generous portions of Spanish tapas and entrées draw diners to this whitewashed adobe house up the hill near San Antonio de Escazú. Wooden-bench tables are distributed along a wraparound porch with views of the Central Valley; inside, settings are arranged in small-to-medium rooms. Antonio and Olga, the passionate Asturian owners, will bring you up to speed with what's best that night and even pull out recipes to share. Presentation isn't the strong suit here: straight-up good food is, as are reasonable prices. Start with a pitcher of sangria and begin sampling; the extensive menu includes dishes such as Spanish omelet. ⊠ *Del Cruce del Barrio El Carmen, 100 m east and 50 m south, San Antonio de Escazú* ☎ *2228–1850* ⊟ *AE, D, DC, MC, V* ⊗ *Closed Mon.–Wed.*

$$
\$\$\$
$$

FRENCH

✕ **Le Monastère.** This monastery-theme formal restaurant high in the San Rafael hills has a great view of the Central Valley. The dining room is dressed up in antiques, with tables set for a five-course meal; waiters don short friar tunics over their standard black pants and white shirts, which makes the atmosphere too theatrical for some tastes, but the classic French dishes are outstanding. The more casual La Cava Grill dining area serves platters of grilled meat. La Cava Bar, beneath the dining room, has tasty appetizers, and live music Thursday to Saturday, and is open into the wee hours. ⊠ *1½ km/1 mi southwest of the Paco Shopping Center in San Rafael de Escazú; take old road west to Santa Ana, turn left at Paco and follow signs, always bearing right* ☎ *2228–8515* ⊕ *www.monastere-restaurant.com formal* ⊟ *AE, D, DC, MC, V* ⊗ *Closed Sun. No lunch.*

$$
\$\$\$
$$

ITALIAN

✕ **Restaurante Cerutti.** The diva of the Central Valley's Italian eateries, this little restaurant promises minimalist elegance in a lovely adobe house built in 1817. The extensive menu, focusing on modern Italian cuisine, ranges from roasted scallops with Spanish chorizo to ravioli stuffed with duck and Italian ham. Core dishes are complemented by a variety of selections that change every month or so. No one disputes that the quality of the food is high—with prices to match. ⊠ *Southeast corner of El Cruce, San Rafael de Escazú* ☎ *2228–9954* ⊕ *www.ceruttirestaurante. com* ⊟ *AE, D, DC, MC, V* ⊗ *Closed Sun.*

$$
\$\$\$
$$

INDIAN

✕ **Taj Mahal.** This burst of northern Indian flavor is such a rarity in Central America that we can overlook the slightly less-than-factual claim that the restaurant is the isthmus's only such option. Richly swathed in warm fuchsias, red ochres, and golds, the mansion's dining area sprawls

Costa Rica's oxcarts are folkloric symbols and a common canvas for local artisans.

through a handful of small, intimate rooms and out to a gazebo in the tree-covered backyard. The price-to-portion ratio is a little high, particularly for North Americans used to good, cheap Indian food, but the sharp tandoori dishes, curries, and *biryanis* (seasoned rice dishes) are a welcome vacation from ubiquitous European and American fare. Vegetarians may swoon at the options. Helpful waiters, in black or maroon traditional Punjabi dress, are frank about recommendations. The restaurant offers free shuttle transport to and from hotels in Escazú, Santa Ana, and San Antonio de Belén. ⊠ *1 km/½ mi west of Paco mall on old road to Santa Ana* ☎ *2228–0980* ⊕ *www.thetajmahalrestaurant. com* ⊟ *AE, D, DC, MC, V* ☺ *Closed Mon.*

WHERE TO STAY

$$ 🏠 **Casa de las Tías.** The gamut of city services is at your doorstep, but you're blissfully apart from them at this tranquil bed-and-breakfast in San Rafael de Escazú. The name means "The Aunts' House," which is appropriate for this yellow house with a front porch and picket fence at the end of a short road. A few old photos of the ladies themselves complete the effect. The rooms and furnishings feel slightly aged, but make up for it in charm, and the large backyard and gardens give the illusion of being far from a major commercial street. **Pros:** tranquility without sacrificing convenience; service that goes the extra mile; excellent breakfast. **Cons:** walls could be a little thicker; slightly dated feel. ⊠ *100 m south and 150 m east of El Cruce; turn east just south of Restaurante Cerutti* ☎ *2289–5517* ⊕ *www.hotels.co.cr/casatias.html* 🛏 *4 rooms, 1 junior suite* ⌂ *In-room: no a/c, Wi-Fi. In-hotel: laundry service, no-smoking rooms, no kids under 12* ⊟ *AE, MC, V* ⦿*BP.*

$ ⊡ **Costa Verde Inn.** When they need to make a city run, many beach-living expats head straight for this quiet B&B on the outskirts of Escazú. Rooms make nice use of local hardwoods and traditional South American art, and the main building serves as a gathering place with a large sitting area, comfortable chairs, and a fireplace. The inn is surrounded by gardens, and at night you can see the lights of San José twinkling to the east, though just three of the rooms take advantage of the view. The inn is at the end of a narrow driveway with an unassuming gate, but you'll see a sign if you've found the right place, so ring the bell. **Pros:** inviting public areas; excellent value. **Cons:** large student groups in summer; can be difficult to find; pool is for plungers, not swimmers. ⊠ *From southeast corner of second cemetery (the farthest west), 300 m south* ☎ *2228–4080* ⊕ *www.costaverdeinn.com* ⥱ *19 rooms, 3 apartments, 3 studios* ⌂ *In-room: no a/c, kitchen (some), refrigerator. In-hotel: pool* ⊟ *AE, D, DC, MC, V* ⏀⎮ *BP.*

> **PICNIC TIME**
>
> Escazú's Saturday-morning farmers' market makes a terrific place to stock up on some fresh fruit and vegetables if you're preparing a do-it-yourself lunch or just want to snack. Vendors start lining the street just north of the church about dawn, and things begin to wind down by late morning.

$$ ⊡ **Posada El Quijote.** Perched on a hill in the Bello Horizonte neighborhood, with a great view of the city, this bed-and-breakfast strikes the right balance between a small inn and a private residence. Being here feels like visiting a friend—albeit a friend with great taste. The quiet, homey feel draws low-key, mature travelers. The best view is from the sundeck, just off a spacious living room with a couch, a fireplace, and lots of modern art. The apartments and the two "deluxe" rooms have comparable views. Smaller "standard" rooms overlook the surrounding gardens, and aren't nearly as nice. The staff is extremely helpful. It's a bit hard to find, so you may want to take a taxi or call for directions. **Pros:** peaceful, friendly place to spend first or last night; excellent staff. **Cons:** need a car to get around; can be difficult to find. ⊠ *Bello Horizonte de Escazú, first street west of Anonos Bridge 1 km/½ mi up hill* ☎ *2289–8401, 813/287–9996 in North America* ⊕ *www.quijote.co.cr* ⥱ *8 rooms, 2 apartments* ⌂ *In-room: no a/c. In-hotel: laundry service, Wi-Fi hotspot, some pets allowed* ⊟ *AE, D, DC, MC, V* ⏀⎮ *BP.*

NIGHTLIFE

Escazú is the Central Valley's hot spot for nightlife—many Josefinos head here for the restaurants, bars, and dance clubs that cater to a young, cell phone–toting crowd. You can't miss the bright lights as you swing into town off the Próspero Fernández Highway. One of the more popular watering holes with the under-30 set is **Henry's Beach Cafe** (⊠ *500 m west of El Cruce, Plaza San Rafael, 2nd fl.* ☎ *2289–6250),* which features televised sports by day, varied music by night, and an islands decor of beach paintings and surfboards. Costa Ricans refer to this style of bar as an "American bar," which is fairly accurate. A young, sophisticated crowd keeps **Il Panino** (⊠ *Centro Comercial Paco* ☎ *2228–3126* ⊕ *www.jazzcafecostarica.com* ✉ *$6–$8* ☉ *Closed Sun.)* buzzing. It's a great place to start or end an evening. Music fans on the west side of town cheered the 2008 opening of **Jazz Café Escazú** (✉ *Next to Confort Suizo, across the highway from Hospital Cima; first exit after the toll booths* ☎ *2288–4740* ⊕ *www.jazzcafecostarica.com* ⊟ *$6–$8* ⊘ *Closed Sun.*). The boxy club hosts an eclectic live-music lineup similar to that of its popular sister venue in San Pedro and has double the capacity. The high-end **Itskatzú** complex, 1 km (½ mi) east of Multiplaza, has a number of restaurants and bars ranging from the low-brow (Hooters) to sophisticated sushi and live Cuban music.

SHOPPING

★ If you get the shopping bug and absolutely must visit a mall while on vacation, Escazú is the place to do it. **Multiplaza,** on the south side of the Autopista Próspero Fernández, approximately 5 km (3 mi) west of San José, is a big, luxurious one. **Biesanz Woodworks** (✉ *Bello Horizonte, 800 m south of Escuela Bello Horizonte* ☎ *2289–4337* ⊕ *www.biesanz.com*) is where local craftsmen ply their trade and expat artist Barry Biesanz creates unique, world-class items from Costa Rican hardwoods, which are turned (a form of woodworking) on-site. It's difficult to find, so take a taxi or call for directions from your hotel.

SANTA ANA

17 km/10 mi southwest of San José.

As metro development, with the accompanying condos and shopping malls, marches westward, it's hard to tell where Escazú ends and the once-tranquil agricultural community of Santa Ana begins. But the town center, with its rugged stone church surrounded by homes and businesses, has changed little in the past decade. The church, which was built between 1870 and 1880, has a Spanish-tile roof, carved wooden doors, and two pre-Columbian stone spheres flanking its entrance. Its rustic interior—bare wooden pillars and beams and black iron lamps— seems appropriate for an area with a tradition of ranching. Because it is warmer and drier than the towns to the east, Santa Ana is one of the few Central Valley towns that doesn't have a good climate for coffee—it is Costa Rica's onion capital, however—and is instead surrounded by pastures and patches of forest; it isn't unusual to see men on horseback here.

GETTING HERE AND AROUND

From San José, turn left at the western end of Paseo Colón, which ends at the Parque La Sabana. Take the first right, and get on the highway. Get off at the sixth exit; bear left at the flashing red lights, winding past roadside ceramics and vegetable stands before hitting the town center, about 2 km (1 mi) from the highway. The trip takes about 25 minutes. Blue buses to Santa Ana leave from San José's Terminal Coca-Cola every eight minutes. To get to places along the Autopista Próspero Fernández or Piedades, take buses marked "Pista" or "Multiplaza." Those marked "Calle Vieja" leave every 15 minutes and pass through Escazú on the old road to Santa Ana. Buses run from 5 AM to 11 PM.

CLOSE UP

Speaking Costa Rican

Spanish in Costa Rica tends to be localized. This is a land where eloquent speech and creative verbal expression are highly valued. For example, here the response to a "thank-you" is the gracious, uniquely Tico *"Con mucho gusto"* ("With much pleasure") instead of *"De nada"* ("It's nothing"), which is used in much of Latin America. In other cases, informality is preferred: the conventional *Señor* and *Señora,* for example, are eschewed in favor of the more egalitarian *Don* and *Doña,* used before a first name. Even President Oscar Arias is called "Don Oscar." Exercise caution when selecting from the list *below,* however. Although young Costa Rican men address everyone as *maje* (dude), you'll get a withering look if you, a visitor, follow suit.

adios good-bye; but also used as "hello" in rural areas
agarrar de maje to pull someone's leg
birra beer
brete work
cachos shoes
chunche any thingamajig
clavar el pico to fall asleep
estar de chicha to be angry
estar de goma to have a hangover

harina money
jupa head
macho, macha a person with blond hair
maje buddy, dude, mate
mamá de Tarzán know-it-all
maría a woman's name; also a taxi meter
matar la culebra to waste time
montón a lot
paño towel
pelo de gato cat hair; or fine, misty rain that falls during December
peso colón *pinche* a tight-fisted person
ponerse hasta la mecha to get drunk
porfa please
pura vida fantastic, great
rojo red; also a 1,000-colón note
soda an inexpensive local restaurant
torta a big mistake or error
tuanis cool
tucán toucan; also a 5,000-colón note
upe anyone home?
con mucho gusto used in response to "thank you" instead of "de nada"
muy bien, gracias a Dios very well, thank goodness
muy bien, por dicha very well, luckily
si Dios quiere God willing

SANTA ANA ESSENTIALS

Bank/ATM Banco de Costa Rica (✉ *100 m west of church* ☎ *2203–4281*). **Banco Popular** (✉ *Southwest corner of church* ☎ *2203–7979*). **Banco Nacional** (✉ *Northwest corner of church* ☎ *2282–2479*).

Internet Internet Café El Sol (✉ *Southwest corner of church, across from Banco Popular* ☎ *2282–8059*).

Medical Assistance Farmacia Sucre (✉ *25 m south of church* ☎ *2282–1296*).

Post Office Correos (✉ *Northwest corner of church*).

WHERE TO EAT AND STAY

$$$ ✕ **Bacchus.** Take a Peruvian chef trained in France and an Italian owner,
ECLECTIC and you get Bacchus, a welcome addition to the local dining scene. The cuisine is a mix of French and Italian dishes such as duck breast in a port sauce, baked mushroom-and-polenta ragout, and a variety of

pizzas. Modern art decorates the simple but elegant interior, and outdoor seating is available. An extensive wine list and reasonable prices make it a great pick for dinner. ⊠ *200 m east and 100 m north of church* ☎ *2282–5441* ▭ *AE, D, DC, MC, V.*

$$–$$$ ⊡ **Alta.** The view from this colonial-style hotel perched on a hillside
★ above Santa Ana is impressive, but then, so is the hotel. The sloping stairway entrance lined with tall columns and greenery is reminiscent of a narrow street in southern Spain, an effect reinforced by the barrel-tile roof and ochre-stucco walls; the narrow hallways feel like an old castle. Guest rooms are spacious, with colonial-style furniture and bathrooms with hand-painted tiles; ask for one on the fourth or fifth floor to take advantage of the view. The restaurant, La Luz ($$$), has a hardwood floor, a beamed ceiling, and plenty of windows for admiring the distant hills and the pool and gardens below. The eclectic and unusual menu includes baked goat cheese salad, macadamia-encrusted fish, and Moroccan chicken. **Pros:** classy service; panoramic views; excellent value for price. **Cons:** lower-floor rooms lose out on the view; little to do within walking distance. ⊠ *2½ km/1½ mi west of Paco shopping center, on old road between Santa Ana and Escazú, Alto de las Palomas* ☎ *2282–4160; 888/388–2582 in North America* ⊕ *www.thealtahotel.com* ⤵ *18 rooms, 5 suites* ⚶ *In-room: safe, refrigerator, Internet, Wi-Fi. In-hotel: restaurant, room service, bar, pool, gym, laundry service* ▭ *AE, D, DC, MC, V* |○| *CP.*

$$ ⊡ **Hotel Posada Canal Grande.** This small Italian-owned hotel tucked into the hills to the west of Santa Ana is a great value. Each room is different, and most have wicker beds. Second-floor rooms, each with a balcony over the pool, have excellent views, but the first-floor rooms aren't bad either. Two four-poster beds are placed in the shade by the pool, just to lounge on. On a clear day you can see the Gulf of Nicoya to the west. Poolside chatter is in French, Spanish, and German as much as it is in English. **Pros:** great value; international feel. **Cons:** spartan bathrooms; dining options limited. ⊠ *On the Próspero Fernández highway to Ciudad Colón, 500 m north of Piedades de Santa Ana bus terminal* ☎ *2282–4089* ⊕ *www.hotelcanalgrande.com* ⤵ *12 rooms* ⚶ *In-room: no a/c, safe, refrigerator. In-hotel: restaurant, bar, pool, laundry service, Wi-Fi hotspot, Internet terminal, no-smoking rooms, some pets allowed* ▭ *AE, D, DC, MC, V* |○| *BP.*

SHOPPING

★ Large glazed pots with ornate decorations that range from traditional patterns to modern motifs are the specialties at **Cerámica Las Palomas** (⊠ *Old road to Santa Ana, opposite Alta Hotel* ☎ *2282–7001*). Flowerpots and lamps are also common works, and the staff will eagerly show you the production process, from raw clay to art.

GOLF

Although it sits inside a residential complex of the same name, **Valle del Sol** (⊠ *1,700 m west of HSBC* ☎ *2282–9222* ⊕ *www.valledelsol. com* ⤓ *$94 for 18 holes with cart* ⊙ *Mon. 8–6, Tues.–Sun. 6:30–6*) is Costa Rica's preeminent public golf course. Call to reserve tee times at this 7,000-yard, par 72, 18-hole course. Collared shirts and blouses are required; denim shorts and trousers are prohibited.

NORTH OF SAN JOSÉ

As you set out from San José to explore the towns to the north, you first encounter nothing but asphalt, hotels, and malls—not especially scenic. Santo Domingo and San Antonio de Belén blend into the outskirts of San José, and it's only when you get to the heart of these small towns that you feel you've arrived in Central America. Farther north, Alajuela and Heredia are bustling provincial capitals with charismatic central parks. Throughout this area, tucked into the urban scenery and lining volcanic slopes, are fields of that great Costa Rican staple, coffee.

SAN ANTONIO DE BELÉN

17 km/10 mi northwest of San José.

San Antonio de Belén has little to offer visitors but its rural charm and proximity to the international airport. The latter led developers to build several of the San José area's biggest hotels here. The town also lies on the route of entry for Alajuela's Butterfly Farm, and it's a convenient departure point for trips to the western Central Valley, Pacific coast, and northern region. If you stay at the Marriott, you likely won't even see the town, just the busy highway between San José and Alajuela.

GETTING HERE AND AROUND

From San José, turn right at the west end of Paseo Colón onto the Pan-American Highway (Carretera General Cañas). The San Antonio de Belén exit is at an overpass 6 km (4 mi) west of the Heredia exit, by the Real Cariari Mall. Turn left at the first intersection, cross over the highway, and continue 1 km (½ mi) to the forced right turn, driving 1½ km (1 mi) to the center of town. San Antonio is only 10 minutes from the airport.

SAN ANTONIO DE BELÉN ESSENTIALS

Bank/ATM Banco de Costa Rica (⊠ *50 m north of rear of church* ☎ *2239–1149*). BAC San José ATM (⊠ *200 m west of soccer field*).

Internet Belén Web Café (⊠ *West end of soccer field* ☎ *2239–4181*).

Medical Assistance Farmacia Sucre (⊠ *North side of church* ☎ *2239–3485*).

Post Office Correos (⊠ *3 blocks west and 25 m north of church*).

Taxis Asotaxis Belén (☎ *2293–4712*).

WHERE TO STAY

$$$ ⚟ **Doubletree by Hilton Cariari.** This low-rise hotel (formerly the Meliá Cariari, and many still refer to it by that name) was the metro area's original luxury hotel, and it remains popular for its excellent service and out-of-town location. Just off the busy General Cañas Highway, about halfway between San José and the international airport, the Cariari is surrounded by thick vegetation that buffers it from traffic noise. When Doubletree by Hilton took over in 2008, it began an ambitious renovation project, revamping a number of rooms, replacing all beds, and generally sprucing up the place. Spacious, carpeted guest rooms in back overlook the pool area. The relaxed poolside bar, with cane chairs and colorful tablecloths,

North of San José

0   5 mi

0   5 km

and nearby casino, are popular spots. Overall, it feels slightly more low-key and less grandiose than the nearby Marriott. **Pros:** resort experience close to both San José and the airport; kid-friendly. **Cons:** tricky car access; close to busy highway. ⊠ *Autopista General Cañas, ½ km/ ¼ mi east of intersection for San Antonio de Belén, Cariari, San Antonio de Belén* ☎ *2239–0022; 800/222–8733 in North America* ⊕ *www.cariarisanjose.doubletree.com* ⇆ *198 rooms, 24 suites* ⚑ *In-room: safe, refrigerator, Wi-Fi. In-hotel: 2 restaurants, bars, pool, gym, laundry service, parking (free), no-smoking rooms* ▭ *AE, D, DC, MC, V.*

$$ **El Rodeo.** This quiet hotel bills itself as a "country hotel," though this is more in image than fact—El Rodeo's proximity to the airport and major business parks is the real draw. Spacious rooms, most with polished hardwood floors, high ceilings, and narrow balconies, overlook small gardens and rooms in the adjacent building. An open-air lounge on the second floor has a pool table and wicker furniture. The new Grand Café serves breakfast each morning. The large wooden El Rodeo Steakhouse Restaurant ($$) in front of the hotel is quite popular with Ticos, who pack it on weekends. Decorated with saddles, steer skulls, and other ranching paraphernalia, the restaurant serves an array of grilled meats, from the Argentinean churrascos to T-bones, as well as several fish and shrimp dishes. All rooms here are nonsmoking. **Pros:** proximity to airport; newly renovated facilities; spacious rooms. **Cons:** generic feel.

✉ *Road to Santa Ana 2 km/1 mi east of Parque Central* ☎ *2293–3909* ⊕ *www.elrodeohotel.com* ↪ *22 rooms, 7 suites* ⚬ *In-room: safe, refrigerator, Wi-Fi. In-hotel: restaurant, tennis court, pool, laundry service, Internet terminal, no-smoking rooms* ▤ *AE, D, DC, MC, V* ⑪ *BP.*

$$$–$$$$ ⌂ **Marriott Costa Rica Hotel.** The stately Marriott offers comprehensive ★ luxury close to the airport. Towering over a coffee plantation west of ☾ San José, the thick columns, wide arches, and central courtyard are re-creations straight out of the 16th century, and hand-painted tiles and abundant antiques complete the historic appearance. Guest rooms are more contemporary, but they're elegant enough, with hardwood furniture. Some have sliding glass doors that open onto tiny balconies; new rooms feature flat-screen TVs. The place is always abuzz with upscale tourists, business travelers, and participants in the many events that take place at the facilities. **Pros:** excellent service; lavish grounds; close to airport. **Cons:** tendency to nickel-and-dime guests; impersonal feel. ✉ *¾ km/ ½ mi west of Bridgestone/Firestone, off Autopista General Cañas* ☎ *2298–0000; 800/236–2427 in North America* ⊕ *www.marriott.com* ↪ *290 rooms, 9 suites* ⚬ *In-room: safe, refrigerator, Internet. In-hotel: 3 restaurants, bar, tennis courts, pools, gym, laundry service, Internet terminal, Wi-Fi hotspot, parking (free)* ▤ *AE, D, DC, MC, V* ⑪ *EP.*

ALAJUELA

20 km/13 mi northwest of San José.

Because of its proximity to the international airport (5–10 minutes away) many travelers spend their first or last night in or near Alajuela, but the beauty of the surrounding countryside persuades some to stay longer. Alajuela is Costa Rica's second–most populated city, and a mere 30-minute bus ride from the capital, but it has a decidedly provincial air compared with San José. Architecturally, it differs little from the bulk of Costa Rican towns: it's a grid of low-rise structures painted in dull pastel colors.

GETTING HERE AND AROUND

To reach Alajuela, follow directions to San Antonio de Belén *(above)*. Continue west on the highway past the San Antonio turnoff and turn right at the airport. Buses travel between San José (✉ Avda. 2, Cs. 12–14, opposite the north side of Parque La Merced), the airport, and Alajuela, and run every five minutes from 4:40 AM to 10:30 PM. The bus stop in Alajuela is 400 meters west, 25 meters north of the central park (✉ C. 3 and Avda. 1). Buses leave San José for Zoo Ave from La Merced church (✉ C. 14 and Avda. 4) daily at 8, 9, 10, 11 AM, and noon, returning on the hour from 10 AM to 3 PM.

ALAJUELA ESSENTIALS

Bank/ATM Banco de Costa Rica (✉ *Southwest corner of Parque Central* ☎ *2440–9039).* **Banco Nacional** (✉ *West side of Parque Central* ☎ *2441–0373).*

Hospital Hospital San Rafael (✉ *1 km/½ mi northeast of airport, on main road to Alajuela* ☎ *2436–1001).*

Internet nternet Inter@ctivo (✉ *In front of BAC San José bank, 100 m north of Parque Central* ☎ *2431–1984).*

Medical Assistance Farmacia Chavarría (✉ *Southwest corner of Parque Central* ☏ *2441–1231*). **Farmacia Catedral** (✉ *Northeast corner of Parque Central* ☏ *2441–3555*).

Post Office Correos (✉ *200 m north and 100 m east of Parque Central*).

Taxis Cootaxa (☏ *2443–3030*).

EXPLORING

Royal palms and massive mango trees fill the **Parque Central** (✉ *C. Central, Avdas. 1–Central*), which also has a lovely fountain imported from Glasgow and concrete benches where locals gather to chat. Surrounding the plaza is an odd mix of charming old buildings and sterile concrete boxes, including a somewhat incongruous McDonald's.

The large, neoclassical **Alajuela Cathedral** (✉ *C. Central, Avdas. 1–Central* ☏ *2443–2928*) has columns topped by interesting capitals decorated with local agricultural motifs, and a striking red metal dome. The interior is spacious but rather plain, except for the ornate cupola above the altar. It's open daily 5 AM–6 PM.

Alajuela was the birthplace of Juan Santamaría, the national hero who lost his life in a battle against the mercenary army of U.S. adventurer William Walker when the latter invaded Costa Rica in 1856. The **Parque Juan Santamaría** (✉ *C. Central and Avda. 2*) has a statue of the young Santamaría. After a 2005 restoration, Juan should keep his youthful good looks for years to come—which, sadly, is more than can be said for the abandoned-looking, weedy concrete lot he stands on.

Juan Santamaría's heroic deeds are celebrated in the **Juan Santamaría Museum** (Museo Juan Santamaría) housed in the old jail, one block north of Parque Central. It's worth a short look if you have the time; Santamaría's story is an interesting one. ✉ *Avda. 3, Cs. Central–2* ☏ *2441–4775* ✉ *Free* ☉ *Tues.–Sun. 10–5:30.*

☾ Spread over the lush grounds of **Zoo Ave** is a collection of large cages holding toucans, hawks, and parrots (the macaws range free), not to mention crocodiles, caimans, a boa constrictor, turtles, monkeys, wildcats, and other interesting critters. The zoo, the best in Costa Rica, runs a breeding project for rare and endangered birds, all of which are destined for eventual release. It has 115 bird species, including such rare ones as the quetzal, fiery-billed aracari, several types of eagles, and even ostriches. An impressive mural at the back of the facility shows Costa Rica's 850 bird species painted to scale. ✉ *La Garita de Alajuela. Head west from Alajuela center past cemetery, turn left after stone church in Barrio San José, continue on 2 km/1 mi; or head west on Pan-American Hwy. to Atenas exit, then turn right* ☏ *2433–8989* ✉ *$15* ☉ *Daily 9–5.*

★ Observe and photograph butterflies up close at **The Butterfly Farm** (*La*
☾ *Finca de Mariposas*). The farm's several microclimates keep comfortable some 40 species of tropical butterflies. Come when it's sunny if you can—they don't flutter around when it rains. This is the original butterfly farm, but there are other butterfly gardens near Volcán Poás at La Paz Waterfall Gardens and in Monteverde. The facility holds an annual mural contest, turning not only its own buildings but surrounding corner

Alajuela

SANTA BARBARA

TAMBOR

TUETAL NORTE

ALAJUELA

see inset

TO TACARES, GRECIA, SARCHI, ARENAL

TO SAN PEDRO

TO LA GARITA

TO INTERSECTION MANOLOS, ATENAS

Zoo Ave ◆

TO SAN ISIDRO, POÁS VOLCANO

TO SAN ANTONIO DE BELÉN

TO HEREDIA

TO SAN JOSÉ

Aeropuerto Internacional Juan Santamaría

Hospital San Rafael ◆

KEY

1 *Restaurants*
1 *Hotels*

0 — 1 mile
0 — 1 km

N

Avenida Antonio Arroyo
Soccer Stadium ◆
Juan Santamaría Museum
Tribunales de Justicia ◆
Catedral
Parque Central
Cemetery
TO ZOO AVE
TO BUTTERFLY FARM
Calle Ismael Chavern
Calle El Mesón

Restaurants ▼

Bar y Restaurante
El Mirador **3**
Delicias de Mi Tierra **1**
La Princesa Marina **2**

Hotels ▼

Buena Vista Hotel **5**
Hampton Inn & Suites
Airport–San José **7**
Hotel La Rosa
de América **1**
Hotel Los Volcanes **8**

Orquídeas Inn **2**
Pura Vida Hotel **4**
Siempreverde B&B **6**
Xandari Resort
Hotel & Spa **3**

A National Hero

When the Costa Ricans drove U.S. invader Walker's army from their country, in 1856, they chased his troops to Rivas, Nicaragua. The army of filibusters took refuge in a wooden fort. Juan Santamaría, a poor, 24-year-old drummer with a militia from Alajuela, volunteered to burn it down to drive them out. Legend says that Santamaría ran toward the fort carrying a torch, and that although he was shot repeatedly, he managed to throw it and to burn the fort down. His bravery wasn't recognized at the time, probably because of his modest origins, but in 1891 a statue depicting a strong and handsome soldier carrying a torch was placed in Alajuela, thus immortalizing Santamaría. For this occasion, Ruben Darío, the great Nicaraguan writer, dedicated a poem to him. The entire account may be apocryphal; some historians doubt there ever *was* such a person. But don't tell that to the average Tico. April 11 is now a national holiday in Costa Rica, called Juan Santamaría Day, which celebrates the Costa Rican victory at the Battle of Rivas.

stores and houses into canvases for talented Costa Rican artists. You can get here via tours from San José that depart from the capital at 7:20, 10, and 2. Regardless of your mode of transport, you can wander around the gardens on your own, or take one of the two-hour guided walks that begin at 8:45, 11, 1, or 3. ☒ *From San José, turn south (left) at the intersection just past Real Cariari Mall, follow the road to the north side of the church of San Antonio de Belén, take a left at the corner, then follow the butterfly signs* ☎ *2438–0400* ⊕ *www.butterflyfarm.co.cr* ✉ *$15, $35 with transportation from San José* ☉ *Daily 8:30–5.*

★ Considering the amount of coffee you'll drive past in the Central Valley, you might want to devote an hour or so of your vacation to learning about the crop's production. **Doka Estate,** a working coffee plantation for more than 70 years, offers a comprehensive tour that takes you through the fields, shows you how the fruit is processed and the beans are dried, and lets you sample the local brew. The best time to take this tour is during the October-to-February picking season. ☒ *10 km/6 mi north of Alajuela's Tribunales de Justicia; turn left at San Isidro and continue 6 km/ 4 mi, follow signs, San Luis de Sabanilla* ☎ *2449–5152; 800/946–3652 in North America* ⊕ *www.dokaestate.com* ✉ *$16; transportation from San José, Alajuela, Heredia, Escazú, or San Antonio available* ☉ *Tours: daily at 9, 10, 11, 1:30, 2:30, and 3:30; weekends last tour at 2:30.*

EN ROUTE If you head straight through Alajuela, with the Parque Central on your right, you'll be on the road to Poás Volcano; you should pass the Tribunales de Justicia (the county courthouse) on your right as you leave town. If you turn left upon reaching the Parque Central, and pass the town cemetery on your right, you'll be on the old road to Grecia. About 3 km (2 mi) northwest of town on that road, you'll come upon an old concrete church on the right, which marks your arrival in Barrio San José, a satellite community of Alajuela. A left turn after the church will take you to a lovely rural area called **La Garita** (the Guardhouse), from which the road continues west to Atenas and the Central Pacific beaches. La Garita is a popular weekend destination for Tico families, who head here for the abundant restaurants.

WHERE TO EAT

$$

ECLECTIC

✕ **Bar y Restaurante El Mirador.** Perched on a ridge several miles north of town, El Mirador has a sweeping view of the Central Valley that is impressive by day but more beautiful at dusk and night when the basin is filled with twinkling lights. Get a window table in the dining room, or one on the adjacent porch if it isn't too cool. The menu, which includes *lomito* (tenderloin) and *corvina* (sea bass) served with various sauces, and several shrimp or chicken dishes, plays second fiddle to the view. You could just stop in around sunset for drinks and appetizers. Free transportation from most Alajuela hotels is sometimes available. There are at least two other restaurants nearby with similar names and views—this one is on the main road, close to the Buena Vista Hotel. ⊠ *Road to Poás 5 km/3 mi north of Tribunales de Justicia* ☎ *2441–9347* ⌂ *Reservations essential weekends* ☰ *MC, V.*

¢

COSTA RICAN

✕ **Delicias de Mi Tierra.** A string of *típico* restaurants lines this road, but the "Delights of My Land" is our favorite. Tasty and traditional Tico favorites are served here: *pozol* (corn-and-pork soup), *casado campesino* (stewed beef with rice, beans, corn, potatoes, and plantains), and *chorreada con natilla* (a corn-bread pancake with sour cream). Long wooden tables and benches are surrounded by cane walls, decorative oxcart wheels, dried gourds, and tropical plants—the kind of decor trying so hard to be traditional that it's anything but. Ordering a few *entraditas* (appetizers) is a good way to sample dishes, as is the *parrillada de campo* (country barbecue), a platter with grilled chicken, beef, pork, rice, beans, fried plantains, and salad, or the larger *fiesta de gallos,* a mixed platter of corn tortillas with various fillings. There are also cheap but hearty breakfasts. Get here early for dinner, as closing time is 8 PM. ⊠ *1½ km/1 mi west of the Barrio San José church* ☎ *2433–8536* ☰ *AE, D, DC, MC, V.*

$

SEAFOOD

✕ **La Princesa Marina.** This large open-air eatery (part of a chain) at the intersection of the old Alajuela–Grecia road and the road to La Garita is popular with Ticos, who pack it on weekends to feast on inexpensive seafood. The selection is vast, with 10 types of fish, shrimp, or octopus ceviche, fish fillets served with various sauces, three sizes of shrimp prepared a dozen ways, whole fried fish, lobster tails, and several *mariscadas* (mixed seafood plates). Pastas, rice dishes, beef, and chicken are some other choices, but the seafood is your best bet. The decor is utilitarian—bare tables, ceiling fans, and dividers of potted plants separating the sections—but you avoid that feeling of being in a contrived tourist venue. ⊠ *Barrio San José, north of church* ☎ *2433–7117* ⊕ *www.princesamarina.com* ☰ *AE, D, DC, MC, V.*

WHERE TO STAY

$–$$

🛏 **Buena Vista Hotel.** Perched high above Alajuela, this hotel's superb staff makes up for the somewhat dated, uninspired decor. It does have the "good view" it is named for, but few of its rooms share in that vista, which is best appreciated from the back lawn. Three balcony rooms on the second floor in back have decent views of the Central Valley, but even better are the views of Poás Volcano from the three rooms above the lobby. Most rooms, however, overlook the lawns or pool area. They are fairly standard—carpeted and sparsely decorated, with small baths and TVs—with none of the pizzazz of similarly priced options. The restaurant behind the lobby serves international dishes and grilled items. **Pros:** excellent service; family-friendly. **Cons:** uninspired ambience; mediocre restaurant; farther from the airport than other options. ✉ *6 km/4 mi north of Alajuela's Tribunales de Justicia on road to Poás* ☎ *2442–8595; 800/506–2304 in North America* ⊕ *www.hotelbuenavistacr.com* ⤴ *11 rooms, 4 junior suites, 9 deluxe suites, 1 master suite* ⚬ *In-room: no a/c, no phone, Wi-Fi. In-hotel: restaurant, bar, pool, no-smoking rooms* ⊟ *AE, MC, V* ⏀ *BP.*

$$$ ⛉ **Hampton Inn & Suites Airport-San José.** A longtime favorite for first-night and last-night stays, this U.S. chain outlet lets you ease into and ease out of Costa Rica in familiar surroundings. Closer to the airport you cannot get: it's just across the highway. **Pros:** airport proximity; U.S. amenities. **Cons:** some noise from planes in the evening; sameness of a chain hotel. ✉ *Blvd. del Aeropuerto* ☎ *2442–3320; 800/426–7866 in North America* ⊕ *www.hamptoninncostarica.com* ⤴ *100 rooms* ⚬ *In-room: refrigerator (some), Internet. In-hotel: restaurant, pool, gym, Internet terminal, Wi-Fi hotspot, no-smoking rooms* ⊟ *AE, D, DC, MC, V* ⏀ *CP.*

$$ ⛉ **Hotel La Rosa de América.** This small hotel tucked off the road to La Garita is a simple and relaxed place to unwind. The Canadian owners add a welcoming energy and a personalized touch to a place that would otherwise be simply serviceable. There are six buildings, most divided into two units, arranged around the pool and gardens. The white-wall rooms are simple, but it's a quiet place to sleep. Calling ahead for directions is a good idea, but once you're here, you'll have easy access to nearby restaurants and Zoo Ave. All rooms here are nonsmoking. You'll receive a slight discount if you pay in cash. **Pros:** great for families; helpful owners; close to a number of restaurants. **Cons:** lacks flair of other options in this price range; should have car to stay here. ✉ *1 km/½ mi east of Zoo Ave* ☎ *2433–2741* ⊕ *www.larosadeamerica.com* ⤴ *12 rooms* ⚬ *In-room: no a/c, no phone, safe (some). In-hotel: pool, laundry service, Internet terminal, no-smoking rooms* ⊟ *AE, D, DC, MC, V* ⏀ *BP.*

¢–$ ⛉ **Hotel Los Volcanes.** Budget travelers looking for airport proximity will find this urban oasis an excellent value. Descendants of the Catalan family that thrived in this heritage house in 1920 still live next door, and historic photos of the mansion in its heyday line the earth-tone walls inside. The spacious rooms have low-slung, wide beds that make the ceilings seem sky-high—but avoid the room next to the washer and dryer. Breakfast is served in a courtyard shaded by a fig tree. Plenty of restaurants are within walking distance, the airport is a 10-minute taxi ride away, and just a few blocks away is the bus stop for La Garita, Poás, and most destinations in central and northwest Costa Rica. **Pros:** airport proximity; good value; historic ambience. **Cons:** some rooms are noisy; no views. ✉ *Avda. 3, Cs. 2–Central, or 100 m north, 25 m east of the northwest corner of Parque Central, across from the Juan Santamaría Museum* ☎ *2441–0525* ⊕ *www.hotellosvolcanes.com* ⤴ *11 rooms, 7 with bath* ⚬ *In-room: no a/c (some), safe (some), Wi-Fi. In-hotel: laundry service, Internet terminal, no-smoking rooms* ⊟ *MC, V* ⏀ *BP.*

4

The Alajuela Cathedral's painted domed cupola was rebuilt after the 1991 earthquake.

$$ 🏨 **Orquideas Inn.** A favorite with young couples and families, the friendly Orquideas proves that affordable does not have to equal generic. From a classy Spanish-style main building to a bar dedicated to Marilyn Monroe, this place has style. Deluxe rooms, on a hill with a view of three volcanoes, are spacious, with bamboo furniture, but can smell a bit musty. Smaller rooms have terra-cotta tile floors and Guatemalan fabrics that have seen better days; those on the garden side are quieter, and worth the extra $10. The newest addition to Orquideas' accommodation mix is a two-bedroom geodesic dome, set off in the garden and perfect for families or groups. A sumptuous breakfast buffet is served on the bar's patio. The restaurant's ($$) eclectic selection ranges from straightforward Costa Rican *cuisine* to over-the-top presentations (ceviche served in a half coconut, for one) that have to be seen (and tasted) to be believed. **Pros:** spirited environment; great for first or last night; excellent service. **Cons:** rooms are ready for a face-lift; roadside rooms noisy. ⊠ *2½ km/1½ mi northwest of the Princesa Marina* ☎ *2433–7128* ⊕ *www.orquideasinn. com* ⋐ *20 rooms, 6 suites, 1 dome* ♻ *In-room: safe, Wi-Fi. In-hotel: restaurant, bar, pool, laundry service* ⊟ *AE, D, DC, MC, V* ⑩ *BP.*

$$ 🏨 **Pura Vida Hotel.** Extremely well-informed, helpful owners and prox-
★ imity to the airport (15 minutes) make this a good place to begin and end a trip. Thanks to its location on a ridge north of town, several of this hotel's rooms have views of Poás Volcano, and all of them offer tranquility and abundant birdsong. The two rooms in the main house have the best views, but *casitas* (little houses) scattered around the large garden offer more privacy. Bright and cheery bungalows have small terraces with chairs where guests, typically well traveled, lounge. Continental breakfasts and delicious dinners (by reservation) are served on

a covered terrace behind the house. Ask about their books-for-schools program. **Pros:** owners active in the local community; stellar breakfast. **Cons:** large dogs may turn off those with less-than-fuzzy feelings for animals; stairs to climb. ⊠ *Tuetal 2 km/1 mi north of Tribunales de Justicia; veer left at Y* ☎ *2430–2929* ⊕ *www.puravidahotel.com* ⟿ *2 rooms, 4 bungalows* ⌂ *In-room: no a/c, no phone, safe, refrigerator (some), no TV, Internet. In-hotel: restaurant, laundry service, no-smoking rooms* ⊟ *AE, MC, V* ⎮⎮ *CP.*

$$ ⊡ **Siempreverde B&B.** A night at this isolated bed-and-breakfast in the heart of a coffee plantation might be as close as you'll ever come to being a coffee farmer or to truly getting away from it all. The attractive wooden house has seven sparsely decorated rooms upstairs, with hardwood floors and small windows; ask for the Cuarto Azul (the Blue Room). There's also a living room, a kitchen, a lounge, and a terrace in back where breakfast is served. Photos of the coffee harvest decorate the walls, and just beyond the yard and manicured gardens that surround the house, neat rows of coffee plants stretch off into the distance. **Pros:** off-the-beaten-path feel; plenty of tranquility. **Cons:** isolated location; tour groups pass by for breakfast most mornings. ⊠ *12 km/7½ mi northwest of Tribunales de Justicia de Alajuela; turn left at high school* ☎ *2449–5562* ⊕ *www.siempreverdebandb.com* ⟿ *7 rooms* ⌂ *In-room: no a/c, no phone, no TV* ⊟ *AE, MC, V* ⎮⎮ *BP.*

$$$–$$$$ ⊡ **Xandari Resort Hotel & Spa.** The tranquil and colorful Xandari is a strik-
Fodor's Choice ingly original inn and spa, tailor-made for honeymooners and romantic
★ getaways. Its bold design is the brainchild of a talented couple—he's an architect, she's an artist. Contemporary pueblo-esque villas along a ridge overlooking Alajuela and San José are spacious, with plenty of windows, colorful paintings, large terraces, and secluded lanais (sunbathing patios). It's the kind of place that makes you want to take pictures of your hotel room. Some villas stand alone and some share a building, but nearly all of them have spectacular views. So does the restaurant ($$), which serves tasty, often organic, low-fat food. A 4-km (3-mi) trail through the hotel's forest reserve winds past five waterfalls. **Pros:** amazing service; ideal setting for romance; guilt-free gourmet delights. **Cons:** some noise from other rooms; should have car to stay here. ⊠ *5 km/ 3 mi north of Tribunales de Justicia; turn left after small bridge, follow signs* ☎ *2443–2020; 866/363–3212 in North America* ⊕ *www.xandari. com* ⟿ *22 villas* ⌂ *In-room: no a/c, safe, refrigerator, no TV, Wi-Fi. In-hotel: restaurant, bar, pools, spa, laundry service, Internet terminal, no-smoking rooms* ⊟ *AE, MC, V* ⎮⎮ *CP.*

SANTO DOMINGO

18 km/11 mi northeast of Escazú, 7 km/4½ mi northwest of San José.

Between Heredia and San José, the town of Santo Domingo de Heredia has plenty of traditional architecture and a level of tranquility that belies its proximity to the capital, a mere 15-minute drive away if the traffic gods smile upon you. Established in the early 19th century, Santo Domingo is surrounded by coffee farms and several smaller, even quieter communities. It has two Catholic churches, including one of the country's two basilicas. The Iglesia del Rosario, which faces the town's sparsely planted Parque Central, was built in the 1840s and is open for Mass every morning from 7 to 10. The larger Basílica de Santo Domingo, which stands across from a soccer field in the northeast end of town, is open for evening Mass from 5 to 7, and is a venue for classical music concerts throughout the year, including the July-to-August International Music Festival.

GETTING HERE AND AROUND

For the 30-minute trip from downtown San José, head north on C. Central 4 km (2½ mi) to the central park in Tibás; continue 100 meters (328 feet) and turn left. Follow this road another 2½ km (1¼ mi) to Santo Domingo. From the west end of Paseo Colón, turn right onto the Pan-American Highway (aka the Carretera General Cañas), then right off the highway just before it heads onto an overpass, after the Hotel Irazú (on the right). Keep to this road for about 2 km (1 mi) to the first intersection after it becomes one-way. Turn right at the lights, continue 3 km (2 mi), passing INBioparque, until the road Ts; a left here brings you into town. One of the Heredia bus routes leaves from C. 1, Avdas. 7–9 every three to five minutes and passes through Santo Domingo.

ESSENTIALS

Bank/ATM **Banco Nacional** (⊠ *Across from south side of Iglesia del Rosario* ☎ *2244–0439*).

Post Office **Correos** (⊠ *Avda. Central, Cs. 2 and 4*).

EXPLORING

🄲 Santo Domingo's main attraction is **INBioparque**, which does a good job of explaining the country's various ecosystems. It's a useful, if slightly expensive, primer before you head out to the hinterlands. Wander trails through climate-controlled wetlands and out to tropical dry forest. The forests may not look much different, but your English-speaking guide will explain the subtleties. Along the way, stop at the butterfly farm, snake and insect exhibits, and bromeliad garden. The tour is packed with information—perhaps too much—but if you're visiting Costa Rica for its ecology, it's a worthwhile lesson. Kids love the virtual aerial flyover of Central America introduced by Costa Rican-American NASA astronaut Franklin Chang. A restaurant serves typical Costa Rican fare, and the gift shop has souvenirs and books on natural history. Reservations are required for tours. ⊠ *Road between Santo Domingo and Heredia, 400 m north and 250 m west of Shell gas station* ☎ *2507–8107* ⊕ *www. inbioparque.com* 🄳 *$23* 🕓 *Tues.–Fri. 8–3 (last admission at 2), weekends 9–4:30 (last admission at 3:30). Tours at 9, 11, and 1.*

WHERE TO STAY

$$ 🏨 **Hotel Bougainvillea.** This hotel is a top choice for business travelers and small-scale conferences, but its extensive grounds, which bump up against coffee farms, are ideal for lazy strolls or families with energetic kids. You might even forget that you're only 20 minutes from San José. The spacious and carpeted but otherwise unremarkable rooms are furnished with local hardwoods. Rooms on the second and third floors have large balconies; get one with a view of the gardens behind

The verdant Central Valley is Costa Rica's bread basket.

the hotel. The 8-acre garden, shaded by large trees, holds an extensive bromeliad collection. Pre-Columbian pottery and paintings by Costa Rican artists decorate the lobby and restaurant ($$), which serves a small but excellent selection of Continental cuisine. An hourly shuttle takes you to the Hotel Villa Tournón in San José. All rooms here are nonsmoking. **Pros:** lush and open spaces; of the urban hotels, one of the better bird-watching sites. **Cons:** slightly institutional smell and feel in the hallways. ⊠ *2 km/1 mi east of Santo Domingo de Heredia, Santo Tomas* ☎ *2244–1414; 866/880–5441 in North America* ⊕ *www.hb.co. cr* ⤳ *77 rooms, 4 suites* ⌂ *In-room: no a/c, Wi-Fi (some). In-hotel: restaurant, bar, tennis courts, pool, laundry service, Wi-Fi hotspot, Internet terminal, no-smoking rooms* ⊟ *AE, D, DC, MC, V* ⎺⦿⎺ *EP.*

HEREDIA

4 km/3 mi north of Santo Domingo, 11 km/6 mi northwest of San José.

Heredia is the capital of the important coffee province of the same name, and contains a few of the country's best-preserved colonial structures. Founded in 1706, the city bears witness to how difficult preservation can be in an earthquake-prone country; most of its colonial structures have been destroyed by the tremors and tropical climate—not to mention modernization. Still, the city and neighboring towns retain a certain historic feel, with old adobe buildings scattered amid the concrete structures. The nearby villages of Barva and Santo Domingo de Heredia have more colonial and adobe buildings, and the roads that wind through the hills above those towns pass through charming scenery and rural enclaves, making them excellent routes for exploration.

GETTING HERE AND AROUND

The narrow routes to Heredia are notoriously clogged at almost all times; avoid them during rush hours if possible. Turn right at the west end of Paseo Colón. Follow Pan-American Highway 2 km (1 mi); take the second exit, just before the highway heads onto an overpass and just after the Hotel Irazú (on the right). To get to the center of Heredia, follow that road for 5½ km (3½ mi), then turn left at the Universidad Nacional; continue north past the university instead of turning to reach the Britt Coffee Tour, Museo de Cultura Popular, Sacramento, Barva, and points beyond. Buses run between San José (300 m east of Hospital San Juan de Dios) and Heredia every 5 to 10 minutes daily (between 5 AM and 10 PM), following the above car route. The steady stream of buses leaving from C. 1, Avdas. 7–9 every three to five minutes passing through Santo Domingo are sometimes a better bet during rush hour, particularly the *directo* buses that start after 3:30 PM; these buses also run from midnight to 3:30 AM on the hour. If you're without a car, a taxi is the best way to get to Café Britt or Barva.

ESSENTIALS

Bank/ATM Banco Popular (✉ *200 m east of northeast corner of Parque Central* ☎ *2260–9407*). **Banco Nacional** (✉ *Southwest corner of Parque Central* ☎ *2277–6900*).

Internet Internet Cosmos (✉ *300 m east of Parque Central* ☎ *2262–4775*).

Pharmacy Farmacia Chavarria (✉ *Southwest corner of Parque Central* ☎ *2263–4670*).

Post Office Correos (✉ *Northwest corner of Parque Central*).

EXPLORING

Heredia is centered on tree-studded **Parque Central,** one of the country's loveliest central parks, which is surrounded by a few historic buildings. The park has a cast-iron fountain imported from England in 1879 and a simple kiosk where the municipal band plays Sunday-morning and Thursday-night concerts. ✉ *C. Central and Avda. Central.*

The impressive **Cathedral of the Immaculate Conception** (Catedral de la Inmaculada Concepción) is a whitewashed stone church built between 1797 and 1804 to replace an adobe temple dating from the early 1700s. Its thick stone walls, small windows, and squat buttresses have kept it intact through two centuries of quakes and tremors. It has a pale interior with marble floors and stained-glass windows, and is flanked by tidy gardens. There are Sunday services at 6 AM, 9 AM, 11 AM, and 6 PM. ✉ *Eastern end of Parque Central* ☎ *2237–0779* ☉ *Daily 6–6.*

To the north of the Parque Central stands a strange, decorative tower called the **Little Fort** *(Fortín),* which was built as a military post in the 1870s by the local oligarch Fadrique Gutiérrez. It never did see action and now serves as a symbol of the province, one of the few military monuments in this army-less country. The tower is closed to the public. The old brick building next to the Fortín is the Town Hall (Palacio Municipal). ✉ *C. Central and Avda. Central.*

Two blocks south of the Parque Central is Heredia's **Old Market** (Mercado Viejo), which has fewer souvenirs for sale than San José's Mercado Central but is less cramped and safer. On the next block to the southeast is the **New Market** (Mercado Nuevo), which holds dozens of *sodas* (simple restaurants). ⊠ *C. Central and Avda. 6* ⊗ *Mon.–Sat. 7–6.*

At the edge of a middle-class neighborhood between Heredia and Barva is the **Museum of Popular Culture** (Museo de Cultura Popular), which preserves a farmhouse built in 1885 with an adobe-like technique called *bahareque.* Run by the National University, the museum is furnished with antiques and surrounded by a garden. An adjacent open-air restaurant serves inexpensive Costa Rican lunches on weekends. Just walking around the museum is instructive, but calling ahead to reserve a hands-on cultural tour (such as one on tortilla making) really makes it worth the trip. ⊠ *Between Heredia and Barva; from Musmanni bakery in Santa Lucia de Barva, 100 m north 1 km/½ mi east; follow signs* ☎ *2260–1619* ⊕ *www.ilam.org/cr/museoculturapopular* ⌂ *$2* ⊗ *Weekdays 9–4, Sun. 10–5; closed Sat.*

★ The producer of Costa Rica's most popular export-quality coffee, **Café Britt,** gives a lively tour that highlights Costa Rica's history of coffee cultivation through a theatrical presentation that is admittedly a bit hokey. Your "tour guides" are professional actors, and pretty good ones at that, so if you don't mind the song and dance, it's fun. Take a short walk through the coffee farm and processing plant, and learn how professional coffee tasters distinguish a fine cup of java. One major difference between this tour and that of Doka Estate in Alajuela is that Doka takes you through the mill. Britt, ever the innovator, provides a similar tour add-on by request. A separate "Expert Coffee Lovers Tour" gives a more academic view of the subject and takes you into the world of professional coffee tasters. ⊠ *From Heredia, take road to Barva; follow signs* ☎ *2277–1500; 800/462–7488 in North America* ⊕ *www.coffeetour.com* ⌂ *$20 tour only, $27 with transportation, $35 with transportation and lunch;$47 Expert Coffee Lovers Tour* ⊗ *Tours: Dec.–May, daily at 11 and 3; June–Nov., daily at 11; Expert Coffee Lovers Tour, daily at 11.*

WHERE TO EAT

$-$$ ✕ **L'Antica Roma.** The food here more than makes up for the less-than-
ITALIAN tasteful red curtains, gold walls, and faded images of the Colosseum. The ample menu offers more than 40 pizza varieties, all baked in a wood-burning oven, and homemade fresh pasta, such as three-mushroom ravioli. Two TVs with sports are suspended indoors; the tables out on the wrought-iron-enclosed patio lend themselves better to conversation. ⊠ *C. 7 and Avda. 7, across from the Hotel Valladolid* ☎ *2262–9073* ▭ *AE, D, DC, MC, V.*

WHERE TO STAY

$$$$ ⊞ **Finca Rosa Blanca Country Inn.** There's nothing common about this
Fodor's Choice exclusive bed-and-breakfast overlooking coffee farms; new additions
★ update the Gaudí-esque hideaway's reputation as one of the country's top sumptuous splurges. The main building retains its soaring ceiling and white-stucco arches, set among tropical flowers and shaded by massive fig trees. All rooms—each with its own style—have been spruced

up, from the addition of Jacuzzi bathtubs to new 100% bamboo sheets. The spacious two-story suite is out of a fairy tale, with a spiral staircase leading up to a window-lined tower bedroom. The owners work hard to make the hotel as eco-friendly as possible, using composting, solar panels, and other methods. The hotel is one of only four in the country to receive a top rating for sustainable tourism. Prix-fixe gourmet dinners are available at the new El Tigre Vestido restaurant ($$$$, and expensive for what it offers), and guests can relax in the new bar or full-service spa. All rooms here are nonsmoking. **Pros:** eco-consciousness; indulge with style; service par excellence. **Cons:** some units short on closet and drawer space; overpriced restaurant can be difficult to find. ✉ *800 m north of Café Britt Distribution Center in Santa Barbara de Heredia, Barrio Jesus* ☎ *2269–9392* ⊕ *www.fincarosablanca.com* ⤴ *11 junior suites, 2 master suites, 2 villas* ♿ *In-room: no a/c, safe, kitchen (some), refrigerator (some), no TV, Internet, Wi-Fi. In-hotel: restaurant, bar, pool, spa, laundry service, Internet terminal, no-smoking rooms* ☰ *AE, MC, V* ⍟ *BP.*

$$ ▦ **Hotel Valladolid.** This is hands-down the best hotel in downtown Heredia. The tall (for Heredia) and narrow building has just 11 modern rooms, designed for business travelers and visiting professors at the nearby National University, although the typical guests are now just as likely to be vacationers. The tile floors and white walls aren't exactly inspired but are just fine for a night's sleep. **Pros:** central location; friendly staff. **Cons:** Heredia's charms lie in the outskirts, not in town; a few rooms show their age. ✉ *C. 7 and Avda. 7, 400 m north and 100 m west of the main entrance of La Universidad Nacional* ☎ *2260–2905* ⊕ *www.hotelvalladolid.net* ⤴ *11 rooms, 1 suite* ♿ *In-room: safe, refrigerator, kitchen (some) Wi-Fi. In-hotel: bar, room service, laundry service* ☰ *AE, D, DC, MC, V* ⍟ *CP.*

EN ROUTE
At the center of **Barva de Heredia,** a small community about 3 km (2 mi) north of Heredia proper, is the **Parque Central,** surrounded by old adobe shops with Spanish-tile roofs on three sides and a white-stucco church to the east. The stout, handsome church dates from the late 18th century; behind it is a lovely little garden shrine to the Virgin Mary. On a clear day you can see verdant Volcán Barva *(⇨ Chapter 5)* towering to the north, and if you follow the road that runs in front of the church and veer left at the Y, you will wind your way up the slopes of that volcano to Vara Blanca, where you can either drive north to the La Paz Waterfall Gardens or continue straight to Poás Volcano National Park *(⇨ Chapter 5).* If instead you veer right at the Y and drive up the steep, narrow road, you'll pass through San José de la Montaña and Paso Llano to reach Sacramento, where the road turns into a rough dirt track leading to the Barva sector of Braulio Carrillo National Park *(⇨ Chapter 5).* If you turn left when you reach Barva's central plaza, you'll head to San Pedro and Santa Barbara, where roads head south to Alajuela and north to Vara Blanca.

Continued on page 166

Picking coffee beans from plant

COFFEE, THE GOLDEN BEAN

Tour a working coffee plantation and learn about the product that catapulted Costa Rica onto the world's economic stage, built the country's infrastructure, and created a middle class unlike any other in Central America.

Costa Rica B.C. (before coffee) was a poor, forgotten little colony with scant infrastructure and no real means of making money. Coffee production changed all of that and transformed the country into one of the wealthier and more stable nations in Central America. Coffee remains Costa Rica's bread and butter—the industry employs one-fourth of Costa Rica's population full- or part-time—and coffee plantations are sprinkled throughout the Central Valley and Northern Plains. All cultivate fine Arabica beans (by government decree, the inferior Robusta variety is not grown here). Visit one and learn what makes the country tick.

By Jeffrey Van Fleet

HISTORY IN A CUP

Coffee plantations near Poas Volcano, Central Valley.

DRINKING THE GOOD STUFF

Here's the kicker for you, dear coffee-loving visitor: It's tough to find a decent cup in Costa Rica. True to the realities of developing-country economics, the good stuff goes for export, leaving a poorer quality bean behind for the local market. Add to that that the typical household here makes coffee with heaps of sugar. Your best bet for a good cup is an upscale hotel or restaurant, which is attuned to foreign tastes and does use export-quality product. The decorative foil bags you see in souvenir shops and supermarkets are also export-quality and make terrific souvenirs.

The country's first leaders saw this new crop as a tool with which to engineer a better life for their people. After gaining independence, new laws were created to allow average Costa Ricans to become coffee-growing landowners. These farmers formed the foundation of a middle-class majority that has long distinguished the country from the rest of Latin America. Costa Rica's infrastructure, institutional organizations, and means of production quickly blossomed—young entrepreneurs established small import-export houses, growers banded together to promote a better infrastructure, and everyone plowed their profits into improving the country's primitive road system.

SOCIAL TRANSFORMATION

As the coffee business became more profitable, prominent families were sending their children abroad to study, and doctors, lawyers and other skilled professionals in search of jobs began arriving by the

COFFEE TIMELINE

Native workers harvesting coffee beans in 1800s

1720	Coffee arrives in New World.
1791	Coffee plants introduced to Costa Rica.
1820	First coffee exports go to Panama.
1830	Legislation paves way for coffee profits to finance government projects.
1860	Costa Rican coffee first exported to United States.
1890	Atlantic Railroad opens, allowing for easier port access.

Enjoying a cup of coffee in Montezuma, Nicoya Peninsula

boatload. Returning students and well-educated immigrants brought a new world view that contributed to the formation of Costa Rica's liberal ideology.

MODERN TIMES

Development gobbled up land in the Central Valley by the last half of the 20th century, and coffee production began to spread to other areas of the country. A worldwide slump in coffee prices in the 1990s forced many producers out of the business. Prices have risen since 2002, and the government looks to smooth out any fluctuations with added-value eco-certification standards and innovative marketing.

Today, some 70% of the country's *número uno* agricultural crop comes from small family properties of under 25 acres owned by 250,000 farmers. They seasonally employ over four times that number of people, and kids in rural areas still take class time off to help with the harvest.

CAFÉ CHEAT SHEET

café solo: black

con azúcar: with sugar

con crema: with cream

con leche: with milk

descafeinado: decaffeinated (not easy to find here)

■

grano entero: whole beans

molido: ground

tostado claro or *tueste claro:* light roast

tostado oscuro or *tueste oscuro:* dark roast

Oxcarts built in the early 1900s to transport coffee.

1897	Coffee barons construct San José's ornate Teatro Nacional.
1992	Costa Rica adopts new environmental laws for coffee industry.
1997	Tourism displaces coffee as Costa Rica's top industry.
Today	Costa Rica turns to eco-certification and fair-trade marketing of coffee.

COSTA RICA'S BEAN COUNTRY

Coffee plantations from Cervantes to Orosi Central Valley

Costa Rica possesses all the factors necessary—moderately high altitude, mineral-rich volcanic soil, adequate rainfall but distinct rainy and dry seasons—to be a major coffee player. Costa Rican growers cultivate only Arabica coffee beans. The industry eliminated the inferior Robusta variety in 1989 and hasn't looked back. The Costa Rican Coffee Institute certifies eight regional coffee varieties.

The coffee-growing cycle begins in April or May, when rains make the dark-green bushes explode in a flurry of white blossoms. By November, the fruit starts to ripen, turning from green to red. The busy harvest begins as farmers race to get picked "cherries" to *beneficios* (processing mills), where beans are removed, washed, machine-dried, and packed in burlap sacks either for export or to be roasted for local consumption.

Coffee plantations, Central Valley

❶ Aficionados wax poetic about the bean that come from **Tarrazú,** the high-altitude Los Santos Region in the Southern Pacific. It has good body, high acidity, and a chocolaty flavor.

❷ Coffee grown in **Tres Ríos,** east of San José, has high acidity, good body, and a nice aroma.

❸ Altitude of the **Central Valley** (around San José, Heredia and Alajuela) affects the size and hardness of the coffee bean and can influence certain components, particularly the acidity. This is an important characteristic of Arabica coffee.

❹ **Valle Occidental,** in the prosperous western Central Valley, gives you hints of apricots and peaches.

Arabica coffee beans

Coffee beans | Coffee bean pickers | Hand picking Coffee beans

Coffee plant

Siquirres

Moín

6 TURRIALBA

Puerto Viejo
de Talamanca

Cahuita

Bribri

Sixaola

PANAMA

CORDILLERA DE TALAMANCA

San Isidro

Buenos
Aires Salitre

7

BRUNCA

Palmar Paso Real
Norte

Ciudad
Cortés

Palmar
Sur

San Vito

Ciudad
Neily

Drake Rincón Golfito Río
Claro

Osa Puerto Paso
Peninsula Jiménez Canoas

Zancudo

Carate Pavones

Matapalo

Pan-American Hwy

5 Tasters describe **Orosi** coffee, from the southeastern Central Valley, as "floral."

6 The lower altitudes of nearby **Turrialba** give its product a medium body.

7 The high-altitude **Brunca** region, near San Vito in southern Costa Rica, produces

coffee with excellent aroma, good body, and moderate acidity.

8 Guanacaste is a diverse region that includes Monteverde and the central Nicoya Peninsula. Here they produce a medium-body coffee.

PLANTATIONS WITH TOURS

Wonder where your cup of morning coffee originates? The following purveyors give informative tours of their facilities and acquaint you with the life and times of the country's favorite beverage.

CAFÉ BRITT Barva, Heredia *(see the Central Valley chapter)* Café Britt incorporates a small theater production into its tour, presenting the history of Costa Rican coffee in song and dance. Britt also presents a separate, more academic tour giving you a participatory glimpse into the world of professional coffee tasters.

DOKA COFFEE ESTATE San Luis de Sabanilla, Alajuela *(see the Central Valley)* Doka Coffee Estate offers a comprehensive tour through the entire growing and drying process and lets you sample the local brew. The best time to take this tour is during the October-to-February picking season.

DON JUAN COFFEE TOUR Monteverde *(see the Northern Plains)* A personalized excursion with a small group is the hallmark of this tour to a coffee plantation a few miles outside the town of Santa Elena.

MONTEVERDE COFFEE TOUR Monteverde *(see the Northern Plains)* Monteverde Coffee offers you some hands-on experience. Depending on the time of year, you can help with picking, drying, roasting or packing.

All of the above tours guide you through the plant-to-cup process in English or Spanish, taking you from picking to drying to roasting to packing to brewing.

Reservations are essential and you should plan on spending a half-day for any of these outings. The whole package will set you back about $30 per person.

CARTAGO AND IRAZÚ VOLCANO

Cartago, due east of San José, was the country's first capital, and thus has scattered historical structures and the remarkable Basílica de Los Angeles. To the north of Cartago towers massive Irazú Volcano, which is covered with farmland and topped by an impressive crater.

CARTAGO

22 km/14 mi southeast of San José.

Cartago is Costa Rica's oldest community, but earthquakes have destroyed most of its structures from the colonial era. Cartago was left behind in 1823, when the seat of government was moved to the emerging economic center of San José. You'll see some attractive old buildings as you move through town, most of them erected after a 1910 earthquake. Most visitors see Cartago on their way to or from the Orosi Valley or Turrialba, and there is little reason (or place) to stay the night. The Orosi Valley, a short drive away, has better choices.

GETTING HERE AND AROUND

For the 25-minute drive from San José, drive east on Avenida 2 through San Pedro and Curridabat to the highway entrance, where you have three road options—take the middle one marked Cartago. Shortly before Cartago, a Y intersection marks the beginning of the route up Irazú, with traffic to Cartago veering right. Buses between San José and Cartago leave every 10 minutes daily (25 m north of the Hotel Balmoral or 300 m south of the Teatro Nacional) from 5 AM to midnight; buses to Paraíso leave weekdays from the same terminal every half hour. Cartago buses to San José pick up 200 meters north of the Parque Central. Buses to Orosi leave Cartago every 15 to 30 minutes from 5:30 AM to 10 PM, 100 meters (328 feet) east, 25 meters (82 feet) south of the southwest corner of Las Ruinas.

CARTAGO ESSENTIALS

Bank/ATM BAC San José (⊠ *100 m south of Las Ruinas* ☎ *2295–9797*). **Scotiabank ATM** (⊠ *Northwest corner of Las Ruinas*).

Hospital Hospital Max Peralta (⊠ *200 m south, 150 m east of Las Ruinas* ☎ *2550–1999* ⊕ *www.hmp.sa.cr*).

Pharmacy Farmacia Central (⊠ *Just south of Las Ruinas* ☎ *2551–0698*).

Post Office Correos (⊠ *Avda. 2, Cs. 15–17*).

Taxis Taxis El Carmen (☎ *2551–0836*).

EXPLORING

Churches in some form or another have stood at the site of the present-day Parque Central since 1575 and have been knocked down by earthquakes and reconstructed many times. Undeterred by complete destruction in 1841, the citizens of Cartago began work on a Romanesque cathedral some years later, but the devastating earthquake of 1910 halted work and put an end to the last attempt at building a structure on the site. **Las Ruinas** (⊠ *Avda. 2, Cs. 1–2*) , or "the Ruins," of

Cartago, Irazú and Turrialba Volcanos

this unfinished house of worship now stand in a pleasant park planted with tall pines and bright impatiens. You won't be able to go inside, but the site is spectacular from outside as well. Among the many legends attributed to the ruins is the gruesome story of the priest of one of the earlier churches at the site, who, after falling in love with his sister-in-law, was murdered by his brother. His ghost, dressed as a priest but headless, still haunts the grounds. Although the park is billed as a Wi-Fi hot spot, we recommend not pulling out your laptop in such a public place—nothing to do with alleged hauntings.

Our Lady of the Angels Basilica (*Basílica de Nuestra Señora de los Angeles;* ⊠ *C. 16, Avdas. 2–4, 7 blocks east of central square* ☎ 2551–0465) is a hodgepodge of architectural styles from Byzantine to Baroque, with a dash of Gothic. The interior is even more striking, with a colorful tile floor, intricately decorated wood columns, and lots of stained glass. The church is open daily 6 AM to 7 PM. The basilica is also the focus of an annual pilgrimage to celebrate the appearance of La Negrita, or the Black Virgin, Costa Rica's patron saint.

WHERE TO EAT

Although you can find decent pasta and pizza, haute cuisine just doesn't exist here. Instead, Cartago gives you a fine opportunity to eat some *comida típica.* On just about any street downtown you'll find a *soda*

La Negrita

On the night of August 1 and well into the early-morning hours of August 2, the road to Cartago from San José clogs with worshippers, some of whom have traveled from as far away as Nicaragua to celebrate the 1635 appearance of Costa Rica's patron saint, La Negrita (the Black Virgin). The feast day draws an estimated 1 million pilgrims each year, not bad for a country of just 4 million people. At a spring behind the church, people fill bottles with water believed to have curative properties. Miraculous healing powers are attributed to the saint, and devotees have placed thousands of tiny symbolic crutches, ears, eyes, and legs in a room to the left of the altar. Tour buses and school groups, along with shops selling the saint's likeness, make the scene a bit of a circus.

(simple café), and the women in the kitchen will serve you the same style of food they cook at home for their own families. There are literally dozens of places of comparable quality. One rule of thumb: the busier the better—the locals know where to eat well.

VOLCÁN IRAZÚ

31 km/19 mi northeast of Cartago, 50 km/31 mi east of San José.

Volcán Irazú is Costa Rica's highest volcano, at 3,422 meters (11,260 feet). Its presence is a mixed blessing: The ash fertilizes the Central Valley soil, but the volcano has caused considerable destruction through the centuries. ☎2551–9398; 8200–5025 *for ranger station* ⬛*$7* ⊙ *Daily 8–3:30.*

GETTING HERE AND AROUND

Follow directions to Cartago (⇨ *above*), but shortly before the city a Y intersection marks the beginning of the road up Irazú; traffic to Cartago veers right, then left immediately past the first lights. From downtown Cartago, a 45-minute trip, take the road to Irazú at the northeast corner of the Basilica. Signs from Cartago lead you to the park. Buses head to Volcán Irazú from San José (✉ Avda. 2, Cs. 1–3) daily at 8 AM and return at 12:30 PM.

WHERE TO EAT

$ ✕ **Restaurant 1910.** Decorated with vintage photos of early-20th-century
COSTA RICAN buildings and landscapes, this restaurant documents the disastrous 1910 earthquake that rocked this area and all but destroyed the colonial capital of Cartago. The menu is predominantly Costa Rican, with such traditional specialties as *trucha* (trout), and rice with chicken. One of the less common dishes is *corvina* (sea bass) fillet with béarnaise sauce. The *típico* buffet is a great introduction to Costa Rican cooking. ✉ *Road to Parque Nacional Volcán Irazú; 300 m north of Cot–Pacayas turnoff* ☎ *2536–6063* ⬛ *AE, MC, V* ⊙ *No dinner Sun.*

Cartago's Basilica de Nuestra is the focus of the annual pilgrimage to celebrate the appearance of the Black Virgin.

$

COSTA RICAN

Fodor'sChoice

★

☾

✕ **Restaurante Noche Buena.** If you've raced up Irazú to catch the clear early-morning views, a late breakfast or early lunch at this bright road-side stop is a great excuse to linger in the area. Sample stick-to-your-ribs *gallo pinto* (a traditional dish made with rice and beans), *tres leches* (literally "three milks," a light and airy cake), and—not to be missed—the best fried yucca around. The pale wood floors and walls inside have a studied rustic charm, but the ample patio is a fresher option; neither has particularly impressive views. The Costa Rican owner, Federico Gutiérrez, has added a 3-km (2-mi) trail to waterfalls and a high-tech, interactive volcano museum ($4) that shouldn't be missed. Get here early, as the restaurant closes at 3 on weekdays and 4:30 on weekends. ⊠ *At Km 24.5, road to Parque Nacional Volcán Irazú* ☎ *2530–8013* ⊕ *www.nochebuena.org* ⊟ *AE, D, DC, MC, V* ☾ *No dinner.*

THE OROSI VALLEY

If you have a day to spend near San José, this route past coffee planta-tions, small towns, and verdant landscapes, with countless breathtaking views, makes a classic day trip, popular with locals on the weekend but still off the beaten path. The region is one of the few areas in Costa Rica that still has remnants (ruins and churches) of the 17th-century Spanish colonial era. A good road makes a loop around the valley, easy to do if you have your own vehicle, or if you go on a guided tour—it's a staple of most San José tour operators' offerings. Public transporta-

Bulls dressed in their finest for an oxcart parade in Cartago.

tion is trickier here: Buses travel clockwise and counterclockwise, but neither route completes the loop.

ESSENTIALS

Bank/ATM Banco Nacional (✉ *300 m south of soccer field, Orosi* ☎ *2533-1390* ✉ *West side of central park, Paraíso* ☎ *2574-7274*).

Internet PC Orosi (✉ *200 m south of church, Orosi*).

Pharmacy Farmacia Sucre (✉ *200 m west of central park, Paraíso* ☎ *2574-7286*). **Farmacia Tabor** (✉ *Southeast corner of soccer field, Orosi* ☎ *2533-3395*).

Post Office Correos (✉ *125 m north of central park, in the Edificio Flor María, Paraíso*).

EXPLORING

At the basílica in the center of Cartago, turn right, and then left onto the busy road to Paraíso and Orosi. After 6 km (4 mi), a blue sign on the right marks the short road to the lush gardens of the **Jardín Botánico Lankester** (✉ *West entrance to Paraíso* ☎ *2552-3247* ⊕ *www. jardinbotanicolankester.org* ✉ *$7.50* ⊙ *Daily 8:30-4:30*), one of the world's foremost orchid collections, with more than 1,100 native and introduced species of orchids. Bromeliads, heliconias, and aroids also abound, along with 80 species of trees, including rare palms. The best time to come is February through April, when the most orchids are in bloom. The garden's gift shop is one of the few places in Costa Rica to buy orchids that you can take home legally. (They come in small bottles and don't flower for four years, so you'll need some serious patience.)

Head east toward Paraíso and then into the town itself. Hang a right at the central park. Some 2 km (1 mi) beyond is the **Sanchiri Mirador,** one of the valley's best miradores (lookout points). But our favorite vantage point is at a point on the road just beyond Sanchiri where the earth appears to drop away and the valley comes into view as you make the steep descent to the town of Orosi. Here's a case for letting someone else do the driving.

The town of Orosi, in the heart of the valley, has but one major attraction: the squat but beautifully restored 1743 **Iglesia de San José de Orosi** (⊠ *Across from soccer field* ☎ *2533–3051* ▣ *Museum $1* ⊗ *Church Tues.–Sun. 9–noon and 1–5; museum Tues.–Fri. 1–5, weekends 9–5)),* the country's oldest house of worship still in use, and one of the only structures still remaining from the colonial era. It has a low-slung whitewashed facade; the roof is made of cane overlaid with terra-cotta barrel tiles. Inside are an antique wooden altar and ancient paintings of the Stations of the Cross and the Virgin of Guadalupe, all brought to Costa Rica from Guatemala. A religious-art museum next door has officially posted hours and yet does not always adhere to them.

Continue past the dam into the small hamlet of Ujarrás, then follow the signs to the site of the ruins of Costa Rica's first church, **Iglesia de Ujarrás** (⊠ *In a small park, 1 km/½mi from Restaurante Típico Ujarrás* ☎ *2574–8366* ▣ *Free* ⊗ *Daily 6–6)* Built between 1681 and 1693 in honor of the Virgin of Ujarrás, the church, together with the surrounding village, was abandoned in 1833 after a series of earthquakes and floods wreaked havoc here, at the lowest point of the Orosi Valley. An unlikely Spanish victory in 1666 over a superior force of invading British pirates was attributed to a prayer stop here. A final 6-km (4-mi) drive to Paraíso from Ujarrás completes the road that loops the valley.

South of Orosi, the road becomes a rugged track following the Río Grande de Orosi past coffee plantations, elegant fincas (farmhouses), and seasonal barracks for coffee pickers before it's hemmed in by the steep slopes of thick jungle. At the bottom of the loop road, follow signs for **Tapantí National Park** (⊠ *14 km/8 mi south of Orosi,* ☎ *2551–2970* ▣ *$6* ⊗ *Weekdays 8–4, weekends 7–5)* Though it's worth the trip for just an hour or two of exploring, you could easily fill a day in the park. Stretching all the way to the Talamanca Mountains, the reserve encompasses 47 square km (18 square mi) of largely pristine, remote cloud forest, refuge for more than 400 bird species, including the emerald toucanet, violaceous trogon, and most of the country's hummingbirds. The rangers' office and visitor center are on the right just after the park entrance. You can leave your vehicle at a parking area 1½ km (1 mi) up the road. From here loop trails head off into the woods on both sides. One trail passes a picnic area and several swimming holes with (cold) emerald waters. The other trail is along a forested hillside. About 1½ km (1 mi) up from the parking area is an entrance to the La Pava Trail on the right, leading down a steep hill to the riverbank. If you continue ½ km (¼ mi) past the trailhead, you arrive at a 91-meter (300-foot) stair trail leading to a lookout. Get an early start. The park clouds over markedly by afternoon.

Iglesia de San José de Orosi is the county's oldest church that is still in use.

WHERE TO EAT

$ ✕ **Gecko's.** This textbook backpacker hangout is affiliated with a Dutch-
ECLECTIC Canadian-owned Spanish school and hostel in Orosi. The café is bright
and open, with groovy music and free-spirited clothes for sale. The
creative menu ranges from traditional Costa Rican food to *Kroket*
(deep-fried meat roll on a bun) and shish kebab. Helpful staff run a
tourist-information desk inside. ✉ *400 m south of church* ☏ *2533–3640*
⊟ *No credit cards.*

$ ✕ **La Casona del Cafetal.** The valley's best lunch stop is on a coffee planta-
COSTA RICAN tion overlooking the Cachí Reservoir. It's firmly on the beaten path, which
means frequent visits from tour groups. The spacious brick building has
a high barrel-tile roof, with tables indoors and on a tiled portico on the
lake side. Casados and other Costa Rican staples accompany inventive dishes such as *corvina guarumos* (bass stuffed with mushrooms).
Expect a wait on weekends, when diners come from miles around for the
18-lunch buffet. After lunch, take a stroll down to the lake or check out
the gift shop. ✉ *2 km/1 mi south of Cachí Dam* ☏ *2577–1414* ⊕ *www.
lacasonadelcafetal.com* ⊟ *AE, D, DC, MC, V* ☺ *No dinner.*

WHERE TO STAY

$$–$$$ 🏨 **Hotel Río Perlas Spa & Resort.** Thermal springs fill one of the pools at
this hotel squeezed into a small valley. The place has a condo community feeling, with a driveway running the length of the property and the
rooms divided among many smaller buildings. Rooms are nice, but not
especially luxurious; they have tile floors and wood furniture. Ask for
one of the wooden cabins at the back of the property. There is a replica
of the Orosi church here, too. **Pros:** lots of activity, springs nice to bask

in after a day of sightseeing. **Cons:** basic rooms; lost of activity, so not an option if you seek peace and quiet. ✉ *6 km/3 mi south of Paraíso, turn right at bridge, then 2½ km/1½ mi; look for large sign* ☎ *2533–3341, 800/286–2922 in North America* ⊕ *www.rioperlasspaandresort.com* ↘ *65 rooms* ⚲ *In-room: no a/c. In-hotel: restaurant, pool, Internet terminal* ☰ *AE, D, DC, MC, V* ⦿ *BP.*

$ ⊞ **Kiri Mountain Lodge.** This small, family-run hotel has easy access to the park and its own 175-acre private reserve close to waterfalls and most of the same wildlife seen at Tapantí. The number of bird species in the lodge's gardens alone is impressive, especially hummingbirds. Rooms are small and simple, with tile floors and tiny bathrooms, but their porches have views of a jungle-laden hillside. The restaurant serves a small selection of Costa Rican food; fresh trout, raised in nearby ponds, is the best option. You can also catch your own trout and have them cook it for you. **Pros:** secluded location; friendly owners. **Cons:** basic rooms; need a car to stay here. ✉ *Turnoff 2 km/1 mi before Tapantí park entrance* ☎ *2533–2272* ⊕ *www.kirilodge.net* ↘ *6 rooms* ⚲ *In-room: no a/c, no phone, no TV. In-hotel: restaurant* ☰ *MC, V* ⦿ *BP.*

$–$$ ⊞ **Orosi Lodge.** Run by a German couple who have built a warm rapport with the community, the little lodge blends in with Orosi's pretty, old-town architecture: whitewashed walls are trimmed in blue, ceilings are high, and natural wood is used throughout. Some furnishings, such as the clay lamps in the rooms, are done by local artisans. Common areas are colorful, with paintings and sculpture by local artists. Double beds have two twin-size comforters. Second-floor rooms have views of the Orosi Valley and Irazú Volcano. A bright, spacious chalet can sleep up to five. The hip coffee shop brews a great cup of joe, and Latin music usually plays from a 1960s jukebox in the foyer. ✉ *350 meters south, 100 meters west of soccer field* ☎ *2533–3578* ⊕ *www.orosilodge.com* ↘ *6 rooms, 1 chalet* ⚲ *In-room: no a/c, kitchen (some) no phone, refrigerator, no TV. In-hotel: restaurant* ☰ *AE, MC, V* ⦿ *EP.*

SHOPPING

Stop in at the unique artisan shop **Casa del Soñador** (*House of the Dreamer* ✉ *2 km/1 mi south of the Cachí Dam* ☎ *2577–1186 or 2577–1983*), established by local wood sculptor Macedonio Quesada. Though Macedonio died years ago, his sons Miguel and Hermes and a former apprentice are still here, carving interesting, often comical little statues out of coffee roots.

THE TURRIALBA REGION

The agricultural center of Turrialba and the nearby Guayabo ruins lie considerably lower than the Central Valley, so they enjoy a more moderate climate, a transition between the cooler Central Valley and the sweltering Caribbean coast. There are two ways to reach this area from San José, both of which pass spectacular scenery. The more direct route, accessible by heading east through both Cartago and Paraíso, winds through coffee and sugar plantations before descending abruptly into Turrialba. For the second route, turn off the road between Cartago and the summit of Irazú near the town of Cot, heading toward Pacayas. That narrow route twists along the slopes of Irazú and Turrialba volcanoes past some stunning scenery—stately pollarded trees lining the road, riotous patches of tropical flowers, and metal-girder bridges across crashing streams. As you begin the descent to Turrialba town, the temperature rises and sugarcane alternates with fields of neat rows of coffee bushes.

TURRIALBA

58 km/36 mi east of San José.

The relatively well-to-do agricultural center of Turrialba suffered when the main San José–Limón route was diverted through Guápiles in the late 1970s. The demise of the famous Jungle Train that connected these two cities was an additional blow. But today, because of the beautiful scenery and a handful of upscale nature lodges, ecotourism is increasingly the focus of the town's efforts. The damming of the Reventazón River has cut down on the number of tourists, but significant numbers of kayakers and rafters flock here to run the Pacuare. Turrialba has two major factories: Conair, which you'll see on the road to Siquirres, and a Rawlings factory, which makes all the baseballs used in the major leagues. (Rawlings, unfortunately, does not offer tours.) Though pleasant enough and with a youthful vibe from the nearby university and the white-water folk, Turrialba doesn't have much to offer, but the surrounding countryside hides some spectacular scenery and patches of rain forest. Finally, there's Volcán Turrialba, which you can ascend on foot or horseback.

GETTING HERE AND AROUND

The road through Cartago continues east through Paraíso, where you turn left at the northeast corner of the central park to pick up the road to Turrialba. Marked by signs, this road leads north to Guayabo National Monument. Buses between San José and Turrialba leave hourly (5:15 AM to 10:30 PM) from Calle 13, Avenida 6, just west of the downtown court buildings. Direct buses depart from the Turrialba terminal (at the entrance to Turrialba) for San José on the hour; on the half hour to Cartago, and every two hours to Siquirres.

ESSENTIALS

Bank/ATM Banco Nacional (✉ *C. 1 at Avda. Central* ☎ *2556–1211*).
Banco de Costa Rica (✉ *Avda. 0, C. 1* ☎ *2556–0472*).

Hospital Hospital Dr. William Allen (✉ *Avda. 2, 100 m west of C. 4* ☎ *2558–1300*).

Internet Dimensión >Internet (✉ *East side of central park* ☎ *2556–1586*).

Pharmacy Farmacia San Buenaventura (✉ *50 m south of west side of central park* ☎ *2556–0379*).

Post Office Correos (✉ *Avda. 6 at C. Central 50 m north of central park*).

Taxis Transgalo (☎ *2556–9393*).

EXPLORING

Although you can't easily drive up to its summit as you can at Poás and Irazú, **Volcán Turrialba** is worth visiting, albeit with some precautions these days. The easiest way to arrange the excursion is to call the **Volcán**

Turrialba Lodge (📞 2273–4335) and request a guide. You can ascend the 6 km (4 mi) from the lodge on foot or horseback in one to two hours (allow up to four hours for the round-trip, plus exploring time), and at 3,340 meters (10,958 feet) with luck you'll see clear down to the Caribbean coast. The volcano has showed ever-increasing activity since 2007. At this writing visits are limited to a 20-minute max—a protective measure implemented in response to heightened rumbling. Volcanologists are concerned about the heavy content of sulfur dioxide in fumes emanating from the volcano, a phenomenon that has taken its toll on plant and animal life here. Be prepared for periodic park closures. ⚠ If you suffer from any type of heart or respiratory condition or are pregnant, stay away. On the road that runs from Pacayas to Turrialba through Santa Cruz, there is a signed turnoff at La Pastora, west of Santa Cruz, that leads up the mountain. The drive up is 15 km (9 mi) and starts paved, but the road gets worse the higher you go. In most cases you'll need a 4WD to make the last section before the trailhead, which is in a very small community called La Central de Turrialba. The road veers left toward the Volcán Turrialba Lodge, and a very washed-out road leads right, toward the summit. If you want to take the latter route, you can park on the left just after the school; usually someone is around to charge you a few dollars for the privilege, but as elsewhere in the country, this in no way guarantees your car's safety. We recommend parking at Volcán Turrialba Lodge—they don't charge, they'll point out the way, and you can rest up with some snacks and hot chocolate at the restaurant when you're finished. Get an early start and dress for the weather—it can get chilly up here even during the day. A park employee sometimes hangs out at the top to collect the $1 entrance fee and hand out maps.

CORRUPTION CRACKDOWN

Long a proponent of do-as-I-say, not-as-I-do anticorruption policies, Costa Rica got tough on bigwigs in 2004. Two former presidents were taken into custody for allegedly accepting bribes in a telecommunications deal. A third—José María Figueres—lives in Switzerland and faces arrest if ever he returns to Costa Rica. The sight of former leaders being led away in handcuffs has shaken many Costa Ricans' faith in their democracy, but others see it as a positive sign that no one is above the law.

OFF THE BEATEN PATH

A good place for bird-watching, the **Tropical Agricultural Research and Higher Education Center** (Centro Agronómico Tropical de Investigación y Enseñanza), better known by its acronym, CATIE, is one of the leading tropical research centers in Latin America. You might catch sight of the yellow-winged northern jacana or the purple gallinule in the lagoon near the main building. The 10-square-km (4-square-mi) property includes landscaped grounds, seed-conservation chambers, greenhouses, orchards, experimental agricultural projects, a large swath of rain forest, labs and offices, and lodging for students and teachers. Behind the administration building lies the lake that once was rapids on the Reventazón River. The CATIE staff is working to improve visitor access; two-hour guided tours (call ahead to reserve) of the impressive botanical garden have been added, and forest trails are planned for the future. Groups of 10 or

White-Water Thrills

You're struggling to hang on and paddle, you can't hear a thing over the roar, and you were just slammed with a mighty wall of water. Sound like fun? Then you're in the right place. The **Río Pacuare** and the **Río Reventazón** draw rafters and kayakers from all over the world to Turrialba. Right next to Turrialba, the Reventazón has Class II, III, and IV rapids. The Pacuare, farther from Turrialba, has a spectacular 29-km (18-mi) run with a series of Class III and IV rapids. The scenery includes lush canyons where waterfalls plummet into the river and expanses of rain forest.

Nearly every outfitter has day trips, but some also have multiday trips that include jungle hikes. Costa Rica Nature Adventures and Ríos Tropicales (⇨ *Central Valley Planner, above*) even have their own lodges on the river. Age requirements for children vary by outfitter; Costa Rica Expeditions runs a family trip on the gentler Pejibaye River that kids as young as five can enjoy. The typical trip starts with a van ride to the put-in; including a breakfast stop, it usually takes about 2½ hours from hotel to river. After the first half of the run, guides flip one of the rafts over to form a crude lunch table. Then you continue up the river to Siquirres, and pile back in the van for the ride home.

It would be unwise to choose your company based merely on price:

Those with bargain rates are probably skimping somewhere. Good outfitters require you to wear life vests and helmets, have CPR-certified river guides with near-fluent English skills, and have kayakers accompany the rafts in case of emergencies. A 5:1 guest-to-guide ratio is good; 10:1 is not. Local Turrialba companies have better prices and allow you to book a trip at the last minute. Hotels and travel agencies book trips with larger outfitters, who can pick you up from nearly anywhere in the Central Valley. Prices range from about $75 to $100.

People fall out of the raft all the time, and it is no big deal. The worst-case scenario is getting caught underwater or under the raft, but surprisingly, most fatalities are heart-attack victims, so don't participate if you're high-risk. You should also be able to swim. Almost every long-standing company has had a death—it is an unfortunate reality of the business. Don't hesitate to ask about safety records. The vast majority of trips, however, are pure exhilarating fun.

In 2006 the government decided to keep long-stalled plans to dam the Pacuare on ice for the time being, but reserves the right to revive them in the future. This would be the last nail in the coffin for the rafting industry (the Reventazón was dammed in the 1960s) and would destroy one of nature's real gems.

more now may add on lunch at the new café (Costa Rican and Spanish plates) and/or a fruitful tasting session of bounty from the garden ($4 per person extra). ⊠ *3 km/2 mi outside Turrialba, on road to Siquirres* ☏ *2556–2700* ⊕ *www.catie.ac.cr* ✉ *$15 with guide; $25 for full facility tour, $10 per person for groups of more than 5* ☉ *Weekdays 7–3, weekends by reservation.*

"For a fun ride, try rafting the Pacuare River in October or November when the water is high." —Photo by Linda137, Fodors.com member

On the slopes of Turrialba Volcano is **Guayabo National Monument**, Costa Rica's most significant archaeological site. It's interesting, but definitely no Machu Picchu. Records mentioning the ruins go back to the mid-1800s, but systematic investigations didn't begin until 1968, when a local landowner out walking her dogs discovered what she thought was a tomb. Archaeologists began excavating the site and unearthed the base wall of a chief's house in what eventually turned out to be the ruins of a large community (around 10,000 inhabitants) covering 49 acres, 10 of which have been excavated. The city was abandoned in AD 1400, probably because of disease or war. Guided tours (about two hours) in Spanish or English are provided by freelance guides who wait at the entrance. They'll take you through the rain forest to a *mirador* (lookout) from which you can see the layout of the excavated circular buildings. Only the raised foundations survive, since the conical houses themselves were built of wood. As you descend into the ruins, notice the well-engineered surface and covered aqueducts leading to a trough of drinking water that still functions today. Next you'll pass the end of an 8-km (5-mi) paved walkway used to transport the massive building stones; the abstract patterns carved on the stones continue to baffle archaeologists, but some clearly depict jaguars, which were revered as deities. The hillside jungle is captivating, and the trip is further enhanced by bird-watching possibilities: 200 species have been recorded. If you arrive from the east via the Santa Teresita (Lajas) route, you can make it in any car, but via the alternative Santa Cruz route you'll need a 4WD vehicle to get here. ⊠ *Drive through the center of Turrialba to a girdered bridge; take road northeast 16 km/10 mi (about 20 minutes' driving); take a left at the well-marked turnoff, continue another 3 km/2 mi to the* *monument. If you've taken the sce-nic Irazú foothills route to Turrialba and have a 4WD, the Santa Cruz route—11 km/7 mi (about 35 min-utes' driving)—is an option. Turn left on rough road from Santa Cruz; climb 5 km/3 mi, past the Escuela de Guayabo; turn right at the sign for the monument; the road descends 6 km/4 mi to the site* ☎ *2559–1220* ✉ *$4* ☉ *Daily 8–3:30.*

> ### KEEPING COOL
>
> The Central Valley's climate is often a great surprise to first-time visitors—it's not at all the steamy tropics you've imagined. It's usu-ally cool enough at night to go without air-conditioning, so don't be surprised if many hotels don't have it.

OUTDOOR ACTIVITIES

The two best ways to reach the summit of Turrialba Volcano are on foot or on horseback. **Volcán Turrialba Lodge** (☎ 2273–4335) arranges guided horseback and hiking trips.

WHITE-WATER OUTFITTERS

Most outfitters are based in San José, and many offer both rafting and kayaking. Tico's River Adventures, Costa Rica Ríos (multiday pack-ages only), and Rainforest World are in Turrialba. **Costa Rica Expeditions** (☎ 2257–0766 ⊕ *www.costaricaexpeditions.com*). **Costa Rica Nature Adventures** (☎ 225–3939; 2224–0505; 800/283–5032 *in North America* ⊕ *www.costaricanatureadventures.com*). **Costa Rica Ríos** (☎ 2556–9617 *or* 888/434–0776 ⊕ *www.costaricarios.com*). **Exploradores Outdoors** (☎ 2222–6262; 646/205–0828 *toll-free* ⊕ *www.exploradoresoutdoors.com*). **Rain-forest World** (☎ 2556–0014 *or* 8357–7250 ⊕ *www.rforestw.com*). **Ríos Tropicales** (☎ 2233–6455 *or* 866/722–8273 ⊕ *www.riostropicales.com*).

WHERE TO EAT

¢–$
COSTA RICAN
✕ **La Garza Bar y Restaurante.** Similar to La Feria in scope but slightly more atmospheric and with a bar, La Garza also runs the gamut from hamburgers to chicken but has a better seafood selection. (Sorry, vegetar-ians, "beetsteak" is a misprint.) This is a good place for a late dinner, as it's open until 11. ✉ *Northwest corner of park* ☎ *2556–1073* ▭ *AE, D, DC, MC, V.*

$
COSTA RICAN
✕ **Restaurante La Feria.** A permanent exhibition of national art and the Turrialba expertise of owner Don Roberto (if you speak Spanish) make this a worthwhile stop. This family-style restaurant has the usual mid-scale Costa Rican fare, ranging from fast food to filet mignon. Casados and gallo pinto compete with more familiar chicken and seafood dishes. Even paella is on the menu (with three hours' notice). ✉ *Just west of Hotel Wagelia, at entrance to town* ☎ *2556–0386* ▭ *AE, D, DC, MC, V* ☉ *No dinner Tues.*

WHERE TO STAY

$$–$$$$
★
▣ **Casa Turire.** Set near sugar plantations and overlooking an artificial lake, this timeless hotel is an elegant base for nearby adventure day trips. The building looks like a manor house that has survived myste-riously intact from the turn of the 20th century. In fact, it's the prod-uct of more recent imaginations. From the royal palms that line the driveway to the tall columns and tile floors, Casa Turire is an exercise in attention to detail. High-ceiling guest rooms have hardwood floors

Costa Rica's first church, Iglesia de Ujarrás was abandoned in 1833 after a series of earthquakes and floods wreaked havoc.

and furniture, small balconies, and bright bathrooms with tubs. The central courtyard is a civilized spot in which to relax after a day's adventure, and the restaurant serves reasonably priced international cuisine. The master suite is exceptional, built on two floors with a huge wraparound balcony. A model farm on the property gives kids hands-on time with animals. **Pros:** excellent value; beautiful grounds; good base for adventure trips. **Cons:** mediocre restaurant; need a car to stay here. ⊠ *8 km/5 mi south on Carretera a la Suiza from Turrialba* ☎ *2531–1111* ⊕ *www.hotelcasaturire.com* ⟲ *12 rooms, 4 suites* ♿ *In-room: no a/c (some), safe, DVD. In-hotel: restaurant, room service, bar, pool, bicycles, laundry service, Internet terminal, Wi-Fi hotspot* ▭ *AE, MC, V* ⦿| *BP.*

$$ **Rancho Naturalista.** Customized guided bird-watching within a 160-acre private nature reserve is the reason to stay here. The ranch is a birder's paradise, and the narrow focus may be too much for those not interested in our feathered friends. More than 400 species of birds and thousands of different kinds of moths and butterflies live on the reserve and nearby sites, and a resident ornithologist helps you see and learn as much as you want. The two-story lodge is upscale modern with rustic touches, as are the separate cabins. Good home cooking is served in the indoor and outdoor dining rooms, both of which have beautiful views of Volcán Irazú and the Turrialba Valley. Guided tours, meals, horseback riding, and your birding guide are all included in the price. **Pros:** birder's paradise; hiking trails for guests; warm atmosphere. **Cons:** rooms can be musty with dated feel; not a great base for adventure day trips; need a car to stay here. ⊠ *20 km/12 mi southeast of Turrialba, 1½ km/1 mi south of Tuís, then up a rough road* ☎ *2433–8278 for*

*reservations, 888/246–8513 in North America; 2554–8100 for direc-
tions* ⊕ *www.ranchonaturalista.net* ☞ *15 rooms, 13 with bath* ♿ *In-
room: no a/c, no phone, no TV, Internet. In-hotel: restaurant, laundry
service, no-smoking rooms* ⊟ *No credit cards* ⦿ *FAP.*

$ ▦ **Turrialtico.** Dramatically positioned on a hill overlooking the valley
east of Turrialba, this hotel has impressive views of the surrounding
countryside; it's the best budget option in the area. An open-sided restaurant occupies the ground floor, above which are handsome rooms
with hardwood floors. Ask for one on the west side—these have dazzling views of Turrialba and, if there are no clouds, Volcán Irazú. The
restaurant serves a small selection of authentic Costa Rican and international dishes. The only problem is that the rustic wooden construction
makes the rooms anything but soundproof. **Pros:** rich views at budget
prices; good opportunity to mingle with Ticos. **Cons:** thin walls; less
service-oriented than other options; need a car to stay here. ✉ *8 km/5 mi
east of Turrialba on road to Siquirres* ☎ *2538–1111* ⊕ *www.turrialtico.
com* ☞ *14 rooms, 6 cabins* ♿ *In-room: no a/c, no phone, no TV (some),
Wi-Fi (some). In-hotel: restaurant, bar, laundry service, Wi-Fi hotspot,
Internet terminal* ⊟ *AE, D, DC, MC, V* ⦿ *BP.*

$ ▦ **Volcán Turrialba Lodge.** On the slope of the volcano, usually acces-
sible only by 4WD vehicle (which the lodge will arrange for a fee),
the lodge has simple but comfortable rooms, most with a wood-burning stove. Rates include three meals. You'll eat well: the proprietors
serve healthful Costa Rican food. Even more compelling are the tours.
Mountain-biking and horseback-riding trips can be arranged, as well
as a 10-hour trek from the Volcán Turrialba to Guápiles via Braulio
Carrillo National Park. This place is not for everyone—it gets chilly
at over 10,000 feet—but it's a unique mountain escape and a great
value. A variety of packages, with one, two, or all three meals, is yours
for the booking. ■TIP→ **Day-trippers are welcome. Pros:** good value;
proximity to volcano; friendly staff. **Cons:** gets chilly; options limited
on rainy days; need a car to stay here. ✉ *20 km/12 mi east of Cot, turn
right at Pacayas on road to Volcán Turrialba, 4 km/2½ mi on dirt road*
☎☎ *2273–4335* ⊕ *www.volcanturrialbalodge.com* ☞ *28 rooms* ♿ *In-
room: no a/c, no phone, no TV. In-hotel: restaurant, bar, pool* ⊟ *AE,
MC, V* ⦿ *BP, FAP, MAP.*

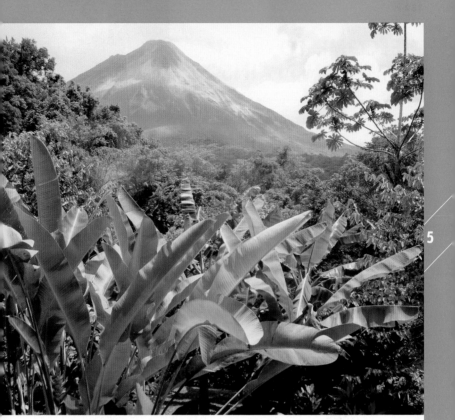

The Northern Plains

WORD OF MOUTH

"Here is a beautiful view of the Arenal Volcano, the most active volcano in Costa Rica. We stayed at a nearby hotel and had a room with a volcano view, as well as skies so clear we could see the summit."

—Photo by Msoberma, Fodors.com member

WELCOME TO NORTHERN PLAINS

TOP REASONS TO GO

★ **Walk in a cloud:** Explore Monteverde's misty world on treetop walkways up to 41 meters (138 feet) off the ground.

★ **Windsurfing:** Lake Arenal is one of the top windsurfing spots on earth; winds can reach 50 to 60 MPH December through April.

★ **Arenal Volcano:** You can hear the rumblings of the world's third most active volcano for miles around, and, on clear nights, watch crimson rock and gas ooze down its flanks.

★ **Watching wildlife:** Waterbirds, monkeys, turtles, crocodiles, jaguars, and sloths abound in the 25,000-acre Caño Negro National Wildlife Refuge.

★ **Walk down to the waterfall:** The reward for a tough hike down to Cataratas de la Fortuna is a magnificent series of waterfalls.

1 Monteverde Cloud Forest Area. Home to the rainiest of cloud forests, the Monteverde Cloud Forest Area is also the canopy-tour capital of Costa Rica. Hanging bridges, treetop tram tours, and zip lines: it's got it all. As if that's not enough, horseback riding, rappelling, and nature hikes are also available.

2 The Far North. Caño Negro National Wildlife Refuge, in the Far North, is great for fishing, bird-watching, and communing with nature.

3 The Sarapiquí Loop. The Sarapiquí Loop circles Braulio Carrillo National Park, rare for its easy-to-access primary rain forest. The loop's highlight is Poás Volcano; its turquoise crater lake and steaming main crater make it the favorite volcano of many visitors.

GETTING ORIENTED

Geographically, the Zona Norte (Northern Zone), as it is known locally, separates neatly into two alluvial plains. The rich, lush terrain runs from the base of the Cordillera Central in the south to the Río San Juan, on the border with Nicaragua in the north. Most visitors begin their visit to Costa Rica in San José, many then heading north to La Fortuna, using it as a base for exploring the volcano, waterfall, and Caño Negro, and participating in activities like sportfishing, windsurfing, and kitesurfing at Lake Arenal, and rafting on the Sarapiquí River.

Río San Juan

35 Acapulco

Santa Domingo   Boca   Altamira   Pangola
Arenal

Puerto Viejo de Sarapiquí

4

Angeles
La Fortuna   Platanar   Chiles   Braulio Carrillo National Park
35

3   Puerto Viejo Loop

San Isidro   Quesada   San Miguel Angeles

4

Poás Volcano ◆

Naranjo

Grecia

CR2   Alajuela

SAN JOSÉ

4 Northwest of San José. Northwest of San José are one of the country's best crafts communities, Sarchí, and some luxurious countryside lodges.

5 Arenal Volcano. The Arenal Volcano area is one of the hottest tourist destinations in Costa Rica. La Fortuna is the closest town to the volcano; among many nearby diversions are the Tabacón Hot Springs. Tilarán, west of Lake Arenal, is the place to be if you're a windsurfer.

NORTHERN PLAINS PLANNER

The Northern Plains: Plainly Kid-Friendly

Perhaps no region of Costa Rica offers as many activities of interest to the under-18 set. Young children especially will "ooh" (and "eeewwww") at various area animal exhibits devoted to bats (Monteverde, La Virgen de Sarapiquí), frogs (Monteverde, Braulio Carrillo National Park, La Virgen de Sarapiquí, La Paz Waterfall Gardens), butterflies (Monteverde, La Fortuna, La Paz Waterfall Gardens), and snakes (Grecia, Monteverde, La Virgen de Sarapiquí, Braulio Carrillo National Park, La Paz Waterfall Gardens). Guided nature hikes abound; shorter treks can be entertaining and cater to younger ones' shorter attention spans. Most sure-footed and confident teenagers can participate in adult activities. We recommend white-water rafting and canopy tours.

A few operators around here will tell you that kids older than eight can participate in canopy tours. We're skeptical of such claims, even if their brochures show children happily zipping from platform to platform. The gondola-like trams (Braulio Carrillo National Park, Monteverde) are far safer ways to see the rain forest canopy.

Rain Forests Are . . . Rainy

We frequently overhear comments such as "I didn't know it would be so rainy in the rain forest." You heard it here first: that's why they call it the rain forest! During the rainy season it's not unusual for it to rain for several days straight, and even during the dry season, brief showers will come up without notice. Be sure to bring a poncho or rain jacket and waterproof footwear.

The Early Bird Catches the Sun

In the rainy season it's almost a given that you'll get a bit damp on your canopy tour, hike, or horseback ride, and most tour operators provide ponchos. But to avoid a thorough soaking, plan activities for the morning. Rains usually begin around 2 PM, like clockwork, from July through December, although they can be more prolonged in September and October. The clearest time of day is normally before 8 AM.

Safety First

This region is Costa Rica's capital of adventure tourism—it gave birth to the canopy tour—so any risks up here are far more likely to be natural than criminal. Before you set out rafting, zip-lining, rappelling, or bungee jumping, be brutally frank with yourself about your abilities, your physical condition, and your fear levels. (It's almost impossible to turn back on many excursions once you've started.) Even an activity as innocuous as hiking or horseback riding poses a certain amount of risk, and you should never go alone. Nature here is not an amusement park. As Dorothy says in The Wizard of Oz, "Toto, I don't think we're in Kansas anymore."

Remember also that little government oversight over adventure tourism exists here. Pay close attention during any safety briefings and orientation. Don't be afraid to ask questions, and don't be afraid to walk away if something seems off to you.

When to Go

Climate is difficult to pinpoint in this vast region. The Northern Plains links the rainier Caribbean in the east to drier Guanacaste in the west. It's a pretty good rule of thumb to say that precipitation decreases from east to west. Grecia, Sarchí, and Naranjo enjoy a climate similar to Costa Rica's higher-elevation Central Valley, with pleasant springlike days year-round, and well-defined rainy and dry seasons.

Throughout the entire region, the warm and humid rainy season normally takes place June to December. But rains can occur outside the official wet season since the area's low elevation frequently hosts battles between competing weather fronts. Expect highs of 26°C to 32°C (80°F to 90°F) and lows of 15°C to 20°C (60°F to 70°F). Nights are cool and comfortable.

At almost 1,524 meters (5,000 feet), Monteverde has a significantly different climate: it's cool, damp, and breezy much of the time, with average highs around 20°C (70°F) and lows around 13°C (55°F), and high winds in January and February.

Visibility changes daily (and hourly), so your chances of seeing the Arenal and Poás craters are more or less the same year-round, though you may have more luck from February to April, the hottest and driest time of the year.

Early December to April is considered a weather-related high season, although many places in Arenal and Monteverde are beginning to impose high-season rates in July and August to correspond with prime North American and European vacation times.

Dining and Lodging Prices

WHAT IT COSTS IN DOLLARS

	¢	$	$$	$$$	$$$$
Restaurants	under $5	$5–$10	$10–$15	$15–$25	over $25
Hotels	under $50	$50–$75	$75–$150	$150–$250	over $250

Restaurant prices are per person for a main course at dinner. Hotel prices are for two people in a standard double room in high season, excluding service and tax (16.4%).

How Much Time?

Although not centrally located, the Northern Plains can be easily tacked onto stays in other regions of Costa Rica. Fairly decent—decent for Costa Rica, that is—transportation links the region to San José, the Central Valley, and the North Pacific. (Always the exception, Monteverde sits isolated, approached only by rugged roads from all directions.)

If your stay here is limited to two or three days, make La Fortuna your base. Don't miss the volcano, the Tabacón Hot Springs, or Caño Negro Wildlife Refuge.

Most tour operators who have volcano hikes end the day at one of the various thermal springs in the area. "Half-day" tours to Caño Negro actually take most of a day, from around 7:30 AM to 4 PM.

A week in the Northern Plains is more than enough time to experience a great deal of this area—especially if you're longing to get out and get moving. Give yourself four days in La Fortuna/Arenal for rafting trips on area rivers, horseback rides, and kitesurfing or windsurfing on Lake Arenal. Devote the rest of your week to Monteverde Cloud Forest.

Driving yourself between Monteverde and Arenal means negotiating some pretty horrendous roads. Tour operators can arrange for boat or even horse transfers.

5

CAÑO NEGRO

Think a smaller version of Florida's Everglades and you'll have a good picture of the Refugio Nacional de Vida Silvestre Caño Negro.

This lowland rain forest reserve in the far northern reaches of Costa Rica near the Nicaraguan border covers 98 square km (38 square mi). It looks remote on the map, but is easily visited on an organized day tour if you're up this way. In 2007 Caño Negro was designated the core of a new UNESCO biosphere called Agua y Paz (Water and Peace), which encompasses more than 2 million acres of wildlife habitat in Costa Rica and Nicaragua.

Caño Negro has suffered severe deforestation over the years, but most of the length of the Río Frío, its principal river, is still lined with trees. The park's vast lake, which floods according to seasonal rains, is an excellent place to watch waterfowl. On land, pumas, tapirs, ocelots, cougars, and the always-elusive jaguar make up the mammal life found here—consider yourself fortunate if you spot that last one. Caimans snap everywhere in the knee-deep marshy waters, too.

BEST TIME TO GO

It gets *hot* here, with March and April brutally so, but the January–March dry season is the best time to spot the reserve's migratory bird population. Opportunities abound the rest of the year too, though. No matter what the season, bring sunscreen, water, insect repellant, and a brimmed hat.

FUN FACT

In addition to other bird species, the reserve is the best place to spot the Nicaraguan grackle. This New World blackbird is only found in Nicaragua and Northern Costa Rica. It's medium-sized, with a long, graduated tail and fairly long bill and legs.

BEST WAYS TO EXPLORE

BOAT TOURS

In the dry season you can ride horses, but a visit here chiefly entails a wildlife-spotting boat tour. You could drive up here on your own—roads to the area are in good shape—but once here, you'd need to arrange for boat transportation. Visiting with a tour company out of La Fortuna—it's a 90-minute ride one way—is the easiest way to see the park.

BIRD-WATCHING

This is the best place in the country to see water birds. Just sit back in your tour boat and survey the passing parade. You're sure to see anhingas spreading their wings to dry; both glossy and white ibis recognizable by their long curved beaks; roseate spoonbills often mistaken for flamingos; and the jabiru, king of the storks. Herons and kingfishers lurk on the banks, ready to spear fish; while jacanas, with their huge feet, forage in the water lettuce, looking as though they are actually walking on water. Above the water, watch for gray-colored snail kites, which true to their name, are hunting for snails.

CAIMAN LAND

Famous for its caimans, Caño Negro still boasts a sizeable population. They're smaller than crocodiles, though—at most 8 feet long—and they are relatively unthreatening since they're too small to eat large mammals (this includes humans). It's a thrill to see them sunning on a bank or to see their spectacled eyes floating just above the water line. Unfortunately, the caimans here are under serious threat from hunters who sneak across the Nicaraguan border and slaughter them by the hundreds for their skins. The proof is sadly on display in the souvenir shops in Nicaragua, where you will see purses and belts made from caiman hides.

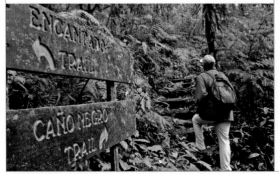

TOP REASONS TO GO

BIRD-WATCHING

The reserve is one of Costa Rica's lesser sung bird-watching and wildlife-viewing destinations. Caño Negro is growing in popularity, but, for now, a visit here still gives you that "I'm in on a secret the rest of the world doesn't know about" satisfaction.

FISHING

It's not all about wildlife viewing here: Caño Negro is also one of Costa Rica's prime freshwater fishing destinations, with snook and marlin yours for the catching and the bragging rights during the July—March season. (There's barely enough water in the lake the other months of the year, so fishing is prohibited then.) The two lodges inside the reserve can hook you up.

GREAT TOURS

It's easy to get here from the Arenal area, with top-notch operators and their teams of knowledgeable guides organizing day tours from La Fortuna and so-called "evening" tours that actually get you here by the very warm midafternoon and depart around dusk.

5

VOLCÁN ARENAL

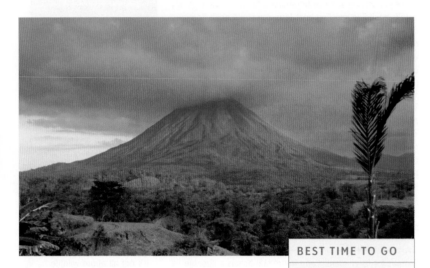

The mile-high Volcán Arenal, Costa Rica's youngest and most active volcano, dominates the region's landscape.

Volcanologists estimate Arenal's age at around 4,000 years and it was dormant for at least 400 years until 1968. It may be local folklore, but residents before then referred to Arenal as simply "the mountain" and apparently, despite its conical shape, did not realize it was a volcano. On July 29, 1968, an earthquake shook the area, and 12 hours later Arenal blew.

Since then, Arenal has been in a constant state of activity—thunderous, rumbling eruptions are sometimes as frequent as one per hour. These earthshaking events remind everyone what it really means to coexist with the world's third most active volcano. Night is the best time to view the action: on a clear evening you can see rocks spewing skyward. Although everyone refers to "lava," "pyroclastic flow," a mix of incandescent rock and gas, is a more apt description of what the volcano churns out. Call it what you will: the spectacle rarely fails to impress.

BEST TIME TO GO

To be honest, viewing Arenal can be hit or miss any time of year. January through April, especially in the early morning, usually means fewer clouds to obscure daytime views. The dry season's clear evenings give the best spectacle of the volcano's flows. Patience is a virtue here.

FUN FACT

Researchers at INBio, the National Biological Institute in Santo Domingo, north of San José have been hard at work around the volcano. They see promise in the lichens growing on Arenal's slopes as a source of new antibiotics.

BEST WAYS TO EXPLORE

VOLCANIC TIPS

Two words: "from afar." Under no circumstances should you hike even the volcano's lower slopes on your own. Lava rocks and volcanic gas have killed trekkers who got too close, most recently in 2000. The tour operators we recommend know where the danger lies and take appropriate precautions. Wait until around 2 PM to see if the weather will cooperate, and then book your afternoon volcano hike.

Beyond that, take a liberal interpretation of "exploring" the volcano, and gaze at its majesty from the distance and safety of several area hotels, restaurants, and hot springs that afford postcard views.

HIKING

For intrepid hikers who want to get a little closer to the action, the Las Heliconias trail, which starts at the park reception center, wends through secondary forest and passes by the cooled lava flow from the 1968 eruption. The Los Tucanes trail also leads to the lava fields, but it's more of an uphill hike, beginning near the entrance to the Arenal Observatory Lodge. There's also a hiking trail up to Cerro Chatto, a lopsided, extinct crater, partially filled with water, creating a pretty lake. Since volcano activity and lava flow can change suddenly, check with the park rangers to see which trails are currently safe to hike.

BIRD-WATCHING

If you decide to hike the park's Los Tucanes trail, chances are you'll see at least one of the five species of toucan that have been recorded here: chestnut-billed and keel-billed toucans, the yellow-eared and emerald toucanet, and the collared araçari. You'll never look at a box of Fruit Loops the same after seeing the real thing. Hummingbirds also abound on the volcano's slope. Look for anything tiny and purple.

TOP REASONS TO GO

A PERFECT VOLCANO

Look up *volcano* in the dictionary. You half expect to see a picture of Arenal. Its perfect cone, red-hot flow, plumes of ash, and menacing location close to the tourist town of La Fortuna practically define the term.

SPORTS AND ADVENTURE

No other attraction in Costa Rica has given rise to a list of accompanying entertainment offerings quite so extensive. Come here to pay your respects to Arenal, and you'll find enough other area activities to keep you occupied for days. (You'll also appreciate the backup on those occasions when clouds obscure your view of the volcano.)

ALL BUDGETS WELCOME

We lament that budget and even moderate travelers are being priced out of the market in certain regions of Costa Rica. Not so here. Choose from everything from backpackers' digs to luxury hotels in the area around Arenal. Feel free to stay for days, no matter what your budget.

POÁS VOLCÁNO

Towering north of Alajuela, the verdant Poás Volcáno is covered with a quilt of farms and topped by a dark green shawl of cloud forest.

That pastoral scene disappears once you get to the summit, and you gaze into the steaming, bubbling crater with smoking fumaroles and a gurgling, gray-turquoise sulfurous lake. You'll swear you're peering over the edge of a giant witches' cauldron. That basin, a mile in diameter and nearly 1,000 feet deep, is thought to be the largest active volcanic crater in the world.

Poás is one of Costa Rica's five active volcanoes—it has erupted 40 times since the early 1800s—and is one of those rare places that permit you to see volcanic energy this close with minimal risk to your safety. Authorities closely monitor Poás's activity following several eruptions in March 2006, the first significant increase in activity since 1994. Access is normally open at this writing, but park officials close the route up here on those occasions of any activity they deem "irregular."

BEST TIME TO GO

The peak is frequently shrouded in mist, and you might see little beyond the lip of the crater. Be patient and wait awhile, especially if some wind is blowing—the clouds can disappear quickly. Aim to get here before 10 AM. The earlier in the day you go, the better.

FUN FACT

Forgot your umbrella? (It gets wet up here.) Duck under a *sombrilla de pobre* (poor man's umbrella) plant. These giant leaves can grow to diameters of 4 to 5 feet—plenty big enough to shelter a few hikers caught out in the rain.

BEST WAYS TO EXPLORE

VOLCANIC TIPS

A paved road leads all the way from Alajuela to Poás's 8,800-foot summit. The 2009 earthquake wrecked the eastern-approach road from Varablanca, so check before you try that route. No one is allowed to venture into the crater or walk along its edge. ■TIP➜ Take periodic breaks from viewing: Step back at least every 10 minutes, so that the sulfur fumes don't overcome you. Be sure to bring a sweater or a jacket—it can be surprisingly chilly up here.

HIKING

From the summit, two trails head into the forest. The second trail, on the right just before the crater, winds through a thick mesh of shrubs and dwarf trees to the eerie but beautiful Botos Lake (**Laguna Botos**), which occupies an extinct crater. It takes 30 minutes to walk here and back, but you'll be huffing and puffing if you're not used to this altitude, almost 9,000 feet above sea level.

BIRD-WATCHING

Although birding can be a little frustrating here because of cloud and mist, more than 330 bird species call Poás home. One of the most comical birds you'll see in Costa Rica is usually spotted foraging in plain sight on the ground: the big-footed finch whose oversized feet give it a clownish walk. Its cousin, the yellow-thighed finch, is easy to recognize by its bright-yellow, er…thighs. Arrive early and bird around the gate before the park opens, and stop along the road to the visitors center wherever you see a likely birding area. In the underbrush you may find spotted wood-quail or the elusive, buffy-crowned wood-partridge. The trees along the road are a favorite haunt of both black-and-yellow and long-tailed silky flycatchers.

TOP REASONS TO GO

LAVA AND ASH

"Up close and personal with nature" takes on a whole new meaning here. Costa Rica forms part of the Pacific Rim's so-called "Ring of Fire," and a visit to the volcano's summit gives you a close-up view of a region of the earth that is still in formation.

MORE THAN A VOLCANO

The park is not just about its namesake volcano. A few kilometers of hiking trails wind around the summit and let you take in the cloud forest's lichens, ferns, and bromeliads.

A+ FACILITIES

You're on your own in many Costa Rican national parks, which have little by way of facilities. This park is a pleasant exception, with an attractive visitor's center containing exhibits, cafeteria, gift shop, and restrooms.

LOCATION, LOCATION, LOCATION

Poás's proximity to San José, the western Central Valley and many destinations *in this chapter* makes it an easy half-day trip. Mix and match a volcano visit with several other area attractions.

ECO-LODGES IN THE NORTHERN PLAINS

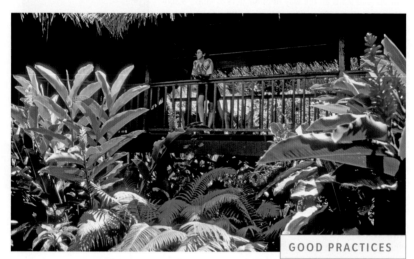

This territory as a whole doesn't garner the attention in eco-circles that other parts of Costa Rica do, but the country has no more diverse region than the Northern Plains.

Cloud forests, rain forests, volcanoes, thermal springs, white-water rivers, waterfalls, coffee and banana plantations, and rolling farmland combine to create the vast landscape that stretches across the northern third of Costa Rica. That translates into a variety of environmentally themed pursuits unmatched anywhere else in the country. The mists of Monteverde define *cloud forest*, and the original Quaker settlers stamped their environmental consciousness on the area. La Fortuna and environs have parlayed the presence of the nearby Arenal Volcano into a myriad of activities. The Sarapiquí region is one of the lesser-known (but no less impressive) rain forest regions with a growing selection of small lodges. (And don't forget that this region gave Costa Rica the zip-line canopy tour, one of its best-known and most popular tourist activities.) The tourist industry up here knows what the region has to offer and is keen to preserve what is green. Hotel owners and tour operators are just as eager to show it off to you.

GOOD PRACTICES

Consider public or semi-public transportation for negotiating the Northern Plains. No question: distances are vast, and your own wheels *do* offer you the greatest convenience. It's surprisingly easy, though, to take shuttle transport, base yourself in Arenal or Monteverde, and use occasional taxis to get around once you arrive. Many tour operators in both places are happy to pick you up at your hotel, too.

Also, ask if your hotel recycles. In Monteverde, the answer will usually be yes, but it'll be less likely in other places. If enough guests keep requesting it, more lodgings just might hop on the eco-bandwagon.

TOP ECO-LODGES IN THE NORTHERN PLAINS

ARCO IRIS LODGE, MONTEVERDE

The German management here eschews the overused word ecotourism, insisting that many in Costa Rica view the concept as simply e¢otouri$m. But if any lodging were entitled to use the term in its marketing, it would be this one. Comfortable cabins are scattered around the grounds here, and though you're right in the center of town, Arco Iris has managed to create a country feel. (The 135 bird species sighted on the property contribute to that ambience.) That, along with the organic foods, active recycling program, biodegradable materials, and involvement in the community, makes this one of our favorite Costa Rican eco-lodges—even if it doesn't call itself that.

LAGUNA DEL LAGARTO LODGE, CIUDAD QUESADA

It doesn't get mentioned in the pantheon of better-known Costa Rican eco-lodges, but this smallish property near the Nicaraguan border offers a variety of nature-themed activities to rival any of the big guys. Accommodation is rustic in this remote locale, but impact on the environment has been minimal. The 1,250-acre rain forest here makes for terrific bird-watching—380 species have been catalogued so far—hiking, and canoeing. Laguna del Lagarto gives back to its community, and has succeeded in bringing employment to a poorer, often forgotten corner of Costa Rica.

LA SELVA, PUERTO VIEJO DE SARAPIQUÍ

You would expect any lodging that functions as a working biological station and where research biologists make up the primary clientele to be eco-friendly. La Selva does not disappoint. The Durham, North Carolina–based Organization for Tropical Studies operates the facility along with two other similar stations in Costa Rica, and offers a fascinating program of nature-themed activities for you, the nonprofessional guest. Keep one caveat in mind, though: scientists take priority in procuring space in the rustic but comfortable cabins.

PLANTING TREES

"Costa Rica" equals "forest" in the minds of most visitors. Truth be told, about half the country has been deforested, much of it occurring in this region. The reasons are mostly understandable: coffee, bananas, and dairy cattle make the Northern Plains the country's breadbasket; for decades, trees have been cleared for farmland. Enter the *A Que Sembrás un Árbol* program. Loosely translated, that means "May you plant a tree." It forms part of the United Nations' international Planting for the Planet program, whose goal is to plant 3.5 billion trees worldwide each year. Costa Rica's contribution to the agenda aims for an annual figure of 7 million trees, around one-third of which are targeted for this region. Like most environmental initiatives here, the program began at the grassroots level, with area students kicking off the tree planting, soliciting support from area businesses, and petitioning the government to become officially involved.

THE NORTHERN PLAINS

By Jeffrey Van Fleet

The vast expanse that locals call the Zona Norte (Northern Zone) packs in more variety of activities than any other part of the country. You'll find almost everything in this region that Costa Rica has to offer, except beaches.

Spend any amount of time here and you can partake of—take a deep breath—volcano-viewing, horseback riding, canoeing, kayaking, rafting, rappelling, windsurfing, wildlife-viewing, bird-watching, bungee jumping, shopping, zip-lining, cloud and rain forest hiking, swimming, and hot-springs soaking. Good transportation links to and within the region make it easy to explore.

GETTING HERE

NatureAir and SANSA have daily flights from their respective airports in San José to La Fortuna (FTN). Most travelers to this region fly into San José's Aeropuerto Internacional Juan Santamaría or Liberia's Daniel Oduber Airport. Monteverde and Arenal are equidistant from both. Base your choice of airport on which other areas in Costa Rica you plan to visit in addition to this one.

Buses in this region are typically large, clean, and fairly comfortable, but often crowded Friday through Sunday. Don't expect air-conditioning. Service tends toward the agonizingly slow: even supposedly express buses marked *directo* (direct) often make numerous stops.

Road access to the northwest is by way of the paved two-lane Pan-American Highway (Carretera Interamericana, or CA1), which starts from the west end of Paseo Colón in San José and runs northwest to Peñas Blancas at the Nicaraguan border. Turn north at Naranjo or San Ramón for La Fortuna; at Lagarto for Monteverde; and at Cañas for Tilarán. Calle 3 heading north from downtown San José becomes the Braulio Carrillo Highway and provides the best access to Puerto Viejo de Sarapiquí and environs.

GETTING AROUND

This region manages to mix some of the country's smoothest highways with some of its most horrendous roads. (The road to Monteverde is legendary in the latter regard, but the final destination makes it worth the trip.) Four-wheel-drive vehicles are best on the frequently potholed roads. If you don't want to pay for 4WD, at least rent a car with high clearance. (Many rental agencies insist you take a 4WD vehicle if you mention Monteverde as part of your itinerary.) You'll encounter frequent one-lane bridges; if the triangular CEDA EL PASO faces you, yield to oncoming traffic.

It is possible to rent a car in La Fortuna or Monteverde, but for a far better selection, most visitors pick up their rental vehicles in San José or Liberia.

NORTHWEST OF SAN JOSÉ

The rolling countryside northwest of San José and west of Alajuela holds a mix of coffee, sugarcane, and pasture, with tropical forest filling steep river valleys and ravines. The Pan-American Highway makes a steady descent to the Pacific coast through this region, which is also traversed by older roads that wind their way between simple agricultural towns and past small farms and pastoral scenery. West of San Ramón the valley becomes narrow and precipitous as the topography slopes down to the Pacific lowlands. An even narrower valley snakes northward from San Ramón to the northern lowlands beyond.

GRECIA

26 km/16 mi (45 mins) northwest of Alajuela, 46 km/29 mi (1 hr) northwest of San José.

Founded in 1838, the quiet farming community of Grecia is reputed to be Costa Rica's cleanest town—some enthusiastic civic boosters extend that superlative to all Latin America—but the reason most people stop here is to admire its unusual church.

GETTING HERE AND AROUND

From San José continue west on the highway past the airport—the turnoff is on the right—or head into Alajuela and turn left just before the Alajuela cemetery. Buses leave Calle 20 in San José for Grecia every 30 minutes from 5:30 AM to 10 PM. From Alajuela, buses to Grecia/Ciudad Quesada pick up on the southern edge of town (C. 4 at Avda. 10).

ESSENTIALS

Bank/ATM BAC San José (⌗ *100 m north of Central Park*). Banco Nacional (⌗ *Northwest corner of Central Plaza* ☎ *2494–3600*).

EXPLORING

The brick-red, prefabricated iron **Church of Our Lady of Mercy** (Iglesia de las Mercedes) was one of two buildings in the country made from steel frames imported from Belgium in the 1890s (the other is the metal schoolhouse next to San José's Parque Morazán), when some prominent Costa Ricans decided that metal structures would better withstand the periodic earthquakes that had taken their toll on so much of the country's architecture. The frames were shipped from Antwerp to Limón, then transported by train to Alajuela—from which the walls of the church were carried by oxcarts. Although the park fronting the church is a Wi-Fi hot spot, we advise against pulling out your laptop in such a public setting. ⊠ *Avda. 1, Cs. 1–3* ☎ *2494–1616* ☉ *Daily 8–4.*

☃ On a small farm outside Grecia, the **World of Snakes** (Mundo de las Serpientes) is a good place to see some of the snakes that you are unlikely—and probably don't want—to spot in the wild. Sequestered in the safety of cages here are some 50 varieties of serpents, as well as crocodiles, iguanas, poison dart frogs, and various other cold-blooded creatures. Admission includes a 90-minute tour. ⊠ *Poro 2 km/1 mi east of Grecia, on road to Alajuela* ☎ *2494–3700* ⊕ *www.theworldofsnakes.com* ✉ *$11, $6 ages 7–15, free under 7* ☉ *Daily 8–4.*

OUTDOOR ACTIVITIES

BUNGEE JUMPING

A 79-meter-tall (265-foot-tall) bridge that spans a forested gorge over the Río Colorado is the perfect place to get a rush of adrenaline in a tranquil, tropical setting. Even if you aren't up for the plunge, it's worth stopping to watch a few mad souls do it. **Tropical Bungee** (⊠ *Pan-American Hwy.2 km/1 mi west of turnoff for Grecia, down a dirt* road on the right ☎ 2248–2212 or 8842–0050 ⊕ www.bungee.co.cr ⊗ Daily 8–11:30 and 1–4) organizes trips to the bridge. The first jump is $65 and the second is $30. Transportation is free if you jump; $10 if you don't. Reservations are essential. If this is your last hurrah in Costa Rica, a van can take you and your bags straight to the San José airport after your jump.

WHERE TO STAY

$$–$$$
Fodor's Choice
★

🏨 **Vista del Valle Plantation Inn.** Honeymooners (and many posters to Fodors.com) frequent this bed-and-breakfast on an orange and coffee plantation outside Grecia overlooking the canyon of the Río Grande. Cottages are decorated in minimalist style with simple wooden furniture and sliding doors that open onto small porches. Each has its own personality; the Nido, removed from the rest and with the nicest decor, is the most romantic. The hotel's forest reserve has an hour-long trail leading down to a waterfall. Breakfast is served by the pool or in the main house, where you can relax in a spacious living room. The food is quite good, and special dietary requests are accommodated with advance notice. It's a mere 20-minute drive from the airport. **Pros:** attentive staff; secluded cabins; healthful food served. **Cons:** car is necessary for staying here. ✉ On highway 1 km/½ mi west of Rafael Iglesia Bridge; follow signs ☎ 2451–1165 ⊕ www.vistadelvalle.com ➹ 10 cottages ⇔ In-room: no a/c, no phone, no TV. In-hotel: restaurant, pool, Internet terminal, Wi-Fi hotspot ▭ AE, MC, V ⍑◎�㇇ BP.

PAINTED OXCARTS

Coffee has come to symbolize the prosperity of the Central Valley and the nation. Nineteenth-century coffee farmers needed a way to transport this all-important cash crop to the port of Puntarenas on the Pacific coast. Enter the oxcart. Artisans began painting the carts in the early 1900s. Debate continues as to why: the kaleidoscopic designs may have symbolized the points of the compass, or may have echoed the landscape's tropical colors. In any case, the oxcart has become the national symbol. Give way when you see one out on a country road, and marvel at the sight.

5

SARCHÍ

8 km/5 mi west of Grecia, 53 km/33 mi (1½ hrs) northwest of San José.

Tranquil Sarchí rambles over a collection of hills surrounded by coffee plantations. It's Costa Rica's premier center for crafts and carpentry. People drive here from all over central Costa Rica to shop for furniture, and tour buses regularly descend upon the souvenir shops outside town. The area's most famous products are its brightly painted oxcarts— replicas of those traditionally used to transport coffee.

GETTING HERE AND AROUND

To get to Sarchí from San José, take the highway well past the airport to the turnoff for Naranjo; then veer right just as you enter Naranjo. Direct buses to Sarchí depart from Alajuela (C. 8, between Avdas. 1 and 3) every 30 minutes 6 AM–9 PM; the ride takes 90 minutes.

ESSENTIALS

Bank/ATM Banco Nacional (✉ *South side of soccer field* ☎ *2454–3044*).

Post Office Correos (✉ *50 m west of central plaza*).

EXPLORING

Sarchí's **Parque Central** resembles the central park of any other Costa Rican small town—the facade of its church is frequently compared to a wedding cake—but the park's real attraction is the world's largest oxcart, constructed and brightly painted by longtime local factory Taller Eloy Alfaro e Hijos and enshrined in the *Guinness Book of World Records*. The work logs in at 18 meters (45 feet) and weighs 2 tons. Since no other country is attached to oxcarts quite the way Costa Rica is, we don't look for that record to be broken anytime soon. ✉ *Center of Sarchí.*

Costa Rica's only real oxcart factory left, **Eloy Alfaro and Sons Workshop** *(Taller Eloy Alfaro e Hijos)*, was founded in 1923, and its carpentry methods have changed little since then, although the "e Hijos" portion of the family (the sons) runs the operation these days. The two-story wooden building housing the wood shop is surrounded by trees and flowers—mostly orchids—and all the machinery on the ground floor is powered by a waterwheel at the back of the shop. Carts are painted in the back, and although the factory's main product is a genuine oxcart—which sells for about $2,000—there are also some smaller mementos that can easily be shipped home. ✉ *200 m north of soccer field* ☎ *2454–4131* ⊙ *Weekdays 8–4.*

If you enjoy plants, the **Else Kientzler Botanical Garden** *(Jardín Botánico Else Kientzler)* is well worth a break from your shopping. The site exhibits some 2,000 plant species, tropical and subtropical, over its sprawling 17 acres. The German owner named the facility, affiliated with an ornamental-plant exporter, after his plant-loving mother. About half of the garden's pathways are wheelchair accessible. ✉ *800 m north of soccer field* ☎ *2454–2070* ⊕ *www.elsegarden.com* ✉ *$15* ⊙ *Daily 8–4.*

SHOPPING

Sarchí is the best place in Costa Rica to buy miniature oxcarts, the larger of which are designed to serve as patio bars or end tables and can be broken down for easy transport or shipped to your home. Another popular item is a locally produced rocking chair with a leather seat and back.

Fodor's Choice
★

The nicest of the many stores south of town is the **Chaverrí Oxcart Factory** *(Fábrica de Carretas* ✉ *Main road 2 km/1 mi south of Sarchí* ☎ *2454–4411)*, and you can wander through the workshops in back to see the artisans in action. (Despite the name, much more is for sale here than oxcarts.) Chaverri is a good place to buy wooden crafts; nonwood products are cheaper in San José. Chaverri also runs a restaurant next door, **Las Carretas** (☎ *2454–1633)*, which serves a variety of local food all day until 6 pm and has a good lunch buffet.

Sarchí's answer to a shopping mall, the **Plaza de la Artesanía** (✉ *2 km/1 mi south of Sarchí* ☎ *2454–3430)* gathers 34 artisan and souvenir shops under one roof. If you can't find it here, it probably doesn't exist.

Taking the plunge. Bungee jumping at the Colorado River Bridge, Grecia.

SAN RAMÓN

23 km/14 mi west of Sarchí, 59 km/37 mi (1½ hrs) northwest of San José.

Having produced a number of minor bards, San Ramón is known locally as the City of Poets. San Ramón hides its real attractions in the countryside to the north, on the road to La Fortuna, where comfortable lodges offer access to private nature preserves. There's not much to see in San Ramón other than its church.

GETTING HERE AND AROUND

San Ramón is on the Pan-American Highway west of Grecia. To reach the hotel we list north of town, head straight through San Ramón and follow the signs. Buses leave hourly for San Ramón from San José's Terminal de Puntarenas. From Alajuela, buses to San Ramón/Ciudad Quesada pick up on the southern edge of town (⌧ C. 4 at Avda. 10).

ESSENTIALS

Bank/ATM HSBC (⌧ *150 m north of Palí supermarket* ☎ *2445–3602).* **Scotiabank** (⌧ *Pan-American Highway, entrance to San Ramón* ☎ *2447–9190).*

Internet Cybercafé San Ramón (⌧ *100 m east of Banco Central* ☎ *2447–9007).*

EXPLORING

Aside from its poets, the massive **Church of San Ramón** (Iglesia de San Ramón), built in a mixture of the Romanesque and Gothic styles, is the city's claim to fame. In 1924 an earthquake destroyed the smaller adobe church that once stood here, and the city lost no time in creating a replacement—this great gray concrete structure took a quarter of a century to complete, from 1925 to 1954. To ensure that the second church would be earthquake-proof, workers poured the concrete around a steel frame that was designed and forged in Germany (by Krupp). Step past the formidable facade and you'll discover a bright, elegant interior. ⊠ *Across from Parque Central* ☎ *2445–5592* ☉ *Daily 6–11:30* AM *and 1:30–7* PM.

FINDING YOUR WAY

No sun to help you get your bearings? Just remember that the entrance to most Catholic churches in Costa Rica faces west, so that the congregation can face east toward Rome. Churches in La Fortuna, and the Central Valley's Orosi and Turrialba are notable exceptions.

WHERE TO EAT AND STAY

$ ✕ **La Colina.** Here's the only Costa Rican restaurant whose food has been

COSTA RICAN   transported into outer space: Retired Costa Rican–American astronaut Franklin Chang, a fan of La Colina's *cajetas especiales*, a sweet orange-coconut dish, took some with him on one of his NASA missions. This roadside diner, with its requisite plastic chairs, has an eclectic menu. Start your meal with a delicious ceviche, moving on to the famous rice and chicken or, for the more adventurous, *lengua en salsa* (tongue in tomato sauce). Meals begin with complimentary chips and pickled vegetables. ⊠ *Highway to Puntarenas 2 km/1 mi west of San Ramón* ☎ *2445–4956* ☰ *AE, D, DC, MC, V.*

$$$ ⊡ **Villa Blanca.** This charming hotel is on a working dairy and coffee

★   farm constructed and once owned by former Costa Rican president Rodrigo Carazo. The farmhouse contains the reception desk, bar, and restaurant; down the hill are lovely casitas, each a replica of a traditional adobe farmhouse complete with whitewashed walls, tile floors, cane ceilings, and fireplaces. Resident guides lead nature walks through the adjacent cloud-forest reserve, which is excellent bird-watching territory. Horses are available for exploring the rest of the farm. **Pros:** attentive service; many activities; secluded location. **Cons:** far from sights; need car to stay here. ⊠ *20 km/12 mi north of San Ramón on road to La Fortuna* ☎ *2461–0300, 877/256–8399 in North America* ⊕ *www.villablancacr.com* ↵ *34 casitas* ⬧ *In-room: no a/c, no phone, refrigerator, no TV, Wi-Fi (some). In-hotel: restaurant, bar, spa, Internet terminal, Wi-Fi hotspot* ☰ *AE, D, DC, MC, V* ◯◻ *BP.*

EN ROUTE   The small town of **Zarcero**, 15 km (9 mi) north of Sarchí on the road to Ciudad Quesada, looks like it was designed by Dr. Seuss. Evangelisto Blanco, a local landscape artist, modeled cypress topiaries in fanciful animal shapes—motorcycle-riding monkeys, a lightbulb-eyed elephant—that enliven the park in front of the town church. The church interior is covered with elaborate pastel stencil work and detailed religious paintings by the late Misael Solís, a well-known local artist. Sample some cheese if you're in town, too; Zarcero-made cheese is one of Costa Rica's favorites.

THE ARENAL VOLCANO AREA

Whether you come here from San José or Liberia, prepare yourself for some spectacular scenery—and a bumpy ride. As you bounce along on your way to Arenal, you may discover that "paved" means different things in different places, and that potholes are numerous. Any discomfort you experience is more than made up for by the swaths of misty rain forest and dramatic expanses of the Cordillera Central. Schedule at least 3½ hours for the trip.

CIUDAD QUESADA (SAN CARLOS)

55 km/33 mi (1 hr) northwest of Zarcero.

Highway signs point you to CIUDAD QUESADA, but it's simply "San Carlos" in local parlance. Like so many other places in Costa Rica, the landscape is splendid, but what passes for architecture varies from ordinary to downright hideous. San Carlos is where everyone in the region comes to shop, take in a movie, get medical care, and generally take care of the necessities. There's also an enormous bus terminal (with shopping center and multiplex movie theater) where you can make connections to almost anywhere in the northern half of the country. If you're traveling from San José to points north, your bus will stop here even if it's a so-called express. This lively mountain market town–provincial capital serves a fertile dairy region and is worth a stop for a soak in the soothing thermal waters in the area.

5

GETTING HERE AND AROUND

Ciudad Quesada lies 55 km (33 mi) off the Pan-American Highway north of Zarcero. Buses from San José leave Terminal Atlántico Norte on the hour, from 5 AM to 7 PM. The trip takes around three hours. The Ciudad Quesada bus terminal is a couple of kilometers from the center of town; taxis wait at the terminal to take you into town. Driving is straightforward in this part of the country, as long as you don't get stuck behind a slow-moving truck transporting sugarcane to the Central Valley. Try to get an early start if you're driving yourself; the road between Zarcero and Ciudad Quesada begins to fog over by early afternoon.

VOLCANIC BEGINNINGS

Many people who settled the Northern Plains came to the then-isolated region in the 1940s and '50s from other parts of the country to take part in government-sponsored homesteading programs. Thanks to rich volcanic soil, the agricultural region became one of the most productive in Central America. More recently, since the 1968 Arenal eruption (the first eruption in nearly 500 years), Ticos have been drawn by jobs in the ever-expanding tourism industry. In the far northern section of the region, close to the border, a great number of residents are Nicaraguan.

ESSENTIALS

Bank/ATM BAC San José (⊠ *100 m north and 125 m west of cathedral*).
Banco Nacional (⊠ *Across from north side of cathedral* ☎ *2401–2000*).
Scotiabank (⊠ *Across from Mercado de Artesanía* ☎ *2461–9660*).

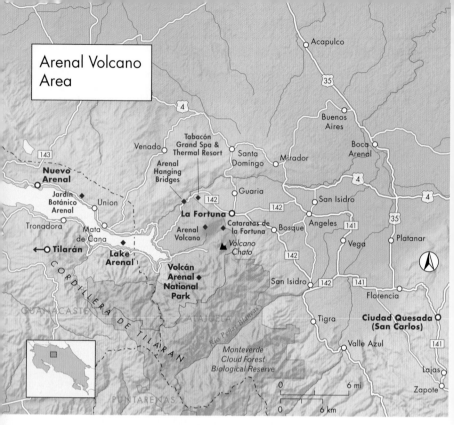

Arenal Volcano
Area

Internet Internet Café (✉ *150 m north of park* ☎ *2460–3653*).

Medical Assistance Hospital de San Carlos (✉ *2 km/1 mi north of park* ☎ *2460–1176*).

Post Office Correos (✉ *Across from Escuela Chávez*).

EXPLORING

Termales del Bosque lets you soak those tired muscles, as you watch the birds, for a more reasonable price than most of the other hot springs in the region. ✉ *Hwy. 140, 7 km/4½ mi east of Ciudad Quesada* ☎ *2460–4740* ⊕ *www.termalesdelbosque.com* 💲 *Day pass $15* ⊙ *Daily 8AM–10PM.*

WHERE TO STAY

$ ⊞ **Laguna del Lagarto Lodge.** One of Costa Rica's smaller eco-lodges, ★ this hideaway in a 1,250-acre rain forest near the Nicaraguan border gives shelter to 380 bird species and counting. Rustic cabins come with single beds. Buffet-style meals are served on a patio with river and forest views. Rates include one guided walk on the 10 km (6 mi) of forest trails, a tour of the butterfly garden, and use of canoes. Recommended extras include horseback riding and a boat trip up to the border on the San Carlos River. (Bring your passport, since San Carlos River is officially Nicaraguan territory.) Ask about transfers available (at extra cost) from various points, including San José. The knowledge-able personnel here speak German, in addition to the requisite English and Spanish. **Pros:** small size; attentive service; great excursions. **Cons:** rough road to get here; spartan rooms. ⊠ *7 km/4 mi north of Boca Tapada, 135 km/78 mi northeast of Ciudad Quesada* ☎ *2289–8163* ⊕ *www.lagarto-lodge-costa-rica.com* ⇨ *20 rooms, 18 with bath* ☖ *In-room: no a/c, no phone, no TV. In-hotel: restaurant, bar, laundry service* ▤ *MC, V* ⏸ *EP.*

CAUTION

The ubiquitous OFFICIAL TOUR-IST INFORMATION signs around La Fortuna and Monteverde aren't "official" at all, but are merely storefront travel agencies and tour operators hoping to sell you tours.

LA FORTUNA

50 km/30 mi (45 mins) northwest of Ciudad Quesada, 75 km/45 mi (90 mins) north of San Ramón, 17 km/11 mi east of Arenal Volcano, 190 km/118 mi (3 hrs by car; 25 mins by plane) northwest of San José.

At the foot of massive Arenal Volcano, the small community of La Fortuna attracts visitors from around the world. Nobody comes to La Fortuna—an ever-expanding mass of hotels, tour operators, souvenir shops, and *sodas* (small, family-run restaurants)—to see the town itself. Instead, thousands of tourists flock here each year to use it as a hub for visiting the natural wonders that surround it. The volcano, as well as waterfalls, vast nature preserves, great rafting rivers, and an astonishing array of birds, are to be found within an hour or less of your hotel. La Fortuna is also the best place to arrange trips to the Caño Negro National Wildlife Refuge *(⇨ below)*.

After the 1968 eruption of Arenal Volcano, La Fortuna was transformed from a tiny, dusty farm town to one of Costa Rica's tourism powerhouses, where visitors converge to see the volcano in action. Volcano-viewing can be hit or miss, though, especially during the rainy season (May–November). One minute Arenal looms menacingly over the village; the next minute clouds shroud its cone. Early morning, especially in the dry season, is always the best time to catch a longer gaze.

NAVIGATING LA FORTUNA
Taxis in and around La Fortuna are relatively cheap, and will take you anywhere; a taxi to the Tabacón resort should run about $10. Get a cab at the stand on the east side of Parque Central.

GETTING HERE AND AROUND

Choose from two routes from San José: for a slightly longer, but better road, leave the Pan-American Highway at Naranjo, continuing north to Zarcero and Ciudad Quesada. Head northwest at Ciudad Quesada to La Fortuna; or for a curvier but shorter route, continue beyond Naranjo on the Pan-American Highway, turning north at San Ramón, arriving at La Fortuna about 90 minutes after the turnoff. Either route passes through a mountainous section that begins to fog over by afternoon. Get as early a start as possible. NatureAir and SANSA fly daily to La Fortuna (FTN); flights land at an airstrip at the hamlet of El Tanque,

7 km (4 mi) east of town. Van transport ($5 one-way) meets each flight to take you into La Fortuna.

Gray Line has daily shuttle bus service between San José, La Fortuna and Arenal ($35), and Monteverde ($35). Interbus also connects San José with La Fortuna, Ciudad Quesada, San Ramón, and Monteverde (all $39) daily, with connections from here to a few of the North Pacific beaches. Public buses depart five times daily from San José's Terminal Atlántico Norte. Travel time is four hours. Although billed as an express route, the bus makes many stops.

Desafío Adventures provides a fast, popular three-hour transfer between Monteverde and La Fortuna via taxi, boat, then another taxi, for $25 each way.

ESSENTIALS

Bank/ATM BAC San José (⊠ *75 m north of gas station*). **Banco de Costa Rica** (⊠ *Money exchange booth; across from south side of churc*). **Banco Nacional** (⊠ *Central Plaza* ☏ *2479–9355*).

Bus Contacts Gray Line Tourist Bus (☏ *2220–2126* ⊕ *www.graylinecostarica. com*). **Interbus** (☏ *2283–5573* ⊕ *www.interbusonline.com*).

Internet Expediciones Fortuna (⊠ *Across the street from Central Plaza* ☏ *2479–9104*).

Medical Clinic Seguro Social (⊠ *300 m east of Parque Central* ☏ *2479–9643*).

Pharmacy FarmaTodo (⊠ *50 m north of La Fortuna's gas station* ☏ *2479–8155*).

Post Office Correos (⊠ *Across from north side of church*).

Rental Cars Alamo (⊠ *100 m west of church, La Fortuna* ☏ *2479–9090* ⊕ *www.alamocostarica.com*). **Mapache** (⊠ *800 m west of church, La Fortuna* ☏ *2479–0010* ⊕ *www.mapache.com*). **Poás** (⊠ *25 m south of church, La Fortuna* ☏ *2479–8027* ⊕ *www.poasrentacar.com*).

Tour Information Desafío Adventures (⊠ *Behind church, La Fortuna* ☏ *2479–9464* ⊕ *www.desafiocostarica.com*).

EXPLORING

MAIN ATTRACTIONS

⟳ Getting to **Fortuna Waterfall** (*Cataratas de la Fortuna*) requires a strenu-

Fodor's Choice ous walk down ½ km (¼ mi) of precipitous steps, but it's worth the

★ effort. Allow 25 to 50 minutes to reach the falls. Swimming in the pool under the waterfall is usually safe. Wear sturdy shoes or water sandals with traction, and bring snacks and water. You can get to the trailhead from La Fortuna by walking or taking an inexpensive taxi ride. Arrang-ing a tour with an agency in La Fortuna is the easiest option. ⊠ *Yellow entrance sign off main road toward volcano 7 km/4 mi south of La Fortuna* ☎ *$6* ⊙ *Daily 8–4*.

Arenal Hanging Bridges is actually a series of trails and bridges that form a loop through the primary rain forest of a 250-acre private reserve, with great bird-watching and volcano-viewing. Fixed and hanging bridges allow you to see the forest at different levels. It's open rain

La Fortuna

TO
MONTEVERDE, NUEVO
ARENAL, TILARAN

Lake Arenal Dam

Lake
Arenal

VOLCÁN ARENAL
NATIONAL PARK

Volcán Arenal
(5,356 ft/1,633 meters)

Baldi
Termae

Volcán Chato
(3,608 ft/1,100 meters)

Cataratas de
La Fortuna

LA FORTUNA

Arenal
Bungee

Gas
Station

TO
SAN JOSÉ

Río Burío

KEY

① *Restaurants*

① *Hotels*

0   1/4 mi

0   1/4 km

Restaurants   ▶

Don Rufino **6**
La Choza de Laurel ...**2**
La Vaca Muca **1**
Las Brasitas **3**
Rancho La Cascada ...**4**
Soda La Parada **5**

Hotels   ▶

Arenal Country Inn **2**
Arenal Nayara **6**
Arenal Observatory
Lodge **11**
Cabinas

Los Guayabos **8**
Cabinas Oriuma **3**
Hotel Bosques
de Chachagua **1**
Hotel San Bosco **4**
The Lost Iguana Resort ...**10**
Montaña de Fuego **7**

La Pradera **5**
Tabacón Grand Spa
& Thermal Resort **9**

"Our best day in Costa Rica—canyoneering and waterfall rappelling near the active Arenal Volcano." —Photo by sportster, Fodors.com member

or shine, and there are things to do in both climates. Shuttle service from La Fortuna can be arranged. ⊠ *Arenal Dam, 4 km/2½ mi west of Tabacón* ☎ *2479–9686 or 2290–0469* ⊕ *www.hangingbridges.com* ✉ *$22; natural history tour $34; bird tour $40, shuttle $12* ☉ *Daily 7–4:30; evening tour at 5:30.*

ALSO WORTH SEEING

The town's squat, pale, concrete **Church of San Juan Bosco**, unremarkable on its own, wins Costa Rica's most-photographed-house-of-worship award. The view of the church from across the central park, with the volcano in the background, makes a great photo of the sacred and the menacing. ⊠ *West side of Parque Central.*

OFF THE BEATEN PATH

In 1945 a farmer in the mountain hamlet of Venado fell in a hole, and thus discovered the **Venado Caverns** *(Cavernas de Venado)*. The limestone caves contain eight chambers extending about 2½ km (1½ mi). Sunset Tours *(⇨ Outdoor Activities, below)* runs trips. If you're nonclaustro-phobic, willing to get wet, and don't mind bats—think carefully—this could be the ticket for you. ⊠ *45 mins north of La Fortuna and 20 mins southeast of San Rafael* ☎ *2479–9415* ☉ *Daily 7–8* ✉ *$40.*

OUTDOOR ACTIVITY

Fodor's Choice
★

Desafío Adventures (⊠ *Behind church* ☎ *2479–9464* ⊕ *www.desafiocostarica. com*) can take you rafting, horseback riding, hiking, canyoning, and rap-pelling. **Jacamar Naturalist Tours** (⊠ *Across from Parque Central* ☎ *2479– 9767* ⊕ *www.arenaltours.com*) launches a variety of tours. **Sunset Tours** (⊠ *Across from south side of church* ☎ *2479–9800; 866/417-7352 in North America* ⊕ *www.sunsettourcr.com*) pioneered excursions to the

Caño Negro Wildlife Refuge and Venado Caverns and is one of the country's best tour operators.

The **Danaus Ecocenter** (*Ecocentro Danaus*), a small ecotourism project outside of town, exhibits 300 species of tropical plants, abundant animal life—including sloths and caimans—and butterfly and orchid gardens. It's also a great place to see Costa Rica's famed red poison dart frogs up close. A two-hour guided evening tour begins at 6 pm and should be reserved in advance. ✉ *4 km/2½ mi east of La Fortuna* ☎ *2479–7019* ⊕ *www.ecocentrodanaus.com* 🍴 *$6, evening tour $30* ⊙ *Mon.–Sat. 8–4, Sun. 9–3.*

BUNGEE JUMPING
You don't even need to leave town to plummet from a 39-meter (130-foot tower). **Arenal Bungee** (✉ *500 m east of church* ☎ *2479–7440* ⊕ *www. arenalbungee.com* ⊙ *Daily 9:30–8:30*), on the east edge of La Fortuna, offers a bungee jump (into a pool if you like) for $50. For another $50, the facility's Rocket Launcher catapults you into the air, with bungeelike recoils to follow. The Big Swing ($50), the third activity here, takes you on a 25-meter-high (85-foot-high), 180-degree arc through the air. You can mix and match activities, too, or do all three for $100. The site is open after dark, but remember that La Fortuna does not face the flow side of Arenal. Twilight is an especially beautiful time to ascend to the top of the tower to catch the sun setting behind the volcano.

CANOPY TOURS
Arenal Volcano Theme Park, a canopy tour–bridge walk complex near La Fortuna, is operated by the Sky Trek–Sky Walk folks in Monteverde. Alpine-style gondolas transport you to the site, from which you can descend via a zip-line canopy tour or hike through the cloud forest along a series of suspended bridges. ✉ *12 km/7 mi west of La Fortuna, El Castillo* ☎ *2479–9944* ⊕ *www.skyadventures.travel* 🍴 *$66, $55 tram only, shuttle $10* ⊙ *Daily 7–4.*

FISHING
Lake Arenal is enormous and stocked with game fish, including tilapia, *guapote* (Central American rainbow bass), and *machaca* (Central American shad). Most tour operators and hotels can set you up with guides. Rates begin at $150. **Jacamar Naturalist Tours** (⇨ *above*) has morning and afternoon sportfishing trips to Lake Arenal and Caño Negro Lagoon.

HORSEBACK RIDING
★ If you're interested in getting up to Monteverde from the Arenal–La Fortuna area without taking the grinding four-hour drive, there's an alternative: **Desafío Adventures** (✉ *Behind church* ☎ *2479–9464* ⊕ *www. desafiocostarica.com*) has a five-hour guided horseback trip ($85). The trip involves taxi or van service from La Fortuna to the southern shore of Lake Arenal, and from that trail's end you ride to Monteverde, circumventing poorly maintained trails. A boat ride across Lake Arenal is included. You leave La Fortuna at 8:30 AM and arrive in Monteverde around 2:30 PM. You can also take the trip in reverse. Desafío will provide a driver to transport your rental vehicle, but you must arrange to include that driver in your rental agreement. ■ TIP➔ Many other agencies,—many of them nothing more than a guy and a horse—lead riding tours between La

Fortuna and Monteverde, but along treacherous trails, and some riders have returned with stories of terrified horses barely able to navigate the way. Stick with Desafío.

The ride from La Fortuna to the Fortuna Waterfall is appropriate for both novice and experienced riders. **Chaves Horse Tours** (☎ 8354–9159 or 2479–9023) has guided horseback tours to the waterfall. **Desafío** (⇨ above) leads guided horseback tours to the falls.

RAFTING AND KAYAKING

Several La Fortuna operators offer Class III and IV white-water trips on the Río Toro. The narrow river requires the use of special, streamlined boats that seat just four and go very fast. The easier Balsa, Peñas Blancas, Arenal, and San Carlos rivers have Class II and III rapids and are close enough to town that they can be worked into half-day excursions. **Canoa Aventura** (☎ 2479–8200 ⊕ www.canoa-aventura.com) can design a canoeing trip with ample wildlife viewing on the Río Peñas Blancas and also has daylong canoe tours of the Caño Blanco Wildlife Refuge. Tours are appropriate for beginners, with a selection of easy floats if you're not feeling too adventurous, and instruction is provided, but the folks here can tailor excursions if you're more experienced.

★ **Desafío Adventures** (✉ Behind church ☎ 2479–9464 ⊕ www.desafiocostarica. com) pioneered rafting trips in this region, and has day trips on the Río Toro for experienced rafters ($85), half-day rafting and kayaking outings on the nearby Balsa river ($65) ideal for beginners, as well as a leisurely wildlife-viewing float on the Peñas Blancas ($45). **Ríos Tropicales** (✉ 1 km/ ½ mi west of La Fortuna ☎ 2479–0075 ⊕ www.flowtrips.com) does the standard trips on the Toro, Peñas Blancas, and Arenal rivers.

RAPPELLING

Rappel down four waterfalls and one rock wall ranging in height from 18 to 45 meters (60 to 150 feet) with **Pure Trek Canyoning** (☎ 2479–1313; 866/569–5723 in North America ⊕ www.puretrekcostarica.com). Two guides lead small groups—10 is the maximum size—on a four-hour tour ($90) that departs at 7 AM or noon to a private farm near La Fortuna, with plenty of wildlife-watching opportunities along the way. The excursion includes transportation, all gear, breakfast (for the morning tour), and a light lunch.

EN ROUTE Increased development on the highway between La Fortuna and the Tabacón resort has led to a noticeable increase in traffic. It is hardly the proverbial urban jungle, and it is one of the country's prettiest stretches of road, but you should drive with caution. Cars dart in and out of driveways. Visitors congregate along the side of the road (likely a sloth-spotting). Drivers gaze up at the volcano that looms over the highway. Keep your eyes on the road.

ADVENTURE ALTERNATIVE

If you're feeling more community-minded than adventurous, **Desafío Adventures** (✉ Behind church ☎ 2479–9464 ⊕ www. desafiocostarica.com) has a day-long tour (🍽 $75) that takes you to an area animal-rescue center, women's arts-and-crafts cooperative, organic medicinal-plant farm, and recycling center. Lunch is included.

WHERE TO EAT

$$
ECLECTIC

✕ **Don Rufino.** The town's most elegant-looking restaurant is really quite informal. The L-shaped bar fronting the main street has become a popular expat and tourist hangout and lends a relaxed air to the place. No need to dress up here: this is La Fortuna, after all. The friendly waitstaff might suggest tilapia in bacon-and-tomato sauce or spinach ricotta to the accompaniment of coconut rice. ⊠ *Across from gas station* ☎ *2479–9997* ⊕ *www.donrufino.com* ▭ *AE, D, DC, MC, V.*

$
COSTA RICAN

✕ **La Choza de Laurel.** Tantalizing rotisserie chicken, and pretty cloves of garlic and bunches of onions dangling from the roof draw in passersby to this old favorite, open-air Costa Rican–style restaurant a short walk from the center of town. The place opens early, perfect for a hearty breakfast on your way to the volcano. ⊠ *300 m northwest of church* ☎ *2479–7063* ⊕ *www.lachozadelaurel.com* ▭ *AE, D, DC, MC, V.*

$
COSTA RICAN

✕ **La Vaca Muca.** The food is good and the servings are generous at this small café just outside La Fortuna. The exterior is draped with foliage, and the interior has turquoise paneling, glass tables, and bamboo and candles aplenty. Go for the steak, or if you're in the mood for something more basic, try the casado heaped with chicken, beef, or fish; rice; beans; fried egg; fried plantain; and cabbage salad. Stroll through the small orchid and butterfly garden next door ($7) after you're through. ⊠ *2 km/1 mi west of La Fortuna* ☎ *2479–9186* ▭ *MC, V.*

$
COSTA RICAN

✕ **Las Brasitas.** Chicken turns over wood on a rotisserie in a brick oven at this pleasant restaurant on the road heading out of town toward the volcano. Try the succulent chicken when it ends up in the tasty fajitas or any of the other ample-size Mexican dishes. Service is good, and you have your choice of three open-air dining areas arranged around a garden. Two are secluded and intimate; the third is less so, being closer to the road. ⊠ *200 m west of church* ☎ *2479–9819* ⊕ *www.lasbrasitas.com* ▭ *AE, D, DC, MC, V.*

$
COSTA RICAN

✕ **Rancho la Cascada.** You can't miss its tall, palm-thatch roof in the center of town. The festive upstairs contains a bar, with large TV, neon signs, and flashing lights. Downstairs the spacious dining room—decorated with foreign flags—serves basic, midprice Costa Rican fare. Its location right in the center of town makes it a favorite for tour groups. ⊠ *Across from northeast corner of Parque Central* ☎ *2479–9145* ▭ *AE, D, DC, MC, V.*

¢
COSTA RICAN

✕ **Soda la Parada.** Here's a case study in what tourism does to a place: La Fortuna's only 24-hour eatery was once a hole-in-the-wall joint across from the bus stop. It has now expanded greatly and even has sit-down dining. It is still a convenient place to grab a quick and cheap meal, and to stock up on snacks for long bus rides. ⊠ *Across from Parque Central and regional bus stop* ☎ *2479–9547* ▭ *AE, MC, V.*

5

WHERE TO STAY

$$ ⊞ **Arenal Country Inn.** It doesn't quite approximate an English country inn, although it is charming. Each brightly furnished modern room has two queen-size beds and a private patio. The lush grounds have great views of the Arenal Volcano. A big breakfast is served in the restaurant, an open-air converted cattle corral. You can take lunch and dinner there as well. **Pros:** good value; friendly staff. **Cons:** several blocks from center of town; removed from sights. ⊠ *1 km/½ mi south of church of La Fortuna, south end of town* ☎ *2479–9670; 2283–0101 in San José* ⊕ *www.arenalcountryinn. com* ☞ *20 rooms* ⚬ *In-room: safe, refrigerator. In-hotel: restaurant, bar, pool, laundry service* ▤ *AE, DC, MC, V* ‖◎‖ *BP.*

RICE & BEANS

"More tico than gallo pinto" is an old saying here, but just how Costa Rican is the country's signature dish? Nicaraguans also claim it as their own, and the rivalry has led to five Guinness Book of World Records bids for the largest batch. Costa Rica captured the first title in 2003, only to have Nicaragua top it a mere 12 days later. Costa Rica recaptured the prize in 2005. After three years of grumbling, in 2008, Nicaragua snatched the title back with a 22,000-dish batch of rice and beans. Costa Rica more than doubled that amount at a March 2009 event with a whopping 50,000 servings. Nicaragua, it's your serve.

$$$ ⊞ **Arenal Nayara.** This upscale lodge has expansive grounds scattered with cabins, all strategically aligned to provide balcony views of the volcano. Each is decorated in bright tropical colors and comes with dark-wood furnishings, four-post canopy beds, plasma TVs, DVD players, whirlpool tubs, and two showers, one indoors and one outdoors. Those are amenities rarely seen up here, and rarely seen in Costa Rica at all, for that matter. All rooms here are non-smoking. **Nayara offers frequent Web-only promotions. Pros:** luxurious rooms; great volcano views; good restaurant. **Cons:** massive grounds navigable only by golf cart shuttles; can be difficult to find. ⊠ *5 km/3 mi west of La Fortuna* ☎ *2479–1600, 866/311–1197 in North America* ⊕ *www.arenalnayara.com* ☞ *24 rooms* ⚬ *In-room: safe, refrigerator, DVD. In-hotel: restaurant, room service, bar, tennis court, pool, spa, laundry service, Wi-Fi hotspot, no-smoking rooms* ▤ *AE, D, DC, MC, V* ‖◎‖ *EP.*

$–$$ ⊞ **Arenal Observatory Lodge.** You're as close as anyone should be to an active volcano at the end of the winding road leading to the lodge—a mere 1¾ km (1 mi) away. The isolated lodge was founded by Smithsonian researchers in 1987. It's fairly rustic, emphasizing that outdoor activities are what it's all about. Rooms are comfortable and simply furnished (comforters on beds are a cozy touch), and most have stellar views. Five of the rooms here are wheelchair accessible, as are a couple of miles of the property's trails. After a hike, take a dip in the infinity-edge pool or 12-person hot tub, which face tall pines on one side and the volcano on the other. The dining room, which serves tasty and hearty food, has great views of the volcano and lake. **Pros:** best volcano views; secluded location; numerous activities. **Cons:** rough road to get here; isolated location. ⊠ *3 km/2 mi east of dam on Laguna*

A leisurely stroll across a suspension bridge in Monteverde.

de Arenal; from La Fortuna, drive to Tabacón resort and continue 4 km/2½ mi past resort to turnoff at base of volcano; turn and continue for 9 km/5½ mi ☎ *2479–1070; 2290–7011 in San José* ⊕ *www.arenalobservatorylodge.com* ⤵ *43 rooms, 38 with bath; 2 suites* ⚒ *In-room: no a/c, no phone, safe, no TV. In-hotel: restaurant, bar, pool, laundry service* ▭ *AE, D, DC, MC, V* ⬦ *BP.*

$ 🏠 **Cabinas Los Guayabos.** A great budget alternative to the more expensive lodgings lining the road to the volcano is this group of basic but spotlessly clean cabins managed by a friendly family. The units have all the standard budget-lodging furnishings, but each comes with its own porch facing Arenal—ideal for viewing the evening spectacle. **Pros:** good budget value; friendly owners; great volcano views. **Cons:** rustic rooms; best to have car to stay here. ⊠ *9 km/5½ mi west of La Fortuna* ☎ *2479–1444* ⊕ *www.hotellosguayabos.com* ⤵ *8 cabins* ⚒ *In-room: no phone, refrigerator* ▭ *V* ⬦ *EP.*

¢   🏠 **Cabinas Oriuma.** Right in the center of town, Oriuma is a popular choice for budget travelers and tour groups. The modern rooms are sparkling clean. The second-floor balcony is a pleasant spot to relax and read, watch the happenings in the Parque Central across the street, or plan your next adventure. **Pros:** good budget value; close to center of town. **Cons:** some rooms get street noise; boxy design. ⊠ *15 m north of Parque Central* ☎ *2479–9111* ✉ *oriuma@ice.co.cr* ⤵ *24 rooms* ⚒ *In-room: no a/c (some), no phone, safe* ▭ *MC, V* ⬦ *EP.*

$$ 🏠 **Hotel Bosques de Chachagua.** At this working ranch, intersected by a brook, you can see *caballeros* (cowboys) at work, take a horseback ride into the rain forest, and look for toucans from the open-air restaurant, which serves local meat and dairy products. Each cabina (cottage) has

a pair of double beds and a deck with a picnic table. Large, reflective windows enclosing each cabina's shower serve a marvelous purpose: birds gather outside your window to watch their own reflections while you bathe and watch them. The lodge is 3 km (2 mi) up a rough track—4WD is a must in rainy season—on the road headed south from La Fortuna to La Tigra. **Pros:** secluded location; many activities. **Cons:** rustic rooms; far from sights. ⊠ *12 km/7 mi south of La Fortuna* ☎ *2468–1011* ⊕ *www.chachaguarainforesthotel.com* ⏍ *9 rooms, 22 cabinas* △ *In-room: no a/c, no phone, no TV. In-hotel: restaurant, bar, pool* ☰ *AE, D, DC, MC, V* ⫯◉⫯*BP.*

$$ ⫯⫯ **Hotel San Bosco.** Covered in blue-tile mosaics, this two-story hotel is certainly the most attractive and comfortable in the main part of town. Two kitchen-equipped cabinas (which sleep 8 or 14 people) are a good deal for families. The spotlessly clean, white rooms have polished wood furniture and firm beds and are linked by a long veranda lined with benches and potted plants. **Pros:** good value; close to center of town. **Cons:** some rooms get street noise; boxy design. ⊠ *220 m north of La Fortuna's gas station* ☎ *2479–9050, 800/393–0902 in North America* ⊕ *www.hotelsanboscocr.com* ⏍ *34 rooms* △ *In-room: no phone, refrigerator (some), Wi-Fi. In-hotel: pool, Internet terminal* ☰ *AE, D, DC, MC, V* ⫯◉⫯*BP.*

$$ ⫯⫯ **La Pradera.** "The Prairie" is a simple roadside hotel with comfortable guest rooms that have high ceilings, spacious bathrooms, and verandas. Two rooms have whirlpool tubs. Beef eaters should try the thatch-roof restaurant next door. The steak with jalapeño sauce is a fine, spicy dish. **Pros:** good value; good restaurant. **Cons:** spartan rooms; lackadaisical staff. ⊠ *2 km/1 mi west of La Fortuna* ☎ *2479–9597* ⊕ *www.lapraderadelarenal.com* ⏍ *28 rooms* △ *In-room: no phone, refrigerator (some), Wi-Fi. In-hotel: restaurant, bar, pool, laundry service* ☰ *MC, V* ⫯◉⫯*BP.*

$$$–$$$$ ⫯⫯ **The Lost Iguana Resort.** Despite its relative isolation—you're several kilometers beyond Tabacón—the Lost Iguana hums with activity, and is a favorite among Fodors.com posters. Buildings here scale a hillside a short drive up a rugged road above the Arenal Dam. Each unit comes with a huge picture window that leads out onto an individual balcony with stupendous volcano views. Rooms are decorated with locally made art and bamboo-frame beds. Suites come with vaulted ceilings, private garden showers, and private whirlpools. A few cottages tuck away on the grounds and make ideal getaways for families. The location makes this a good bet if you have your own vehicle, but taxis can ferry you to and from area attractions, too. **Pros:** secluded location; great volcano views; many activities. **Cons:** removed from sights; rough final stretch of road to get here. ⊠ *31 km/19 mi west of La Fortuna on highway toward Nuevo Arenal* ☎ *2479–1555; 2267–6148 in San José* ⊕ *www.lostiguanaresort.com* ⏍ *42 rooms* △ *In-room: no a/c (some) safe (some), kitchen (some), refrigerator (some), Wi-Fi. In-hotel: restaurant, room service, bar, pools, spa, laundry service, no kids under 6 (except in houses)* ☰ *AE, MC, V* ⫯◉⫯*EP.*

$$–$$$ ⫯⫯ **Montaña de Fuego.** On a manicured grassy roadside knoll, this highly
Fodor's Choice ★ recommended collection of cabins affords utterly spectacular views of Arenal Volcano. (If you don't stay here, Montaña de Fuego's Acuarela

Restaurant dishes up tasty Costa Rican cuisine and throws in the same stupendous views.) The spacious, well-made hardwood structures have large porches, and rooms have rustic decor. The friendly management can arrange tours of the area. ■TIP→ Montaña de Fuego offers periodic Internet-only discounts when you book via its Web site. **Pros:** great volcano views; many activities for guests only; good restaurant. **Cons:** some cabins face highway noise; sometimes difficult to find space. ⊠ *8 km/5 mi west of La Fortun* ☎ *2479–1220; 877/383–4612 in North America* ⊕ *www.montanafuegohotel.com* ➚ *66 cabinas* ⚴ *In-room: safe (some), kitchen (some), refrigerator. In-hotel: restaurant, bars, pools, spa, laundry service, Internet terminal, Wi-Fi hotspot* ☰ *AE, DC, MC, V* ⦿ *BP.*

$$$–$$$$ ⚏ **Tabacón Grand Spa & Thermal Resort.** Without question, Tabacón, with
★ its impeccably landscaped gardens and hot-spring rivers at the base of Arenal Volcano, is one of Central America's most famous and compelling resorts, and a 2008 remodeling of all units here cemented that status. The hot springs and small but lovely spa customarily draw visitors inland from the ocean with no regrets. All rooms have tile floors, a terrace or patio, and big bathrooms. Some have volcano views; others overlook the manicured gardens. The suites are some of the country's finest lodgings, with tile floors, plants, beautiful mahogany armoires and beds, and two-person whirlpool baths. The hotel's intimacy is compromised by its scale and its popularity with day-trippers—a reservations system for day passes has improved that situation greatly—but it has some private areas for overnight guests only, including a dining room and pool. All rooms here are nonsmoking, although smoking is permitted in public areas. A two-night minimum stay is required. ■TIP→ Tabacón offers frequent Internet-only discounts if you book directly through its Web site. **Pros:** luxurious hot springs; great volcano views; good restaurant. **Cons:** crowded with tour groups; chain-hotel design; music sometimes too loud. ⊠ *13 km/8 mi northwest of La Fortuna on highway toward Nuevo Arenal* ☎ *2460–2020; 2519–1900 in San José; 877/277–8291 in North America* ⊕ *www.tabacon.com* ➚ *114 rooms, 11 suites* ⚴ *In-room: safe, refrigerator, DVD, Internet. In-hotel: 2 restaurants, room service, bars, pools, gym, spa, Wi-Fi hotspot, no-smoking rooms* ☰ *AE, D, DC, MC, V* ⦿ *BP.*

NIGHTLIFE

People in La Fortuna tend to turn in early, though there are a few clubs and discos for night owls. **Volcán Look Disco** (⊠ *5 km/3 mi west of La Fortuna* ☎ *2479–9616*), which bills itself as the largest Costa Rican disco outside San José, erupts with dancing and music on weekends. Pizzeria **Vagabundo** (⊠ *3 km/2 mi west of La Fortuna* ☎ *2479–9565*) turns into a lively bar in the evening, with foosball and billiards in the back room.

VOLCÁN ARENAL NATIONAL PARK

Shimmering Lake Arenal, all 125 square km (48 square mi) of it, lies between green hills and a rumbling volcano. It's Costa Rica's largest inland body of water. Many visitors are surprised to learn it's a man-made lake, created in 1973 when a giant dam was built. A natural depression was flooded, and a 32-km-long by 14.4-km-wide

(20-mi-long by 9-mi-wide) lake was born. The almost constant winds from the Caribbean make this area a windsurfing mecca. Outfitters in La Fortuna, Nuevo Arenal, and Tilarán run fishing, windsurfing, and kitesurfing trips on the lake. Desafío, an operator based in La Fortuna and Monteverde, has a half-day horseback trip between the two towns, with great views of the lake *(⇨ see Exploring in La Fortuna, above)*.

> **IN MEMORIAM**
>
> Those yellow hearts with halos painted on the pavement mark spots where people have died in car accidents or vehicles have struck and killed pedestrians. An alarming number of them dot streets and roads around the country. Drive (and walk) with utmost caution.

NUEVO ARENAL

40 km/25 mi (1 hr) west of La Fortuna.

Much of the original town of Arenal, at one of the lowest points near Lake Arenal, was destroyed by the volcano's 1968 eruption, and the rest was destroyed in 1973, when Lake Arenal flooded the region. The *nuevo* (new) town was created about 30 km (19 mi) away from the site of the old. It doesn't have much to interest tourists, but is about halfway between La Fortuna and Tilarán, making it a good stop for a break, and an even better base with a couple of truly lovely lodgings nearby.

GETTING HERE AND AROUND

The route from La Fortuna to Nuevo Arenal around the north shore of Lake Arenal is in better shape than it has been in years, with only a couple of short atrocious sections to negotiate. Expect smooth sailing west of the Tabacón resort as far as the Arenal Dam, beyond which you should stick to daylight travel only. Watch out for the raccoonlike coatimundis (*pizotes* in Spanish) that scurry along the road. Longtime human feeding has diminished their ability to search for food on their own, and the cookies and potato chips they frequently get make matters worse. Public buses run twice daily from La Fortuna to Nuevo Arenal and beyond to Tilarán.

ESSENTIALS

Bank/ATM Banco Nacional (✉ West side of church ☎ 2694–4122).

Internet Tom's Pan (✉ 300 m south of gas station ☎ 2694–4547).

Post Office Correos (✉ Next to Guardia Rural).

WHERE TO STAY

$ 🏠 **Chalet Nicholas.** John and Cathy Nicholas (and their resident Great Danes) have converted their hillside home into a charming bed-and-breakfast with stunning views of the lake and volcano. The two rosewood rooms downstairs have tile floors. Up a spiral staircase lies the L-shaped, all-wood double loft with three beds and a back porch that overlooks the large garden. All rooms have volcano views. Birds abound: 100 species have been catalogued on the grounds. The entire property is nonsmoking. **Pros:** attentive owners; great breakfasts; good

Fodor's Choice ★

The perfect way to end the day: a nice soak in the hot springs in Arenal Volcano National Park.

value. **Cons:** best for dog lovers; need car to stay here. ✉ *3 km/2 mi west of Nuevo Arenal* 🖶🖶 *2694–4041* ⊕ *www.chaletnicholas.com* ⤸ *3 rooms* ⚙ *In-room: no a/c, no phone, no TV. In-hotel: restaurant, no-smoking rooms* ▭ *No credit cards* ⅋ *BP.*

$$$–$$$$ ⊡ **La Mansión Inn Arenal.** Halfway between La Fortuna and Nuevo Arenal, the elegant La Mansión Inn sits at the point where the volcano begins to disappear from sight, but the lake views (and the sunsets) remain as spectacular as ever. Individual cottages scatter around the 25-acre grounds on Arenal's north shore. Brightly colored wrought-iron furnishings decorate every split-level unit. As befits such a secluded place, bird-watching opportunities abound. ▪ **TIP→** The hotel offers frequent Web-only packages. **Pros:** luxurious furnishings; stupendous lake views. **Cons:** far from sights; need car to stay here. ✉ *Road between Nuevo Arenal and La Fortuna* 🖶 *2692–8018; 877/660–3830 in North America* ⊕ *www.lamansionarenal.com* ⤸ *18 cottages, 3 suites* ⚙ *In-room: no a/c (some), no phone, refrigerator, DVD (some), no TV (some). In-hotel: restaurant, bar, pools, spa, laundry service, Wi-Fi hotspot* ▭ *AE, D, DC, MC, V* ⅋ *BP.*

$$ ⊡ **Villa Decary.** There's everything to recommend at this hillside lodging
Fodor's Choice   overlooking Lake Arenal, but it all goes back to owners Jeff and Bill and
★   their attentive service. Rooms have large picture windows and private balconies—great places to take in the ample bird-watching opportunities—and bright yellow-and-blue spreads and drapes. Higher up the hill, spacious bungalows afford an even better view. The hotel accepts payment in American Express traveler's checks, too. All rooms here are nonsmoking. **Pros:** attentive owners; great breakfasts; good value. **Cons:** need car to stay here. ✉ *2 km/1 mi east of Nuevo Arenal* 🖶 *2694–4330,*

800/556–0505 in North America ⊕ www.villadecary.com ⟋ 5 rooms,
3 bungalows ⟋ In-room: no a/c, no phone, no TV. In-hotel: restaurant,
Wi-Fi hotspot, no-smoking rooms ☰ MC, V ❙◎❙ BP.

TILARÁN

Heading west around Laguna de Arenal, you pass a couple of small villages and arrive at the quiet whitewashed town of Tilarán, on the southwest side of the lake. A windmill farm in the hills high above the town attests to its being the windiest place in the country, and it's used as a base by bronzed windsurfers. For those days when you get "skunked" (the wind fails to blow), horseback riding and mountain biking can keep you busy. A lakeside stroll is a pleasant way to while away a few hours.

GETTING HERE AND AROUND

22 km/14 mi (45 mins) southwest of Nuevo Arenal, 62 km/38 mi
(1½ hrs) west of La Fortuna.

The road from La Fortuna via Nuevo Arenal is in reasonable shape these days, with a few short potholed stretches. Give yourself sufficient time—say, two hours—for the trip, and make the trip during daylight hours. Public buses travel to and from La Fortuna twice daily, and from a small terminal at Calle 20 and Avenida 3 in San José five times daily.

ESSENTIALS

Bank/ATM Banco Nacional (✉ *Central Plaza* ☎ 2695–5610). **CooTilarán**
(✉ *150 m north of cathedral* ☎ 2695–6155).

Hospital Clínica Tilarán (✉ *200 m west of Banco Nacional* ☎ 2695–5093).

Post Office Correos (✉ *115 m west of municipal stadium*).

OUTDOOR ACTIVITIES

WINDSURFING AND KITESURFING

The best selection of wind- and kitesurfing equipment for rent or purchase can be found at **Tilawa Wind Surf** (✉ *Hotel Tilawa 8 km/5 mi north of Tilarán* ☎ *2695–5050* ⊕ *www.windsurfcostarica.com*). It's the only outfitter here open year-round. Beginner's lessons start at $100.

Rent wind- and kitesurfing equipment at **Tico Wind** (✉ *30 km/18 mi west of Nuevo Arenal* ☎ *2692–2002* ⊕ *www.ticowind.com*) during the December to April season. It offers beginner's lessons starting at $50, or enroll in a multiday course for $200.

WHERE TO STAY

$–$$ **Hotel Tilawa.** This Costa Rican homage to the Palace of Knossos on Crete has neoclassical murals, columns, and plant-draped arches that somehow don't seem dramatically out of place. The large rooms have two queen-size beds with Guatemalan bedspreads and natural wood ceilings; the bathrooms are especially spacious. Sailing tours in a 39-foot catamaran, the windsurfing and kitesurfing school and shop, and the skateboarding park make this a practical place to base yourself if you want an active vacation. Packages include the use of windsurfing gear. The open-air patio restaurant dishes up steaks and seafood.

Pros: many activities; stupendous lake views. Cons: isolated location; lackluster staff. ✉ *8 km/5 mi north of Tilarán* ☎ *2695–5050* ⊕ *www. hotel-tilawa.com Tilarán* ⇌ *20 rooms* ⚲ *In-room: no a/c, no TV. In-hotel: restaurant, bar, pool, spa, water sports, bicycles, laundry service* ⊟ *MC, V* ⏏*EP.*

MONTEVERDE CLOUD FOREST AREA

Monteverde is a rain forest, but you won't be in the tropics, rather in the cool, gray, misty world of the cloud forest. Almost 900 species of epiphytes, including 450 orchids, are found here; most tree trunks are covered with mosses, bromeliads, ferns, and other plants. Monteverde spans the Continental Divide, extending from about 1,500 meters (4,920 feet) on the Pacific slope and 1,350 meters (4,430 feet) on the Atlantic slope up to the highest peaks of the Tilarán Mountains at around 1,850 meters (6,070 feet).

MONTEVERDE CLOUD FOREST BIOLOGICAL RESERVE

★ *10 km/6 mi (30 mins) south of Santa Elena, 35 km/22 mi (2 hrs) southeast of Tilarán, 167 km/104*

Close to several fine hotels, the private Reserva Biológica Bosque Nuboso Monteverde is one of Costa Rica's best-kept reserves, with well-marked trails, lush vegetation, and a cool, damp climate. The collision of moist winds with the Continental Divide here creates a constant mist whose particles provide nutrients for plants growing at the upper layers of the forest. Giant trees are enshrouded in a cascade of orchids, bromeliads, mosses, and ferns, and in those patches where sunlight penetrates, brilliantly colored flowers flourish. The sheer size of everything, especially the leaves of the trees, is striking. No less astounding is the variety: 2,500 plant species, 400 species of birds, 500 types of butterflies, and more than 100 different mammals have so far been catalogued at Monteverde. A damp and exotic mixture of shades, smells, and sounds, the cloud forest is also famous for its population of resplendent quetzals, which can be spotted feeding on the *aguacatillo* (similar to avocado) trees; best viewing times are early mornings from January until September, and especially during the mating season of April and May. Other forest-dwelling inhabitants include hummingbirds and multicolor frogs.

For those who don't have a lucky eye, a short-stay aquarium is in the field station; captive amphibians stay here just a week before being released back into the wild. Although the reserve limits visitors to 160 people at a time, Monteverde is one of the country's most popular destinations. We do hear complaints (and agree with them) that the reserve gets too crowded with visitors at times. As they say, the early bird catches the worm, and the early visitor has the best chance at spotting wildlife. Allow a generous slice of time for leisurely hiking to see the forest's flora and fauna; longer hikes are made possible by some strategically placed overnight refuges along the way. At the reserve entrance you can buy self-guide pamphlets and rent rubber boots; a

Monteverde Cloud Forest Area

map is provided when you pay the entrance fee. You can navigate the reserve on your own, but a guided tour (7:30 and 11:30 AM and 1 PM) is invaluable for getting the most out of your visit. There's also another option: take advantage of their two-hour guided night tours starting each evening at 7:15 (reservations required), and the reserve provides transport from area hotels for an extra $3. ✉ *10 km/6 mi south of Santa Elena* ☎ *2645–5122* ⊕ *www.cct.or.cr* 🎫 *$17 ($9 for students with International Student Identity Card) plus $17 with guide services; $17 night tour* ☽ *Daily 7–4.*

DID YOU KNOW?

Monteverde's Quakers, or more officially, the Society of Friends, no longer constitute the majority here these days, but their imprint on the community remains strong. (Don't expect to see anyone dressed like the man on the Quaker Oats box.) The Friends' meetinghouse, just south of the Cheese Factory on the road to the reserve, welcomes visitors at meetings of worship, 10:30 AM Sunday and 9 AM Wednesday. Most of the time is spent in quiet reflection.

What Is a Cloud Forest?

Cloud forests are a type of rain forest, but are very different from the hot, humid lowland forests with which most people are familiar. First of all, they're cooler. Temperatures in Monteverde Cloud Forest, for example, are in the 18°C (65°F) range year-round, and feel colder because of the near-constant cool rain. Cloud forests—also known as montane forests—occur at elevations of around 1,950 to 3,450 meters (6,500 to 11,500 feet). At this altitude, clouds accumulate around mountains and volcanoes, providing regular precipitation as well as shade, which in turn slows evaporation. Moisture is deposited directly onto vegetation, keeping it lush and green.

The trees here, on top of high ridges and near the summits of volcanoes, are transformed by strong, steady winds that sometimes topple them and regularly break off branches. The resulting collection of small, twisted trees and bushes is known as an elfin forest. The conditions in cloud forests create unique habitats that shelter an unusually high proportion of rare species, making conservation vital. Monteverde is Costa Rica's most touristed cloud forest, but not its only one. Other cloud forests are in nearby Santa Elena Reserve, the Los Angeles Cloud Forest Reserve near San Ramón (⇨ *above*), and around San Gerardo de Dota (⇨ *Chapter 6*).

GETTING HERE AND AROUND

Buses from San José leave twice daily from the Terminal Atlántico Norte (⊠ C. 12 at Avda. 9), at 6:30 AM and 2:30 PM, stopping in the center of Santa Elena and at various locations on the way up the mountain as far as the Cheese Factory. Buses from Santa Elena leave for San José at 6:30 AM and 2:30 PM daily. Taxis from Santa Elena are $7. Buses from Tilarán to Santa Elena leave once a day, at 12:30 PM. The roads to the area are some of the worst in the country.

MONTEVERDE AND SANTA ELENA

Monteverde is 167 km/104 mi (5 hrs) northwest of San José. Santa Elena is 6 km/4 mi (30 mins) north of Monteverde and 35 km/22 mi (2 hrs) southeast of Tilarán.

The area's first residents were a handful of Costa Rican families fleeing the rough-and-ready life of nearby gold-mining fields during the 1940s. They were joined in the early 1950s by Quakers, conscientious objectors from Alabama fleeing conscription into the Korean War. A number of things drew them to Costa Rica: just a few years earlier it had abolished its military, and the Monteverde area offered good grazing. But it was the cloud forest that lay above their dairy farms that soon attracted the attention of ecologists. Educators and artisans followed, giving Monteverde and its "metropolis," the village of Santa Elena, a mystique all their own. In any case, Monteverde looks quite a bit different than it did when the first wave of Quakers arrived. New hotels have sprouted up everywhere, traffic grips the center of town, and a small shopping mall has gone up. A glut of rented all-terrain vehicles contributes to the increasing din that disrupts Monteverde's legendary peace and quiet. Some define this as progress. Others lament the gradual chipping-away at what makes one of Costa Rica's most special areas so, well, special. Locals have taken to posting signs that exclaim "¡PAR- QUEO, NO! ¡PARQUE SÍ!" ("PARKING LOT, NO! PARK, YES!"). We side with them. You can still get away from it all up here, but you'll have to work harder at it than you used to. In any case, you'll not lack for things to do if seeing nature is a primary reason for your visit.

Note that a casual reference to "Monteverde" generally refers to this entire area, but officially the term applies only to the original Quaker settlement, which is by the dairy-processing plant just down the mountain from the reserve entrance. If you follow road signs exclusively, you'll end up a bit outside the town of Santa Elena.

> **CAUTION**
>
> The San José–Monteverde public bus route is notorious for theft; watch your bags, and never let your passport and money out of your sight—or off your person.
>
> Never take advice from the street "guides" who meet incoming buses in Monteverde and La Fortuna. They claim to want to help you find accommodations and tours, when in reality they receive kickbacks for sending tourists to less-than-desirable hotels or to unqualified "tour guides."

The only way to see the area's reserves, including the Monteverde Cloud Forest, is to hike them (⇨ *Hiking in Outdoor Activities, below*).

NAVIGATING MONTEVERDE AND SANTA ELENA There will be times you wish you had your own vehicle, but it's surprisingly easy to get around the Monteverde area without a car. Given the state of the roads, you'll be happy to let someone else do the driving. However, if you do arrive by rental car, the road up the mountain from Santa Elena is paved as far as the gas station near the entrance to the Hotel Belmar. Taxis are plentiful; it's easy to call one from your hotel, and restaurants are happy to summon a cab to take you back to your hotel after dinner. Taxis also congregate in front of the church on the main street in Santa Elena. Many tour companies will pick you up from your hotel and bring you back at the end of the day, either free or for a small fee.

GETTING HERE AND AROUND

Getting here means negotiating some of the country's legendarily rough roads, but don't let that deter you from a visit. Years of promises to pave the way up here have collided with politics and scarce funds, but many residents remain just as happy to keep Monteverde out of the reach of tour buses and day-trippers. ("Do we really want this to be a shore excursion for cruise ships?" some residents ask.) Your own vehicle gives you the greatest flexibility, but a burgeoning number of shuttle-van services connect Monteverde with San José and other tourist destinations throughout the country.

If your bones can take it, a very rough track leads from Tilarán via Cabeceras to Santa Elena, near the Monteverde Cloud Forest Biological Reserve, doing away with the need to cut across to the Pan-American Highway. You need a 4WD vehicle, and you should inquire locally about the current condition of the road. The views of Nicoya Peninsula,

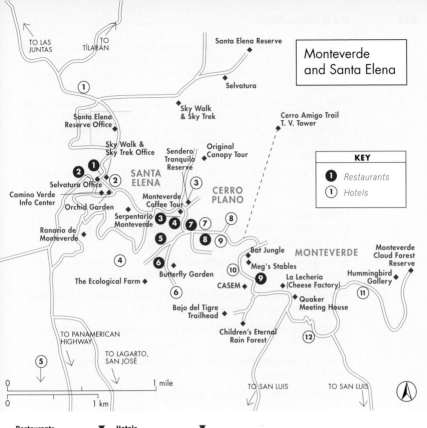

Monteverde
and Santa Elena

TO LAS JUNTAS
TO TÍLARÁN

Santa Elena Reserve

Selvatura

KEY

1 Restaurants
① Hotels

Sky Walk & Sky Trek

Cerro Amigo Trail
T. V. Tower

Santa Elena
Reserve Office

Sky Walk &
Sky Trek Office

Sendero
Tranquilo
Reserve

Original
Canopy Tour

SANTA
ELENA

Selvatura Office

CERRO
PLANO

Camino Verde
Info Center

Monteverde
Coffee Tour

Orchid Garden

Serpentario
Monteverde

Ranario de
Monteverde

Bat Jungle

MONTEVERDE

Monteverde
Cloud Forest
Reserve

Meg's Stables

The Ecological Farm

Butterfly Garden

La Lechería
(Cheese Factory)

Hummingbird
Gallery

CASEM

Bajo del Tigre
Trailhead

Quaker
Meeting House

TO PANAMERICAN
HIGHWAY

TO LAGARTO,
SAN JOSÉ

Children's Eternal
Rain Forest

0   1 mile
0   1 km

TO SAN LUIS   TO SAN LUIS

Restaurants ▼	Hotels ▼
Cafe Flor de Vida 4	Arco Iris Lodge 2
Chimera 8	El Bosque Lodge 10
De Lucía 5	El Establo Mountain Hotel 7
El Márquez 1	Fonda Vela 12
Morphos 7	Hotel Belmar 8
Pizzeria de Johnny 3	Hotel El Sapo Dorado 3
Sofía 6	Hotel Montaña Monteverde 9
Stella's Bakery 7	Montverde Inn 6
Tree House 2	Monteverde Lodge 4
	El Sol 5
	Swiss Hotel Miramontes 1
	Trapp Family Lodge 11

Lake Arenal, and Arenal Volcano reward those willing to bump around a bit. Note, too, that you don't really save much time—on a good day it takes about 2½ hours as opposed to the 3 required via Cañas and Río Lagarto on the highway.

Gray Line has daily shuttle bus service between San José, La Fortuna and Arenal ($27), and Monteverde ($38). Interbus also connects San José with La Fortuna, Ciudad Quesada, San Ramón, and Monteverde (all $29) daily, with connections from here to a few of the North Pacific beaches.

Desafío Adventures provides a fast, popular three-hour transfer between Monteverde and La Fortuna. The taxi-boat-taxi service costs $25 one-way.

ESSENTIALS

Bank/ATM Banco Nacional (⊠ *50 m north and 50 m west of bus station, Santa Elena* ☎ *2645–5027*).

Bus Information Gray Line Tourist Bus (☎ *2220–2126* ⊕ *www.graylinecostarica.com*). **Interbus** (☎ *2283–5573* ⊕ *www.interbusonline.com*).

Internet Historias Internet Café (⊠ *Road to Jardín de Mariposas, 75 m down from Pizzería de Johnny, Cerro Plano* ☎ *2645–6914*).

Medical Clinic Seguro Social (⊠ *150 m south of soccer field, Santa Elena* ☎ *2645–5076*).

Pharmacy Farmacia Vitosi (⊠ *Across from Super Compro supermarket, Santa Elena* ☎ *2645–5004*).

Post Office Correos (⊠ *Center of Santa Elena*).

Rental Cars Hertz (⊠ *Cerro Plano, Monteverde* ☎ *2645–6555* ⊕ *www.hertz.com*).

Tourist Information Centro de Visitantes Monteverde (⊠ *Across from Super Compro supermarket, Santa Elena* ☎ *2645–6565*). **Desafío Adventures** (⊠ *Across from Super Compro supermarket* ☎ *2645–5874* ⊕ *www.monteverdetours.com*).

OUTDOOR ACTIVITIES

ZIP-LINE TOURS

Fodor'sChoice ★ **Selvatura**, a cloud forest park outside of Monteverde Reserve, has the only zip-line tour built entirely inside the cloud forest. It has 15 lines and 18 platforms. Mix and match packages to include the complex's hanging bridges, hummingbird and butterfly gardens, and reptile exhibition. *(See more on Selvatura, below.)* ⊠ *Office across from church, Santa Elena* ☎ *2645–5929* ⊕ *www.selvatura.com* ✉ *$45.*

Sky Trek has 11 cables that are longer than those of the Original Canopy Tour—the longest more than 750 meters (2,500 feet). The zip lines here extend between towers above the canopy, rather than between trees, and you'll more likely notice the effects of the wind on this one. ⊠ *Office across from Banco Nacional, Santa Elena* ☎ *2645–5238* ⊕ *www.skyadventures.travel* ✉ *$60, shuttle $1.*

Continued on page 228

"This is our 5 year old on his first zipline through the rainforest of Manuel Antonio."
—Jill Chapple, Fodors.com member

CANOPY TOURS

Costa Rica invented the concept of the canopy tour, and the idea has spread across the globe. Zip lining through the treetops is a once-in-a-lifetime experience, and exploring the jungle canopy is the best way to see the most eye-catching animals.

A canopy tour is an umbrella term describing excursions that take you to the jungle's ceiling. The experience is distinctly Costa Rican and is one of the country's signature activities for visitors. There are two types of tour: one gives you a chance to see animals (from bridges and platforms), and the other lets you swing through the trees like them (on zip lines). We know of around 80 tours nationwide but recommend only about a third of that number. You'll find tour information in every chapter of this book, even in San José.

By Jeffrey Van Fleet

WHAT EXACTLY IS A CANOPY TOUR?

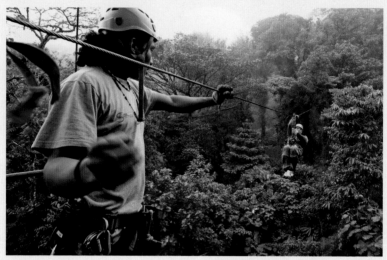

Canopy cable ride at Monteverde cloud forest

WHAT TO EXPECT

Plan on a half-day for your canopy tour, including transportation to and from your hotel, and a safety briefing for zip line excursions. Most zipline tours begin at fixed times and reservations are always required, or at least advised. Hanging-bridges tours are far more leisurely and can be done at your own pace. The occasional mega-complex, such as Monteverde's Selvatura, offers both types of tours. For most, it's one or the other.

BRIDGES AND TRAMS

These are canopy tours in a literal sense, where you walk along suspension bridges, ride along in a tram, or are hoisted up to a platform to get a closer look at birds, monkeys, and sloths. They're also called hanging-bridges tours, sky walks, or platform tours. If seeing nature at a more leisurely pace is your goal, opt for these, especially the bridge excursions. They're peaceful and unobtrusive. Early mornings are

the best time for animal sightings—at 50–250 feet above ground, the views are stupendous—and the weather is usually better.

ZIP LINES

This type of tour is a fast-paced, thrilling experience. You're attached to a zip line with a safety harness, and then you "fly" at about 30 miles per hour from one tree platform to the next. (You may be anywhere from 60–300 feet above the forest floor.) Tree-to-tree zip lines date from the 19th century and have been a bona fide activity for visitors to Costa Rica since the mid-1990s when the first tour opened in Monteverde. When most people say "canopy tour" they're referring this type of excursion. These tours are tremendous fun, but don't plan on seeing the resplendent quetzal as you zip from platform to platform. (Your shouts of exhilaration will probably scare them all away.) An average fitness level—and above-average level of intrepidness—are all you need.

TOP CANOPY TOURS BY REGION

KEY

🪜 Bridge
🚠 Tram
🧗 Zip

TOUR OPERATOR	LOCATION	TYPE		
Arenal Rain Forest Reserve	Arenal	Zip	Bridge	Tram
Canopy Safari	Manuel Antonio	Zip	Bridge	
Canopy del Pacífico	Malpaís	Zip		
Cocozuma	Montezuma	Zip		
Crazy Monkey Canopy	Gandoco-Manzanillo	Zip		
Hacienda Poco Azul	La Virgen, Sarapiquí	Zip		
Hotel Villa Lapas	Tárcoles	Zip	Bridge	
Natural Wonders Tram	Monteverde			Tram
Original Canopy Tour	Atenas	Zip		
Original Canopy Tour	Drake Bay	Zip	Bridge	
Original Canopy Tour	Veragua, Limón	Zip		
Rain Forest Aerial Tram	Braulio Carrillo National Park			Tram
Rain Forest Aerial Tram	Jacó			Tram
Rincón de la Vieja Canopy	Rincón de la Vieja National Park	Zip		
Selvatura	Monteverde	Zip	Bridge	
Tití Canopy Tour	Manuel Antonio	Zip		
Urban Canopy	San José	Zip	Bridge	
Waterfall Canopy Tour	Jacó	Zip	Bridge	
Wing Nuts Canopy Tour	Sámara	Zip		
Witch's Rock Canopy Tour	Papagayo	Zip	Bridge	

SAFETY FIRST

(top left) Zip lining Aventuras del Sarapiqui. (bottom right) Brown-Throated Three-Toed Sloth. (right) Sky Tram, Rainforest Canopy Tour, Arenal

PLAYING IT SAFE

Flying through the air, while undeniably cool, is also inherently dangerous. Before you strap into a harness, be certain that the safety standards are first rate. There's virtually no government oversight of the activity in Costa Rica. Here is a list of questions you should ask before you book:

1. How long has the company been in business?

2. Are they insured?

3. Are cables, harnesses, and other equipment manufacturer-certified?

4. Is there a second safety line that connects you to the zip line in case the main pulley gives way?

5. What's the price? Plan on paying $50 to $80— a low price could indicate a second-rate operation.

6. Are participants clipped to the zip line while on the platform? (They should be.)

KEEP IN MIND

■ Listen closely to the guides' pre-tour safety briefing and obey their instructions.

■ Never argue with the guide when s/he is making a decision to preserve your safety.

■ Don't attempt to take photos in flight.

■ Gauge your abilities frankly. Remember, once you start, there's no turning back.

■ If anything seems "off" or makes you uncomfortable, walk away.

☺ The **Original Canopy Tour** near Santa Elena was the first zip-line tour in Costa Rica, with 10 platforms in the canopy, and lasting 2½ hours. You arrive at most of the platforms using a cable-and-harness traversing system and climb 12.5 meters (42 feet) inside a strangler fig tree to reach one. ⊠ *Cerro Plano* ☎ *2291– 4465 in San José for reservations* ⊕ *www.canopytour.com* ☜ *$45.*

> **I LOVE A PARADE**
>
> Tread carefully when you see a tiny green parade on the ground before you. It's a troop of leaf-cutter ants carrying compost material to an underground nest.

HANGING BRIDGES AND TRAMS

☺ **Natural Wonders Tram** is an hour-long ride through the rain forest canopy in a two-person carriage on an elevated track. You control the speed of your carriage. Alternatively, a 1½-km (1-mi) walk gives you a ground-level perspective. The site opens for night visits ($25) with advance reservations. ⊠ *Off main road between Santa Elena and Monteverde, on turnoff to Jardín de Mariposas* ☎ *2645–5960* ⊕ *www.telefericomonteverde.com* ☜ *$20* ☾ *Daily 8–5.*

☺ **Tree Top Walkways**, inside of Selvatura, takes you to heights ranging from
★ 50 meters (150 feet) up to 170 meters (510 feet) on a 3-km (2-mi) walk. These are some of the longest and strongest bridges in the country and run through the same canopy terrain as the zip-line tour. ⊠ *Office across from church, Santa Elena* ☎ *2645–5929* ⊕ *www.selvatura.com* ☜ *$25.*

☺ **Sky Walk** allows you to walk along five hanging bridges, at heights of up to 41 meters (138 feet), connected from tree to tree. Imposing towers, used as support, mar the landscape somewhat. Reservations are required for guided tours. A tram, similar to that found at the Arenal Rain Forest reserve, is under construction at this writing. ⊠ *Across from Banco Nacional, Santa Elena* ☎ *2645–5238* ⊕ *www.skyadventures. travel* ☜ *$30* ☾ *Daily 7–4.*

HORSEBACK RIDING

★ Long-established **Desafío Adventures** (⊠ *Across from Super Compro supermarket, Santa Elena* ☎ *2645–5874* ⊕ *www.monteverdetours.com*) leads four-hour horseback tours to the San Luis Waterfall, an area not often taken in by Monteverde visitors, and also has shorter excursions on farms around Santa Elena. For the Monteverde–La Fortuna trip ($65), you travel by car and boat, with a three-hour horseback ride on a flat trail along Lake Arenal. Farms for resting the animals are at each end. It's infinitely more humane for the horses (and you) than the muddy, treacherous mountain trails used by dozens of other individuals who'll offer to take you to Arenal. Tour prices range from $25 to $48.

■ TIP→ The ride from Monteverde to La Fortuna can be dangerous with outfitters that take inexperienced riders along steep trails. Desafío should be your only choice for getting from Monteverde to La Fortuna on horseback.

Escorted half-day horseback-riding tours ($40) with **Caballeriza El Rodeo** (⊠ *West entrance of town of Santa Elena, at tollbooth* ☎ *2645–5764* ✉ *rodeo@racsa.co.cr*) are on a private farm. Excursions are for everyone from beginner to experienced rider. A two-hour sunset tour ($25) begins at 4 PM. Family-operated **El Palomino** (⊠ *Just outside Santa Elen*

☏ 2645–5479) gives escorted afternoon half-day horseback-riding tours on farm areas around Santa Elena. Transportation from your hotel is included.

On a horseback tour with **Gold Tours** (✉ *Monteverde Homestay, 150 m northeast of school, Cerro Plano* ☏ 2645–6914) you visit a 1920s gold mine. The excursion ($40) includes a demonstration of the panning methods used during those heady days, and on the trip back a visit to a *trapiche*, a traditional sugarcane mill. Everyone from small children to seasoned experts can participate on these guided horseback-riding trips ($15–$50) with **Meg's Stables** (✉ *Main road, across from CASEM* ☏ 2645–5419). Reservations are a good idea in high season, and essential if you want an English-speaking guide. A tour to the San Luis waterfalls is geared toward experienced riders.

■ TIP→ **Book horseback trips in the morning during rainy season (July–December). Rains usually begin around 2 PM.**

EXPLORING

MAIN ATTRACTIONS

☾ If your time in Monteverde is limited, consider spending it at **Selvatura**, a kind of nature theme park—complete with canopy tour and bridge walks—just outside the Santa Elena Reserve. A 100-bird hummingbird garden, an enormous enclosed 50-species *mariposario* (butterfly garden), a *herpetario* (frog and reptile house), and insect exhibition sit near the visitor center. Transportation from area hotels is included in the price. You can choose from numerous mix-and-match packages, depending on which activities interest you, or take it all in, with lunch and guide included, for $125. Most visitors get by for much less, given that you couldn't take in all there is to do here in one day. ✉ *Office across from church, Santa Elena* ☏ 2645–5929 ⊕ *www.selvatura.com* 🗷 *Prices vary, depending on package* ☾ *Daily 8:30–4:30.*

☾ Forty species of butterflies flit about in four enclosed botanical gardens at the **Butterfly Garden** (Jardín de Mariposas). Morning visits are best, since the butterflies are most active early in the day. Your entrance ticket includes an hour-long guided tour. ✉ *Near Monteverde Inn; take right-hand turnoff 4 km/2½ mi past Santa Elena on road to Monteverde, continue for 2 km/1 mi* ☏ 2645–5512 ⊕ *www.monteverdebutterflygarden. com* 🗷 *$9, $3 for kids under 12* ☾ *Daily 9:30–4.*

Several conservation areas that have sprung up near Monteverde make attractive day trips, particularly if the Monteverde Reserve is too busy. The 765-acre **Santa Elena Reserve** just west of Monteverde is a project of the Santa Elena high school, and has a series of trails of varying lengths and difficulties that can be walked alone or with a guide. The 1.4-km (¾-mi) Youth Challenge Trail takes about 45 minutes to negotiate and contains an observation platform with views as far away as the Arenal Volcano—that is, if the clouds clear. If you're feeling hardy, try the 5-km (3-mi) Caño Negro Trail, clocking in at around four hours. There's a shuttle service to the reserve with fixed departures and returns. Reservations are required, and the cost is $2 each way. ✉ *6 km/4 mi north of Santa Elena* ☏ 2645–5390 ⊕ *www.reservasantaelena.org* 🗷 *$12, plus $15 with guide services* ☾ *Daily 7–4.*

5

ALSO WORTH SEEING

☾ Butterflies, frogs, and snakes already have their own Monteverde-area exhibits. The **Bat Jungle** gives its namesake animal equal time with guided tours into the life of one of the planet's most misunderstood mammals. An adjoining museum documents the history of the region, in particular, its early settlement by the Quakers. ✉ *Across from Casem Monteverde* ☎ *2645–6566* ☜ *$10* ☽ *Daily 9:30–8:30.*

☾ The 54,000-acre **Children's Eternal Rain Forest** (Bosque Eterno de los Niños) dwarfs the Monteverde and Santa Elena reserves. It began life as a school project in Sweden among children interested in saving a piece of the rain forest, and blossomed into a fund-raising effort among students from 44 countries. The reserve's **Bajo del Tigre trail** makes for a gentle, self-guided 1½-km (1-mi) hike through secondary forest. Along the trail are 27 stations at which to stop and learn about the reserve, many with lessons geared toward kids. A separate guided twilight walk ($15) begins at 5:30 PM and lasts two hours, affording the chance to see the nocturnal side of the cloud forest; reservations are required. Much of the rest of the reserve is not open to the public, but the Monteverde Conservation League offers stays at San Gerardo and Poco Sol, two remote field stations within the forest. The $34 packages include dormitory accommodation and meals. ✉ *100 m south of CASEM* ☎ *2645–5003* ⊕ *www.acmcr.org* ☜ *Forest $7; transportation from area hotels $2* ☽ *Daily 8–4:30.*

The **Ecological Farm** (Finca Ecológica) is a private wildlife refuge with four trails on its 75 acres, plus birds, sloths, agoutis, coatimundis, two waterfalls, and a coffee plantation. If you can't make it all the way up to the Monteverde Reserve for the evening hike, there's a top-notch guided, two-hour twilight walk that begins each evening at 5:30. Reservations are required. ✉ *Turnoff to Jardín de Mariposas, off main road between Santa Elena and Monteverde* ☎ *2645–5869* ☜ *$9, twilight walk $15* ☽ *Daily 7–5.*

★ Bite your tongue before requesting Costa Rica's ubiquitous Café Britt up here. Export-quality Café Monteverde is the locally grown product. The **Monteverde Coffee Tour** lets you see the process up close from start to finish, from shade growing on the area's Turín plantation, 7 km (4 mi) north of Santa Elena; transport to the *beneficio,* the processing mill where the beans are washed and dried; and finally to the roaster. Reservations are required, and pickup is from area hotels. ☎ *2645–7090* ⊕ *www.crstudytours.com* ☜ *$25* ☽ *Tours at 8 AM and 1 PM.*

The **Orchid Garden** (Jardín de Orquídeas) showcases more than 450 species of orchids, one of which is the world's smallest. The Monteverde Orchid Investigation Project manages the gardens. ✉ *150 m south of Banco Nacional* ☎ *2645–5308* ⊕ *www.monteverdeorchidgarden.com* ☜ *$7* ☽ *Daily 8–5.*

The 200-acre **Sendero Tranquilo Reserve** is managed by the Hotel Sapo Dorado and bordered by the Monteverde Cloud Forest Biological Reserve and the Guacimal River. Narrow trails are designed to have as little impact on the forest as possible (only groups of two to six are allowed). A guide leads you through primary and secondary forest and

CLOSE UP

Bird Country

Nearly 850 bird species have been identified in Costa Rica, more than in the United States and Canada combined. Consequently, bird-watchers flock here by the thousands. The big attractions tend to be eye-catching species like the keel-billed toucan, but it is the diversity of shape, size, coloration, and behavior that makes bird-watching in Costa Rica so fascinating.

Tropical superstars: Parrots, parakeets, and macaws; toucans and toucanets; and the elusive but legendary resplendent quetzal are a thrill for those of us who don't see them every day.

In supporting roles: Lesser-known but equally impressive species include motmots, with their distinctive racket tails; oropéndolas, which build hanging nests; and an array of hawks, kites, and falcons.

Color me red, blue, yellow, . . . : Two of the most striking species are the showy scarlet macaw and the quirky purple gallinule; tanagers, euphonias, manakins, cotingas, and trogons are some of the country's loveliest plumed creatures, but none of them matches the iridescence of the hummingbirds (⇨ below).

Singing in the rain: The relatively inconspicuous clay-color robin is Costa Rica's national bird. It may look plain, but its song is melodious, and because the males sing almost constantly toward the end of the dry season—the beginning of their mating season—local legend has it that they call the rains.

The big and the small of it: The hummingbird is a mere 6¼ cm (2½ inches) tall and weighs just over 2 grams, whereas the jabiru, a long-legged stork, can grow to more than 1.2 meters (4 feet) tall and weigh up to 14 pounds.

Parrots, parakeets, and macaws; toucans and toucanets; and the elusive but legendary resplendent quetzal: Costa Rica hosts 51 members of the hummingbird family, compared with just one species for all of the United States east of the Rocky Mountains.

"Snow birds": If you're here between October and April, don't be surprised if you see some feathered friends from home. When northern birds fly south for the winter, they don't all head to Miami. Seasonal visitors like the Kentucky warbler make up about a quarter of the amazing avian panorama in Costa Rica.

Bird-watching can be done everywhere in the country. And don't let the rainy season deter you: seasonal *lagunas* (lagoons) such as Caño Negro and the swamps of Palo Verde National Park, which disappear during the dry months, are excellent places to see birds.

5

an area that illustrates the effects of deforestation. Because of the emphasis on minimal environmental impact, animals here tend to be more timid than at some other reserves. ⊠ *3 km/2 mi north of Monteverde Reserve entrance, Cerro Plano* ☎ *2645–5010* ⊕ *www.sapodorado.com* 🖃 *$35* ☉ *Tours depart daily at 7:30 AM and 1 PM; reservations required.*

🜄 At the **Serpentarium of Monteverde** *(Serpentario Monteverde)*, greet 40 species of live Costa Rican reptiles and amphibians with glass safely

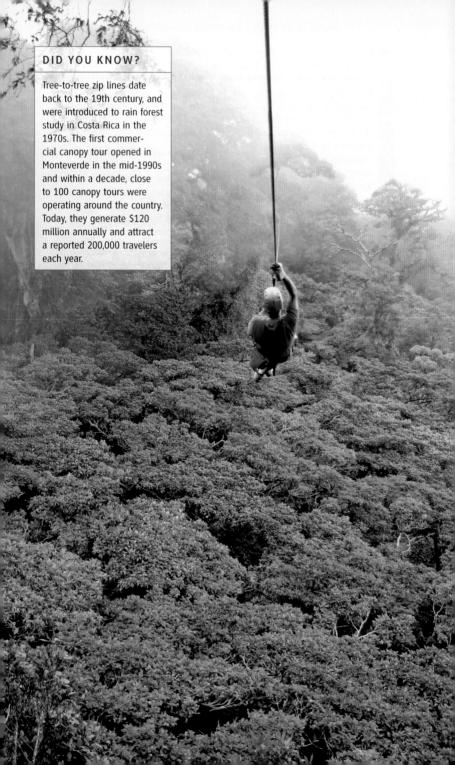

between you and them. Guided tours in English or Spanish are included in your admission price. ✉ *Just outside Santa Elena on road to Monteverde* ☎ *2645–6002* ⊕ *www.snaketour.com* ✐ *$8* ⊗ *Daily 8–8.*

NEED A BREAK?

Long before tourists flocked up here, dairy farming was the foundation of Monteverde's economy. Quakers still operate what is locally referred to as the Cheese Factory, or **La Lechería** (✉ ½ *km/¼ mi south of CASEM, halfway between Santa Elena and Monteverde Reserve* ☎ *2645–2850; 2645–7090 tours*). The factory store sells local cheeses and ice cream. Stop in for a cone. It's open Monday–Saturday 7:30–5 and Sunday 7:30–4. If you have more time, take a two-hour tour of the operation Monday–Saturday at 9 or 2. Tours are $8 and wind up with a cheese-sampling session. Reserve in advance. If you're not heading up the mountain, these folks also operate a stand across from the Treehouse restaurant on the main street in Santa Elena.

WHERE TO EAT

$
ECLECTIC

✕ **Chimera.** Karen Nielsen, owner of nearby Sofía, also operates this all-tapas (appetizers) offering, where you can mix and match small plates from the à la carte menu. Prices do add up quickly, but two or three menu items will make a filling meal out of such diverse mini-dishes as sea bass with passion-fruit cream, or coconut shrimp in mango-ginger sauce. Excellent dessert choices include a chocolate mousse or vanilla ice cream with pineapple-ginger-rum syrup, and a terrific selection of tropical-style cocktails and European and South American wines. A scant nine tables dot the place. Arrive before 7 if you want a guaranteed table, although the wait is never too long. ✉ *Cerro Plano* ☎ *2645–6081* ▤ *AE, D, DC, MC, V.*

$$$
MIDDLE EASTERN

✕ **De Lucía.** Cordial Chilean owner José Belmar is the walking, talking (in five languages) menu at this elegant restaurant, always on hand to chat with guests. All entrées are served with grilled vegetables and fried plantains, and include sea bass with garlic sauce, and orange chicken. The handsome wooden restaurant with red mahogany tables is given a distinct South American flavor by an array of Andean tapestries and ceramics. An excellent dessert choice is *tres leches* (three milks), a richer-than-rich cake made with condensed, whole, and evaporated milk. ✉ *Turnoff to Jardín de Mariposas, off main road between Santa Elena and Monteverde, Cerro Plano* ☎ *2645–5337* ▤ *AE, MC, V.*

$
SEAFOOD

✕ **El Márquez.** Seafood is an unexpected treat up here in the mountains, and it's fresh: the owner gets shipments from Puntarenas several times weekly. The place is nothing fancy—expect plastic tables and chairs, with lots of local flavor—but when area residents want a special restaurant meal, this is where they come. Portions are big, but prices aren't. You could have trouble finishing the generous mixed seafood platter with shrimp, crab, and octopus in a white-wine sauce, or the jumbo shrimp with a sauce of mushrooms and hearts of palm. ✉ *Next to Suárez veterinary clinic, Santa Elena* ☎ *2645–5918* ▤ *AE, MC, V.*

$
VEGETARIAN

✕ **Morphos.** Casual Morphos serves meat dishes and quite a few vegetarian options. Inside this second-floor restaurant are stone walls, log-hewn chairs, artwork, and huge wooden light fixtures in the shape of the famed blue butterfly from which the restaurant takes its name. A large window lets you survey all that goes on in town. This tiny place fills up quickly—make reservations a week in advance. ⊠ *Across from Super Compro supermarket, Santa Elena* ☎ *2645–5607* ⊟ *MC, V.*

$$
ITALIAN
✕**Pizzería de Johnny.** Everyone makes it to this stylish but informal place with candles and white tablecloths. The Monteverde pizza, with the works, is the most popular dish, and pastas, sandwiches, and a decent wine selection round out the menu. ⊠ *Road to Monteverde Reserve, 1½ km/1 mi southeast of Santa Elena* ☎ *2645–5066* ⊟ *AE, D, DC, MC, V.*

$$$
ECLECTIC
Fodor'sChoice
★
✕**Sofía.** Here's one of the area's most stylish restaurants, but this is still Monteverde, so you can leave your fancy clothes at home. Waiters in crisp black aprons scurry attentively around the three dining rooms with ample window space. We like Sofía for its variety of about a dozen main courses: a mix of chicken, beef, pork, seafood, and vegetarian entrées. Try the chimichanga with corvina and shrimp and a side of coconut rice. There's an extensive wine and cocktail selection, too. ⊠ *Turnoff to Jardín de Mariposas, off main road between Santa Elena and Monteverde, Cerro Plano* ☎ *2645–7017* ⊟ *AE, D, DC, MC, V.*

$
CAFÉ
✕**Stella's Bakery.** This local institution is one of the few spots that open at 6 AM. It's a good place to get an early-morning fix before heading to the Monteverde Reserve. Pastries, rolls, muffins, natural juices, and coffee are standard breakfast fare. Take them with you if you're running short of time. Lunch consists of light sandwiches, soups, and pastas. Make it a very early dinner here; the place closes at 6 PM. ⊠ *Across from CASEM, Monteverde* ☎ *2645–5560* ⊟ *AE, D, DC, MC, V.*

$
ECLECTIC
✕**Tree House.** The name describes the place: this two-story restaurant on Santa Elena's main street is built around a 60-year-old fig tree. Tree branches shelter first-floor tables from the afternoon mist, but not entirely. If that's a problem, grab a table on the covered upper floor. The menu mixes pastas and seafood with Costa Rican cuisine. For a taste of everything, try the *típico* platter. The service here is "leisurely" or "slow," depending on your perspective. Spending at least $6 here gets you 30 minutes of free Internet use at the bank of computers downstairs. ⊠ *Across from AyA, Santa Elena* ☎ *2645–5751* ⊟ *AE, D, DC, MC, V.*

WHERE TO STAY

$–$$$
★
🛏 **Arco Iris Lodge.** You're almost right in the center of town, but you'd never know it. This tranquil spot has cozy cabins set on 4 acres of birding trails. Cabin decor ranges from rustic to plush, but all lodgings come with porches. Start your day with a delicious breakfast buffet, including homemade bread and granola. You need not be a honeymooner to stay in the sumptuous three-level honeymoon cabin, secluded off on a corner of the property, with private patio, whirlpool tub, and DVD player. The laid-back German management can provide good advice about how to spend your time in the area. **Pros:** attentive owner and staff; terrific breakfasts; ecology-minded place. **Cons:** back of bank blocks views; steep walk if on foot. ⊠ *50 m south of Banco Nacional, Santa Elena* ☎ *2645–5067* ⊕ *www.arcoirislodge.com* ↜ *20 cabins, 1 suite* ⊘ *In-room: no a/c, no phone, safe (some), DVD (some), no TV (some). In-hotel: laundry service, Internet terminal* ⊟ *MC, V* ¶◯¶ *EP.*

$ □ **El Bosque Lodge.** Convenient to the Bajo del Tigre nature trail and Meg's Stables, El Bosque's quiet, simple rooms are grouped around a central camping area. A bridge crosses a stream and leads to the hotel. Brick-oven pizzas are served on the veranda. **Pros:** good budget value; seclusion, especially in rooms away from road. **Cons:** basic rooms; lackluster staff. ⊠ *2½ km/ 1½ mi southeast of Santa Elena on road to Monteverde Reserve, Monteverde* ☎ *2645–5158* ⊕ *www.bosquelodge.net* ⤶ *27 rooms* ⌂ *In-room: no a/c, no TV, Internet. In-hotel: restaurant, bar, laundry service, Internet terminal* ⊟ *AE, DC, MC, V* ⴼ◎*EP.*

THE UBIQUITOUS SODA

In Costa Rica the word *soda* has nothing to do with a carbonated beverage. (That's a *gaseosa* here.) Instead, a soda is a small, often family-run restaurant frequented by locals that you'll find in every town and city. Don't expect anything as fancy as a menu. A board usually lists specials of the day. The lunchtime *casado* (literally, "married")—a "marriage" of chicken, pork, or beef with rice, beans, cabbage salad, and natural fruit drink—sets you back about $2. No one will bring you a bill; just pay the cashier when you're finished.

$$$ □ **El Establo Mountain Hotel.** "The Stable" began life as just that, a stable near the road, remodeled and apportioned into comfortable rooms with basic furnishings. Over the years, ever-upward expansion has turned this place into a sprawling operation. A newer pink building perches on the hill with large suites with wood-and-stone walls. Some contain lofts; all come with amenities rarely seen up here, such as bathtubs, phones, and enormous windows with views of the Gulf of Nicoya. The two newest buildings, higher on the hill, have rooms with hot tubs, private balconies, and even more commanding views. This is, by far, the area's largest hotel complex—you'll need the minivan shuttle to transport you up and down the hill. In that regard, El Establo is somewhat "un-Monteverde," but its guests undeniably have fun with its many facilities, including a guests-only canopy tour. Oh, and those original stable rooms? They're not in use anymore. **Pros:** luxurious furnishings; many activities. **Cons:** massive grounds; lacks intimacy of other Monteverde lodgings. ⊠ *3½ km/2 mi northwest of Monteverde* ☎ *2645–5110; 877/623–3198 in North America* ⊕ *www.hotelelestablo.com* ⤶ *155 rooms* ⌂ *In-room: no a/c, safe, refrigerator. In-hotel: 2 restaurants, bars, tennis courts, pool, gym, spa* ⊟ *AE, D, DC, MC, V* ⴼ◎*BP.*

$$ □ **El Sol.** A charming German family tends to guests at one of those quintessential get-away-from-it-all places just 10 minutes down the mountain from—and a noticeable few degrees warmer than—Santa Elena. Two fully furnished *ojoche*-wood cabins perch on the mountainside on the 25-acre farm. Every vantage point in the cabins—the living area, the bed, the desk, the shower, and even the toilet—has stupendous views. The property has 3 km (2 mi) of trails, a stone-wall pool, and a Finnish sauna. Meals can be arranged and taken in the main house or brought to your cabin. **Pros:** great views; whimsically decorated cabins. **Cons:** need car to get here; far removed from sights. ⊠ *4 km/2½ mi southwest of Santa Elena* ☎ *2645–5838* ⊕ *www.elsolnuestro.com* ⤶ *2*

5

cabins ⚅ *In-room: no a/c, no phone, no TV. In-hotel: restaurant, pool*
▤ *No credit cards* ¶Ⓞ¶ *EP.*

$$ 🏨 **Fonda Vela.** Owned by the Smith brothers, whose family was among
Fodor'sChoice the first American arrivals in the 1950s—their father's paintings grace
★ the lodging's public areas—these steep-roof chalets have large bedrooms
with white-stucco walls, wood floors, and huge windows. Some have
views of the wooded grounds; others, of the far-off Gulf of Nicoya.
The most innovatively designed of Monteverde's hotels is also one of
the closest to the reserve entrance. Both restaurants ($$$) prepare local
and international recipes with flair, served indoors or on the veranda.
The place is a longtime favorite of those who post to Fodors.com Latin
America discussion board. **Pros:** rustic luxury; secluded location; terrific
restaurant. **Cons:** far from town; rough road to get here. ✉ *1½ km/1 mi*
northwest of Monteverde Reserve entrance, Monteverde ☎ *2645–5125*
⊕ *www.fondavela.com* ⤳ *40 rooms* ⚅ *In-room: no a/c, refrigerator. In-*
hotel: 2 restaurants, bar, laundry service, Internet terminal ▤ *AE, D,*
DC, MC, V ¶Ⓞ¶ *BP, EP, FAP, MAP.*

$$ 🏨 **Hotel Belmar.** Built into the hillside, Hotel Belmar resembles two tall
Swiss chalets and commands extensive views of the Golfo de Nicoya
and the hilly peninsula. The amiable Chilean owners have designed both
elegant and rustic rooms, paneled with polished wood; half the rooms
have balconies. In the restaurant ($$–$$$) you can count on adventur-
ous and delicious *platos del día* (daily specials) of Costa Rican and
international fare. **Pros:** good value; friendly staff. **Cons:** far from town;
steep walk if on foot. ✉ *4 km/2½ mi north of Monteverde* ☎ *2645–5201*
⊕ *www.hotelbelmar.net* ⤳ *28 rooms* ⚅ *In-room: no a/c, no TV. In-*
hotel: restaurant, bar, laundry service, Wi-Fi hotspot, Internet terminal
▤ *AE, MC, V* ¶Ⓞ¶ *EP.*

$$ 🏨 **Hotel El Sapo Dorado.** After beginning its life as a nightclub, the
"Golden Toad" became a popular restaurant and then graduated into
a very pleasant hotel. Geovanny Arguedas's family arrived here to farm
10 years before the Quakers did, and he and his wife, Hannah Lowther,
have built secluded hillside cabins with polished paneling, tables, fire-
places, and rocking chairs. The restaurant ($$) is well known for its pas-
tas, pizza, vegetarian dishes, and sailfish from Puntarenas. **Pros:** rustic
luxury; attentive service. **Cons:** trails between cabins get muddy in rainy
season; no screens on some windows, steep walk if on foot. ✉ *6 km/4 mi*
northwest of Monteverde Reserve entrance, Monteverde ☎ *2645–5010,*
800/407–3903 in North America ⊕ *www.sapodorado.com* ⤳ *30 rooms*
⚅ *In-room: no a/c, no phone, refrigerator, no TV. In-hotel: 2 restau-*
rants, bar, Internet terminal ▤ *AE, D, DC, MC, V* ¶Ⓞ¶ *CP.*

$$ 🏨 **Hotel Montaña Monteverde.** The area's first lodging—it dates from
1979—underwent a 2007 makeover worthy of a reality TV show. Some
of the hotel's seclusion has been lost as a result, but the sparkle of the
updated furnishings makes up for it. Each room comes with shower
and tub, flat-screen TV, brightly colored drapes and spreads, and large
windows with super views. On the topic of views, the terrace restaurant
also offers superb vistas of the far-off Gulf of Nicoya. **Pros:** luxurious
furnishings; new remodeling. **Cons:** a little farther outside Santa Elena
than some might want; a few front rooms get noise from road. ✉ *Cerro*

Plano ☎ 2645–5046 ⊕ *www.monteverdemountainhotel.com* ✍ 42
rooms ⚐ *In-room: no a/c, safe, refrigerator (some). In-hotel: restaurant,
room service, bar, Internet terminal* ⊟ *AE, D, DC, MC, V* ⦿ *EP.*

$$–$$$
Fodor's Choice
★

⌂ **Monteverde Lodge.** The well-established Costa Rica Expeditions operates this longtime favorite close to Santa Elena. Rooms have vaulted
ceilings, bathtubs—an amenity rarely seen here—and great views. A
table abuts the angled bay window overlooking the 15 acres of grounds,
a perfect place to have a cup of coffee and bird-watch from indoors.
The restaurant and bar congregate around an enormous but cozy lobby
fireplace. Relax in the whirlpool tub in the enormous solarium, a perfect place to unwind after a day of tromping through the reserves. Or
take in the evening slide presentation, showcasing cloud forest life.
These folks also offer packages that include meals, guided walks, and
round-trip transportation from San José. **Pros:** rustic luxury; attentive
service; many activities. **Cons:** ground-floor rooms can be noisy; not
centrally located relative to Santa Elena or reserve. ⊠ *200 m south of
Ranario de Monteverde, Santa Elena* ☎ 2645–5057; 2257–0766 *in San
José,* 800/866–2609 *in North America* ⊕ *www.costaricaexpeditions.
com* ✍ 27 *rooms* ⚐ *In-room: no a/c, safe, no TV. In-hotel: restaurant,
bar, Internet terminal* ⊟ *AE, D, DC, MC, V* ⦿ *EP, FAP, MAP.*

¢
⌂ **Monteverde Inn.** One of the cheapest inns in the area is quite far from
the Monteverde Reserve entrance, on a 28-acre private preserve. The
bedrooms are basic, but they have stunning views of the Gulf of Nicoya
as well as hardwood floors, firm beds, and powerful, hot showers.
Home cooking is served by the chatty David and María Savage and family. **Pros:** good rock-bottom budget value; friendly owners; good views.
Cons: spartan rooms. ⊠ *50 m past Butterfly Garden on turnoff road,
Cerro Plano* ☎ 2645–5156 ⊕ *www.pensionmonteverdeinn.com* ✍ 13
rooms ⚐ *In-room: no a/c, no phone, no TV, Wi-Fi. In-hotel: restaurant*
⊟ *No credit cards* ⦿ *BP, MAP.*

$
⌂ **Swiss Hotel Miramontes.** Switzerland meets the cloud forest at this
Swiss-owned and -operated small inn. Each room has a private porch.
Guests have access to a private orchid garden with more than 300 varieties. If you're tired of rice and beans, the restaurant serves a variety of
Swiss, Austrian, Italian, and French dishes. **Pros:** pleasant, small operation, friendly owners. **Cons:** not many frills; far from sights. ⊠ *1 km/
½ mi south of Santa Elena* ☎ 2645–5152 ⊕ *www.swisshotelmiramontes.
com* ✍ 8 *rooms* ⚐ *In-room: no a/c, safe (some). In-hotel: restaurant,
bar* ⊟ *MC, V* ⦿ *BP.*

$$
⌂ **Trapp Family Lodge.** The enormous rooms, with wood paneling and
ceilings, have lovely furniture marvelously crafted from—you guessed
it—wood. The architectural style is appropriate, as the lodge is sur-
rounded by trees, just a 10-minute walk from the park entrance, mak-
ing it the closest lodge to the reserve. (This means, though, that the trip
into town is longer.) The friendly Chilean owners are always around
to provide personalized service. Other than a small hutlike enclosure
near the entrance, the entire property is nonsmoking. **Pros:** rustic lux-
ury; good value; closest lodging to reserve entrance. **Cons:** far from
town; rough road to get here. ⊠ *Main road from Monteverde Reserve,
Monteverde* ☎ 2645–5858; 305/712–5634 *in North America* ⊕ *www.*

trappfamilylodgecr.com ↩ *26 rooms* ⚑ *In-room: no a/c, refrigerator, no TV (some). In-hotel: restaurant, bar, laundry service, Internet terminal, no-smoking rooms* ≡ *AE, D, DC, MC, V* ⦿❘*EP.*

SHOPPING

ARTS AND CRAFTS

Atmosphera (⊠ *Turnoff to Jardín de Mariposas, Cerro Plano* ☎ *2645–6555*) specializes in locally made primitivist wood carvings. **Bromelia's** (⊠ *100 m east of CASEM, Monteverde* ☎ *2645–6272*) bills itself as a bookstore, but sells colorful batiks, masks, and jewelry, too. The **Cooperativa de Artesanía de Santa Elena y Monteverde** (*CASEM* ⊠ *Next to El Bosque Lodge, Monteverde* ☎ *2645–5190*), an artisans' cooperative made up of 89 women and 3 men, sells locally made crafts. The prices are higher than at most other places. **Coopesanta Elena** (⊠ *Next to CASEM* ☎ *2645–5901*) is the distributor for packages of the area's gourmet Café Monteverde coffee and accoutrements. The **Hummingbird Gallery** (⊠ *Outside entrance to Monteverde Reserve* ☎ *2645–5030*) sells books, gifts, T-shirts, great Costa Rican coffee, prints, and slides by nature specialists Michael and Patricia Fogden, as well as watercolors by nature artist Sarah Dowell.

NIGHTLIFE

"Wild nightlife" takes on its own peculiar meaning here. You can still get up close with nature after the sun has gone down. Several of the reserves have guided evening walks—advance reservations and separate admission are required—and the Ranario, Serpentario, and Bat Jungle keep evening hours. Noted area biologist Richard LaVal presents a slide show called **Sounds and Scenes of the Cloud Forest** at the Monteverde Lodge nightly at 6:15 ($5). Advance reservations are required. Beyond that, you'll probably while away the evening in a restaurant or your hotel dining room chatting with fellow travelers. Monteverde is an early-to-bed, early-to-rise kind of place.

CAÑO NEGRO REFUGE AREA

Long a favorite among fishing enthusiasts and bird-watchers, this remote area is off the beaten track and may be difficult to get to if your time in Costa Rica is short. You can cross into Nicaragua, via Los Chiles, but there are almost no roads in this part of southern Nicaragua, making access to the rest of the country nearly impossible. The border crossing at Peñas Blancas, near the north Pacific coast, is far more user-friendly (⇨ *Crossing into Nicaragua at Peñas Blancas, in Chapter 6*).

CAÑO NEGRO NATIONAL WILDLIFE REFUGE

Fodor's Choice   *91 km/57 mi (1½ hrs) northwest of La Fortuna.*

★   Caño Negro doesn't grab the same amount of attention in wildlife-viewing circles as other destinations in Costa Rica, but the reserve is a splendid place to watch waterfowl and resident exotic animals. ⊠ *180 km/108 mi north of La Fortuna* ⊑ *$7* ☉ *Daily 7–4.*

GETTING HERE AND AROUND

The highway from La Fortuna to Los Chiles is one of the best-maintained in the northern lowlands. You can catch public buses in San José at Terminal Atlántico Norte twice a day, a trip of about five hours, with many stops. Public buses also operate between La Fortuna and Los Chiles. If they have room, many tour companies (Sunset Tours included) will allow you to ride along with them on their shuttles, for a cost of around $10. If you're not staying way up here, an organized tour of the reserve is the best way to get to and from it.

OUTDOOR ACTIVITIES

Several La Fortuna–area tour companies have trips to Caño Negro. **Sunset Tours** (☎ 2479–9800; 866/417–7352 in North America ⊕ www. sunsettourscr.com) pioneered tours to the reserve, and runs top-notch, informative daylong or half-day tours, among the best in the country, to Caño Negro for $80 to $100, with higher rates in effect if you stay at one of the more far-flung Arenal lodgings. Bring your jungle juice: the mosquitoes are voracious. **Jacamar Naturalist Tours** (☎ 2479–9767 ⊕ www.arenaltours.com) is a well-established tour operator with three-hour boat trips ($65) on the Río Frío in the Caño Negro reserve.

Now you see it, now you don't: Caño Negro's lake forms during the rainy season when the Río Frío floods its banks. By February, dry conditions begin to shrink the lake, and by April, all that's left are a few spotty lagoons.

WHERE TO STAY

$$ ☰ **Caño Negro Natural Lodge.** That such an upscale property exists in this remote place might amaze you, but this Italian-designed, family-operated resort on the east side of the reserve is never pretentious. Rooms have high ceilings, colorful drapes and bedspreads, and huge showers; some rooms have bunk beds. There are two- and three-day packages available for anglers and non-anglers alike. The lodge has a variety of meal options; most guests opt for taking all meals here, since there are few other restaurants in town. Horseback riding can be arranged and miniature golf, croquet, and badminton are a few of the on-site diversions. **Pros:** secluded location; close to reserve. **Cons:** need car to get here. ⊠ *Caño Negro village* ☎ *2471–1000; 2265–1204 in San José* ⊕ *www.canonegrolodge.com* ⟿ *42 rooms* △ *In-room: no phone, safe, no TV. In-hotel: restaurant, room service, bar, pool, laundry service* ⊟ *AE, MC, V* ⊚ *CP.*

$$ ☰ **Hotel de Campo.** All are welcome here, though the lodge is best known for its fishing tours, equipment and boat rental, and nearby lake filled with tarpon and bass. Seven white bungalows of high-quality wood each contain two bright, sparkling rooms with terra-cotta tile floors, and are arranged around the wooded property. The produce from the lodge's citrus orchard ends up on your breakfast plate. In addition to credit cards and cash, the lodge accepts American Express traveler's checks. **Pros:** secluded location; close to reserve. **Cons:** need car to get here. ⊠ *Caño Negro village* ☎ *2471–1012* ⊕ *www.hoteldecampo.com* ⟿ *14 rooms* △ *In-room: no a/c, no phone, no TV. In-hotel: restaurant, bar, pool* ⊟ *AE, MC, V* ⊚ *BP.*

THE SARAPIQUÍ LOOP

The area immediately north of the San José metro area doesn't leap to mind when discussing ecotourism in Costa Rica, but it should. The Sarapiquí River gave its name to this region at the foot of the Cordillera Central mountain range. To the west is the rain forest of Braulio Carrillo National Park, and to the east are Tortuguero National Park and Barra del Colorado National Wildlife Refuge. These splendid national parks share the region with thousands of acres of farmland, including palm, banana, and pineapple plantations, as well as cattle ranching. Cheap land and rich soil brought a wave of Ticos to this area a half century ago. Until the construction of Highway 126 in 1957, which connects the area to San José, this was one of the most isolated parts of Costa Rica, with little or no tourism. Government homesteading projects brought many residents, who cleared massive swaths of the rain forest for cattle grazing and agriculture. Now, ironically, old-growth lowland rain forest, montane cloud forest, and wetlands exist only within the borders of the national parks and several adjoining private reserves. A growing selection of nature lodges has set up shop here, and you can enjoy their

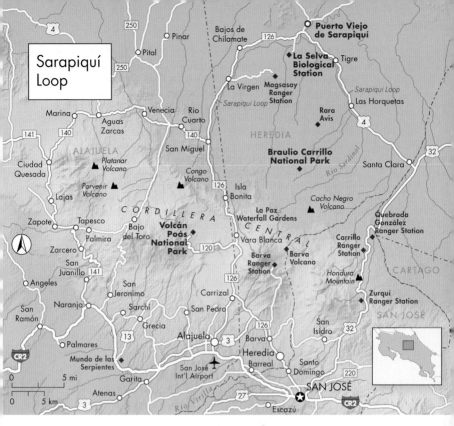

offerings 60 to 90 minutes after you leave the capital. (Just try getting to the Osa Peninsula on the Southern Pacific coast in that same time.)

VOLCÁN POÁS NATIONAL PARK

Fodor's Choice ★ *37 km/23 mi (45 mins) north of Alajuela, 57 km/35 mi (1 hr) north of San José.*

Arenal may be Costa Rica's most famous volcano, but you can walk right up to the crater here at Poás. That gives it an edge in the "cool volcano visit" department.

GETTING HERE AND AROUND

Taxis from San José are around $100 (and around $50 from Alajuela). From the Pan-American Highway north of Alajuela, follow the signs for Poás. The road is in relatively good condition. One public bus departs daily at 8 AM from San José (⊠ Ave. 2, Calle 12–14), and returns at 2 PM. A slew of tours from San José take in the volcano and combine the morning excursion with an afternoon at the La Paz Waterfall Gardens, or tours of Café Britt near Heredia or the Doka Estate near Alajuela. (⇨ *Chapter 4*). (⊠ From Alajuela, drive north through town and follow signs ☎ 2482–2424, 192 (national parks hotline) in Costa Rica ☎ $10 ☉ Daily 8:30–3:30.)

EXPLORING

★ Five magnificent waterfalls are the main attractions at **La Paz Waterfall Gardens,** on the eastern edge of Volcán Poás National Park, but they are complemented by the beauty of the surrounding cloud forest, an abundance of hummingbirds and other avian species, and the country's biggest butterfly garden. A concrete trail leads down from the visitor center to the multilevel, screened butterfly observatory and continues to gardens where hummingbird feeders attract swarms of these multicolor creatures. The trail then enters the cloud forest, where it leads to a series of metal stairways that let you descend into a steep gorge to viewing platforms near each of the waterfalls. A free shuttle will transport you from the trail exit back to the main building if you prefer to avoid the hike uphill. Several alternative paths lead from the main trail through the cloud forest and along the river's quieter upper stretch, providing options for hours of exploration—it takes about two hours to hike the entire complex. (Enter by 3 PM to give yourself adequate time.) The visitor center has a gift shop and open-air cafeteria with a great view. The gardens are 20 km (12 mi) northeast of Alajuela, and are a stop on many daylong tours from San José that take in the Poás volcano or area coffee tours. ✉ *6 km/4 mi north of Vara Blanca* ☎ *2482–2720* ⊕ *www.waterfallgardens.com* ✉ *$35, $47 with lunch, $65 with round-trip transportation from San José* ☉ *Daily 8–5.*

OUTDOOR ACTIVITIES

HORSEBACK RIDING

Guided horseback tours with **Poás Volcano Lodge** (✉ *6 km/4 mi east of Chubascos restaurant, on road to Vara Blanca* ☎ *2482–2194*) are available in the cloud forest of Finca Legua, a private reserve 5 km (3 mi) north of the lodge. Daily tours ($65), which include lunch, run from 9 AM to 2 PM. Make reservations.

WHERE TO EAT AND STAY

$ ✕ **Chubascos.** Amid tall pines and colorful flowers on the upper slopes
COSTA RICAN   of Poás Volcano, this popular restaurant has a small menu of traditional
Fodor's Choice   Tico dishes and delicious daily specials. Choose from the full selection of
★   casados and platters of *gallos* (homemade tortillas with meat, cheese, or potato fillings). The *refrescos* (fresh fruit drinks) are top-drawer, especially the ones made from locally grown *fresas* (strawberries) and *moras* (blackberries) blended with milk. ✉ *1 km/½ mi north of Laguna de Fraijanes* ☎ *2482–2280* ▭ *AE, D, DC, MC, V* ☉ *Closed Tues.*

$ ✕ **Jaulares.** Named after the *jaul,* a tree common in the nearby cloud for-
COSTA RICAN   est, this spacious restaurant specializes in grilled meat, though there are also several fish dishes and *chicharrones* (deep-fried meaty pork rinds). All the cooking is done with wood, which adds to the rustic ambience of terra-cotta floors, bare wooden beams, and sylvan surroundings. The house specialty, *lomito Jaulares* (Jaulares tenderloin), is a strip of grilled meat served with *gallo pinto* (rice and beans) and a mild *salsa criollo* (creole sauce). Though primarily a lunch spot, Jaulares stays open until midnight on weekends for concerts—Latin music on Friday night and rock on Saturday night. Four basic cabinas in back are an inexpensive overnight option, though you'll need to reserve them early for concert nights. ✉ *2 km/*

1 mi north of Laguna de Fraijanes ☎ *2482–2155* ⊕ *www.jaulares.com* ⊟ *AE, D, DC, MC, V.*

$$$$ ⊞ **Peace Lodge.** These rooms overlooking the misty forest of La Paz
★ Waterfall Gardens seem like something out of the *Lord of the Rings*, with their curved, clay-stucco walls, hardwood floors (note that all but the top floors can be noisy because of creaky stairs), stone fireplaces (gas), and four-poster beds made of varnished logs, complete with mosquito-net canopy. They are proper abodes for elfin kings, especially the spacious, grottolike bath-

rooms with two showers, a whirlpool tub, tropical gardens, and private waterfall. Most hotels settle for a room with a bath. Peace Lodge gives you a bath with a room. And as if that weren't enough, you can soak in your second whirlpool tub on a porch with a cloud-forest view. Being able to explore the waterfall gardens before they open is another perk; room rates include admission. The cuisine here is a couple of notches below the accommodations. The entire place is an old favorite of posters to the Fodors.com discussion boards. **Pros:** many activities included in rates; whimsical furnishings; rates include admission to Waterfall Gardens. **Cons:** popular with tour groups; sometimes difficult to find space. ⊠ *6 km/4 mi north of Vara Blanca* ☎ *482–2720; 225–0643 in San José; 954/727–3997 in North America* ⊕ *www.waterfallgardens.com* ⌁ *17 rooms, 1 villa* ⚲ *In-room: no a/c, no phone, refrigerator. In-hotel: restaurant* ⊟ *AE, D, DC, MC, V* ◯ *EP.*

$–$$ ⊞ **Poás Volcano Lodge.** The rustic architecture of this former dairy farmhouse, with rough stone walls and pitched beam roof, fits perfectly into the rolling pastures and forests that surround it. The interior mixes Persian rugs with textiles from Latin America, and Guaitil Indian pottery with North American pieces. The oversize sunken fireplace may be the lodge's most alluring feature. All rooms are different, so if possible, look at a few before you decide: one has an exquisite stone bathtub. The less expensive rooms, though not as opulent, have a more dependable supply of hot water. A small dairy farm and garden supply the kitchen with ingredients for the hearty breakfasts. **Pros:** cozy rooms; close to volcano. **Cons:** rustic rooms. ⊠ *6 km/4 mi east of Chubascos restaurant, on road to Vara Blanca* ☎ *2482–2194* ⊕ *www.poasvolcanolodge.com* ⌁ *11 rooms, 9 with bath* ⚲ *In-room: no a/c, no phone, no TV. In-hotel: restaurant, laundry service, Wi-Fi hotspot, Internet terminal* ⊟ *AE, D, DC, MC, V* ◯ *BP.*

SHOPPING

The **Neotrópica Foundation** sells nature-theme T-shirts, cards, and posters in the national park's visitor center and devotes a portion of the profits to conservation projects.

Certificate of Sustainable Tourism

One trip to Costa Rica and you'll swear everything here is eco-lodges, ecotourism, eco-this, eco-that. But *sustainability*, the buzzword in Costa Rican tourism these days, also has to do with conserving cultural, as well as natural, resources. The Certification for Sustainable Tourism (CST) program, administered jointly by the Costa Rican Tourism Institute, National Chamber of Tourism, Ministry of the Environment, and University of Costa Rica, recognizes businesses that adhere to those ideals. Those that submit to a rigorous assessment are evaluated on their employment of local people, respect for local culture, contribution to the economic and social well-being of the community, and preservation of natural resources. Businesses that rely heavily on foreign investment and whose earnings are mostly repatriated outside Costa Rica don't make the cut (but probably don't submit to an evaluation in the first place).

Instead of stars, 107 hotels have earned one to five leaves for their efforts. At this writing, Finca Rosa Blanca, north of Heredia in the Central Valley; Lapa Ríos, at Cabo Matapalo on the South Pacific; Sí Como No, at Manuel Antonio on the Central Pacific; The Harmony Hotel in Nosara in the North Pacific; and Hotel Villa Blanca, near San Ramón in the Northern Plains, are the only five lodgings to hold five leaves. The resorts and hotels that are recognized are not all small "mom-and-pop" places: the Four Seasons on the Papagayo Peninsula and Arenal's Tabacón have been recognized as well. Nor are they only places in the middle of the rain forest: San José's large but unobtrusive Clarion Hotel Amón Plaza is among several city lodgings proudly displaying awards.

Although other countries have their own rating systems for eco-friendly lodgings, many of these suffer from corrupt policies that allow ratings to be bought. The CST is one of the best and most thorough awards programs in the world. In fact, the World Tourism Organization has adopted it as its model, and countries from Mexico to Malawi now employ similar standards. You'll find a list of Costa Rica's CST holders at the program's Spanish-English-French Web site, ⊕ *www. turismo-sostenible.co.cr.*

BRAULIO CARRILLO NATIONAL PARK

30 km/19 mi (45 mins) north of San José.

In a country where deforestation is still rife, hiking through Parque Nacional Braulio Carrillo is a rare opportunity to witness dense, primary tropical cloud forest. The park owes its foundation to the public outcry provoked by the construction of the highway of the same name through this region in the late 1970s—the government bowed to pressure from environmentalists, and somewhat ironically, the park is the most accessible one from the capital thanks to the highway. Covering 443 square km (171 square mi), Braulio Carrillo's extremely diverse terrain ranges from 55 meters (108 feet) to about 2,896 meters (9,500 feet) above sea level and extends from the central volcanic range down the Caribbean slope to La Selva research station near Puerto Viejo de Sarapiquí. The park protects a series of ecosystems ranging from the cloud forests on the upper slopes to the tropical wet forest of the Magsasay sector; it is home to 6,000 tree species, 500 bird species, and 135 mammal species.

For all its immense size and proximity to the capital, visitor facilities in the park are limited. Your exposure will most likely take place when you pass through on the way to the Caribbean, or when you stay at any of the lodgings that fringe Braulio Carrillo. Penetrating the park's depths is a project only for the truly intrepid:

The **Zurquí ranger station** is to the right of the highway, ½ km (¼ mi) before the Zurquí Tunnel. Here a short trail loops through the cloud forest. Hikes are steep; wear hiking boots to protect yourself from mud, slippage, and snakes. The main trail through primary forest, 1½ km (1 mi) long, culminates in a *mirador* (lookout point), but alas, the highway mars the view. Monkeys, tapirs, jaguars, kinkajous, sloths, raccoons, margays, and porcupines all live in this forest, and resident birds include the resplendent quetzal and the eagle. Orchids, bromeliads, heliconias, fungi, and mushrooms live closer to the floor. Another trail leads into the forest to the right, beginning about 17 km (11 mi) after the tunnel, where it follows the Quebrada González, a stream with a cascade and swimming hole. There are no campsites in this part of the park. The **Carrillo ranger station**, 22 km (14 mi) northeast along the highway from Zurquí, marks the beginning of trails that are less steep. Farther north on this highway, near the park entrance/exit toward Guápiles, is the **Quebrada González** ranger station. To the east of Heredia, a road climbs **Barva Volcano** *(⇨ below)* from San Rafael. ☎ 2290–8202 *Sistemas de Areas de Conservación; 192 (national parks hotline)* 🖆 *$10* ☼ *Daily 7–4.*

The 2,896-meter (9,500-foot) summit of **Barva Volcano** is the highest point in Braulio Carrillo National Park. Dormant for 300 years now, Barva is massive: its lower slopes are almost completely planted with coffee fields and hold more than a dozen small towns, nearly all of which are named after saints. On the upper slopes are pastures lined with exotic pines and the occasional native oak or cedar, giving way to the botanical diversity of the cloud forest near the top. The air is usually cool near the summit, which combines with the pines and pastures to evoke the European or North American countryside.

Barva's misty, luxuriant summit is the only part of Braulio Carrillo where camping is allowed, and it's a good place to see the rare resplendent quetzal early in the morning. Because it's somewhat hard to reach, Barva receives a mere fraction of the crowds that flock to the summits of Poás and Irazú. A two- to four-hour hike in from the Barva ranger station takes you to the main crater, which is about 162 meters (540 feet) in diameter. Its almost vertical sides are covered in sombrillas de pobre, a plant that thrives in the highlands, and oak trees laden with epiphytes (nonparasitic plants that grow on other plants). The crater is filled with an otherworldly black lake. Farther down the track into the forest lies a smaller crater lake. ■TIP→ **Bring rain gear, boots, and a warm shirt. Stay on the trail when hiking anywhere in Braulio Carrillo; even experienced hikers who know the area have lost their way up here, and the rugged terrain makes wandering through the woods very dangerous. In addition, muggings of hikers have been reported in the park. (This is the closest national park to San José and its attendant urban problems.) Go with a ranger if possible.**

For access to the volcano, start from Sacramento, north of Heredia. North of Barva de Heredia the road grows narrow and steep. At Sacramento the paved road turns to dirt, growing worse as it nears the Barva ranger station. We recommend a 4WD vehicle, especially during the rainy season. From the ranger station you can take a 4WD vehicle over the extremely rocky road to the park entrance (dry season only), or hike up on foot. The walk through the cloud forest to the crater's two lakes takes two to four hours, but your efforts should be rewarded by great views (as long as you start before 8 AM, to avoid the mist). ✉ *Access via the park's Barva ranger station* ☎ *2283–5906; 192 (national parks hotline) in Costa Rica* 💲 *$10 (in addition to $6 Braulio Carrillo Park entrance)* ☉ *Tues.–Sun. 7–4.*

San Rafael de Heredia, 2 km (1 mi) northeast of Heredia, is a quiet, mildly affluent coffee town with a large church notable for its stained-glass windows and bright interior. The road north from the church winds its way up Barva Volcano to the Hotel La Condesa, ending atop the Monte de la Cruz lookout point.

GETTING HERE AND AROUND
From San José, travel northeast on Calle 3, which becomes the Guápiles Highway (Hwy. 32), toward Limón. This highway winds through the park, entering at the main ranger station, Zurquí, and exiting at the Quebrada González ranger station. The Barva station is on the west side of the park, north of Zurquí, and is the easiest to access. From Heredia, drive north to Sacramento on Highway 114. The station is 4 km (2½ mi) northeast of Sacramento on a trail that's accessible on foot or by 4WD (except during heavy rains).

Any bus going to Guapiles, Siquirres, and Puerto Viejo de Sarapiquí can drop you off at the Zurquí ranger station. Buses ($2) depart from San José Monday through Saturday from the Atlántico Norte bus station (for Guápiles) or the Gran Terminal del Caribe (for Siquirres or Puerto Viejo de Sarapiquí) several times daily. A cab from San José costs $40 to $50. A number of tour companies offer one-day tours from San José.

OUTDOOR ACTIVITIES
HIKING
The upper slopes of **Barva Volcano** have excellent hiking conditions: cool air, vistas, and plentiful birds. The crater lakes topping the volcano can be reached only on foot, and if you haven't got a 4WD vehicle, you'll also have to trek from Sacramento up to the entrance of Braulio Carrillo National Park. The trails are frequently muddy; ask about their

Paz Waterfall Gardens attracts 24 different species of hummingbirds and has a huge butterfly garden.

condition at the ranger station. The **Sendero Botello** trail, on the east side of the park (entrance near the Quebrada González ranger station off the Guápiles Highway), is a better choice for casual hikers.

WHERE TO STAY

$$–$$$ ⬚ **Hotel & Villas La Condesa Monte de la Cruz.** The stone fireplace surrounded by armchairs and a small bar in the La Condesa lobby is one of the many facets of the hotel that suggest a lodge you'd expect to find in a more northern latitude. In the central courtyard, topped by a giant skylight, is one of the hotel's two restaurants. A tropical garden is similarly enclosed in the pool area. Guest rooms are carpeted and tastefully furnished, and each has a picture window. Suites have bedroom lofts, sitting areas, and the hotel's best views. **Pros:** rustic luxury; easily reached from San José. **Cons:** isolated; not much within walking distance. ⊠ *Next to Castillo Country Club 10 km/6 mi north of San Rafael de Heredia* ☎ *2267–6000* ⊕ *www.hotellacondesa.com* ⬞ *70 rooms, 36 suites* ♿ *In-room: no a/c, safe, kitchen (some), refrigerator, Wi-Fi. In-hotel: 2 restaurants, bar, pool, laundry service, spa, Internet terminal* ⊟ *AE, D, DC, MC, V* ⅋️ *BP.*

$ ⬚ **Hotel Chalet Tirol.** The Austrian design here doesn't seem out of place amid the pines, pastures, and cool air of Volcán Barva's upper slopes. The replica of a cobbled Tirolean town square—complete with fountain and church—may be a bit much, but the cozy, bright, two-story wooden chalets are charming, as is the restaurant, with its ivy, wooden ceiling, and elegant murals. High-quality French cuisine makes this a popular weekend destination for Costa Ricans. The suites have fireplaces and are more private than the chalets. ⊠ *Main road, 10 km/6 mi north of San Rafael de Heredia* ☎ *2267–6222* ⬞ *13 suites, 10 chalets* ♿ *In-room: no* *a/c. In-hotel: restaurant, bar, tennis court, laundry service* ☰ *AE, DC, MC, V* ⑩ *BP.*

$ 🔲 **Las Ardillas.** Surrounded by old pines on a country road, these unpretentious log cabins are inviting retreats for those looking to lock themselves up in front of a fireplace and tune out the world. The small on-site spa is a good reason to venture from the comfortable, romantic rooms. The restaurant specializes in meats roasted over a wood fire and has a nice selection of Spanish wines. All rooms have modest wood furniture and queen-size beds. **Pros:** secluded location; good restaurant. **Cons:** rustic rooms; chilly here at night. ✉ *Main road, Guacalillo de San José de la Montaña* ☎ *2260–1003* ⊕ *www.grupoardillas.com* ↗ *8 cabins* ☄ *In-room: no a/c, no phone, kitchen, no TV (some). In-hotel: restaurant, bar, spa* ☰ *MC, V* ⑩ *BP.*

> **A WAY OF LIFE**
>
> *Pura vida* means, literally, "pure life," and is used by Costa Ricans to express agreement, greeting, leave-taking, and basically anything positive. If someone asks, "¿Pura vida?" (basically, "How's it going?" or "Everything okay?"), the response could also be "¡Pura vida!" ("Excellent!") It might also be used to wish someone luck or to say, "Have fun!" Once you arrive, you realize that pura vida is also a philosophy of life, and undoubtedly one reason why around 2 million visitors come here each year.

PUERTO VIEJO DE SARAPIQUÍ

6½ km/4 mi north of La Selva.

In the 19th century, Puerto Viejo de Sarapiquí was a thriving river port and the only link with the coastal lands straight east. Fortunes nose-dived with the construction of a full-fledged port in the town of Moín near Limón, and today Puerto Viejo has a slightly run-down air. The activities of the Nicaraguan Contras made this a danger zone in the 1980s, but now that the political situation has improved, boats once again ply the old route up the Sarapiquí River to the San Juan River on the Nicaraguan frontier, from where you can travel downstream to Barra del Colorado or Tortuguero. A few tour companies have Sarapiquí River tours with up to Class III rapids in the section between Chilamate and La Virgen, with plenty of wildlife to see. If you prefer to leave the driving to them, many of the lodges operate boat tours on the tamer sections of the river.

GETTING HERE AND AROUND

The Braulio Carrillo Highway runs from Calle 3 in San José and passes the Zurquí and Quebrada González sectors of Braulio Carrillo National Park. It branches at Santa Clara, north of the park, with the paved Highway 4 continuing north to Puerto Viejo de Sarapiquí. Alternatively, an older winding road connects San José with Puerto Viejo de Sarapiquí, passing through Heredia and Vara Blanca. The former route is easier, with less traffic; the latter route is more scenic but heavily trafficked. (If you are at all prone to motion sickness, take the newer road.) The roads are mostly paved, with the usual rained-out dirt and rock sections;

road quality depends on the time of year, the length of time since the last visit by a road crew, and/or the amount of rain dumped by the latest tropical storm. Heavy rains sometimes cause landslides that block the highway near the Zurquí Tunnel inside the park, in which case you have to go via Vara Blanca. Check conditions before you set out. Get an early start; fog begins to settle in on both routes by midafternoon. ■ TIP➔ There are gas stations on the Braulio Carrillo Highway at the turnoff to Puerto Viejo de Sarapiquí, as well as just outside of town. Fill the tank when you get the chance.

Buses travel several times daily via both routes and leave from San José's Gran Terminal del Caribe.

ESSENTIALS

Bank/ATM Banco Nacional (⊠ *Across from post office* ☎ *2766–6012*).

Internet Internet Sarapiquí (⊠ *Next to Joyería Mary* ☎ *2766–6223*).

Medical Clinic Red Cross (⊠ *West end of town* ☎ *2766–6901*).

Post Office Correos (⊠ *50 m north of soccer field*).

EXPLORING

Bats are not blind, contrary to popular belief, and most have no interest in sucking your blood. These are just a couple of things you learn on the **Bat Tour** at the nonprofit **Tirimbina Rainforest Center**. Also in the "did you know?" category, touching frogs will not give you warts. You'll learn that on Tirimbina's evening Frog Tour. An informative three-hour guided tour during the day is a terrific value. The center encompasses 750 acres of primary forest and 8 km (5 mi) of trails, some of them traversing hanging bridges at canopy level. Reservations are required for all tours. ⊠ *La Virgen de Sarapiquí 17 km/11 mi southwest of Puerto Viejo* ☎ *2761–1579* ⊕ *www.tirimbina.org* ☜ *$15, $22 guided tour, $19 bat tour, $22 frog tour, $24 bird-watching tour* ⊙ *Daily 7–5. Bat tour daily 7:30 PM; frog tour daily 7:30 PM; guided tours daily 8 AM and 2 PM.*

★ Costa Rica's indigenous peoples don't get the visibility of those in Guatemala or Mexico, probably because they number only 40,000 out of a population of 4 million. The **Dr. María Eugenia Bozzoli Museum of Indigenous Cultures** (Museo de Culturas Indígenas Doctora María Eugenia Bozzoli), part of the Centro Neotrópico Sarapiquís, provides a well-rounded all-under-one-roof introduction to the subject. Nearly 400 artifacts of the Boruca, Bribri, Cabécar, Guaymí, and Maleku peoples are displayed, including masks, musical instruments, and shamanic healing sticks. Start by watching a 17-minute video introduction, *Man and Nature in Pre-Columbian Costa Rica.* A botanical garden next door cultivates medicinal plants still used by many traditional groups. In 1999 researchers discovered an archaeological site on the grounds that contains pre-Columbian tombs and petroglyphs dating from the 15th century. The site is still under study. ⊠ *La Virgen de Sarapiquí 17 km/11 mi southwest of Puerto Viejo* ☎ *2761–1418* ⊕ *www.sarapiquis.org* ☜ *$12 (includes guide)* ⊙ *Daily 9–5.*

The newest of Costa Rica's serpentaria is the aptly named **Snake Garden**, with some 50 species of reptiles on display, including all the poisonous snakes (and most of the nonpoisonous ones) found here in Costa Rica, as well as pythons, anacondas, and rattlesnakes from elsewhere in North and South America. You can handle a few specimens (the non-venomous varieties, at least) upon request and under supervision. ⊠ *La Virgen de Sarapiquí, 400 m south of Centro Neotrópico Sarapiquís* ☎ *2761–1059* ⊟ *$7, $5 children under 6* ☉ *Daily 9–5.*

A working dairy farm and horse ranch, the **Hacienda Pozo Azul** runs guided tours of the ecologically sound 360-cattle dairy operation. It also has many adventure tours

(⇨ *Outdoor Activities, below*). ⊠ *La Virgen de Sarapiquí 17 km/11 mi southwest of Puerto Viejo* ☎ *2761– 1360; 877/810–6903 in North America* ⊕ *www.pozoazul.com* ⊟ *$10* ☉ *By reservation.*

> **CAUTION**
>
> Don't confuse Puerto Viejo de Sarapiquí with Puerto Viejo de Talamanca on the south Caribbean coast (⇨ *Puerto Viejo de Tala-manca, in Chapter 9*). Locals refer to both as simply "Puerto Viejo." Buses for both towns depart from San José's Gran Terminal del Caribe with nothing more than a PUERTO VIEJO sign in the station to designate either. Point to the map and ask for clarification before boarding.

Heliconias abound at the aptly named **Heliconia Island** in the Sarapiquí River. Some 70 species of the flowering plant, a relative of the banana, are among the collections that populate 5 acres of botanical gardens here. Expect to see ample bird and butterfly life, too. ⊠ *La Chaves 8 km/5 mi south of Puerto Viejo de Sarapiquí* ☎ *8397–3948* ⊕ *www.heliconiaisland.com* ⊟ *$12, $17 with guide* ☉ *Daily 8–5.*

OUTDOOR ACTIVITIES

Hacienda Pozo Azul (⊠ *La Virgen de Sarapiquí 17 km/11 mi southwest of Puerto Viejo* ☎ *2761–1360; 877/810–6903 in North America* ⊕ *www. haciendapozoazul.com*) is a dairy farm and ranch with biking, horse-back riding, rafting, canopy tours, float tours, and rappelling excursions that allow you to combine several activities in a day. **Hotel Gavilán Río Sarapiquí** (☎ *2766–6743* ⊕ *www.gavilanlodge.com*) runs wildlife- and bird-watching tours from its site near Puerto Viejo de Sarapiquí up to the San Juan River. Passports are required for the trip, since the San Juan lies entirely within Nicaragua.

CANOPY TOUR

The canopy tour ($45) at **Hacienda Pozo Azul** (⇨ *above*) has 12 zip lines, ranging in height from 18 to 27 meters (60 to 90 feet).

HORSEBACK RIDING

Dairy farm **Hacienda Pozo Azul** (⇨ *above*) is also a horse ranch and has riding excursions for all experience levels through the region around La Virgen. A two-hour tour is $35; a half-day is $45. Check out the multiday tours, too, if you're an experienced rider.

MOUNTAIN BIKING

Aventuras de Sarapiquí (☎ *2766–6768* ⊕ *www.sarapiqui.com*) has made-to-order half-day and multiday biking trips for casual and serious riders. **Costa Rica Biking Adventure** (☎ *2235–4982 in San José* ⊕ *www. bikingincostarica.com*) runs one-day mountain-biking tours of the area.

Insanely steep hills and heavy rainfall make this country a mecca for white-water sports.

Hacienda Pozo Azul (⇨ *above*) has half-day, full-day, and two-day rough-and-tumble back-roads bike tours ($45–$75).

RAFTING

The Virgen del Socorro area is one of the most popular "put-in points" for white-water rafters, and offers both Class II and III rapids. Trips leaving from the Chilamate put-in are more tranquil, with mostly Class I rapids. The put-in point depends on the weather and season.

Several operators lead tours on the Sarapiquí River. Old standby **Costa Rica Expeditions** (☎ *2222–0333* ⊕ *www.costaricaexpeditions.com*) offers full-day trips on the Sarapiquí from San José. **Ríos Tropicales** (☎ *2233–6455* ⊕ *www.riostropicales.com*) takes in the Sarapiquí on day excursions from San José.

RAPPELLING

Hacienda Pozo Azul (⇨ *above*) guides you on a 27-meter (90-foot) river canyon descent ($28).

WHERE TO STAY

$$ 🛏 **Centro Neotrópico Sarapiquís.** Overlooking the Sarapiquí River, the ☾ CNS is an environmental educational center, museum, garden, and hotel all rolled into one. Three indigenous-inspired circular *palenque* (indigenous huts) buildings with palm-thatch roofs house the ample-size rooms. All come with a tile floor, pre-Columbian-style decor, wrought-iron fixtures, and a private terrace. There's an extra cost to visit the center's numerous attractions. **Pros:** good value; many activities; whimsical furnishings. **Cons:** no a/c; sometimes difficult to find space. ✉ *La Virgen de Sarapiquí 17 km/11 mi southwest of Puerto Viejo* ☎ *2761–1004; 866/581–0782 in North America* ⊕ *www.sarapiquis.org* ⬦ *36*

rooms ♿ In-room: no a/c, no phone (some), no TV, Internet. In-hotel: restaurant, room service, bar, laundry service, Internet terminal ▭ AE, D, DC, MC, V ℀ EP.

$ ▦ **Hotel Gavilán Río Sarapiquí.** Beautiful gardens run down to the river, and colorful tanagers and three types of toucan feast in the citrus trees. The two-story lodge has comfortable rooms with white walls, terra-cotta floors, and decorative crafts. The food, Costa Rican *comida típica* (typical fare), has earned its good reputation. Prime activities are horseback jungle treks, boat trips up the Sarapiquí River, and bird-watching—more than 100 species have been spotted here. **Pros:** lovely gardens; many activities. **Cons:** rustic rooms; need car to stay here. ✉ 700 m north of Comando Atlántico (naval command) ☎ 2766–6743; 2234–9507 in San José ⊕ www.gavilanlodge.com ⤳ 17 rooms ♿ In-room: no a/c, no phone, no TV. In-hotel: restaurant ▭ AE, D, DC, MC, V ℀ EP.

¢   ▦ **Posada Andrea Cristina.** The Martinez family owns and operates this friendly and comfortable bed-and-breakfast. High-ceiling rooms have private bathrooms and hot water. Two A-frame bungalows share a (cold-water-only) bathroom. All bungalows and rooms have private gardens with hammocks. **Pros:** good value; secluded location; attentive owners. **Cons:** rustic rooms; need car to stay here. ✉ ½ km/¼ mi west of town, La Guaria ☎ 2766–6265 ⊕ www.andreacristina.com ⤳ 6 cabins, 4 with bath ♿ In-room: no a/c ▭ No credit cards ℀ BP.

$$–$$$ ▦ **Selva Verde Lodge.** Built on stilts over the Sarapiquí River, this expan-
★   sive complex stands on the edge of a 2-square-km (1-square-mi) private reserve of tropical rain forest and caters primarily to natural-history tours. The buildings have wide verandas strung with hammocks, and the rooms come with polished wood paneling and mosquito blinds. Activities include guided walks, boat trips, canoeing, rafting, and mountain biking. Room prices include a bird-watching tour. Reserve a few weeks ahead, especially in high season; the place is very popular with tour groups. **Pros:** ecology-minded staff; many activities. **Cons:** popular with tour groups; sometimes difficult to find space; steep walk to reach a few bungalows. ✉ 7 km/4 mi west of Puerto Viejo de Sarapiquí ☎ 2766–6800; 800/451–7111 in North America ⊕ www.selvaverde. com ⤳ 40 rooms, 5 bungalows ♿ In-room: no a/c (some), no phone, safe, refrigerator (some), no TV. In-hotel: restaurant, bar, pool, laundry service ▭ AE, MC, V ℀ BP, FAP.

LA SELVA BIOLOGICAL STATION

⏱   6 km/4 mi south of Puerto Viejo de Sarapiquí, 79 km/49 mi (2–4 hrs) northeast of San José.

At the confluence of the Puerto Viejo and Sarapiquí rivers, La Selva packs about 420 bird species, 460 tree species, and 500 butterfly species into just 15 square km (6 square mi). Spottings might include the spider monkey, poison dart frog, agouti, collared peccary, and dozens of other rare creatures. ■ TIP➔ **If you want to see wildlife without having to rough it too much, skip Rara Avis and come here.** Extensive, well-marked trails and swing bridges, many of which are wheelchair accessible, connect habitats as varied as tropical wet forest, swamps, creeks, rivers, secondary regenerating forest, and pasture. The site is a project of the Organization for Tropical Studies, a research consortium of 65 U.S., Australian, Latin American, and African universities, and is one of three biological stations OTS operates in Costa Rica. To see the place, take an informative three-hour morning or afternoon nature walk with one of La Selva's bilingual guides, who are some of the country's best. Walks start every day at 8 AM and 1:30 PM. You can add a noontime lunch to your walk for $12; schedule it in advance. For a completely different view of the forest, set off on a guided two-hour walk at 5:45 AM or the night tour at 7 PM. If you get a group of at least five together, you can enroll in the daylong Bird-Watching 101 course or one of the nature-photo workshops, which can be arranged anytime—either is $40 per person. Or get a group of at least six together and tag along with one of the resident research scientists for a half-day. Young children won't feel left out either, with a very basic nature-identification course geared to them. Even with all the offerings, La Selva can custom-design excursions to suit your own special interests, too. Advance reservations are required for the dawn and night walks as well as for any of the courses. ⊠ *6 km/4 mi south of Puerto Viejo de Sarapiquí* ☎ *2766–6565; 2524–0607 in San José; 919/684–5774 in North America* ⊕ *www.threepaths.co.cr* ☞ *Nature walk $30, morning and afternoon walks $38, dawn or night walk $40* ☉ *Walks daily at 8 AM and 1:30 PM.*

GETTING HERE AND AROUND

To get here, drive south from Puerto Viejo, and look for signs on the west side of the road. For those without wheels, La Selva is a $4 taxi ride from Puerto Viejo de Sarapiquí.

WHERE TO STAY

$$$ 🛏 **La Selva.** Other lodges provide more comfort for the money, but none can match La Selva's tropical nature experience. The dorm-style rooms have large bunk beds, tile floors, and lots of screened windows. Newer family-style cabins can sleep up to four people and offer a greater level of comfort and privacy. The restaurant, something like a school cafeteria, serves decent food but has a very limited schedule (reserve ahead). It's a good idea to pay the full-board fee, which includes a guided nature walk and three meals a day with your room rate, since there's nowhere else to eat. Priority is given to researchers—this is a working field station—so advance reservations are essential. **Pros:** many activities, ecology-minded staff. **Cons:** rustic room; no a/c; sometimes difficult to procure overnight space. ⊠ *6 km/4 mi south of Puerto Viejo de Sarapiquí* ☎ *2766–6565; 2524–0607 in San José* ⊕ *www.threepaths.co.cr* ☞ *60 bunk beds share 12 baths, 18 cabins* ♿ *In-room: no a/c, no phone, no TV. In-hotel: restaurant, laundry facilities* ▭ *AE, MC, V* ❖*FAP.*

OFF THE BEATEN PATH

South of Puerto Viejo de Sarapiquí, the tiny hamlet of Las Horquetas is a jumping-off point for two lodges, at different ends of the comfort scale:

$$\text{\$\$–\$\$\$}$$ ▢ **Rara Avis.** Toucans, sloths, great green macaws, howler and spider monkeys, vested anteaters, and tapirs may be on hand to greet you when you arrive at Rara Avis, one of Costa Rica's most popular private reserves, one open only to overnight guests. There are three lodging options here. The Waterfall Lodge, near a 59-meter (197-foot) waterfall, has hardwood-paneled rooms with chairs, firm beds, balconies, and hammocks. Despite the prices, accommodation is rustic, with minimal amenities and no electricity. More basic, Las Casitas are three two-room cabins with shared bath and cold water. On the high end, ideal for a rustic honeymoon, is the River Edge Cabin, a 10-minute walk through the forest (it's dark at night, but you're given a flashlight), with private bath and balcony and solar panel–generated electricity. Rates include guides and transport from Las Horquetas. It's time-consuming to get here—your journey from Las Horquetas is on a tractor-pulled cart ($10 one way)—so the recommended stay is two nights. **Pros:** many activities. **Cons:** rough trip to get here; expensive for amenities provided. ⊠ *Las Horquetas* ☎ *2764–1111* ⊕ *www.rara-avis.com* ↗ *16 rooms, 10 with bath* ♿ *In-room: no a/c, no phone, no TV. In-hotel: restaurant* ▭ *MC, V* ¶◎¶ *AI.*

$$\text{\$\$}$$ ▢ **Sueño Azul Resort.** This nature lodge and wellness retreat is the most luxurious property in the area, and a favorite for honeymooners and those attracted by the wide variety of yoga and other "wellness" disciplines. Spacious rooms have high ceilings, two double beds, large bathrooms, and a private porch overlooking either one of the rivers or a small lake. One large junior suite has its own outdoor whirlpool tub. Meals are served in an open-air dining room with a view. A wide range of tours and activities is offered, including rain forest hikes, horseback riding, mountain biking, and fly-fishing, as well as trips to major attractions. The spa and yoga facility are impressive for an area in which these amenities are unheard of. **Pros:** lovely furnishings. **Cons:** no a/c. ⊠ *Just west of Horquetas, off Hwy. 4* ☎ *2764–1000; 2253–2020 in San José* ⊕ *www. suenoazulresort.com* ↗ *65 rooms* ♿ *In-room: safe. In-hotel: restaurant, bar, pool, spa, laundry service* ▭ *AE, D, DC, MC, V* ¶◎¶ *EP.*

North Pacific

WORD OF MOUTH

"We spent a week in Samara in November. There is a trip report here somewhere. We loved it. We stayed at the Treehouse Inn, which is a great, small beachfront property. The town is small, safe, and friendly. There are kayaks (the real ones) for rent on the beach."

—SteveH5863

WELCOME TO NORTH PACIFIC

TOP REASONS TO GO

★ **Beaches:** White sand; black sand; palm-fringed strands; beaches for swimming, partying, surfing, and sunbathing—you can't beat Guanacaste's beaches for sheer variety.

★ **Endangered nature:** Guanacaste's varied national parks protect some of Central America's last remaining patches of tropical dry forest, an unusual ecosystem where you might spot magpie jays or howler monkeys in the branches of a gumbo-limbo tree.

★ **Surfing:** The waves are usually excellent at more than a dozen North Pacific beaches, including Playa Avellanas, Playa Grande, and Playa Negra.

★ **Big wind:** From December to May, the trade winds whip across northern Guanacaste with a velocity and consistency that makes the Bahía Salinas a world-class sailboarding and kitesurfing destination.

★ **Scuba diving:** Forget the pretty tropical fish. Sharks, rays, sea turtles, and moray eels are the large-scale attractions for divers on the Guanacaste coast.

1 **Far Northern Guanacaste.** Dry, hot Far Northern Guanacaste is traditionally ranching country, but it does include the impressive wildernesses of Santa Rosa and Rincón de la Vieja national parks, the latter of which holds one of Costa Rica's five active volcanoes. Farther to the north is Bahía Salinas, second only to Lake Arenal for wind- and kitesurfing.

2 **Tempisque River Basin.** National parks Palo Verde and Barra Honda are the main attractions in the Tempisque River Basin. The former is a prime bird-watching park; the latter has caves and tropical forest ripe for exploration.

3 **Nicoya Coast.** The number and variety of beaches along the Nicoya Coast make it a top tourist destination. Each beach has its specialty, be it surfing, fishing, diving, or just plain relaxing. Hotels and restaurants are in generous supply.

GETTING ORIENTED

Guanacaste Province—a vast swath of land in northwestern Costa Rica—is bordered by the Pacific Ocean to the west and the looming Cordillera de Guanacaste volcanic mountain range to the east. To the south is the Nicoya Peninsula, with almost continuous beaches along more than 100 km (62 mi) of Pacific coastline, as the crow flies. Many roads are unpaved, especially those to the national parks and less developed beaches, so the best way to get around is in a 4WD vehicle. Take a plane, bus, or shuttle van to Liberia and pick up your rental car there.

6

NORTH PACIFIC PLANNER

Weather or Not

The North Pacific region of Costa Rica is known for reliably beautiful weather, awesome beaches for surfing and sportfishing, and plenty of wildlife-watching opportunities. Guanacaste is the driest region of the country, with only 165 centimeters (65 inches) of average annual rainfall; it's also the hottest region, with average temperatures around 30°C to 35°C (86°F to 95°F). Mid-November through mid-January—the shoulder season—is the best time to visit, when the landscape is green, the evening air is cool, and hotels and restaurants are prepped and excited for the tourist influx. The beaches and trails can get packed during the drier months, especially mid-December to February, when school is out in Costa Rica. February through April are the driest months: skies are clear, but the heat is intense and the landscape is brown and parched. Fishing and scuba diving are at their best during this period. May through October are the rainy months, which bring lower prices, fewer crowds, and a lush green landscape—though most afternoons also see major downpours.

Getting Around the Region

Most roads here alternate between being extremely muddy and treacherous during the rainy season, and being extremely dusty and treacherous during the dry season. That said, it can be a real adventure exploring the coastline if you have a 4WD or a hired driver with a good, sturdy car. The major artery in this region is the Pan-American Highway (CA 1), which heads northwest from San José to Liberia, then due north to the Nicaraguan border. It's poorly maintained, with many potholes and hills. Trucks and buses often create heavy traffic. To skip the hours of driving, consider flying into Liberia, whose airport provides easy access to the region. Local hotels and tour companies can help you arrange for ground transportation in many cases. In Guanacaste, it's usually safe to take *pirata* (pirate, or unofficial) taxis, but always negotiate the price before getting into the cab.

What to Do

ACTIVITY	WHERE TO DO IT
Fishing	Playa Flamingo, Tamarindo, Puerto Carrillo, Playas del Coco
Diving	Playa Hermosa, Playa Flamingo, Playa Potrero, Playas del Coco, Ocotal
Surfing	Tamarindo, Playa Langosta, Playa Grande, Playa Avellanas, Playa Negra, Santa Rosa National Park, Playa Guiones
Volcanoes	Rincón de la Vieja National Park
Turtle-watching	Playa Grande, Playa Ostional
Wildlife-watching	Palo Verde National Park, Rincón de la Vieja National Park, Santa Rosa National Park, Barra Honda National Park

Getting the Most Out of the North Pacific

Visiting this region for 10 days to 2 weeks will introduce you to its wonders and leave you with a real taste of the North Pacific. Schedule plenty of beach time for lounging, sunbathing, surfing, diving, and snorkeling. Logistically, you also need to take into consideration slow travel over bumpy roads. A beach with lots of restaurants and nightlife can keep you entertained for a week or more, whereas a more solitary beach might merit only a couple of days. Also plan to visit some protected areas to enjoy canopy tours, wildlife-viewing, and hiking. Outdoorsy types should consider spending a few days around Rincón de la Vieja National Park for its amazing hiking, bird-watching, and horseback riding. Other parks to consider are Palo Verde National Park, Santa Rosa National Park, and Barra Honda National Park. Most North Pacific beaches are just a few hours drive from the Arenal Volcano area (⇨ Chapter 3), so the region can be combined with the Northern Plains. Macaw Air flies directly from Tamarindo or Liberia to Puerto Jiménez, where you can spend a few days in a jungle lodge off the grid in the Osa Peninsula, a contrast to developed Nicoya beaches.

Recommended Tour Operators

Swiss Travel Service (☎ 2282–4898 ⊕ *www.swisstravelcr. com*) specializes in Guanacaste. Despite the name, it's operated by Costa Ricans with lots of local experience. Custom-design a guided private or small-group tour.

The excellent **Horizontes Nature Tours** (☎ 2222–2022 ⊕ *www.horizontes.com*) has independent, private tours with your own guide/driver and small-group tours.

Dining and Lodging Prices

WHAT IT COSTS IN DOLLARS

	¢	$	$$	$$$	$$$$
Restaurants	under $5	$5–$10	$10–$15	$15–$25	over $25
Hotels	under $50	$50–$75	$75–$150	$150–$250	over $250

Restaurant prices are per person for a main course at dinner. Hotel prices are for two people in a standard double room in high season, excluding service and tax (16.4%).

Where to Stay?

A wide range of lodging options awaits you in the North Pacific, so choose wisely. If your goal is to take leisurely swims and lounge quietly on the beach with a cocktail in hand, then avoid the beaches that are renowned for surfing waves. Superexpensive resorts like the Four Seasons are generally well balanced with budget hotels that charge less than $50 per night. As in all of Costa Rica, the places we recommend most highly are the small owner-operated hotels and bed-and-breakfasts that blend in with unspoiled nature and offer one-on-one attention from the staff and owners. Most hotels will be able to connect you with local tour operators and knowledgeable staff members who can help show you the best aspects of each destination, whether it's a local park with howler monkeys, a great family-run restaurant on the beach, or a thrilling canopy tour.

Word of Mouth

"There is a nice hike [in Rincón de la Vieja] that goes by the hot mud pots and other interesting things. You'll have to cross some streams. You can access the trail from the main park entrance. The hike to the top [of the crater] is pretty strenuous. We weren't allowed up the time we tried because of high winds."

—Suzie2

PALO VERDE NATIONAL PARK

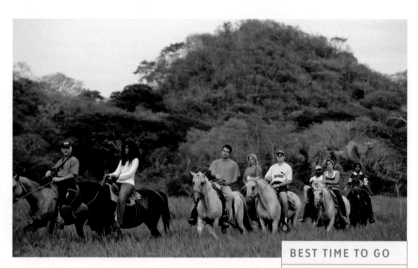

One of the best wildlife- and bird-watching parks in the country, Palo Verde extends over 198 square km (76 square mi) of dry deciduous forest, bordered on the west by the wide Tempisque River.

With fairly flat terrain and less dense forest than a rain forest, wildlife is often easier to spot here. Frequent sightings include monkeys, coatis, peccaries, lizards, and snakes. (Keep an eye out for the harlequin snake. It's non-poisonous but mimics the deadly coral snake coloring.)

The park contains seasonal wetlands at the end of the rainy season that provide a temporary home for thousands of migratory and resident aquatic birds, including herons, wood storks, jabirus, and flamingo-like roseate spoonbills. Crocodiles ply the slow waters of the Tempisque River year-round, and storks nest on islands at the mouth of the river where it empties into the Gulf of Nicoya. Trails are well marked, but the weather here can be very hot and windy. Mosquitoes, especially in the marshy areas, are rampant.

BEST TIME TO GO

The best time of year to go is at the beginning of the dry season, especially in January and February, when the seasonal wetlands are shrinking and birds and wildlife are concentrated around smaller ponds. Set off early in the morning or after 3 in the afternoon, when the sun is lower and the heat is less intense.

FUN FACT

The park is named after the lacy, light-green Palo Verde bush, also known as the Jerusalem thorn. Even when it loses its leaflets, this tree can still photosynthesize through its trunk, so it can withstand the droughts common to this area.

BEST WAYS TO EXPLORE

PARK STRATEGIES

Unlike many of the other national parks, you can drive 7 km (5 mi) of fairly rough road from the park entrance to the Organization for Tropical Studies (OTS) research station, where most of the trailheads begin. From that point, the best way to see the park is on foot. Plan to spend a couple of nights in the dormitory-style park lodge so that you can get an early-morning start. You'll want to start early because this is a very, very hot area. Hike open areas in the cooler mornings and then choose shaded forest trails for hikes later in the day. Make sure you have a good sun hat, too.

BIRD-WATCHING

The greatest number of creatures you're likely to see here are birds, close to 300 recorded species. Many of them are aquatic birds drawn to the park's vast marshes and seasonal wetlands. The most sought-after aquatic bird is the jabiru stork, a huge white bird with a red neck and long black bill. You'll most likely see it soaring overhead—it's hard to miss. Other birds endemic to the northwest, which you may find in the park's dry-forest habitat, are streaked-back orioles, banded wrens, and black-headed trogons.

There's a raised platform near the OTS station with a panoramic view over a bird-filled marsh. Be prepared to climb a narrow metal ladder.

RIVER CRUISE

A river does run through the park, so a delightful and less strenuous wildlife-viewing option is to cruise down the Tempisque River on a chartered boat with a guide who'll do the spotting for you. Without a boat, you are limited to observing the marshy areas and riverbanks from a long distance. Be sure the boat you choose has a bilingual naturalist on board who knows the English names of birds and animals.

TOP REASON TO GO

BIRDS, BIRDS, BIRDS
Even if you're not used to looking at birds, you'll be impressed by the waves of migratory waterbirds that use this park as a way station on their migratory routes. Think of the 2001 documentary *Winged Migration,* and you'll have an idea of the numbers of birds that flock here.

LOTS OF WILD ANIMALS
Hiking the forest trails is hot work, especially in the dry season. But the wildlife-viewing here makes it worthwhile. Watch for monkeys, peccaries, large lizards, and coatis. Take plenty of water with you wherever you walk, and use repellent or wear long sleeves and pants.

OUTDOOR ADVENTURES
The Organization for Tropical Studies has a number of activities that are good for just about any type of group. Choose from guided nature walks, mountain biking, boat tours, and even an occasional nighttime tour. Accommodations can be a little rugged here, but that's half the fun.

6

RINCÓN DE LA VIEJA NATIONAL PARK

Rincón de la Vieja National Park is Costa Rica's mini-Yellowstone, with volcanic hot springs and bubbling mud pools, refreshing waterfalls, and cool forest trails. Often shrouded in clouds, the volcano dominates the landscape northwest of Liberia, rising above the sunbaked plains.

It has two windswept peaks, Santa María, 1,916 meters (6,323 feet) high on the east slope, and Rincón de la Vieja at 1,895 meters (6,254 feet) on the west. The latter slope has an active crater that hardy hikers can climb up to, and easily accessible fumaroles on its lower slope that constantly let off steam. The park protects more than 177 square km (54 square mi) of the volcano's forested slopes. The wildlife list includes more than 250 species of birds, plus mammals such as white-tailed deer, coyotes, howler and capuchin monkeys, armadillos, and the occasional harlequin snake (not poisonous). The Las Pailas entrance has the most accessible trails, including an easy loop trail that wends past all the interesting volcanic features.

BEST TIME TO GO

Good times to visit are January through May, during the dry season. January can be very windy, but that means temperatures stay cool for hiking. May to November—the green season—is when the fumaroles and boiling mud pots are most active, but the crater is often covered in clouds so it's not the best time to hike to the top. Trails can get crowded during school break (mid-December through February). Get here early if you plan a long hike or a climb to the crater, since the park entrance closes at 3 PM. The park is closed on Monday all year.

BEST WAYS TO EXPLORE

HIKING

The only way to explore the park trails is on foot, along well-marked paths that range from easy loops to longer, more demanding climbs. The ranger station at the Las Pailas entrance provides maps of the park trails and washrooms before you set off. The easiest hike is the Las Pailas loop, which starts just past the ranger station; it takes about two hours to hike. If you want to venture farther afield, follow the signs for the La Cangreja trail. After passing through dense, cool forest, you'll emerge through an avenue of giant agave plants into an open, windy, meadow. Your reward is the cool waterfall and swimming hole at the end of the trail. There are also warm springs in the rocks surrounding the pool, so you can alternate between warm and cool water in this natural spa.

BIRD-WATCHING

Wherever you walk in this park, you are bound to hear the three-note song of the long-tailed manakin. It sounds something like "Toledo," and that's what the locals call this bird. Along with their lavish, long tail feathers, the males are famous for their cooperative courting dance: two pals leap back and forth over each other, but only the senior male gets any girl who falls for this act. The hard-to-spot rock wren lives closer to the top of the volcano. Birding is excellent most of the year here except for January when the weather is dry but often too windy to distinguish between a fluttering leaf or a flittering bird.

ON HORSEBACK

Saddle up to explore the lower slopes of the volcano, just outside the park borders. Local ranches and lodges organize daylong trail rides to waterfalls and sulfur springs. Your nose will tell you when you are approaching the springs—it's not the picnic lunch gone bad, it's the distinctive rotten-egg smell of sulfur.

TOP REASON TO GO

GEOLOGICAL WONDERS

The 3-km (2-mi) Las Pailas loop trail showcases the park's famous geothermal features. Along the trail you'll see fumaroles with steam hissing out of ground vents, a *volcancito* (baby volcano), and boiling mud fields named after pots (*pailas*) used for boiling down sugarcane.

CLIMBING TO THE CRATER

The hike to the crater summit is the most demanding, but also the most dramatic. The trail climbs 8 km (5 mi) through shaded forest, then up a sunbaked, treeless slope to the windswept crater, where temperatures plummet. Be sure to check wind and weather conditions at the ranger station before attempting this hike.

BIRDING

The park's forest, alive with the haunting songs of the long-tailed manakin and the loud whinnies of the ivory-billed woodcreeper, is prime bird-watching territory. For intrepid birders, the winding trail leading to the crater is home to the rock wren, which can only be found on these slopes.

6

SANTA ROSA NATIONAL PARK

Renowned for its wildlife, Santa Rosa National Park protects the largest swath of extant lowland dry forest in Central America, about 91,000 acres. *Dry* is the operative word here, with less than 162 centimeters (64 inches) of rainfall a year.

If you station yourself near watering holes in the dry season—January to April—you may spot deer, coyotes, coatis, and armadillos. The park also has the world's only fully protected nesting beach for olive ridley sea turtles. Treetop inhabitants include spider, capuchin, and howler monkeys, as well as hundreds of bird species. The deciduous forest here includes giant kapok, Guanacaste, and mahogany trees, as well as calabash, acacia, and gumbo-limbo trees with their distinctive peeling bark. The park is also of historical significance to Costa Rica because it was here, in 1856, that an army of Costa Rican volunteers decisively defeated an invading force of mercenaries led by an American adventurer named William Walker.

BEST TIME TO GO

Dry season is the best time to visit if you want to see wildlife. The vegetation is sparse, making for easy observation. It's also the best time to drive to the park's beaches. Be aware: it can get very hot and very dry, so take plenty of water if you plan on hiking. In the rainy season, trails can become mud baths.

FUN FACT

Moving from sparse, sunlit secondary forest into the park's shady primary forest areas, you can experience an instant temperature drop of as much as 5°C (9°F). It's a little like walking into a fridge, so wear layers.

BEST WAYS TO EXPLORE

GETTING AROUND

Only the first 12 km (7 mi) of the park's roads are accessible by vehicles. The rest of the park's 20 km (12 mi) of trails are for hiking only. It's easy to drive to the La Casona headquarters along a paved road and pick up a loop hiking trail, but beyond that point you need a four-wheel-drive vehicle. During the rainy season, the roads beyond La Casona are impassable even to four-wheel-drive vehicles. Get an early start for any hikes to take advantage of cooler temperatures.

A HISTORICAL TOUR

Costa Rica doesn't have many historical sites—relics of its colonial past have mostly been destroyed by earthquakes and volcanic eruptions. So La Casona, the symbolic birthplace of Costa Rica's nationhood, is a particularly revered site. Most Costa Ricans come to Santa Rosa on a historical pilgrimage. Imagine the nation's horror when the place was burned to the ground in a fire purposely set in 2001 by disgruntled poachers, who had been fined by park rangers. The government, school children, and private businesses came to the rescue, raising the money to restore the historic hacienda and replace the exhibits of antique farm tools and historical photos.

TURTLE-WATCHING

Thousands of olive ridley sea turtles emerge from the sea every year, from July to December, to dig nests and deposit eggs on the park's protected beaches at Playa Nancite and Playa Naranjo. Green sea turtles and the huge leatherbacks also clamber ashore, but in much smaller numbers. If you're a hardy outdoors type, you can hike the 12 km (8 mi) to Playa Naranjo and pitch your tent near the beach. Unlike most other turtle-nesting beaches with organized tours, this is a natural spectacle you'll get to witness far from any crowds.

TOP REASONS TO GO

EXPLORE THE FOREST

The short (about a half a mile) La Casona nature-trail loop, which starts from the park headquarters, is a great way to get a sampling of dry tropical forest and to spot wildlife. Look for signs leading to the *Indio Desnudo* (Naked Indian) path, named after the local word for gumbo-limbo trees.

WILDLIFE-WATCHING

Wildlife is easy to spot here thanks to the low-density foliage of this tropical dry forest. Scan the treetops and keep an eye out for spider, white-faced capuchin, and howler monkeys. If you're lucky you might even spot an ocelot.

SERIOUS SURFING

Off Playa Naranjo lies the famous Witch's Rock, a towering rock formation famous for its surfing breaks. If you're interested in checking it out but don't feel like walking for miles, take a boat from Playa del Coco, Playa Hermosa, or Playa Tamarindo.

6

ECO-LODGES IN THE NORTH PACIFIC

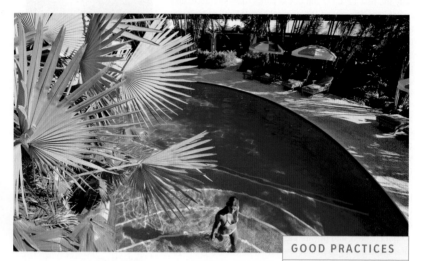

On the mainland, sweeping plains bordered by volcanoes hold remnants of Central America's tropical dry forest. On the Pacific-edged Nicoya Peninsula, conservationists try to protect turtle-nesting beaches from the encroachments of ever-grander resort hotels and vacation houses.

These tropical dry forests change from relatively lush landscapes during the rainy season to desertlike panoramas in the dry months. The national parks of Santa Rosa, Rincón de la Vieja, Palo Verde, and Barra Honda all protect vestiges of dry forest, as do the private reserves of Hacienda Guachipelín and Rincón de la Vieja Mountain Lodge, where guests can explore on horseback. Visitors can experience the region's wetlands and waterways by riverboat tours and raft. The Nicoya Peninsula is also the site of Las Baulas National Marine Park, where massive leatherback sea turtles lay their eggs on Playa Grande from October to March; and Ostional National Wildlife Refuge, where thousands of olive ridley turtles clamber ashore on moonlit nights from July to January.

GOOD PRACTICES

After a decade of uncontrolled development in the North Pacific province of Guanacaste, *Guanacastecation* became a pejorative watchword in Costa Rica for unsustainable development.

Playas Junquillal, Negra, Nosara, and Punta Islita are some of the notable exceptions to overdevelopment, managing to maintain a balance between nature and commercial development. Eco-minded tourists who are planning a beach vacation may want to visit these less-developed areas and reward lodge owners who have worked hard to keep their pieces of paradise as sustainable as possible.

TOP ECO-LODGES IN THE NORTH PACIFIC

HARMONY HOTEL

Steps from Playa Guiones in Nosara, this former surfer hotel has been transformed into a low-key, luxury resort with a sustainable mind-set. From permaculture-inspired landscaping with native plants and the use of biodegradable cleaning products and toiletries, to solar-heated hot water and conscientious recycling and waste-management policies, the hotel owners cover all the sustainable stops. Hotel employees, most of them local hires, also volunteer in the town schools, mentoring and teaching English classes and computer literacy.

LAGARTA LODGE

Perched high on a hill, Lagarta Lodge has a wonderful view of distant Ostional National Wildlife Refuge bordering the Pacific. With only six guest rooms, the hotel minimizes its environmental impact by keeping a sharp eye on its consumption of water and energy, as well as on waste management and recycling. Its eco-friendly hospitality practices have garnered it two leaves in the national Green Leaf sustainability program. By far the most salient eco-aspect of the lodge, though, is its 90-acre private Nosara Biological Reserve, with trails crisscrossing a huge mangrove forest bordering the Nosara River and snaking through primary forest on the steep slopes leading from the lodge down to the river.

BORINQUEN MOUNTAIN RESORT & SPA

This luxury resort of stylish villas on the western slope of Rincón de la Vieja doesn't fit the typical eco-lodge profile. But the hotel's eco-conscious policies have won it three leaves in the Green Leaf sustainability program. As well as putting sustainable practices to work, staff members teach the local community about the importance of recycling, waste separation, and organic gardening. The hotel uses earth-friendly, biodegradable products; conserves energy consumption and water use; and helps support community schools with proceeds from recycling refunds.

NESTING LEATHERBACK TURTLES

You simply cannot believe how big a leatherback turtle is. Weighing in at 550 kilos (more than 1,200 pounds), females come ashore under cover of night to lay clutches of up to 100 golf ball–size eggs in nests they dig out of the sand with their flippers. People will go to great lengths in the hopes of catching this incredible sight. Your best chance is at Playa Grande in Las Baulas National Marine Park. As night falls, groups of visitors, each shepherded by a local guide, hunker down at the park entrance, waiting for the summons to sprint down the beach to take their turn, standing silently and witnessing the monumental egg laying. A decade ago, it was almost a sure thing to find at least one laying turtle on the beach during the nesting season. But today, some groups will come away disappointed, a sad reminder of how in the past 25 years, shore development and commercial fishing have reduced sea turtle populations by 99%.

6

NORTH PACIFIC

Updated by
David Duden-
hoefer and
Heidi Leigh
Johansen

Beautiful weather and a windswept coastline bring surfers to the North Pacific area of Costa Rica, an abundance of marine life and stellar diving spots lure underwater aficionados, and a sturdy flow of tourism paired with a laid-back attitude make this an all-around top spot to experience Costa Rica's charms.

GETTING HERE AND AROUND

Aeropuerto Internacional Daniel Oduber Quirós (LIR) in Liberia is an international gateway to the coast. Tamarindo, Playa Nosara, Playa Sámara, Playa Carrillo, and Punta Islita also have airstrips. Flying in from San José to these airports is the best way to get here if you are already in the country. If your primary destination lies in Guanacaste or Nicoya, make sure you or your travel agent investigates the possibility of flying directly into Liberia instead of San José, which saves some serious hours on the road.

SANSA and Nature Air have scheduled flights between San José and destinations on the Nicoya Peninsula. Macaw Air flies small planes between Liberia and Tamarindo, as well as between destinations on the Nicoya Peninsula and to other destinations, including Quepos and Puerto Jiménez.

The northwest is accessed via the paved two-lane Pan-American Highway (CA 1), which begins at the top of Paseo Colón in San José. Take the bridge across the Tempisque River to get to the Pacific beaches south of Liberia. Paved roads run down the spine of the Nicoya Peninsula all the way to Playa Naranjo, with many unpaved and potholed stretches. Once you get off the main highway, dust, mud, potholes, and other factors come into play, depending on which beach you visit. The roads to Playa Flamingo, Playa Conchal, Playa Brasilito, Tamarindo, Playa Grande, Playa Sámara, Playas del Coco, Hermosa, and Ocotal are paved all the way; every other destination requires some dirt-road maneuvering.

You can ride in a comfortable, air-conditioned minibus with Gray Line Tourist Bus, connecting San José, Liberia, Playa Flamingo, Playa Conchal, Playa Potrero, Playa Brasilito, Playa Hermosa, Playas del Coco, Ocotal, Tamarindo, Rincón de la Vieja, and Playa Langosta. Fares range from $35 to $45, depending on destination. The Gray Line Tourist Bus from San José to Liberia and Tamarindo begins picking up passengers from hotels daily around 8 AM. The return bus leaves the Tamarindo and Flamingo areas around 8:30 AM and 3:30 PM. Interbus has door-to-door minivan shuttle service from San José to all the major beach destinations (Papagayo, Canas, Flamingo, Tamarindo, Cocos, Ocotal, Nicoya, and Sámara), for $35 to $49 per person. Reserve at least one day in advance.

ESSENTIALS

Bus Contacts Gray Line Tourist Bus (2220–2126 ⊕ *www.graylinecostarica. com*). **Interbus** (📞 2283–5573 ⊕ *www.interbusonline.com*).

FAR NORTHERN GUANACASTE

The mountains, plains, and coastline north of Liberia up to the border of Nicaragua make up Far Northern Guanacaste. Liberia, the capital of Guanacaste province, is the closest town to Costa Rica's second-largest airport. You'll most likely pass through it on your way to the beaches southwest of the city or to the nearby national parks of Guanacaste, Santa Rosa, or Rincón de la Vieja. This last park is home to Volcán Rincón de la Vieja, an active volcano that last erupted in 1991.

Northwest of Rincón de la Vieja, on the coast, Parque Nacional Santa Rosa (Santa Rosa National Park) is a former cattle ranch where Costa Ricans defeated the invading mercenary army of American William Walker in 1856. Together with adjacent Guanacaste National Park, Santa Rosa protects the country's largest remnant of tropical dry forest, as well as an important nesting beach for olive ridley sea turtles, which lay their eggs in the sand between July and November. Closer still to the Nicaraguan border is the town of La Cruz, overlooking the lovely Golfo de Santa Elena, and the remote beaches and windswept hotels of Bahía Salinas.

RINCÓN DE LA VIEJA NATIONAL PARK

25 km (15 mi) northeast of Liberia.

★ Parque Nacional Rincón de la Vieja is Costa Rica's mini-Yellowstone, with volcanic hot springs and boiling, bubbling mud ponds. The park protects more than 140 square km (54 square mi) of the volcano's upper slopes, which are covered with forest. Often enveloped in clouds, the volcano dominates the scenery to the east of the Pan-American Highway. It has two peaks: Santa María (1,916 meters [6,323 feet]) and the barren Rincón de la Vieja (1,895 meters [6,254 feet]). The latter has an active crater and fumaroles on its lower slope that constantly let off steam, making an eruption unlikely anytime soon. The wildlife here is diverse: more than 250 species of birds, including long-tailed manakins and blue-crowned motmots; plus mammals such as white-tailed deer, coyotes, howler and capuchin monkeys, and armadillos. There are two main entrances: Santa María and Las Pailas; the latter is the most common place to enter the park because it has the most accessible trails and there are several hotels along the road leading up to it. ■TIP→ If you want to explore the slopes of the volcano, go with a guide—the abundant hot springs and geysers have given unsuspecting visitors some very nasty burns. In addition, the upper slopes often receive fierce and potentially dangerous winds—before ascending, check at either ranger station for conditions. The park does not have guides; we recommend the guides at Hacienda Guachipelín and Rincón de la Vieja Volcano Mountain Lodge (⇨ below). You must sign in and pay at the ranger station. Many of the attractions people visit in Rincón de la Vieja are accessible without actually entering the park, since the ranches that border it also hold significant forest and geothermal sites. ☎ 2666–5051 ☞ $10 ☉ Tuesday to Sunday 7–5, last entry at 3 PM.

GETTING HERE AND AROUND

There are two park entrances on the volcano's southern slope: the less traveled one at Hacienda Santa María on the road leading northeast from Liberia (one hour); and the one at Las Pailas, past Curubandé off the Pan-American Highway. To get to the Las Pailas entrance from

CLOSE UP

More Texan than Tropical

Guanacaste, Costa Rica's "Wild West," looks different from the rest of Costa Rica. It was originally covered in dry tropical forests, but beginning in early colonial times, and then picking up speed in the 1950s (when cattle ranching became big business), the dry forest was cleared to create vast cattle ranges. Harder-to-access forests covering the volcanic slopes survived. The resulting flat, sunbaked landscape makes the inland parts of the province look a little like the American Southwest. Cowboy culture still takes center stage during seasonal fiestas and a few rodeos. But these days more and more *sabaneros* (cowboys) are trading in their horses for pickup trucks.

Liberia, take the first entrance road 5 km (3 mi) northwest of Liberia off the Pan-American Highway. The turnoff is easy to miss—follow signs for Hacienda Guachipelín or the town of Curubandé. It's a rough 23-km (14-mi) dirt road, and you have to pay a small toll. The Santa María entrance is 25 km (15 mi) northeast of Liberia along the Colonia Blanca route, which follows the course of the Río Liberia. The turnoff from the Pan-American Highway to the hotels on the western slope of the volcano is 12 km (7 mi) northwest of Liberia, turning right at the road signed for Cañas Dulces. A 4WD vehicle is recommended, though not essential, for all these slow and bone-rattling rides.

OUTDOOR ACTIVITIES

Borinquen Mountain Resort & Spa (⊠ *12 km/7½ mi northwest of Liberia on the Pan-American Hwy., then 23 km/14 mi north on the dirt road that passes Cañas Dulces* ☎ *2690–1900* ⊕ *www.borinquenhotel.com*) offers a day package ($95 that begins with a horseback ride and a 90-minute canopy tour, followed by lunch and free time in the hotel's hot springs and natural steam bath. **Buena Vista Lodge & Adventure Center** (⊠ *Western slope of volcano 10 km/6 mi north of Cañas Dulces* ☎ *2690–1414, in Liberia 2665-7759* ⊕ *www.buenavistalodgecr.com*), west of the park, lies on a large ranch contiguous with the park where visitors enjoy horseback riding, waterfall hikes, a canopy tour, hanging bridges, a 480-meter (1,600-foot) (long, not steep) waterslide through the forest, and hot springs. Tours are $25 to $45 per person; a combo ticket is $80, including lunch. **Hacienda Guachipelín Adventure Tours** (⊠ *Road to Rincón de la Vieja National Park* ☎ *2666–8075 or 2256-5693* ⊕ *www. guachipelin.com*) has horseback riding, river tubing, hot springs and mud baths, and guided waterfall and volcano hikes. The popular canyon tour includes rock climbing, rappelling, zip lines, suspension bridges, and a Tarzan swing. A one-day, all-you-can-do adventure pass is $80, including lunch. Playa Hermosa–based Mainor Lara Bustos of **Tours Your Way** (☎ *8820–1829* ⊕ *www.tours-your-way.com*) guides tours to Rincón de la Vieja or Palo Verde for $80, including transportation, entrance fees, lunch, and snacks.

6

CANOPY TOURS

The zip-line canopy tour ($40) with **Buena Vista Lodge & Adventure Center** (⇨ *above*) has cables that are up to 27 meters (90 feet) off the ground and up to 135 meters (450 feet) long. **Rincón de la Vieja Canopy** (✉ *Rincón de la Vieja Volcano Mountain Lodge* ☎ 2200–0238 ⊕ *www. guanacastepuravida/com*) runs four-hour horseback and canopy tours ($45), which include a 16-platform zip line, a ride to the Los Azufrales sulfur springs, or a forest hike to a waterfall with a box lunch.

HIKING

Nearly all the lodges and outfitters in the area offer guided hikes through the park to the fumaroles, hot springs, waterfalls, summit, or the edge of the active crater.

If you're doing a self-guided hike, stop for trail maps and hiking information at the park stations at both entrance gates. The 8-km (5-mi) **trail to the summit** heads up into the forest from the Las Pailas park entrance, then emerges onto a windy, exposed shale slope that's slippery and hard going, and has poor visibility owing to clouds and mist. It's a trip for serious hikers, best done in dry season with preparation for cold weather at the top. A less strenuous option is the fascinating 3-km (2-mi) **loop through the park**, which takes about two hours to complete, starting at the Las Pailas entrance. Along the well-marked trail you'll see fumaroles exuding steam, a *volcáncito* (little volcano), and Las Pailas, the boiling mud fields named after pots used for boiling down sugarcane. If you tread softly in the nearby forest, you may spot animals such as howler, capuchin, and spider monkeys, as well as raccoonlike coatis looking for handouts. ■ TIP→ Remember the cardinal rule of wildlife encounters: don't feed the animals. Another popular hike out of Las Pailas is a four-hour, 10-km (6-mi) **La Cangreja Waterfall loop**, passing through beautiful primary forests and windswept savannas. The *catarata* (waterfall) has a cool swimming hole below; the surrounding rocks have pockets of hot springs.

HORSEBACK RIDING

Borinquen Mountain Resort & Spa (⇨ *above*) offers horseback tours ($80) on a 494-acre ranch that holds patches of forest and ridges with views of nearby Rincón de la Vieja that can be combined with a hike to waterfalls, or a canopy tour. The tour combos include lunch and use of hot springs, and range in price from $80 to $95.

Buena Vista Mountain Lodge & Adventure Center (⇨ *above*) has horseback trips to hot springs ($40) and to Borinquen Waterfall ($40). If not everyone in your party is a horse lover, tractor transport ($35) is available to the hot springs as well. **Rincón de la Vieja Volcano Mountain Lodge** (⇨ *above*) has guides for hiking or horseback riding near the park. **Hacienda Guachipélin** (⇨ *above*) is a working ranch with more than 100 horses and miles of trails to three waterfalls, tropical dry forest, and hot springs. Fees range from $25 to $40.

WHERE TO STAY

$$$–$$$$ ⊡ **Borinquen Mountain Resort & Spa.** The spacious villas on this 12,000-acre ranch overlook lawns shaded by tropical trees on the volcano's windy west slope. They are the nicest accommodations in the area, with

sloping wooden ceilings, large porches, and plenty of amenities, but they are by far the most expensive as well. Elegant deluxe bungalows have king-size canopy beds, whereas the junior suites have amazing views. Though 90 minutes from the park entrance, the ranch holds most of the same natural attractions, including three waterfalls and patches of forest that hold monkeys, parrots, deer, and other wildlife. The spa has volcanic mud baths, hot springs, and a wooden sauna heated by steam from a fumarole, all included in room rates. Activities include hiking, horseback riding, ATV trips, a canopy tour, and a trip to the park in a Land Rover followed by a hike. The rooms are separated from the restaurant and spa by steep climbs, but the staff can transport you in a golf cart. **Pros:** attractive, well-equipped bungalows; peaceful environment; lots of outdoor activities. **Cons:** far from park entrance; overpriced; restaurant a notch below accommodations. ⊠ *13 km/8 mi northwest of Liberia on Pan-American Hwy., then 29 km/18 mi north on the dirt road toward Cañas Dulces* ☎ *2690–1900* ⊕ *www.borinquenhotel.com* ⤵ *22 villas, 17 bungalows* ⌂ *In-room: refrigerator. In-hotel: restaurant, bar, pool, spa, laundry service, Internet terminal, Wi-Fi hotspot* ☰ *AE, DC, MC, V* �ⓄⅠ *BP.*

$ ▦ **Hacienda Guachipelín.** Day-trippers come here, perhaps one of the best
★ values in the Rincón area, for hair-raising adventure tours *(⇨ Outdoor Activities, above)*, but this 3,706-acre working ranch is also famous for its horses—more than 100 of them—and its nature trails leading to several waterfalls, hot springs, and mud baths. Rugged ranch hands swaggering around give the place a real cowboy flavor. Rooms are large and pleasantly furnished, with windows front and back to let in cool mountain air. The newer rooms, numbers 32 and up, are more colorful and larger, though a bit of a walk from the restaurant. Avoid rooms 24 to 31, right beside the corral, unless you enjoy the aroma of horses; try to get one between 32 and 39, which have volcano views from the front terrace. Hearty buffet meals are served in the open-air restaurant, which has valley views. Dairy and beef products come fresh from the hacienda's own herd; vegetarians may have trouble finding meat-free dishes. Large groups often stay here, but you can always find a quiet trail on the vast, partially forested property. The hotel's spa offers an array of treatments, from mud wraps to massages. **Pros:** near park entrance; lots of activities; good value. **Cons:** caters to lots of large groups and day visitors; no a/c in some rooms. ⊠ *17 km/10 mi northeast of the Pan-American Hwy., on road to Las Pailas park entrance* ☎ *2666–8075 or 2442–1828* ⊕ *www.guachipelin.com* ⤵ *52 rooms* ⌂ *In-room: no a/c, no phone, safe, no TV. In-hotel: restaurant, bar, pool, spa, laundry service, Internet terminal* ☰ *AE, DC, MC, V* ⓄⅠ *BP.*

$ ▦ **Rincón de la Vieja Mountain Lodge.** This is the closest you can stay to the Las Pailas park entrance, which makes it a good spot for hikers and nature lovers who aren't terribly demanding. Hiking and horse trails lead to a hot sulfuric pool, and farther through the forest, to a blue lake and waterfall, and the volcano's crater deep in the park. The sunny log cabins (room numbers 39 and up), with colorful tiled bathrooms and porches with hammocks, are the best choices. Avoid the rows of connected older rooms (1 to 28), which are dark and gloomy. The dining room is claustrophobic, with mediocre food served buffet-style, but the alfresco bar is lively in the evening, usually filled with small groups of international ecotourist types. The grounds are shaded by giant malinche trees, and there is a tiny dipping pool. **Pros:** close to park; lots of tour options; reasonably priced. **Cons:** rustic rooms; mediocre food. ⊠ *21 km/12 mi northeast of Pan-American Hwy.; 5 km/3 mi north of Hacienda Guachipelín; 2 km/1 mi south of Las Pailas park entrance* ☎ *2200–0238* ⊕ *www.guanacastepuravida.com* ⟲ *42 rooms* ⌂ *In-room: no a/c, no phone, no TV. In-hotel: restaurant, bar, Wi-Fi* ⊟ *AE, MC, V* ⟠ *BP.*

SANTA ROSA NATIONAL PARK

35 km/22 mi northwest of Liberia.

Renowned for its wildlife, which is easy to spot in the dry season, thanks to sparser foliage, Santa Rosa protects the largest swath of tropical dry forest in Central America. Camping expeditions serving bird-watchers, naturalists, and backpackers often venture deep into the interior, but it's possible to experience a good bit of its impressive flora and fauna on a full-day or half-day visit. Treetop inhabitants include spider, capuchin, and howler monkeys, as well as hundreds of bird species. If you station yourself next to water holes during the dry season, you may also spot deer, coyotes, coatis, or armadillos. Typical dry-forest vegetation includes kapok, Guanacaste, mahogany, calabash, acacia thorn, and gumbo-limbo trees.

Santa Rosa's wealth of flora and fauna is due in part to its remoteness, since much of it is still inaccessible to the common tourist. To get anywhere in the park, you must have a vehicle—preferably 4WD. The park headquarters, a historic ranch house and museum called La Casona, and a nearby camping area are 8 km (5 mi) from the Pan-American Highway via a paved road. Within this dense, shady forest, temperatures drop by as much as 5°C (9°F).

In rainy season the park's rough road to the beach cannot be accessed by even 4WD vehicles, but several short trails head into the forest from its first, flat stretch, and day hikers can easily explore the first stretch of the steep part on foot. Park off the road just before it descends into the forest. From the park headquarters it's 13 km (8 mi) to **Playa Naranjo,** where famed Witch's Rock surf break is located (surfers often get there by boat). **Playa Nancite**—the site of one of the world's only completely protected olive ridley turtle *arribada,* or mass nesting (accessible primarily to biologists and students; permit required)—is an additional 5 km (3 mi) by footpath north of Playa Naranjo. ⊠ *Km 269, Pan-American Hwy. 35 km/22 mi north of Liberia* ☎ *2666–5051* ⟲ *$10* ☉ *Daily 8–4:30.*

GETTING HERE AND AROUND

The turnoff for Santa Rosa National Park from the Pan-American Highway is well marked, about 30 minutes out from Liberia. From Liberia you can hop on a bus heading north to La Cruz and get off at the park entrance, but you'll have to hitchhike or hike 8 km (5 mi) in the hot sun to La Casona from here.

OUTDOOR ACTIVITIES

HIKING

The short (about half a mile) **La Casona nature-trail loop** from the park headquarters is worth taking to get a brief sampling of the woods. Look for the INDIO DESNUDO, or "Naked Indian," path, named after the local word for gumbo-limbo trees. ■TIP→ Carry plenty of water and insect repellent.

Several other short trails lead off the road **to the beaches** before it becomes impassable to vehicles. The hike to Playa Naranjo (13 km [8 mi] west of La Casona) and Playa Nancite (5 km [3 mi] north of Naranjo) requires good physical condition and lots of water. You can get a map of the trails at the park entrance.

> **WALKERS LAST STAND**
>
> Santa Rosa Park was the site of the 1856 triumph over American invader William Walker in the famous Battle of Santa Rosa— one of the few historic military sites in this army-less country. The rambling colonial-style ranch house called La Casona was the last stand of a ragged force of ill-equipped Costa Ricans who routed the superior mercenary army of the notorious Walker. Disgruntled poachers burned La Casona to the ground in 2001, but it has since been rebuilt.

SURFING

★ **Witch's Rock** towers offshore over a near-perfect beach break off Playa Naranjo in Santa Rosa National Park. If you are interested in surfing Witch's Rock, take a boat tour from Playas del Coco, Playa Hermosa, or Playa Tamarindo, to the south.

WHERE TO STAY

There are basic, dormitory-style lodgings and a camping area near the park's administrative center and at a biological station at Playa Naranjo. You can also camp within Santa Rosa National Park at the very basic and remote campsites at the beaches of Naranjo and Murcielego. Call the park headquarters (☎ 2666–5051 or 2666–0630) for information. Most people visit the park on day trips from Liberia, or nearby Cuajiniquil.

PLAYA BAHÍA JUNQUILLAL

26 km/16 mi northwest of Santa Rosa National Park entrance.

This 2½-km (1½-mi), tree-fringed, Blue Flag beach is as close as you can get to white-sand beach in this part of Guanacaste. The warm, calm water makes it one of the best swimming beaches on the Gulfo de Santa Elena. Not to be confused with the Playa Junquillal on the western coast of the Nicoya Peninsula farther south, this beach is part of the Guanacaste National Wildlife Refuge to the north of Santa Rosa. Stay for the day or camp out in the well-kept, shaded camping area with cold-water showers, grills, and picnic tables. You can snorkel if you've got your own gear. ⊠ *18 km/11 mi west of Pan-American Hwy. Cuajiniquil turnoff.*

GETTING HERE AND AROUND

From the Pan-American Highway, take the road signed for Cuajiniquil, 43 km (26 mi) northwest of Liberia and 8 km (5 mi) north of Santa Rosa National Park. Follow the paved road 14 km (8 mi) to the beach turnoff, along a dirt road for another 4 km (2½ mi). From the Bahía Salinas area, take the scenic dirt road (4WD recommended); then follow the road near Puerto Soley (signed for Cuajiniquil) 7 km (4 mi) to the beach entrance. It's about 30 minutes from the Pan-American turnoff and one hour from Bahía Salinas.

WHERE TO STAY

$ ☆ **Santa Elena Lodge.** This simple family-run lodge on the outskirts of Cuajiniquil provides the closest accommodations to both Playa Bahía Junquillal and Santa Rosa National Park, making it a good option for nature lovers and anyone who wants to stray from the vacationing crowds. The owner, Manuel Alán, is a former fisherman who switched to tourism a few years ago, converting his family home into a bed-and-breakfast. The rooms have varnished hardwood walls and ceilings, plenty of windows, and small bathrooms—rooms 5 and 6 are the nicest, since they overlook the garden. Breakfast is served in back, whereas lunch and dinner are available at the adjacent seafood restaurant. Manuel rents no bikes, kayaks, and snorkeling equipment, and offers an array of tours that include horseback riding, a hike through the Murcielago sector of Santa Rosa National Park, a boat tour of a mangrove estuary, and whale-watching from August to February. **Pros:** friendly; near beach and park; lots of outdoor options. **Cons:** little English spoken; basic accommodations; close to road. ⊠ *Cuajiniquil 10 km/6 mi west of Pan-American Hwy., 8 km/5 mi east of Junquillal* ☎ *2679–1038* ⊕ *www.santaelenalodge.com* ↝ *10 rooms* ᗒ *In-room: no phone, no TV. In-hotel: restaurant, water sports, laundry service, Internet terminal* ═ *AE, DC, MC, V* ⊠*BP.*

LA CRUZ

40 km/25 mi northwest of Liberia.

North of Santa Rosa National Park on the west side of the highway is the turnoff to La Cruz, a scruffy, bustling little town. For travelers, it's noteworthy only for the stunning views of Bahía Salinas from its bluff and its proximity to the nearby windswept beaches on the south shore of Bahía Salinas, in the hamlet of Jobo, and in the Golfo de Santa Elena. The Nicaraguan border lies just north of La Cruz at Peñas Blancas. ■TIP➜ **All travelers are stopped at two checkpoints south of La Cruz for passport and cursory vehicle inspection. Police vigilance is heightened in the region.**

GETTING HERE AND AROUND

La Cruz is a straight-shot, one hour's trip north of Liberia on the Pan-American Highway. Buses leave Liberia for La Cruz, or you can flag down a bus that says LA CRUZ on its windshield anywhere along the highway north of Liberia.

Guanacaste National Park

The 325-square-km (125-square-mi) Parque Nacional Guanacaste, bordering the east side of the Pan-American Highway 30 km (18 mi) north of Liberia, was created in 1989 to preserve rain forests around Cacao Volcano (1,633 meters [5,443 feet]) and Orosi Volcano (1,464 meters [4,879 feet]), which are seasonally inhabited by migrant wildlife from Santa Rosa. The park isn't quite ready for tourism yet. There are very few facilities and no well-marked trails; if you want to hike, it's best to hire a professional guide. In rainy season, roads are impassable; a 4WD vehicle is required year-round. The park is a mosaic of interdependent protected areas, parks, and refuges; the goal is to eventually create a single Guanacaste mega-park to accommodate the migratory patterns of animals, from jaguars to tapirs. Much of the park's territory is cattle pasture, which, it is hoped, will regenerate into forest. Today the park has more than 300 different birds and more than 5,000 species of butterflies.

To really explore the park, you must stay in the heart of it, at one of three biological stations. They are mostly reserved for students and researchers, but you can request accommodations from the **park headquarters** (☎ 2666–5051).

ESSENTIALS

Bank Banco Nacional (✉ Pan-American Hwy. across from Ursa gas station ☎ 2679–9389). **Banco Popular** (✉ 1 block east of Central Park ☎ 2679–9352).

Hospital Hospital Area de Salud La Cruz (✉ Main highway at entrance to town ☎ 2679–9311).

Pharmacy Farmacia La Cruz (✉ 1 block north of Central Park ☎ 2679–8048 ⊗ Mon. to Sat. 7 am to 9 pm; Sun. 9 to 6.).

Internet Internet Café (✉ Beside Banco Popular).

Post Office Correo (✉ Behind police station on west side of Central Park).

CROSSING INTO NICARAGUA AT PEÑAS BLANCAS

Costa Rica and Nicaragua share a busy border crossing at Peñas Blancas, 18 km (11 mi) north of La Cruz along a paved highway. ■ TIP➔ Rental vehicles may not leave Costa Rica. Tica Bus and Transnica bus companies (⇨ Bus Travel in Travel Smart Costa Rica) travel direct between San José and Managua via this route. You can also take a Tralapa bus to the border from other points in Costa Rica. You'll make your crossing, then catch a Nicaraguan bus or taxi to Rivas, 35 km (22 mi) farther, which is the regional hub for buses departing to other parts of Nicaragua. The fee to cross the border is $7 (paid on the Nicaraguan side), plus a $2 surcharge if you cross from noon to 2 PM or on weekends. Nicaraguan shuttle taxis transport people between the border posts. Returning to Costa Rica is basically the same process in reverse; you are charged a $1 municipal tax and $2 exit tax to leave Nicaragua by land. The crossing is open daily 6 AM–8 PM; get there with time to spare or you *will* be stranded. Banks on both sides of the border change their own currency and U.S. dollars. Colones are not accepted or exchanged in Nicaragua; likewise for córdobas in Costa Rica. Overland border crossing procedures can be confusing if you don't speak Spanish.

BAHÍA SALINAS

15 km/9 mi west of La Cruz.

The large windswept bay at the very top of Costa Rica's Pacific coast is the second-windiest area in the country, after Lake Arenal, making it ideal for windsurfing and kitesurfing. Strong breezes blow from November to May, when only experienced surfers are out on the water and the water grows steadily cooler. The south (bay) side has the strongest winds, and choppy, colder water from January to May.

In July and August the wind is more appropriate for beginners, whereas any time of year you can enjoy the area's diving and beaches. On the sheltered Golfo de Santa Elena, to the west, are two beaches that rank among the most beautiful in all of Costa Rica: Playa Rajada and Playa Jobo, a far cry from the overdeveloped beaches of Guanacaste's gold coast farther to the south.

GETTING HERE AND AROUND

From a high point in La Cruz, the road to Salinas descends both in altitude and condition. It's only 15 km (9 mi) southwest to Hotel Ecoplaya, but the road can be jilted and broken, so may take up to 45 minutes or an hour. Signs direct you to Puerto Soley and El Jobo, an end-of-the-road hamlet, about 2 km (1 mi) past the turnoff for Ecoplaya. Playa Copal is about 13 km (8 mi) along the same road from La Cruz.

EXPLORING

Playa Copal (⊠ *About 2 km/1 mi east of the branch road that leads to Ecoplaya*) is a narrow, dark-beige beach that wouldn't be worth visiting except for the fact that it is one of the main venues for kitesurfing. There are villas and rooms for rent. A couple of kilometers to the east, Playa Papaturro also has kitesurfing and simple accommodations.

Gorgeous, horseshoe-shaped **Playa Rajada** (⊠ *5 km/3 mi west of Ecoplaya Beach Resort or 3 km/2 mi north of the town of El Jobo*) is a wide sweep of almost-white, fine-grain sand. Shallow, warm waters make it perfect for swimming, and an interesting rock formation at the north end invites snorkelers. It's also a favorite beach for watching sunsets.

THIEVES ON THE BEACHES

The North Pacific's idyllic landscapes and friendly people belie an ever-present threat of theft. Though a tiny minority, Costa Rica's thieves manage to ruin a lot of vacations by absconding with backpacks, cameras, wallets, and passports, the last of which necessitates a trip to San José. Keep your valuables in your hotel safe and don't ever leave anything in an unattended car, even while checking into your hotel. Hotel parking lots are popular spots for local kleptomaniacs, as are beaches.

Semana Santa

Don't underestimate how completely Costa Rica shuts down for Holy Week, the week preceding Easter. Cities become ghost towns—San José turns beguilingly peaceful—save for religious processions. Many businesses close the entire week; little opens on Thursday or Friday. Tourists, local and international, flock to the beaches. Make reservations months in advance if you plan to be here during that week, and expect greatly inflated room rates. Know that Holy Thursday and Good Friday are, by law, dry days. Bars and liquor stores must close, and no one, including restaurants or your hotel dining room, is permitted to sell alcohol.

★ **Playa Jobo** (⊠ *3 km/2 mi walk or drive, west from Ecoplaya Beach Resort*) is a gem with fine sand and calm water. It's fringed with acacia trees that have sharp thorns, so keep your distance. There's a shady parking area about 150 meters (500 feet) off the beach where you have to leave your car.

OUTDOOR ACTIVITIES

Inshore fishing is quite good in the bay during windy months, when snapper, roosterfish, wahoo, and other fighters abound. Scuba divers also encounter plenty of big fish from December to May, though visibility can be poor then. From May to December the snorkeling is good around the rocky points and Isla Bolaños. **Ecoplaya Beach Resort** (⊠ *La Coyotera Beach 15 km/10 mi west of La Cruz on a rough dirt road* ☎ *2676–1010* ⊕ *www.ecoplaya.com*) organizes local adventure tours that include kayaking to Isla Bolaños (a tiny island that is a refuge for such seabirds as the brown pelican), inshore fishing, horseback riding, hiking, and snorkeling and windsurfing, as well as farther-afield adventure tours to Santa Rosa National Park, Hacienda Guachipelín, and the historic city of Granada, in nearby Nicaragua.

KITESURFING AND WINDSURFING

The **Kite Surfing School** (☎ *8826–5221* ⊕ *www.bluedreamhotel.com*) on Playa Papaturro (9 km [5½ mi] west of La Cruz, turn left at sign for Papaturro) is run by Nicola Bertoldi, a multilingual instructor with lots of experience; eight hours of beginner's kitesurfing lessons cost $240, including equipment (minimum 2 people). The school has 10 inexpensive rooms on a ridge with ocean views and a restaurant, called Blue Dream Hotel. **Cometa Copal Kite Surfing Centre and School** (☎ *2676–1192*), on Playa Copal (10 km [6 mi] west of La Cruz), is run by an American who provides kitesurfing lessons and rents equipment.

WHERE TO STAY

$$ 🏠 **Ecoplaya Beach Resort.** Set between La Coyotera Beach and a mangrove estuary, this small resort has a sprawling collection of villas and two-story concrete buildings (with several types of spacious rooms) that

dot ample grounds. Be warned—it's in a high-wind zone. Even with glass buffers and windbreak trees and shrubs, the large swimming pool usually has waves. The 1-km-long (½-mi-long) beach has coarse brown sand flecked with broken shells, and the water is extremely shallow and murky during the windy months. Jobo, Copal, and Rajada beaches are just a short drive away. The hotel organizes activities and tours that include fishing, windsurfing and snorkeling, horseback riding, and full-day tours to the province's national parks, or historic towns in nearby Nicaragua. Since the resort is also a time-share, it's often packed with Costa Rican families and is full during the holidays. The restaurant, set beneath a massive thatch roof, serves good food, though the service is inconsistent. **Pros:** friendly; quiet; lots of activities. **Cons:** timeworn; service inconsistent; pool gets packed during holidays. ⊠ *La Coyotera Beach 15 km/10 mi west of La Cruz on a rough dirt road* 🕾 *2676–1010; 2228–7146 in San José* ⊕ *www.ecoplaya.com* ⌁ *26 villas, 18 rooms* ⌂ *In-room: safe, kitchen (some). In-hotel: restaurant, bar, pool, beachfront, water sports, laundry service* ⊟ *AE, MC, V* ⍥ *FAP.*

‹ 🖫 **Pura Vida Residence.** An affordable base for exploring the area, this Italian-built and -managed hilltop residence overlooks Playa Copal, the premier beach for windsurfing and kitesurfing. Studio rooms are in a white concrete building on a ridge overlooking a small pool. Fully equipped villas are perfect for groups. High ceilings, lots of cool stone and tile, and huge windows to catch the winds off the bay help you keep your cool despite the lack of air-conditioning in the rooms and some of the villas. The small restaurant above those rooms serves the best food in the area ($), such as fresh pastas, baked whole fish, risottos, stuffed calamari, and a selection of pizzas. It's a great lunch option, since the view from its rustic wooden tables is impressive. **Pros:** good value; near surfing beach. **Cons:** isolated; weather-worn. ⊠ *Playa Copal 13 km/ 8 mi west of La Cruz* 🕾 *8389–6794* ⊕ *www.progettopuravida.com* ⌁ *7 rooms, 5 villas* ⌂ *In-room: no a/c (some), no phone, kitchen (some), no TV. In-hotel: restaurant, pool* ⊟ *No credit cards* ⍥ *EP.*

LIBERIA

214 km/133 mi (4–5 hrs) northwest of San José.

Once a dusty cattle-market town, Liberia is now galloping toward modernization. Though you can spot the occasional *sabanero* (cowboy) on horseback, the capital of Guanacaste province is well on its way to becoming one big shopping mall, complete with fast-food restaurants and a multiplex theater. The whitewashed adobe houses for which Liberia was nicknamed the "White City" are the only traces of its colonial past. Today Liberia is essentially a good place to have a meal and make a bank stop, though it can serve as a base for day trips to Santa Rosa and Rincón de la Vieja national parks. The drive from San José takes between four and five hours, so it makes sense to fly directly into Liberia if you're going only to the North Pacific. It's easy to rent a car near the airport.

Liberia

KEY

- **1** Restaurants
- **①** Hotels

Restaurants ▶

Burger King/ATM	**1**
El Café Liberia	**3**
La Toscana	**2**
Restaurante y Marisquería Paso Real	**4**

Hotels ▶

Best Western Hotel Las Espuelas	**①**

The *avenidas* (avenues) officially run east–west, whereas the *calles* (streets) run north–south. Liberia is not too big to walk easily, but there are always taxis lined up around the central park.

GETTING HERE AND AROUND

From San José, follow the Pan-American Highway west past the Puntarenas exit, then north past Cañas to Liberia. The road is paved but is poorly maintained in places. It's a heavily traveled truck and bus route, and there are miles and miles where it is impossible to pass, but many drivers try, making this a dangerous road. Hourly direct buses leave San José for Liberia each day, and there are half a dozen daily flights, so it might be worth busing or flying to Liberia and renting a car from here.

ESSENTIALS

Bank/ATM Banco de Costa Rica (✉ *C. Central at Avda. 1; diagonally across from Central Park* ☎ *2666–9002*).

Bancredito (✉ *Avda. Central, 2 blocks north of highway*).

Hospital Liberia Hospital (✉ *North end of town* ☎ *2399–0399*).

Pharmacy Farmacia Lux (✉ *C. 4 and Avda. Central* ☎ *2666–0061* ☉ *Weekdays and Sat. 8–10*).

Internet Ciber Enl@ce (✉ *C. 4 and Avda. Central* ☉ *Daily 8*AM*–10*PM).

Post Office Correo (✉ *300 m west of highway, 200 m north of Avda. Central*).

Rental Cars Alamo (✉ *2 km/1 mi northeast of Liberia airport, Liberia* ☎ *2668–1111; 800/462-5266 in U.S.*) **Budget** (✉ *1 km/½ mi southwest of Liberia airport, Liberia* ☎ *2668–1118*)). **Economy** (✉ *3½ km/2 mi southwest of Liberia airport, Liberia* ☎ *2666–2816 or 2666–7560*). **Hola Rentacar** (✉ *6 km/4 mi southwest of Liberia airport, Liberia* ☎ *2667–4040*). **Payless Car Rental** (✉ *5 km/3 mi southwest of Liberia airport, Liberia* ☎ *2667–0511*).

☙

EN
ROUTE
Yes, that is a life-size dinosaur standing beside the highway 20 minutes north of Puntarenas. It is one of 26 lifelike models of extinct and endangered animals arranged along a 1½-km (1-mi) forest trail at Parque MegaFauna Monteverde (✉ *Pan-American Hwy.* ☎ *2645–5029*). Along with the spectacular models outdoors, the $4 entrance fee includes an impressive insect museum. The park is open daily 8 AM to 4:30 PM.

WHERE TO EAT

¢
CAFÉ
✕ **El Café Liberia.** The smell of roasting coffee is the best advertisement for this sophisticated café in the center of Liberia. New Peruvian and Colombian owners have kept some of the former French-Canadian owner's excellent dishes, including refreshing soups—the mint pea is a winner—savory quiches, and hot sandwiches. Save room for homemade desserts. The casual bar is a cool place to relax, sip a glass of wine, and browse through the paperbacks in the book exchange. ✉ *Ca. 8, 75 m south of Banco Nacional* ☎ *2665–1660* ▭ *M, V* ☉ *Closed Sun.*

Making a Difference

National park or reserve entrance fees help support the preservation of Costa Rica's wildlife and places. You can also make your visit beneficial to the people living nearby by hiring local guides, horses, or boats; eating in local restaurants; and buying things (excluding wild-animal products) in local shops. You can go a few steps further by making donations to local conservation groups or to such international organizations as Conservation International, the Rainforest Alliance, and the World Wide Fund for Nature, all of which support important conservation efforts in Costa Rica. It's also helpful to explore private preserves off the beaten path and to stay at lodges that contribute to environmental efforts and to nearby communities. By planning your visit with an eye toward grassroots conservation efforts, you join the global effort to save Costa Rica's tropical ecosystems and help ensure that the treasures you traveled so far to see remain intact for future generations.

6

$ × **La Toscana.** Billing itself as "spaghetteria, pizzeria, grigliata, and cafe,"
ITALIAN this restaurant uses real Italian ingredients. Properly aged Parmigiano cheese and prosciutto from Parma give authenticity to the 20 types of wood-oven pizzas. Tender tuna carpaccio and ensalada caprese are tasty starters. Risottos are the chef's specialty; a nutty, brown, three-mushroom version is cooked perfectly *al dente* and flavored with truffle oil—rare in these parts. ⊠ *Centro Comercial Santa Rosa, across from Burger King, on road to airport* ☎ 2665–0653 ⊟ *AE, DC, MC, V.*

$–$$ × **Restaurante y Marisquería Paso Real.** A Liberia institution, this second-
SEAFOOD floor restaurant's terrace overlooks Liberia's Parque Central, which makes for great people-watching. Fresh, tangy ceviches or seafood-laden *sopas de mariscos* (seafood soup) are great light lunches. Save the *filet gratinado al brandy con camarones* (fish fillet topped with grilled shrimp and smothered in a brandy cream sauce) for when you're really hungry. Service is efficient and pleasant. It's open daily 11 AM to 9:30 PM. ⊠ *Avda. Central, south side of main square* ☎ 2666–3455 ⊟ *AE, MC, V.*

WHERE TO STAY

$$ ⊞ **Best Western Las Espuelas.** From the gigantic Guanacaste tree that shades its parking lot to the local paintings and indigenous stone statues that decorate its lobby, this motel just south of town has more character than one might expect. Rooms are a little institutional, but the grounds are verdant and the rectangular pool is quite large. Two suites, by the pool, have private whirlpool tubs. Rooms facing the highway can be a little noisy; numbers 17 and up are quieter. The restaurant, which resembles a coffee shop, serves complimentary buffet breakfasts, but you're best off heading into town for dinner. **Pros:** reasonable rates; big pool. **Cons:** highway noise; mediocre rooms; insects sometimes a problem. ⊠ *Pan-American Hwy. 2 km/1 mi south of Liberia* ☎ 2666–0144 ⊕ *www.bestwestern.co.cr* ↪ *44 rooms, 2 suites* ⚙ *In-*

room:. In-hotel: restaurant, bar, pool, laundry service, Wi-Fi hotspot
≡ *AE, D, MC, V* ⦿| *BP.*

THE NICOYA COAST

Strung along the coast of the Nicoya Peninsula are sparkling sand beaches lined with laid-back fishing communities, and hotels and resorts in every price category. As recently as the 1970s, fishing and cattle ranching were the area's mainstays. Development is barreling ahead full speed, though, bringing with it sophisticated restaurants, hotels, and shops, along with congestion, construction chaos, water pollution, and higher prices. Roads are only starting to catch up, so you'll find the interesting anomaly of a trendy restaurant or upscale hotel plunked at the end of a tortuous dirt road. The key to enjoying Nicoya is to slow down. You'll soon be as mellow as the locals.

PAPAGAYO PENINSULA

The Papagayo Peninsula, a crooked finger of land cradling the west side of Bahía Culebra (Snake Bay), is the site of a government-sponsored development program modeled after Cancún. Five large hotels are already situated around Papagayo Bay, and many others are slated to be built here. Although the hotels are modeled on their Caribbean counterparts, the beaches are distinctly Costa Rican, with brown sand and aquamarine water that grows cool from January to April. Isolation is the name of the game, which means that getting out of man-made "paradise" to explore anything off-property often entails a pricey tour.

High season here coincides with dry season. There's guaranteed sun January to April, but there's also intense heat, and the landscape becomes brown and brittle. In the rainy season (August to December), the landscape is greener and more lush. Sparkling water and spectacular sunsets are beautiful year-round.

GETTING HERE AND AROUND

All hotels here have airport pickup. To get to the Four Seasons from the Liberia airport (the hotel refuses to put up directional signs in order to "protect its privacy"), drive 10 km (6 mi) south of Guardia, over the Río Tempisque Bridge, then take the turn on the right signed for Papagayo Allegro Resort. Follow this road about 20 km (12 mi) to its end at the entrance to the resort.

OUTDOOR ACTIVITIES

CANOPY TOUR

Taking advantage of one of the few remaining patches of dry tropical forest on the Papagayo Peninsula, **Witch's Rock Canopy Tour** (☎ *8371–3685* ✎ www.*witchsrockcanopytour.com*) gives you your money's worth: 23 platforms, with a thrilling 450-meter (1,485-foot) cable zip between two of them; four hanging bridges; a waterfall in rainy season; and hiking trails. The 1½-hour tour is $75 per person.

Nicoya Coast

Papagayo
Peninsula
Puerto
Culebra
Playa Panamá
Playa Hermosa
Panama
Guardia
CR1
164
Playas del Coco
Playa Ocotal
Sardinal
Bagaaces

Playa Pan de Azúcar
Filadelfia

0   8 mi
0   8 km

Playa Penca
Potrero
Playa Potrero
Playa Flamingo
Belén
Ortega
Playa Conchal
Brasilito
Santo Ana
Puerto Viejo
Playa Real
Palo Verde
National Park

Matapalo
Huacas
21

Salinas
Villa
155
Santa Barbara
Puerto Moreno
Playa Grande
Real
Lagunilla
GUANACASTE

Tamarindo
and Playa
Langosta
see detail map
Playa Tamarindo
Tamarindo
Caimito
Santa
Cruz

Playa Langosta
Vientisiete
de Abril
Barra Honda
National Park

Playa Avellanas
160
Nicoya
18

Playa Negra
Vigia

Playa Junquillal
21
Mansion
Chumico

Playa Lagarto
Hojancha

Lagarto
160
Carmona

San Juanillo
150

Playa Ostional
Ostional
Nosara

Playa Nosara

Ostional National Wildlife Refuge
Playa Pelada
Garza
Puerto
Carrillo

Playa Guiones
160

Sámara
Playa
Carrillo
Punta Islita

WHERE TO STAY

$$$$ ☒ **Four Seasons Resort Costa Rica.** By far one of the most luxurious hotels in Costa Rica, the Four Seasons is extremely secluded (it's nearly 30 minutes from the main road). Service, provided by a cream-of-the-crop, bilingual staff, is faultless. The decor is tasteful and arty. Huge rooms have king-size beds, marble baths, and screened-in living-room terraces. The breezy 18-hole Arnold Palmer signature golf course has breathtaking views—and prices ($195 per round). The state-of-the-art spa is impressive but a little sterile. Dishes created at the dinner-only Di Mare restaurant are worth their wildly expensive price tags, but the rest of the hotel's food has been disappointing. **Pros:** impeccable service; lovely beach. **Cons:** isolated; expensive. ☒ *25 km/15 mi west of Guardia; follow signs to Papagayo Allegro Resort and continue to end of road* ☏ *2696–0000* ⊕ *www.fourseasons.com/costarica* ⊃ *123 rooms, 36 suites, 21 villas* ⌂ *In-room: safe, refrigerator, Wi-Fi. In-hotel: 4 restaurants, room service, bars, golf course, pools, gym, spa, beach-front, water sports, children's programs (ages 4–12), laundry facilities, Internet terminal, no-smoking rooms* ▭ *AE, DC, MC, V* ⦿*EP.*

PLAYA HERMOSA

27 km/17 mi southwest of Liberia airport.

Beautiful Playa Hermosa is one of the last laid-back beach towns on this part of the coast. It's the kind of place where the beach is still the town's main thoroughfare, filled with joggers, people walking their dogs, and families out for a stroll. Not to be confused with the mainland surfers' beach of the same name south of Jacó, this Playa Hermosa is experiencing heavy development pressures, with new crops of sunny villas and high-rise condos filling up with American and Canadian expatriates. Luckily, though, the full length of the beach has long been occupied by small hotels, restaurants, and homes, so the newer hotel behemoths and other developments are forced to set up shop off the beach or on other beaches in the area.

Hermosa's mile-long crescent of dark gray volcanic sand attracts heat, so the best time to be out on the beach is early morning or late afternoon, in time for the spectacular sunsets. The beach fronts a line of trees, so there's a welcome respite from the heat of the sun. The crystal-clear water—it's a Blue Flag beach—is usually calm, with no strong currents and with comfortable temperatures of 74°F to 80°F (23°C to 27°C). Sea views are as picturesque as they get, with bobbing fishing boats, jagged profiles of coastline, rocky outcroppings, and at night the twinkling lights of the Four Seasons Resort across the bay. At the beach's north end, low tide creates wide, rock-lined tidal pools.

GETTING HERE AND AROUND

From the Comunidad turnoff of Highway 21, heading from Liberia, Playa Hermosa is about 15 km (9 mi) northwest. The paved road forks after the small town of Sardinal, the right fork heading into Hermosa and the left leading to Playas del Coco. Local directions usually refer to the first and second entrance roads to the beach, the first entrance being the southern one. There is no through beachfront road, so you have to approach the beach from either of these two roads. Transportes La Pampa buses leave from Liberia for Playa Hermosa daily at 5:30, 7:30, and 11:30 AM and 1, 3:30, 5:30, and 7:30 PM. A taxi to Playas del Coco costs about $12 and takes about an hour.

ESSENTIALS

Playa Hermosa has few resources. Get what you need in Liberia or Playas del Coco, just to the south.

Internet Villa Acacia (✉ *Second entrance to Playa Hermosa; south on beach road* ☎ *2672–1000*).

OUTDOOR ACTIVITIES

Aqua Sport (✉ *Beach road; heading south, take second entrance to Playa Hermosa and follow signs* ☎ *2672–0050* ⊕ *www.costa-rica-beach-hotel.com*) organizes fishing, surfing, and snorkeling trips and rents every kind of boat and board. **Charlie's Adventure** (✉ *Hotel Condovac, north end of beach* ☎ *2672–1041 or 2672–0275*) organizes ATV tours ($85), horseback riding ($55), and sunset sails ($55), as well as boat tours of Hermosa Bay ($75, including drinks). **Velas de Papagayo** (✉ *Hotel Playa Hermosa Bosque del Mar* ☎ *2223–8010* ⊕ *www.*

velasdepapagayo.com) runs morning and sunset cruises of Papagayo Bay that include snorkeling, drinks, and snacks ($100). **Hotel El Velero** (✉ *100 m north of Aqua Sport* ☎ *2672–1017* ⊕ *www.costaricahotel. net*) will take you out for a five-hour sunset cruise on a 38-foot sailing yacht ($60 per person). Daytime tours include snorkeling, cave exploring, canopy touring, and diving.

DIVING AND SNORKELING

Average temperatures of 75°F to 80°F (23°C to 27°C), 20 to 60 feet (32 to 95m) of visibility, and frequent sightings of sea turtles, sharks, manta rays, moray eels, and very big fish make Hermosa a great place to dive. There is little coral in the area, but rock reefs attract large schools of fish, and countless critters lurk in their caves and crannies.

Charlie's Adventure (⇨ *above*) organizes snorkeling and diving trips. **Diving Safaris** (✉ *Second entrance road to Playa Hermosa, almost at beach on right side* ☎ *2672–1259* ⊕ *www.costaricadiving.net*) has a range of scuba activities, from beginner training to open-water PADI certification courses. Multitank dives are organized at more than 20 sites. Guides and trainers are very good, and their safety standards have the DAN (Divers Alert Network) seal of approval. This dive shop has also earned the coveted five-star, gold-palm status from PADI. Prices range from $80 for two-tank morning dives to $425 and up for the PADI open-water certification course.

FISHING

The fishing at Playa Hermosa is mostly close to the shores, and yields edible fish like *dorado* (mahimahi), amberjack, roosterfish, snapper, and yellowfin tuna. Local restaurants are happy to cook your catch for you. You can rent a boat with **Aqua Sport** (⇨ *above*). **Charlie's Adventure** (⇨ *above*) runs fishing trips. **Papagayo Gulf Sport Fishing** (☎ 2670–1564 ⊕ *www.papagayofishing.typepad.com*) also runs various fishing tours in the area, as well as snorkeling and surfing tours and water taxis around the bay.

WHERE TO EAT

A few of Playa Hermosa's best restaurants are at hotels (⇨ *Where to Stay, below*).

$ ✕ **Ginger.** This tapas restaurant, in a modernistic glass-and-steel tree
ECLECTIC house cantilevered on the side of a hill, is a big hit. The chef has cre-
★ ated an Asian-fusion menu with a few Mediterranean dishes. It includes such intriguing appetizer-size offerings as chicken satay with a macadamia-nut rub, mahimahi with a ginger mango sauce, and a taco basket filled with seared pepper-crusted tuna and pickled ginger slaw. Portions are small, but layers of condiments and garnishes make them surprisingly satisfying. The fun thing to do is order several dishes and share. ✉ *Main highway, south of Hotel Condovac* ☎ *2672–0041* ⚐ *Reservations essential* ▭ *MC, V* ⊗ *Closed Mon.*

WHERE TO STAY

$$$ ⌂ **Casa Conde del Mar.** Spread over verdant grounds just behind rela-
★ tively pristine Playa Panama—a mile north of Playa Hermosa—this is
☾ the place to head for privacy and relaxation. Rooms are in one-story buildings with a traditional Costa Rican decor: Spanish tile roof; red-

tile floors; high, sloping ceilings; and covered front terraces offering a glimpse of the sea through the forest that lines the nearby beach. Standard rooms are spacious and equipped with amenities you might expect from any big luxury hotel, whereas the suites are bigger, and more elegant. The master suites have a Jacuzzi in the bathroom and pullout couch in the living room. There's a large pool with a waterfall and swim-up bar, and an elegant, airy restaurant ($$) that serves pizza, pastas, and other Italian fare as well as local seafood and beef. The people at the tour desk offer an array of tours, and placid, tree-lined Playa Panama is mere steps away. **Pros:** spacious rooms; immaculate grounds; quiet. **Cons:** not much nightlife; remote. ⊠ *Playa Panama 2 km/1 mi north of Playa Hermosa* ☎ *2226–0808 or 2672–1001* ⊕ *www.grupocasaconde.com* ⤴ *96rooms, 8 suites, 2 master suites; 3 handicapped accessible suites* ⚐ *In-room: safe, Wi-Fi. In-hotel: restaurant, room service, bars, pool, beachfront, laundry service, Internet terminal* ▭ *AE, DC, MC, V* ⦿ *BP.*

$$ ⛱ **Hotel El Velero.** This laid-back hotel is right on the beach, and though ☾ nothing fancy, it's an excellent option if you're watching your expenses. The open-air bar and restaurant, hemmed by exuberant greenery and a small pool, is often hopping with local expats and visitors exchanging fishing, boating, and real-estate stories. The Canadian general manager is an ebullient host, full of local lore and advice. Attractive rooms have tropical decor with terra-cotta tiles, bamboo furniture, and large windows. Those on the second floor are nicer, with high, sloping wooden ceilings. Only two rooms have ocean views, but you're likely to spend plenty of your time in one of the many chairs and hammocks overlooking the beach, some of which are a shell's toss from the surf at high tide. The hotel runs daily snorkeling and sunset cruises on its own handsome 38-foot sailboat. In the restaurant, jumbo shrimp and always-fresh mahimahi are fixtures. Come on Wednesday or Saturday for beach barbecues. In high season, there's live music on Saturday night. Drinks are two-for-one every day during happy hour, 4 to 6 PM. **Pros:** on the beach; competitive rates; friendly; informal. **Cons:** tiny pool; most rooms have lousy views; can be noisy. ⊠ *Second entrance to Playa Hermosa, on beach road* ☎ *2672–0036* 🖷 *2672–0016* ⊕ *www. costaricahotel.net* ⤴ *22 rooms* ⚐ *In-room: safe. In-hotel: restaurant, bar, pool, water sports, laundry service* ▭ *AE, MC, V* ⦿ *EP.*

$$ ⛱ **Hotel La Finisterra.** From its perch 250 meters (825 feet) up the ridge that defines the southern end of Playa Hermosa, this hotel enjoys a commanding view of the beach and bay. The restaurant ($$), which overlooks the pool and sea, is popular with local expats, who come for the Peruvian-style ceviche, octopus sautéed in a tomato sauce, macadamia-encrusted sea bass, and Mediterranean chicken. The rooms, above the restaurant, are simple but comfortable, with two doubles or one king-size bed, picture windows, and nature paintings by local artists. Rooms on the north side of the building have the best view, though the vista from the common balcony and pool area below are even more impressive. **Pros:** good food; friendly staff; great view. **Cons:** steep road up from beach; small pool. ⊠ *First entrance to Playa Hermosa, left before Hotel Playa Hermosa, 250 m/825 feet up hill* ☎ *2672–0227* ⊕ *www.lafinisterra.com* ⤴ *10 rooms*

☯ *In-room: no phone, no TV, Wi-Fi. In-hotel: restaurant, pool, Wi-Fi hotspot* = *AE, MC, V* 🀤| *BP.*

$$ \quad \square$$ **Hotel Playa Hermosa Bosque del Mar.** Century-old trees shade this low-lying hotel on the southern end of Playa Hermosa. The most popular activity here is lounging in hammocks strung around the garden, but floating in the blue-tile pool surrounded by lush landscaping is a close second. Flashes of sunlit ocean, just a few barefoot steps away, periodically penetrate the cool greenery, and now and then an iguana, bird, or monkey rustles the foliage above. Rooms complement the surrounding nature, with trees growing through porches, stained-wood furniture, earth tones, and ceramic bathrooms. Beachfront rooms are the nicest, since you can open the screened windows at night and catch the breeze and the sound of the ocean. The restaurant serves truly fresh fish and beef tenderloin raised on the owner's own ranch. **Pros:** recently remodeled; great food. **Cons:** spotty service; few bathroom amenities. ⊠ *End of first entrance to Playa Hermosa* ☎ *2672–0046* ⊕ *www.hotelplayahermosa.com* ↶ *20 rooms, 12 deluxe suites* ☯ *In-room: safe, refrigerator. In-hotel: restaurant, bar, beachfront, water sports, Wi-Fi hotspot* = *AE, DC, MC, V* 🀤| *EP.*

$$ \quad \square$$ **Villa del Sueño.** Although the handsome garden restaurant ($$$) is the main attraction at this elegant hotel, the spacious rooms are quite nice, too, though it's about a block from the beach. Rooms have up-to-date bathrooms, comfortable mattresses, and tropical color schemes. The smaller "standard" rooms around the pool are a good deal, and they open onto small terraces with chairs. Larger "superiors" above the restaurant sleep more people, but aren't as nice. If you need more room, spring for a one- or two-bedroom suite in the development across the street, which have kitchenettes, large balconies, or terraces, and are steps away from a larger pool. The restaurant has formal food and polished service, but a casual atmosphere. Filet mignon with a brandy-and-peppercorn sauce, perfectly cooked mahimahi in shrimp sauce, and garlicky butterfly shrimp are among the options. **Pros:** excellent restaurant; good value. **Cons:** not on the beach; can be noisy. ⊠ *First entrance to Playa Hermosa, 350 m west of main highway* ☎ *2672–0026* ⊕ *www.villadelsueno.com* ↶ *14 rooms, 14 suites* ☯ *In-room: safe, kitchen (some), refrigerator (some), no TV (some). In-hotel: restaurant, room service, bar, pools, laundry service, Internet terminal, Wi-Fi hotspot, no-smoking rooms* = *AE, MC, V* 🀤| *EP.*

NIGHTLIFE

Hotel El Velero (⊠ *Second entrance to Playa Hermosa, then 100 m north of Aqua Sport on beach road*) hosts beach barbecues with live music on Wednesday and Saturday nights in high season. The crowd is 30-ish and up. In high season there's live music on Tuesday, Friday, and Sunday nights at **Villa del Sueño** (⊠ *First entrance to Playa Hermosa, 350 m west of main highway*).

SHOPPING

You can shop for a beach picnic at **Aqua Sport** (⊠ *Second entrance to Playa Hermosa; follow signs heading south on beach road*) minimarket and liquor store and buy souvenirs in the gift shop. The gift shop at **Villa del Sueño** (⊠ *First entrance to Playa Hermosa, 350 m west of*

Continued on page 297

Choosing a Beach

From pulverized volcanic rock and steady waves to soft white sand and idyllic settings, all of the beaches along Nicoya's coast have their own distinct merits. Playa Brasilito has restaurants so close to the ocean the surf spray salts your food; Playas Hermosa and Sámara are family-friendly spots with swimmable waters; and Playas Langosta and Pelada are made for contemplative walks.

NORTHERN NICOYA PENINSULA

Playa Tamarindo

1 Popular all-inclusive resorts line the beaches of the **Papagayo Peninsula**.

2 **Playa Hermosa** is one of the few Costa Rican beaches with calm, crystal-clear waters.

3 Surfing, diving, and fishing are the name of the game at **Playas del Coco** and its scruffy beach town.

4 **Playa Ocotal** is a quiet beach with great views and good snorkeling.

5 **Playa Pan de Azúcar** is difficult to access, but practically deserted once you get there.

6 **Playa Potrero** is the jumping-off point for diving trips to the Catalina Islands.

7 Busy white-sand **Playa Flamingo** is ideal for swimming and sunning.

8 Shells sprinkle the sand at chilled-out **Playa Conchal**, near a small fishing village.

9 Lively **Tamarindo** is a hyped up surfing and water-sports beach with wild nightlife.

BEACHES KEY

- Diving
- Snorkeling
- Fishing
- Surfing
- Kayaking
- Sailing
- Swimming
- Blue Flag Ecological Award

0 — 8 miles
0 — 12 km

Gulf of Papagayo

Papagayo Peninsula **1**

Puerto Culebra

Bahía Culebra

Playa Panamá

Panama

Playa Hermosa **2**

Sardinal

Playas del Coco **3**

El Coco

Playa Ocotal **4**

Nuevo Colon

Playa Pan de Azúcar

5 Potrero

Tempate

6 **Playa Potrero**

Playa Flamingo **7**

Isla Sta. Catalina

Brasilito

155

Llano

Portegolpe

Playa Conchal **8**

Brasilito

Huacas

Playa Real

Matapalo

Salinas

Playa Grande

Villarreal

155

Las Baulas Marine National Park

Tamarindo

Playa Tamarindo **9**

Playa Langosta

CENTRAL NICOYA PENINSULA

(top) Playa Avellanas (bottom) Sunset at Sámara

❶ Black-sand **Playa Langosta** is great for walks up its estuary and watching dramatic sunsets.

❷ **Playa Avellanas** is a no frills backwater surf spot.

❸ **Playa Negra** has some of Costa Rica's best surfing waves.

❹ Peaceful and pretty **Playa Junquillal** is all about relaxation.

❺ Hemmed in by rocks, **Playa Pelada** is a calm beach staked out by territorial Tico surfers.

❻ Long, clean **Playa Guiones** has a coral reef and is backed by dense jungle.

❼ **Sámara's** gentle waters make it perfect for kayaking and swimming.

❽ Perhaps the most beautiful beach in the country, **Playa Carrillo** fronts an idyllic half-moon bay.

❾ Rocky **Punta Islita** has interesting tidal pools to explore.

SOUTHERN NICOYA PENINSULA

(top) Montezuma (bottom) Surfing at Malpaís

❶ Crescent-shaped **Tambor** is flanked by all inclusive resorts.

❷ **Montezuma's** off-beat town is as much a draw as its bayside beach.

❸ Some of the largest surfing waves in Costa Rica are at **Malpaís**.

MAKING THE BEST OF YOUR BEACH VACATION

■ Tamarindo, Nosara, and Sámara are good for beginning surfers. Playas Grande, Avellanas, and Negra are best left to those with experience; other surfing waters are somewhere in between.

■ Tamarindo, Nosara, Sámara, and Tambor are beaches with air service to San José.

Horseback riding at Tamarindo Beach

■ The beach road connecting most Nicoya Peninsula beaches is hard to stomach any time of year, and virtually impassable during the August through December rains. Take easier inland routes instead.

■ Riptides are seriously dangerous and hardly any Costa Rican beaches have lifeguards; get information from your hotel about where to swim.

main highway) has original oil paintings, exotic crafts from around the world, locally made mother-of-pearl jewelry, and unique ivory bracelets made of local Brahma cow bones. **Kaltak Art and Craft Market** (⊠ *South of airport on road to Santa Cruz*) has five rooms of high-quality crafts and gifts, including organic-cotton blouses and dresses and traditional leather-and-wood rocking chairs, which they will ship for you.

PLAYAS DEL COCO

25 km/16 mi southwest of Liberia airport.

Messy, noisy, colorful, and interesting, Playas del Coco is first and foremost a fishing port, with a port captain's office, a fish market, and an ice factory for keeping the catch of the day fresh—not for cooling margaritas, although many are enjoyed here. The town (called "El Coco" by locals) is not particularly scenic. The dark-sand beach is mostly a workplace, and it hasn't yet met the Blue Flag standards of cleanliness. The main street becomes a sea of mud when it rains and a dust bowl when it doesn't. So why do visitors flock here? Although fresh seafood, myriad souvenir shops, and plenty of bars draw some tourism, the primary reasons to come to Playas del Coco are the diving, fishing, and surfing at remote breaks such as Ollie's Point and Witch's Rock. Because El Coco is mere minutes from Playa Hermosa, however, you can just as easily enjoy those sports while staying at that more pleasant beach. If you like to party, and want some local color, Coco's slightly down-at-the-heels ambience can be appealing.

GETTING HERE AND AROUND

The easy drive from the Liberia airport to Playas del Coco takes about 30 minutes. The paved highway turns into a grand, divided boulevard as you enter town and then dissolves into the dusty main street that leads directly to the beach. If you don't have a car, the best way to get here from Playa Hermosa is in a taxi, for about $12 each way.

ESSENTIALS

Bank/ATM Banco Nacional (⊠ *Main street, at entrance to town*).

Hospital Public Health Clinic (⊠ *Next to Hotel Coco Verde* ☎ *2670–0987*).

Post Office Correo (⊠ *Beachfront, beside police station*).

OUTDOOR ACTIVITIES

DIVING AND SNORKELING

Half-a-dozen dive shops populate this small town. The standard price for a two-tank dive is $80; Catalina Island dives are $110. This coast doesn't have the coral reefs or the clear visibility of the Caribbean coast, but it does have a lot of plankton (hence the lower visibility) that feeds legions of fish, some of them really, really big. Manta rays and sharks (white-tipped, nurse, and bull varieties) are among the stars of the undersea show. It takes about 20 to 45 minutes to reach most dive sites.

Most of the dive shops have instruction, including **Summer Salt Dive Center** (⊠ *Main street* ☎ *2670–0308* ⊕ *www.summer-salt.com*). **Deep Blue Diving Adventures** (⊠ *Main street, in Hotel Coco Verde parking lot* ☎ *2670–1004* ⊕ *www.deepblue-diving.com*) is a reliable option. **Rich**

Coast Diving (✉ *Main street, across from A&A office* ☎ *2670–0176* ⊕ *www.richcoastdiving.com*) has enthusiastic guides and instructors and limits tours to five divers per instructor and 15 divers per boat.

FISHING

Fishing charter boats go out 24 to 64 km (15 to 40 mi) seeking yellowfin tuna, mahimahi, grouper, and red snapper close-in, and sailfish, marlin, and roosterfish offshore (beyond 64 km [40 mi]). Boats, moored here and in nearby Ocotal, can pick you up from a beach near your hotel. **TranquilaMar** (☎ *2670–0833* ⊕ *www.tranquilamar.com*) has four 28-foot Cummins diesel-power boats moored in nearby Ocotal. They can pick you up at any local beach. Just bring sunscreen and your hat, says the owner. Trips are $450 for a half day and $650 for a full day. **Blue Marlin Service Sportfishing** (✉ *Main street* ☎ *2670–0707 or 8348–6510* ⊕ *www.sportfishingbluemarlin.com*) has 11 boats, ranging from a 25-foot boat for close-in fishing ($325 half day) to a luxury 52-footer for a full day offshore ($2,200).

GOLF

The brand-new **Papagayo Golf & Country Club** (✉ *10 km (6 mi) southeast of Playas del Coco* ☎ *2697–0169 or 2697–1313* ⊕ *www.papagayo-golf.com*) is an 18-hole, par-72 course. It's also affordable; you can play the whole course for $95, including golf cart and a cooler with ice, or play 9 holes for $55. There's a restaurant and bar, and a tournament every Sunday morning.

SURFING

★ Legendary **Witch's Rock and Ollie's Point** surfing spots are a one-hour boat ride away from Playas del Coco off the coast of Santa Rosa National Park. You can surf as long as you pay the $6 park entrance fee.

You can sign up for a surfing trip with any beach-town tour operator, but local authorities allow excursions to Witch's Rock and Ollie's Point to originate only from the main dock at Playas del Coco, in boats owned by local boat owners, in order to curb overcrowding and undue environmental stress.

WHERE TO EAT AND STAY

$$–$$$
SEAFOOD

✕ **Restaurante Papagayo Seafood.** The food here is straightforward, reliably fresh, and flavorful. Start with fish ceviche, or seafood soup generously packed with shrimp, squid, fish, and crab. Then sink your teeth into the catch of the day (including lobster, most notably), prepared any one of a dozen ways, or Papagayo seafood au gratin, which is a mix of sautéed seafood in a tarragon cream sauce. Meat lovers can order from the menu of the contiguous Papagayo Steakhouse, which has local and USDA beef, as well as a kids' menu. Seating is available downstairs, between the stuffed fish and potted plants, or on the cooler, quieter second floor. ✉ *Main street, across from Hotel Coco Beach* ☎ *2670–0298* ▭ *AE, DC, MC, V.*

$$
♻

🏨 **La Puerta del Sol.** Facing a formal garden with sculpted shrubs and a lovely pool just two blocks from the beach, this tranquil enclosure of stylish suites has modern, airy Mediterranean-style guest rooms shot through with hot, tropical colors. Each room has high ceilings, plenty of windows, and gleaming white, tiled bathrooms. King-size beds roost

THE ECOLOGICAL BLUE FLAG

The tourist industry here estimates that three-quarters of visitors to Costa Rica make a beach excursion. With that in mind, the national water utility, Acueductos y Alcantarillados, in conjunction with the Instituto Costarricense de Turismo, began evaluating and ranking water and environmental quality in coastal communities in 1996. Those that achieved at least a 90 percent score were awarded a Bandera Azul Ecológica (ecological blue flag) to fly as a symbol of excellence. The program, modeled on one begun in Spain in 1986, awards flags as prizes for communities, rather than to individual hotels. Participants are required to form a Blue Flag committee, a move that brings together diverse sectors of an area's population, many of which otherwise fiercely compete for tourist dollars. The program has prompted communities to put resources into improving environmental quality of life for themselves and for their guests.

Only 10 beaches earned a flag that first year, a fact that Costa Rica sheepishly decided not to publicize, not wanting to call attention to the high number of communities that didn't make the cut. When 19 succeeded the following year, the results went public. Blue Flag locales receive year-round inspections of water quality—both ocean and drinking water—trash cleanup, waste management, security, signage, and environmental education. (Winners dare not rest on their laurels: a few know the shame of having their flags yanked.) In 2002, the competition was opened to inland communities; 2006 saw schools recognized; eco-friendly businesses were added in 2008, including the Rain Forest

Aerial Tram; and rivers became eligible for inclusion in 2009.

Blue flags fly proudly in the following locations covered in this book:

Central Valley
Carrizal (Alajuela).

Northern Plains
La Fortuna, Las Horquetas, San Rafael de Heredia, Vara Blanca.

North Pacific
Bahía Junquillal, Nosara (Playa Guiones), Ostional, Playa Avellanas, Playa Carrillo, Playa Conchal, Playa Flamingo, Playa Grande, Playa Hermosa, Playa Junquillal, Playa Langosta, Playa Pan de Azúcar, Playa Panamá, Punta Islita.

Central Pacific
Barú, Isla Tortuga, Malpaís, Manuel Antonio (Playa Manuel Antonio, Playa Espadilla Sur, Puerto Escondido, Playa Gemelas), Puntarenas, Punta Leona (Playa Blanca, Playa Limoncito, Playa Mantas).

South Pacific
Ballena National Marine Park (Playa La Colonia, Playa Piñuela, Playa Ballena, Punta Uvita), San Gerardo de Rivas, San Marcos de Tarrazú.

Caribbean
Cahuita (Puerto Vargas, Playa Blanca, Playa Negra), EARTH, Gandoca-Manzanillo Wildlife Refuge, Puerto Viejo de Talamanca (Playa Chiquita, Playa Cocles, Punta Uva), Rain Forest Aerial Tram.

6

atop adobe platforms, whereas single beds nearby double as sofas by day. Pasha, the resident Newfoundland dog, can usually be found lolling around the reception area, and there are various pet cats prowling in the garden. The restaurant, El Sol y La Luna, is excellent. **Pros:** intimate; comfortable. **Cons:** a walk to the beach; small. ⊠ *180 m to right (north) off main road to town* ☎ *2670–0195* ⊕ *www.lapuertadelsolcostarica. com* ⤳ *9 rooms* ⚬ *In-room: safe, refrigerator. In-hotel: restaurant, pool, gym, laundry service, Wi-Fi hotspot* ☰ *MC, V* ⦿ *BP.*

NIGHTLIFE

Most local expats prefer**Coconutz** (⊠ *Main road, across from Hotel Coco Beach*), which is usually packed around happy hour (4 to 6), when they often have live music. They also have pool tables, lots of big TVs for games, and bar food. At the **Lizard Lounge** (⊠ *Main road, west of Hotel Coco Beach*) there's dancing every night on a big thatch-roof dance floor. The reggae, techno, and rap beats appeal to a very young crowd. **Zouk Santana** (⊠ *Main road, west of Hotel Coco Beach*) is a split-level lounge with a funky ambience that combines bars, couches, and small dance floors for moving to the eclectic mix of music.

SHOPPING

If you can't find it at **Galería & Souvenirs Susy** (⊠ *Main street, next to Coco Beach Hotel*), chances are they don't make it in Costa Rica. Along with a huge selection of interesting notebooks and albums made of botanical materials, the place also sells locally made shell belts.

PLAYA OCOTAL

3 km/2 mi north of Playas del Coco.

One of the most dramatic beaches in the country, this serene crescent is ringed by rocky cliffs. The sparkling, clean turquoise water contrasts with the black sand. It's only ½ km (mi) long, but the vistas are endless, with offshore islands and the jagged profile of the Santa Elena Peninsula 34 km (21 mi) away. Right at the entrance to the Gulf of Papagayo, it's a good place for sportfishing enthusiasts to hole up between excursions. There's good diving at Las Corridas, just 1 km (½ mi) away, and excellent snorkeling in nearby coves and islands, as well as right off the beach around the rocks at the east end of the beach.

GETTING HERE AND AROUND

The drive is 10 minutes from Playas del Coco on a paved road to the gated entrance of Playa Ocotal. The road winds through a heavily populated Tico residential area, so be on the lookout, especially at night, for bicyclists without lights, children, dogs, cows, and horses on the road. There are no buses from Playas del Coco to Ocotal, but it's about $7 by taxi.

OUTDOOR ACTIVITIES

DIVING AND SNORKELING

The rocky outcrop at the north end of the beach near Los Almendros is good for close-to-shore snorkeling. The dive shop at the **Ocotal Beach Resort** (⊠ *3 km/2 mi south of Playas del Coco* ☎ *2670–0321* ⊕ *www. ocotaldiving.com*) is the only PADI Instruction Development Center

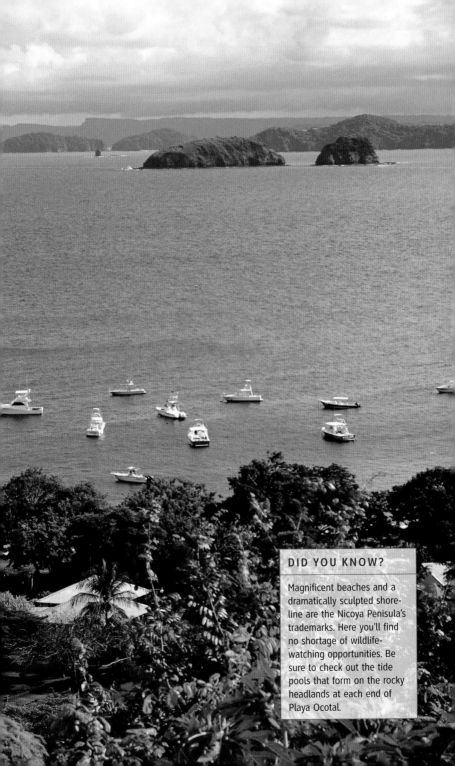

DID YOU KNOW?

Magnificent beaches and a dramatically sculpted shoreline are the Nicoya Penisula's trademarks. Here you'll find no shortage of wildlife-watching opportunities. Be sure to check out the tide pools that form on the rocky headlands at each end of Playa Ocotal.

in Costa Rica, offering the highest-level diving courses and five diving boats. The shop has excellent equipment, safety standards, and instruction. A regular dive costs $78; equipment rental is $26. The shop also rents snorkeling equipment for $12 per day. Or you can take a snorkeling boat tour for $0, including gear.

FISHING

Ocotal Beach Resort (⇨ *above*) has a sportfishing operation with three 32-foot Morgan hulls powered by twin 260-horsepower Cummins engines ($525 half day; $803 full day for up to four fishers). Marlins are catch-and-release, but you can keep—and eat—the mahimahi, yellowfin tuna, grouper, and amberjack you catch.

HIKING

Take an exhilarating and engrossing morning walk ($20, minimum 2 people) in the hills of Ocotal with retired vet and very active naturalist **Will Abrams** (☎ 2670–0553). The energetic, knowledgeable Kentucky native entertains and educates with stories about the secret lives of trees, plants, and animals spotted along the way.

WHERE TO EAT AND STAY

$$$

COSTA RICAN

✕ **Picante.** It's hot and it's tropical, and, as the name warns (*picante* means "spicy"), everything here makes your taste buds tingle. The menu spices up (literally) local fish and tropical fruits in dishes like grilled mahimahi with a picante mango sauce. (There's also a milder kids' menu.) The large terrace restaurant is poolside, facing the gorgeous beach backed by a cookie-cutter condominium development at Bahía Pez Vela. The cheap dinette furniture is out of sync with the innovative food, but you'll forgive the furniture faux pas when you taste the homemade brownies and coconut flan. Their Sunday brunch (10–2) is quite popular. ⊠ *At the beach, Bahía Pez Vela 1½ km/1 mi south of Ocotal* ☎ 2670–0901 ▭ *MC, V.*

$$
★

🏨 **Hotel Villa Casa Blanca.** For romance, you can't beat this Victorian-style, all-suites bed-and-breakfast in a hillside building buried in a bower of tropical plantings. Four-poster beds, plush furniture, and Victorian detailing set the mood. The honeymoon suites have deep soaking tubs built for two. The pool is small but pretty. There's no room service, but the obliging staff can arrange for local restaurants to deliver dinners *á deux*, to be enjoyed by candlelight at the pool or on the terrace. Waffles, pancakes, muffins, and savory dishes provide fuel in the morning. Breakfast entertainment is provided by various pet parrots that are vociferous as well as notorious moochers. Judging by the guest comments, people love them. **Pros:** romantic; fabulous breakfasts. **Cons:** small rooms; sometimes dingy. ⊠ *Inside gated entrance to El Ocotal Beach Resort* ⊕ *Apdo. 176–5019, Playas del Coco* ☎☎ 2670–0448 ⊕ *www.hotelvillacasablanca.com* ➥ *12 suites* ⌂ *In-room: no phone, safe, no TV. In-hotel: pool, laundry service, Internet terminal, Wi-Fi hotspot, no-smoking rooms* ▭ *AE, MC, V* ⊙| *BP.*

$$$

🏨 **Ocotal Beach Resort.** This resort has the best sea views hereabouts and is one of the best dive and sportfishing resorts in the country. All rooms have ocean views, but those with the nicest views are on the hilltop, even though they may be a bit cramped with furniture. Down the hill to the beach, comfortable triangular bungalows each have two separate suites that share a semiprivate pool. Swimming pools dot the property; be prepared, though, for a steep hike to the biggest one down at the beach, or call for a golf cart to take you there. The best feature of the restaurant, which specializes in Mediterranean and Asian flavors, is the 270-degree view from the terrace. **Pros:** lots of excursions; great infrastructure; lovely view. **Cons:** resort-y; spotty service. ⊠ *3 km/2 mi south of Playas del Coco, down newly paved road* ☎ *2670–0321* ⊕ *www.ocotalresort.com* ⬳ *42 rooms, 5 suites, 12 bungalow suites* ⬧ *In-room: safe. In-hotel: 2 restaurants, room service, bars, tennis court, pools, spa, diving, laundry service, Internet terminal, Wi-Fi hotspot* ⊟ *AE, MC, V* ⍓*BP.*

NIGHTLIFE

Enjoy a quiet margarita with an ocean view at **Father Rooster Sports Bar & Grill** (⊠ *Next door to El Ocotal Beach Resort 3 km/2 mi south of Playas del Coco*) on the beach. The action heats up later in the evening with big-screen TV, music, pool, beach volleyball, and Tex-Mex bar food. During peak holiday weeks, crowds of partiers descend on the bar to dance by torchlight.

PLAYA PAN DE AZÚCAR

8 km/5 mi north of Flamingo Beach.

Playa Pan de Azúcar (literally "Sugar Bread Beach," though most people call it simply Sugar Beach) has a quality that can be hard to come by in this area: privacy. With only one built-up property, the entire stretch of soft, light-colored sand feels practically deserted. The north end of the beach has some good snorkeling when the sea is calm—usually around low tide—and the swimming out from the middle of the beach is relatively safe. But if the swell is big, children and weak swimmers shouldn't go in past their waist. Playa Penca, a short walk south along the beach, can be a good swimming beach as well. A large part of the attraction here is the forest that hems the beach, where you may see howler monkeys, black iguanas, magpie jays, trogons, and dozens of other bird species.

GETTING HERE AND AROUND

Getting to this beach is an adventure in itself. It's still a very bumpy road 20 minutes from Flamingo Beach. If you have a 4WD vehicle and an excellent sense of direction, you can attempt to drive (dry season only) the 16-km (11-mi) Monkey Trail, which cuts through the mountains from Coco to Flamingo. But even some Ticos get lost on this route, so keep asking for directions along the way. There are no buses to Playa Pan de Azúcar; a taxi from Playa Flamingo costs about $20.

OUTDOOR ACTIVITIES

Most of the operators who work out of Flamingo *(⇨ below)* can pick up guests at the Hotel Sugar Beach for skin diving, sportfishing, sailing, horseback riding, and other excursions. The Hotel Sugar Beach *(⇨ below)* offers outrigger tours to a secluded beach 40 minutes to the north, which has a large reef and calm water for snorkeling.

WHERE TO STAY

$$–$$$ **Hotel Sugar Beach.** The theme of this secluded hotel with a shimmering
     pool and thin, curving beach is harmony with nature. Its owners have
Fodor's Choice   gone to great lengths to protect the surrounding environment, as the
★   abundant wildlife on its 25 acres of protected forest attests. Spacious
one- and two-bedroom suites, with high ceilings and private terraces
with idyllic sea views, are great for couples and families (kids under 12
stay free). If you like serenity and want to spend a little less on lodging, opt for a standard room in one of the duplexes scattered through
the forest. Each room is decorated in earth tones, with elegant wicker
furniture, a wooden door with a hand-carved local bird or animal, and
a veranda with a garden or ocean view (the best ocean views are from
rooms 21 and 22). The open-air rotunda restaurant serves good seafood
dishes ($$$), and there's a kids' menu. The hotel's recycling, energy and
water conservation, and community service programs are exemplary.
Pros: friendly; natural setting; practically private beach. **Cons:** waves
and rocks can make the ocean dangerous for kids. ⊠ *8 km/5 mi north of
Playa Flamingo* ☎ *2654–4242* ⊕ *www.sugar-beach.com* ⊅ *22 rooms, 6
suites, 2 houses* ♿ *In-room: safe, kitchen (some), refrigerator. In-hotel:
restaurant, room service, bar, pool, water sports, laundry service, Inter-
net terminal, Wi-Fi hotspot* ⊟ *AE, D, MC, V* ⊺○⊺ *BP.*

PLAYA POTRERO

4 km/2½ mi north of Flamingo.

The small town of Potrero is a classic Tico community, with a church,
school, and supermarket arranged around a soccer field. But Potrero
Beach stretches for 4 km (2½ mi) all the way south from the village to
the skyline of Flamingo. Development is picking up speed, with large
houses and condominium developments springing up on any hill with
a view. There's a large Italian contingent here, adding some style and
flavor to area hotels. The brown-sand beach is safe for swimming, but
Potrero is neither the prettiest, nor cleanest, of this region's beaches.
The best area for swimming is midway between Flamingo and Potrero
town, near the hotel Bahía del Sol. The best beach view and best breeze
are from a bar stool at Bar Las Brisas. About 10 km (6 mi) offshore lie
the Catalina Islands, a barrier-island mecca for divers and snorkelers,
which dive boats based in Flamingo can reach in 10 minutes.

GETTING HERE AND AROUND

Just before crossing the bridge at the entrance to Flamingo, take the
right fork signed for Playa Potrero. The road, which is alternately
muddy or dusty, is rough and follows the shoreline. Local buses run
from Flamingo to Potrero, but it's so close that you're better off tak-
ing a taxi.

OUTDOOR ACTIVITIES

DIVING

Marked as Santa Catarina on some maps, the **Catalina Islands,** as they
are known locally, are a major destination for dive operations based all
along the coast. These barrier islands are remarkable for their diversity,
and appeal to different levels of divers. On one side, the islands have

20- to 30-foot drops, great for beginners. The other side has deeper drops of 18 to 24 meters (60 to 80 feet), better suited to more experienced divers. The top dive sites around the Catalina Islands are **The Point** and **The Wall.** From January to May, when the water is colder, you are almost guaranteed manta-ray sightings at these spots. Cow-nosed and devil rays are also spotted here in large schools, as well as bull and white-tipped sharks, several types of eels, and an array of reef fish. Dive operators from Playa Hermosa south to Tamarindo offer trips to these islands. Reserve through your hotel.

Costa Rica Diving (✉ *1 km/½ mi south of Flamingo on the main highway* ☎ *2654–4148* ⊕ *www.costarica-diving.com*) has been specializing in Catalina Islands dives for more than 16 years, with two-tank, two-location trips limited to five divers costing $85. The German owners also offer courses and are noted for their precision and high safety standards.

WHERE TO EAT

¢–$ ✕ **Bar Las Brisas**. The perfect beach bar, Las Brisas is a shack with a view
MEXICAN of the entire sweep of Playa Potrero. The kitchen serves up fairly basic bar fare and some fresh seafood such as rice with shrimp, and a grilled mahimahi sandwich. The fish tacos are outstanding—breaded strips of fish smothered in lettuce, tomato, and refried beans and encased in both a crisp taco and a soft tortilla shell. Wednesday is ladies' night, when the joint really jumps. The place is decorated with old surfboards, rusty U.S. license plates, and wall murals. ✉ *100 m west of soccer field, across from supermarket* ☎ *2654–4047* ▭ *V.*

$ ✕ **El Castillo Gourmet Eatery**. You won't find a better peanut-butter cookie
ECLECTIC in the country. This bakery/restaurant is also famous for its gooey cinnamon buns and pizza, which you can pick up to eat on the beach or back at your hotel. A mix of Latin and American food—from breakfast eggs Benedict through sandwiches and salads, Tex-Mex standards, shrimp skewers, and fish-and-chips—is served at casual terrace tables shaded by an ancient fig tree. The only drawback is the location on a busy corner, since the traffic tends to kick up a lot of dust. There's live music on Friday night, and karaoke on Saturday night. ✉ *Across from Bahía del Sol* ☎ *2654–4271* ▭ *MC, V.*

WHERE TO STAY

$$–$$$ ⌂ **Bahía del Sol**. It has the premier location on the beach, with rooms
★ surrounding lush gardens shaded by tropical trees. But this luxury hotel doesn't rest on its well-situated laurels. The service matches the unbeatable surroundings. At the restaurant ($$$), next to the gorgeous palm-fringed pool, smartly uniformed waiters serve jumbo shrimp, lobster, fresh fish, and various meat dishes prepared in an eclectic mix of ways, from blackened tuna to Moroccan lamb. Seating is under a massive thatch roof or at several tables on the lawn overlooking the beach. Rooms are spacious and elegant, with Costa Rican wicker and wood furniture, patterned ceramic-tile floors, and paintings by Costa Rican artists. They open onto a portico with chairs, hammocks, and views of the garden; deluxe rooms also have a back patio with a Jacuzzi hemmed by greenery. Spacious one- and two-bedroom suites also have kitchens and living

rooms. **Pros:** on the beach; lovely grounds; excellent restaurant; friendly. **Cons:** noise from nearby bars; rooms could use updating. ⊠ *South end of Potrero Beach, across from El Castillo* ☎ *2654–4671* ⊕ *www.potrerobay. com* ⤳ *12 rooms, 16 suites* ⌂ *In-room: safe, refrigerator, Wi-Fi. In-hotel: restaurant, room service, bar, pool, beachfront, bicycles, laundry service, Internet terminal, Wi-Fi hotspot* ⊟ *AE, MC, V* �𝌆 *BP.*

$ ⌗ **Bahía Esmeralda Hotel & Restaurant.** Although it's not on the beach, this Italian-run hotel has style at an affordable price. It's a great place for families or groups. Ochre-color villas are spread out around pretty pool gardens and lawn. Large glass doors bring in lots of light, and the fans hung from high wooden ceilings keep things cool. The well-equipped apartments sleep four, six, or eight people, and have handsome fabrics and bathrooms tiled in cool green. An alfresco restaurant serves breakfast and light Italian dishes. The friendly owner-manager is always on the premises. It's a five-minute walk through the village to the beach. **Pros:** friendly service; economical. **Cons:** not on the beach. ⊠ *1 block east of Potrero village* ☎ *2654–4480* ⊕ *www.hotelbahiaesmeralda.com* ⤳ *4 rooms, 8 apartments,2 suite. 2 villass* ⌂ *In-room: no phone, kitchen (some). In-hotel: restaurant, pool, laundry service, Wi-Fi hotspot* ⊟ *AE, MC, V* �𝌆 *BP rooms, EP apartments.*

PLAYA FLAMINGO

80 km/50 mi southwest of Liberia.

Flamingo was the first of the northern Nicoya beaches to experience the wonders of overdevelopment, a fact immortalized in the concrete towers that straggle up the hill above Flamingo Bay. The place is still abuzz with real-estate activity, and any ledge of land with a view is a building site. The beach, hidden away to the southwest of the town, is one of the loveliest strands in Costa Rica, with light-beige sand sloping into a relatively calm sea and buttonwood trees separating it from the road. This beach is great for swimming, with a fine-sand bottom and no strong currents, though there are a few submerged rocks in front of the Flamingo Beach Resort, so you should swim a bit farther south. There's sometimes a bit of surf, so if the waves are big, keep your eye on little paddlers. There is little shade along the beach's kilometer-long stretch, and no services, though there are restaurants in the beach resort and the adjacent town. To find the beach, go straight as you enter town, instead of going up the hill, and turn left after the Flamingo Beach Resort.

Flamingo is perhaps most famous for its large sportfishing fleet, temporarily moored out in the bay while the government grants a new concession to update and operate the marina here. Lured by boatloads of single-for-the-week fishermen, working girls abound here, adding a faint salacious whiff to the nightspots.

GETTING HERE AND AROUND

To get to Playa Flamingo from Liberia, drive 45 km (28 mi) south to Belén and then 35 km (22 mi) west on a good, paved road. The trip takes about three hours. If you're coming from the Playas del Coco and Ocotal area, you can take a 16-km (10-mi) shortcut, called the Monkey Trail, starting near Sardinal and emerging at Potrero. It's then

4 km (2½ mi) south to Flamingo. Attempt this only in dry season and in a 4WD. You can also take a bus from Liberia (⇨ *Bus Travel in Travel Smart Costa Rica*).

ESSENTIALS

Bank/ATM **Banco de Costa Rica** (✉ *50 m. south of Supermercado Massi* ☎ *2654–4984*).

Pharmacy **Santa Fe Medical Center & Pharmacy** (✉ *Halfway up hill*).

Internet **Shark Point at Costa Rica Diving** (✉ *1 km/½ mi south of town* ☎ *2654–4148* ⊙ *Daily 9–6*).

OUTDOOR ACTIVITIES

Flamingo offers the quickest access to the **Catalina Islands**, visible from its beach, where big schools of fish, manta rays, and other sea creatures gather. Coastal reefs to the north are visited on day trips that combine snorkeling with time on undeveloped beaches. **Aquacenter Diving** (✉ *Below Flamingo Marina Resort* ☎ *2654–4141* ⊕ *www.aquacenterdiving. com*) runs two-tank dives at the Catalina Islands ($79 and snorkeling trips ($49), as well as offering a range of PADI certification courses.

BOATING

Lazy Lizard Catamaran Sailing Adventures (☎ *2654–5900* ⊕ *www. lazylizardsailing.com*) offers a morning or afternoon snorkeling and sunbathing tour on a 34-foot catamaran. The four-hour tours start at 8:30 AM (minimum of 8 people) and 2 PM and cost $55, with snorkeling equipment, kayaks, drinks, and food included.

Sail off for an afternoon of snorkeling, snacking, and sunset drinks on **Samonique III** (☎ *2654-5280, 8703-6162* ⊕ *www.costarica-sailing.com*), a *trés jolie* 52-foot French ketch ($75 per person, minimum of five; children under 12, half-price). The ship sails daily at 2 and returns at 6:30 PM.

FISHING

Although the marina is still closed down while officials consider bids to rebuild it, there are plenty of sportfishing boats bobbing in Flamingo Bay. Larger boats have moved to moorings in the new Papagayo Marina near the Four Seasons Hotel. In December the wind picks up and many of the smaller, 31-foot-and-under boats head to calmer water farther south. But the wind brings cold water and abundant baitfish, which attract marlin (blue, black, and striped), Pacific sailfish, yellowfin tuna, wahoo, mahimahi, grouper, and red snapper. January to April is consequently prime catch-and-release season for billfish. One of the established fishing operations that sticks around all year is **Billfish Safaris** (✉ *Lower level, Mariner Inn, at entrance to town* ☎ *2654–5244* ⊕ *www.billfishsafaris.com*). Its 42-foot boat with twin 450-horsepower diesel engines can go anywhere in any kind of sea. Trips on a smaller 35-foot boat are also available. Half-day trips are $1,100–$1,750 for up to seven anglers; full-day trips run $1,350–$2,200. You can also go out night fishing for snapper and grouper ($120 per person).

The reclusive zebra moray eel likes to hide it's entire body in in rock or corral holes.

WHERE TO EAT

$$$
FRENCH
★

✕ **Mar y Sol.** Come early to catch the sunset from the second-floor tapas lounge here, then linger over a fine French-accented dinner at this elegant, torchlighted terrace restaurant perched on a hillside. The chef/owners Alain and Jean Luc Taulere represent the fifth and sixth generations of a family of French restaurateurs, so of course there are escargots. More interesting, though, are their fusions of French traditions with tropical flavors in dishes such as crispy duck with a *mora* (blackberry) sauce. Seafood is a specialty, with passion fruit shrimp ceviche for starters, followed by grilled mahimahi with a mango salsa and buerre blanc sauce, or seared tuna with an Asian reduction, wakame, and wasabi mashed potatoes. The coco del mar is a not-to-be-missed platter of seafood, Caribbean–style, served with a spicy sauce in a fresh coconut. There's an extensive wine cellar to match the sophisticated menu, and they serve two-dozen wines by the glass. Service is smoothly professional. ✉ *150 m uphill (west) from the Banco de Costa Rica* ☎ *2654–4151* ▭ *AE, MC, V* ☉ *Closed Sept. and Oct.*

$
SEAFOOD

✕ **Marie's Restaurant.** A Flamingo institution, serving beachgoers and locals for more than two decades, this popular restaurant serves an array of sandwiches and salads, as well as reliably fresh seafood in large portions at reasonable prices. Settle in at one of the wooden tables beneath the ceiling fans and massive thatched roof for a traditional Costa Rican ceviche, avocado stuffed with shrimp, or heart of palm and pejivalle (palm fruit). The main fare includes whole-fried red snapper, shrimp and fish kebabs, and a delicious *plato de mariscos* (shrimp, lobster, and fish served with garlic butter, potatoes, and salad). Save room for Marie's signature banana-chocolate bread pudding. At breakfast, try unusual papaya pancakes, French toast made with cream cheese and jam, or Marie's special omelet with cheese, onion, sweet pepper, bacon, and ham. ⊠ *Main road, near north end of beach* ☎ *2654–4136* ▭ *AE, MC, V.*

WHERE TO STAY

$$ 🛈 **Flamingo Beach Resort.** This three-story concrete hotel has a great location overlooking beautiful Flamingo Beach, and though few of its rooms have ocean views, they are all mere steps away from the sand and surf. Formerly a family-friendly inn, it has recently been expanded, re-modelled and upgraded. You can't beat its beach-accessible location, or the huge, centerpiece swimming pool with 25-meter lap lanes along one side. The kids' pool has a sunburn-preventive thatch roof, and is close enough to the swim-up bar that you could save a toddler without spilling your piña colada. There's a dive shop on-site as well as water-sports equipment, and there are several pool tables and children's activities. Rooms are standard size, with high ceilings and private balconies or terraces. Get a pool view, preferably on the second or third floor; those with higher numbers have ocean views. The restaurants are not exciting, so don't take the all-inclusive option. There are good restaurants within walking distance or a quick shuttle trip away. **Pros:** beachfront; big pool; good value. **Cons:** inconsistent service; mediocre food. ⊠ *Hotel entrance on left past Marie's Restaurant* ☎ *2654–4444; 2283–8063 in San José* ⊕ *www.resortflamingobeach. com* ⌁ *120 rooms, 11 suites* ⌂ *In-room: safe, kitchen (some), refrigerator. In-hotel: restaurant, room service, bars, tennis court, pools, gym, casino spa, beachfront, diving, children's programs (ages 2–12), laundry service, Wi-Fi hotspot* ▭ *AE, MC, V* |O| *AI, BP.*

$$–$$$ 🛈 **Flamingo Marina Resort.** Though a short walk from Flamingo beach, this collection of hillside villas has lots to do. There are four pools, tennis courts, a beach, a dive shop, and a tour desk. The fashionably decorated rooms, color-washed in a mango hue, have terra-cotta lamps, hand-carved wooden furniture, and shell-shaped sinks. The luxurious condos have modern kitchens and spacious sitting areas with leather couches. Nearly all rooms and condos have large verandas with views of the sea and Playa Potrero. **Pros:** spacious rooms; sea views; ample grounds. **Cons:** not on main beach; no nightlife. ⊠ *Hill above Flamingo Bay* ⌖ *Apdo. 321–1002, San José* ☎ *2654–4141* ⊕ *www. flamingomarina.com* ⌁ *22 rooms, 6 suites, 80 condos* ⌂ *In-room: safe, kitchen (some). In-hotel: restaurant, room service, bar, pools, beachfront, diving, laundry service, Internet terminal, Wi-Fi* ▭ *AE, DC, MC, V* |O| *EP in condos, BP in rooms.*

$ 🛈 **Hotel Guanacaste Lodge.** On the outskirts of Flamingo, a short drive from the beach, this Tico-run lodge offers basic accommodations for a fraction of what the town's big hotels charge. Ten simple, duplex bungalows have high-beamed ceilings, wood furniture, walk-in closets, and spacious bathrooms. Each room has a picture window looking out onto a garden that holds the pool, a thatched shelter, and a cascading

---

THE GUANACASTE TREE

Massive and wide spreading, with tiny leaflets and dark brown, earlike seedpods, the Guanacaste tree is common through this region, and is Costa Rica's national tree.

6

fountain. **Pros:** very private; friendly. **Cons:** no in-room phones; simple. ⊠ *200 m south of the Potrero-Flamingo crossroads* ☎ *2654–4494* ⊕ *www.guanacastelodge.com* ⤳ *8 rooms* ☖ *In-room: no phone. In-hotel: restaurant, pool* ⊟ V ⫿ BP.

NIGHTLIFE

The **Mariner Inn Bar** (⊠ *Bottom of hill, entering Flamingo*) is often boisterous and thick with testosterone, as fishermen trade fish tales. If you're interested in fishing of a different sort, or just like to watch, restaurant/disco/casino **Amberes** (⊠ *Halfway up hill in Flamingo*) is the late-night meeting place.

PLAYA CONCHAL

8 km/5 mi south of Flamingo.

Lovely, secluded Playa Conchal is named for the bits of broken shells that cover its base of fine white sand (the Spanish word for shell is concha). It's an idyllic strand of sugary sand sloping steeply into aquamarine water and lined with an array of trees. The point that defines Conchal's northern end is hemmed by a lava-rock reef that is a popular snorkeling area—locals rent equipment on the beach—whereas the beach's southern extreme is often deserted. Although the sprawling Paradisus Playa Conchal resort covers the hinterland behind the beach, you don't need to stay at that all-inclusive resort to enjoy Conchal, since it's a short walk, or drive, south to Brasilito.

GETTING HERE AND AROUND

The drive south from Flamingo is 10 minutes on a paved highway. Both town and beach are just 1 km (½ mi) north of the entrance to Paradisus Playa Conchal. To reach Playa Conchal, turn left at the end of the town square and follow the dirt road across a stretch of beach and over a steep hill; the beach stretch is impassable at high tide. Buses run from Flamingo to Conchal three times daily, at 7:30 and 11:30 AM and 2:30 PM. A taxi from Flamingo is about $6.

ESSENTIALS

The closest bank and ATM are in Flamingo.

Hospital Costa de Emergencias (⊠ *Crossroads at Huacas* ☎ *2653–6440*).

Pharmacy Farmacia El Cruce (⊠ *Crossroads at Huacas* ☎ *2653–8787* ☾ *Daily 8 AM–10 PM*).

EXPLORING

A small, scruffy fishing village just 1 km (½ mi) north of Conchal, **Brasilito** has ramshackle houses huddled around its main square, which doubles as the soccer field. It's cluttered, noisy, and totally Tico, a lively contrast to the controlled sophistication of the Playa Conchal resort and residential development. Fishing boats moor just off a wide beach, about 3 km (2 mi) long, with golden sand flecked with pebbles and a few rocks. The surf is a little stronger here than at Flamingo Beach, but the shallow, sandy bottom keeps it swimmable. The sea is cleaner off nearby Playa Conchal, which is also a more attractive beach. A few casual *marisquerias* (seafood eateries) and a couple of notable restaurants line Brasilito's beach.

OUTDOOR ACTIVITIES
GOLF

One of the best golf courses in the country, the Paradisus Playa Conchal megaresort's **Reserva Conchal Golf Club** (✉ *Paradisus Playa Conchal, entrance, less than 1 km/½ mi south of Brasilito* ☎ *2654–4123*) is an 18-hole, par-71 course designed by Robert Trent Jones Jr. The course is reserved for hotel guests only, who can try out their swing on 18 holes for $150, cart included.

WHERE TO EAT AND STAY

$$ ✕ **El Camarón Dorado.** Much of the appeal of this open-air bar-restaurant
SEAFOOD whose name translates as "The Golden Shrimp" is its shaded location on Brasilito's beautiful beach. Some tables are practically on the beach, with the surf lapping just yards away, making it the perfect spot for sunset drinks. The white-plastic tables and chairs are not up to the standards of the food, which is mostly locally caught fish and seafood served in bountiful portions. The house specialties include mahimahi prepared various ways, *arroz a la marinera* (rice with seafood), grilled lobster, and either jumbo, or the smaller pinky shrimp *al ajillo* (sautéed with garlic). If you have a reservation, a van can pick you up from Flamingo or Tamarindo hotels. ✉ *200 m north of Brasilito Plaza* ☎ *2654–4028* ▭ *AE, DC, MC, V.*

$–$$ ✕ **Il Forno.** For a break from seafood, try lunch or dinner at this roman-
ITALIAN tic Italian garden restaurant. There are 17 versions of thin-crust pizzas, plus fine homemade pastas and risotto. Vegetarians have lots of choices (if you can get past the thought that veal is on the menu), including an eggplant lasagna and interesting salads. They also serve some tasty seafood and meat dishes. At dinner, fairy lights and candles glimmer all through the garden, and some private tables are set apart under thatched roofs. Spanish and Italian wines are available by the glass or bottle. ✉ *Main road, 200 m east of the bridge in Brasilito* ☎ *2654–4125* ▭ *No credit cards* ☉ *Closed Mon. and Oct.*

¢ ⌂ **Hotel Brasilito.** Backpackers and travelers who don't need amenities will love this vintage, two-story, wooden hotel's seafront location, if not its no-frills rooms. Those rooms are a bit devoid of decor, though they do have hot water and either air-conditioning or a fan. Be prepared for some noise: kids playing, dogs barking, and motors revving. Ask for one of the two larger rooms above the restaurant; they share a veranda with unobstructed sea views. You can't beat the price for seaside rooms. Outback Jack's ($$), the Australian restaurant that occupies the open-air lobby, is a colorful, lively spot that specializes in grilled meat and seafood. **Pros:** inexpensive; across the street from beach; good restaurant. **Cons:** very basic rooms; can be noisy. ✉ *Between soccer field and beach, Brasilito* ☎ *2654–4237* ⊕ *www.brasilito.com* ↪ *13 rooms* ⌂ *In-room: no a/c (some), no phone, no TV. In-hotel: restaurant, beachfront, laundry service, Wi-Fi hotspot* ▭ *MC, V* ⎢○⎢ *EP.*

$$$$ ⌂ **Paradisus Playa Conchal Beach & Golf Resort.** So vast that guests ride around in trucks covered with striped awnings and the staff gets around on bicycles, this all-inclusive resort, the top of the line of the Spanish Melía hotel chain, is luxurious, if lacking a bit in personality. The grounds encompass almost 4 square km (1½ square mi) that include a

distant, picture-perfect beach. But in the labyrinthine guest village, the ocean disappears and the only views are of gardens and other buildings exactly like yours. The split-level Spanish Colonial–style villas have huge marble bathrooms and elegant sitting rooms. More than 120 "Royal Service" rooms are closer to the beach and have a private concierge. There's a kids' club and the largest—and perhaps warmest—pool in Central America. Grownups can amuse themselves sailing, snorkeling, kayaking, gambling at the casino, playing the gorgeous 18-hole golf course, or rejuvenating at the spa. If you're into the beach, try to get booked into a building between 1 and 5, or 33 and 40. More expansive Royal Service rooms are far from the beach. **Pros:** lovely rooms; beach access; abundant activities. **Cons:** expensive; massive; most rooms far from beach. ⊠ *Entrance less than 1 km/½ mi south of Brasilito* 🕾 *2654–4123* ⊕ *www.paradisus-playa-conchal.com* ➽ *292 villas, 122 Royal Service villas* ᜒ *In-room: safe, refrigerator, Wi-Fi. In-hotel: 7 restaurants, room service, bars, golf course, tennis courts, pools, gym, spa, beachfront, water sports, bicycles, children's programs (ages 3–12), laundry service, Internet terminal, Wi-Fi hotspot* ⊟ *AE, DC, MC, V* ⫶◎⫶ *AI.*

NIGHTLIFE

Live music, both acoustic guitar and rowdier dance bands, keeps **The Happy Snapper** (⊠ *On main street across from beach in Brasilito*) hopping from Wednesday to Saturday nights. Owner Mike Osborne often mans the bar and spikes the drinks with his own brand of wry humor.

EN ROUTE Gas stations are few and far between in these hinterlands. If you're heading down to Tamarindo from the Flamingo/Conchal area, fill up first. Your best bet is the 24-hour Oasis Exxon, 3 km (2 mi) east of Huacas.

TAMARINDO

82 km/51 mi southwest of Liberia.

Once a funky beach town full of spacey surfers and local fishermen, Tamarindo has become a pricey, hyped-up hive of commercial development and real estate speculation, with the still-unpaved roads kicking up dust and mud alternately, depending on the season. On the plus side, there's a dizzying variety of shops, bars, and hotels, and probably the best selection of restaurants of any beach town. Strip malls and high-rise condominiums have obscured views of the still-magnificent beach, and some low-life elements are making security an issue. But once you're on the beach, almost all the negatives disappear (just keep your eyes on your belongings). Wide and flat, the sand is packed hard enough for easy walking and jogging. How good it is for swimming and surfing, however, is questionable, since the town has twice lost its Blue Flag clean-beach status (because of overdevelopment and the total absence of water treatment). The water quality is especially poor during the rainy months, when you'll want to do your swimming and surfing at nearby Playa Langosta, or Playa Grande. ■TIP➔ **Strong currents at the north end of the beach get a lot of swimmers into trouble, especially when they try to cross the estuary without a surfboard.**

Surfing is the main attraction here, and there's a young crowd that parties hard after a day riding the waves. Tamarindo serves as a popular base for surfing at the nearby Playas Grande, Langosta, Avellanas, and Negra. There are plenty of outdoor options in addition to surfing, though, among them diving, sportfishing, wildlife-watching, and canopy tours. You can play 18 rounds at the nearby Hacienda Pinilla golf course, or simply stroll the beach and sunbathe.

GETTING HERE AND AROUND

Both Nature Air and SANSA fly to Tamarindo from San José. Macaw Air flies between Liberia and Tamarindo and to other Nicoya Peninsula towns. By car from Liberia, travel south on the highway to the turnoff for Belén, then head west and turn left at the Huacas crossroads to Tamarindo. Stretches of the paved road from Belén are in deplorable states of disrepair. There are no direct bus connections between Playa Grande or Playa Avellanas and Tamarindo. A taxi is the way to go from nearby towns if you don't have wheels. The **Tamarindo Shuttle** (☎ 2653–1326) ferries passengers between the various beaches in a comfortable van.

ESSENTIALS

Bank/ATM **Banco Nacional** (✉ Across from Tamarindo El Diria Hotel).

Internet **Internet Café** (✉ Road to Hotel Pasatiempo, next to ABC Realty).

Medical Assistance **Farmacia Tamarindo** (✉ Main road into town ☎ 2653–1239) **Emergencias 2000** (✉ 100 m. east of CitiBank ☎ 8380–4125 or 2653-2282 ⊕ www.lifeguardcostarica.com).

Rental Cars **Alamo** (✉ Hotel Diría, main road, Tamarindo ☎ 2653–0727). **Budget** (✉ Hotel Zullymar, main road, Tamarindo ☎ 2653–0756). **Economy** (✉ Main road entering Tamarindo, next to Restaurant Coconut, Tamarindo ☎ 2653–0752). **Hola Rentacar** (✉ Hotel El Milagro, Tamarindo ☎ 2653–2000).

Taxis **Olman Taxi** (☎ 8347-8553 [cell]) A taxi from the airport to the center of Tamarindo costs about $5.

OUTDOOR ACTIVITIES

BOATING

Rocky Isla El Capitán, just offshore, is a close-in kayaking destination, full of sand-dollar shells. Exploring the tidal estuaries north and south of town is best done in a kayak at high tide, when you can travel farther up the temporary rivers. Arrange kayaking trips through your hotel. **Iguana Surf** (✉ *on beach, 100 m north of El Diría Hotel* ☎ *2653–0148* ⊕ *www.iguanasurf.net*) has an office with information on guided kayaking tours of the San Francisco Estuary and a full roster of local tours, including snorkeling. Sail off into the sunset aboard a 50-foot traditional schooner with cruise company **Mandingo Sailing** (☎ *8831-8875, 2653–2323 after 7* PM ⊕ *www.tamarindosailing.com*). Soft drinks, beer and wine, and bocas (snacks) are included on the three-hour cruise. The boat leaves at 3 PM from in front of El Pescador restaurant on the beach ($80 per person).

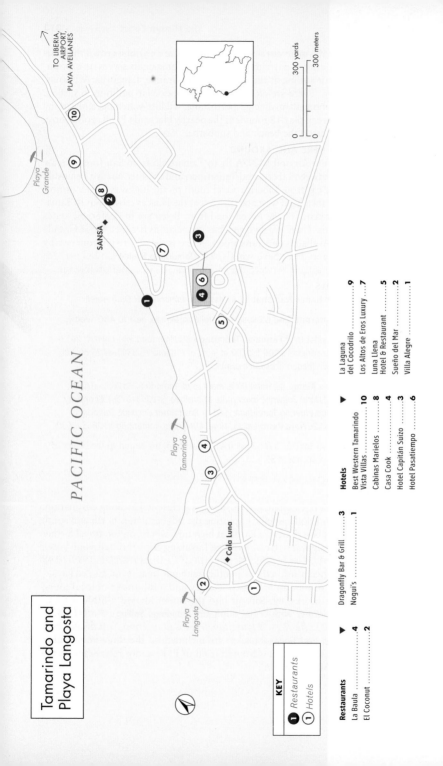

Tamarindo and Playa Langosta

PACIFIC OCEAN

Playa Langosta

Playa Tamarindo

Playa Grande

♦ Cala Luna

SANSA ♦

TO LIBERIA, AIRPORT, PLAYA AVELLANES

0   300 yards
0   300 meters

KEY

▶ *Restaurants*
① *Hotels*

Restaurants ▶

La Baula **4**
El Coconut **2**
Dragonfly Bar & Grill **3**
Nogui's **1**

Hotels ▶

Best Western Tamarindo
Vista Villas **10**
Cabinas Marielos **8**
Casa Cook **4**
Hotel Capitán Suizo **3**
Hotel Pasatiempo **6**
La Laguna
del Cocodrilo **9**
Los Altos de Eros Luxury **7**
Luna Llena
Hotel & Restaurant **5**
Sueño del Mar **2**
Villa Alegre **1**

FISHING

A number of fishing charters in Tamarindo cater to saltwater anglers. The most experienced among them is **Tamarindo Sportfishing** (☎ 2653–0090 ⊕ *www.tamarindosportfishing.com*), run by Randy Wilson, who has led the way in developing catch-and-release techniques that are easy on the fish. Wilson has roamed these waters since the 1970s, and he knows where the big ones lurk. His 38-foot *Talking Fish* is equipped with a marlin chair and a cabin with a shower, and costs $1,500 for a full day, $850 for a half. A fishing trip for up to four anglers on one of two 28-foot boats costs $825 to $975 for a full day; $550 to $675 for a half.

GOLFING

Mike Young, who has designed some of the best golf courses in the southern United States, designed the par-72 championship course at **Hacienda Pinilla** (✉ *10 km/6 mi south of Tamarindo via Villa Real* ☎ *2680–7062 or 2680–3000* ⊕ *www.haciendapinilla.com*). It has ocean views and breezes, and plenty of birds populate the surrounding trees. Guests pay $185 ($75 after 2 PM) for 18 holes in high season.

SURFING

Iguana Surf (✉ *son beach. 100 m. north of El Diriá Hotel* ☎ *2653–0148* ⊕ *www.iguanasurf.net*) rents surfboards and boogie boards and offers lessons (for ages 3 to 88). **Maresias Surf Shop** (✉ *Next to Banco Nacional* ☎ *2653–0224* ⊕ *www.maresiasurfcostarica.com*) has equipment, lessons, and lots of local knowledge. Check out **Tamarindo August Surf Shop** (✉ *Tamarindo Vista Villas* ☎ *2653–0221*) for boards to buy or rent, surfing gear, swimsuits, and sunblock. The shop operates a kids' surfing school as well as offering adult lessons and guided surfing tours. **High Tide Surf Shop** (✉ *Road to Langosta, about 200 m west of Hotel Pasatiempo* ☎ *2653–0108*) has high-end surfing equipment and clothing and a large selection of beachwear in a second-story shop.

WILDLIFE TOURS

ACOTAM (☎ *2653–1687*), a local conservation association, conducts turtle-viewing tours with local guides for $35, including park entrance fee. The group picks you up at your hotel and briefs you at their headquarters on the estuary that separates Tamarindo and Playa Grande. An open boat then takes you across the estuary, where you wait at the park station until a turtle has been spotted. The turtle-nesting season runs from mid-October to February. They also offer mangrove tours year-round.

WHERE TO EAT

$$
ECLECTIC
★

✕ **Dragonfly Bar & Grill.** A low-key, natural ambience with tree-trunk columns, sculptural hanging lamps, and a cool soundtrack make this immensely popular, friendly restaurant a great place to spend an evening. The chef offers a limited but enticing menu of innovative dishes that combine the flavors of Asia and Latin America, with a few Mediterranean accents. Settle in and tingle your taste buds with spicy shrimp rolls, or a roasted beet, Gorgonzola, and walnut salad. Then sink your incisors into a pork chop over roasted garlic potato puree, or a Thai-style crispy fish cake with curried sweet corn. There are various vegetarian options, and the daily fish specials are always a good bet. ✉ *100 m* *east of Hotel Pasatiempo* ☎ *2653–1506* ⊕ *www.dragonflybarandgrill. com* ⊟ *AE, DC, MC, V* ✆ *Closed Sun. and Sept./Oct. No lunch.*

$$$$
SEAFOOD

✕ **El Coconut.** The red, black, and dark-wood interior of this high-gloss, dinner-only restaurant with giant stone sculptures and a coconut tree growing through the roof feels like a lacquered Japanese *bento* box. Seafood is the main event, with the catch of the day—usually mahimahi—served half a dozen ways, but they also serve a good tenderloin, with a choice of sauces, and the classic surf and turf. The innovative jumbo shrimp or lobster in a pineapple, raisin, and ginger sauce are delicious, and the list of sauces for the fish includes the traditional Norwegian *sandelfjords smor* (a cream sauce with lime)—the owner is from Norway. Service is smooth and more formal than at most beach restaurants, and they have a good wine list, but the food and drink are much more expensive here than at the competition. ⊠ *Main street, 150 m south of Tamarindo Vista Villas* ☎ *2653–0086* ⊟ *AE, MC, V* ✆ *Closed Mon. No lunch.*

$
PIZZA
☾

✕ **La Baula.** Popular with the locals, this alfresco pizzeria on a quiet side street has plenty of cars parked outside most nights. Families are especially fond of La Baula—the Costa Rican name for the "leather-back turtle"—because of its reasonable prices and adjacent playground. Everyone enjoys the consistently delicious thin-crust pizzas, though if you don't like pizza, stay away. It's about the only thing on the menu, which consists of two-dozen pies and a mixed salad. They also offer a tasty little tiramisu. ⊠ *100 m north of Hotel Pasatiempo* ☎ *2653–1450* ⊟ *AE, MC, V* ✆ *No lunch.*

$$
SEAFOOD

✕ **Nogui's.** Pleasing a loyal legion of local fans since 1974, Nogui's offers a hearty Costa Rican menu and an ocean view. It is one of Tamarindo's best options for lunch, with a good selection of sandwiches and huge salads. It's also a good spot for dinner, when they offer a full seafood menu and various meat dishes. The recipes and presentation are nothing fancy, but the seafood is fresh and the price is right. Instead of the ubiquitous rice and beans on the side, Nogui's has a puree of *tiquisque*, a potato-like tuber. The homemade pies are legendary, notably the coconut cream. They also serve a signature margarita made with tamarind fruit. After 5 PM the restaurant on Nogui's second floor offers the same menu with a higher ocean view and balmy breezes. ⊠ *South side of Tamarindo Circle, on beach* ☎ *2653–0029* ⊟ *AE, MC, V* ✆ *Closed Wed. and 2 wks in Oct.*

WHERE TO STAY

$$

⊞ **Best Western Tamarindo Vista Villas.** If you're into surfing, this is where you want to be. Even though it's across the street from the beach, it's quite close to Tamarindo's beach break, and a quick paddle to the river-mouth break and Playa Grande. Around the pool and bar the talk is all about waves. There's a surf school and a surf shop, and surfing legends Robert August and Wing Nuts, of *Endless Summer* movie fame, are frequent guests. The large villas with kitchens have a bedroom with a double bed and two futon couches; they are slowly being redecorated. Avoid rooms 101 to 107, which face the pool's supporting wall. Poolside rooms can be noisy when the pool is filled with frolicking kids. The hotel has a helpful tour desk. **Pros:** near beach break; villas view ocean. **Cons:**

A group of local musicians rocking out in Tamarindo.

not on the beach; spotty service. ⊠ *Main road entering Tamarindo, on left* ☎ *2653–0114; 800/536–3241 in U.S.* ⊕ *www.tamarindovistavillas. com* ⥲ *12 rooms, 17 villas* ♿ *In-room: safe, kitchen (some). In-hotel: restaurant, room service, bar, pool, water sports, laundry service, Wi-Fi hotspot* ⊟ *AE, MC, V* ⊚ *CP.*

¢ ⊞ **Cabinas Marielos**. Rooms at this well-situated, locally owned hotel are among the best of the budget category in Tamarindo. Two wings, decorated with floral motifs in the style of the artisans of Sarchí, are well back from the busy main road, on grounds with colorful gardens, coconut palms, and other trees. The beach and surf break are a short walk away. Rooms are quite basic, with cold-water showers and either a fan or air-conditioning. Guests sometimes share meals in the well-equipped common kitchen. The atmosphere is surprisingly serene, and the friendly staff can arrange turtle-watching, horseback riding, and other tours. **Pros:** cheap; near beach; relatively quiet. **Cons:** basic rooms; no hot showers. ⊠ *Across main dirt road from beach, on left after Best Western* ☎ *2653–0141* ⊕ *www.cabinasmarieloscr.com* ⥲ *24 rooms* ♿ *In-room: no a/c (some), no phone, safe, refrigerator (some), no TV. In-hotel: no-smoking rooms* ⊟ *AE, MC, V* ⊚ *EP.*

$$$ ⊞ **Casa Cook**. With just a few rooms on the quiet, southern end of
★ the beach, this friendly, family-run place is one of Tamarindo's most secluded lodging options. Two cabinas on the beach have sleeping areas separated by 5-foot-high walls from living rooms with futon couches and kitchenettes. Narrow front terraces have ocean views through a high iron fence—security first—with hammocks hung between the trees on the other side of the gate. Behind those bungalows is a small tile pool hemmed by gardens, and the casita, which occupies the ground

floor of the building that holds the owners' apartment. Though less private than the cabinas, the casita is slightly larger, with two futon couches, a kitchen, and glass doors that open onto the pool area. There are several restaurants and a supermarket within walking distance. **Pros:** small; secluded, beachfront; friendly. **Cons:** often full; extremely tiny. ⊠ *Road to Playa Langosta, 100 m before Hotel Capitán Suizo* ☎ *2653–0125* ⊕ *www.casacook.net* ⌐ *2 cabinas, 1 casita, 1 apartment* ⟁ *In-room: no phone, safe, kitchen. In-hotel: pool, beachfront, water sports, laundry service, Wi-Fi hotspot, no-smoking rooms, no kids under 12* ☰ *AE, MC, V* ⓘ *EP.*

$$$–$$$$
Fodor's Choice
★

▦ **Hotel Capitán Suizo.** For folks who like nature, intimacy, and a beautiful beach setting, this is the best choice in town. Nestled in the forest on the relatively quiet southern end of Tamarindo's beach, elegant balconied rooms and airy bungalows surround a lovely pool shaded by large trees and greenery. Second-floor rooms have high, angled ceilings and lots of screens, which keeps them relatively cool despite their lack of air-conditioning. Lower rooms are smaller and darker, but have air-conditioning, and terraces with views of the forested grounds, which are home to iguanas, raccoons, howler monkeys, and an array of birds. All rooms are decorated with fascinating vintage sepia photos depicting early-20th-century Costa Rican life. The two-level bungalows have king-size four-poster beds, futon couches, sensuous bathrooms with sunken whirlpool tubs, and outdoor garden showers—only two have an ocean view. The four-bedroom apartment has a kitchen and whirlpool tub. A beautifully decorated terrace restaurant overlooking the pool and beach serves contemporary cuisine and hosts lively beach barbecues on Friday night. Service is friendly and polished. **Pros:** beachfront; secluded; friendly; lovely gardens and pool. **Cons:** sand fleas and mosquitoes can be a problem; pricey. ⊠ *Right side of road toward Playa Langosta* ⟁ *Apdo. 22–5159, Villa Real, Guanacaste* ☎ *2653–0075* ⊕ *www.hotelcapitansuizo.com* ⌐ *22 rooms, 8 bungalows, 1 apartment* ⟁ *In-room: no a/c (some), safe, refrigerator, no TV. In-hotel: restaurant, room service, bar, pool, beachfront, water sports, bicycles, laundry service, Internet terminal, Wi-Fi hotspot* ☰ *AE, MC, V* ⓘ *BP.*

$$
▦ **Hotel Pasatiempo.** Come for Sunday football, open mike on Tuesday night, or great eggs Benedict any morning. One way or another, you are bound to pass some time at this friendly, laid-back place. This is one of the last relatively tranquil hotels in the sea of Tamarindo construction. Duplex bungalow rooms are scattered around lushly landscaped grounds and the pool, next to which towers the restaurant's thatch roof. Each unit, named after a Guanacaste beach, has a small patio with a hammock or swinging chair and a hand-painted beach mural; newer deluxe rooms are nicer and more secluded. Suites are good for young families, since they have one bedroom and small daybeds in the living room. The Oasis Restaurant ($$) serves a mix of above-average bar food and pizza, along with more sophisticated fare, such as macadamia-encrusted mahimahi with a mango sauce, or chicken in a Stroganoff sauce. **Pros:** lush grounds; relatively quiet. **Cons:** several blocks from beach; noisy Sunday to Tuesday. ⊠ *Off dirt road to Playa Langosta, 180 m from beach behind Tamarindo Circle* ☎ *2653–0096*

⊕ *www.hotelpasatiempo.com* ⟿ *22 rooms, 2 suites* ⟳ *In-room: no phone, saf, Wi-Fie. In-hotel: restaurant, bar, pool, laundry service, Internet terminal, Wi-Fi hotspot* ▭ *AE, MC, V* ⦿*BP.*

$–$$ ⚎ **La Laguna del Cocodrilo.** This hotel's name, which translates as "The Crocodile's Lagoon," refers to a pond between the hotel and the beach that is frequented by one of those giant lizards. A short trail leads from past that pond to the north end of Playa Tamarindo and the estuary. Standard rooms here should be avoided, since they are too close to Tamarindo's main road and are dark, but the ocean views and junior suites are a good deal, especially since they're practically on the beach. The only problem is their proximity to the restaurant and bar, which stays open till 11 PM, so this isn't the place for early-to-bed types. No matter where you stay, though, you should dine at the hotel's restaurant ($$$), where tables are scattered amid tropical greenery and coconut palms decorated with light spirals. The tasty seafood inventions here include red snapper stuffed with a Cognac mousse, potato-wrapped sea bass, and a decent bouillabaisse. The French bakery in front serves good breakfasts, light lunches, and sweets. **Pros:** almost beachfront; good restaurant. **Cons:** standard rooms dark; can be noisy. ⊠ *Main street, on right entering town* ☎ *2653–0255* ⊕ *www.lalagunadelcocodrilo.com* ⟿ *10 rooms, 2 suites, 1 studio* ⟳ *In-room: no phone, safe, refrigerator. In-hotel: restaurant, bar* ▭ *MC, V* ⦿*EP.*

$$$$ ⚎ **Los Altos de Eros Luxury Inn & Spa.** This intimate adults-only inn is the place to be for honeymooning couples with enough money left over after the wedding to pamper themselves. Rooms, with queen or king beds, are elegant and comfortable, opening out onto a large pool with expansive views as far as the ocean. But the main draw here is the spa, built into the side of a mountain and staffed by a team of professional therapists, offering such sybaritic pleasures as volcanic mud wraps, honey-cucumber-lime facials, papaya body polishes, and relaxing massages. Day packages are available for nonguests. Gourmet breakfast and lunch are included, as is dinner two nights a week. Other evenings, you can take a free shuttle into nearby Tamarindo to experience the local dining scene. Early-morning yoga classes and hikes around the 70-acre property keep you active. **Pros:** secluded; small; romantic; no kids under 8. **Cons:** scheduled mealtimes; pricey. ⊠ *Cañafistula, 14 km/ 8½ mi southeast of Tamarindo* ☎ *8850–4203; 786/866–7039 in U.S.* ⊕ *www.losaltosdeeros.com* ⟿ *4 rooms, 1 suite* ⟳ *In-room: safe, refrigerator. In-hotel: restaurant, bar, pool, gym, spa, Wi-Fi hotspot* ▭ *MC, V* ☯ *Closed Oct.* ⦿*MAP.*

$$ ⚎ **Luna Llena Hotel & Residence.** This place looks a little like a Fellini film set of a fantasy tropical village. Bright-yellow conical thatch-roof huts on different levels circle a small pool and tropical gardens. Interiors are colorful and whimsical, with unusual fabrics, furniture, and walls painted by co-owner Simona Daniela, who, along with husband Pino Trimarchi, adds Italian panache to the place. They also serve good Italian food in their on-site restaurant, plus sushi in the Sushi Club by the pool. Four bright double rooms on the second floor have queen-size beds, high ceilings, spacious bathrooms, and colorful, creative decors. Bungalows with their own kitchens are great for families. The ground floor holds a kitchenette, bathroom, and a queen bed, whereas a steep, curving stair leads to a wooden loft with two single beds. The hotel is a 10-minute walk from the beach, in a relatively quiet area. **Pros:** secluded; lush grounds. **Cons:** several blocks away from beach; small pool. ⊠ *From road to Playa Langosta, first left (uphill); 1 block past Iguana Surf* ☎ 2653–0082 ⊕ *www.hotellunallena.com* ⤴ *5 rooms, 7 bungalows* ♿ *In-room: safe, kitchen (some). In-hotel: 2 restaurants, room service, pool, laundry service, Internet terminal, Wi-Fi hotspot* ▤ *AE, MC, V* ⦾ *CP.*

NIGHTLIFE

Tamarindo is one of the few places outside of San José where the night-life really jumps. In fact, it has the dubious distinction of being featured on Entertainment Television's explicit *Wild On* series, which spotlights the rowdiest party scenes around the world.

Although party-hearty hot spots come and go with the tides, Tamarindo does have some perennial, low-key options. For a pleasantly sedate Friday evening, try barbecue on the beach at the **Hotel Capitán Suizo** (⊠ *Right side of road toward Playa Langosta; veer left before circle*), starting at 6:30 with a cocktail, then on to a lavish barbecue buffet and live folk music and dancing ($29, reserve in advance). Friday nights at **Crazy Monkey Bar** (⊠ *Tamarindo Vista Villas, main road entering Tamarindo*) is ladies' night. The live music attracts a crowd of locals who really know how to move. **Aqua Discoteque** (75 m north of Hotel El Diría, ⊕ *www. aquadiscoteque.com*) is a sophisticated new dance spot in town, with a waterfall in the middle of the dance floor and an ocean-front patio. It's open Monday, Wednesday, Friday and Saturday nights, from about 10 pm, with changing DJs and live bands.

SHOPPING

Most stores in the strip malls lining the main road sell the same souvenirs. It's hard to leave town without at least one sarong in your suitcase. At **Calypso** (⊠ *Main Street at Tamarindo El Diria Hotel* ☎ 2653–1436), Parisian Anne Loriot has raised the bar on beach fashion with fabulous Indonesian- and Mexican-style coverups and elegant, cool dresses, all available in real women's sizes.

★ You'll also find original clothing and jewelry at **Azul Profundo** (⊠ *Main street, Plaza Tamarindo* ☎ 2653–0395), designed by a talented young Argentine woman. All her jewelry is made with real and semiprecious stones.

☾ For a good selection of swimsuits and a wide range of kiddie beach-wear, check out **Tienda Bambora** (⊠ *On beach, south side of Tamarindo Circle* ☎ 2653–0865).

PLAYA LANGOSTA

2 km/1 mi south of Tamarindo.

Playa Langosta is actually two beaches divided by the San Francisco Estuary, the mouth of which is a knee-high wade at low tide, and a deep river with dangerous currents around high tide. To the north is residential Langosta, where every foot of beachfront has been built up. It is sort of a bedroom community of Tamarindo, just five minutes away by car. To the south of the estuary is pristine Langosta, a protected annex of Las Baulas National Marine Park, where leatherback turtles nest at night and beachcombers roam by day. Luckily, most of the development on the northern half is tucked behind the buttonwood trees, so you can enjoy an unsullied dramatic beachscape, with surf crashing against rocky outcroppings. The beach here is rather narrow, since the coast is lined with rocks, and the light-gray sand is rather coarse. There's a wider, less rocky stretch in front of the Barceló Resort, where you can walk across the San Francisco Estuary at low tide to stroll and swim on the beach's southern half. If you walk a ways up that shallow tidal river at low tide, you may see snowy egrets, baby blue herons, tail-bobbing spotted sandpipers, and, if your eyes are sharp, tiny white-lored gnat-catchers, endemic to these parts.

GETTING HERE AND AROUND

The dirt road from Tamarindo is alternately dusty or muddy, but reliably rough. Or you can walk along the beach, at low tide, all the way from Tamarindo Beach. Most car-free visitors get picked up from Tamarindo by their hotels. Or you can take a taxi.

OUTDOOR ACTIVITIES

Tour operators in Tamarindo, just a few miles north, offer activities in the Playa Langosta area.

WHERE TO STAY

$$$–$$$$
Fodor's Choice
★

Sueño del Mar. The name of this place means "Dream of the Sea," and the front gate opens into a dreamy world of intimate gardens, patios, frescoes, hand-painted tiles, and a jungle of Latin American *objets d'art*. This nearly flawless bed-and-breakfast occupies an adobe-style house with spacious double rooms, two larger casitas with kitchens and loft bedrooms, and a second-floor suite. The downstairs rooms are a little dark, but are full of interesting, often amusing folk art, and have Balinese showers that open to the sky. All rooms but the suite have queen-size beds, and the casitas have couches that convert into two single beds. If privacy is paramount, opt for the breezy honeymoon suite, a sensuous sultan's lair with rich, red fabrics, rugs, and hanging glass lamps and an ocean view. A lavish breakfast is served on the patio next to a tiny garden pool. Or you can take your morning coffee on the beach, with chairs and hammocks amid the trees and driftwood—it's also the perfect spot for sunsets. At low tide a large snorkeling pool forms in the rocks that surround the beach, but the swimming area is a 10-minute walk to the south. **Pros:** intimate; well appointed. **Cons:** small pool; awful roads nearby. ⊠ *130 m south of Capitán Suizo, veer right for 45 m, then right again for about 90 m to entrance gate, across from back of Cala Luna Hotel* ⌂ *Sueño del Mar, detras de Cala Luna Hotel, Playa Langosta, Guanacaste* ☎ *2653–0284* ⊕ *www.sueno-del-mar.com* ⤵ *3 rooms, 1 suite, 2 casitas* ⚴ *In-room: no phone, kitchen (some), no TV, Wi-Fi. In-hotel: restaurant, pool, beachfront, water sports, laundry service, Internet terminal, no-smoking rooms* ☰ *MC, V* ⍥ *BP.*

$$$　　⛱ **Villa Alegre**. A visit here is like coming to stay with friends who just
★　　happen to have a really terrific house on the beach. Owned by con-
genial and helpful Californians Barry and Suzye Lawson, this homey
but sophisticated Spanish-style bed-and-breakfast overlooks a small
forest reserve and a somewhat rocky section of Langosta Beach, which
is visible only from the terrace and pool. Rooms, villas, and casitas
are furnished with souvenirs from the Lawsons' international travels,
including Japan, Russia, and Guatemala. The Mexican honeymoon
suite has a Frida Kahlo–esque canopy bed and a huge outdoor bath-
room/patio. Spacious villas have kitchens, living rooms with several
futons, and terraces overlooking the forest. Lavish breakfasts are
served family-style at 8:30 on a terrace overlooking the small pool—
they're a chance to meet other guests and to ask the Lawsons for travel
advice or other help, which they happily provide. The hotel often plans
and hosts weddings; ceremonies take place at a huge boulder on the
beach dubbed Marriage Rock. **Pros:** lovely grounds; friendly. **Cons:**
dark rooms; pricey; no kids under 12 (depends on whether you think
this is a pro or con!). ✉ *Playa Langosta, 300 m south of Hotel Capi-
tán Suizo* ☎ *2653–0270* ⊕ *www.villaalegrecostarica.com* ⟿ *4 rooms,
2 villas, 1 casita* ♿ *In-room: no phone, no TV, Wi-Fi. In-hotel: pool,
beachfront, laundry service, Internet terminal, no-smoking rooms*
═ *AE, MC, V* ⍟ *BP.*

PLAYA GRANDE

21 km/13 mi north of Tamarindo.

Down the (long, paved) road from Tamarindo, but only five minutes
by boat across a tidal estuary, lies beautiful Playa Grande. The beach
has thus far escaped the overdevelopment of nearby Tamarindo, and
is consequently lined with thick vegetation instead of hotels and strip
malls. It is one of the world's most important nesting beaches for the
giant leatherback sea turtle, and is consequently protected within a
national park, though admission is free unless you go on a turtle tour
during the nesting season (October 20 to February 15). The beach's
protected status is in part because a surfer who arrived here more than
30 years ago was so upset by the widespread turtle-egg poaching that he
adopted a conservationist's agenda. Louis Wilson, owner of Las Tortu-
gas Hotel, spearheaded a campaign to protect the nesting *baulas* (leath-
erback turtles) that eventually resulted in the creation of Las Baulas
Marine National Park. The long Blue Flag beach is also a paradise for
surfers and sunbathers by day, and the forest that lines it holds howler
monkeys and an array of birds, whereas the mangrove estuary on the
north end of the beach has crocodiles. The only problem with Playa
Grande is the abundance of mosquitoes during the rainy months, espe-
cially near the estuary, so bring plenty of repellent.

Playa Grande isn't immune to development, though; developers have
sold hundreds of lots, and there are at least 100 finished houses. The
ongoing battle to protect the beach continues. The good thing is that
the homes are well back from the beach, thanks to a legislated buffer
zone and a decree that no lights can be visible from the beach, to avoid

Continued on page 328

BIRD-WATCHING

by Dorothy
McKinnon

Even if you've never seen yourself as a bird-watcher, Costa Rica will get you hooked. Waking you before dawn, calling to you throughout the day, and serenading you through tropical nights, birds are impossible to ignore here.

Luckily, Costa Rica has a wealth of world-class ornithologists and local bird guides that can answer all your questions. Even licensed naturalist guides have some birding expertise, so virtually every tour you take in the country will include some bird-watching.

The sheer variety and abundance of birds here makes bird-watching a daily pastime—with less than 0.03% of the planet's surface, Costa Rica counts some 875 bird species, more than the United States and Canada combined. You don't have to stray far from your hotel or even need binoculars to spot, for instance, a kaleidoscopic-colored Keel-billed Toucan, the one of Fruit Loops cereal fame. But armed with a pair of binoculars and a birding guide, the sky is literally the limit for the numbers of birds you can see.

Part of the thrill of walking along a jungle trail is the element of surprise: What is waiting around the path's next curve? Catching sight of a brilliantly colored bird is exciting, but being able to identify it after a couple of encounters is even more thrilling. For kids, spotting birds makes a great game. With their sharp, young eyes, they're usually very good at it—plus it's wildly educational.

About 10% of Costa Rica's birds are endemic, so this is a mecca for bird-watchers intent on compiling an impressive life list.

BEST BIRDING DESTINATIONS

The most sought-after bird is the aptly named Resplendent Quetzal, sporting brilliant blue, green, and red plumage and long tail feathers. The best places to spot it are the new **Los Quetzales National Park** in the Cerro de la Muerte highlands, the **San Gerardo de Dota valley**, and the **Monteverde Cloud Forest Reserve**.

Another bird high on many bird-watchers' lists, is the Scarlet Macaw, the largest of the parrot family here. You'll see pairs performing aerial ballets and munching in beach almond trees in **Corcovado National Park**, along the **Osa Peninsula's coastline**, and around **Carara National Park** in the Central Pacific region.

The **Tempisque River delta's** salty waters, at the north end of the Gulf of Nicoya, are famous for its wealth of water birds, notably Wood Storks, Glossy Ibis, and Roseate Spoonbills. A little farther north, in **Palo Verde and Cano Negro National Parks**, look for the rarest and largest of wading birds, the Jabiru.

The network of jungle-edged natural canals in **Tortuguero National Park**, in the northern Caribbean, is home to a host of herons, including the spectacular Rufescent Tiger-Heron and the multi-hued Agami Heron.

More than 50 species of hummingbirds hover around every part of the country. Look for them around feeders at lodges in the **Cerro de la Muerte area, Monteverde**, and the **Turrialba region**.

WHEN TO GO: The best time to bird is November to May, when local species are joined by winter migrants. Breeding season, which varies by species throughout the year, is the easiest time to spot birds, as males put on displays for females, followed by frequent flights to gather nesting material and then food for the chicks. Also keep your eye on fruit-bearing trees that attract hungry birds.

BIRD-WATCHING 101

Quetzal in Valley of the Quetzals; Krasinsky, Fodors.com member

Binoculars are the most important piece of equipment. They don't have to be a very expensive pair, but they should have good light-gathering lenses and be waterproof. A magnification of 7 to 8 is ideal; any higher and your range of vision becomes very limited.

A good guidebook is essential. The standard "bible" has been a comprehensive tome written by Dr. Alexander Skutch, but beginners (and experienced birders) will probably find the new field guide, written by Richard Garrigues and illustrated by Robert Dean, much more useful—and lighter to carry. It has range maps for every bird and lists the most obvious field marks to help you identify each species. Gift shops and hotels also sell plastic-laminated, one-page guides for local birds that can get you started.

The most important advice for new birders is to find the bird with your naked eye and then bring your binoculars to your eyes, without losing your focus on the bird. Look for beak shape; characteristic rings around the eye; bars, stripes, spots, and mottling on plumage; and, of course, colors on feathers, eyes, beaks, legs, and feet.

10 EASY-TO-IDENTIFY BIRDS FOR BEGINNERS

❶ Blue-Crowned Motmot
Unmistakable with those long tail feathers that look like tennis racquets, this gorgeous turquoise and green bird perches low in trees often close to a stream. They're usually silent but their call is easy to identify: a repeated, low "whoop."

❷ Keel-Billed Toucan
Half a dozen of these rainbow-colored, huge-billed birds often travel together, hunting for berries and fruits. Look for them in Cecropia trees, and listen for the loud, rapid beat of their wings.

❸ Great Kiskadee
You can tell the kiskadee from the similar looking flycatchers by its *pecho amarillo* (yellow breast), black-and-white-striped head, reddish tinted wings, and its call—it really does say *Kiss-kah-deeee*!

❹ Orange-fronted Parakeet
Found in forest canopy on the Pacific side of the country, these highly social and noisy little birds feed in flocks of up to 100. The adults are mainly green, and have shorter tails than their crimson-fronted cousins. The head is distinctive, with a blue crown, and orange forehead. Sadly, the population has been decreasing for a number of years thanks to the pet trade.

❺ Rufous-tailed Hummingbird
Stake out hibiscus hedges or any flowering shrub for the country's most common hummingbird. An iridescent green color, with a long red beak and reddish-brown tail, it makes a loud "tse, tse" chipping sound as it goes about its business.

6

❻ Scarlet Macaw

Look for this huge scarlet, yellow, and blue parrot in the beach almond trees that edge South Pacific beaches. They usually travel in pairs and you'll probably hear their raucous squawks before you see them.

❼ Blue-Gray Tanager

Abundant everywhere—cities, towns, gardens, and countryside—this bluish-gray bird, always seen in pairs, loves fruit. You'll often find them at feeding platforms and in fruiting fig trees.

❽ Black Vulture

Almost every large black bird you see circling high in the sky will be a vulture; these have white-tipped wings. You'll also see them hopping along the roadside feasting on roadkill.

❾ Roadside Hawk

This raptor sits quietly on low perches in trees alongside fields and roads, waiting to pounce on lizards, large insects, and small mammals. It has a gray head, a yellow beak and legs, and a brown and white striped chest.

❿ Cherrie's Tanager (aka Passini's Tanager)

The unmistakable scarlet-rumped, velvety-black male travels with a harem of olive-and orange-colored females, making a lot of scratchy noises as they hunt insects in dense shrubbery.

disturbing the turtles. A few hotels and restaurants make this a pleasant, tranquil alternative to Tamarindo. And if you want to go shopping, Tamarindo is only a boat ride away. ■TIP➞ Recent trip reports suggest that crime in the Playa Grande area has increased of late. Take reasonable precautions, choose a hotel with room safes, bring very few valuables, and stay alert.

GETTING HERE AND AROUND

The road from Tamarindo is paved for the duration of the 30-minute drive. Palm Beach Estates, where most hotels are, is about 3 km (2 mi) south of the main Playa Grande entrance on a dirt road. Alternatively, you can take a small boat across the Tamarindo Estuary for about $2 per person and walk 30 minutes along the beach to the surf break; boats travel between the guide kiosk at the north end of Tamarindo and either Villa Baulas or Hotel Bula Bula in Playa Grande.

EXPLORING

Both **Las Baulas Marine National Park** *(Parque Nacional Marino Las Baulas)*, which protects the long Playa Grande, and the **Tamarindo Wildlife Refuge,** a mangrove estuary with some excellent bird-watching, have been under some developmental pressure of late.

TURTLE-WATCHING

Playa Grande hosts the world's largest visitation of nesting giant leatherback turtles. From October 20 to February 15, during the peak nesting season, the beach is strictly off-limits from 6 PM to 6 AM. You can visit only as part of a guided tour, waiting your turn at the park entrance, beside Hotel Las Tortugas, until spotters find a nesting turtle. At their signal, you'll walk down the beach as silently as you can, where in the darkness you'll witness the remarkable sight of a 500-pound creature digging a hole in the sand large enough to deposit up to 100 golf ball–size eggs. About 60 days later, the sight of hundreds of hatchlings scrambling toward open water in the early morning is equally impressive. Turtle-watching takes place around high tide, which can be shortly after sunset, or in the early morning. From December to mid-February, try to reserve your tour a week ahead of time, or stop by the ranger station early the morning of the day you want to do the tour, since they allow only 40 people on the beach per night, half of which can register that day. Plan on spending one to four hours at the ranger station waiting for a turtle to come up, during which you can watch a video on the turtles in English (the guides speak mostly Spanish). ⊠ *Playa Grande, 100 m east of main beach entrance* ☎ *2653–0470* ⛵ *$20, includes guided tour* ☉ *Oct. 20–Feb. 15 by reservation made between 8 AM and 5 PM.*

OUTDOOR ACTIVITIES

■TIP➞ Unless you are a strong swimmer attached to a surfboard, don't go in any deeper than your waist here. There is calmer water for snorkeling about a 20-minute walk north of Las Tortugas, at a black-sand beach called Playa Carbón.

All the hotels can arrange boat tours of the estuary, where you may see crocodiles, monkeys, herons, kingfishers, and an array of other birdlife; go either early in the morning or late in the afternoon, and bring insect repellent. **Hotel Las Tortugas** (⊠ *Las Baulas Marine National*

Park ☎ *2653–0423* ⊕ *www.lastortugashotel.com*) has a full menu of nature tours, including guided nature walks, and canoeing on the estuary; they also explain how to get to Playa Carbón, the nearest snorkeling spot.

SURFING

Playa Grande is renowned for having one of the most consistent surf breaks in the country. Only experienced surfers should attempt riding this beach break, which often features big barrels and offshore winds. The waves are best at high tide, especially around a full moon. **Hotel Las Tortugas** (⇨ *above*) rents boards for $20 a day. **Hotel Bula Bula** (✉ *Palm Beach Estates 2 km/1 mi east of Playa Grande* ☎ *2653–0975* ⊕ *www. hotelbulabula.com*) rents both long- and shortboards for $25 a day.

WHERE TO EAT

$$$

CONTINENTAL

✕ **Hotel Cantarana.** World-Toques Star Chef René Kalobius brings to the table 30 years of cooking experience in Spain, Germany, and Southeast Asia. The menu changes depending on availability of local ingredients—think lots of seafood—and on the chef's inspired meat dishes, but is always classically Continental, with both Spanish and tropical flavors and elegant presentation. ✉ *Palm Beach Estates 2 km/1 mi east of park headquarters* ☎ *2653–0486* ⊕ *www.hotel-cantarana.com* ▭ *MC, V, closed Sun.*

$$$

ECLECTIC

★

✕ **Upstairs@the Ripjack.** Located a block from the beach, this place usually has an ocean breeze to complement the ceiling fans, which are best enjoyed from the hammock in the corner. They have rooms for rent downstairs, but most people who head here come to eat, or party at the long bar, which occupies about a third of the restaurant. The food is quite good, and the menu ranges from sesame-crusted tuna with tempura vegetables to grilled tenderloin with mash potatoes, a goat cheese and chimichurri sauce. The lunch menu has a good selection of salads and sandwiches. Save room for a mud pie, or cheesecake with strawberries. There's free Wi-Fi, too. ✉ *100 m south of park headquarters* ☎ *2653–0480* ⊕ *www.ripjackinn.com* ▭ *AE, DC, MC, V* ☺ *Closed Wed.*

WHERE TO STAY

$$

🛏 **Hotel Bula Bula.** At the eastern edge of the estuary near Palm Beach Estates, Bula Bula has its own dock and boat for ferrying guests and restaurant patrons the short distance to and from Tamarindo. The hotel forms a 45-degree angle to the curvy pool bordered by a garden. (Be careful of the cactus!) Rooms have king-size beds and high ceilings, and open onto a portico with wicker rocking chairs, with walls painted in brilliant colors and hung with Central American art. They don't offer a lot of privacy, but the friendly American owners provide complimentary sarongs, fluffy pool towels, coffeemakers, DVD players, and other amenities. They can arrange a two-hour boat tour of the estuary, or rentals of nearby houses. The menu at the alfresco Great Waltini's Restaurant & Bar ($$–$$$) reads like that of a U.S.-style eatery: seafood enchiladas, peel-and-eat shrimp, pork chop, filet mignon, and New York strip steak. They have good fresh seafood specials. Save room for the homemade tres leches dessert. **Pros:** friendly; good food; lots of amenities. **Cons:** rooms small for price; 10-minute walk from beach;

6

Costa Rica's shores are visited by the green turtle, the olive ridley, the hawksbill, the loggerhead, and the leatherback turtle.

far from surf break. ⊠ *Palm Beach Estates 3 km/2 mi east of Playa Grande* ☎ *2653–0975; 877/658–2880 in U.S.* ⊕ *www.hotelbulabula. com* ⇆ *10 rooms* ♿ *In-room: no phone, refrigerator, coffee-maker, safe. In-hotel: restaurant, bar, pool, laundry service, Wi-Fi hotspot* ⊟ *AE, MC, V* ⦙⦿⦙ *BP.*

¢–$ 🏨 **Hotel El Manglar.** If you like cooking for yourself, consider the apartments at this pretty hotel. Painted in tropical colors, the rooms have a Provençal touch, with French doors and lace curtains. Sitting rooms, kitchens, and terraces give you lots of room to relax, and there is even a grill on the terrace. The cheaper upstairs guest rooms are much more basic, with minimalist decor and loft bedrooms with fans instead of air-conditioners. There's also a two-bedroom family apartment. The hotel has a pretty garden and a pool inlaid with bright mosaic tile. It's a short walk from the beach. **Pros:** quiet; near beach. **Cons:** foam mattresses; no restaurant (but breakfast available); far from surf break. ⊠ *Palm Beach Estates 2 km/1 mi south of Playa Grande, south of Hotel La Cantarana* ☎☎ *2653–0952* ⊕ *www.hotel-manglar.com* ⇆ *5 rooms, 4 apartment, 1 family apartments* ♿ *In-room: no a/c (some), no phone, safe, kitchen (some), no TV (some). In-hotel: pool* ⊟ *No credit cards.*

¢–$$ 🏨 **Hotel Las Tortugas.** With a prime location on the beach, steps away
★ from Playa Grande's famous surf break, this place is perfect for surfers, nature lovers, and sun worshippers. The name, which means "The Turtles," is no accident; this hotel was designed with turtles in mind. Owner/conservationist Louis Wilson made sure, for instance, that room

and restaurant lights don't shine on the beach, because light disorients the turtles. Rooms are spacious, with good beds, stone floors, and colorful tile bathrooms. Most have either a terrace or a balcony. Las Tortugas accommodates all budgets, with rooms ranging from spacious suites to dorm-style rooms in an annex that Louis built for student groups and volunteers. They also offer an array of apartments up the hill, some with kitchenettes, that rent by the night, week, or month. All of this adds up to the best value in Playa Grande, and one of the best deals on the Pacific coast. The main surf break is just to the south of the hotel, and turtle tours start at the nearby ranger station. Rip currents are a danger on the beach here, which is why many guests prefer the pool shaped like a leatherback turtle (the turtle's head is the kiddie pool). Lush gardens slung with hammocks round out the grounds' appeal. The restaurant ($$$) serves a good selection of fresh seafood and grilled meat dishes. **Pros:** on the beach; friendly owners; good value. **Cons:** busy spot; spotty service at times. ⊠ *Entrance to Las Baulas Marine National Park, 33 km/20 mi north of Tamarindo>* ☎ *2653–0423* ⊕ *www.lastortugashotel.com* ↝ *11 rooms, 8 dorms, 17 apartments* ⬧ *In-room: no phone, safe (some), kitchen (some), refrigerator (some), no TV. In-hotel: restaurant, bar, pool, beachfront, water sports, laundry service, Internet terminal, Wi-Fi hotspot* ▭ *MC, V* ⍾ *EP.*

PLAYA AVELLANAS

17 km/11 mi south of Tamarindo.

Traditionally a far cry from Tamarindo's boom of real-estate development, this relatively undeveloped beach's main claim to fame is surfing. As you bump along the rough beach road, most of the cars you pass have surfboards on top. Nevertheless, Avellanas (pronounced ah-vey-ya-nas) is a lovely spot for anyone who likes the sea and sand, though you shouldn't go in deeper than your waist when the waves are big, because of rip currents. Tamarindo escapees have been slowly encroaching on Avellanas for years, building private houses and a smattering of small hotels, but the inauguration of a massive Marriott here in 2008 marked the beginning of major development. The beach itself is a beautiful, 1-km (½-mi) stretch of pale-gold sand with rocky outcroppings at its southern end, a small river mouth, and a mangrove swamp behind its northern half. Unfortunately, security is an issue here, as at most Costa Rican beaches; posted signs warn visitors not to leave anything of value in parked cars or unattended on the beach.

GETTING HERE AND AROUND

You have to drive 30 minutes inland from Tamarindo to Villa Real, where you turn right for the 13-km (8-mi) trip down a bumpy road to reach Playa Avellanas. There are rivers to cross in rainy season, when you may want to drive via Paraíso and Playa Negra. If you're without a car, take the **Tamarindo Shuttle** (☎ *2653–1326*) van, $10 to $20 one-way for one to four people.

OUTDOOR ACTIVITIES
SURFING

Locals claim there are eight breaks here when the swell is big, which means Avellanas doesn't suffer the kind of overcrowding the breaks at Playas Negra and Langosta often do. Tamarindo-based surf schools can arrange day trips here. You can rent boards and find kindred surfing spirits at **Cabinas Las Olas** (⊠ *Main road, on right* ☏ 2652–9315), $2.50 an hour or $25 a day.

WHERE TO EAT AND STAY

$–$$

VEGETARIAN

★

✕**Lola's.** In deference to Lola, the owners' pet pig that used to freely roam the beachfront but is now sadly deceased, the menu at this hip beach café is heavily vegetarian. It has exactly the kind of ambience one comes to Costa Rica for, with tables scattered along the beach amid palms and Indian almond trees, hammocks swinging in the wind, palm fronds rustling, and surfers riding the glistening waves in front. Seating, or more precisely, lolling, is all on the sand at low hardwood tables and reclining chairs, or on colorful cushions on rattan mats. A new second-floor lounge specializes in Asian appetizers. Along with the fresh-fruit smoothies and ultrathin vegetarian pizzas, the menu includes organic chicken and "responsible fish" (fish caught in nets that don't also trap turtles). Seared ahi tuna with sun-dried tomato and olive tapenade served on ciabatta bread is a winner, as are the ceviche, fish-and-chips, and assorted salads. You can arrange in advance for private beach dinners by candlelight. They're open from 8 AM to sunset. ⊠ *At main entrance to Playa Avellanas* ☏ *2652–9097* ▤ *No credit cards* ⊗ *Closed Mon. No dinner.*

$

▦ **Cabinas Las Olas.** Frequented mainly by surfers, this place is a good option for anyone seeking beach access and relative solitude. The hotel's spacious glass-and-stone bungalows are scattered across a leafy property behind Playa Avellanas, which guests reach via an elevated boardwalk through a protected mangrove estuary. Each cabina has a queen and a single bed, high wooden ceiling, and covered terrace with a hammock. There's no air-conditioning, but high ceilings, a shady location, and good cross ventilation keep the rooms cool at night. Monkeys, iguanas, and other critters lurk in and around the extensive, forested grounds. The restaurant, under the shade of a giant Guanacaste tree, serves a good selection of Costa Rican and continental cuisine at reasonable prices ($$) for breakfast, lunch, and dinner. **Pros:** near beach; in forest; secluded. **Cons:** mosquitoes a problem in rainy season; simple rooms. ⊠ *1 km/½ mi before Avellanas, on right* ☏ *2652–9315* ⊕ *www. cabinaslasolas.co.cr* ⟿ *10 rooms* ♿ *In-room: no a/c, no phone, safe, no TV. In-hotel: restaurant, water sports, laundry service, Wi-Fi hotspot* ▤ *AE, MC, V* ⊗ *Closed 15 days in Oct.* ⏣*EP.*

PLAYA NEGRA

3 km/2 mi south of Playa Avellanas.

Surfer culture is apparent here in the wave of beach-shack surfer camps along the beach road. But there's also a big residential development here called Rancho Playa Negra, with more upscale development on the drawing boards. Contrary to the name, the beach is not black, but rather beige with dark streaks. It's not a great swimming beach, because it tends to have big waves and is lined with rocks, though there is one short stretch of clear sand to the south of the hotel, and at low tide a large tidal pool forms in front of the hotel. The spindly buttonwood trees that edge the beach provide sparse shade.

A SURF CLASSIC

Americans—surfer Americans, at least—got their first look at Playa Negra in 1994's *The Endless Summer II*, a film by legendary surf documentarian Bruce Brown.

GETTING HERE AND AROUND

From Playa Avellanas, continue south 10 minutes on the rough beach road to Playa Negra. If it's rainy season and the road is too rough, you can approach along a slightly more civilized route from Santa Cruz. Drive 27 km (16½ mi) west, via Veintisiete de Abril, to Paraíso, then follow signs for Playa Negra for 4 km (2½ mi). Taxis are the easiest way to get around if you don't have a car.

OUTDOOR ACTIVITIES

SURFING

Surfing cognoscenti dig the waves here, which are almost all rights, with beautifully shaped barrels. It's a spectacular, but treacherous, rock-reef break for experienced surfers only. There's also a small beach break to the south of the rocks where neophytes can cut their teeth. Both breaks can be ridden from mid- to high tide. The point break is right in front of the **Hotel Playa Negra** (⊠ *4 km/2½ mi northwest of Paraíso on dirt road, then follow signs carefully at forks in road* ☎ *2652–9134 or 2652–9298* ⊕ *www.playanegra.com*), which can arrange surfing classes ($25 per hour), and rents boards ($20 per day).

WHERE TO STAY

$$ ★ **Hotel Playa Negra.** Brilliantly colored thatch-roof cabinas are sprinkled across sunny lawns strewn with tropical plantings at this gorgeous oceanfront place. Each hut has curvaceous tile bathrooms plus built-in sofas that can double as extra beds. There's no air-conditioning, but conical thatch roofs keep the cabinas cool. Ocean tidal pools, swimming holes, and rock reefs provide plenty of opportunities for lazy afternoon exploration. This is paradise for surfers, with a good swell running right in front of the hotel. The round restaurant serves typical food with a few continental dishes under a giant thatch roof, but the ocean view is more of an attraction than the food. There's also an air-conditioned Internet café in the beach boutique, which arranges kayaking and horseback tours. **Pros:** in front of reef break; friendly. **Cons:** not a great swimming beach; concrete-floor rooms. ⊠ *4 km/2½ mi northwest of Paraíso on dirt road (watch signs for Playa Negra), then follow signs carefully at forks in road* ☎ *2652–9134* 🖶 *2652–9035* ⊕ *www.playanegra.com* 🛌 *10 cabinas* ♨ *In-room: no a/c, no phone, safe, no TV. In-hotel: restaurant, bar, pool, beachfront, water sports, laundry service* ⊟ *AE, DC, MC, V* ⊙ *Restaurant closed Sept. 15–Nov. 1* 🍽 *EP.*

PLAYA JUNQUILLAL

4 km/2½ mi south of Paraíso, 34 km/22 mi southwest of Santa Cruz.

☾ Seekers of tranquility need look no farther than Junquillal (pronounced hoon-key-*yall*). A short drive to the south of Playa Negra, this wide swath of light brown sand stretches over 3 km (2 mi), with coconut palms lining much of it and hardly a building in sight. Two species of sea turtle nest here, and a group of young people collect and protect their eggs, releasing the baby turtles after sunset. Although it qualifies as a Blue Flag beach, the surf here is a little strong, so watch children carefully. There's a kids' playground right at the beach, and a funky little restaurant with concrete tables amid the palms. It's also a perfect beach for taking long, romantic strolls. Surfers head here to ride the beach break near Junquillal's northern end, since it rarely gets crowded. A surprisingly cosmopolitan mélange of expats has settled in this area, as the selection of goods in the small supermarket in town confirms, but Junquillal is still barely on the tourist map. Its handful of hotels consequently offers some of the best deals on the North Pacific coast.

GETTING HERE AND AROUND
In rainy season, the 4-km-long (2½-mi-long) beach road from Playa Negra to Playa Junquillal is sometimes not passable. The alternative is driving down from Santa Cruz one hour on a road that's paved most of the way. The Castillos bus company runs a bus to Junquillal from the central market in Santa Cruz four times a day (at 5 and 10:30 AM, and 2:30 and 5:30 PM); the trip takes about 40 minutes. A taxi from Santa Cruz costs about $25; from Tamarindo, $35.

ESSENTIALS
The closest town for most services is Santa Cruz, 34 km (22 mi) northeast.

Hospital Clínica (✉ *Veintisiete de Abril* ✢ *16 km/10 mi northeast of Playa Junquillal*).

OUTDOOR ACTIVITIES
HORSEBACK RIDING
At German-run **Paradise Riding** (☎ *2658–8162* ⊕ *www.paradiseriding. com*) the 16 horses are in tip-top shape, as is the impressive tack room, with top-quality saddles lined up in a neat row. There are two-hour trail rides (about $55), or you can set off for a whole day of riding. The maximum number of riders they can handle is 8. You'll saddle up at the friendly owner's house, across from the entrance to Guacamaya Lodge.

WHERE TO EAT
$
COSTA RICAN

✕ **Restaurante Playa Junquillal.** This funky, open-air restaurant with concrete tables amid the coconut palms is a classic Costa Rican beach bar. It regularly fills up in the evening, when local expats gather to watch the sunset. The lunch options include a small selection of appetizers, a fish sandwich, and the typical Costa Rican casado (fish fillet, or barbecued steak with rice and beans). At dinner, you can also get a fish fillet, or shrimp sautéed with garlic, barbecued chicken, or beef, and a few vegetarian options. It's basically just a good spot for a drink and snack on the beach. ✉ *Main entrance to Playa Junquillal* ☎ *2658–8432* ▭ *MC, V.*

WHERE TO STAY

$–$$ **Guacamaya Lodge.** Spread across a breezy hill with expansive views of the surrounding forest and the sea above the treetops, the Guacamaya is a real find. Spacious cabinas surround a generous-size pool, lawn, and tropical plants. The large restaurant ($–$$) shaded by a conical thatch roof serves excellent Continental cuisine, including such Swiss specialties as *Rösti* (hash browns with bacon and cheese) and *Zürcher Geschnetzeltes* (beef medallions and mushrooms in a creamy sauce), various pastas, fresh seafood dishes, and a good salad selection. Meals come with deliciously dense homemade bread. The spacious duplex bungalows with plenty of windows and small terraces are a real deal. Screened windows let in the cooling evening breezes, so you probably won't need the quiet air-conditioners in each room. Well-equipped studios in a two-story building have kitchenettes, big bathrooms, and covered porches; those on the second floor are more spacious and have better views. The modern house, with a full kitchen and a large covered veranda, is perfect for rental by families. There's also a kids' pool, a playground, and a resident little girl happy to have playmates. The place fills up fast, so book early. **Pros:** good value; clean; friendly. **Cons:** 1,000 feet from the beach. ✉ *275 m east of Playa Junquillal* ✆ *Apdo. 6, Santa Cruz* ☎ *2658–8431* ⊕ *www.guacamayalodge.com* ⇆ *6 cabinas, 4 studios, 1 villa* ⚿ *In-room: no phone, kitchen (some), no TV. In-hotel: restaurant, bar, tennis court, pool, laundry service, Internet terminal, Wi-Fi hotspot* ▭ *AE, MC, V* ⊘ *Closed Sept. and Oct.* ⦿ *EP.*

¢   **Hotel TaTanka.** This attractive Italian-run hotel has tasty food and very comfortable rates. Ten big rooms are lined up under a tile-roof veranda facing a kidney-shaped pool. They have Mayan-style wall paintings, arty bamboo closets, and large tiled bathrooms. Wood-oven pizzas and homemade pastas—the *spaghetti a la carbonara* is *delicioso*—are served in a huge alfresco restaurant with elegant furniture. The beach is a three-minute walk away. **Pros:** inexpensive; near beach. **Cons:** rooms a bit dark; musty. ✉ *Main Junquillal road, just south of Guacamaya Lodge* ☎ *2658–8426, 1-866-498-0824 toll-free* ⊕ *www.hoteltatanka.com* ⇆ *10 rooms* ⚿ *In-room: safe, no phone, no TV. In-hotel: restaurant, pool, laundry service, Internet terminal, Wi-Fi* ▭ *MC, V* ⊘ *Closed last two weeks of Oct.; restaurant closed Mon.* ⦿ *BP.*

$$ **The Hotel Villa Serena.** Serenely spread across verdant grounds a short walk from the beach, this hotel is certainly aptly named. The rooms are slightly old, but bright and spacious, with high wooden ceilings, big bathrooms, and soothing pastels and local art on the walls. They open onto narrow terraces with wooden chairs, most of which overlook the gardens; only rooms 1 and 2 have ocean views. A large, rectangular pool is surrounded by coconut palms, and across the street is a small shelter at the edge of the beach, perfect for watching the sunset. The second-floor bar and restaurant ($$$) also have a nice ocean view. The menu ranges from fish-and-chips to filet mignon, with daily seafood specials. Coffee is delivered to rooms in the morning, and free snorkeling gear and kayaks are available to guests. **Pros:** closest rooms to beach; quiet. **Cons:** only TV is at the bar; bugs. ⊠ *Main Junquillal road, south of main beach access* ☎ *2658–8430* ⊕ *www.land-ho.com/villa* ⊊ *12 rooms* ⬧ *In-room: no phone, no TV. In-hotel: restaurant, bars, pool, gym, spa, water sports, laundry service, Wi-Fi hotspot* ⊟ *AE, DC, MC, V* ⍾○⍾ *EP.*

> **CAUTION**
>
> To approach Nosara along the coast from Junquillal to the north, you have to ford many rivers, including the Río Ostional, which is sometimes impassable during the wet season. This beach road requires 4WD. If you have a compact car, or it has been raining a lot, you are better off driving via Nicoya on the paved road.

NOSARA

28 km/17 mi southwest of Nicoya.

One of the last beach communities for people who want to get away from it all, Nosara's attractions are the wild stretches of side-by-side beaches called Pelada and Guiones, with surfing waves and miles of sand on which to stroll, and the tropical dry forest that covers much of the hinterland. The town itself is inland and not very interesting, but the surrounding flora and fauna keep nature lovers entertained. Regulations here limit development to low-rise buildings 600 feet from the beach, where they are, thankfully, screened by trees. Americans and Europeans, with a large Swiss contingent, are building at a fairly rapid pace, but there appears to be an aesthetic sense here that is totally lacking in Tamarindo and Sámara.

For years, most travelers headed here for the surf, but the Nosara Yoga Institute, which offers instructor training, and daily classes for all levels, is increasingly a draw for health-conscious visitors. Bird-watchers and other nature enthusiasts can explore the tropical dry forest on hiking trails, on horseback, or by boating up the tree-lined Nosara River. The access roads to Nosara are abysmal, and the labyrinth of woodsy roads around the beaches and hard-to-read signs make it easy to get lost, which is why most hotels here provide local maps for their guests.

GETTING HERE AND AROUND

From Nicoya, drive south, almost to Sámara, but take the very first road signed for Nosara, 1 km (½ mi) south of the big gas station before Sámara. This high road is rough for about 8 km (5 mi), but there are bridges over all the river crossings. When you join up with the beach road near Garza, you still have a very bumpy 10 km (6 mi) to go. The roads into Nosara are in really bad shape, so a 4WD vehicle is definitely recommended. Budget about one hour for the trip. You can also fly directly to Nosara on daily scheduled SANSA and Nature Air flights,

Beginning surfers love Sámara's almost placid water and its undeveloped palm-fringed beach.

or take an air-conditioned shuttle van from San José. Several major rent-a-car companies have offices in Nosara.

ESSENTIALS

Bank/ATM Banco Popular (✉ *In strip mall next to Café de Paris on road to Playa Guiones* ☎ *2682–0267*).

Hospital Centro Médico Nosara (✉ *In front of strip mall next to Café de Paris, on road to Playa Guiones* ☎ *2682–1212*).

Pharmacy Farmacia Nosara (✉ *In front of strip mall next to Café de Paris, on road to Playa Guiones* ☎ *2682–1148* ⏱ *Mon.–Sat. 8–noon and 1:30–5*).

Internet Café de Paris (✉ *At entrance to Playa Guiones* ☎ *2682–0087*).

Post Office Correo (✉ *Next to soccer field*).

Rental Cars Alamo (✉ *Café de Paris shopping center, main road, Nosara* ☎ *2682–0052*).

Taxis Independent drivers provide taxi service. **Abel's Taxi** (☎ *8812–8470*) is reliable.

EXPLORING

With some of the most consistent surf on the Pacific coast, **Playa Guiones** attracts a lot of surfboard-toting visitors. But the breezy beach, with vegetation rising up from the high-tide mark for its length, is also a haven for shell seekers, sun lovers, and anyone who wants to connect with nature. The only building in sight is the bizarre Hotel Nosara, which was originally the only choice for lodging in town, but which is now a rambling private residence complete with observation tower. Otherwise, this glorious beach has 7 km (4 mi) of hard-packed sand, great for jogging and riding bikes. Because there's a 9-foot tide, the beach is expansive at low tide but rather narrow at high tide, when waves usually create strong currents that can make the sea deadly for nonsurfers. Most hotels post tide charts. Guiones is at the south end of the Nosara agglomeration, with three public accesses. The easiest one to find is about 300 meters (1,000 feet) past the Hotel Harmony, heading straight at the intersection.

North along the shore, Playa Guiones segues seamlessly into crescent-shape **Playa Pelada**, where the water is a little calmer. There are tide pools to explore and a blowhole that sends water shooting up when the surf is big. Lots of trees provide shade. This is the locals' favorite vantage point for watching sunsets. Olga's Bar, a ramshackle Tico beach bar, is a great place for a cool beer; or sip a sunset cocktail at the funky La Luna Bar & Grill, next door.

Ostional National Wildlife Refuge *(Refugio Nacional de Fauna Silvestre Ostional)* protects one of Costa Rica's major nesting beaches for olive ridley turtles. Locals have formed an association to run the reserve on a cooperative basis, and during the first 36 hours of the *arribadas* (mass nesting) they are allowed to harvest the eggs, on the premise that eggs laid during this time would likely be destroyed by subsequent waves of mother turtles. Though turtles nest here year-round, the largest arribadas, with thousands of turtles nesting over the courses of several nights, occur from July to December, though smaller arribadas take place between January and May. They usually take place around high tide, the week of a new moon. People in Nosara usually know when an arribada has begun. The mandatory guided tours of the nesting and hatching areas cost $10 per person. Stop at the kiosk at the entrance to the beach to arrange a tour. ⊠ *7 km/4½ mi north of Nosara* ☎ *2682–0428 or 2682–0400* ☜ *$10 for tour.*

★ **Nosara Biological Reserve** (Reserva Biológica Nosara) is a treasure. The 90-acre private reserve includes trails through a huge mangrove wetland and old-growth forest along the Nosara River. A concrete walkway passes over an eerily beautiful mangrove swamp, with fantastical stilt roots and snap-crackling sound effects from respiring mollusks. More than 270 bird species have been spotted here, and there's an observation platform for watching birds. There are always crabs, lizards, snakes, and other creatures rustling in the grass and howler monkeys and iguanas in the trees. Pick up a self-guided trail map from the Hotel Lagarta Lodge when you pay your admission fee, or better yet, hire the resident nature guide; call ahead if you want to hire a guide. The best times to do the hike, which takes about two hours, are early in the morning or late in the afternoon, which means you can follow your trek with breakfast, or sunset cocktails at the Hotel Lagarta Lodge. ⊠ *Trailhead 168 steps down from Hotel Lagarta Lodge, top of hill at the north end of Nosara* ☎ *2682–0035* ☜ *$6, free for kids under 15, $12 with guide (reserve 1 day in advance).*

MASSAGE AND YOGA

The Nosara Yoga Institute (✉ *Southeast end of town, on main road to Sámara* ☎ *2682–0071; 866/439–4704 in U.S.* ⊕ *www.nosarayoga.com*) focuses on teacher certification, but also offers several daily 90-minute yoga classes to the public ($10), weeklong workshops, and retreats. Relaxing massages in a jungle setting ($55 per hour) are available by appointment at **Tica Massage** (✉ *Across from the Hotel Harmony* ☎ *2682–0096*), plus spa services such as facials and salt glows.

OUTDOOR ACTIVITIES

> ### HELP ON THE ROAD
>
> The more remote the area, the more likely that someone will stop to help you change a tire or tow you out of a river. Usually, Good Samaritans won't accept any payment and are more trustworthy than those who offer to "help" in the States. Near Ostional, there's a farmer named Valentin who regularly pulls cars out of the flooded river with his tractor. So he is known as Valentin *con chapulin* (with a tractor).

Iguana Expeditions (✉ *Gilded Iguana, Playa Guiones* ☎ *2682–4089* ⊕ *www.iguanaexpeditions.com*) organizes kayaking on the Nosara River, a hike to a waterfall, horseback riding, fishing, surfing, and nature tours. The **Harbor Reef Surf Resort** (✉ *Follow signs from Café de Paris turnoff, Playa Guiones* ☎ *2682–0059 or 2682–1000* ⊕ *www.harborreef.com*) has an excellent tour desk that can arrange fishing, surfing, nature tours, and river expeditions.

BIRD-WATCHING

On river trips with **Nosara Boat Tours** (✉ *Boat moored at bottom of hill leading to Hotel Lagarta Lodge, follow signs to the boca [mouth] of Nosara River* ☎ *2682–0610* ⊕ *www.nosaraboattours.com*), you glide up the Nosara and Montaña rivers in a flat-bottom catamaran with an almost noiseless electric motor. Wading herons, egrets, roseate spoonbills, ospreys, and kingfishers are common sights. The German-born naturalist guide also knows where river otters play and crocodiles hunker down in mud caves along the riverbank. Trips are $30 per person ($20 for kids under 14).

HORSEBACK RIDING

German equestrienne Beate Klossek and husband Hans-Werner take small groups of up to six people on 3½-hour horseback nature tours through the jungle and along the beach ($50 to $80 per person, according to group size) with **Boca Nosara Tours** (✉ *150 m below Hotel Lagarta Lodge, at mouth of Nosara River* ☎ *2682–0280* ⊕ *www.bocanosaratours.com*). Horses are well mannered and well treated. There are smaller saddles for kids over eight.

SURFING

If you ever wanted to learn to surf, Nosara is the place. Guiones is the perfect beginners' beach, with no rocks to worry about. Local surf instructors say that the waves here are so consistent that there's no week throughout the year when you won't be able to surf. In March and April, the Costa Rican National Surf Circuit comes here for surf trials. Especially recommended for beginners, **Safari Surf School** (✉ *Road to Playa Guiones; ask for directions at Casa Tucán* ☎ *2682-0573, 2682-0113* ⊕ *www.*

safarisurfschool.com) is run by two surfing brothers from Hawaii, one of whom lives here year-round. A one-hour private lesson costs $45, equipment included. The school is closed in September and October. **Corky Carroll's Surf School** (⊠ *Near Casa Romántica, on the Playa Guiones road* ☎ *2682–0384, 888-454-7873 toll-free in U.S.* ⊕ *www. surfschool.net*) has its own hotel for surfing students. **Coconut Harry's Surf Shop** (⊠ *Main road, across from Café de Paris* ☎ *2682–0574* ⊕ *www.coconutharrys.com*) has boards ($15 to $20 per day), gear, and lessons ($45 per hour, board included). **Nosara Surf Shop** (⊠ *Café de Paris, road to Playa Guiones* ☎ *2682–0186* ⊕ *www.nosarasurfshop.com*) offers lessons ($40 per hour), and rents boards by the day ($15 to $20) and has lots of gear, too.

> **CAUTION**
>
> Many restaurants do not include the legally required 13% tax and 10% service in their menu prices, but tack them onto the bill at the end. It might be indicated somewhere on the menu that tax and tip are not included, but that's not always the case. If you're not sure, ask.

WHERE TO EAT

$$ ✕ **Café de Paris**. The French-Swiss owners have turned this corner res-
ECLECTIC   taurant into a chic, alfresco eatery. Fresh-baked pastries and desserts are a major draw. Sweet and savory croissants are excellent, as is the divine chocolate tart. In addition to the tried-and-true wood-oven piz-zas, nachos, and hearty sandwiches, they have such Continental treats as fish and vegetables baked in papillote, jumbo shrimp flambé, and lamb stew with mushrooms. ⊠ *Main road at Playa Guiones entrance* ☎ *2682–0087* ⊟ *AE, MC, V.*

$$ ✕ **Giardino Tropicale**. Famous for its crispy-crust, wood-oven pizzas loaded
ITALIAN   with toppings as well as the bowls of homemade chili-pepper sauce that
★   grace every table, this thatch-roof multilevel restaurant casts a wide net to include daily fresh seafood and fish specials. Sit on one of the upper decks by day, and you'll dine amid the treetops. Service is always fast and very friendly. ⊠ *Giardino Tropicale Hotel, main street, past entrance to Playa Guiones* ☎ *2682–0258* ⊟ *AE, MC, V* ☻ *No lunch.*

$$ ✕ **Marlin Bill's**. Sink your teeth into classic rib-eye steak, pork chops,
AMERICAN   and lobster in American-size portions at this open-air restaurant with a distant ocean view. Lighter choices include eggplant parmigiana and delicious "dorado fingers"—battered fish fillet strips served with tartar sauce. The decor is decidedly fishy, with fishy art on the walls. Fishing and real estate talk over beer and chicken wings keeps the U-shaped bar abuzz. The restaurant is closed 3 PM–6 PM and Sundays, unless there is an NFL football game on TV. ⊠ *Hilltop above main road, near Coconut Harry's Surf Shop* ☎ *2682–0458* ⊟ *MC, V* ☻ *Closed Sun.*

WHERE TO STAY

$–$$ ☷ **Casa Romántica Hotel**. The name ("Romantic House") says it all: the
★   Spanish Colonial–style house has a balustraded veranda upstairs and a graceful arcade below. The young Swiss owners renovated the origi-nal rooms and built new rooms in separate wings. All are bright, with big bathrooms and shared terraces with views of the glorious gardens. There's a kidney-shaped pool next to a thatch shelter with hammocks,

and a short path through the surrounding forest leads to the beach. The small patio restaurant where the complimentary buffet breakfast is served becomes a truly romantic, candlelighted restaurant ($–$$) at night, when the menu includes such Continental favorites as chicken cordon bleu, beef Stroganoff, a creamy shrimp curry, and daily fish and seafood specials. **Pros:** near beach; good restaurant; good value. **Cons:** rooms not spectacular; can be noisy. ⊠ *100 m west of Giardino Tropicale, on left,* ☎☎ *2682–0272* ⊕ *www.casa-romantica.net* ⤳ *10 rooms* ⚖ *In-room: no a/c (some), no phone, safe, refrigerator, no TV, Wi-Fi. In-hotel: restaurant, pool, beachfront, laundry service* ⊟ *MC, V* ⦿⦙ *BP.*

$–$$ 🛏 **Giardino Tropicale Hotel.** In the lush gardens downhill from the popular restaurant (⇨ *above*), shaded by large trees, are comfortable cabinas and a sparkling 56-foot swimming pool—the only good lap pool in town. The handsome suites have everything you need to make breakfast: electric kettles, coffeemakers, refrigerators, and sinks. Two spacious apartments also have full kitchens. The four smaller cabinas have solar-heated hot water, ceiling fans, coffeemakers, and refrigerators; use of air-conditioning costs extra. Inexpensive, hearty breakfasts are served by the pool, and the restaurant is one of the best in town. **Pros:** good value; environmentally friendly; helpful owners. **Cons:** road noise; extra charge for a/c; short walk to beach. ⊠ *Main street, past entrance to Playa Guiones* ☎ *2682–4000* ⊕ *www.giardinotropicale.com* ⤳ *4 cabinas, 4 suites, 2 apartments* ⚖ *In-room: no phone, kitchen (some), refrigerator, no TV (some). In-hotel: restaurant, pool, Wi-Fi hotspot* ⊟ *AE, DC, MC, V* ⦿⦙ *EP.*

$ 🛏 **The Gilded Iguana.** This lively hotel/bar/restaurant has been a Nosara fixture for more than 15 years. Televised sports, live music, and lots of friendly regulars make the open-air bar a popular place. The on-site tour desk can arrange almost any outing you can imagine. Six large, air-conditioned rooms are lined up behind a small, kidney-shaped pool with a refreshing waterfall. For traditionalists, the original rooms have more character, in a shaded wooden building with louvered, screened windows letting in fresh breezes in lieu of air-conditioning. **Pros:** economical; laid-back. **Cons:** spotty service; needs updating. ⊠ *Playa Guiones, Nosara* ☎ *2682–0259* ⊕ *www.thegildediguana.com* ⤳ *10 rooms, 2 suites* ⚖ *In-room: no a/c (some), no phone, refrigerator, no TV. In-hotel: restaurant, bar, pool, laundry service, Wi-Fi* ⊟ *MC, V* ⦿⦙ *EP.*

$$ 🛏 **Harbor Reef Surf Resort.** Lose yourself in the junglelike garden grounds centered around two small pools, one presided over by a concrete crocodile, the other by a tiny waterfall. Your wake-up call is the bellowing of a resident howler monkey, and you can bird-watch at breakfast. Rooms and suites cater to surfers of every age, with plenty of space for boards and gear inside, but the decor is rudimentary. "Surf city" rooms have two queen beds in slightly separate alcoves, whereas larger suites are great for families, with two bedrooms, two baths, a loft with twin beds, and a kitchen. The surf break at Playa Guiones is a 300-meter (1,000-foot) walk away. The open-air restaurant ($–$$) serves an American menu, with fresh fish, steak, chicken, pastas, and some Tex-Mex dishes. A large souvenir shop and a beachwear shop are on the grounds. Owner Randy Bombard has a wealth of information about the area. **Pros:** attractive grounds; near beach; good restaurant. **Cons:** bland rooms; pricey. ✉ *Follow signs from Café de Paris turnoff 2682–1000* ⊕ *www.harborreef.com* ↘ *9 rooms, 12 suites, 4 houses* ⌂ *In-room: no phone, kitchen (some), refrigerator, Wi-Fi. In-hotel: restaurant, bar, pools, laundry service, Internet terminal, Wi-Fi hotspot* ▭ *AE, DC, MC, V* ¡○¡ *CP.*

$$$ 🖼 **The Harmony Hotel.** Surf's up. *Upscale,* that is. This formerly frayed
★   surfer's haunt has been reborn as an ultracool hipster's retreat. The American owners are surfers, but of an age where comfort and quiet are more appealing than partying. The rooms surround a huge garden that holds a gorgeous, chlorine-free pool and sundeck—an oasis of tranquility. Every room, villa, and bungalow has soft sage-and-cream-color walls, a king-size bed dressed in white linen, and natural and polished wood trim and furniture. Enclosed back decks with hammocks expand what are otherwise standard-size rooms. The slightly larger duplex bungalows in back offer a little more privacy for an extra $60. The retro '60s lounge bar with basket chairs and adjacent restaurant add to the sophisticated ambience, but chic is not cheap—this place is markedly more expensive than its neighbors. For the health-conscious traveler there's a "healing center" complete with spa, yoga classes, and juice bar. The best surf breaks are just 180 meters (600 feet) away, down a shaded path. **Pros:** near beach; room rate includes a free yoga class; chic; nice details. **Cons:** pricey; not overly kid-friendly. ✉ *From Café de Paris, take road almost all the way to Playa Guiones, on right* ☎ *2682–4114, 2682-1073* ⊕ *www.harmonynosara.com* ↘ *10 rooms, 13 bungalows. 1 suite* ⌂ *In-room: safe, refrigerator, no TV, Wi-Fi. In-hotel: restaurant, bar, pool, spa, beachfront, laundry service, no-smoking rooms* ▭ *AE, DC, MC, V* ¡○¡ *BP.*

$ 🖼 **Hotel Lagarta Lodge.** A birders' and nature lovers' Valhalla, this mag-
★   nificent property on a promontory has amazing views of the forest, river, and coast north of Nosara. The private Nosara Biological Reserve is directly below the lodge. A 10-minute walk down a steep path takes you through a monkey-filled forest to beautiful Playa Guiones and surfing waves. The bright, spacious rooms are simple but comfortable, with balconies and terraces perfect for admiring the sweeping vista. Swiss managers Regina and Amadeo Amacker oversee the eagle's-nest lobby-restaurant ($–$$, reservations essential), which features a Swiss-inspired menu that is strong on fresh fish and seafood, such as skewered prawns with bacon, and poached fish with a lemon sauce. There is also a cocktails-and-canapés Sunset Bar that you must visit even if you stay elsewhere. The breakfast buffet is delicious, with fresh breads and homemade jams. Both the garden and reserve are maintained without any chemical fertilizers, insecticides, herbicides, or the use of electric machinery. **Pros:** amazing views and grounds; close to nature. **Cons:** not on the beach; plain rooms. ✉ *Top of hill at north end of Nosara* ☎ *2682–0035* ⊕ *www.lagarta.com* ↘ *6 rooms* ⌂ *In-room: no a/c, no phone, no TV. In-hotel: restaurant, bar, pool, Internet terminal, Wi-Fi* ▭ *MC, V* ¡○¡ *EP.*

$$ 🖼 **Luna Azul.** Sequestered in the hills above Playa Ostional, several
★   miles north of Nosara, Luna Azul is a tranquil, tasteful spot full of clever design and healthful attributes—supplied by the zoologist and

homeopathist Swiss owners. Abundant birds and wildlife, thanks to the surrounding private nature reserve, make this an excellent spot for nature lovers; it is also the most convenient lodge for seeing turtles nesting. Rooms are spacious, and the bathrooms are elegant, with hot-water showers open to nature. Three separate rooms have very private decks, cooled by overhead fans; four others have their own gardens. Acupuncture and homeopathic treatments and massages are available. The chic seafood restaurant overlooking the small tile pool and treetops draws customers from Nosara, with perfectly prepared seafood, fresh fish, tenderloin, and organic chicken. The only drawback to this picture-perfect place is that it's hard to get to when the Lagarto River swells in rainy season, but you can always reach it via Veintisiete de Abril, near Tamarindo. **Pros:** isolated in a picturesque environment; good restaurant. **Cons:** off the beaten path. ⊠ *1 km (½ mi) north of Ostional, 5 km (3 mi) north of Nosara* ☎ *8821–0075, 2682-1400* ⊕ *www.hotellunaazul.com* 🔁 *3 bungalows, 4 rooms* ⚒ *In-room: no phone, safe, refrigerator, no TV. In-hotel: restaurant, bar, pool, laundry service, Wi-Fi* ▤ *AE, DC, MC, V* ⊗ *Closed Oct.* ⧖ *BP.*

NIGHTLIFE

The Gilded Iguana (⊠ *Playa Guiones* ☎ *2682–0259*) has live acoustic music on Tuesday night that draws a big crowd.

Sunset is the main event in the evening, and people gather to watch it at **Olga's Bar** (⊠ *Playa Pelada* ☎ *No phone*), a ramshackle beach shack. Saturday night, the popular **Tropicana** (⊠ *Downtown Nosara, beside the soccer field* ☎ *No phone*) is where the action is.

SHOPPING

Arte Guay (⊠ *Commercial center, just past Café de Paris on road to Playa Guiones* ☎ *2682–0757*) has local crafts and beachwear. Along with surfing wear and gear, **Coconut Harry's Surf Shop** (⊠ *Main road, across from Café de Paris*) has an interesting selection of jewelry and bottled hot sauces made by Harry himself. (The Iguana Atomic Hot Sauce will rip your tongue out!)The **Chenoa Boutique** (⊠ *Commercial center, just past Café de Paris on road to Playa Guiones*) has an interesting selection of jewelry, handbags, and beachwear.

SÁMARA

36 km/23 mi southwest of Nicoya, 26 km/16 mi south of Nosara.

The drive to Sámara from Nicoya may be one of the most scenic in Costa Rica, passing rolling hills and green vistas before descending to a wide, south-facing bay hemmed by palm-shaded sand. Long a favorite summer-home spot with well-off Costa Ricans, Sámara's combination of safe swimming water and relative proximity to San José make it popular among working-class Ticos as well. The town of Sámara has an abundance of budget accommodations, which makes it a good destination for travelers with limited budgets. It can be a lively place on weekends, with bars on the beaches and handicraft vendors on the main drag, but it isn't the cleanest of beaches (no Blue Flag), and those seeking solitude should head to the beach's western or eastern ends. Though

Soft music and cocktails on the beach at the La Vela Latina in Sámara.

it lacks the rip currents that make many Costa Rican beaches dangerous, Sámara has pollution problems, and thus is not the best beach for swimming from September to December, when daily rains flush plenty of things you wouldn't want to swim with into the sea.

Sámara's wide sweep of light-gray sand is framed by two forest-covered hills jutting out on either side. It's the perfect hangout beach, with plenty of natural shade, bars, and restaurants to take refuge in from the sun. There is, however, a sandy roadway running through the coconut palms and Indian almond trees that line the beach, so be sure to look both ways when you move between the surf and margaritaville. The waves break out on a reef that lines the entrance of the cove, several hundred yards offshore, which keeps the water calm enough for safe swimming but leaves enough surf to have fun in. The reef holds plenty of marine attractions for diving and snorkeling excursions. Isla Chora, at the south end of the bay, provides a sheltered area that is especially popular for kayakers and snorkelers—it even has a tiny beach at lower tides.

GETTING HERE AND AROUND

The road from Nicoya is paved all the way for the scenic one-hour drive to Sámara. ■ TIP➜ Potholes are spreading, so keep your eyes on the road instead of the beautiful views. A rough beach road from Nosara is passable in dry season (it's more direct, but takes just as long); do not attempt this road when it rains. To get from Nosara to Sámara via the paved road, drive south, 5 km (3 mi) past Garza. At the T in the road, ignore the road toward Sámara (the beach road) and take the road to the left, toward Nicoya. This will take you uphill to merge with the main Nicoya–Sámara highway. Sámara-bound buses leave Nicoya from a stop 300 meters east of the central park. They depart hourly from 5 AM to 3 PM and then at 4:30, 6:30, 8, and 9:45 PM.

ESSENTIALS

Bank/ATM Banco Nacional (✉ *50 m west of church* ☎ *2656–0089*).

Hospital Clinica (1 km west of Sámara in Cangreja, ☎ *2656-0166*).

Pharmacy Farmacia Sámara (✉ *North end of soccer field* ☎ *2656–0123*).

Internet Se@net (✉ *Across from soccer field* ☎ *2656–0302* ☉ *Daily 8–7*).

Post Office Correo (✉ *Beside church, across from soccer field*).

Rental Cars Alamo (✉ *Calle Principal, Sámara* ☎ *2656-0958*). **Budget** (✉ *100 m east of Hotel Giada, Sámara* ☎ *2656-0078*).

OUTDOOR ACTIVITIES

Sámara is known more for gentle water sports such as snorkeling and kayaking than for surfing, although there are a couple of surf schools in town. There are also two high-flying adventures here: zip-line tours and ultralight flights and flying lessons. ATV tours, tearing along dirt roads, are popular with travelers who are particularly fond of dust, or mud, according to the season. For information on area activities, visit the town's official Web site at ⊕ *www.samarabeach.com.*

Tío Tigre Tours (✉ *50 m east of school and 100 m north* ☎ *2656–1060*) has a full line of guided outdoor activities, including kayaking ($20), snorkeling ($20), horseback riding ($35), and dolphin- and whale-watching tours ($45). **Sámara Travel Center** (✉ *Main street, across from Century 21* ☎ *2656–0922*) offers an array of local tours and bus and plane tickets to other parts of the country, and rents bikes and motorcycles.

CANOPY TOURS

Wing Nuts Canopy Tour (✉ *In the hills above Sámara* ☎ *2656–0153*) has a three-hour, 12-platform zip-line tour through a patch of tropical forest just south of town, with ocean views from some of the platforms ($55).

DIVING AND SNORKELING

The reef offshore is the best place to snorkel. Kayakers also paddle out to Isla Chora to snorkel on the leeward side of the island. The lone dive shop here, French-run **Pura Vida Dive** (✉ *Sámara, 600 m west of church* ☎ *2656–0643* ⊕ *www.puravidadive.com*), takes a maximum of five divers ($90 each) about 8 km (5 mi) out to explore rock formations off Playa Buena Vista and Playa Carrillo. Turtles, white-tipped sharks, and lots of big fish are the star sightings. The company also rents scuba equipment and arranges snorkeling trips.

KAYAKING

Plastic sit-on-top kayaks can be rented at Villas Playa Sámara (⇨ *below*), which is quite close to Isla Chora and the reef. **C&C Surf Shop** (✉ *On beach across from Casa del Mar* ☎ *2656–0590* runs kayak snorkeling tours to Isla Chora and the nearby reef ($30). **Tío Tigre** (⇨ *above*) offers various kayaking tours.

SURFING

The surf is relatively gentle at Sámara, so it's a good place for beginners. The challenging waves for more experienced surfers are farther south, at Playa Camaronal, which has both left and right breaks. **C&C Surf Shop** (⇨ *above*) has a beachfront surf school ($30 per lesson), and rents boards ($3 per hour).

ULTRALIGHT FLIGHTS

Flying Crocodile Lodge (⊠ *Playa Buena Vista 6 km/4 mi northwest of Sámara* ☎ *2656–8048* ⊕ *www.flying-crocodile.com*) gives ultralight flights and flying lessons ($75 for 20-minute tour).

WHERE TO EAT

$$$ ✕ **El Lagarto.** With varnished wooden tables scattered across the sand
STEAK   amid ficus and Indian almond trees, close enough to the sea to hear
★   the surf above the mix of Latin music on the stereo, El Lagarto has Sámara's best ambience by far. But its big draw is the food—fresh local seafood and high-quality meat grilled to perfection on a massive, open-air barbecue. The name means "The Crocodile," but you won't find croc steaks on the menu. You can, however, sink your teeth into juicy tenderloin, lamb chops, mahimahi, prawns, tuna, veal ribs, mussels, chicken breast stuffed with mushrooms and cheese, portobello mushrooms, or a whole-grilled lobster. You won't find any barbecue sauce on the meat here; everything is simply brushed with extra-virgin olive oil seasoned with a bit of garlic, salt, and pepper to complement the flavor of the wood. Dinners include grilled vegetables and potatoes; a salad is à la carte. They have a kids' menu, an ample wine list, and an extensive cocktail selection, not to mention banana splits. ⊠ *200 m west and 200 m south of Banco Nacional* ☎ *2656–0750* ⊟ *AE, DC, MC, V* ⊗ *No lunch. Closed Oct.*

$ ✕ **El Manglar.** Hidden on a rutted side street, this informal Italian eatery
ITALIAN   beneath a large thatch roof doesn't look like much, but there are usually
★   plenty of cars parked in front, since it's a favorite of local expatriates. Italian cooks are in the kitchen, preparing fresh pasta, fish, and meat dishes to order, or sliding superthin, crispy pizzas out of the oven. They make the best pizza in town, with two-dozen varieties to choose from. The ricotta-and-spinach ravioli with porcini mushrooms and zucchini have made many a mouth water, as have the homemade gnocchi—but ask for the mahimahi ravioli, which isn't on the menu but is often available, smothered in creamy shrimp sauce. Nearly everything fresh, which means you have to wait a little longer here than at the competition. ⊠ *200 m west and 150 m south of Banco Nacional* ☎ *2656–0096* ⊟ *MC, V* ⊗ *No lunch. Closed 2 wks in May.*

$ ✕ **Pizza & Pasta a Go-Go.** An ample selection of high-quality Italian food,
ITALIAN   including 25 fabulous pizzas, 26 pastas, generous salads, and a lengthy Italian wine list, is just one reason to drop in at this sidewalk trattoria. Unlike the checkered tablecloths you'd find elsewhere, here you have glass tabletops showcasing shells, or plain wooden tables by the pool. Save room for a tiramisu that transcends the tropics and delivers your taste buds to Italy. ⊠ *Hotel Giada lobby, main strip, 150 m north of beach* ☎ *2656–0132* ⊟ *AE, MC, V.*

WHERE TO STAY

¢–$ 🏨 **Hotel Casa del Mar.** Less than a block from the beach, this pleasant, well-tended hotel is one of Sámara's best values. The bright, tidy rooms have dark-wood furniture, white walls, and ceramic floors. Eleven of the rooms have aair-conditioning and private bath, and some have queen-size beds. Six of the rooms lack air-conditioning and share baths, but they share a common balcony with an ocean view, and sea breezes help to cool them. The hotel has a giant cold-water whirlpool in a small garden and a big cage holding a parrot named Lolita. Breakfast is included in the rate for rooms with private bath only. **Pros:** helpful staff; easy on the wallet. **Cons:** not right on the beach; no swimming pool. ✉ *Main strip, 45 m east of school* ☎ *2656–0264* ⊕ *www.casadelmarsamara.com* ➲ *17 rooms, 11 with bath* ♿ *In-room: no a/c (some), no phone, refrigerator (some), no TV (some). In-hotel: no-smoking rooms* ▭ *AE, MC, V* ⟨○⟩ *BP.*

¢–$ 🏨 **Hotel Giada.** Giada means "jade" in Italian, and this small hotel in the heart of town has been decorated with the artistic Italian owners' precious, polished creations. Watermelon, terra-cotta, and yellow washes give the walls an antique Mediterranean look, and the terraces of the back rooms overlook a curvaceous blue pool surrounded by tropical greenery. The rooms have whimsical bamboo furniture and sea creatures on the hand-painted bathroom tiles. Pizza & Pasta a Go-Go (⟹ *above*), the hotel's restaurant, is an excellent Italian restaurant. The hotel's drawback is noise from the restaurant and the street, which is why roadside rooms should be avoided; ask for a room overlooking the pool. **Pros:** affordable; friendly. **Cons:** not right on the beach; small rooms. ✉ *Main strip, 250 m from beach* ☎ *2656–0132* ⊕ *www. hotelgiada.net* ➲ *24 rooms* ♿ *In-room: safe, refrigerator (some). In-hotel: restaurant, pool* ▭ *AE, DC, MC, V* ⟨○⟩ *BP.*

¢–$ 🏨 **Hotel Las Brisas del Pacífico.** One of the few beachfront hotels in Sámara, Las Brisas has been here for nearly two decades, and much of the place shows its age. The standard rooms, in two rows of white, Spanish-style bungalows hugging the bottom of a steep hill, can be hot and stuffy. "Sky rooms," in the two-story building at the top of the hill, are more expensive, but much nicer, with ocean-view balconies and a nearby pool, as well as a separate parking lot, so that you don't have to climb up and down the steep hill. Newer "on-top" rooms above the office are closer to the beach and have balconies, but most view the restaurant's roof. You'll want to eat everything but breakfast in town. The receptionist can arrange diving trips and other outings. **Pros:** great location; two nice pools. **Cons:** rooms and grounds somewhat neglected; service inconsistent. ✉ *South of town* ☎ *2656–0250* ⊕ *www.brisas.net* ➲ *34 rooms* ♿ *In-room: no a/c (some), no phone, safe. In-hotel: restaurant, bar, pools, beachfront, laundry service, Wi-Fi hotspot* ▭ *AE, D, MC, V* ⟨○⟩ *BP.*

$$ 🏨 **Villas Kalimba.** You may never want to leave this tranquil oasis hidden ★ behind scrolled white-and-orange walls. The architecture is Mexican, but the style is all Italian. Ochre-washed villas with hammocks and dining tables on their front porches circle an exuberant garden and pool with a cool waterfall. Rooms have state-of-the-art kitchens, and you can dine alfresco at a long wooden table on your own tiled terrazza. All the

6

Idyllic Playa Carrillo is perfect for swimming, snorkeling, or just sunning.

comforts of a luxury home—king-size bed, cable TV, a personal portable phone—are here, just across the street from the beach. Barbecues and pasta dinners for guests are offered several times a week beneath a Spanish-tile roof by the pool. **Pros:** spacious villas; lovely garden; quiet. **Cons:** not on beach; uninspired dining. ⊠ *200 m east of the Sámara Police Station, along beach road* ☎ *2656–0929* ⊕ *www.villaskalimba.com* ⤳ *6 villas, 2 casas* ⌂ *In-room: kitchen, safe, Wi-Fi. In-hotel: pool, laundry service, Wi-Fi* ⊟ *MC, V* ⊺◉⊺ *EP.*

\$\$\$ 🏨 **Villas Playa Sámara.** Families come back to this property year after year for good reason: there's lots to do, the villas are spacious and practical, and the setting is fabulous. It is spread along the picture-perfect southern end of the beach, where the ocean is cleaner than it is near town, and shallow and safe enough for swimming. The spacious, Spanish-style one-, two-, and three-bedroom villas of white stucco are sprinkled across the property's gardens and wide lawns. They have kitchens and dining areas with daybeds that are perfect for kids (under 12 stay free), and shaded terraces with either a hammock or chairs, but they are quite timeworn and lack such basics as a phone and a TV. Most have ocean views through the palms, but the duplex villas 2A/B and 11A/B are especially close to the beach, and thus cost an extra \$20; 17 A/B is a close second. The restaurant food is not terrific; it's best to cook for yourself or dine in town. **Pros:** great location; spacious villas; ample grounds. **Cons:** villas timeworn; cleaning inconsistent. ⊠ *Off main road 2 km/1¼ mi south of town* ☎ *2656-1111* ⊕ *www.villasplayasamara.com* ⤳ *59 villas* ⌂ *In-room: no phone, kitchen, no TV (some). In-hotel: restaurant, bar, pool, beachfront, water sports, bicycles, laundry service, Internet terminal, Wi-Fi hotspot* ⊟ *AE, MC, V* ⊺◉⊺ *EP.*

NIGHTLIFE

The liveliest, noisiest beach bar is **Las Olas** (✉ *On beach, 200 m west and 200 m south of Banco Nacional* ☎ *2656–1100*). Three pool tables, bright lights, and a pulsing Latin soundtrack attract a mix of locals and young backpackers. **Tutifruti** (✉ *50 m west of police station*), on the beach, is the local dance club. It opens only on Friday and Saturday, when it gets packed with young Costa Ricans. **Shake Joe's** (✉ *On beach, center of town*) is the place for music, drinks, and an international menu.

★ **La Vela Latina** (✉ *Across from Villas Kalimba, on beach*) is the cool place for grown-up soft music and cocktails on the beach.

SHOPPING

Souvenir stands set up along the main street and at the entrance to the beach. Most shops here have pretty much the same beachwear and souvenirs for sale. **Tienda Licia** (✉ *Main street*) has a wall hung with pretty glass fish and butterfly ornaments made by a San José artist. Arts-and-crafts gallery **Dragonfly Galería** (✉ *Across the street from Licia*) sells local paintings and carvings, and shell, feather, and bead jewelry. It also paints temporary henna tattoos.

PLAYA CARRILLO

7 km/4 mi southeast of Sámara.

Fodor's Choice ★ With its long, reef-protected beach backed by an elegant line of swaying palms and sheltering cliffs, Playa Carrillo (interchangeably called Puerto Carrillo) is a candidate for the most picturesque beach in Costa Rica. Unmarred by a single building, it's ideal for swimming, snorkeling, walking, and lounging—just remember not to sit under a loaded coconut palm. There are some concrete tables and benches, but they get snapped up quickly. This is a popular beach with locals, and it gets quite busy on weekends. The main landmark here is the Hotel Guanamar, high above the beach. Unfortunately the former private fishing club and previously grand hotel has been bought and sold so often that its charm has faded. But its bar still has the best view.

GETTING HERE AND AROUND

You can fly into Playa Carrillo on SANSA or Nature Air and land at the airstrip, or head south 15 minutes on the smooth, paved road from Sámara. If you're not staying at a hotel in Carrillo, you'll have to park your car either in a sunbaked concrete lot halfway along the beach or on the grassy median at the south end of the beach. You can also leave the driving to Interbus (⇨ *North Pacific Essentials, at end of chapter*) and get here in an air-conditioned van.

ESSENTIALS

Sámara is the closest town for banks and other services.

EXPLORING

☼ Most nature lovers are no fans of zoos, but **La Selva Zoo & Bromeliad Garden,** a small zoo with mostly rescued small animals, is a great chance to see them up close in chest-high corrals under the shade of trees. The zoo's focus is on hard-to-see nocturnal animals, so the best time to visit is at sunset when the roly-poly armadillos and big-eyed kinkajous are starting to stir. There are also skunks, spotted pacas, raccoons, and scarier species like bats, boas, poison dart frogs, caimans, and crocodiles. A bromeliad and orchid collection is artistically arranged around the zoo. If you come early in the day, your ticket is also good for a return evening visit. ⊠ *Road behind Hotel Esperanza* ☎ *2656-2236* 🖃 *$14 adults, $8 children* ⏱ *Daily 8* AM–7 PM.

OUTDOOR ACTIVITIES

FISHING

From January to April, the boats moored off the beach take anglers on fishing expeditions. Experienced local skipper Rob Gordon lives right in Puerto Carrillo and runs fishing trips on the five-passenger **Kitty Kat** (☎ *2656–0170 or 8359–9039* ⊕ *www.sportfishcarrillo.com*), a recently re-fitted, custom-built 28-foot boat with twin diesels ($950 full day, $500–$650 half day). He offers catch-and-release marlin and sail fishing as well as good-eating dorado, yellowfin tuna, and wahoo. Captain Rob also offers sunset cruises. There are also dolphins and occasional whales to watch if the fishing is slow.

PUNTA ISLITA

8 km/5 mi south of Playa Carrillo in dry season, 50 km/31 mi south of Carrillo by alternative route in rainy season.

Punta Islita is named for a tiny tuft of land that becomes an island at high tide, but the name is synonymous in Costa Rica with Hotel Punta Islita, one of the country's most luxurious and gorgeous resorts. The curved beach is rather rocky but good for walking, especially at low tide when tidal pools form in the volcanic rock. Another interesting stroll is through the small village, which has become a work in progress, thanks to a community art project led by renowned Costa Rican artists who use town buildings as their canvas. Everything—from outdoor activities to food—revolves around, and is available through, the resort.

GETTING HERE AND AROUND

During the dry season, it's a quick trip south of Playa Carrillo in a 4WD vehicle, but in the rainy season, it's often impossible to cross the Río Ora, so you have to make a much longer detour along rough dirt roads with spectacular mountain views. Most guests consequently fly into the hotel's private airstrip.

WHERE TO STAY

$$$$
Fodor's Choice
★

🖼 Hotel Punta Islita. Overlooking the ocean from a forested ridge, this secluded hotel is luxury incarnate. Hidden around the hillside are villas, casitas, suites, and spacious rooms, each with a private porch and a hammock. Beds have rough-hewn wooden bedposts, and bathrooms are tiled, with deep tubs. Casitas have their own private plunge pools or outdoor whirlpools and private gardens, one of the main attractions for the many honeymooners. A massive thatched dome covers the restaurant and opens onto an infinity-edge pool with a swim-up bar. If you overdo it with the activities here—including golfing, mountain biking, and zip-line tours—stop by the spa for massage treatments using local herbs. **Pros:**

gorgeous views; lots of activities. **Cons:** isolated; mediocre beach. ⊠ *8 km/5 mi south of Playa Carrillo* ⊕ *Apdo. 242–1225, Plaza Mayor, San José* ☎ *2231–6122 in San José, 2656-2020, hotel, toll-free U.S. 1-866-446-4053* ⊕ *www.hotelpuntaislita.com* ➲ *14 rooms, 8 suites, 8 casitas, 17 villas* ⚒ *In-room: DVD (some). In-hotel: 2 restaurants, bars, driving range, tennis courts, pools, gym, spa, beachfront, laundry service, Wi-Fi hotspot, no-smoking rooms* ⊟ *AE, DC, MC, V* ⏿ *BP.*

THE TEMPISQUE RIVER BASIN

The parks in and around the Río Tempisque are prime places to hike, explore caves, and spot birds and other wildlife. The town of Nicoya is the commercial and political hub of the northern Nicoya Peninsula. By road, Nicoya provides the best access to Sámara, Nosara, and points south and north and is linked by a smooth, well-paved road to the artisan community of Guaitil and the northern Nicoya beach towns.

The Friendship Bridge, built with donated funds from Taiwan and more commonly referred to as the Río Tempisque Bridge, crosses the Río Tempisque just north of where passengers used to weather long waits for a ferry. To get to the bridge, head north from San José on the Pan-American Highway, turn left about 48 km (30 mi) north of the Puntarenas turnoff, and drive 27 km (17 mi) west.

PALO VERDE NATIONAL PARK

52 km/32 mi south of Liberia.

One of the best wildlife- and bird-watching parks in Costa Rica, Palo Verde is bordered on the west by the Río Tempisque. Extending over 198 square km (76 square mi), the park protects a significant amount of deciduous dry forest. The terrain is fairly flat—the maximum elevation in the park is 268 meters (879 feet)—and the forest is less dense than a rain forest, which makes it easier to spot the fauna. The park holds seasonal wetlands that provide a temporary home for thousands of migratory birds toward the end of the rainy season, whereas crocodiles ply the Tempisque's waters year-round. From September through March you can see dozens of species of migratory and resident aquatic birds, including herons, wood storks, jabirus, and elegant, flamingo-like roseate spoonbills. ■TIP→ A raised platform near the ranger station, about 8 km (5 mi) past the park entrance, gives you a vantage point over a marsh filled with ducks and jacanas. But be prepared to climb a narrow metal ladder. Lodging in rustic dormitory facilities ($10) and meals ($5 breakfast; $7 for lunch or dinner) can be arranged through the park headquarters. ⊠ *29 km/18 mi southwest of Bagaces* ☎ *2200–0125* ➲ *$10* ⊙ *Daily 8–dusk; entrance gates open 8–noon and 1–4.*

GETTING HERE AND AROUND
To get to Palo Verde from Liberia, drive south along the Pan-American Highway to Bagaces, then turn right at the small, easy-to-miss sign for Palo Verde, along a rough dirt road for 28 km (17 mi). Count on an hour to drive the distance from the main highway to the park entrance; it's a very bumpy road. You'll have to pay the $10 park entrance fee to

6

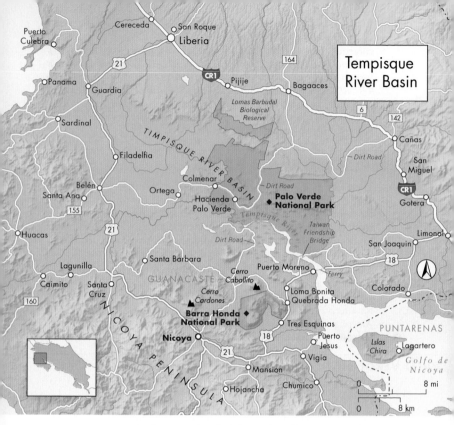

Tempisque
River Basin

get to the Organization for Tropical Studies station. The OTS station is about 7 km (5 mi) beyond the park entrance; the park headquarters is just another kilometer farther. The gatekeeper takes lunch from noon to 1 PM. The drive should take a total of about three hours.

EXPLORING

Just 3 km (2 mi) north of the Palo Verde road at Bagaces, take the dirt road signed for **Llanos de Cortés** to get to this hidden waterfall less than 2 km (1 mi) off the highway. About half a kilometer along the dirt road you'll see on your right a large rock with CATARATAS scrawled on it. Follow this bumpy road about 1.3 km (0.8 mi) to its end and then clamber down a steep path to the pool at the bottom of a spectacular, wide, 50-foot waterfall. This is a great place for a picnic. ■TIP→ Don't leave anything of value in your car.

Sad but sobering, one of the few places left in the country where you are guaranteed to see large wild cats, including a jaguar, is **Las Pumas Rescue Shelter** (⊠ 4½ km/3 mi north of Cañas on main highway ☎ 2669–6044 ⊕ www.laspumas.org) (Centro de Rescate Las Pumas). The small enclosures also hold jaguarundis, pumas, margays, ocelots, and oncillas. Some small animals and birds are rehabilitated and released into the wild. The larger cats are probably here for life, as it's dangerous for them to be released. The refuge relies on contributions. It's open daily 8 to 4.

OUTDOOR ACTIVITIES

The **Organization for Tropical Studies** (☎ *2524–0607* ⊕ *www.ots.ac.cr*), a nonprofit, scientific consortium, offers overnight packages with a guided walk, meals, and lodging in rustic, bunk-bedded double rooms with private bath ($85 per person). Their biological research station overlooks the Palo Verde wetlands, and they also offer a boat tour plus longer hikes as affordable add-ons to the package.

BIRD-WATCHING

The best bird-watching in Palo Verde is on the wetlands in front of the Organization for Tropical Studies' (OTS) biological station. The OTS has expert guides who can help you see and identify the varied birds in the area, but if you have good binoculars and a bird book, you can identify plenty of species on your own. A boat excursion to Isla Pájaros south of the Río Tempisque is interesting for birders. Toward the end of rainy season this 6-acre island near Puerto Moreno is an exciting place to see hundreds of nesting wood storks, cormorants, and anhingas. You can get close enough to see chicks being fed in nests. ■TIP➔ The best time to go is very early in the morning, to avoid heat and to guarantee the most bird sightings. **Aventuras Arenal** (☎ *2479–9133* ⊕ *www.arenaladventures.com*) guides have good eyes and usually know the English names for birds. The company specializes in ecological tours. Tours depart from docks along the Río Tempisque, including the dock at Palo Verde. **CATA Tours** (☎ *2674–0180; 2296–2133 in San José*) runs wildlife- and bird-watching boating adventures down the Río Bebedero into Palo Verde.($50 per person for two, $35 per person for three or more persons.) Arrange hotel pickup from Nicoya beaches and Papagayo Peninsula when you book.

Safaris Corobici (☎ *2669–6191* ⊕ *www.nicoya.com*) is a small company that specializes in the Class I and II floats down the Río Corobicí ($37 to $60; children under 14 half price) that start from (and end at) the Restaurante Rincón Corobicí, at Km 193 on the Pan-American Highway 5 km (3 mi) north of Cañas.

WILDLIFE-WATCHING

On a calm adventure trip with **Safaris Corobici** (✉ *Main highway to Liberia at Km 193, south of Corobicí* ☎ *2669–6191* ⊕ *www.nicoya.com*), two- or three-hour float trips ($37 to $60) cover wildlife-rich territory not far from Palo Verde. **Ríos Tropicales** (☎ *2233–6455* ⊕ *www.riostropicales.com*) lets you paddle down the easy Class I and II rafting route on the Río Corobicí. Those two- to three-hour trips ($50 excluding ground transportation) are great for bird- and monkey-watching and are safe enough for kids ages seven and older.

WHERE TO STAY NEAR PALO VERDE

$ **La Ensenada Lodge.** This is the most comfortable base for bird-watching and nature appreciation near the Río Tempisque. Part of a national wildlife refuge, the property is also a 1,000-acre cattle ranch and salt producer. The salt flats and nearby shallow waters attract wading birds (and crocodiles that snack on them). The Isla Pájaros Biological Reserve, the country's largest breeding ground for black-crowned night herons, is a short boat ride away. The wood cabins are

Rafting on the Corobici River, North Guanacaste.

comfortable, with verandas and big screened windows that let the light and breeze in. But because most of them are duplexes, they don't afford a lot of privacy, so see if you can get a freestanding one. The rancho restaurant serves buffet-style Italian and Costa Rican meals, including beef raised on the ranch. **Pros:** wildlife; interesting setting. **Cons:** very simple rooms; large tour groups at times. ⊠ *13 km/8 mi southwest of Pan-American Hwy. along a dirt road, 40 km/25 mi north of the Puntarenas turnoff* ☎ *2289–6655* ⊕ *www.laensenada.net* ⇌ *26 cabin rooms* ⚭ *In-room: no a/c, no phone, no TV. In-hotel: restaurant, bar, pool, laundry service* ▭ *No credit cards* �� *EP.*

BARRA HONDA NATIONAL PARK

100 km/62 mi south of Liberia, 13 km/8 mi west of Río Tempisque Bridge.

GETTING HERE AND AROUND

From the Río Tempisque Bridge, drive west along a paved highway. Then follow a dirt road (signed off the highway) for 10 km (6 mi) to the park entrance. There are buses that come here from the town of Nicoya, but they don't leave until 12:30 and 4 PM, a little late to start a hike. You can also take a taxi from Nicoya to the park entrance or go with one of many tour companies in beach towns on the Nicoya Peninsula.

EXPLORING

Barra Honda National Park Once thought to be a volcano, 390-meter (1,184-foot) **Barra Honda Peak** actually contains an intricate network of caves, a result of erosion after the ridge emerged from the sea. Some caves on the almost 23-square-km (14-square-mi) park remain unexplored, and they're home to abundant animal life, including bats, birds, blindfish, salamanders, and snails.

Every day from 7 AM to 1 PM local guides take groups rappelling 18 meters (58 feet) down into **Terciopelo Cave,** which shelters unusual formations shaped (they say) like fried eggs, popcorn, and shark's teeth. You must wear a harness with a rope attached for safety. The tour costs $22 including equipment rental, guide, and entrance fee. Kids under 12 are not allowed into this cave, but they can visit the kid-size La Cuevita cavern ($6), which also has interesting stalagmites. Both cave visits include interpretive nature hikes.

> ## THE FIRST GUANACASTECOS
>
> The Chorotega tribe first settled the Guanacaste area and grew corn and fished. Chief Nicoya was the Chorotegan leader who greeted the conquistadors in 1523 and bequeathed his name to the town and peninsula.

If you suffer a fear of heights, or claustrophobia, the cave tour is not for you, but Barra Honda still has plenty to offer, thanks to its extensive forests and abundant wildlife. You can climb the 3-km (2-mi) Los Laureles trail (the same trail that leads to the Terciopelo cave) to Barra Honda's summit, where you'll have sweeping views over the surrounding countryside and islet-filled Gulf of Nicoya. Wildlife you may spot on Barra Honda's trails includes howler monkeys, white-faced monkeys, skunks, coatis, deer, parakeets, hawks, dozens of other bird species, and iguanas. Local guides charge $6 for hiking tours. An off-site park office (⊠ *Across from colonial church, Nicoya* ☎ *2686–6760*) provides information and maps of the park. It's open weekdays 8 AM–4. It's a good idea to hire a local guide from the **Asociación de Guias Ecologistas.** The park has camping facilities. ⊠ *13 km/8 mi west of Río Tempisque Bridge* ☎ *2659–1551* 🖅 *$10* 🕙 *Daily 7:30–4.*

NICOYA

27 km/15 mi west of the Río Tempisque Bridge.

Once a quaint provincial town, Guanacaste's colonial capital is now bustling because of tourism and real estate booms along the nearby coast. With all the commercial bustle, Nicoya is rapidly losing what small-town charm it once had. But there are still a few historical remnants around the central park. A noticeable Chinese population, descendants of 19th-century railroad workers, has given Nicoya numerous Chinese restaurants. The town has Internet cafés and ATMs that take international cards.

GETTING HERE AND AROUND

The town of Nicoya is 40 minutes west of the Río Tempisque Bridge on a paved road. If you're running out of gas, oil, or tire pressure, the Servicentro Nicoyano on the north side of Nicoya, on the main road, is open 24 hours.

ESSENTIALS

Bank/ATM Banco de Costa Rica (⊠ *West side of central park* ☎ *2685–5110*). **Coopmani ATH** (⊠ *Main street, beside Fuji Film store*).

Hospital Hospital de L'Anexion (⊠ *Main road into town from highway* ☎ *2685–8400*).

Pharmacy Farmacia Clinica Medica Nicoyana (⊠ *Main street, near Restaurante Nicoya* ⊙ *Weekdays 8–7:30, Sat. 8–6*).

Post Office Correo (⊠ *Southwest corner of park*).

Taxis Taxi Service (☎ *2686–2466*).

EXPLORING

Nicoya's only colonial landmark is the whitewashed, mission-style **Church of San Blas**. Originally built in 1644, the church was reconstructed after the original was leveled by an 1831 earthquake. The spare interior is made grand by seven pairs of soaring carved-wood columns. Inside are folk-art wood carvings of the Stations of the Cross arrayed around the stark white walls, a small collection of 18th-century bronze mission bells, and some antique wooden saints. Arched doorways frame verdant views of park greenery and distant mountains. ⊠ *North side of central park* ☎ *No phone* ☜ *By donation* ⊙ *Erratic hours.*

OUTDOOR ACTIVITIES

Hiking in Barra Honda is the main outdoor adventure here.

WHERE TO EAT AND STAY

$ ✕ **Restaurante Nicoya.** There are many Chinese restaurants from which to
CHINESE choose in Nicoya. This one is the most elegant, with hanging lanterns, a colorful collection of international flags, and an enormous menu with 85 Asian dishes, such as stir-fried beef with vegetables. The fresh sea bass sautéed with fresh pineapple, chayote, and red peppers is excellent. ⊠ *Main road, 70 m south of Coopmani Bldg.* ☰ *AE, DC, MC, V* ⊙ *Closed daily 3–5.*

$ ☷ **Hotel de Lujo Río Tempisque.** There aren't many reasons to stay overnight in Nicoya, but if you get stuck here, this recently expanded "luxury" lodge is the best option. The rooms here, with high wooden ceilings and big picture windows, are comfortable by any standards. Huge white-tile bathrooms have mirrored closets and showers big enough for two. The best thing about the place, though, is its tranquil location north of town, and its ample gardens and small pool. **Pros:** quiet; convenient. **Cons:** simple; not memorable. ⊠ *Highway north to Santa Cruz, outside Nicoya* ☎ *2686–6650* ↘ *106 rooms* ♿ *In-room: no phone, refrigerator. In-hotel: restaurant, pool* ☰ *AE, MC, V* ❍❙ *EP.*

¢ ☷ **Hotel Mundiplaza.** This hotel is the town's most modern. On the second floor above a medical clinic, it doesn't have much personality. But if you need a bed for the night, it has fresh rooms with all the modern conveniences. There's also a small restaurant and Internet café in the same building. ⊠ *Main road into Nicoya, near hospital* ☎ *2685–3535* ↘ *25 rooms* ♿ *In-room: no phone* ☰ *AE, DC, MC, V* ❍❙ *EP.*

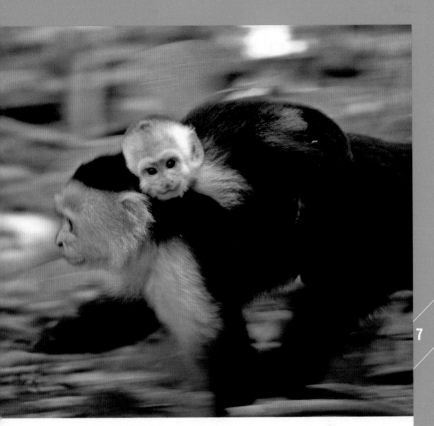

Central Pacific

WORD OF MOUTH

"At the end of a hike through Manuel Antonio, we finally reached a beach where a troop of white-faced capuchins had gathered. They entranced everyone as they ran along low-hanging branches, tantalizingly close."

—Photo by Gwen Morris, Fodors.com member

WELCOME TO CENTRAL PACIFIC

TOP REASONS TO GO

★ **Nature and wildlife:** Explore seaside flora and fauna at Manuel Antonio National Park, Curú National Wildlife Refuge, and Cabo Blanco Absolute Nature Reserve.

★ **Fishing:** Deep-sea fishing at Quepos, Tambor, Jacó, or Herradura is a chance to hook a sailfish, marlin, wahoo, or yellowfin tuna.

★ **Sunsets:** Whether you view it from the beach in Malpaís or while sipping hilltop cocktails in Manuel Antonio, this region has some of the country's best venues for watching the sunset.

★ **Surfing:** This is Costa Rica's surf central. Jacó, Malpaís, and Playa Hermosa swarm with surfers, from beginners to pros.

★ **Adventure sports:** Snorkel among colorful fish, get muddy on ATV mountain rides, and zip through treetops near Jacó, Manuel Antonio, or Montezuma.

1 Southern Nicoya Tip. On the Southern Nicoya Tip, across the gulf from the "mainland," towns are more tranquil and more spread out. Beaches and surfing dominate.

GETTING ORIENTED

Most of the Central Pacific is mountainous, and beach towns are backed by forested peaks. Humid evergreen forests, oil-palm plantations, and cattle pastures blanket the land. The coastal highway connects all towns from Tárcoles to the southern Pacific. The hub town of Jacó makes a good base for visiting surrounding beaches and wildlife areas. Farther south are Quepos and its neighbor, Manuel Antonio, followed by smaller towns barely touched by tourism. Across the Gulf of Nicoya, the more tranquil southern tip of the Nicoya Peninsula is also surrounded by impressive mountains, but with dry tropical forests that change radically from the rainy to the dry season.

7

Carara
Biological
Reserve **3**

SAN JOSÉ

Pavona

PUNTARENAS

Esterillos
Este   Parrita

Esterillos   Playa   Paquita
Oeste   Bejuco   Quepos

Manuel Antonio   Rey

Manuel Antonio   **4**
National Park   34

0   10 mi

0   10 km

2 Inland. Humid evergreen forests, coffee fields, and cattle pastures blanket the Inland portions of the Central Pacific.

3 Carara National Park. Carara National Park is home to a very impressive collection of plants and animals.

4 Coast. From Tárcoles, the highway along the Coast connects lively tourist hubs Jacó, Quepos, and Manuel Antonio, and on down to the South Pacific. This is the place to surf, do a multitude of active tours, laze on the beach, and explore Manuel Antonio National Park.

CENTRAL PACIFIC PLANNER

Beating the Crowds

The dry season here is the high season: visitors (lots of them) arrive December through May, pushing hotel prices up and crowding the beaches. During Holy Week and the last week of the December, rooms are even harder to come by. A great time to visit the area is during July and August, which see warm, sunny days with the occasional light shower. If you are in the area in high season and want to visit one of the parks, get an early start and arrive by 7 AM.

Choosing a Place to Stay

The Central Pacific has a good mix of high-quality hotels, nature lodges, and *cabinas* (low-cost Tico-run hotels, often laid out like motels), including some of the country's priciest lodgings. As a rule, prices drop 20% to 30% during the rainy season. Reserve as far in advance as possible during the busy dry season. Near Manuel Antonio National Park, Manuel Antonio is the more activity-rich, attractive, and expensive place to stay (though we've culled the best budget options).

Do It Your Own Way

This popular area is also easily reachable. If you're not pressed for time, and you'd like to experience more than just resorts, beaches, and, depending on when you go, crowds, then rent a car or travel by bus, shuttle, or private driver instead of flying from San José. Your rewards will be plenty: beautiful landscapes, typical rural towns, and easygoing Ticos. Distances from San José are not overwhelming, and the ferry ride across the Gulf of Nicoya has great views of the mountainous coast and its islands. Buses are timely and economical, but if you prefer an air-conditioned ride, shuttles leave from San José and can drop you off at your hotel's doorstep. Most travelers heading to the southern tip of the Nicoya Peninsula arrive by car via the ferry from Puntarenas to Paquera. You can also fly into Tambor's airstrip and taxi to your beach from here.

What to Do

ACTIVITY	WHERE TO DO IT
Fishing	Quepos, Manuel Antonio, Playa Herradura, Tambor, Jacó
Snorkeling	Isla Tortuga, Manuel Antonio, Montezuma
Surfing	Jacó, Playa Hermosa, Malpaís
Wildlife-viewing	Manuel Antonio National Park, Río Tárcoles, Cabo Blanco Absolute Nature Reserve, Curú National Wildlife Refuge, Carara National Park
Yoga	Montezuma, Malpaís, Jacó, Manuel Antonio
Zip-line tours	Malpaís, Montezuma, Jacó, Playa Herradura, Playa Hermosa, Manuel Antonio, Quepos

Recommended Tour Operators

Costa Rica 4u (CRT ☎ 2508–5000 ⊕ *www.costarica4u.com*) has a variety of Central Pacific tours, plus car rentals, private drivers, shuttle vans, and a 4WD off-the-beaten-path "adventure" transfer between San José and Manuel Antonio.

Cruise West (☎ 888/851–8133 ⊕ *www.cruisewest.com*) runs four 11- to 15-day cruises that visit coastal reserves in Panama and Costa Rica.

King Tours (☎ 8819–1920, 2643–2441, or 800/213–7091 ⊕ *www.kingtours.com*) arranges trips to the top Central Pacific attractions, including Manuel Antonio National Park and Carara National Park.

Ríos Tropicales (☎ 2233–6455 or 866/722–8273 ⊕ *www.riostropicales.com*), a high-quality adventure tour company, runs a four-day, three-night sea-kayaking trip ($600) based at Curú National Wildlife Refuge and meanders among the islands of the Gulf of Nicoya. White-water rafting trips on rivers near Manuel Antonio cost $70 to $99.

Dining and Lodging Prices

WHAT IT COSTS IN DOLLARS

	¢	$	$$	$$$	$$$$
Restaurants	under $5	$5–$10	$10–$15	$15–$25	over $25
Hotels	under $50	$50–75	$75–$150	$150–$250	over $250

Restaurant prices are per person for a main course at dinner. Hotel prices are for two people in a standard double room in high season, excluding service and tax (16.4%).

Planning the Days and Nights

Nightlifers of all ages, Ticos as well as travelers, flock to Jacó to party until sunrise, making it the country's liveliest beach town. Jacó draws everyone from partying college kids to groups of men seeking to savor the local beer. Be aware that Jacó also attracts a fair number of ladies of the night.

South of Quepos along the coastal highway lie tranquil beaches, where time seems to stand still, a real contrast with the busy Manuel Antonio area. Dominical makes a great surf spot after Jacó, whereas Punta Uvita has a vast beach and more wildlife than people. From the southern tip of Nicoya, head up the west coast to hop along the endless stretch of beaches. Or ferry back to the mainland to explore Monteverde's cloud forest.

Timing

A week gives you enough time to visit several beaches on the central coast or get a good grasp of the tip of Nicoya.

Word of Mouth

"As a first timer, you should plan on at least a day trip to MA. It's a good place to get your feet wet seeing some wildlife in a very user-friendly situation."

—artiejay

CARARA NATIONAL PARK

One of the last remnants of an ecological transition zone between Costa Rica's drier northwest and more humid southwest, Carara National Park holds a tremendous collection of plants and animals.

Squeezed into its 47 square km (18 square mi) is a mixed habitat of evergreen and deciduous forest, river, lagoon, and marshland. Much of the park's terrain is blanketed with dramatic primary forest, massive trees laden with vines and epiphytes. This is a birder's and plant-lover's haven. The sparse undergrowth makes terrestrial wildlife and ground birds easier to see, but of course nothing is guaranteed. Your chances of seeing wildlife increase dramatically the earlier you get here. The most famous denizens—apart from the crocodiles in the adjoining Río Tarcoles—are the park's colorful and noisy scarlet macaws, which always travel in pairs. An oxbow lake (a U-shaped body of water that was once part of a river) adds an extra wildlife dimension, attracting turtles and waterfowl—and the crocodiles that dine on them. Bring lots of drinking water; this park can get very hot and humid.

BEST TIME TO GO

Dry season, January to April, is the best time to visit. The trails get very muddy during the rainy season and may even close in the wettest months. This small park can feel crowded at the trailheads, so arrive early and walk far. Bird-watchers can call the day before to arrange early admission.

FUN FACT

The crowning glory of Carara is the successful conservation program that has doubled its scarlet macaw population. You can't miss these long-tailed, noisy parrots—look for streaks of brilliant blue and red in the sky.

BEST WAYS TO EXPLORE

HIKING

The best and really only way to explore this park is on foot. Rubber boots or waterproof shoes are essential in the rainy season, and still a good idea, even in the drier months. Trails are well marked and maintained but the ground is often muddy—this is rain forest, after all. The shortest—and most popular—loop trail can be done in only 15 minutes. But if you venture farther afield, you'll quickly be on your own, except for the wildlife you're bound to encounter. The longer trail that connects with the Quebrada Bonita loop takes one to three hours to hike. There is also a short wheelchair-accessible route that starts at the main entrance. It goes deep enough into the forest to give visitors a sense of its drama and diversity.

BIRD-WATCHING

With more than 350 species recorded here, Carara is on every bird-watcher's must-visit list. It's an especially good place to see elusive ground birds, such as antpittas (a small ground-dwelling bird that eats ants), early in the morning and late in the afternoon. Around the lake and in the marshy areas, you may also spot roseate spoonbills, northern jacanas, and stately boat-billed herons. The park's most famous fliers are the scarlet macaws. Once almost absent from the area, a decades-long conservation program has revitalized the local population.

WILDLIFE-WATCHING

Carara is famous for an amazing variety of wildlife, given its relatively small area. Keep alert (and quiet) while walking and you'll have a good chance of spotting big and small lizards, coatimundis (a member of the raccoon family), and sloths. You're almost guaranteed to see white-faced monkeys and, with luck, howler and spider monkeys, too. You may even surprise a nine-banded armadillo snuffling along the ground, or a northern tamandua (anteater) patrolling low branches.

TOP REASON TO GO

WILDLIFE

For most visitors, wildlife is the park's main attraction. You can count on seeing monkeys and lots of lizards as you walk the trails. Although they are a little harder to spot, look for anteaters, sloths, and armadillos.

BIRDS

With a varied habitat that attracts both forest and water birds, Carara is a treasure trove for birders. Even if you're not a birder, you'll get a thrill hearing the raucous crowing of beautiful scarlet macaws as they soar over the forest canopy.

THE JUNGLE

The forest here is simply magnificent. Even if you don't spot a single bird or animal, you will experience the true meaning of jungle. Carara has one of the most diverse collections of trees in the country. Breathe deeply, be alert to the symphony of forest sounds, and bask in a totally natural world.

7

MANUEL ANTONIO NATIONAL PARK

At only 7 square km (3 square mi), Manuel Antonio National Park—Costa Rica's smallest park—has an impressive collection of natural attractions: wildlife, rain forest, white-sand beaches, and rocky coves with abundant marine life.

The forest is dominated by massive gumbo-limbo trees, recognizable by their peeling bark. It's home to both two- and three-toed sloths, green and black iguanas, agoutis (similar to the guinea pig, but with longer legs), three species of monkeys, and more than 350 species of birds.

Trails are short, well maintained—and heavily traveled. Make no mistake about it: this is no undiscovered wilderness. In fact, Manuel Antonio is Costa Rica's second-most-visited attraction. There are 5 km (3 mi) of coastline, and it's one of the few parks where you can combine nature walks with swimming off idyllic beaches. There's absolutely no commercial beach development, so the beaches are picture-perfect pristine.

BEST TIME TO GO

Visit any day but Monday, when the park is closed, and any month but September or October, when it's very wet. Come early, ideally between 7 and 8 AM, because park rangers allow only 600 to 800 people at a time inside.

FUN FACT

The park's territory is too small to support all of its monkeys, so forested corridors and suspended bridges have been built to allow the monkeys to come and go.

BEST WAYS TO EXPLORE

HIKING

Don your hiking shoes and set off on the main trail from the ranger station. You'll immediately find yourself in rain forest and then emerge onto sparkling Playa Espadilla Sur. Another trail leads to Playa Manuel Antonio, which has a good coral reef for snorkeling. These two beaches lie on either side of a *tombolo*, a sandy strip that connects the mainland to rocky Punta Catedral, which used to be an island. Farther east, where fewer visitors venture, Playa Escondido is rocky and secluded. Trails from the entrance to Punta Catedral and Playa Escondido are in good shape. Trails farther east are progressively rougher going. Sturdy walking sandals are good enough for most of the trails, but light hiking boots or closed shoes will help you avoid nasty encounters with biting ants.

WILDLIFE-WATCHING

Manuel Antonio is famous for its monkeys, especially the noisy white-faced monkeys that pester tourists at the beach. A troop of rarer squirrel monkeys also lives here, one of the few places in the country where you can still find them. These tiny monkeys—*mono tití* in Spanish—are an endangered species. Catching sight of them is a real wildlife coup. The smallest of Costa Rica's four monkey species, these little guys have squirrel-like bushy tails but they only use them for balance—they can't swing from them.

Watch, too, for less active creatures, such as the more-or-less stationery sloth, especially along the park's Sloth Trail. They sleep much of the day, curled up high in the trees. Look for clumps of green and brown and watch carefully to see if they move.

You'll see many more animals and birds with a guide than without one. You can hire an official guide at the park entrance. If you're interested in seeing birds, be sure to hire a guide carrying a scope, so you can get close-up views of faraway birds.

TOP REASON TO GO

MONKEYS

Along with the ubiquitous white-faced monkeys performing for visitors on the beaches, you'll also find howler monkeys (*congos*) draped over tree branches in the forest, and more rarely, the endangered, diminutive squirrel monkey.

BEACHES

Gorgeous beaches without any commercial clutter or noise are one of the best reasons to visit Manuel Antonio. Bring your own snorkeling gear, snacks, and drinks since there's nowhere to buy them. There are very basic toilet facilities and cold-water, open-air showers.

PELICANS

Just off Playa Espadilla, you can swim out to some rocks and tread water while pelicans dive for fish, oblivious to visitors who bob quietly in the water.

VIEWS

For a fabulous coastal view, take the steep path that leads up to Punta Catedral's rocky hill, draped with thick jungle. You'll pass a lookout point from which you can gaze out at the Pacific and the park's islets.

7

ECO-LODGES IN THE CENTRAL PACIFIC

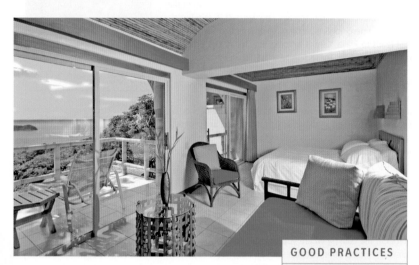

The Central Pacific is more renowned for its hedonistic Pacific beaches and resort nightlife than for wildlife or ecotourism. But there are some small pockets of original forest and habitat, and a couple of greener lodging choices.

An ecological transition zone between the dry forests of the North Pacific and the rain forests of the South Pacific, the Central Pacific is home to animals and plants of both regions. It is one of the easiest places to get a good look at the American crocodile, many of which gather near the bridge over the Tarcoles River. It's also easy to spot scarlet macaws in and around nearby Carara National Park, which protects the largest expanse of forest left in the region. Nearby Rainmaker Reserve is another good place to experience wildlife. At Manuel Antonio Park farther down the Pacific coast, you can see wildlife and enjoy an ocean swim at the same time. Over on the Nicoya Peninsula, the smaller Curú National Wildlife Reserve and Cabo Blanco Absolute Nature Reserve (its name says it all) are farther off the beaten path but worth a visit if wild is what you seek.

GOOD PRACTICES

No matter how many warning signs are posted, visitors still feel compelled to feed the animals. At Manuel Antonio National Park, the white-faced monkeys have become a nuisance down at the beach, begging for food and even stealing backpacks and ripping food packages open. They are very cute, but they can also be quite mean and deliver nasty bites to the hands that feed them.

It's not only animal behavior, but also animal health that has been compromised. The white-faced monkeys in Manuel Antonio show elevated levels of cholesterol from all the fried chips they have been fed over decades!

TOP ECO-LODGES IN THE CENTRAL PACIFIC

HOTEL SÍ COMO NO

From its meticulous recycling policy and energetic reduction of waste and energy consumption to its innovative conservation programs, Sí Como No has led the way in sustainable tourism. Perched on a hillside in the center of developed Manual Antonio, this luxury hotel is not a classic "eco-lodge." But owner Jim Damalas has worked hard to minimize the hotel's environmental impact. Guests may notice another more ephemeral but no less important policy here: good-natured hospitality. By creating a harmonious workplace, the hotel has retained well-trained, happy staff, who in turn do their best to make guests happy, too.

The hotel's most notable contribution to local ecotourism is the nearby Butterfly Garden and a 30-acre wildlife refuge. Sí Como No also promotes local culture in Quepos and its surrounding farm villages. The hotel is a member of the Green Hotels of Costa Rica and has attained the country's highest sustainability award: Five Green Leaves.

ARENAS DEL MAR BEACH AND NATURE RESORT

One of the newest hotels in the Central Pacific, this luxury hotel has an impressive eco pedigree. It is the brainchild of Teri and Glenn Jampol, owners of Finca Rosa Blanca in the Central Valley, one of the first lodges in the country to achieve five-leaf sustainability status. Their goal here was to create a five-star luxury resort that is also a five-leaf sustainable hotel. The first most obvious eco-aspect guests encounter is the reception center in a forest clearing, where you leave your car behind and ride an electric golf cart to the main open-air lobby.

You may also not be able to see your room for the trees. For 20 years, the Jampols reforested and allowed these formerly farmed slopes to regenerate before they began building, often wrapping terraces around established trees. The result is a totally natural landscape, home to lots of wildlife.

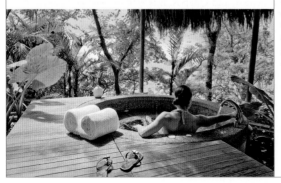

FROM OUR WRITER

"Conserving natural habitat is not only a good idea, ecologically speaking, but also makes for potentially unpredictable and memorable wildlife sightings. On a visit to Arenas del Mar Beach and Nature Resort, in Manuel Antonio, I was relaxing by one of the hotel's two swimming pools, watching white-faced monkeys scrambling among branches over the nearby restaurant roof, throwing down half-eaten fruits and the occasional partially vivisected grasshopper (headless but still squirming).

Suddenly, my peripheral vision caught sight of a coatimundi emerging from the forest at the farside of the pool. He dove into the pool, dog-paddled diagonally across, climbed out, and made a beeline into the forest. It was a surprise to me to learn that coatis could even swim. This one was obviously so at home here that he thought nothing of using the hotel pool as a cool shortcut."

—Dorothy MacKinnon

7

Updated by
Jeffrey Van
Fleet

The Central Pacific region of Costa Rica is a long swath of gorgeous land, from sublime coastline dotted with national parks to inland stretches of ranches, coffee plantations, small villages, and forested mountains. There's a reason this is a popular place to visit: the region has a lot of "Pura Vida" to offer.

GETTING HERE AND AROUND

The 30-minute flight between San José and Quepos, on Nature Air or SANSA, can save you the three-hour drive or bus trip. Flights from San José to Tambor, on Nature Air or SANSA, take 20 minutes—a fraction of the time it takes to drive to Puntarenas and ferry over, and from here it's a reasonable taxi trip to Montezuma and Malpaís.

Residents of this region rejoiced at the 2010 opening of Highway 27, connecting San José to the Pacific port of Caldera, near Puntarenas. The 77-km. (46-mi) highway, 35 years on the drawing board, varies from four to three to two lanes, but eliminates the former tortuous, winding drive through the mountains, and puts the coast just one hour from the capital. Exits lead to Atenas and farther west to Orotina. From where a two-lane highway leads southeast to Jacó and Manuel Antonio. The coastal highway, or Costanera, heads south from Orotina to Tárcoles, Jacó, Hermosa, Bejuco, and Quepos. It is well marked and paved. An asphalt road winds its way over the hill between Quepos and Manuel Antonio National Park. It takes about 1½ hours to drive to Jacó and 2½ to Quepos.

Buses are very inexpensive and easy to use. From San José to Puntarenas you'll pay about $5 and from San José to Quepos or Manuel Antonio you'll pay about $8.

Comfortable, air-conditioned alternatives to regular bus service exist. Gray Line offers hotel-to-hotel shuttle service between San José and Jacó ($27) and Manuel Antonio ($35). Interbus offers similar shuttle service between San José and Jacó ($29), Manuel Antonio ($39), Tambor ($39). Montezuma ($39), and Santa Teresa and Malpaís ($49). You can request that vans to Jacó drop you off at Carara National Park.

Vans to Manuel Antonio can drop you off at Playa Hermosa's hotels. There is also once-daily service connecting Jacó and Manuel Antonio to the major North Pacific beaches, Monteverde, and Arenal; rates range from $35 to $45.

ESSENTIALS

Bus Contacts Gray Line (☎ 2220–2126 or 2643–3231 ⊕ www.graylinecostarica.com). **Interbus** (☎ 2283–5573 ⊕ www.interbusonline.com).

THE SOUTHERN NICOYA TIP

Reached by a one-hour ferry ride from Puntarenas, the southern tip of the Nicoya Peninsula is one of Costa Rica's less-developed regions, where some of the country's most gorgeous beaches, rain forests, waterfalls, and tidal pools lie at the end of some of its worst roads. Within the region are quiet, well-preserved parks where you can explore pristine forests or travel by boat or sea kayak to idyllic islands for birdwatching or snorkeling. Other outdoor options include horseback riding, gliding through the treetops on a canopy tour, or surfing on some of the country's most consistent waves. In the laid-back beach towns of Montezuma, Santa Teresa, and Malpaís, an international cast of surfers, nature lovers, and expatriate massage therapists live out their dreams in paradise.

PUNTARENAS

82 km/50 mi west of San José.

A launching pad for ferries heading southeast to the coast of the Nicoya Peninsula, Puntarenas could easily be relegated to what you see from your car as you roll through town. Unless you're waiting to catch the ferry, there's really no reason to stay in Puntarenas. Parts of its urban beach look almost like a Dumpster. How this stretch of shoreline got a Blue Flag for cleanliness is a mystery. Nonetheless, it's a city with a past as an affluent port town and principal vacation spot for San José's wealthy, who arrived by train in the last century. Once the port was moved and roads opened to other beaches, Puntarenas's economy crashed. Recent attempts by politicians and hotel owners to create tourism-boosting diversions have been unsuccessful thus far. But if you have some downtime here, head for the Paseo de los Turistas, a beachfront promenade lined with concrete benches. From this narrow spit of sand—*punta de arenas* literally means "point of sand"—which protrudes into the Gulf of Nicoya, you get impressive sunsets and vistas of the Nicoya Peninsula.

GETTING HERE AND AROUND

The drive from San José to Puntarenas takes just over one hour. From San José, take the new Highway 27 to the port of Caldera, then head north to Puntarenas. From here it's another 15 minutes to the ferry dock. Buses run every hour between San José and Puntarenas. If you travel to Puntarenas by bus, take a taxi to the ferry dock.

Ferries shuttle passengers between Puntarenas and Paquera on the Nicoya Peninsula, where they are met by buses bound for Cóbano, Montezuma, and Santa Teresa. The passenger and car ferries run by **Naviera Tambor** (☎ 2661–2084) depart both Puntarenas and Paquera at 5, 7:30, and 10 AM, and 12:30, 3, 5:30, and 10 PM. The trip takes about 60 minutes.

Asociación de Desarrollo Integral Paquera (☎ 2641–0118) runs a small passenger-only ferry that departs from behind Puntarenas Mercado daily at 11:30 AM and 4 PM, with return trips at 7:30 AM and 2 PM. The trip takes 90 minutes.

ESSENTIALS

Bank/ATM Banco de Costa Rica (*BCR* ✉ *100 m north of municipal market*). **Banco Nacional** (✉ *200 m west of municipal market* ☎ *2661–0233*). **Mutual Alajuela ATH** (✉ *Across from Ferretería Tung Sing, near municipal market*).

Hospital Hospital Monseñor Sanabria (✉ *8 km/5 mi east of Puntarenas* ☎ *2663–0033*).

Pharmacy Farmacia Andrea (✉ *75 m east of Victoria Park* ☎ *2661–2866*).

Internet Millennium Cyber Café (✉ *Paseo de Los Turistas, east of Hotel Tioga* ☎ *2661–4759*).

Post Office Correos (✉ *Avda. 3, near Parque Victoria*).

Tourist Information La Camara de Turismo (✉ *Plaza de las Artesanías, in front of Muelle de Cruceros* ☎ *2661–2980* ⊙ *Weekdays 8–12:30 and 1:30–5:30; weekends when cruise ships are in port*). **La Oficina de Información Turística** (✉ *Near car ferry terminal* ☎ *2661–9011* ⊙ *Daily 8–5*).

WHERE TO EAT AND STAY

$–$$
ECLECTIC

✕ **Gugas.** Simple but elegant, Gugas receives high praise from locals for its fine dining alfresco. "Chicken of the Sea" (fish stuffed with shrimp and spices), pasta dishes, vegetarian options, seafood, and meat plates are all on the menu of this German-owned restaurant. ✉ *100 m north of the cruise-ship port or 100 m from the bus terminal, across from the fishing pier* ☎ 2661–4231 ▭ *AE, D, DC, MC, V.*

$$
COSTA RICAN

✕ **Restaurante La Yunta.** In a 1928 wooden building that originally served as a vacation home for San José's upper class, this old-fashioned steak house is presided over by mounted ox heads (*yunta* means "a yoked pair of oxen"). Seating is on a large veranda with a view of the ocean and of passersby strolling down the Paseo de los Turistas. The specialty is *churrasco* (tenderloin), but the diverse menu includes seafood dishes like lobster and sea bass cooked 10 different ways. The liquor list is impressively long. ✉ *West end of Paseo de los Turistas, east of Hotel Tioga* ☎ 2661–3216 ▭ *AE, D, DC, MC, V.*

$$

▦ **Hotel Las Brisas.** Close to the ferry docks, this white, three-story motel-style building wraps around its pool, where the views of the sun setting over the Nicoya Peninsula are terrific. Superior rooms have balconies with views of the ocean, and a few of them also have Jacuzzis. Standard rooms on the third floor cost a little bit more, but they are worth it for the ocean view. Pictures of Greece taken by the owner hang in the hallways and a few rooms. The restaurant menu ($$–$$$) reflects the

The Southern
Nicoya Tip

owners' nationalities with Greek-influenced seafood and meat and some Mexican dishes. **Pros:** ocean views; decent restaurant. **Cons:** expensive, considering location; plain rooms. ✉ *West end of Paseo de los Turistas* ☎ *2661–4040* ⊕ *www.lasbrisashotelcr.com* ⤻ *19 rooms* ⚒ *In-room: safe (some), Wi-Fi In-hotel: restaurant, room service, bar, pool, gym, laundry service, Wi-Fi* ▭ *AE, D, DC, MC, V* ⦿ *BP.*

$$ ☷ **Hotel Tioga.** Across the street from a tree-filled park and the cleanest part of the city's beach, Hotel Tioga opened in 1959 and is run by the original owner's son. Face-lifts over the years have modernized it a bit, but it's still rather timeworn. Glimpses of the past hang in hallways of the first to third floors with black-and-white photographs of Puntarenas in the early 1900s. Your best bets are the 11 "executive" guest rooms upstairs, with balconies overlooking the gulf, pleasantly decorated with colorful, tropical prints and heavy varnished dark-wood furniture. Rooms around the courtyard, which holds a small pool, can be noisy. The second-floor restaurant is open to cool breezes off the gulf. **Pros:** good value; across street from beach. **Cons:** timeworn; a bit cramped; busy on weekends. ✉ *Paseo de los Turistas, 8 blocks west of dock* ☎ *2661–0271* ⊕ *www.hoteltioga.com* ⤻ *52 rooms* ⚒ *In-room: safe. In-hotel: restaurant, room service, bar, pool, gym, laundry service, Wi-Fi hotspot* ▭ *AE, D, DC, MC, V* ⦿ *BP.*

CLOSE UP

A Darker Side of Tourism

Despite Costa Rica's relative affluence in Central America—in large part because of its thriving tourism industry—the fact remains that 10% of the country's population still lives in poverty. And although burgeoning tourism has benefited portions of the population, it has manifested itself in less fortunate ways in more impoverished sectors of society by giving rise to a sex-for-sale trade that some experts say rivals that in Thailand.

The case is bleak for impoverished Costa Ricans, but is worst for women and young girls. Forty percent of girls do not attend school, and 41% of births in Costa Rica are to unwed mothers. Prostitution is legal for those over 18 in Costa Rica, but pimping is not, and prostitution of minors certainly is not. There are no statistics on the number of minors involved in prostitution, but it's clear from the many Web sites promoting travel to Costa Rica as a sex-tourism paradise with plenty of young girls available that the problem is ongoing. In 1996 the National Institute for Children (PANI) targeted Limón, San José, and Puntarenas as the places where poor children are most susceptible to entering into prostitution.

In 2004 the U.S. Human Trafficking Report listed Costa Rica as one of the world's worst offenders in the trafficking of women and children into prostitution. To their credit, current administrations have taken steps to combat the problem of the underage sex trade, a refreshing change from predecessor, Miguel Angel Rodríguez, who famously denied in an interview on the ABC News program *20/20* in 2001 that such a problem existed. Steps taken thus far have included crackdowns on brothels, closer surveillance, harsher penalties for offenders, and a Web site that lists photos of missing children.

EN ROUTE If you take the ferry from Puntarenas to the southern tip of the Nicoya Peninsula, you'll arrive at a ferry dock 5 km (3 mi) north of the small community of **Paquera**. The only reason to stop here is to pick up supplies or fill up your tank on the way to the beach.

CURÚ NATIONAL WILDLIFE REFUGE

7 km/4½ mi south of Paquera, 1½ to 2 hrs southwest of Puntarenas by ferry.

Established by former farmer and logger-turned-conservationist Frederico Schutt in 1933, Refugio Nacional de Vida Silvestre Curú was named after the indigenous word for the pochote trees that flourish here. Trails lead through the forest and mangrove swamps where you see hordes of phantom crabs on the beach, howler and white-faced capuchin monkeys in the trees, and plenty of hummingbirds, kingfishers, woodpeckers, trogons, and manakins (including the coveted long-tailed manakin). The refuge is working to reintroduce spider monkeys and scarlet macaws into the wild. Some very basic accommodations, originally designed for students and researchers, are available by the beach ($8 per person); call ahead to arrange for lodging, guides, horseback riding, and early-morning bird-watching walks. ✉ *7 km/4½ mi south of Paquera on road to Cóbano, left side of road* ☎ *2641–0100* ⊕ *www.curuwildliferefuge.com* 🎟 *$8* ⏱ *Daily 7–3.*

The land that is now Curú National Wildlife Refuge was once owned by the Pacific Lumber Company, which logged the area's rosewood, cedar, and mahogany trees. Thanks to its protected status, the area is now home to more than 230 species of birds, 78 species of mammals, and 500 species of plants.

HABLA INGLÉS?

Although some Central Pacific areas like Jacó and Manuel Antonio are very touristy, don't assume everyone speaks English. Taxi and bus drivers often won't understand your directions in English. To make traveling smoother, write down the name of the place you're headed to or ask someone at your hotel's reception desk to write out directions in Spanish, which you can pass on with a smile to your driver.

GETTING HERE AND AROUND

From the town of Paquera it's a short drive to Curú National Wildlife Refuge. You can also take a bus bound for Cóbano, asking the driver to drop you off at the refugio.

OUTDOOR ACTIVITIES

Curú Tourism (✉ *Main road, across from Esso station* ☎ *2641–0004* ⊕ *www.curutourism.com*) gives horseback tours of the refuge ($16) and also has a ride to sparkling-white Quesera Beach ($16). The company also offers inexpensive kayaking trips ($26) and tours to Isla Tortuga ($23).

Paquera is the closest city to Tambor, but if you're headed to Montezuma or Malpaís, you'll pass through **Cóbano,** 12 km (7½ mi) southwest of Tambor. The town has a supermarket, gas station, and Banco Nacional with the area's only ATM.

PLAYA TAMBOR AREA

27 km/17 mi south of Paquera.

Known for massive, all-inclusive hotels and housing developments, Playa Tambor runs along the large half-moon Bahía Ballena, whose waters are more placid than those of other beaches on Nicoya's southern tip. Playa Tambor is one of the country's least attractive beaches, although there are two small but lovely ones to the south. The tiny fishing village hasn't developed as much as Montezuma or Malpaís, which makes it a better destination for those who want to get away from the crowds. It can serve as a convenient base for fishing excursions, horseback-riding trips, and day trips to Curú National Wildlife Refuge and Isla Tortuga.

GETTING HERE AND AROUND

You can fly directly to Tambor from San José on SANSA and Nature Air. Taxis meet every flight and can take you to a nearby hotel ($10 to $15), to Montezuma ($30), or to Malpaís ($40).

Isla Tortuga, just off the coast near Curú National Wildlife Refuge.

ESSENTIALS

Internet Compu-Office del Pacífico (✉ *In small strip mall on left after Costa Coral Hotel, coming from Paquera* ☎ *2683–0582* ⊘ *9–7*).

OUTDOOR ACTIVITIES

Unlike other beach towns, Tambor doesn't have tour operators on every corner or rental shops of any kind—not even for a basic bike. The receptionist at your hotel can set up tours of the area's diverse natural attractions.

FISHING In the open sea off the Gulf of Nicoya, sailfish, marlin, tuna, and wahoo are in abundance from November to March. Local fishermen in small boats are your best guides to finding fish in the gulf, including snapper, sea bass, and jacks, almost year-round. Prices for inshore fishing range from $250 for half-day trips to $500 for full-day excursions. Tambor's best deep-sea fishing boat is the 29-foot *Phoenix*, owned by **End of the Line Sportfishing** (✉ *Road from Paquera, just before Playa Tambor's entrance* ☎ *2683–0453* ✉ *endofthelinefishing@yahoo.com*). Captain Robert Ranck offers full-day excursions ($750) or half-day trips that last around five hours ($450). The boat carries six people. Lunch, drinks, and fishing gear are included.

HIKING An easy and quick excursion from Tambor is the 1-km (½-mi) hike south of town to the secluded beach of Palo de Jesús. From the town's dock, follow the road south until it becomes a shady trail that winds its way over rocks and sand around Punta Piedra Amarilla. The trees along the way resound with squawks of parakeets and the throaty utterings of male howler monkeys.

HORSEBACK RIDING — Both the Hotel Tambor Tropical and the Tango Mar have their own stables and offer a selection of horseback tours that can take you down trails through the rain forest or down to the beach to see an array of wildlife. Set off early in the morning or late in the afternoon, when it is cooler and you are more likely to see birds and animals. Tours range from $30 to $60, depending on the duration.

WHERE TO EAT

$–$$
SWISS

✕ **Beach Combers.** Between the row of private residences built along Playa Tambor is this restaurant that serves a dozen different pasta dishes, cheese fondue, and chicken *cordon bleu,* among other international plates. Surrounded by thick foliage, tables are arranged on an open-air terrace area beneath a white stucco building. The restaurant is a couple of minutes from town on foot along the beach. ✉ *In Tambor, across from the ocean on the main street.* ☎ 2683–0152 ▭ MC, V.

$$
ITALIAN
★

✕ **Trattoria Mediterránea.** This colorful restaurant in an old wooden house is often packed with local epicureans who come to savor the homemade pastas, thin-crust pizzas, and fresh seafood. The young Italian owner, Maurizio, welcomes guests with complimentary bruschetta made with fresh-baked bread, and everything is made to order, so the food can take awhile to arrive. They offer a selection of about a dozen pizzas and authentic dishes such as linguine *con gamberi* (with shrimp), *scaloppini con esparagi* (chicken medallions with asparagus) and *pescado de la trattoria* (baked fish with olive oil, lemon, garlic, and spices). ✉ *On left after main entrance to Playa Tambor* ☎ 2683–0400 ⟋ *Reservations essential* ▭ MC, V ☉ *Closed Mon. (and Tues. in low season) and end of Sept. to end of Oct. No lunch.*

WHERE TO STAY

$

🛏 **Costa Coral del Pacifico.** On the road from Paquera, a few meters from Tambor's entrance, stands this festive blue-and-orange hotel with spacious and tastefully decorated Mexican-theme rooms. Those with terraces face the pool and hot-tub area, and all have well-kept kitchenettes. The top floor holds a restaurant and bar, with karaoke on Thursday night. The beach lies about 300 meters (1,000 feet) away. This place makes for a good overnight stop on your way to or from Paquera. **Pros:** wonderful staff; clean. **Cons:** very out of the way; little English spoken. ✉ *Road to Cóbano, 200 m from Tambor's cemetery, left-hand side* ☎ 2683–0105 or 2683–0280 ⇘ *10 rooms* ⟐ *In-room: kitchen. In-hotel: restaurant, bar, pool, laundry service* ▭ MC, V ⎟◯⎟ BP.

$$$

🛏 **Tambor Tropical.** Though a stone's throw from the beach, this small hotel isn't a great place for beach lovers, because it isn't a great beach. But it is a convenient base for anyone interested in sportfishing or horseback riding, or for those who simply seek an intimate setting in which to loll by the pool. The attractive, spacious suites have floors, ceilings, walls, and even toilet seats made of varnished tropical hardwoods. The large windows running across the front give them a great view of the sea and surrounding gardens—second-floor rooms have the best. Platform beds provide sunrise views. The sea breeze and ceiling fans cool the rooms better than air-conditioning, and the lack of televisions inspires rest and relaxation. Meals are served by a lovely, blue-tile pool or in the thatch dining room during the rainy months; on Monday they have a

7

popular barbecue. **Pros:** lovely rooms; tranquil. **Cons:** not on nice beach; no a/c in rooms. ⊠ *Main street of Tambor, turn left at beach* ☏ *2683–0011, 866/890–2537 in U.S.* ⊕ *www.tambortropical.com* ⊅ *12 suites* ☖ *In-room: no a/c, no phone, kitchen, no TV, Wi-Fi. In-hotel: restaurant, room service, bar, pool, beachfront, laundry service, no kids under 16* ▭ *AE, MC, V* ⊚*| BP.*

$$$ $$$$ ⚅ **Tango Mar Resort.** This idyllic resort south of Tambor was featured on ⚉ the TV series *Temptation Island.* The 150-acre grounds include a small Fodor's Choice 9-hole golf course, exuberant gardens, tropical forests, and stunning ★ Playa Quitzales, a beach lined with coconut palms and lush foliage. There is a large rock reef just offshore, and an impressive waterfall on the beach a short hike away. Colorful villas with two to five bedrooms and ample porches overlook the beach. Smaller suites are housed in raised octagonal wooden bungalows with whirlpool tubs and ocean views. The standard rooms are in a three-story concrete building that is a stone's throw from the surf. Two restaurants serve Costa Rican and Continental cuisine. On-site activities include snorkeling, horseback riding, hiking through a private nature reserve, and golf (greens fee $20). They also offer a dozen tours to nearby attractions, as well as sportfishing excursions. **Pros:** gorgeous setting; friendly; quiet; lots of activity options. **Cons:** not the place for partyers; hard to get to. ⊹ *3 km/2 mi south of Tambor* ⊡ *Apdo. 1–1260, Escazú* ☏ *2683–0001, 800/297–4429 in North America* ⊕ *www.tangomar.com* ⊅ *18 rooms, 17 suites, 4 villas* ☖ *In-room: safe, kitche(some), refrigerator. In-hotel: 2 restaurants, bars, golf course, tennis courts, pools, spa, beachfront, water sports, bicycles, laundry service, Internet terminal, Wi-Fi hotspot* ▭ *AE, D, DC, MC, V* ⊚*| BP.*

ISLA TORTUGA

⚉ *90 mins by boat from Puntarenas.*

Soft white sand and casually leaning palms fringe this island of tropical dry forest off the southern coast of the Nicoya Peninsula. Sounds heavenly? It would be if there weren't quite so many people. Tours from Jacó, Herradura, San José, Puntarenas, and Montezuma take boatfuls of visitors to drink from coconuts and snorkel around a large rock. You'll see a good number of colorful fish, though in the company of many tourists. But it does make for an easy day trip out to sea. On the boat ride from Playa Tambor or Montezuma you might spot passing dolphins. A 40-minute hiking trail wanders past monkey ladders, strangler figs, bromeliads, orchids, and the fruit-bearing *guanabana* (soursop) and *marañón* (cashew) trees up to a lookout point with amazing vistas. Though state owned, the island is leased and inhabited by a Costa Rican family. Day trips here cost $17 to $99, depending on the duration and departure point.

GETTING HERE AND AROUND

Every tour operator in Playa Tambor and Montezuma *(⇨ below)* offers trips to Isla Tortuga, one of the area's biggest attractions, or you can kayak from the nearby Curú National Wildlife Refuge. Admission to the island is $7 (included in tour prices).

OUTDOOR ACTIVITIES

KAYAKING   **Curu Tourism** (✉ *Main road, across from Esso station* ☎ *2641–0004* ⊕ *www.curutourism.com*) arranges year-round kayak excursions to Isla Tortuga for $23, including entrance fee to the island. Snorkeling equipment is available for an additional fee. **Calypso Cruises Island Tours** (☎ *2256–2727, 800/887–1969 in North America* ⊕ *www.calypsocruises. com*) takes you to Isla Tortuga from San José, Jacó, Manuel Antonio, or anywhere in between with bus and boat transportation included ($119, kids under six $65).

MONTEZUMA

7 km/4½ mi southeast of Cóbano, 45 km/28 mi south of Paquera, 18 km/11 mi south of Tambor.

Beautifully positioned on a sandy bay, Montezuma is hemmed in by a precipitous wooded shoreline that has prevented the overdevelopment that has affected so many other beach towns. Its small, funky town center is a pastel cluster of New Age health-food cafés, trendy beachwear shops, jaunty tour kiosks, noisy open-air bars, and older *sodas* (casual eateries). Most hotels are clustered in or around the town's center, but the best ones are on the coast to the north and south, where the loudest revelers are the howler monkeys in the nearby forest. The beaches north of town, especially Playa Grande, are lovely.

Montezuma has been on the international vagabond circuit for years, attracting backpackers and alternative-lifestyle types. At night, the center of town often fills up with tattooed travelers and artisans who drink in the street and entertain each other and passersby. When college students are on break, the place can be a zoo.

North and south of the town center, however, are always quiet, and the attractions here include swaths of tropical dry forest, waterfalls, and beautiful virgin beaches that stretch across one national park and two nature preserves. One especially good walk (about 2½ hours) or horseback ride leads to a small waterfall called El Chorro that pours into the sea, where there is a small tidal pool at lower tides.

GETTING HERE AND AROUND

Most people get here via the ferry from Puntarenas to Paquera, which is an hour's drive from Montezuma. The quickest way to get here, however, is to fly to nearby Tambor (⇨ *Air Travel in Travel Smart Costa Rica*). One of the taxis waiting at the airstrip will take you to Montezuma for $35, about a 1½-hour drive. There are also one-hour water taxis ($35) that travel every morning between Herradura, near Jacó, and Montezuma, departing from Montezuma at 6:30 and 9:30 AM, and Herradura at 7:45 and 10:45 AM.

ESSENTIALS

ATM Banco Nacional (✉ *Main road, Cóbano* ☎ *2642–0210*).

Internet Surf the Banana Internet Café (✉ *Main road, next to El Sano Banano* ☎ *2642–0944*).

Post Office Librería Topsy (✉ *Next door to school*).

Jumping through one of the two waterfalls in Montezuma.

OUTDOOR ACTIVITIES

In Montezuma it seems that every other storefront is occupied by a tour operator. The town's oldest and most experienced tour company, **Cocozuma Traveller** (✉ *Main road, next to El Sano Banano* ☎ *2642–0911* 🌐 *www.cocozumacr.com*), offers horseback riding to a beachfront waterfall ($40), a full-day snorkeling trip to Isla Tortuga with lunch ($50) and various sportfishing options ($170–$750).

★ Hiking is one of the best ways to explore Montezuma's natural treasures, including beaches, lush coastline, jungles, and waterfalls. There are plenty of options around town or in nearby parks and reserves. Just over a bridge, 10 minutes south of town, a slippery path patrolled by howler monkeys leads upstream to two waterfalls and a fun swimming hole. If you value your life, don't jump or dive from the waterfalls. Guides from any tour operator in town can escort you, but save your money. This one you can do on your own. To reach the beachfront waterfall called **El Chorro,** head left from the main beach access and hike about two hours to the north of town along the sand and through the woods behind the rocky points. The trip takes you across seven adjacent beaches, on one of which there is a small store where you can buy soft drinks. Bring water and good sunblock. El Chorro can also be reached on a horseback tour with a local tour operator.

WHERE TO EAT

$$ ✕ **Cocolores.** Follow the line of multicolor lanterns to this open-air eatery. The simple wooden tables are on a patio bordered with gardens or,
ECLECTIC during the drier months, on the beach. The Italian and Argentine owners serve an eclectic menu ranging from shrimp curry to seafood pasta

to tenderloin with porcini mushrooms. They also have a good selection of pizzas. ⊠ *Behind Hotel Pargo Feliz* ☎ *2642–0348* ⊟ *No credit cards* ⊗ *Closed Mon. and Oct. No lunch June–Dec.*

$$
ECLECTIC
✕ **El Sano Banano Restaurant.** Freshly caught seafood, organic chicken, sushi, Thai dishes, and a half-dozen pasta dishes are included on the menu at Montezuma's first natural-food restaurant. Named after the dried bananas sold by the owners, the eatery serves mostly vegetarian fare, including some excellent salads. On the terrace, which is a popular people-watching spot, you can enjoy a delicious Mocha Chiller, made with frozen yogurt, or a wide variety of coffee drinks. A battalion of ceiling fans keeps the air moving in the spacious, adobe-style dining room. A free movie is shown nightly at 7:30 in the dining room, which is a popular diversion, but don't expect a romantic dinner during this time. Rooms to rent on the second floor are a comfortable option if the other hotels are full. ⊠ *Main road* ☎ *2642–0944* ⊕ *www. elbanano.com* ⊟ *AE, MC, V.*

$$$
ITALIAN
Fodor'sChoice
★
✕ **Playa de los Artistas.** This open-air restaurant with driftwood tables scattered along the beach specializes in modern Mediterranean-style seafood, meat dishes, and pizza. Flickering lanterns combine with crashing surf to create a romantic and relaxed dinner experience. Portions are plentiful and dramatically presented on huge platters. The eclectic menu changes daily, and on weekends they fire up a barbecue. An outdoor, coffee-wood oven gives a tropical aroma to pizza, fish, and pork. Meals are accompanied with freshly baked, savory focaccia. ⊠ *275 m south of town, near Los Mangos Hotel* ☎ *2642–0920* ⊟ *No credit cards* ⊗ *Closed Sun., hours may vary May–Nov.*

$$$
ECLECTIC
★
✕ **Ylang-Ylang Restaurant.** One of Montezuma's best restaurants, Ylang-Ylang is nestled between the beach and the jungle. The lunch menu—a selection of sushi, salads, and sandwiches—makes it well worth the 10-minute walk down the beach. The inventive dinner menu ranges from a Thai-style teriyaki tuna steak and stir-fries to penne in a seafood sauce. There are also various vegan and raw live dishes. Whatever you choose, you'll want to save room for one of the scrumptious desserts, such as the tiramisu espresso crepe. At night, they provide free transportation from the Sano Banano, in town. ⊠ *On beach, ½ km/¼ mi north of town, at Ylang-Ylang Beach Resort* ☎ *2642–0636* ⊟ *AE, D, DC, MC, V.*

WHERE TO STAY

$–$$
🏠 **Hotel Amor de Mar.** About ½ km (¼ mi) south of town, this ruggedly handsome hotel sits across from the entrance to Montezuma's famous waterfall. A grassy lawn stretches to the rocky seashore, where you can cool off in a natural tidal pool at low tide or lounge about in one of the palm-shaded hammocks. The place has a peaceful and intimate atmosphere in which to savor the homemade breakfasts served each morning. Wood-panel rooms are rustic but comfortable; second-floor rooms have more windows. Two rooms share a bathroom and are considerably cheaper. The two-story oceanfront houses next door have four bedrooms, making them great for larger groups. **Pros:** beautiful property; friendly. **Cons:** most of the rooms are small; can be a little worn. ⊠ *300 m south of town, past bridge* ☎ *2642–0262* ⊕ *www.amordemar.*

7

com ⚓ *11 rooms, 9 with bath; 2 houses* ⚓ *In-room: no a/c (some), no phone, safe, no TV. In-hotel: restaurant* ▭ *MC, V* ⦿ *EP.*

$$ 🏨 **Hotel El Jardín.** Spread across a hill several blocks from the beach, this hotel has rooms with ocean, pool, and garden views. True to its name, the rooms are scattered around a lush garden populated with bright red ginger flowers and faux stone indigenous sculptures. Teak paneling and furniture, stained-glass pictorial panels, and terraces with hammocks give this hotel style as well as comfort. If you don't mind the climb, ask for an upper room and you'll get a better view. There's no formal breakfast, but fresh fruit and coffee are laid out in the reception area each morning. **Pros:** central location; good value. **Cons:** noise from bars in town; pricey. ✉ *West end of main road* ☎ *2642–0074* ⊕ *www. hoteleljardin.com* ⚓ *15 rooms, 2 villas* ⚓ *In-room: no phone, refrigerator, no TV, Wi-Fi. In-hotel: pools* ▭ *AE, D, DC, MC, V* ⦿ *EP.*

¢–$$ 🏨 **Hotel Los Mangos.** Within sight and sound of the sea, these affordable ★ octagonal wood bungalows are spread across a shady mango grove. Hammocks and rocking chairs furnish the wraparound decks on each. Less attractive, though cheaper, are the rooms in a two-story, orange-and-blue building by the road. Here you'll find verandas and rocking chairs facing the sea. Four of the second-floor rooms share baths, for half the price. The secluded, scenic pool with a waterfall overlooks the ocean. Memorable yoga classes are given in an open-air pavilion. **Pros:** great pool; lots of wildlife. **Cons:** noisy; needs updating. ✉ *Near entrance to waterfall trail, ½ km/¼ mi south of town* ☎ *2642–0384* ⊕ *www.hotellosmangos.com* ⚓ *10 rooms, 6 with bath; 9 bungalows* ⚓ *In-room: no a/c, no phone, safe (some), refrigerator (some), no TV. In-hotel: pool* ▭ *AE, D, DC, MC, V* ⦿ *EP.*

$$ 🏨 **Nature Lodge Finca los Caballos.** A dirt road leads to this cozy equestrian paradise high on a hill, just a short ride from Montezuma center. Horses graze on the 14-acre estate when they aren't taking guests to nearby waterfalls, mountains, or beaches. The open-air restaurant and pool terrace have bird's-eye views of the ocean and the surrounding valley. The small, simple rooms have pastel walls decorated with stencils of lizards and frogs; all have hammocks in front. Only four have forest views, so ask for one of these when you reserve. Massages and other spa services are available to guests. **Pros:** clean rooms; relaxing ambience. **Cons:** not a great location; no screens on the windows. ⊹ *3 km/2 mi north of Montezuma on main road* ☎ *2642–0124* ⊕ *www.naturelodge.net* ⚓ *12 rooms* ⚓ *In-room: no a/c, no phone, safe, refrigerator, no TV. In-hotel: restaurant, bar, pool, laundry service, Wi-Fi hotspot, no-smoking rooms* ▭ *MC, V* ☯ *Closed Oct.* ⦿ *BP*

$$$–$$$$ 🏨 **Ylang-Ylang Beach Resort.** Secluded and quiet, this tropical resort with
Fodor's Choice a holistic slant is a 10-minute beach walk from town. Nestled between
★ the sea and a lush forest, the geodesic-dome bungalows are snug but charming, with outdoor showers and terraces. Some have sea views and cozy loft sleeping areas. Facing the beach, a three-story building has two-story suites with balconies and simple but colorful standard rooms below. Rustic "jungalows"—large tents with beds and decks—offer a back-to-nature experience, but they share bathrooms. The grounds are covered with trees that hold iguanas, howler monkeys, tricolor

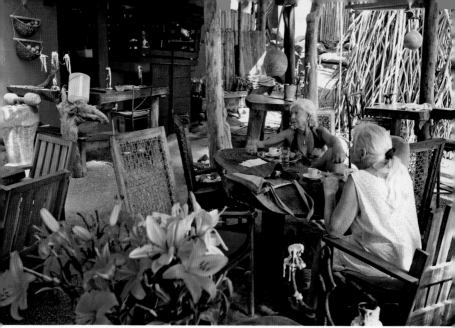

Enjoying a snack at Playa De Los Artistas restaurant in Montezuma.

squirrels, and an array of birds. Adding to the romance is a jungle-fringed pool with a waterfall. Yoga classes and spa services are offered, and a restaurant with tables under the stars serves some of the tastiest fusion dishes in Montezuma. **Pros:** gorgeous, natural setting; great restaurant; friendly. **Cons:** jungalows offer limited privacy; some rooms are small. ⊠ *700 m north of school in Montezuma* ⊕ *El Sano Banano, Montezuma* ☎ *2642–0636, 888/795–8494 in North America* ⊕ *www. elbanano.com* ↪ *3 rooms, 3 suites, 8 beachfront bungalows, 6 tents* ♿ *In-room: no a/c (some), no phone, safe, refrigerator (some), no TV. In-hotel: restaurant, bar, pool, beachfront, spa, water sports, laundry service, Internet terminal, Wi-Fi* ▭ *AE, MC, V* ❙⊘❙ *MAP.*

NIGHTLIFE

Though options are extremely limited, Montezuma's nightlife scene is growing. Locals and foreigners mix at pool tables or late-night clubs, a refreshing change from larger beach towns where the clientele tends to be more segregated. Street-side artisans selling their creations often animate the area with drumming and dancing that draws passersby to stop and shake their hips, too.

Chico's Bar (⊠ *Next to Hotel Moctezuma*) blasts music from its dark, uninviting entrance, but farther back is a brighter, spacious deck with pool tables and dancing. Directly behind is an open-air beach bar with a more laid-back atmosphere. The bar at **Restaurante Moctezuma** (⊠ *Under Hotel Moctezuma* ☎ *2643–0657*) serves the cheapest beers in town. At night, tables in the sand are lighted by candles and moonlight.

SHOPPING

Beachwear, banana paper, wooden crafts, and indigenous pottery are some of what you find in colorful shops in the town's center. During the dry season, traveling artisans from around the world unfold their street-side tables just before the sun begins to set; candles light up the handmade leather-and-seed jewelry, dream catchers, and knit tops. For some intellectual stimulation at the beach, head to **Librería Topsy** (⊠ *Next door to school* ☎ *2642–0576*), where you can buy, exchange, or rent a book—one whole room is devoted to a lending library. Some foreign newspapers are available.

WORD OF MOUTH

"Our drive to Manuel Antonio was great. We ended up driving on the new highway, which was wonderful—nice smooth road (a bit longer mileage-wise but worth it to us). Manuel Antonio is a wonderful park in which to view wildlife, especially with a guide. At the entrance we were delighted to see our first sloth hanging in plain view. A great way to start our tour!"

—gpkbrand

CABO BLANCO ABSOLUTE NATURE PRESERVE

10 km/6 mi southwest of Montezuma, about 11 km/7 mi south of Malpaís.

Conquistadores named this area Cabo Blanco on account of its white earth and cliffs, but it was a more benevolent pair of foreigners—Nicolas Wessberg and his wife, Karen, arriving here from Sweden in the 1950s—who made it a preserve (Reserva Natural Absoluta Cabo Blanco, in Spanish). Appalled by the first clear-cut in the Cabo Blanco area in 1960, the pioneering couple launched an international appeal to save the forest. In time their efforts led not only to the creation of the 12-square-km (4½-square-mi) reserve but also to the founding of Costa Rica's national park service, the National Conservation Areas System (SINAC). Wessberg was murdered on the Osa Peninsula in 1975 while researching the area's potential as a national park. A reserve just outside Montezuma was named in his honor. A reserve has also been created to honor his wife, who dedicated her life to conservation after her husband's death.

Informative natural-history captions dot the trails in the moist evergreen forest of Cabo Blanco. Look for the sapodilla trees, which produce a white latex used to make gum; you can often see V-shaped scars where the trees have been cut to allow the latex to run into containers placed at the base. Wessberg catalogued a full array of animals here: porcupine, hog-nosed skunk, spotted skunk, gray fox, anteater, cougar, and jaguar. Resident birds include brown pelicans, white-throated magpies, toucans, cattle egrets, green herons, parrots, and blue-crowned motmots. A fairly strenuous 4-km (2½-mi) hike, which takes about two hours in each direction, follows a trail from the reserve entrance to **Playa Cabo Blanco**. The beach is magnificent, with hundreds of pelicans flying in formation and paddling in the calm waters offshore—you can wade right in and join them. Off the tip of the cape is the 7,511-square-foot

Isla Cabo Blanco, with pelicans, frigate birds, brown boobies, and an abandoned lighthouse. As a strict reserve, Cabo Blanco has restrooms and a visitor center but no other tourist facilities. Rangers and volunteers act as guides. ⊠ *10 km/6 mi southwest of Montezuma via Cabuya* ☎ *2642–0093* ☒ *$8* ⊘ *Wed.–Sun. 8–4.*

GETTING HERE AND AROUND

Roads to the reserve are usually passable only in the dry season, unless you have a 4WD. From Montezuma or Malpaís, take the road to Cabuya. Taxis can take you to or from Montezuma, but buses toward the park also leave from Montezuma daily at 8 and 9:50 AM and 2 PM, returning at 9 AM, and 1 and 4 PM.

MALPAÍS AND SANTA TERESA

12 km/7½ mi southwest of Cóbano, 52 km/33 mi south of Paquera.

This remote fishing area was once frequented only by die-hard surfers in search of some of the country's largest waves and by naturalists en route to the nearby Cabo Blanco Absolute Nature Preserve. The town and its miles of beach are accessible only down a steep and bumpy dirt road. But now hotels, restaurants, and shopping centers are springing up at an alarming rate, especially toward the Santa Teresa side. Still, the abundant forest, lovely beaches, and consistent surf make this a great place to spend some time.

Coming from Montezuma, the road hits an intersection, known locally as El Cruce, marked by hotel signs and a strip mall on the right. To the left is the rutted route to tranquil Malpaís, and to the right is the road to Santa Teresa, with plenty of hotels, restaurants, and shops. Playa Carmen, straight ahead, is the area's best place for surfing, though swimmers will want to be careful of rip currents there. Malpaís and Santa Teresa are so close that locals disagree on where one begins and the other ends. You could travel up the road parallel to the ocean that connects them and not realize you've moved from one town to the other.

GETTING HERE AND AROUND

From Paquera it's a 90-minute drive to Malpaís via Cóbano. After Cóbano, the road quickly deteriorates. It can become quite muddy in the rainy season, so you'll want a 4WD vehicle. There are no direct buses between Paquera and Malpaís; to get here you have to change buses in Cóbano. Taxis waiting at Tambor's airstrip will take up to four people to Malpaís for $40. The trip between Jacó and Malpaís takes about two hours, thanks to the daily boat service from Montezuma. **Tropical Tours** (⊠ *North of El Cruce* ☎ *2640–1900*) can set you up with a shuttle to San José ($35), or a taxi and boat from Malpaís and to Jacó ($55).

ESSENTIALS

ATM Banco Nacional (⊠ *Centro Comercial Playa Carmen* ☎ *2640–0598*).

Internet Tropical Tours (⊠ *50 m north of El Cruce* ☎ *2640–1900*) has two Internet cafés in Santa Teresa.

Pharmacy Farmacia Amiga (⊠ *Centro Comercial Playa Carmen* ☎ *2640–0463*).

OUTDOOR ACTIVITIES

Canopy del Pacífico (⊠ *In front of fishermen's village* ☎ *2640–0360* ⊕ *www.canopydelpacifico.com*) is the only canopy tour in the area ($35 for a two-hour, nine-platform tour). You can walk, glide, or rappel through 64 acres of forest. **Tropical Tours** (⊠ *North of El Cruce* ☎ *2640–1900*) can set you up with a horseback-riding jaunt, or day trip to Isla Tortuga.

SURFING   From November to May, the Malpaís area has some of Costa Rica's most consistent surf, as well as clear skies and winds that create idyllic conditions. **Playa Carmen** is the area's most consistent surf spot for all levels, and has dozens of beach breaks scattered along its shores. The sea grows rough and dirty during the May to December rainy season, with frequent swells that make it impossible to get out. **Playa Santa Teresa** is a better option when the waves at Playa Carmen are too gnarly. In Malpaís, at **Mar Azul,** more advanced surfers can try the break over a rock platform. **Corduroy to the Horizon** (⊠ *20 m east of Playa Carmen* ☎ *2640–0173*), Malpaís's original surf shop, rents surfboards ($10 per day); arranges lessons ($30 per hour); and sells wax, boards, and beachwear.

WHERE TO EAT

$$$ ✕ **Nectar.** Resort Florblanca's alfresco restaurant by the pool has some
SEAFOOD   tables that provide calming sea views through the tropical foliage. Fresh
★   seafood is the specialty here, with inventive daily specials that focus on the day's catch. Asian and Mediterranean influences shine through in dishes ranging from spicy prawn fettuccine, to succulent pork ribs, to seared tuna with sweet Thai rice and braised bok choy. There's always a pizza of the day and a small sushi menu. ⊠ *Resort Florblanca* ✛ *2 km/ 1 mi north of soccer field* ☎ *2640–0232* ⌂ *Reservations essential* ▭ *AE, D, DC, MC, V.*

$ ✕ **Pizzeria Playa Carmen.** This restaurant's location, under the trees on
PIZZA   the area's most popular beach, makes it the perfect choice for lunch. It's extremely casual, so you don't even have to put on a shirt. Oven-baked pizza is the house specialty, and these thin-crust pies are big enough for two people, especially if you start with one of the oversize salads. The kitchen also serves shrimp scampi, various pastas, and other dishes. ⊠ *Playa Carmen, east of El Cruce* ☎ *2640–0110* ▭ *MC, V* ⊘ *Closed Tues. and Sept.–Nov.*

$$$ ✕ **Soma.** This small, tranquil restaurant within the Milarepa hotel
SEAFOOD   serves delicious and creative Asian-inspired plates based on fresh local
★   ingredients. The menu changes each night, but usually has fresh tuna, mahimahi, or other seafood, plus a chicken or beef dish. Any of the

dishes can be prepared without meat, so vegetarians can choose from a wide selection. Tables are arranged under an open-air poolside deck a short walk from the beach. ⊠ *Milarepa* ✛ *2 km/1 mi north of soccer field* ☎ *2640–0023 or 2640–0663* ✍ *Reservations essential* ⊟ *MC, V* ⊗ *Closed Oct.*

WHERE TO STAY

$$ 🖳 **Blue Jay Eco-Lodge.** Perched along a forested mountainside, these wooden bungalows feel like tree houses; you'll hear howler monkeys and an array of birdsong from your bed. Steep trails lead to the rustic aeries built on stilts, with screens for walls on three sides, comfortable beds, and balconies hung with hammocks. Once you drag your luggage up the hill, you will be rewarded with great views from the upper rooms. Blankets buffer you against the sometimes cool, breezy nights. Blue Jay's three lower cabins are larger, but lack the arboreal charm of the rest. Breakfast is in the open-air restaurant, next to an attractive, blue-tile pool. Head to the nearby beach, or climb the mountain trail behind the cabins, to look for birds. **Pros:** natural setting; good value. **Cons:** not well maintained; steep terrain. ⊠ *From El Cruce, 800 m south toward Malpaís* ☎ *2640–0089* ⊕ *www.bluejaylodgecostarica. com* ⤳ *10 cabins* ᗱ *In-room: no a/c, no phone, safe, no TV. In-hotel: restaurant, pool, laundry service, no-smoking rooms, some pets OK* ⊟ *AE, D, DC, MC, V* ⍉*BP.*

$$$$ 🖳 **Florblanca.** Named for the white flowers of the frangipani trees grow-
Fodor'sChoice ing between the restaurant and the beach, this collection of luxurious
★ villas is scattered through the forest mere steps from the surf. It's a tasteful, friendly resort dedicated to relaxation and rejuvenation. The wonderfully decorated and spacious villas have an Asian feel, especially in the outdoor Balinese-inspired bathrooms with rain showers and sunken tubs. Airy living rooms open onto porches with large hammocks. Most villas have one air-conditioned bedroom with a king-size bed; two-bedroom villas have a second room with twin beds. Only three villas have sea views through the trees, so request one of these when you book. Free yoga classes are given in a studio that faces the ocean, and the massage therapist at the beachfront spa will happily work out your kinks. The only TV is in a comfortable lounge. **Pros:** gorgeous villas and grounds; friendly; great yoga classes. **Cons:** very expensive; on rocky stretch of beach; insects sometimes a problem. ✛ *2 km/ 1 mi north of soccer field* ⍋ *Apdo. 131–5361, Cóbano* ☎ *2640–0232* ⊕ *www.florblanca.com* ⤳ *10 villas* ᗱ *In-room: safe, refrigerator, no TV, Wi-Fi. In-hotel: restaurant, room service, bar, pools, gym, spa, beachfront, water sports, bicycles, laundry service, Internet terminal, no kids under 14* ⊟ *AE, D, DC, MC, V* ⍉*EP.*

$$ 🖳 **Luz de Vida.** This laid-back, beachfront lodge owned by a group of
⟳ Israeli surfers is a good value. Simple bungalows, spread around forested grounds, have sloping wooden ceilings, lofts, a couch, or extra beds downstairs (kids under 10 stay free). Smaller standard rooms in two-story concrete buildings close to the road are not nearly as good a deal. The pool has a waterfall and is surrounded by trees, gardens, and thatch parasols. The open-air restaurant, nearby, has an ocean view and serves everything from falafel to filet mignon. Good waves break

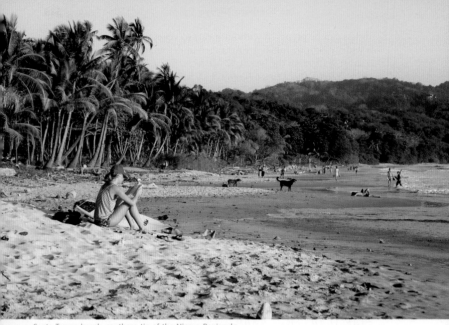
Santa Teresa beach, southern tip of the Nicoya Peninsula.

right in front of the hotel, so when the staff offers to arrange surfboard rentals and lessons, be sure to take them up on it. **Pros:** beachfront; nice grounds; friendly. **Cons:** service inconsistent; standard rooms too close to road. ⊠ *From El Cruce, 800 m south toward Malpaís* ☎ *2640–0568* ⊕ *www.luzdevida-resort.com* ⤴ *6 bungalows, 8 rooms* ⚄ *In-room: safe, refrigerator. In-hotel: restaurant, bar, pool, beachfront, water sports, laundry service, Wi-Fi* ☰ *MC, V* �ⓘ⎮ *EP.*

$$$
★

Ⅲ **Milarepa.** Named after a Tibetan Buddhist saint who gained enlightenment in just one lifetime, Milarepa is a perfect place for peaceful renewal, whether romantic or spiritual. The four bamboo bungalows are spaced apart to ensure privacy and are furnished in ascetic but exquisite taste, with carved Indonesian wooden beds draped with mosquito netting, and bamboo armoires. Bathrooms are open to the sky, with alcoves for Buddhist deities. Each bungalow has a veranda looking out onto the beach, shaded by a grove of palms and lined with volcanic rocks. Beachfront bungalows cost a bit more than those with ocean views set farther back. A large pool lies next to Soma (⇨ *above, the hotel's excellent restaurant [$$$]).* **Pros:** secluded; small; beachfront; great restaurant. **Cons:** loosely managed; insects can be a problem; on rocky section of beach. ✛ *2 km/1 mi north of school, beside Resort Florblanca* ☎ *2640–0023* ⊕ *www.milarepahotel.com* ⤴ *4 cottages* ⚄ *In-room: no a/c, no phone, safe, no TV. In-hotel: restaurant, bar, pool, beachfront, water sports, laundry service, Wi-Fi hotspot, no-smoking rooms* ☰ *MC, V* �ⓘ⎮ *BP.*

$
☼
★

Ⅲ **Ritmo Tropical.** Tranquil, comfortable, and nicely priced, this small hotel a short walk from the beach is the best deal in Malpaís. Red-tile-roof bungalows here are simple yet tasteful, with high wooden ceilings, large bathrooms, lots of windows, and front terraces. Some cabins, arranged in a semicircle around the large pool and gardens, have views of the sea and the jungle. A couple of rooms in back are even cheaper than the others. The reasonably priced Italian restaurant ($) in front of the property serves two-dozen types of pizza, fresh fish with a selection of sauces, and tasty pasta dishes such as farfalle with fish and shrimp curry sauce.

> ### BASE CAMP
>
> Visitors to Costa Rica prefer using Atenas as their first- and last-night base camp instead of San José, because Atenas is smaller, friendlier, and more tranquil. The international airport is geographically closer to Atenas, but the hilly roads make the ride slightly longer than on San José's express highway.

Pros: very clean rooms; economical. **Cons:** variety in room type; a walk to town. ⊠ *100 m south of El Cruce on road toward Malpaís* ☎ *2640–0174* ⊕ *www.hotelritmotropical.net* ⤳ *7 bungalows* ⚑ *In-room: no a/c, no phone, safe, no TV, Wi-Fi. In-hotel: restaurant, bar, pool, laundry service* ▤ *MC, V* ¶◯¶ *EP.*

INLAND

Beaches may be this region's biggest draw, but the countryside holds some splendid scenery, from the steep coffee farms around Atenas to the tropical forests of the lowlands. In the wilderness of Carara National Park and surroundings, you might encounter white-faced capuchin monkeys in the trees or crocodiles lounging on a riverbank. The region is extremely biologically diverse, making it an excellent destination for bird-watchers and other wildlife enthusiasts.

ATENAS

42 km/26 mi west of San José.

Known for its excellent climate, Atenas is a pleasant, friendly town surrounded by a hilly countryside of coffee and cane fields, cattle ranches, and patches of forest. The small city is off the tourist circuit, which means that here, unlike other highly popular destinations, you'll walk alongside more locals than foreigners and get a more authentic idea of the country. Gazing at the tree-covered peaks and exploring the coffee farms are the main activities in this traditional town. Atenas's center has a concrete church, some well-kept wooden and adobe houses, and a park dominated by royal palms.

GETTING HERE

Atenas lies about one hour west on the route between San José and beaches such as Herradura, Jacó, and Manuel Antonio. Take the Pan-American Highway past the airport and turn right at the overpass with the signs for beach resorts and Zoo Ave. Turn left from the exit and stay on the main road. Buses to Atenas leave frequently from the Coca-Cola terminal in San José and arrive near the center of town.

ESSENTIALS

Bank/ATM Banco de Costa Rica (✉ *200 m west of Catholic church* ☎ *2446–6034*). **Banco Nacional** (✉ *Northern corner of central park* ☎ *2446–5157*).

Hospital Clínica Pública (✉ *150 m south of the fire station* ☎ *2446–5522*).

Pharmacy Farmacia Don Juan (✉ *West corner of Catholic church* ☎ *2446–5055*).

Internet C@fé K-puchinos (✉ *Northwest corner of Parque Central* ☎ *2289–0082*).

Post Office Correos (✉ *50 m southeast of northeast corner of market*).

WHERE TO EAT AND STAY

$

LATIN AMERICAN

✕ **Mirador del Cafétal.** An obligatory stop even if it's just for a cup of coffee, this open-air restaurant next to the road between Atenas and Jacó is a great spot to enjoy the view of steep hillsides covered with coffee trees. The best view is from the long countertops with stools that line the edge of the building, but the wooden tables and chairs might be more comfortable. The food is a mix of Costa Rican and Mexican cuisine, including burritos, chicken with rice, and *sopa azteca* (a tomato-base soup). The restaurant's own brand of coffee is sold by the pound. ✉ *Road to Jacó* ✛ *6 km/3 mi west of Atenas* ☎ *2446–7361* ▭ *AE, MC, V.*

$$

▦ **El Cafetal Inn.** This charming bed-and-breakfast feels and looks more like a home than a hotel, since they go out of their way to help with your travel plans. On a hilltop coffee farm, the two-story concrete lodge has comfortable accommodations with fabulous vistas. Most rooms have balconies, and those on the corners of the second floor have curved windows offering panoramic views. They also have a bungalow near the pool, and two small houses for rent nearby. Breakfast, which includes homegrown coffee roasted on the premises, is served on the back garden patio. The fact that it lies just 25 minutes from the airport makes this a tranquil place to begin or end a Costa Rica trip. **Pros:** superb food; lovely grounds. **Cons:** not all rooms have views. ✛ *8 km/5 mi north of Atenas; heading west from San José on highway to Puntarenas, turn left (south) just before bridge 5 km/3 mi west of Grecia, Santa Eulalia de Atenas* ☎ *2446–5785* ⊕ *www.cafetal.com* ✍ *14 rooms, 1 bungalow, 2 houses* ♿ *In-room: no a/c, no phone, no TV. In-hotel: restaurant, bar, pool, laundry service, no-smoking rooms* ▭ *AE, MC, V* ⊙ *BP.*

CARARA NATIONAL PARK

43 km/25 mi southwest of Atenas, 85 km/51 mi southwest of San José.

On the east side of the road between Puntarenas and Playa Jacó, Parque Nacional Carara protects one of the last remnants of an ecological transition zone between Costa Rica's drier northwest and the more humid southwest. It consequently holds a tremendous collection of plants and animals. Much of the 47-square-km (18-square-mi) park is covered with primary forest on steep slopes, where the massive trees are laden with vines and epiphytes. The sparse undergrowth makes wildlife easier to see here than in many other parks, but nothing is guaranteed. If you're lucky, you may glimpse armadillos, basilisk lizards, coatis, and any of several monkey species, as well as birds such as blue-crowned motmots, chestnut-mandibled toucans, and trogons.

The first trail on the left shortly after the bridge that spans the Río Tárcoles (a good place to spot crocodiles) leads to a horseshoe-shaped *laguna meandrica* (oxbow lake). The small lagoon covered with water hyacinths is home to turtles, crocodiles, and waterfowl such as the northern jacana, roseate spoonbill, and boat-billed heron. It is a two- to four-hour hike from the trailhead to the lagoon and back, depending on how much bird-watching you do. ■TIP→ **Cars parked at the trailhead have been broken into. If you don't see a ranger on duty at the sendero laguna meandrica trailhead, avoid leaving anything of value in your vehicle. You may be able to leave your belongings at the main ranger station (several miles south of the trailhead), where you can also buy drinks and souvenirs and use the restroom. Otherwise, visit the park as a day trip from a nearby hotel.**

Two trails lead into the forest from the parking lot. The shortest one can be done in 15 minutes, whereas the longer one that connects with the Quebrada Bonita loop takes one to three hours to hike. The latter can be quite muddy during the rainy months, when you may want rubber boots. Carara's proximity to San José and Jacó means that tour buses arrive regularly in high season, scaring some animals deeper into the forest. Come very early or late in the day to avoid crowds. Bird-watchers can call the day before to arrange admission before the park opens. Camping is not permitted.

Local travel agencies and tour operators arrange transport to and guides through the park (⇨ *Park Tours, below*). The park itself has guides, but you must arrange in advance. ⊠ *East of Costanera just south of bridge over Rio Tárcoles* ☎ *8383–9953* ⊒ *$10* ☉ *Daily 7–4.*

GETTING HERE

Take the new Highway 27 west of San José beyond Orotina and follow the signs to Jacó and Quepos. The reserve is on the left after you cross Río Tárcoles. From San José, hop on a bus to Jacó, Quepos, or Manuel Antonio and ask to be dropped off near the park entrance, about a two-hour drive.

PARK TOURS

Johnny Marin at **Jaguar Riders** (☎ *2643–0180 or 8393–6626*), in Jacó, has been guiding people through the forests of Carara for years. **Costa Rica Expeditions** (☎ *2222–0333* ⊕ *www.costaricaexpeditions.com*), the country's original ecotour operator, offers day trips to Carara from San José, and includes the park in several of its multiday trips. **Horizontes** (☎ *2222–2022* ⊕ *www.horizontes.com*) , the country's premier nature-tour operator, can arrange visits to Carara as a day trip from San José or as part of a longer tour.

THE COAST

Along a short stretch of Costa Rica's Pacific coast from Tárcoles to Manuel Antonio are patches of undeveloped jungle, the popular Manuel Antonio National Park, and some of the country's most accessible beaches. The proximity of these strands to San José leads Costa Ricans and foreigners alike to pop down for quick beach vacations. Surfers have good reason to head for the consistent waves of Playas Jacó and Hermosa, and anglers and golfers should consider Playa Herradura for its golf courses and ocean access. You might find Herradura and Jacó overrated and overdeveloped. Manuel Antonio could be accused of the latter, but nobody can deny its spectacular natural beauty.

TÁRCOLES

90 km/54 mi southwest of San José.

Crocodile boat tours on the Río Tárcoles are this small town's claim to fame. In fact, you don't actually have to drive to Tárcoles to do the tour, because operators can pick you up in Herradura or Jacó. The muddy river has gained a reputation as the country's dirtiest, thanks to San José's inadequate sewage system, but it amazingly remains an impressive refuge for wildlife. A huge diversity of birds results from a combination of transitional forest and the river, which houses crocodiles, herons, storks, spoonbills, and other waterbirds. This is also one of the only areas in the country where you can see scarlet macaws, which you may spot on a boat tour or while hiking in a private reserve nearby.

GETTING HERE

By car, head West from San José on the new Highway 27 to Orotina and follow the signs to Herradura, Jacó, and Quepos. After crossing the bridge over the Rio Tárcoles, look for the entrance to the town of Tárcoles on the right. On the left is the dirt road that leads to the Hotel Villa Lapas and the waterfall reserve. Any bus traveling to Jacó can drop you off at the entrance to Tárcoles. Let the driver know in advance.

OUTDOOR ACTIVITIES

⟳ On the two-hour riverboat tours through the mangrove forest and Tarcoles River you might see massive crocodiles, Jesus lizards, iguanas, and some of roughly 50 colorful bird species, including the roseate spoonbill and boat-billed heron. Tours reach the river's mouth, providing nice sea views, especially at sunset. ■TIP➔ Around noon is the best time to spot crocs sunbathing; bird enthusiasts prefer afternoon rides to catch scarlet macaws. During the rainy season (May to November), the river may grow too rough for boats in the afternoon.

Two brothers run **Crocodile Man Tour** (✉ *Main road into Tárcoles* ☎ *2637–0771* ⊕ *www.crocodilemantour.com*). The small scars on their hands are the result of the tour's most original (and optional) attraction: feeding fish to the crocs. The boats are small enough to slide up alongside the mangroves for a closer look. Transportation is provided from nearby beaches, but not from San José.

Inland and
Central Pacific Coast

Pacific Ocean

| 0 | 5 mi |
| 0 | 5 km |

CANOPY TOUR **Hotel Villa Lapas** (⊠ *Off Costanera, after bridge over Río Tárcoles* ☎ *2637–0232, 2203-3553* in San José ⊕ *www.villalapas.com*) manages a suspension-bridge nature walk and a zip-line tour. **Sky Way** consists of five suspension bridges spread out over a 2½-km (1½-mi) old-growth-forest nature trail. You can do the trail with a guide ($20). A shuttle picks you up at the Hotel Villa Lapas. **Villa Lapas Canopy** has zip lines through primary forest ($30).

WHERE TO EAT AND STAY

¢–$ ✕ **Soda los Mangos.** This simple place serves casados and fresh fried fish
COSTA RICAN or fish fillets in garlic sauce. Most tables are outdoors except for one beneath the television indoors. ⊠ *Near entrance to Tárcoles* ☎ *2637–0672* ⊟ *No credit cards.*

$$ ✕ **Steve n' Lisa's.** A convenient location, an ocean view, and good food
ECLECTIC make this roadside restaurant overlooking Playa La Pita, just south of the entrance to Tárcoles, a popular pit stop for those traveling between San José and the Central Pacific beaches. Sit on the covered porch or at one of the concrete tables on the adjacent patio, and enjoy the view of the Gulf of Nicoya through the palm fronds. The menu includes breakfast options and a wide selection of lunch and dinner entrées that

CLOSE UP

Diving the Deep at Coco Island

Rated one of the top diving destinations in the world, Isla del Coco is uninhabited and remote, and its waters are teeming with marine life. It's no place for beginners, but serious divers enjoy 30-meter (100-foot) visibility and the underwater equivalent of a big-game park: scalloped hammerheads, white-tipped reef sharks, Galápagos sharks, bottlenose dolphins, billfish, and manta rays mix with huge schools of brilliantly colored fish.

Encompassing about 22½ square km (14 square mi), Isla del Coco is the largest uninhabited island on earth. Its isolation has led to the evolution of dozens of endemic plant and animal species. The rocky topography is draped in rain forest and cloud forest and includes more than 200 waterfalls. Because of Isla del Coco's distance from shore (484 km [300 mi]) and its craggy topography, few visitors to Costa Rica—and even fewer Costa Ricans—have set foot on the island.

Costa Rica annexed Coco in 1869, and it became a national park in 1978. Today only extremely high-priced specialty-cruise ships, park rangers and volunteers, and scientists visit the place Jacques Cousteau called "the most beautiful island in the world." The dry season (November to May) brings calmer seas and is the best time to see silky sharks. During the rainy season large schools of hammerheads can be seen, but the ocean is rougher.

Two companies offer regular 10-day dive cruises to Isla del Coco that include three days of travel time on the open ocean and cost roughly $3,735 to $4,395, depending on the boat and dates. The *Okeanos Aggressor* (☎ 2289–2261, 800/348–2628 in U.S. ⊕ www.aggressor.com) offers 8- and 10-day dive safaris to Coco Island year-round. *Undersea Hunter* (☎ 2228–6613, 800/203–2120 in U.S. ⊕ www.underseahunter.com) runs 10-day dive trips to the island year-round.

ranges from tacos and hot dogs to a pricey surf and turf. ⊠ *On the Costanera ✛ 1 km/½ mi south of Tárcoles turnoff, on right* ☎ *2637–0594* ▤ *AE, D, DC, MC, V.*

$$ $$$ 🏨 **Hotel Villa Lapas.** Within a tranquil rain forest preserve, far from other
☺ hotels (and the beach), Villa Lapas is a great escape for nature lovers, but also has on-site entertainment to keep you busy, such as a large-screen television, a pool table, and foosball. You can cross a suspension bridge to reach a small replica of a Costa Rican colonial village with a restaurant, cantina, church, and gift shops. Follow the river flowing through the protected forest for a pleasant hike. There is a canopy tour on the property *(⇨ see Canopy Tour, above).* The austere rooms are nothing special, but they have terra-cotta floors, hardwood ceilings, and large baths. An all-inclusive meal plan is available, but you're better off eating your lunch and dinner elsewhere. **Pros:** surrounded by forest; lots of activities; birds; kid-friendly. **Cons:** rooms sometimes musty; air-conditioners old; mediocre buffets. ⊠ *Off Costanera, 3 km/ 2 mi after bridge over Rio Tárcoles, turn left on dirt road, up 600 m* ☎ *2637–0232, 2203–3553 in San José* ⊕ *www.villalapas.com* ⤳ *55*

rooms ♿ In-room: safe, no TV (some). In-hotel: 2 restaurants, bars, pool, laundry service, Wi-Fi ▭ AE, D, DC, MC, V ⊙ BP.

EN ROUTE
Even if you choose to bypass Tárcoles and its crocodile tours, you can still get a peek at the huge reptiles as they lounge on the riverbanks: on the Costanera, pull over just after crossing the Río Tárcoles bridge and walk back onto it. Bring binoculars if you have them. ■TIP→ Be sure to lock your car—vehicles have been broken into here.

BETWEEN TÁRCOLES AND PLAYA HERRADURA

Past Tárcoles, the first sizable beach town of the Central Pacific coast is Playa Herradura. In between, you'll pass two exclusive hotels, hidden from view at the end of long winding roads.

About a kilometer (½ mi) south after the entrance to Tárcoles, the Costanera passes a small beach called **Playa La Pita**, which provides your first glimpse of the Pacific if you're coming down from San José or the Central Valley. The beach is rocky, and its proximity to the Rio Tárcoles makes the water murky and unfit for swimming, but it's a nice spot to stop and admire the ocean. From here the road heads inland again, and you'll come across the entrance to Punta Leona, a vast hotel and residential complex. The road then winds its way up a steep hill, atop which is the entrance to the luxury hotel Villa Caletas. On the other side of that ridge is the bay and beach of Herradura.

WHERE TO EAT AND STAY

$$$ ✕ **El Mirador Restaurant.** White tablecloths, glass walls, and yellow-and-blue-checked curtains contribute to the sophisticated but not overly stuffy atmosphere of this restaurant at Villa Caletas. Expensive prix-fixe meals include your choice of appetizer, main dish, and dessert. Appetizers range from the traditional escargots to a shrimp and lobster bisque. The entrées include beef tenderloin with a red wine and espresso sauce, jumbo shrimp sautéed with coconut and vanilla, and a combination of a veal chop and roast duck. A covered terrace below the restaurant is popular for sunset viewing over a cocktail, and the tapas menu is much less expensive than the main restaurant. ✉ *Villa Caletas hotel, off coastal highway ⊕ 3 km/1½ mi south of Punta Leona* ☎ *2637–0505* ▭ *AE, D, DC, MC, V.*

$$–$$$ ▦ **Hotel Punta Leona.** This 740-acre private reserve and resort community is an odd and overwhelming mix of nature, residential development, and vacation spot. Punta Leona's attractions include three beaches, a tropical forest, a butterfly farm, and guided bird-watching hikes. Punta Leona (Lion's Point) made headlines as the setting of the Ridley Scott film *1492: Conquest of Paradise* and more recently for blocking public access to its beaches, which is illegal in Costa Rica. The little "city" contains everything from restaurants and pools to a grocery store and church, plus plenty of amusements, including a zip-line tour, tennis court, and mini–golf course. Frequent shuttles travel between the rooms, restaurants, and beaches. Hotel guests, home owners, and time-share members contribute to crowded beaches on weekends, especially in the dry season, when this place can be a bit of a zoo. **Pros:** ample beachfront; lots of variety in activities. **Cons:** far from town; dingy

7

rooms; spotty service. ✛ *15 km/9 mi south of Tárcoles on west side of road to Jacó* ☎ *2630–1000, 2231–3131 in San José, 888/301–9473 in North America* ⊕ *www.hotelpuntaleona.com* ⤳ *108 rooms, 13 suites, 27 apartments* ⌂ *In-room: safe, refrigerator. In-hotel: 3 restaurants, room service, bars, tennis court, pools, beachfront, water sports, laundry service, Wi-Fi* ⊟ *AE, D, DC, MC, V* ⏀ *BP.*

$$$–$$$$ ⚄ **Villa Caletas.** Perched 365 meters (1,200 feet) above the sea on a
★   promontory south of Punta Leona, this collection of elegant rooms sequestered in the jungle has jaw-dropping views of the surrounding foliage and sea below. Spectacular sunset views should be enjoyed from the bar, even if you stay elsewhere. Freestanding suites and villas are gorgeous, but rooms in the main building are far inferior; if a villa isn't within your budget, do try to get a deluxe room. Victorian, French Colonial, and Hellenistic motifs are combined throughout, with Ionic columns, varied artwork, cookie-cutter trims, and cane chairs. The regular pool is rather small and chilly, but the new Zephyr Palace complex has amazing views and an impressive infinity pool. The closest beach, Playa Caletas, is attractive, but small and rocky. Though a great place for romance or relaxation, this hotel has little to offer kids or active travelers. **Pros:** gorgeous views, forest, and sunsets; good food. **Cons:** abundant insects; little to do; lots of stairs; inconsistent service. ✉ *Off coastal highway* ✛ *3 km/1½ mi south of Punta Leona, on right* ⌂ *Apdo. 12358–1000, San José* ☎ *2637–0505* ⊕ *www.villacaletas.com* ⤳ *10 rooms, 14 villas, 7 junior suites, 13 suites* ⌂ *In-room: refrigerator, safe. In-hotel: 2 restaurants, bar, pool, gym, spa, laundry service, no-smoking rooms* ⊟ *AE, D, DC, MC, V* ⏀ *EP.*

PLAYA HERRADURA

20 km/12 mi south of Tárcoles.

If sportfishing and golf are your priorities, this is a good option. If you're looking for nature, seclusion, a beautiful beach, or a bargain, keep driving. Rocky Playa Herradura, a poor representative of Costa Rica's breathtaking beaches, gets its name from the Spanish word for "horseshoe," referring to the shape of the deep bay in which it lies. Its tranquil waters make it considerably safer for swimming than most central and southern Pacific beaches, and that, coupled with its proximity to San José, has turned it into a popular weekend getaway for Josefinos, who compete for shade beneath the sparse palms and Indian almond trees that line the beach. On the north end of the beach is the Los Sueños development, which includes a large marina, shopping center, hundreds of condos, a golf course, and a massive Marriott hotel.

GETTING HERE

By car, head 20 minutes straight down the Central Pacific highway. The town's entrance is on the right-hand side, where a long paved road leads to the beach. Follow the signs to the Marriott.

OUTDOOR ACTIVITIES

Few activities are available directly in Playa Herradura, but that doesn't mean you have to settle for less. Most of the area's diverse outfitters can pick you up at your hotel for activities near Jacó and Playa Hermosa.

Your hotel's reception desk is often a good source of information.

King Tours (✉ *Main road into Playa Herradura, in front of Los Sueños* ☎ *2643–2441, 8819–1920, or 800/213–7091 in North America* ⊕ *www.kingtours.com*) arranges trips to renowned attractions like Manuel Antonio National Park and Carara National Park, as well as crocodile boat tours, deep-sea and coastal fishing trips, horseback rides, and canopy tours. The company can also book tours to destinations elsewhere in the country, such as Poás and Arenal volcanoes, Monteverde Cloud Forest, and Isla Tortuga. **Costa Rica Dreams** (✉ *Los Sueños Marina* ☎ *2637–8942, 732/901–8625 Ext. 246 in U.S.* ⊕ *www.costaricadreams.com*) is one of the area's oldest and most reputable sportfishing outfitters.

> **THE HAUNTED CART**
>
> If you're out late one night and hear a slow scraping of wheels against the road, it just might be the *carreta sin bueyes* (cart without oxen) of ghostly legend. Its owner reputedly stole building materials from a church, and was condemned to perpetually traverse the country's highways and byways in the cart he used to transport his stolen goods. (The oxen were blameless for their role and escaped the curse.)

WHERE TO EAT AND STAY

$$
SEAFOOD
✕ **Restaurante El Pelícano.** It may not look like much at first glance, but this open-air restaurant across the street from the beach serves some dishes you'd be hard-pressed to find in other casual beach-town places. The decor is limited to green-tile floors, thin wooden columns, lime tablecloths, and soft candlelight. Starters include fish croquettes in a lemon sauce, green pepper stuffed with shrimp and mushrooms, or clams *au gratin*. Grilled tuna in a mango sauce, sea bass in a heart-of-palm sauce, lobster, and tenderloin are a few of the main dishes. ✉ *Turn left at end of main road into Playa Herradura* ☎ *2637–8910* ▭ *AE, D, DC, MC, V.*

$$$$
⬚ **Los Sueños Marriott Ocean and Golf Resort.** This mammoth multimillion-dollar resort in a palatial colonial-style building has a gorgeous view of Herradura Bay. It combines modern amenities with traditional Central American decorative motifs, such as barrel-tile roofing and hand-painted tiles. Rooms here, though attractive and some of the country's most expensive, are nothing special compared with those at smaller hotels in the same price range. They have marble baths, wooden furniture, and tiny balconies. Be sure to get a room with an ocean view, or you'll be contemplating condos. An enormous pool with islands and swim-up bars, a Ted Robinson golf course called La Iguana, a modern marina, and various diversions are designed to keep you on-site and entertained. **Pros:** impeccable grounds; great service; memorable. **Cons:** so-so service; beach can be dirty. ✉ *800 m west of road to Jacó from San José, follow signs at entrance of road to Playa Herradura* ☎ *2630–9000, 888/236–2427 in North America* ⊕ *www.marriott.com* ⤶ *191 rooms, 10 suites* ♿ *In-room: safe, refrigerator, Internet. In-hotel: 6 restaurants, room service, bars, golf course, tennis courts, pool, gym, spa,*

7

beachfront, children's programs (ages 5–15), laundry service, Internet terminal, Wi-Fi, no-smoking rooms ▭ *AE, D, DC, MC, V* ⦿| *BP.*

JACÓ

2 km/1 mi south of Playa Herradura, 114 km/70 mi southwest of San José.

Its proximity to San José has made Jacó the most developed beach town in Costa Rica. Nature lovers and solitude seekers should skip this place, which is known mostly for its nightlife, surf scene, and prostitution. More than 50 hotels and cabinas back its long, gray-sand beach, and the mix of restaurants, shops, and bars lining Avenida Pastor Díaz (the town's main drag) give it a cluttered appearance devoid of any greenery. Any real Costa Rican–ness evaporated years ago; U.S. chain hotels and restaurants have invaded, and you can pretty much find anything you need, from law offices and dental clinics to DVD-rental shops and appliance stores. It does have a bit of everything in terms of tours and outdoor activities, and makes a convenient hub for exploring neighboring beaches and attractions. Theft can be a problem here; watch your things carefully.

GETTING HERE AND AROUND

The drive from San José takes about two hours; take the new Highway 27 west of San José beyond Orotina, and then take the exit to Jacó and Quepos. The exit, on the right after Herradura, is well marked. Buses leave from San José's Coca-Cola station five times daily. **Pacific Travel & Tours** (☎ *2643–2520, 800/397–5716 in North America* ⦿ *www. pacifictravelcr.com*) brings passengers across the Gulf of Nicoya to Montezuma.

ESSENTIALS

Bank/ATM BAC San José (✉ *ll Galeone mall*). **Banco Nacional** (✉ *Avda. Pastor Díaz* ☎ *2643–3621*).

Hospital Ambulance (☎ *2643–1690*). **Clínica Pública** (✉ *In front of Plaza de Deportes* ☎ *2643–1767*).

Pharmacy Farmacia Jacó (✉ *Diagonally across from Mas X Menos supermarket* ☎ *2643–3205*).

Internet Centro de Computación (✉ *Avda. Pastor Díaz, center of town*).

Post Office Correos (✉ *Avda. Pastor Diaz*).

Rental Cars Budget (✉ *Avda. Pastor Díaz* ☎ *2643–2665* ⦿ *www.budget.com*). **Economy** (✉ *Avda. Pastor Díaz* ☎ *2643–1098* ⦿ *www.economyrentacar.com*). **Alamo** (✉ *Avda. Pastor Díaz* ☎ *2643–1752* ⦿ *www.alamo.com*). **Payless** (✉ *Avda. Pastor Díaz* ☎ *2643–3224* ⦿ *www.paylesscarrental.com*).

Taxis Taxi services (☎ *2643–2020, 2643–2121, or 2643–3030*).

Tourist Information Pacific Travel & Tours (✉ *Centro Comercial La Casona [La Casona shopping center]* ☎ *2643–2520, 800/397–5716 in North America* ⦿ *www.pacifictravelcr.com*).

Jacó

PACIFIC
OCEAN

KEY

● *Shopping*

① *Hotels & Nightlife*

EXPLORING

Long, palm-lined **Playa Jacó,** west of town, is a pleasant enough spot in the morning, but can burn the soles of your feet on a sunny afternoon. Though the gray sand and beachside construction make it less attractive than most other Costa Rican beaches, it's a good place to soak up the sun or enjoy a sunset. Playa Jacó is popular with surfers for the consistency of its waves, but when the surf is up, swimmers should beware of dangerous rip currents. During the rainy months the ocean here is not very clean.

OUTDOOR ACTIVITIES

You don't have to physically step into any tour office, because everyone from a reception desk attendant to a boutique salesperson can book you a local adventure. Almost every tour can pick you up at your hotel's doorstep. ■TIP→ Keep in mind that part of your price tag includes the salesperson's commission, so if you hear higher or lower prices from two different people, it's likely a reflection of a shift in the commission. You can try negotiating a better deal directly from the outfitter.

Jaguar Riders (☎ 2643–0180 or 8393–6626) specializes in ATV tours of the mountains east of town and trips to Carara National Park, but can arrange all kinds of personalized excursions. **Fantasy Tours** (✉ *Best Western Jacó Beach Resort* ☎ 2643–2231 or 2220–2126 in San José ⊕ *www.graylinecostarica.com*) deals primarily with large groups, arranging day trips from Jacó to Arenal and Poás volcanoes, Manuel Antonio National Park, Sarchí, Isla Tortuga, and raft trips on the Savegre River. **Pacific Travel & Tours** (✉ *Centro comercial La Casona [La Casona shopping center]* ☎ 2643–2520, 800/397–5716 in North America ⊕ *www.pacifictravelcr.com*) sells an array of tours in and around Jacó.

ATV TOURS Because ATV tours are fairly new here, the vehicles are in good condition. But they're not exactly the most eco-friendly way to see the area's rain forest and wildlife. Some operators will ask you to put up a credit card voucher of roughly $500. **Ricaventura** (✉ *In the center of Playa Jacó, behind Subway* ☎ 2643–5720, 877/561–7263 in North America ⊕ *www.ricaventura.com*) is considered by locals to be the best ATV tour with the longest routes. Ricaventura offers various options: a two-hour sunset tour ($69), a four-hour Carara Park and nearby river tour ($89), a six-hour Pacayal Waterfall trip ($110), and full-day trips ($150).

CANOPY **Waterfalls Canopy Tour** (☎ 2643–3322 ⊕ *www.waterfallscanopy.com*), in
TOURS a private reserve 4 km (2½ mi) from Jacó, is a zip-line tour with a view of rain forest and waterfalls. You can combine the tour, which costs $60 per person, with nature walks and a visit to a butterfly and frog garden, or do it at night.

A modified ski lift offers easy access to the rain-forest canopy, with six-seat gondolas that float through the treetops at the **Rain Forest Aerial Tram** (☎ 2257–5961 ⊕ *www.rainforestram.com*). This tram lies within a 222-acre private reserve 3 km (2 mi) west of Jacó. The company offers guided tours that explain a bit of the local ecology ($55), as well as early-morning bird-watching tours (six-person minimum; $83 per person). There is also a small serpentarium and medicinal plant garden.

HANG GLIDING

A truly unique experience, hang gliding gives you the chance to see not just Jacó, but a huge expanse of Pacific coastline. With **Hang Glide Costa Rica** (☎ 2643–4200 ⊕ *www. hangglidecr.com*) you can take a tandem hang-gliding flight or fly in a three-seat, open cockpit ultralight plane. You are picked up in Jacó and taken to the airstrip 6 km (4 mi) south of Playa Hermosa. Prices start at $69 per person.

HORSEBACK RIDING

Discovery Horseback Tours (☎ 8830–7550 ⊕ *www.horseridecostarica. com*) is owned by a British couple who run 2½-hour trail rides on healthy horses. You'll spend some time in the rain forest and also stop

> ## RIPTIDES
>
> Riptides (or rip currents), common in Jacó and Manuel Antonio's Playa Espadilla, are dangerous and have led to many deaths in the area. If you get caught in one, don't panic and don't try to swim against it. Let the current take you out just past the breakers, where its power dissipates, then swim parallel to shore. Once the current is behind you, swim back to the beach. The best policy is not to go in deeper than your waist when the waves loom large.

at a small waterfall where you can take a dip ($60). **Horse Tours Jacó at Hacienda Agujas** (☎ 2637–0808 or 8838–7940) are serene enough for all ages and skill levels. Late-afternoon tours are on a cattle ranch about 25 minutes north of Jacó, where the trail winds through a rain forest and down a beach. The ride ends with a colorful sunset bang ($65).

KAYAKING AND CANOEING

Kayak Jacó Costa Rica Outriggers (☎ 2643–1233 ⊕ *www.kayakjaco.com*) takes you to waters calmer than those at Jacó Beach. Instead, you'll visit Playa Agujas for sea-kayaking tours and Hawaiian-style outrigger canoe trips ($60). The half-day tours include snorkeling (conditions permitting) at secluded beaches.

SURFING

Jacó has several beach breaks, all of which are best around high tide. Surfboard-toting tourists abound in Jacó, but you don't need to be an expert to enjoy the waves—the swell is often small enough for beginners, especially around low tide. Abundant surf shops rent boards and give lessons. Prices range from $30 to $50 an hour and usually include a board and transportation. If you plan to spend more than a week surfing, it might be cheaper to buy a used board and sell it before you leave (⇨ *Shopping, below*). If you don't have much experience, don't go out when the waves are really big—Jacó sometimes gets very powerful swells, which result in dangerous rip currents. During the rainy season, waves are more consistent than in the dry months, when Jacó sometimes lacks surf.

SWIMMING

The big waves and dangerous rip currents that make surfing so popular here can make swimming dangerous. Lifeguards are on duty only at specific spots, and only sporadically. If the ocean is rough, stay on the beach—dozens of swimmers have drowned here over the years.

When the ocean is calm, especially around low tide, you can swim just about anywhere along Jacó Beach. The sea is always calmer near the beach's northern and southern ends, but the ocean bottom is littered with rocks there, as it is in front of the small rivers that flow into the sea near the middle of this beach.

7

WHERE TO STAY

$-$$ 🏨 **Apartotel Flamboyant.** Though nothing special, this small beachfront
★   hotel is a good deal, especially if you take advantage of the cooking
♻   facilities. Half the rooms have small kitchenettes; the others have air-
conditioning instead. Larger apartments can fit five to six people. Terraces with chairs overlook a garden and pool area, where there's a grill
for your use. Second-floor rooms have balconies with sea views. It's all
just a few steps from the surf and a block east of Jacó's busy main strip.
Pros: beachfront; good value; quiet; centrally located. **Cons:** very simple
rooms; looks a little worn. ⊠ *100 m west of Centro Comercial Il Galeone* ☎ *2643–3146* ⊕ *www.apartotelflamboyant.com* ➲ *20 rooms, 3
apartments* ♿ *In-room: no a/c (some), safe, refrigerator, kitchen (some),
no TV (some), Wi-Fi (some). In-hotel: pool, beachfront, laundry service,
Wi-Fi* ▭ *AE, MC, V* ⧖ *EP.*

$$ 🏨 **Apartotel Girasol.** A great option for families, or small groups of
♻   friends looking for comfort and quiet, Girasol is a quiet beachfront
hotel with a neighborly feel. The cozy apartments face the small pool
and grill area and include a bedroom with a queen and single bed, a
living and dining room with another bed, a complete kitchen, and a
terrace with chairs. A winding pathway crosses the well-maintained
front lawn with an impressive ficus tree in the middle, and leads to a
small gate that opens directly onto the beach, where you should take at
least one evening to enjoy a spectacular sunset. **Pros:** beachfront; quiet
grounds; big apartments. **Cons:** far from town center; often full. ⊠ *100
m west of Motoshop, end of C. Republica Dominicana* ☎ *2643–1591,
800/923–2779 in North America* ⊕ *www.girasol.com* ➲ *16 apartments*
♿ *In-room: safe, kitchen, Wi-Fi. In-hotel: pool, beachfront, laundry
service* ▭ *MC, V* ⧖ *EP.*

$$$ 🏨 **Club del Mar.** Secluded at the beach's southern end, far from Jacó's
Fodor's Choice   crowds, Club del Mar is the area's priciest, and nicest, lodging option.
★   In the main building, above the restaurant, bar, and reception, standard
green-and-cream-hue rooms have private teak balconies with screen
doors that keep the sea breeze circulating. Comfortable condos, clustered in two-story buildings amid massive trees and verdant lawns, are
considerably nicer. One- and two-bedroom apartments have abundant
windows, modern kitchens, and pleasant furnishings; two-bedroom
condos are a bargain for two couples. The nicest condos are those nearest the sea (nos. 13 to 16). Las Sandalias restaurant ($$–$$$) serves
some of the area's finest food (⇨ *above*). **Pros:** beachfront; tranquil;
friendly; lush grounds; tasteful decor. **Cons:** some highway noise reaches
back to condos; some insects. ⊠ *Costanera, 275 m south of gas station* ⌖ *Apdo. 107–4023, Jacó* ☎ *2643–3194, 866/978–5669 in North
America* ⊕ *www.clubdelmarcostarica.com* ➲ *8 rooms, 22 condos, 2
suites* ♿ *In-room: safe, refrigerator (some), kitchen (some). In-hotel:
restaurant, room service, bar, pool, beachfront, water sports, laundry
facilities, Wi-Fi* ▭ *AE, D, DC, MC, V* ⧖ *EP.*

$$–$$$ 🏨 **Docelunas.** Most of Jacó's hotels and visitors huddle around the beach,
but "Twelve Moons" sits a couple of miles from the sea and sand.
With a mountainous green backdrop, this hotel spreads out across 5
acres of lawns shaded by tropical trees and luxuriant gardens. Spacious

teak furniture–filled rooms have large bathrooms with showers, bath-tubs, and double sinks. Yoga classes are given daily in a hilltop, hard-wood-floor room with windows for walls. The full-service spa uses the hotel's own homemade beauty products, and the open-air restaurant ($$–$$$) serves creative seafood, meat, vegetarian, and vegan dishes. ⊠ *On coastal highway from San José, pass the first entrances to Jacó; take dirt road on left with signs for Docelunas* ☎ *2643–2211* ⊕ *www. docelunas.com* ⇆ *20 rooms* ⚒ *In-room: safe, refrigerator, Wi-Fi. In-hotel: restaurant, room service, bar, pool, spa, laundry service, no-smoking rooms* ▤ *AE, D, DC, MC, V* ⦿ *BP.*

$$–$$$

⚒

Fodor'sChoice

★

▦ **Hotel Canciones del Mar.** The poetically named "Songs of the Sea" is a tranquil, intimate, and charming hotel with rooms that are among the closest to the ocean of any hotel in the area. Tastefully and individually decorated, the one- and two-bedroom suites are in a two-story cream-color building, with well-equipped kitchens. Five ocean-view rooms cost a bit more, but the rest have porches overlooking the lush gardens and blue-tile pool. Breakfast and drinks can be enjoyed under a thatch roof next to the beach or in the shade of palms on the beach itself, whereas the rooftop tapas bar is a great spot to watch the sunset. A communal tree house–like space behind the pool makes a pleasant reading or relax-ing spot. **Pros:** close to ocean; rooms have kitchens. **Cons:** too close to Jacó; rooms feel worn. ⊠ *End of C. Bri Bri* ✉ *Apdo. 86–4023, Jacó* ☎ *2643–3273* ⊕ *www.cancionesdelmar.com* ⇆ *15 suites* ⚒ *In-room: safe, kitchen, refrigerator, Wi-Fi. In-hotel: restaurant, room service, bar, pool, beachfront, laundry service* ▤ *AE, MC, V* ⦿ *BP.*

$$–$$$

⚒

▦ **Hotel Tangerí.** One of Jacó's older hotels, the Tangerí has an excellent beachfront location and ample grounds shaded by coconut palms. The accommodations range from spacious rooms by the sea to villas big enough for a large family. The bright but bland standard rooms in a two-story concrete building by the beach are a good deal for couples. Beachfront rooms have balconies or terraces with lovely ocean views through the palms. Ocean-view rooms are over the lawn, and some have a rather distant glimpse of the sea. The villas, complete with kitchens and one to three bedrooms, are set back from the beach; avoid nos. 5, 6, and 8, which are too close to the road. This is a popular spot with Costa Rican families, thanks to its convenient beach access, several pools, a playground, Ping-Pong, and pool table, which means it can be quite busy during the holidays. There's a snack bar by the pool and a steak house ($$$) near the entrance. **Pros:** beachfront; spacious rooms; centrally located. **Cons:** rooms a bit timeworn; musty. ⊠ *Avda. Pastor Díaz, north of river* ☎ *2643–3001, 2222–2924 in San José* ⊕ *www. hoteltangeri.com* ⇆ *14 rooms, 11 villas* ⚒ *In-room: kitchen (some), refrigerator, safe. In-hotel: restaurant, bar, pools, gym, beachfront, laun-dry service, Wi-Fi* ▤ *AE, MC, V* ⦿ *EP, BP, FAP.*

¢

▦ **Las Orquídeas.** Just far enough from the beach and main tourist beat to be a bargain, but close enough to be convenient, this pleasant little hotel provides cleanliness and comfort at reasonable rates. Colorful, narrow rooms have tile floors, two beds, and the basic amenities; air-conditioning costs $10 extra. Small front terraces overlook the gar-dens and small pool, where the predominantly surfer guests tend to

7

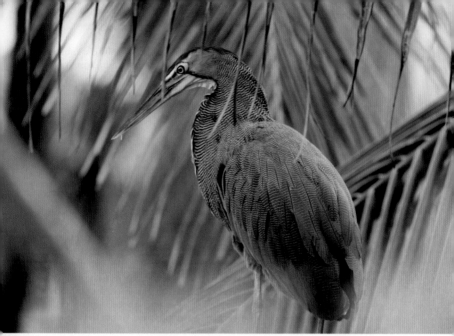

congregate. **Pros:** good location; clean. **Cons:** no frills; no beachfront. ⊠ *East of Frutástica supermarket* ☎ *2643–4056* ⤳ *10 rooms* ♿ *In-room: no phone, safe, refrigerator, Internet. In-hotel: pool, laundry service* ▭ *AE, MC, V* ◎| *EP.*

$$ ⛲ **Mar de Luz.** It may be a few blocks from the beach, and it doesn't look like much from the street, but Mar de Luz is a surprisingly pleasant place full of flowering plants and shady, bird-attracting trees. The Dutch owner is dedicated to cleanliness and providing lots of amenities, such as poolside grills, a kids' game room, plentiful common areas—like the large open-air reading lounge—and inexpensive tours. Rooms vary in decor: the bright, pastel-hue rooms have two queen-size beds and kitchenettes; top-floor rooms have a small living room with checkered sofas and a double bed; the cozy split-level rooms with kitchenettes and stone walls are reminiscent of European bed-and-breakfasts. **Pros:** attentive owner; plenty to do. **Cons:** rooms a bit dark; service can be spotty. ⊠ *East of Avda. Pastor Díaz, behind Jungle bar* ☎ *2643–3000 or 877/623–3198 in North America* ⊕ *www.mardeluz.com* ⤳ *27 rooms, 2 suites* ♿ *In-room: safe, kitchen (some), refrigerator, Wi-Fi (some). In-hotel: room service, pool, laundry service, Internet terminal, no-smoking rooms* ▭ *AE, D, DC, MC, V* ◎| *BP.*

$ ⛲ **Tropical Garden Hotel.** As its name suggests, this hotel's special charm comes from the impressive lush gardens that fill almost every inch of its property, making it one of the most verdant places in Jacó. Meters from the beach and from the main strip, rooms lack style but have very basic kitchenettes and front porches for iguana- and bird-spotting. It's one of Jacó's original hotels (formerly known as Villas Miramar), and the rooms show their age, but it's competitively priced. You receive a small discount for paying in cash. **Pros:** pleasant grounds; economical. **Cons:** timeworn; simple. ⊠ *50 m west of Il Galeone mall, toward the beach* ☎ *2643–3003* ⊕ *www.tropicalgardenhotel.com* ↻ *12 studios, 1 suite* ♿ *In-room: no a/c (some), no phone, safe, kitchen, Internet. In-hotel: pool* ═ *AE, MC, V* �📶*EP.*

NIGHTLIFE AND THE ARTS

Whereas other beach towns may have a bar or two, Jacó has an avenue full of them, with enough variety for many different tastes. After-dinner spots range from restaurants perfect for a quiet drink to loud bars with pool tables to dance clubs or casinos.

BARS For a laid-back cocktail, people-watching, and a tropical feel, head to **Restaurante El Colonial** (⊠ *Avda. Pastor Díaz, across from Il Galeone mall* ☎ *2643–3326*) on the main drag, which has a large circular bar in the center and lots of wicker chairs and tables in the front. Sometimes it has live music. A mix of bar and disco, **Nacho Daddy's** (⊠ *Avda. Pastor Díaz, 1st fl of Il Galeone mall* ☎ *2643–2270*) is Jacó's after-hours nightspot, open from 10 PM to 4 AM. The restaurant **Tabacón** (⊠ *Avda. Pastor Díaz, north of Il Galeone mall* ☎ *2643–3097*) is a nice place for a cocktail, after-dinner drinks, or a late-night meal. It has a big bar in back, pool tables, and live music on weekends. **Jungle** (⊠ *Avda. Pastor Daz, across from Hotel Tangerí, above Subway*) has a large, second-floor bar, has wide-screen TVs, several pool tables, dartboards, a large bar, and a dance floor in back.

CASINOS **Jazz Casino and Sportsbook** (⊠ *Hotel Amapola, 130 m east of the Municipalidad government building, southern end of town* ☎ *2643–2316*), Jacó's first casino, has rummy, slot machines, and craps. There's also a roomy bar area.

SHOPPING

Souvenir shops with mostly the same mass-produced merchandise are crowded one after the other along the main street in the center of town. Most of the goods, like wooden crafts and seed jewelry, are run-of-the-mill souvenir fare, but a few shops have more unusual items. The two neighboring shops at **Cocobolo** (⊠ *Avda. Pastor Díaz, next to Banana Café* ☎ *2643–3486*) are jam-packed with merchandise hanging from the ceiling, walls, and shelves. It's much of what you find in other stores, but with more international and tasteful items and a richer variety. **El Cofre** (⊠ *Avda. Pastor Díaz, across from Banco Nacional* ☎ *2643–1912*) claims to sell only handmade goods and specializes in mostly wooden furniture, including heavy Guatemalan pieces and Indonesian teak; it also sells masks, drums, Moroccan lamps, and even carved doors. Curious religious statues of saints and angels from Central America are big sellers. **Guacamole** (⊠ *Centro Comercial Costa Brava, south of Il Galeone mall* ☎ *2643–1120*) sells beautiful and comfortable batik clothing produced locally, along with Brazilian bathing suits, Costa Rican leather sandals and purses, and different styles of jewelry.

SURFBOARDS AND GEAR **Cartón** (⊠ *Calle Madrigal* ☎ *2643–3762*) sells new and used boards and has a selection of surf wear, sunglasses, and accessories. **Jass** (⊠ *Centro Comercial Ureña* ☎ *2643–3549*) has a good variety of surf gear at decent prices. It sells new and used boards. ■ TIP→ Most shops that sell boards also buy used boards.

PLAYA HERMOSA

5 km/3 mi south of Jacó, 113 km/70 mi southwest of San José.

On the other side of the rocky ridge that forms the southern edge of Jacó Beach is Playa Hermosa, a swath of gray sand and driftwood stretching southeast as far as the eye can see. Despite its name—Spanish for "Lovely Beach"—Playa Hermosa is hardly spectacular. The southern half of the wide beach lacks palm trees or other shade-providing greenery; its sand is scorchingly hot in the afternoon; and frequent rip currents make it unsafe to swim when there are waves. But board riders find beauty in its consistent surf breaks. The beach's northern end is popular because it often has waves when other spots are flat, and the ocean is cleaner than at Jacó. There is also plenty of forest covering the hills, and scarlet macaws sometimes gather in the Indian almond trees near the end of beach. For nonsurfers, outdoor options include horseback and canopy tours in the nearby, forested hills or ultralight and hang-gliding flights over the coast. But all of these can be done from other beaches. As for the town itself, there's really not much, which is part of the attraction for travelers who want to escape Jaco's crowds and concrete towers. Most of the restaurants, bars, and hotels have cropped up one after the other on a thin stretch separating the highway and the beach. From June to December, olive ridley turtles nest on the beach at night, especially when there's not much moonlight.

GETTING HERE

If you have a car, take the coastal highway 5 km (3 mi) past Jacó. You'll see the cluster of businesses on the right. If you don't, take a taxi from Jacó or a local bus toward Quepos.

ESSENTIALS

Internet Goola Café and Internet (✉ *Costanera, north of soccer field* ☎ *2643–3696*).

OUTDOOR ACTIVITIES

You can arrange activities throughout the Central Pacific from Playa Hermosa. Most tour operators and outfitters include transportation in their prices. *For more options than we list here, see Outdoor Activities in Jacó, above, or consult your hotel's reception.* Raul Fernandez of **Playa Hermosa Turtle Tours** (☎ *8817–0385*) takes small groups to look for nesting sea turtles on Playa Hermosa between July and December ($35), as part of a project to collect the eggs and raise them in a hatchery. Tour times vary depending on the tide; he can provide transportation from hotels in Jacó.

CANOPY TOUR   **Chiclets Canopy Tour** (✉ *West of Costanera, ½ km/¼ mi north of Hermosa* ☎ *2643–3271* ⊕ *www.jacowave.com*) runs four guided tours daily that take you through the rain forest canopy ($60). Cables strung between platforms perched high in a dozen trees have views of tropical foliage, wildlife, and the nearby coast.

SURFING Most people who bed down at Playa Hermosa are here for the same reason—the waves that break just a shell's toss away. There are a half-dozen breaks scattered along the beach's northern end, and the surf is always best around high tide. Because it is a beach break, though, the waves here often close out, especially when the surf is big. If you don't have much experience, don't go out when the waves are really big—Hermosa sometimes gets very powerful swells, which result in dangerous rip currents. If you're a beginner, don't go out at all. Surf instructors in Hermosa take their students to Jacó, an easier place to learn the sport.

Reggae-theme **Restaurante Jammin'** (⊠ *Next to Cabinas Las Arenas* ☎ *2643–1853*) offers surf lessons ($45) and buys, rents, and sells boards as they're available. Andrea Díaz, a professional surfer with **Waves Costa Rica** (⊠ *Next to the Backyard* ☎ *2643–7025* ⊕ *www.wavescr.com*), takes surf students to calmer Playa Jacó for two-hour lessons ($55 per person for group sessions; $100 for a private surf package). She also offers surf-camp packages, which include room and board and yoga.

WHERE TO EAT AND STAY

$$ ⤫ **The Backyard.** Playa Hermosa's original nightlife spot, the North American–style Backyard has two seating areas, each with its own bar. Television sets on the wraparound bar in the front room show sports matches and surf videos. A wooden deck in back overlooking the beach is great for lunch and sunset, mostly because of the pleasant sea breezes and view. The usual bar food—Tex-Mex standards and burgers—is complemented by fresh seafood, including ceviche, grilled tuna, lobster, and jumbo shrimp. It's popular especially on Friday and Saturday, when there's live music. ⊠ *Costanera, southern end of town next to the Backyard hotel* (⇨ *below*) ☎ *2643–7011* ⊕ *www.backyardhotel.com* ▭ *AE, D, DC, MC, V*.

ECLECTIC

$$ ⤫ **Jungle Surf Café.** This simple, open-air eatery decorated with a colorful rain forest mural serves some of Hermosa's best food. Seating is on a patio and wooden deck hemmed by tropical trees, with views of the road and soccer field. Breakfasts are hearty—try the banana pancakes—and the eclectic lunch selection ranges from shish kebabs to fish sandwiches. The dinner menu changes nightly, but usually includes big portions of fresh tuna or mahimahi. ⊠ *Costanera, north of soccer field* ☎ *2643–1495* ▭ *No credit cards* ⛽ *BYOB*.

SEAFOOD

$$$ ▦ **The Backyard.** Surfers—not the budget backpacking kind—are the main clientele at this small, cream-color hotel on the beach. Rooms have high ceilings, clay-tile floors, and sliding-glass doors that open onto semiprivate balconies and terraces, most of which have good views of Playa Hermosa. Second-floor rooms have better views, as do the two spacious corner suites with separate bedrooms and large balconies—they're a good deal for small groups. There's a nice little pool surrounded by tropical foliage in back. **Pros:** steps from the surf; nice views from second floor; friendly. **Cons:** expensive; bar next door noisy on weekends. ⊠ *Costanera, southern end of town* ☎ *2643–7011* ⊕ *www.backyardhotel.com* ⤙*6 rooms, 2 suites* ⌂ *In-room: safe, refrigerator, Wi-Fi. In-hotel: restaurant, room service, bar, pool, laundry service* ▭ *AE, D, DC, MC, V* ⥾⦿*CP*.

Continued on page 413

SURFING
COSTA RICA

Costa Rica's big surfing community, consistent waves, and not-too-crowded beaches make surfing accessible to anyone who is curious enough to give it a whirl; surf schools, board rentals, and beachside lessons are plentiful. At the most popular beaches, surf tourism is a regular part of the scene. Many instructors are able to bridge generational divides, giving lessons tailored for anyone from tots to retirees. First timers would be wise to start

by Leland Baxter-Neal

Costa Ricans are known for their laid-back attitude, and this usually translates into a welcoming vibe in the water. Of course, as the waves get more intense, and the surfers more serious, the unspoken rules get stricter, so beginners are advised to stay close to the shore. A good instructor should help keep you out of the way anywhere you go, and if you're on your own, just steer clear of the hot shots until you know the

COSTA RICA'S SURF FINDER

THE PACIFIC COAST

For those new to surfing, destinations on the Pacific coast are more welcoming in a number of ways. There are more beaches, hotels, bars, and surf schools than in the Caribbean, and the waves are friendlier. Access to the Northern and Central Pacific coast is also made easy by (sometimes) paved and well-marked roads. As you head southward down the coast, the route becomes untamed. The remoteness of the Osa Peninsula has guarded a couple of world-class breaks surrounded by some of the country's most untouched jungle.

WHEN TO GO: waves are most consistent from December through April. As you move southward down the coast, the breaks are best from May to November.

THE CARIBBEAN

Costa Rica's truncated Caribbean has comparatively few beaches and they draw only the most dedicated surf seekers. The laid-back culture of that coast seems a perfect match for the surfer vibe. Among the Caribbean waves is perhaps Costa Rica's most famous: Puerto Viejo's Salsa Brava.

WHEN TO GO: Best conditions January through April.

TYPES OF BREAKS

BEACH BREAK: The best type for beginners. Waves break over sandbars and the seafloor. Jacó, Hermosa, and Sámara are all beach breaks.

POINT BREAK: Created as waves hit a point jutting into the ocean. With the right conditions, this can create very consistent waves. Pavones is a point break.

REEF BREAK: Waves break as they hit reef. It can create great (but dangerous) surf. There's a good chance of getting smashed and scraped over extremely sharp coral or rocks. Salsa Brava, in Puerto Viejo, is a reef break.

general

PACIFIC

❶ Tamarindo: Very popular with all levels of surfers. Beach breaks are great to learn on; nice waves are formed at a rock outcropping called Pico Pequeño and at the river mouth at the beach's north end. Neighboring Playa Grande is a big, fast beach break for advanced riders.

❷ Playa Guiones: If not the best surf in the vicinity of Nosara, it's the best for beginners and longboarders, second only to Sámara. Lots of long, fun beach breaks.

❸ Sámara: Protected, mellow beach breaks where the greatest danger

is that the waves are too small. Great for beginners and close to lots of breaks for more advanced surfers.

❹ Mal País: A variety of beach breaks plus a point break that's good when waves get big. Good for beginners and advanced surfers.

❺ Jacó: Unless the surf gets too big, the consistent beach breaks produce forgiving waves that are good to begin and advance on. The south end is best for beginners. Avoid water pollution problems and the occasional crocodile by staying clear of river mouths.

Tamarindo

SAN JOSÉ

Playa Negra · Salsa Brava

Playa Cocles

Jacó · Esteríllos

Playa Hermosa

Manuel Antonio

Dominical

ais

PACIFIC OCEAN

Osa Peninsula

Pavones

7

IN FOCUS SURFING COSTA RICA

Jacó

6 Playa Hermosa:
A steep beach break just south of Jacó with some of the country's best waves and surfers. Waves can get big, mean, and thunderously heavy; beginners should enjoy the show from the shore. Rip currents make swimming much too dangerous.

7 Esteríllos:
Divided into three beaches, going north to south: Oeste, Centro, and Este. A beautiful stretch of coast, uncrowded to the point of desolation.

The surf and currents can be tough for beginners, and Este and Centro have waves much like Hermosa. Oeste has a variety of beach breaks with softer, friendlier waves.

8 Manuel Antonio:
Just outside the national park you'll find a variety of beach breaks. Playitas, at the park's north end, is perhaps the most consistent.

9 Dominical: At the foot of beautiful, forested coastal mountains. A long set of beach breaks that are fun and great for all levels. When waves do get big, beginners should head south to Dominicalito. Rip cur-

Manuel Antonio

rents make Dominical too dangerous for swimming.

10 Pavones: Legendary, remote, and surrounded by rain forest, Pavones is said to be the world's longest, or second-longest, left-breaking wave, with a perfect ride lasting nearly three minutes. But with fickle conditions and a tough drive to get here, it's best for the very experienced and dedicated.

CARIBBEAN

11 Playa Negra:
A largely undiscovered but quality beach break for all skill levels.

12 Salsa Brava:
When the conditions are right, this is arguably Costa Rica's best and most powerful wave; it's placed right over a shallow coral reef. For advanced surfers only.

13 Playa Cocles:
Plenty of beach breaks to pick from, good for all levels. But beware the currents or you'll drift out to sea.

SURF SCHOOL TIPS

Surf lesson

Surfing is for the young and the young of heart. At many of Costa Rica's top surf beaches, a wide range of ages and skill sets can be found bobbing together in the water. With the right board and some good instructions, just about anybody can stand up and have some fun in the waves. We strongly recommend taking a lesson or two, but be sure to take them from an actual surf school (there's one on just about every beach) rather than the eager kid who approaches you with a board. Trained instructors will be much better at adapting their lesson plans to different skill levels, ages, and body types.

If you're a first timer, there are a few things you need to know before getting in the water.

■ **Pick your beach carefully:** Sámara is a good choice, as is Jacó or Tamarindo. You want beach breaks and small, gentle waves. Make sure to ask about rip tides.

■ **Expect introductory lessons to cover the basics:** how to lie on the board, paddle out, duck the incoming waves, and how to pop up onto your surf stance. If you're a natural, you'll be able to hop up and stay standing in the white wash of the wave after it breaks.

■ **Have realistic expectations:** even if you have experience in other board sports, like snowboarding or skateboarding, don't expect to be surfing on the face of the wave or tucking into barrels on your first day.

■ **Choose the right gear:** if you're a beginner, start on a longboard. Be sure to wear a T-shirt or a wet suit to help protect your chest and stomach from getting scraped.

SURF SLANG (or how not to sound like a dork).

Barrel: The area created when a wave breaks onto itself in a curl, creating a surfable tube that's the surfer's nirvana. Also called the green room.

Drop in: To stand up and drop down the face of a wave. Also used when one surfer cuts another off : "Hey, don't drop in on that guy!"

Duck dive: A maneuver where the surfer first pushes his or her board underwater and then dives with it, ducking under waves that have already broken or are about to break. It's difficult with a longboard (see Turtle roll).

Goofy foot: Having a right-foot-forward stance on the surfboard. The opposite is known as natural.

Close out: When a wave or a section of a wave breaks all at once, rather than breaking steadily in one direction. A frustrating situation for surfers, giving them nowhere to go as the wave comes crashing down.

Ding: A hole, dent, crack, or other damage to a board.

Funboard: A little longer than a shortboard with a broad, round nose and tail. Good for beginners looking for some-thing more maneuverable than a longboard.

Outside: The area farther out from where waves are most regularly breaking. Surfers line up here to catch waves.

Shortboard: Usually 6 to 7 feet long with a pointed nose. A tough board to learn on.

Stick: A surfboard.

Turtle roll: A maneuver where the surfer rolls over on the surfboard, going underwater and holding the board upside down. Used by longboarders and beginners to keep from being swept back toward shore by breaking waves.

$–$$ Cabinas Vista Hermosa. Playa Hermosa's original hotel, Cabinas Vista Hermosa sits at the edge of a pleasant grove of coconut palms and almond trees. It can be a bit hard to find. The hotel was renovated in 2007, and the new rooms in a two-story concrete building are simple but comfortable. Pay the extra $20 for an ocean-view room, with sliding doors that open onto a common terrace, since the ones in back overlook the road and parking lot. A separate building on the beach has rustic backpacker rooms that share a bathroom for half the price. The rooms and restaurant overlook two pools, a grill for guest use, and tables on the beach. Common areas have hammocks and diversions like foosball and Ping-Pong. **Pros:** economical; lots of activities. **Cons:** very simple; hard to find. ⊠ *Costanera, 150 m south of soccer field* ☎ *2643–7022* ⊕ *www.vistahermosa.20m.com* ⇨ *10 rooms* ⌂ *In-room: refrigerator, kitchen (some). In-hotel: restaurant, pools, laundry service* ▭ *No credit cards* ¶ *BP.*

PLAYA BEJUCO

27 km/16 mi south of Playa Hermosa, 32 km/19 mi south of Jacó.

Surfers wanting to escape the crowds at Jacó and Playa Hermosa, or anyone simply seeking to stray from the beaten path, need only drive 20 minutes south to this relatively deserted palm-lined beach. One could stroll for an hour along the light-gray swath of sand and hardly encounter a soul. Several vacation homes and two small hotels sit behind the first part of the beach, and behind them is a large mangrove forest where you might see macaws or white-faced monkeys. The surf is as big and consistent as at Playa Hermosa, but with a fraction of the surfers. It's a Blue Flag beach, but like Hermosa, it can develop dangerous rip currents, so swimmers should go in no deeper than their waist when the waves are big. Aside from surfing and beachcombing, there is little to do here, which makes it a good place for people wanting to do nothing at all. The mosquitoes can be quite fearsome during the rainy months.

GETTING HERE

If you have a car, take the coastal highway 27 km (16 mi) south past Playa Hermosa to the turnoff for Playa Bejuco, which is 1 km (½ mi) west of the highway. If you don't, take a taxi from Jacó, or local bus toward Quepos.

OUTDOOR ACTIVITIES

SURFING   There are various high-tide beach breaks scattered along Playa Bejuco. Waves tend to close out here when the swell is big, but then you can try the mouth of the estuary, 1 km (½ mi) south of the hotels. Bejuco is a do-it-yourself beach, with neither surf schools nor board rental nearby, and because the waves break so close to shore, it's not a good spot for beginners.

WHERE TO STAY

$$**   Delfín Beach Front Resort. Every room in this two-story hotel has an ocean view, and the surf breaks right in front of it. Tastefully decorated rooms are standard size, with one king or two queen beds, and a small bathroom. They all have either a large balcony or a terrace; those on the ground floor tend to have better views of the sea, past the skinny coconut palms. The bright, airy restaurant ($$) also overlooks the beach, but the menu is very limited, with tilapia instead of ocean fish, oddly enough. There's a small pool in back, near which hang a few hammocks. **Pros: beachfront; clean rooms. **Cons:** limited selection at restaurant; so-so management. ⊠ *On beach, Playa Bejuco* 🕾 *2778–8054* ⊕ *www. delfinbeachfront.com* ⤴ *12 rooms* ⛉ *In-room: no phone, safe, Internet. In-hotel: restaurant, bar, pool, beachfront, laundry service* ⊟ *AE, D, DC, MC, V* ⓘⓞⓘ *CP.*

$$ 🏨 **Hotel Playa Bejuco Hotel.** Playa Bejuco's less expensive accommoda-
☾   tions are 50 meters (165 feet) away from the beach, so the views are of pool and gardens rather than surf and sand. The rooms are spacious and well equipped, and the hotel is nicely designed with ochre walls, lots of foliage, and a large, blue-tile pool. They cater to families by putting several beds in some rooms, such as the second-floor rooms with one king and a loft with two twin beds. The restaurant ($$–$$$) has an extensive menu that includes sea bass served with various sauces, pastas, pork loin, filet mignon, and jumbo shrimp. **Pros:** big pool; decent restaurant. **Cons:** lacks ocean view. ⊠ *Road to Playa Bejuco, on left* 🕾 *2778–8181* ⊕ *www.hotelplayabejuco.com* ⤴ *20 rooms* ⛉ *In-room: no phone, safe, refrigerator. In-hotel: restaurant, bar, pool, laundry service, Wi-Fi, no-smoking rooms* ⊟ *AE, D, DC, MC, V* ⓘⓞⓘ *BP.*

QUEPOS

23 km/14 mi south of Parrita, 174 km/108 mi southwest of San José.

This hot and dusty town serves as a gateway to Manuel Antonio. It also serves as the area's hub for banks, supermarkets, and other services. Because nearby Manuel Antonio is so much more attractive, there is no reason to stay here, but many people stop for dinner, for a night on the town, or to go sportfishing. Quepos's name stems from the indigenous tribe that inhabited the area until the Spanish conquest wiped them out. For centuries the town of Quepos barely existed, until the 1930s, when the United Fruit Company built a banana port and populated the area with workers from other parts of Central America. The town thrived for nearly two decades, until Panama Disease decimated the banana plantations in the late 1940s. The fruit company then switched to less lucrative African oil palms, and the area declined. Only since the 1980s have tourism revenues lifted the town out of its slump, a renaissance owed to the beauty of the nearby beaches and nature reserves. Forests around Quepos were destroyed nearly a century ago, but the massive Talamanca Mountain Range, some 10 km (6 mi) to the east, holds one of the largest expanses of wilderness in Central America.

GETTING HERE

It's about a three-hour drive from San José to Quepos; follow the directions for Jacó and continue south another 40 minutes. Buses from San José's Coca-Cola bus station drop you off in downtown Quepos. SANSA and Nature Air run multiple flights per day between San José and Quepos, as well as direct flights between Quepos and other tourist destinations.

ESSENTIALS

Bank/ATM BAC San José (⊠ *Avda. Central*). **Banco Nacional** (⊠ *50 m west and 100 m north of bus station* ☎ *2777–0113*).

Hospital Ambulance (☎ *2777–0118*). **Quepos hospital** (✛ *4 km/2½ mi on road to Dominical* ☎ *2777–0020*).

Pharmacy Farmacia Fischel (⊠ *Near bus station, in front of municipal market* ☎ *2777–0816*).

Post Office Correos (⊠ *C. Central*).

Rental Cars Alamo (⊠ *Downtown, 50 m south of Korean school* ☎ *2777–3344, 800/462–5266 in U.S.* ⊕ *www.alamo.com*). **Payless** (⊠ *Main road between Quepos and Manuel Antonio* ☎ *2777–0115* ⊕ *www.paylesscarrental. com*).

Taxis Taxi services (☎ *2777–0425, 2777–1693, or 2777–1068*).

Travel Agency Lynch Travel (⊠ *Downtown, behind bus station* ☎ *2777–1170* ⊕ *www.lynchtravel.com*).

EXPLORING

Spread over Fila Chota, a lower ridge of the Talamanca Range 22 km (13 mi) northeast of Quepos, **Rainmaker** is a private nature reserve that protects more than 1,500 acres of lush and precipitous forest. The lower part of the reserve can be visited on guided tours from Manuel Antonio, or as a stop on your way to or from Quepos. Tours begin at 7:30. There are two tours available: a walk up the valley of the Río Seco, which includes a dip in a pool at the foot of a waterfall; or a hike into the hills above the waterfall and over a series of suspension bridges strung between giant tropical trees. The park also offers an early-morning bird-watching tour and a night hike. The best value is a half-day package ($70) that includes transport from Manuel Antonio or Quepos, a guided tour, a river swim, and breakfast and lunch. The reserve is home to many of Costa Rica's endangered species, and you may spot birds here that you won't find in Manuel Antonio. It isn't as good a place to see animals as the national park, but Rainmaker's forest is different from the park's—lusher and more precipitous—and the view from its bridges is impressive. It's best to visit Rainmaker in the morning, since—true to its name—it often pours in the afternoon. ✛ *22 km/13 mi northeast of Quepos* ☎ *2777–3565, 504/349–9848 in U.S.* ⊕ *www.rainmakercostarica.org* ✉ *$60–$90 for guided tours* ☉ *Mon.–Sat. 7:30–4.*

OUTDOOR ACTIVITIES

There's a tour operator or travel agency on every block in Quepos that can sell you any of about a dozen tours, but some outfitters give discounts if you book directly through them. The dry season is the best time to explore the area's rain forests. If you're here during the rains, do tours first thing in the morning.

CANOPY TOUR   There are many zip-line tours in the area that take you flying through the treetops, but **Canopy Safari** (✉ *Office downtown, next to the Poder Judicial* ☎ *2777–0100* ⊕ *www.canopysafari.com*) has earned a reputation for long and fast-paced rides. The company's privately owned forest is about a 45-minute car ride from Quepos, and the tour ($65) includes gliding down nine zip lines and a swim in a river pool.

FISHING   Quepos is one of the best points of departure for deep-sea fishing in southwestern Costa Rica. The best months for hooking a marlin are from October to February and in May and June, whereas sailfish are abundant from November to May, and are caught year-round. From May to October you're more likely to catch yellowfin tuna, roosterfish, mahimahi, and snapper. **Bluefin Tours** (✉ *Downtown, across from the soccer field* ☎ *2777–0000* ⊕ *www.bluefinsportfishing.com*) has catch-and-release sportfishing, conventional fishing, and fly-fishing on a fleet of 26-, 28-, and 33-foot boats. Full-day charters run $343– to $399. **Costa Mar Dream Catcher** (✉ *Entrance to Quepos, next to Café Milagro* ☎ *2777–4700* ⊕ *www.costamarsportfishing.net*) has the largest fleet of boats in Quepos, with six boats ranging from 25 to 38 feet, and consequently has a wide range of rates. Half- and full-day charters run $500–$1,100. Half-, three-quarter-, and full-day catch-and-release fly and conventional trips ($600–$900 for a full day) with **Luna Tours Sport Fishing** (✉ *Downtown, next to Casino Kamuk* ☎ *2777–0725, 888/567–5488 in U.S.* ⊕ *www.lunatours.net*) are available on 27-, 32-, and 33-foot boats.

KAYAKING AND RAFTING   **Iguana Tours** (✉ *Downtown Quepos, across from soccer field* ☎ *2777–2052* ⊕ *www.iguanatours.com*) specializes in exploring the area's natural beauty through white-water rafting on the Naranjo and Savegre rivers and kayak adventures at sea or in a mangrove estuary. They also offer bird-watching, horseback riding, and canopy tours.

MOUNTAIN BIKING   The area's green mountains are great for biking, but in the dry season it's hot—very, very hot. The rainy season is slightly cooler, but be prepared to get muddy. **Estrella Tour** (✉ *Downtown, across the street from Restaurante El Pueblo* ☎ *2777–1286 or 8843–6612* ⊕ *www.puertoquepos. com/ecotourism/mountain-biking.html*) has an array of bike tours for intermediate and expert riders ranging from a couple of hours to a full day ($40 to $95). They also offer two- and three-day trips ($140 to $310) that include meals and lodging in mountain cabins.

WHERE TO EAT

$$ ✗ **El Gran Escape.** A favorite with sportfishermen ("You hook 'em, we
SEAFOOD   cook 'em"), the Great Escape is the town's best place for seafood. The
★   menu is dominated by seafood entrées, from shrimp scampi to fresh tuna with mushrooms to bouillabaisse and paella. You can also get hearty burgers, or a handful of Mexican dishes, and there's a kids' menu. You won't find any billfish, like marlin or swordfish, on the menu, owing to their conservation policy, but the back wall is covered with pictures of them (and their proud reelers). Weathered fishing caps hang from the

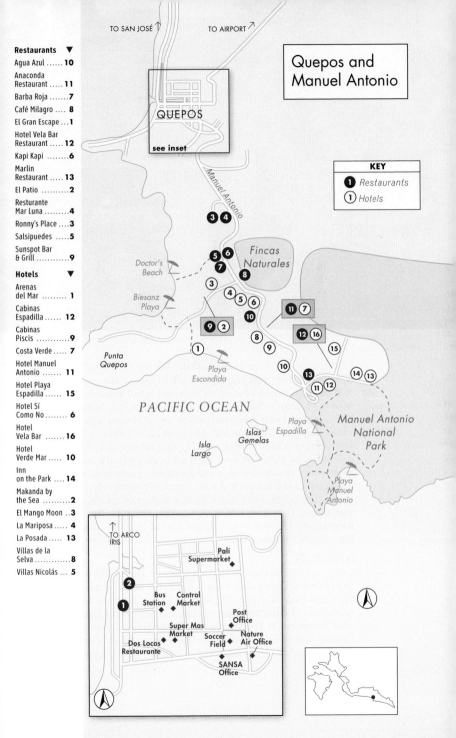

Quepos and Manuel Antonio

TO SAN JOSÉ ↑   TO AIRPORT ↗

QUEPOS

see inset

Manuel Antonio

KEY
❶ Restaurants
① Hotels

Fincas
Naturales

Doctor's
Beach

Biesanz
Playa

Punta
Quepos

PACIFIC OCEAN

Playa
Escondida

Isla
Largo

Islas
Gemelas

Playa
Espadilla

Manuel Antonio
National
Park

Playa
Manuel
Antonio

TO ARCO
IRIS ↑

Palí
Supermarket

Bus
Station   Control
Market

Post
Office

Super Mas
Market   Soccer
Field   Nature
Air Office

Dos Locos
Restaurante

SANSA
Office

"I was in complete awe as my fantastic local Quepos guide led me along a delightful path up in the hills outside of Quepos." —Photo by Colleen George, Fodors.com member

bar's ceiling. ⊠ *150 m north of Hotel Kamuk* ☎ *2777–0395* ⊕ *www. elgranescape.net* ⊟ *AE, D, DC, MC, V* ☺ *Closed Tues.*

$$$

LATIN AMERICAN

★

✕ **El Patio.** It would be easy to miss this small restaurant squeezed between a couple of shops south of the bridge into town, but don't. The nouveau Latin American cuisine includes some delectable innovations on traditional Central American and Caribbean flavors. Start with some chicken tamales, ceviche, or a mango and *chayote* (green squash) salad, then sink your teeth into a slice of pork loin in a *creole mojo* (spicy tomato sauce), shrimp in a rum coconut sauce, or mahi-mahi cooked in a banana leaf with a smoked tomato mojo and a squash puree. The lunch menu has a good selection of salads, sandwiches, and wraps. The nicest tables are in back, around a lush garden and fountain. ⊠ *250 m north of Hotel Kamuk* ☎ *2777–4982* ⊟ *AE, D, DC, MC, V* ☺ *Closed Sun.*

NIGHTLIFE

Large, air-conditioned **El Arco Iris** (⊠ *Over last bridge into Quepos* ☎ *2777–0449*) is the only dance club in the area. Locals and tourists of all ages pack in after midnight, after warming up in other bars. A DJ spins a mix of salsa, merengue, reggae, and pop. Older American expats often congregate at Tex-Mex **Dos Locos Restaurante** (⊠ *Avda. Central at C. Central, near bus station* ☎ *2777–1526*) day and night to people-watch or, on Wednesday and Friday nights, to listen to live music.

MANUEL ANTONIO

3 km/2 mi south of Quepos, 179 km/111 mi southwest of San José.

You need merely reach the top of the forested ridge on which many of Manuel Antonio's hotels are perched to understand why it is one of Costa Rica's most popular destinations. That sweeping view of beaches, jungle, and shimmering Pacific dotted with rocky islets confirms its reputation. And unlike the tropical forests in other parts of the country, Manuel Antonio's humid tropical forest remains green year-round. The town itself is spread out across a hilly and curving 5-km (3-mi) road that originates in Quepos and dead-ends at the entrance to Manuel Antonio National Park. Along this main road, near the top of the hill or on its southern slope, are the area's most luxurious hotels and fine-dining restaurants, surrounded by rain forest with amazing views of the beaches and offshore islands. The only problem with staying in one of those hotels is that you'll need to drive or take public transportation to and from the main beach and national park, about 10 minutes away. More hotel and restaurant options are available at the bottom of the hill, within walking distance of the beach, but they lack the sweeping view.

Manuel Antonio is a very gay-friendly town. Many hotels and bars cater to gay travelers, and all of them offer a warm welcome to anyone walking in the door. The area doesn't especially cater to budget travelers, but there are a few cheap places near the end of the road, and various mid-range lodging options.

GETTING HERE

Manuel Antonio is a 15-minute drive over the hill from Quepos and 25 minutes from the Quepos airport. Between SANSA and NatureAir, there are 10 flights per day linking San José and Quepos, as well as direct flights between Quepos and other tourist destinations. Buses depart from San José's Coca-Cola bus station for Manuel Antonio three times a day, at 6 AM, noon, and 6 PM, traveling the opposite direction at 6 AM, noon, and 5 PM; they pick up and drop off passengers in front of hotels on the main Quepos–Manuel Antonio road. Gray Line offers door-to-door service to and from San José, Jacó, Monteverde, Arenal, and major North Pacific beaches. The trip from San José takes about 3½ hours by car or bus. A local public bus makes the 20-minute trip from Quepos to Manuel Antonio every half hour from 7 to 7, then hourly until 10 PM.

ESSENTIALS

Bank/ATM Banco Proamérica (✉ *Main road, next to Economy Rent a Car*).

Pharmacy Farmacia Manuel Antonio (✉ *Main road, across from Marlin Restaurant* ☎ *2777–5370*). **Farmacia La Económica** (✉ *Main road, across from soccer field* ☎ *2777–2130*).

Internet Cantina Internet (✉ *Main road, across from Costa Verde* ☎ *2777–0548*). **Sí Como No Internet** (✉ *Main road, inside Regalame Art Gallery* ☎ *2777–0777*).

Taxis Taxi services (☎ *2777–0425, 2777–0734, or 2777–1693*).

Rental Cars Economy (✉ *Next to Banca Proamérica* ☏ *2777–5353* ⊕ *www.economyrentacar.com*).

EXPLORING

Fodor'sChoice
★
☪
Parque Nacional Manuel Antonio (Manuel Antonio National Park) proves that good things come in small packages. Costa Rica's smallest park packs in an impressive collection of natural attractions: lots of wildlife, rain forest, white-sand beaches, and rocky coves with abundant marine life. Trails are short, well maintained, and easy to walk. The forest is dominated by massive ficus and gumbo-limbo trees, and is home to

two- and three-toed sloths, green and black iguanas, agoutis, four species of monkeys, and more than 350 species of birds.

Despite being Costa Rica's smallest national park, this is its second most visited, after Poás Volcano. Why? Maybe because it is one of two places in Costa Rica to see adorable squirrel monkeys. It's also one of the best places in Costa Rica to see white-faced capuchin monkeys and three-toed sloths. Make no mistake about it: Manuel Antonio is no undiscovered wilderness. It's one of Costa Rica's most-visited attractions, so if you're looking for an undisturbed natural oasis, this is not it. But what Manuel Antonio does have is great diversity of wildlife, all easily spotted from the well-marked trails. And because animals are so used to humans, this is one of the best places to see them up close.

From the ranger station a trail leads through the rain forest behind Playa Espadilla Sur, the park's longest beach. It's also the least crowded because the water can be rough. The coral reefs and submerged volcanic rocks of white-sand Playa Manuel Antonio make for good snorkeling. The 1-km-long (½-mile-long) beach, tucked into a deep cove, is safe for swimming. At low tide you can see the remains of a Quepos Indian turtle trap on the right—the Quepos stuck poles in the semicircular rock formation, which trapped turtles as the tide receded. Olive ridley and green turtles come ashore on this beach May through November. Espadilla and Manuel Antonio beaches lie on opposite sides of a tombolo, or a sandy strip that connects the mainland to Punta Catedral (Cathedral Point), which used to be an island. The steep path that leads up Punta Catedral's rocky hill draped with thick jungle passes a lookout point from which you can gaze over the Pacific at the park's islands.

Farther east, Playa Escondido (Hidden Beach) is rocky and secluded, but it's also more difficult to access. Before you head out to Escondido, find out when the tides come in so you're not stranded. It's quiet and secluded. Kayaking trips might take you down to Punta Serrucho near the southern border of the park, whose jagged peaks explain its name. (Serrucho means "saw.")

A few tips: Hire a guide—you'll walk away with a better understanding of the flora and fauna and see things you probably would have missed otherwise. Get here as early as possible—between 7 and 8 AM is ideal. Rangers permit only 600 to 800 people inside at a time, and during peak season visitors line up to enter. Early morning is also the best time to see animals. And beware of manzanillo trees (indicated by warning signs)—their leaves, bark, and applelike fruit secrete a gooey substance that irritates the skin. ⊠ *Manuel Antonio* ☎ *2777–5185* 🕭 *$10* 🕑 *Tues.–Sun. 7–4*).

As the road approaches the national park, it skirts the lovely, forest-lined beach of **Playa Espadilla,** which stretches for more than 2 km (1 mi) north from the rocky crag that marks the park's border to the base of the ridge that holds most of the hotels. One of the most popular beaches in Costa Rica, Playa Espadilla fills up with sunbathers, surfers, volleyball players, strand strollers, and sand-castle architects on dry-season weekends and holidays, but for most of the year it is surprisingly quiet. Even on the busiest days it is long enough to provide an escape from the crowd, which tends to gather around the restaurants and lounge chairs near its southern end. Though it is often safe for swimming, beware of rough seas, which create deadly rip currents.

Fincas Naturales, a former teak plantation, has been reforested to allow native trees to spring back among the not-so-native ones. A footpath winds through part of the 30-acre tropical forest, and naturalist guides do a good job of explaining the local ecology and identifying birds. The reserve is home to three kinds of monkeys, as well as iguanas, motmots, toucans, tanagers, and seed-chomping rodents called agoutis. Guided walks are given throughout the day: the first starts at 6:30 AM for bird-watching, then at 9 AM and 1 PM, plus a nighttime jungle trek that departs at 5:30 PM. The quickest and least expensive tour is an hourly walk through displays on butterflies, reptiles, and amphibians. Unfortunately, you can't explore the reserve at your own pace. ⊠ *Entrance across street from Sí Como No Hotel* ☎ *2777–0850* ⊕ *www. wildliferefugecr.com* 🕭 *$15–$45, kids under 12 $10–$35, depending on tour* 🕑 *Daily 7 AM–6 PM.*

OUTDOOR ACTIVITIES

Manuel Antonio's list of outdoor activities is almost endless. Tours generally range from $40 to $90 per person and can be booked through your hotel's reception desk or directly through the outfitter. During the rainy season, some outdoor options might lose their appeal, but clouds usually let loose in the afternoon, so take advantage of sunny mornings.

CANOPY TOURS

★ **Tití Canopy Tours** (☎ *2777–3130* ⊕ *www.titicanopytours.com*) has a relatively slow-paced zip-line tour ($55) through a forest reserve that is contiguous with the national park. Guides go above and beyond to make you feel comfortable and safe, and will help you spot animals.

TOUR
OPERATORS

A small company run by friendly young locals with a good grasp of the area's activities, **Espadilla Tours** (☎2777–5334) can arrange any kind of activity in the Manuel Antonio area, from surf lessons to sunset sails. The Internet café next to the Marlin Restaurant has information.

> ## IN THE THICK OF IT
>
> There's more rain forest on private land than in Manuel Antonio National Park, which means it's not unusual to see many of the animals the park is famous for from the balcony of your hotel room or from your breakfast table. It also means that local landowners play an important role in conserving the area's flora and fauna.

HIKING

Highly visited Manuel Antonio National Park is the obvious place to go, but in private reserves like Fincas Naturales (⇨ above) and Rainmaker (⇨ Quepos, above) you can also gain a rich appreciation of the local forests' greenery and wildlife. ■TIP→ Bring binoculars!

HORSEBACK
RIDING

Brisas del Nara (☎2779–1235 ⊕ www.horsebacktour.com) takes riders of all ages and levels through the protected Cerro Nara mountain zone, 32 km (20 mi) from Manuel Antonio, and ends with a swim in a natural pool at the foot of a 350-foot waterfall. Full-day tours ($65) include three hours on horseback, with breakfast and lunch included; the ride on the half-day tour ($50) lasts two hours, and there's no lunch. **Finca Valmy Tours** (☎2779–1118 ⊕ www.valmytours.com) is known for its attentive service and healthy horses. Its six-hour horseback tours take you through the forested mountains above Villa Nueva, east of Manuel Antonio ($65). Lunch and swimming in a pool below a small waterfall on their property are included.

Beach riding is the specialty of **Rancho Savegre** (☎2779–4430 or 8834–8687 ⊕ www.costaricahorsevacation.com). Trips set out from a cattle ranch about 15 minutes south of Manuel Antonio and include a stop at a waterfall for swimming or trail walking. Of the two half-day tours, only the morning tour includes a meal.

KAYAKING

Iguana Tours (☎2777–2052 ⊕ www.iguanatours.com) runs sea-kayaking trips ($65) to the islands of Manuel Antonio National Park—which require some experience when the seas are high—and a mellower paddle through the mangrove estuary of Isla Damas, where you might see monkeys, crocodiles, and various birds.

SNORKELING
AND DIVING

The islands that dot the sea in front of Manuel Antonio are surrounded by volcanic rock reefs with small coral formations and attract schools of snapper, jacks, barracudas, rays, sea turtles, moray eels, and other marine life. **Oceans Unlimited** (☎2777–3171 ⊕ www.oceansunlimitedcr. com) offers various offshore sites, an all-day diving excursion to Caño Island ($149–$220), PADI certification courses, and snorkeling. Several tour operators in town can put you on an organized snorkel excursion to the calm waters of Biesanz Beach.

SWIMMING

When the surf is up, riptides are a dangerous problem on Playa Espadilla, Manuel Antonio's main beach, which runs parallel to the road to the park's entrance. For a less turbulent swim and smaller crowds, head to **Playa Biesanz** (✉ Near Hotel Parador), which lies within a sheltered cove and also has good snorkeling. Manuel Antonio's safest swimming area is sheltered **Playa Manuel Antonio,** the second beach in the national park. Its white sand makes it attractive for lounging around, and it's also a good place for snorkeling. ■ TIP→ Never leave your valuables unattended while you're swimming.

WHITE-WATER RAFTING

The three white-water rivers in this area have limited seasons. The rains from August to October raise the rivers to their perfect peak. **Río Savegre,** which flows past patches of rain forest, has two navigable stretches: the lower section (Class II to III), which is a mellow trip perfect for neophytes, and the more rambunctious upper section (Class III to IV). It is usually navigable from June to March. **Río Naranjo** (Class III to IV) has a short but exciting run that requires some experience and can be done only from June to December. **Río Parrita** (Class II to III) is a relatively mellow white-water route, and in the dry season it can be navigated only in two-person, inflatable duckies.

Manuel Antonio's original rafting outfitter, **Adventure Manuel Antonio** (☎ *2777–1234* ⊕ *www.adventuremanuelantonio.com*), leads trips down the Savegre and Naranjo on half-day and full-day tours ($98). Naranjo River tours can be combined with kayaking in the nearby estuary. **Ríos Tropicales/h2O Adventures** (☎ *2777–4092* ⊕ *www.h2ocr.com*), the biggest rafting outfitter in the country, runs kayaking excursions and rafting trips on the Savegre and Naranjo ($65 to $86).

WHERE TO EAT

$$$
SEAFOOD
★

✕ **Agua Azul.** This simple second-floor restaurant with a small kitchen in one corner offers a breathtaking view by day and a deliciously inventive selection of seafood at night. The lunch menu is strong on salads and sandwiches, but the dinner options include some of the best entrées in town. In addition to nightly fish and pasta specials, they offer such inventive delicacies as seared tuna over a tequila-and-lime cucumber salad, calamari sautéed with capers and olives, and coconut-crusted mahimahi. ⊠ *Main road, above the Villas del Parque office* ☎ *2777–5280* 🗀 *V* ⊙ *Closed Wed. and Oct.*

$$
ECLECTIC

✕ **Anaconda Restaurant.** Named for the humongous snake whose skin is mounted on the wall behind the bar, this open-air restaurant is hidden in the rain forest. You won't see any anacondas (they are found in South America), but you may spot iguanas, squirrel monkeys, or various species of birds from one of the restaurant's oversize chairs. You are sure to enjoy the view of the coast. The eclectic menu ranges from Japanese-style tuna to Tuscan mahimahi. They also serve excellent pastas and salads. The restaurant is a short drive from the beach, making it an excellent option for a quiet lunch. ⊠ *Costa Verde Hotel* ☎ *2777–1973* 🗀 *AE, D, DC, MC, V.*

$
CAFÉ

✕ **Café Milagro.** The only place in town that serves its own fresh-roasted coffee, Café Milagro is a colorful, cozy choice for breakfast food any time of the day, or to satisfy a chocolate-chip-cookie craving. The North American menu includes bagels, breakfast burritos, baked goods like brownies and muffins, an inventive selection of sandwiches, and a fruit plate with granola. Tables on the front porch overlook the road, but there's also seating in the back garden. ⊠ *Main road to park, across*

7

from La Mariposa ☎ 2777–0794 ⊕ *www.cafemilagro.com* ⊟ *AE, D, DC, MC, V* ⊗ *No dinner.*

$$ ✕ **Hotel Vela Bar Restaurant.** This small, open-air restaurant retains an
ECLECTIC intimate atmosphere behind a hedge of tropical foliage and beneath
a conical thatch roof. They serve a variety of dishes in generous
proportions, including mahimahi with an array of sauces, shrimp
with ginger, and pork chops in pineapple sauce. There are vegetarian
options as well. Service can be slow when it gets busy. ⊠ *Up road
from Marlin Restaurant* ☎ 2777–0413 ⊕ *www.vealbar.com* ⊟ *AE,
D, DC, MC, V.*

$$$ ✕ **Kapi Kapi.** This elegant restaurant at the edge of the forest offers
ECLECTIC Manuel Antonio's best ambience for dinner, with low lighting, ochre
★ walls, dark hardwoods, and potted palms. The name is a greeting in the
indigenous Maleku language, but the menu is the cosmopolitan inven-
tion of a Californian chef. It includes such un–Costa Rican starters as a
lemongrass, chicken, and coconut soup, and "seafood cigars"—a mix
of fresh tuna, shrimp, and mahimahi deep-fried in an egg-roll wrap-
per and served on a cabbage salad. The main courses include such
Asian-inspired dishes as prawns with a tamarindo-coconut-rum glaze
and macadamia-encrusted mahimahi with a plum chili sauce. Only in
dessert does the chef reveal his nationality, with the chocolate s'more
cake. ⊠ *East side of main road, across from Pacifico Colonial condos*
☎ 2777–5049 ⊕ *www.restaurantekapikapi.com* ⬩ *Reservations essential* ⊟ *MC, V* ⊗ *No lunch.*

$$ ✕ **Marlin Restaurant.** The outdoor tables of this two-story concrete res-
COSTA RICAN taurant are pretty much always full, owing to its location on Manuel
Antonio's busiest corner, across the street from the beach. It's a con-
venient place to grab breakfast after an early-morning hike through
the park—be it banana pancakes or a *típico*, with eggs and *gallo pinto*
(black beans and rice). The lunch and dinner menu ranges from the
ubiquitous *arroz con pollo* (rice with chicken) to tenderloin with french
fries, and jumbo shrimp in garlic and lemon butter. The fresh mahimahi
and tuna are always a good bet. Breakfast is also available. ⊠ *Main
road, south of the hill, on corner across from bus stop and beach*
☎ 2777–1134 ⊟ *AE, D, DC, MC, V.*

$$$ ✕ **Restaurante Mar Luna.** Easy to overlook, this simple blue wooden res-
SEAFOOD taurant propped on the hillside is often packed. The decor is limited
to illuminated plastic fish, ceramic mobiles, potted palms, and colorful tablecloths, but the restaurant has a pleasant view of treetops and
the sea below. The fresh seafood, caught each morning by one of the
cooks, is what draws the crowd. You might start with sashimi or seafood soup, and move on to one of the popular entrées: grilled tuna
with peppers and onions, lobster in a brandy sauce, the humongous
mariscada—a sautéed seafood platter for two—or one of the surf-
and-turf options. They have live Latin music Thursday to Saturday,
and a small bamboo bar in front. ⊠ *East side of road, 100 m north
of Manuel Antonio Elementary School* ☎ 2777–5107 ⊟ *AE, MC, V*
⊗ *No lunch.*

$$ ✕ **Ronny's Place.** A spectacular sunset view and friendly, attentive service
COSTA RICAN are this simple, open-air restaurant's best qualities. The small menu

Espadilla Beach, not far from Quepos, is one of the few beaches in Costa Rica with lifeguards.

includes such typical Tico dishes as *sopa negra* (black-bean soup), ceviche, shrimp and fish on a skewer, and filet mignon wrapped with bacon and topped with a mushroom sauce. Ronny's is somewhat secluded down a long dirt road that crosses a green valley on a narrow ridge in front of the sea. ✛ *1 km/½ mi west of main road, down dirt road across from Amigos del Río* ☎ *2777–5120* ⊕ *www.ronnysplace.com* ▭ *AE, D, DC, MC, V.*

$ ✕ **Salsipuedes.** This colorful, friendly tapas bar nestled behind a rock
ECLECTIC formation at the edge of the forest has one of the best sunset views in town, making it a great cocktail and appetizer option. The tapas are fun to share, three to five per couple, depending on how hungry you are. They range from sashimi and grilled tuna or mahimahi to fajitas. Such Costa Rican favorites as *frijolitos blancos* (white beans stewed with chicken) and *chicharrones con yuca* (fried pork and cassava root) are also available. They offer half a dozen full dinners, including larger cuts of fish, and some rice and pasta dishes, plus they're willing to turn any of the tapas dishes into a full meal. ⊠ *Main road, across from Banco Proamérica* ☎ *2777–5019* ▭ *MC, V* ⊗ *Closed Tues. No lunch.*

$$$ ✕ **Sunspot Bar and Grill.** The open-air, poolside restaurant of the exclu-
ECLECTIC sive Makanda by the Sea hotel has tables beneath purple cloth tents
★ overlooking the sea and surrounding jungle. Its kitchen, cleverly hidden beneath the bar, serves up such succulent treats as jumbo shrimp in a ginger sauce and grilled beef tenderloin with a choice of sauces. The menu also includes poultry, lamb, and pasta dishes, along with nightly specials. At lunch they offer great pizzas, salads, and sandwiches. You'll want to put on insect repellent at night. ⊠ *Makanda by the Sea hotel*

⊕ *1 km/½ mi west of La Mariposa* ☎ *2777–0442* ⊕ *www.makanda.
com* ⌦ *Reservations essential* ⊟ *AE, D, DC, MC, V.*

WHERE TO STAY

$$$$

Fodor's Choice

★

🏨 **Arenas del Mar Beach and Nature Resort.** What you don't see is what
you get at this new eco-luxury hotel: no cars, no crowds, no clutter. You
can hardly see the hotel's seven sage-and-beige modern buildings camouflaged on reforested hillsides sloping down to two pristine, almost
deserted beaches. Rooms here are chic and elegant but still "green,"
decorated with gorgeous natural fabrics, king-size beds, and flamboy-
ant local art. Bathrooms are spacious, with round, glass-brick shower
stalls. Huge private terraces, some with ocean view and mosaic-tiled hot
tubs, have comfortable outdoor sitting areas. Two pools, two beaches
to choose from, and a spa all spell luxury. Even the eco element here
is an added luxury, with 12 acres of beach and forest alive with birds,
butterflies, and wildlife. The main restaurant is practically in the trees,
and the menu is innovative and ambitious. There's also a more casual
daytime restaurant at the lower pool nearest the beach. **Pros:** best of
both worlds: luxury and eco-consciousness; best beach access in Manuel
Antonio; wonderful bird-watching and wildlife viewing. **Cons:** very
steep paths and stairs, although electric carts constantly transport
guests. ⊠ *Far west end of Playa Espadilla, down the El Parador road, in
Manuel Antonio* ☎ *2777–2777* ⊕ *www.arenasdelmar.com* ⇨ *38 rooms*
⌂ *In-room: safe, kitchen, Wi-Fi. In-hotel: 2 restaurants, bar, 2 pools,
spa, beachfront, laundry service, Internet terminal, Wi-Fi, parking (free)*
⊟ *AE, MC, V* ¶◎¶ *BP.*

$$

☾

🏨 **Cabinas Espadilla.** Owned by the same family that runs the nearby
Hotel Playa Espadilla, these quiet cabinas close to the beach are more
affordable but have fewer amenities. Rooms open onto porches over-
looking tropical gardens and a wide lawn, shaded by hammock-strung
palm trees, and a large pool. The rooms with kitchenettes cost $10 more,
but are a bit cramped. Guests have access to the hotel's restaurant, ten-
nis court, and forest trail. **Pros:** good value; short walk from beach; nice
grounds. **Cons:** mediocre rooms; not very friendly. ⊠ *On road beside
Marlin Restaurant* ☎ *2777–0903* ⊕ *www.cabinasespadilla.com* ⇨ *16
cabinas* ⌂ *In-room: no phone, safe, kitchen (some), refrigerator, no TV.
In-hotel: tennis courts, pool, laundry service* ⊟ *AE, MC, V* ¶◎¶ *EP.*

¢

🏨 **Cabinas Piscis.** A short walk through the woods from the beach, this
tranquil hotel shaded by tall trees is one of the area's best options for
budget travelers. Most rooms are in a concrete building with a wide
porch; they are simple but spacious, with small bathrooms and lots of
windows. The tiny, lower-price rooms that share a separate, cold-water
bathhouse are marketed to backpackers. Also available are a separate
cabin with a refrigerator, and an open-room, fully equipped *casita* for
four. A small restaurant serves breakfast and light lunches. Bathrooms
do not have hot water. **Pros:** forested property on the beach; inex-
pensive. **Cons:** spartan rooms; soft beds. ⊠ *Road to park, past Hotel
Karahe* ☎ *2777–0046* ⇨ *15 rooms, 10 with bath; 1 casita; 1 cabin*
⌂ *In-room: no a/c, no phone, no TV* ⊟ *MC, V* ¶◎¶ *EP.*

$$–$$$

★

🏨 **Costa Verde.** You're likely to see monkeys, iguanas, and all kinds of
birds on the forest trails surrounding this extensive hotel's buildings,

which are scattered on both sides of the main road. Adult-only studios are spacious, with large balconies and screened walls that let the breeze through. Those in the other buildings are smaller but are air-conditioned. Splurge for a "Studio-Plus," which all have ocean views. Three fully equipped bungalows are also available for groups of up to six. The cheaper "efficiencies" are a mixed lot—only those in Building D, in the jungle overlooking the sea, are recommended; Buildings B and C aren't. Costa Verde's newest addition is a suite ($$$$) converted from a Boeing 727 fuselage. The hotel's Anaconda Restaurant *(⇨ above)* is excellent. The dinner-only La Cantina ($$), across the street, serves good grilled meats and seafood, and has live music. **Pros:** great ocean views; wildlife; restaurants; studios and Building D efficiencies a good value. **Cons:** most efficiencies suffer road noise; no beach access; service inconsistent. ⊠ *Road to park, south side of hill, on left* ☎ *2777–0584, 866/854–7958 in North America* ⊕ *www.costaverde.com* ⌦ *10 efficiencies, 15 studios, 3 bungalows* ⌂ *In-room: no a/c, no phone (some), kitchen. In-hotel: 2 restaurants, bars, pools, laundry service, Internet terminal* ⊟ *AE, MC, V* ¶◎¶ *EP.*

$$$ ⊞ **El Mango Moon.** This bed-and-breakfast's intimate atmosphere and hospitable staff make you feel as if you're staying with a friend rather than at a hotel. The comfy, open living-room area extends to a balcony lined with a wooden counter and stools with views to the mango-shaped pool below and a tranquil cove framed by the rain forest. The cream-color rooms vary in size and amenities; more expensive rooms have semiprivate balconies. Rooms on the top floor can connect for families. Monkey-attracting mango trees surround the building, and a steep 20-minute trail leads to a secluded beach. **Pros:** nice view; tranquil area; friendly. **Cons:** far from main beaches; not much privacy; some rooms dark; relatively expensive. ⊠ *Between La Mariposa and Makanda* ☎ *2777–5323* ⊕ *www.mangomoon.net* ⌦ *9 rooms, 2 suites* ⌂ *In-room: no phone, safe. In-hotel: restaurant, bar, pool, no kids under 12, no-smoking rooms* ⊟ *AE, MC, V* ¶◎¶ *BP.*

$$ ⊞ **Hotel Manuel Antonio.** One of Manuel Antonio's original hotels, this ★ place is close to the national park entrance and across the street from the beach. The rooms, in two-story concrete buildings, have tile floors, simple pastel drapes and bedspreads, and large balconies or terraces, many of which have ocean views. Unfortunately, the ocean view is often obstructed by souvenir vendors' stalls and cars lining the road. The rooms are comfortable but not fancy, equipped with air-conditioning and cable TV, and just steps away from the beach and park. Backpackers can stay in one of the rustic wooden rooms above the restaurant, which lack air-conditioning and TV, but are a third of the price. **Pros:** near beach, park; a real bargain. **Cons:** busy area on weekends; service inconsistent. ⊠ *End of road to park* ☎ *2777–1237 or 2777–1351* ✉ *hotelmanuelantonio@racsa.co.cr* ⌦ *24 rooms* ⌂ *In-room: safe. In-hotel: restaurant, room service, bar, laundry service, no-smoking rooms* ⊟ *AE, MC, V* ¶◎¶ *EP.*

$$$ ⊞ **Hotel Playa Espadilla.** A short walk from the beach, this friendly hotel ↻ spreads across grounds bordered on two sides by the tall trees of Manuel Antonio National Park, and it has a trail through an area of the

7

The Pacific Coast is backed by mangrove, rain, transitional, and tropical dry forests.

park that few people visit. The simple but spacious mint-green rooms with big windows are housed in two-story buildings surrounded by green lawns; for a bit more money, some rooms have good-size kitchens with modern appliances. A small blue-tile pool and patio have a pleasant adjacent bar area with a billiard table. Directly behind are a large, open-air restaurant and a tennis court, but there are better places to dine in the area. **Pros:** surrounded by forest; close to beach. **Cons:** service inconsistent; very small pool. ⊠ *150 m up side road from Marlin Restaurant, first left* ☎ *2777–0903* ⊕ *www.hotelespadilla.com* ⇌ *16 rooms* ⌂ *In-room: safe, refrigerator (some), kitchen (some), Wi-Fi. In-hotel: restaurant, room service, bar, tennis court, pool, laundry service, Wi-Fi, no-smoking rooms* ▭ *AE, D, DC, MC, V* ⊚ *BP.*

$$$–$$$$ ⊡ **Hotel Sí Como No.** This luxury resort goes to great lengths to be eco-friendly, and has earned a level-five Certificate of Sustainable Tourism, the highest level possible. It's also quite family-friendly, with a separate kids' pool, complete with waterslide, and an in-house cinema. Rooms of varying sizes (and prices) are in two-story buildings scattered through the rain forest, decorated in earth tones to complement the surrounding nature. Spring for a spacious deluxe room for a sea view, which you can enjoy from your private balcony. Smaller "superior" rooms, in the ground floors, have less impressive views, whereas standard rooms view the forest. There is live music nightly at the Claro Que Sí restaurant (dinner only; $$$), which specializes in Caribbean-style seafood, and the Rico Tico ($$) grill, which serves lighter fare. A free shuttle makes scheduled trips to the beach, about 3 km (2 mi) away. **Pros:** friendly; nice views; environmentally sustainable; good restaurants. **Cons:** 3 km (2 mi) from beach; standards overpriced; several suites too close to road.

Road to park, just after Villas Nicolás, right-hand side ☎ 2777–0777, 888/742–6667 in North America ⊕ www.sicomono.com ⤶ 38 rooms, 20 suites ⚬ In-room: safe, kitchen (some), refrigerator, no TV. In-hotel: 2 restaurants, bars, pools, spa, laundry service, Wi-Fi hotspot ⊟ AE, MC, V ⊺○⫿ BP.

$ ⊞ **Hotel Vela Bar.** Abutting the jungle not far from Playa Espadilla, this
★ low-key, eclectic hotel has small but attractive rooms and very competitive rates. Though a bit cramped, each room has its own rustic charm, with white stucco walls, simple wooden furniture, and terra-cotta tile or wood floors. Room 7 is particularly nice, thanks to large windows and a bathtub. Shared front terraces with rocking chairs and hammocks overlook lush gardens. Two bungalows with private patios, air-conditioning, and TV sleep four. The restaurant, under a conical thatch roof in front, serves an eclectic mix of seafood and meat dishes with an array of sauces. **Pros:** very affordable; laid-back. **Cons:** basic rooms; spotty service. *⊠ Up road from Marlin Restaurant, on left ☎ 2777–0413 ⊕ www.velabar.com ⤶ 8 rooms, 2 bungalows, 1 apartment ⚬ In-room: no a/c (some), no phone, safe, kitchen (some), refrigerator (some), no TV (some). In-hotel: restaurant, bar, laundry service, Internet terminal ⊟ AE, D, DC, MC, V ⊺○⫿ EP.*

$$ ⊞ **Hotel Verde Mar.** This whimsical little hotel and its helpful staff are in the rain forest, with direct access to the beach and minutes away from the park. The rooms in a long two-story concrete building are on the small side, with one queen bed, but have colorfully artistic interiors, kitchenettes, and large windows with views of the ubiquitous tropical foliage. Suites are a bit bigger than standard rooms and have two queen beds and a walk-in closet. There's a small pool, from which a wooden catwalk leads through the woods to the beach. **Pros:** good value; mere steps from beach; in forest; friendly. **Cons:** rooms smallish; very basic. *⊹ ½ km/¼ mi north of park ☎ 2777–2122, 877/872–0459 in North America ⊕ www.verdemar.com ⤶ 22 rooms ⚬ In-room: no phone, safe, kitchen (some), no TV. In-hotel: pool, Internet, no-smoking rooms ⊟ AE, DC, MC, V ⊺○⫿ EP.*

$$ ⊞ **Inn on the Park.** This family-friendly inn has a quiet location near the
☾ beach and national park. The papaya-color building has three floors with two rooms each. Half are master suites with separate bedrooms, kitchens, and pullout couches, which can be a deal for small families (kids under 12 stay free). Upper rooms share balconies with verdant views. A small pool area with a wooden deck has a grill and tables where complimentary Continental breakfast is served. The rain forest rises up just behind it. **Pros:** good for families; lovely locale. **Cons:** no frills; rooms can be dingy. *⊠ 200 m up side road from Marlin Restaurant ☎ 2777–3791 ⊕ www.innontheparkhotel.com ⤶ 6 rooms ⚬ In-room: safe, kitchen (some, Wi-Fi). In-hotel: pool, laundry service, Internet, no-smoking rooms ⊺○⫿ BP.*

$$$–$$$$ ⊞ **La Mariposa.** The best view in town—a sweeping panorama of verdant
Fodor's Choice hills, the aquamarine ocean, and offshore islands—is Mariposa's claim
★ to fame. A confusing array of accommodations ranges from standard rooms overlooking the rain forest to bright suites with ocean-view balconies, to a penthouse. All are spacious and are in a series of buildings

7

between the jungle and gardens ablaze with colorful flowers. The four-story main building holds the lobby and restaurant, above which are three floors of ocean-view rooms reached by external spiraling stairways, which aren't for people who have trouble with stairs or suffer from vertigo. They are big, though rather plain, and have semiprivate balconies with amazing views; book a bright corner room on an upper floor (No. 31, 35, 36, or 40). Older ocean-view rooms on the hillside have low ceilings, Spanish decor, and big balconies overlooking the coast and park. Newer standard ocean views, down the hill, have lesser vistas, but TV sets. Larger premier rooms offer more privacy and great views, and have daybeds for kids (under 10 stay free), though the modern, new units suffer design flaws. The sundeck and wraparound pool are lovely. Transportation is provided to and from the beach, several times a day. **Pros:** gorgeous views; decent restaurant; central location. **Cons:** 4 km (2½ mi) from beach, ocean-view balconies separated by cane barriers. ⊠ *West of main road, right after Barba Roja* ✆ *Apdo. 4, Quepos* ☎ *2777–0355, 800/572–6440 in U.S.* ⊕ *www.hotelmariposa. com* ⇱ *60 rooms* ⚒ *In-room: safe, kitchen (some), no TV, Internet. In-hotel: restaurant, room service, bars, pools, laundry service, Wi-Fi* ▭ *AE, D, DC, MC, V* ⏀ *BP.*

$$–$$$ ⚏ **La Posada Private Jungle Bungalows.** Nestled on the edge of the national
Fodor's Choice park, this cluster of bungalows is also just a short walk from the beach.
★ Each bungalow has its own name—Fisherman's Wharf, Birds of Paradise, Jungle—and is decorated accordingly. The palm-thatch terraces face the small pool and lush greenery of the rain forest, which is regularly animated by troops of squirrel monkeys and other animals. As the charming North American owner, Michael, says, it's as close as you'll get to sleeping in the park. The main building holds three spacious apartments and a fully equipped *casita* (small house) on the second floor with two bedrooms, two baths, and a futon. Complimentary breakfast and cheap pizza are served in a small restaurant ($) in front. **Pros:** good value; near beach and park; wildlife; friendly. **Cons:** a bit isolated; small pool. ⊠ *250 m up side road from Marlin Restaurant* ✆ *Apdo. 155–6350, Quepos* ☎ *2777–1446* ⊕ *www.laposadajungle. com* ⇱ *4 bungalows, 2 apartments, 1 casita* ⚒ *In-room: no phone, safe, refrigerator, kitchen (some), no TV (some). In-hotel: pool, laundry service, no-smoking rooms* ▭ *MC, V* ⏀ *BP.*

$$$$ ⚏ **Makanda by the Sea.** Hypnotic views of the jungle-framed Pacific
Fodor's Choice Ocean make this secluded rain forest retreat perfect for honeymooners.
★ The bright, spacious, white-and-cream villas are among the country's most tasteful (and expensive). They have a comfortable seating area and king-size bed facing the sliding glass doors that lead to large balconies with ocean views and hammocks. The modern kitchens won't be necessary for breakfast, which is delivered to your room. Windows behind the bed maximize natural light, and the small Japanese-style garden out back adds to the subtle, well-designed touches. The smaller studios are darker, and have less impressive views, but they have access to the lovely, colorful pool and the Sunspot Bar and Grill (⇨ *above*), one of the best restaurants in town. Adventurous hikers can make the 20-minute

trek through the jungle to a tiny, private beach. **Pros:** secluded; tranquil; surrounded by nature; ocean views. **Cons:** far from beach; studios need updating. ✛ *1 km/½ mi west of La Mariposa* ⌂ *Apdo. 29, Quepos* ☎ *2777–0442, 888/625–2632 in North America* ⊕ *www.makanda. com* ⇨ *6 villas, 5 studios* ⌂ *In-room: safe, kitchen, Internet. In-hotel: restaurant, room service, pool, beachfront, laundry service, Internet terminal, no kids under 14* ▭ *AE, D, DC, MC, V* ⵘ*BP.*

$$–$$$ 🏨 **Villas de la Selva.** Hidden from the main road behind a mural of monkeys, this unique hillside hotel has comfortable accommodations and great views of the ocean. Straight down the long stairway, and perched on a cliff facing the ocean, are three airy rooms, each with its own color scheme, kitchenette, and ample terrace. There's also a casita that fits several people. Up the side of the hill, two much smaller rooms with balconies have nice views, but tiny bathrooms. A 300-meter (990-foot) trail leads to the beach. **Pros:** nice views; beach access; good value. **Cons:** unfriendly owner; not much privacy. ⊠ *Road to park, past Costa Verde and La Arboleda hotels* ☎ *2777–1137* ⊕ *www.villasdelaselva. com* ⇨ *6 rooms, 1 casita* ⌂ *In-room: no a/c (some), no phone, safe (some), kitchen (some), refrigerator. In-hotel: pool, laundry service* ▭ *MC, V* ⵘ*EP.*

$$–$$$$
Fodor'sChoice
★
🏨 **Villas Nicolás.** On a hillside about 3 km (2 mi) from the beach, terraced Mediterranean-style privately owned (and rented) villas have impressive views. Villas on the upper levels have ocean views, and those on the lower level overlook the jungle, where you may spot monkeys, iguanas, and an array of birds. (Avoid units 1 and 2, which overlook the hotel next door.) Each room is decorated differently, but the predominant motif is tropical. Most have balconies, some of which are large enough to hold a table, chairs, and hammock. Narrow walkways wind through this tranquil property's lush grounds to the villas and blue-tile pool. During the high season a tiny restaurant by the pool offers breakfasts and light meals. **Pros:** great location; most rooms have great views. **Cons:** some units need updating; inconsistent service. ⊠ *Road to park, across from Hotel Byblos* ⌂ *Apdo. 236, Quepos* ☎ *2777–0481* ⊕ *www.villasnicolas.com* ⇨ *12 villas* ⌂ *In-room: safe, kitchen (some), refrigerator, no TV. In-hotel: pool, laundry service, no-smoking rooms, no kids under 6* ▭ *AE, D, DC, MC, V* ⵘ*EP.*

NIGHTLIFE

BARS The **Billfish Bar** (⊠ *Main road, across from Barba Roja* ☎ *2777–0411*), with large-screen TVs and pool tables, fills up on game nights.

★ **Salsipuedes** (⊠ *Main road, north of Barba Roja* ☎ *2777–5019*), a colorful tapas bar hidden behind tropical foliage, is a great sunset venue. It's one of the few places you can enjoy a quiet drink.

DANCE CLUB **Barba Roja** (⊠ *Main road, across from Hotel Divisamar* ☎ *2777–0331*) has a popular sunset happy hour. The bar becomes a dance club late on Saturday night. **Tutu** (⊠ *Above Gato Negro, Casitas Eclipse* ☎ *No phone*) is Manuel Antonio's late-night gay bar. It's an elegant place, with light reflected off a deep blue pool. **The Lounge** (⊠ *Main road, above La Hacienda Restaurant* ☎ *2777–5143*) is a popular late-night spot, with reggae playing Monday and Wednesday and a mix of Latin rhythms other nights.

SHOPPING

There's no shortage of shopping in this town. The beach near the entrance to the park is lined with a sea of vendors who sell T-shirts, hats, and colorful beach wraps. More authentic handicrafts are sold at night by artisans positioned along the sidewalk in central Manuel Antonio.

La Buena Nota (⊠ *Main road, past Hotel Karahe* ☎ *2777–1002*) has an extensive selection of beachwear, souvenirs, sunscreen, hats, postcards, and English-language books and magazines. **Regáme** (⊠ *Next to Sí Como No Hotel* ☎ *2777–0777*) is primarily an art gallery, with paintings, drawings, pottery, and jewelry by dozens of artists.

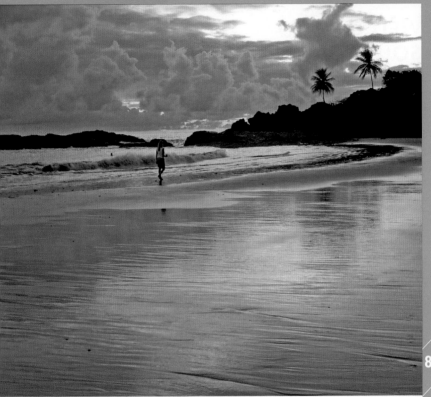

South Pacific

WORD OF MOUTH

"This was taken at sunset on Dominical Beach. The tide goes way out and the sand stays wet. We found this to be one of the most picturesque beaches in Costa Rica."

—Photo by Chad Clark, Fodors.com

WELCOME TO SOUTH PACIFIC

TOP REASONS TO GO

★ **Enormous Corcovado National Park:** The last refuge of such endangered species as jaguars and tapirs.

★ **Mountain hikes:** Hikes that range from easy daytime treks from luxurious lodges to Costa Rica's toughest: 3,810-meter (12,500-foot) Cerro Chirripó.

★ **Kayaking:** Head to the Golfo Dulce or along the Sierpe or Colorado rivers' jungly channels.

★ **Bird-watching:** Yields such beauties as scarlet macaws and the resplendent quetzal.

★ **Wild places to stay:** Relax in the top eco-lodges, thatch-roof beach bungalows, and cozy mountain cabins.

1 Central Highlands. The main road climbs more than 2,134 meters (7,000 feet) over mountains and above the clouds of the Central Highlands before descending into the huge Valle de El General agricultural region. Highlights are fabulous mountain lodges and Chirripó National Park.

2 The Coast. The Coast consists of miles of beaches and small beach communities, including Dominical, a scruffy but lively surfer haven.

3 The Osa Peninsula. The wild Osa Peninsula consists almost entirely of Corcovado National Park, 1,156 square km (445 square mi) of primary and secondary rain forest straight out of a David Attenborough nature documentary.

4 Golfo Dulce. The eastern Golfo Dulce draws anglers to Golfito, slow-paced beach bums to Zancudo, and serious surfers to Pavones.

GETTING ORIENTED

The most remote part of Costa Rica, the South Pacific encompasses the southern half of Puntarenas Province and La Amistad International Biosphere. The region descends from mountainous forests just an hour south of San José to the humid Golfo Dulce and the richly forested Osa Peninsula, 8 to 10 hours from the capital by car.

8

SOUTH PACIFIC PLANNER

Climate and Weather

The climate swings wildly in the south, from frigid mountain air to steamy coastal humidity. In the mountains it's normally around 24°C (75°F) during the day and 10°C (50°F) at night, though nighttime temperatures on the upper slopes of Cerro de la Muerte can be close to freezing. Temperatures in coastal areas are usually 24°C–32°C (76°F–90°F), but it's the humidity that does you in. If you're traveling from San José through the mountains on your way to points south, be sure to pack a warm sweater or jacket.

The dry season, from January through April, has the most reliably dry weather. But the shoulder seasons can be delightful, especially in early December when the landscape is lush and green and crowds of tourists have yet to arrive. The May-to-December rainy season is the worst in the Osa Peninsula, where rains usually last through January. Roads sometimes flood and lodges might close in the rainiest months (October and November). Elsewhere during the rainy season, mornings tend to be brilliant and sunny, with rain starting in midafternoon.

Choosing a Place to Stay

Expect reasonable comfort in unbelievably wild settings. Most accommodations are in small hotels, cabins, and lodges run by hands-on owners, many of them foreigners who fell in love with the place on a visit and stayed. Generally speaking, the farther south and more remote the lodge, the more expensive it is. Bad roads (causing supply problems) and lack of electricity and communications make hotel keeping costly, especially in the Osa Peninsula and Golfo Dulce. When you look at the per-person prices, take into account that most of these places include meals, transport, guides, and unique locations.

The country's premier eco-lodges are almost all in the Southern Zone, ranging from simple tents to sophisticated lodges. But keep in mind that if you yearn to be close to nature, you have to be prepared for encounters of the natural kind in your shower or bedroom. Keep a flashlight handy for nighttime trips to the bathroom and always wear sandals.

A World Apart

Visitors go south to heed the call of the wild. On land, hiking, bird-watching, horseback riding, and wildlife-viewing are the main activities, along with some thrilling tree-climbing, zip-line, and waterfall-rappelling opportunities. On the water, there's surfing, snorkeling, diving, fishing, sea-kayaking, and whale- and dolphin-watching, as well as swimming and beachcombing. There's even a sky option, flying in a two-seater ultralight plane.

What makes many of these activities special in the Southern Zone is that, given the wildness of the locations, the focus is more on nature than on entertainment. No matter what you're doing, you'll come across interesting flora and fauna and natural phenomena. Another key to what sets the Southern Zone apart is the large number of trained naturalist guides. Most eco-lodges have resident guides who know not only where to find the birds and wildlife, but also how to interpret the hidden workings of the natural world around you.

Getting Here and Around

You need at least a week to truly experience any part of the Osa Peninsula. Even if you fly, transfers to lodges are slow, so plan two days for travel alone. Choose one home base and take day trips. In three weeks, though, you can experience the entire Southern Zone: mountains, beaches, and the Osa Peninsula.

For points between San José and San Vito, driving is a viable option, as long as you give yourself lots of time. Direct buses to San Isidro, Golfito, and Puerto Jiménez are cheap and reliable and are reasonably comfortable. The best and fastest way to get to the far south, though, is to fly directly to Golfito, Puerto Jiménez, Drake, Palmar Sur, or Carate. Many lodges arrange flights, taxi, and boat transfers all the way from San José as part of a package. If you want your own car to go exploring, you can rent 4WD vehicles in Puerto Jiménez and Golfito.

If you are driving south, keep in mind that Cerro de la Muerte is often covered with fog in the afternoon, so plan to cross the mountains in the morning. Don't try to cover too much ground on a set schedule. It is simply impossible to underestimate how long it takes to drive the roads or make transportation connections in this part of the country, especially during rainy season when flooding and landslides can close roads and bad weather can delay flights. But remember, getting there is part of the adventure.

Dining and Lodging Prices

WHAT IT COSTS IN DOLLARS

	¢	$	$$	$$$	$$$$
Restaurants	under $5	$5–$10	$10–$15	$15–$25	over $25
Hotels	under $50	$50–$75	$75–$150	$150–$250	over $250

Restaurant prices are per person for a main course at dinner. Hotel prices are for two people in a standard double room in high season, excluding service and tax (16.4%).

Kids Gone Wild

The Southern Zone is like Outward Bound for families, where kids and parents can face challenges—such as no TV or video games!—and have adventures together. Plunge the family into real-life adventures with added natural-history educational value. You might inspire a future herpetologist or marine biologist among your progeny.

Go horseback riding to waterfalls and swimming holes. Steal into the night with infrared flashlights to scout out frogs and other fascinating, nocturnal creepy-crawlies. Enjoy kayaking in a calm gulf where dolphins play. Rappel down a waterfall, climb inside a hollow tree, or zip-line through the trees.

The remoter areas of the South are ideal for kids ages 7 and up. Babies and all their paraphernalia are hard to handle here, and toddlers are tough to keep off the ground where biting insects and snakes live.

Tour Operators

Horizontes Nature Tours (☎ 2222–2022 ⊕ www.horizontes.com) is an expert ecotourist company that arranges custom tours with naturalist guides and ornithologists.

Costa Rica Expeditions (☎ 2257–0766 ⊕ www.costaricaexpeditions.com) is the original ecotourist outfit in Costa Rica, specializing in countrywide nature tours with local naturalist guides.

8

CHIRRIPÓ NATIONAL PARK

Chirripó National Park is all about hiking. The ascent to Mount Chirripó, the highest mountain in Costa Rica, is the most popular and challenging hike in the country. It's also the most exclusive, limited to 35 hikers per day.

From the trailhead to the peak, you gain more than 2,438 meters (8,000 feet) of elevation, climbing through shaded highland forest, then out into the wide-open, windswept wilds of the páramo, scrubby moorland similar to the high Andes. It's a 48-km (30-mi) round-trip, and you need at least three days to climb to the hostel base, explore the summits, and descend. The modern but chilly stone hostel is the only available accommodation, with small rooms of four bunks each, shared cold-water bathrooms, and a cooking area. You need to bring your own sleeping bag, pillow, and provisions. A new generator and some solar panels provide some electricity, but the hostel is still bare-bones rustic. Trails from the hostel lead to the top of Chirripó—the highest point in Costa Rica—and the nearby peak of Terbi, as well as half a dozen other peaks and glacier lakes. ■TIP→ **Pack plenty of warm clothes.**

BEST TIME TO GO

Between sometimes freezing temperatures and more than 381 centimeters (150 inches) of rain a year, timing is of the essence here. The best months are in the dry season, January to May. The park is often closed from September through mid-December, when the trails are too wet and slippery for safety.

FUN FACT

A climb up Chirripó is a rite of passage for many young Costa Ricans, who celebrate their graduation from high school or college with a group expedition.

BEST WAYS TO EXPLORE

HIKING

There's no getting around it: the only way to explore this park is on foot. And the only way is up. It's a tough climb to Mount Chirripó's base camp—6 to 10 hours from the official park entrance, depending on your physical condition—so most hikers head out of San Gerardo de Rivas at the first light of day. You can hire porters to lug your gear up and down for you, so at least you can travel relatively light.

People who live in Costa Rica train seriously for this hike, so be sure you are in good enough shape to make the climb. Smart hikers also factor in a couple of days in the San Gerardo de Rivas area to acclimatize to the high altitude before setting out. The hike down is no picnic, either: your knees and ankles will be stretched to their limits. But it's an adventure every step of the way—and the bragging rights are worth it.

MOUNTAIN HIGHS

The base-camp hostel at Los Crestones is at 11,152 feet above sea level, so you still have some hiking ahead of you if you want to summit the surrounding peaks. Take your pick: Chirripó at 12,532 feet; Ventisqueros at 12,467 feet; Cerro Terbi at 12,336; and, for the fainter of heart, Mt. Uran at a measly 11,811 feet. Mountain hikers who collect "peaks" can add all four mountaintops to their list.

BIRD-WATCHING

Although your eyes will mostly be on the scenery, there are some highland species of birds that thrive in this chilly mountain air. Watch for the Volcano Junco, a sparrow-like bird with a pink beak and a yellow eye ring. Only two hummingbirds venture up this high—the fiery-throated, which lives up to its name; and the volcano hummingbird, which is the country's smallest bird. If you see a raptor soaring above, chances are it's a red-tailed hawk.

TOP REASONS TO GO

DID IT!
The sheer sense of accomplishing this tough hike is the number one reason hikers take on this challenge. You don't have to be a mountain climber but you do need to be in very good shape.

TOP OF THE WORLD
The exhilaration of sitting on top of the world, with only sky, mountain peaks, and heath as far as the eye can see, motivates most visitors to withstand the physical challenges and the spartan conditions in the hostel.

UNIQUE ENVIRONMENT
A climb up Chirripó gives visitors a unique chance to experience extreme changes in habitat, from pastureland through rainforest and oak forest to bleak, scrubby páramo (a high elevation ecosystem). As the habitat changes, so does the endemic wildlife, which thins out near the top, along with the air.

OCEAN VIEWS
On rare, perfectly clear days, the top of Chirripó is one of the few places in the country where you can see both the Pacific and Atlantic oceans.

8

CORCOVADO NATIONAL PARK

For those who crave untamed wilderness, Corcovado National Park is the experience of a lifetime. Covering one-third of the Osa Peninsula, the park is blanketed primarily by virgin rain forest and holds Central America's largest remaining tract of lowland Pacific rain forest.

The remoteness of Corcovado and the difficult access to its interior make it one of the most pristine parks in the country—barely disturbed by human presence—where massive, vine-tangled primary-forest trees tower over the trails, and birds and wildlife abound. Your chances of spotting endangered species are better here than anywhere else in the country, although it still takes a combination of determination and luck. The rarest and most sought-after sightings are the jaguar and Baird's tapir. Corcovado also has the largest population of scarlet macaws in the country. Bordering the park are some of Costa Rica's most luxurious jungle lodges and retreats, all of which are contributing to the effort to save Corcovado's wildlife, which has been under heavy pressure in recent years from poachers.

BEST TIME TO GO

Dry season, January to April, is the best time to visit, but it's also the most popular. With so little accommodation available, it's crucial to reserve well in advance. June through August will be wetter, but may also be a little cooler. The trails are virtually impassable from September to December.

FUN FACT

Warning signs to stay on the trails should be heeded: in 2007, the Minister of Tourism got lost and wandered around in a daze for three days after following a baby tapir off the trail and being attacked by its mother.

BEST WAYS TO EXPLORE

GETTING HERE AND AROUND

The easiest way to visit the park is on a day trip by boat, organized by a lodge or tour company in Drake Bay, Puerto Jiménez, or Sierpe. The well-heeled can fly in on an expensive charter plane to the Sirena air field. But no matter how you get there, the only way to explore is on foot. There are no roads, only hiking trails. If you have a backpack, strong legs, and a reservation for a tent site or a ranger station bunk, you can enter the park on foot at three staffed ranger stations and spend up to five days, deep in the wilds.

HIKING

There are two main hiking routes to Corcovado. When you're planning your itinerary, keep in mind that the hike between any two ranger stations takes at least a day. The hike from La Leona to Sirena is about 16 km (10 mi) and requires crossing a wide river mouth and a stretch of beach best crossed at low tide. Some people plan this hike before dawn to avoid the blistering sun. The 17.4-km (10.8-mi) trail from Los Patos to Sirena is the coolest trail, through forest all the way.

BIRD-WATCHING AND WILDLIFE

The holy grail of wildlife spotting here is a jaguar or a Baird's tapir. You may be one of the lucky few to see one of these rare, elusive animals. In the meantime, you can content yourself with coatis, peccaries, and agoutis on the ground and, in the trees, some endemic species of birds you will only see in this part of the country: Baird's trogon, riverside wren, and black-cheeked ant-tanager, to name a few.

TOP REASONS TO GO

FLORA AND FAUNA

The sheer diversity of flora and fauna and the chance to see wildlife completely in the wild are the main draws here. The number of catalogued species, to date, includes 500 trees (49 of them in peril of extinction), 150 orchids, 370 birds, 140 mammals (17 on the endangered list), 123 butterflies, 116 amphibians, and more than 6,000 insects.

OFF THE BEATEN TRACK

Day visitors get to taste the thrill of being completely off the beaten track, in an untamed natural world. But for campers and guests at the park's main lodge, La Sirena, the chance to spend days roaming miles of trails without hearing a single man-made sound is a rare treat.

TEST YOUR LIMITS

The physical challenges of hiking in high humidity and living very basically, along with the psychological challenge of being completely out of touch with "the real world," appeal to the kind of people who like to test their limits.

8

WHALE MARINE NATIONAL PARK

Great snorkeling, whale-watching, and beach-combing draw visitors and locals to Parque Nacional Marino Ballena (Whale Marine National Park), which protects four relatively tranquil beaches stretching for about 10 km (6 mi), as well as a mangrove estuary, a recovering coral reef, and a vast swath of ocean.

Playa Uvita, fronting the small town of Bahía Ballena, is the longest and most visited beach, and the embarkation point for snorkeling, fishing, and whale-watching tours. Restaurants line the nearby main street of the town. Playa Colonia has a safe swimming beach with a view of rocky islands. Playa Ballena, south of Playa Colonia, is a lovely strand backed by lush vegetation. Finally, tiny Playa Piñuela is the prettiest of the park beaches, in a deep cove that serves as the local port. Along with the tropical fish you'll see while snorkeling, you may be lucky enough to see humpback whales and dolphins. Above the water there are frigate birds and brown boobies, a tropical seabird, nesting on the park's rocky islands.

BEST TIME TO GO

December to April is the best time for guaranteed sunny beach weather, as well as for sightings of humpback whales with their young. The whales also roam these waters in late July through late October. Bottlenose dolphins abound in March and April. Avoid weekends in December to February, and Easter week, if you want the beach to yourself.

FUN FACT

Playa Uvita features a *tombolo*, a long swath of sand connecting a former island to the coast. At low tide, the exposed brown sandbar resembles a whale's tail, in keeping with the bay's name: Bahía Ballena (Whale Bay).

BEST WAYS TO EXPLORE

BEACHCOMBING
The park's beaches are ideal to explore on foot, especially the Blue Flag–designated Playa Uvita, which has the longest and widest stretch of beach. Visitors and locals flock here in the late afternoon to catch spectacular sunsets. Don't forget your camera! At low tide, you can walk out onto the Whale's Tail sandbar. During the day, you'll see moving shells every-where—hermit crabs of every size are constantly scuttling around. Although it all looks idyllic—and it mostly is—don't leave valuables unattended on the beach.

IN, ON, AND OVER THE WATER
Swimming here is relatively safe, but check with the park ranger or your hotel about the best swimming spots. Or just watch where the locals are frolicking in the water. Get a little farther out in the water on a fishing charter and try your hand at reeling in mahimahi, tuna, and mackerel. Whale- and dolphin-watching excursions are also a fun option—bottle-nosed dolphins are most often spotted, but humpback whales, especially mothers with babes, are the stars of the show. If you want to be the captain of your boat, sea kayaks are a popular way to explore the park's mangroves and river estuar-ies. Playa Ventanas, just south of the park's official border, has tidal rock caves you can kayak through. You can also paddle out to close-in islets and look for brown boobies, the tropical seabirds that nest here. For the ultimate bird's-eye view, take an ultralight flight over the park.

CAMPING
If you brought a tent, pitch it here. Camping on the beach is allowed at Playas Ballena, Colonia, and Piñuela. You can't beat the price, as camping is included in the park admission. Costa Ricans are avid—and often noisy—campers, so try to avoid busy weekends and *Semana Santa* (Easter Week).

TOP REASONS TO GO

ALONE TIME
If solitude is what you're after, the park's beaches are relatively uncrowded, except on weekends and school holidays when locals come to relax. Neither Playa Colonia nor Playa Piñuela sees a lot of traffic, so you can have them virtually to yourself almost anytime.

BEACHES
Miles of wide, sandy beach backed by palm trees and distant green mountain ridges make this one of the most scenic and accessible coastlines in the country. Playa Uvita and Playa Ballena, with their warm, swimmable waters and soft sand, attract the most beachgoers.

WHALES AND DOLPHINS
Catching sight of a humpback whale with her youngster swimming alongside is a thrill you won't forget. And watching dolphins cavorting around your excursion boat is the best entertainment on water.

8

ECO-LODGES IN THE SOUTH PACIFIC

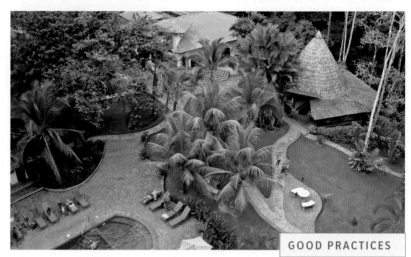

The South Pacific Zone is Costa Rica's last frontier, with a wealth of protected biodiversity. It's also the cradle of the country's ecotourism, including some of the world's best eco-lodges.

Costa Rica's wildest corner has vast expanses of wilderness ranging from the majestic cloud forests and high-altitude páramo of the Talamanca highlands to the steamy, lowland rain forest of Corcovado National Park. Quetzals and other high-elevation birds abound in the oak forests of the San Gerardo de Dota valley, and scarlet macaws congregate in beach almond trees lining the shores of the Osa Peninsula. The Southern Zone has some of the country's most impressive, though least accessible, national parks—towering Chirripó and mountain-studded La Amistad; and Corcovado, where peccaries, tapirs, and, more rarely, jaguars still roam. Stunning marine wonders can be found in the Golfo Dulce, the dive and snorkeling spots around Caño Island Biological Reserve, and Ballena Marine National Park, famous for seasonal whale migrations. The lodges around Drake Bay, together with the off-the-grid lodges of Carate and Cabo Matapalo, provide unequaled immersion in tropical nature.

GOOD PRACTICES

The signage you'll often see in natural areas sums up ecotourism's principal tenets: Leave nothing but footprints; take away nothing but memories.

A few more tips:

Walk softly on forest trails and keep as quiet as you can. You'll spot more wildlife and maintain the natural atmosphere of the forest for other visitors, too.

Stay on marked trails and never approach animals; use your zoom lens to capture close-ups.

Ecotourism is also about getting to know the locals and their culture. Visit a local farm, an artisan's co-op, or a village school.

TOP ECO-LODGES IN THE SOUTH PACIFIC

LAPA RÍOS

Lapa Ríos is the premier eco-lodge in Costa Rica. Along with providing top-notch, sustainable hospitality, the lodge's mission is to protect the 1,000 acres of forest in its private preserve edging Corcovado National Park. Its main weapon is education, through local school programs and community involvement. The lodge owners spearheaded the building of the local school and provide direct employment to more than 45 area families. Lapa Ríos was the first area lodge to offer a free sustainability tour, highlighting innovative eco-friendly practices, including feeding organic waste to pigs to produce methane fuel. As a guest, you'll be thankful for the absence of motor noise—gardeners work exclusively with manual tools.

CASA CORCOVADO

This jungle lodge, bordering Corcovado National Park, gets top eco marks for its energy-saving solar and microhydroelectric systems, and its recycling and waste-management leadership in the area. The lodge financed the building of a recycling center in Sierpe, and all the area's glass and aluminum is now recycled. Guests receive a refillable bottle to use throughout their stay. Owner Steve Lill is cofounder and president of the Corcovado Foundation, a major supporter of local initiatives to preserve wildlife on the Osa Peninsula.

PLAYA NICUESA RAINFOREST LODGE

From its initial construction to its daily operations, this Golfo Dulce lodge, accessible only by boat, has been committed to sustainability. The main lodge and guest cabins were built with fallen wood and recycled materials. Solar power, an organic septic system, composting, and a chemical-free garden also attest to the owners' eco credentials. The kitchen uses local produce and cooks up fish caught in the gulf. Lodge owners Donna and Michael Butler match guests' donations to the Osa Campaign, a cooperative conservation program.

AFTER DARK

The first night in a remote Southern Zone eco-lodge can be unnerving. You may have looked forward to falling asleep to the sounds of nature, but you may not be prepared for the onslaught of night noises: the chirping of geckos as they hunt for insects in the thatch roof, the thwack of flying insects colliding against window screens, and the spine-tingling calls of owls and nightjars. Add in the chorus of croaking frogs and you may have trouble falling asleep. Once you realize that you're safe under your mosquito net, you can start to enjoy the nocturnal symphony. And after the first day of waking up at dawn to the roars of howler monkeys and the chatter of song-birds, you'll be more than ready to crash early the next night. Most guests are asleep by 8 PM and rise at 5 AM, the best time to spot birds and wildlife as they start their day, too. For nighttime visits to the bathroom, be sure to keep a flashlight handy and something to put on your feet if you want to avoid creepy-crawlies.

8

By Dorothy MacKinnon

The South Pacific encompasses everything south of San José, down to the border with Panama, and all the territory west of the Talamanca mountains, sloping down to the Pacific coast. World-class mountain hikes and bird-watching abound in the highlands, just south of the capital.

The beaches attract surfers, fishers, whale-watchers, and beachcombers. But the jewels in the South Pacific crown are the idyllic Golfo Dulce and the wild Osa Peninsula, brimming with wildlife and natural adventures.

GETTING HERE AND AROUND

SANSA and Nature Air have direct flights to Drake Bay, Palmar Sur, and Puerto Jiménez. SANSA has the most flights to Golfito and the only flights to Coto 47 (for San Vito). *For more information about air travel to the South Pacific from San José, see Air Travel in Travel Smart Costa Rica.*

Alfa Romeo Aero Taxi, at the Puerto Jiménez airport (really more of an airstrip), flies small charter planes to Carate, Tiskita, and Corcovado National Park's airstrip at La Sirena. The one-way price is $390 for up to five people.

Owing to the dismal state of the roads and hazardous driving conditions—flooded rivers and potholes—we don't recommend driving to the South Pacific, especially in rainy season. If you decide to drive, make sure your vehicle has 4WD and a spare tire. Give yourself lots of daylight time to get to where you are going. You can also fly to Golfito or the Osa Peninsula and rent a 4WD vehicle locally.

Bus fares from San José range from about $3 to $10, depending on distance and number of stops. The best way to get around the region's roads is by bus—let someone else do the driving. Bus fares are cheap, and you'll meet the locals. But the going is generally slow, buses often leave very early in the morning, and schedules change frequently, so check the day before you want to travel.

Based in Dominical, Easy Ride has two daily shuttle-van services in each direction between San José and the Dominical/Uvita/Ojochal area for $30 to $45 per person. For an extra $5 they will take you to the San José airport.

ESSENTIALS

Bus Contacts Easy Ride (☎ 2253–4444 ⊕ www.easyridecr.com).

THE CENTRAL HIGHLANDS

Less than an hour south of San José the Pan-American Highway climbs up into the scenic Central Highlands of Cerro de la Muerte, famous for spectacular mountain vistas, high-altitude coffee farms, cloud-forest eco-lodges, and challenging mountain hikes.

ZONA DE LOS SANTOS

Santa María de Dota is 65 km/40 mi south of San José. The Route of the Saints is 24 km/15 mi long.

Empalme, at Km 51 of the Pan-American Highway, marks the turnoff for Santa María de Dota, the first of the blessed coffee-growing towns named after saints that dot this mountainous area known as the Zona de Los Santos (Zone of the Saints).

★ The scenic road that winds through the high-altitude valley from Empalme to San Pablo de León is appropriately called **La Ruta de Los Santos** *(Route of the Saints)*. It's well paved to facilitate shipping the coffee produced in the region, which is central to Costa Rica's economy. On the 30-minute (24-km [15-mi]) drive from Empalme to San Pablo de León Cortés, you see misty valleys ringed by precipitous mountain slopes terraced with lush, green coffee plants. The route also captures the essence of a traditional Tico way of life built around coffee growing. Stately churches anchor bustling towns full of prosperous, neat houses with pretty gardens and 1970s Toyota Land Cruisers in a rainbow of colors parked in front.

GETTING HERE From San José, drive an hour and a half southeast on the paved Pan-American Highway, heading toward Cartago, then follow the signs south for San Isidro de El General. The two-lane road climbs steeply and there are almost no safe places to pass heavy trucks and slow vehicles. Make an early start, because the road is often enveloped in mist and rain in the afternoon. At Km 51 turn right at Empalme to reach Santa María de Dota, 14 km (8½ mi) along a wide, curving, paved road.

WHERE TO EAT AND STAY

¢ ✕ **Café de Los Santos.** This pretty café, within sight of the majestic, domed
CAFE San Marcos church, showcases the area's high-altitude *arabica* Tarrazú coffee, the "celestial drink" for which this zone is famous. There are more than 30 specialty coffee drinks, plus homemade sweet and savory pastries, and light lunches. It's open weekdays 9 to 7:30 am, Saturdays 2 to 5:30. Closed Sundays. ✉ *100 m east of church ⊕ 6 km/4 mi west of Santa María de Dota, San Marcos de Tarrazú* ☎ *2546–7881* ▭ *No credit cards*.

$–$$ ▦ **El Toucanet Lodge.** For serenity and mountain greenery, you can't beat this family-run lodge with plenty of pastoral scenery on view from the glassed-in dining room. Each of the six large rooms in three wooden

8

cabins above the main lodge has its own private veranda and tile bathroom with skylight. Two new junior suites have fireplaces, whirlpool baths, and king-size beds. Owners Gary and Edna Roberts are known for hearty breakfasts, baked trout dinners, and creative vegetarian dishes. Gary leads a free quetzal

> **THE FINAL FRONTIER**
>
> The Southern Zone was the very last part of Costa Rica to be settled. The first road, from San José to San Isidro, wasn't begun until the 1950s.

hunt every day at 7 AM along the road, bordering Los Quetzales National Park. He also arranges horseback rides, mountain hikes, and tours of neighboring coffee *fincas* (farms). With at least six hours' notice, he can fire up the natural-stone hot tub for an end-of-day soak under the stars. **Pros:** fresh mountain air; tranquility; low-key; affordable. **Cons:** simple furnishings; limited menu. ⌖ *7 km/4½ mi east of Santa María de Dota along steep, winding paved road, Copey; or from Km 58 of the Pan-American Hwy., turn right at sign for Copey and follow dirt road 8 km/5 mi* ☎ *2541–3131* 🖷 *2541–3045* ⊕ *www.eltoucanet.com* ⇥ *6 rooms, 2 junior suites* ⟳ *In-room: no a/c, no phone, no TV. In-hotel: restaurant* ⊟ *MC, V* ⊗ *Closed Sept.* ⟊⊙⟊ *BP.*

SHOPPING

The best place to buy local coffee is where the farmers themselves bring their raw coffee beans to be roasted and packed into jute bags, the **Coopedota Santa Maria** (⊠ *Main road, just after the bridge as you enter Santa María de Dota* ☎ *2541–2828*). You can buy export-quality coffee at their new coffee shop for about $10 per kilo (2.2 pounds). Choose between *en grano* (whole bean) or *molido* (ground), and between light or dark roast. The shop is open 8 to 6, daily in high season. You can also reserve a short, one-hour tour ($8) or a longer three-hour ($13) of the coffee co-op by calling ahead.

SAN GERARDO DE DOTA

89 km/55 mi southeast of San José, 52 km/32 mi south of Santa María de Dota.

Cloud forests, invigorating, cool mountain air, well-kept hiking trails, and excellent bird-watching make San Gerardo de Dota one of Costa Rica's premier nature destinations. The tiny hamlet is in the narrow Savegre River valley, 9 km (5½ mi) down a twisting, partially asphalted track that descends abruptly to the west from the Pan-American Highway. The peaceful surroundings look more like the Rocky Mountains than Central America, but hike down the waterfall trail and the vegetation quickly turns tropical again. Beyond hiking and bird-watching, activities include horseback riding and trout fly-fishing.

GETTING HERE

The drive from San José takes about three hours, and from Santa María de Dota about one hour. At Km 80 on the Pan-American Highway, turn down the dirt road signed SAN GERARDO DE DOTA. It's a harrowing, twisting road for most of the 9 km (5½ mi), with signs warning drivers to gear down and go slow. Some newly paved sections help to ease the worst curves. Tourist vans often stop along the road when the guides spot birds; grab your binoculars and join them!

OUTDOOR ACTIVITIES

BIRD-
WATCHING
★

This area is a must for bird-watchers, who flock here with small package tours (⇨ *Tours in Travel Smart Costa Rica*). Individual birders can choose from a roster of expert local guides; check with your hotel for recommendations. **Savegre Hotel de Montaña** (☎ *2740–1028* ⊕ *www. savegre.co.cr*) has the best bird guides in the area ($70 for a half day) and organizes hiking tours in the surrounding mountains.

Although you can see many birds from your cabin porch, most bird-watching requires hiking, some of it along steep paths made extra challenging by the high altitude (from 7,000 to 10,000 feet above sea level). Come fit and armed with binoculars and layers of warm clothing. The early mornings are brisk up here, but you'll warm up quickly with the sun and the exertion of walking.

HIKING

Some of the best hiking in the country is in this valley. Expert birder Marino Chacón of Savegre Hotel (⇨ *below*) leads a daylong natural-history hike (about $150 for up to nine people, including transportation and a packed lunch) that starts with a drive up to the *páramo* (high-altitude, shrubby ecosystem) of **Cerro de la Muerte.** The trail begins at the cluster of communication towers, near Km 89, and descends through the forest into the valley. Miles of prime bird-watching/hiking trails wind through the forest reserve belonging to the Chacóns. ■TIP➔ **Night temperatures on the slopes of Cerro de la Muerte can approach freezing— it's called the Mountain of Death for the very simple reason that long-ago travelers attempting to cross it on foot often froze to death during the night. Pack accordingly.**

The most challenging trail in the area is the one that begins at the

★ Hotel Savegre and follows the **Río Savegre** down to a spectacular waterfall. To get to the trailhead, follow the main road past Savegre Hotel to a fork, where you veer left, cross a bridge, and head over the hill to a pasture that narrows to a

> ## THE RESPLENDENT QUETZAL
>
> The damp, epiphyte-laden oak-tree forest around San Gerardo de Dota is renowned for resplendent quetzals, considered by many to be the most beautiful bird in the Western world. Male quetzals in full breeding plumage are more spectacular than females, with metallic green feathers, crimson stomachs, helmetlike crests, and extravagantly long tail feathers. Ask guides or hotel staff about common quetzal hangouts; early morning during the March-to-May nesting season is the best time to spot them.

footpath. Although it is only 2 km (1¼ mi) each way, the hike is steep and slippery, especially near the bottom, and takes about three hours.

WHERE TO STAY

$ 🛏 **Albergue de Montaña Paraíso del Quetzal.** Nestled in a cloud forest just minutes off the main highway, this rustic lodge is, indeed, a paradise for resplendent quetzals and for the visitors who want to see this most beautiful and sought-after bird in Costa Rica. Even if you don't catch sight of a quetzal, the vistas of cloud-enshrouded mountains and valleys will keep you busy, as will the hiking and birding trails through ancient oak forests dripping with moss and epiphytes. Each cozy cabin, set in splendid isolation, has a double bed plus a bunk bed, and lots of blankets. Nighttime temperatures drop into the 40s (around 4°C to 7°C at this altitude (about 2,377 meters [7,800 feet] above sea level), and you'll be happy for the tiny, tiled bathrooms with steaming-hot showers. The main lodge has a wood-burning stove and a deck abuzz with brilliant hummingbirds. Meals are simple *comida tipica* (typical food), cooked on a woodstove. All the family pitches in, cooking, serving, and guiding. This is the first hotel in this world-renowned birding area to receive the country's coveted Blue Flag for eco-friendliness. Per-person rates include dinner and breakfast, and guided hiking and birding tours. **Pros:** scenic views; pristine cloud forest; amazing bird-watching and hikes. **Cons:** very simple lodging and food; steep paths to some cabins; very cold nights. ⊠ *Km 70, Pan-American Hwy., Cerro de la Muerte* ☎ *2200–0241 or 2771–4582* ⊕ *www.paraisodelquetzal.com* ➾ *8 cabins* ⌂ *In-room: no a/c, no phone, no TV. In-hotel: restaurant* ═ *MC, V* ⦿*EP.*

$ 🛏 **Cabañas y Senderos Las Cataratas.** One of the best deals—and meals— in the valley is at this rustic restaurant and cabins run by a Tico family, who all join in (kids, too) to help serve meals. Three simple, wooden cabins, one with a wood-burning fireplace, have red-velvet decor reminiscent of a bordello, but they are cheap and comfortable. There are

A male white-throated mountain-gem hummingbird in a defense posture. Río Savegre, San Gerardo de Dota.

some short, steep forest trails to explore. At the restaurant ($) you can dine on fresh trout—pulled directly out of the adjoining pond when you place your order—with salad, vegetables, dessert, and juice for less than $10. If you haven't got the time or the courage to face the steep road all the way down to San Gerardo, this is a good compromise, only 3 km (2 mi) in from the highway. It's a good idea to call ahead on a weekday, and Bernardo, the owner, will be ready for you. **Pros:** cheap; excellent fresh trout; authentic Tico culture. **Cons:** rustic, simple; call ahead on a weekday to make sure someone is there. ✛ *3 km/2 mi down steep road to San Gerardo de Dota* ☎ *2740–1064 or 2740–1065* 🛏 *3 cabins* ♿ *In-room: no a/c, no phone, no TV. In-hotel: restaurant* 🟰 *MC, V* 🍽 *EP.*

$$–$$$　🏨 **Dantica Lodge and Gallery.** High style at high altitude, this avant-garde lodge clinging to the side of a mountain has unbeatable valley views. Spacious white-stucco casitas with two bedrooms and baths are perfect for families. New casitas in a forest clearing provide the ultimate in seclusion and close-to-nature experiences, including the honeymoon hideaway with sunken whirlpool tub big enough for two, a private garden, and forest trail. All the casitas have living rooms with huge picture windows, private terraces, kitchenettes, and electric heaters, along with fluffy, warm duvets. Some have the added luxury of sunken whirlpool tubs and fireplaces. Mixing modern European style with Colombian antiques, the young Dutch/Colombian owners have an unerring eye for style, reflected in their stunning, glassed-in gallery of Latin American *artesanía* (arts and crafts); even if you don't stay here, check out the gallery. Enjoy a hearty breakfast or light lunch served on exquisite china in a glass-walled house with a heart-stopping view. **Pros:** stylish, comfortable casitas; gorgeous natural setting; 5 km (3 mi) of trails. **Cons:** no dinner served, so bring your own food, go off-property, or order dinner from a nearby restaurant; steep access to forest casitas along narrow trails. ⊠ *Road to San Gerardo de Dota ✛ 4 km/2 mi west of Pan-American Hwy.* ☎ *2740–1067* ⊕ *www.dantica.com* ↩ *7 casitas, 1 suite, 1 house* ☖ *In-room: kitchen, refrigerator. In-hotel: restaurant, no-smoking rooms* ☰ *AE, MC, V* ¡○¡ *BP.*

$$–$$$
Fodor's Choice
★

Savegre Hotel de Montaña. Famous for its miles of bird-watching trails and expert guides, this once-rustic lodge has been upgraded to luxury, including new cabins with handsome wood furniture, fireplaces, and deep bathtubs—unthinkable luxuries back in the 1950s when Don Efrain Chacón first bushwhacked his way through these mountains. Still run by Efrain's children and grandchildren, the main lodge has a big fireplace, a cozy bar, and a veranda buzzing with hummingbirds. Breakfast and lunch can be served on a sunny terrace also abuzz with hummingbirds. Homegrown trout is the restaurant's specialty. You can avoid the twisting drive here by taking a bus to Km 80 on the Pan-American Highway and arranging to get a lift to the hotel ($12). **Pros:** great trails; amazing birdlife; excellent guides. **Cons:** buffet-style meals when hotel has lots of groups; older cabins are very simple and lack privacy; be prepared for very cold nights. *Turn right at sign to San Gerardo de Dota on Pan-American Hwy., about 80 km/50 mi southeast of San José, and travel 9 km/5½ mi down very steep gravel road* ⌖ *Apdo. 482, Cartago* ☎ *2740–1028* ⊕ *www.savegre.co.cr* ↩ *25 cabinas, 20 cabin-suites* ☖ *In-room: no a/c, no TV. In-hotel: restaurant, bar, Internet terminal* ☰ *AE, MC, V* ¡○¡ *BP.*

$–$$
Trogón Lodge. Overlooking the same cloud forest and boulder-strewn river as Savegre Hotel de Montaña, Trogón Lodge is more a relaxing hideaway than a hiking-heavy destination. The green wooden cabins encircle a fantasy garden bursting with color and a riot of roses, calla lilies, and geraniums. Each cabin has two separate rooms with big windows, queen-size beds, and white-tile baths with hot showers and rain-forest showerheads. Gas heaters and extra blankets guard against chilly mountain nights. The only drawback is shared verandas. A honeymoon cabin perched in solitary splendor has a king-size bed and a whirlpool tub with a panoramic view. Meals are served in a restaurant with tree-trunk tables, adjoined by a new bar and dining terrace with a river view. Quetzal-watching, horseback riding, waterfall hikes, and an 11-platform canopy tour are some of the diversions, or you can relax with a massage at the new spa. **Pros:** pretty, lush garden; pleasant, convivial public area. **Cons:** steep, short trails that end at road; little privacy except in honeymoon suite. ✛ *Turn right at sign to San Gerardo de Dota on Pan-American Hwy., about 80 km/50 mi southeast of San José, and follow signs; lodge is 7½ km/4½ mi down a dirt road* ⌖ *Apdo. 10980–1000, San José* ☎ *2740–1051, 2293–8181 in San José* ⊕ *www. grupomawamba.com* ↩ *22 rooms, 1 suite* ☖ *In-room: no a/c, no phone, no TV. In-hotel: restaurant, bar* ☰ *AE, MC, V* ¡○¡ *BP.*

VALLE DE EL GENERAL REGION

The Valle de El General (The General's Valley) is bounded to the north and west by the central highlands of the massive Cordillera de Talamanca and to the south by La Amistad International Park, above San Vito. The valley is named for the Río de El General, one of the many rivers that rise in the Talamancas and run down through the valley, making it ideal for farming. This area includes vast expanses of highland wilderness on the upper slopes of the Cordillera de Talamanca and the high-altitude *páramo* (shrubby ecosystem) of Chirripó National Park, as well as prosperous agricultural communities amid vast, sunbaked fields of pineapple and sugarcane.

SAN ISIDRO DE EL GENERAL

54 km/34 mi south of San Gerardo de Dota.

Although San Isidro de El General has no major attractions, the bustling market town is a good place to have lunch, get cash at one of the many ATMs (most accept Visa/Plus cards), or fill your tank—the main highway into town is lined with service stations, some operating 24 hours. Advice to map readers: There are other San Isidros in Costa Rica, but this is the only San Isidro de El General. Just to confuse matters more, this town also goes by the name Peréz Zeledón.

GETTING HERE AND AROUND

The Pan-American Highway takes you straight into San Isidro. It's 129 km (80 mi) south of San José and about 1½ hours' drive south of the San Gerardo de Dota highway exit. Truck traffic can be heavy. Buses to Dominical leave San Isidro from the Quepos bus terminal, 100 meters south and 200 meters east of the cathedral, near the main highway. Buses to San Gerardo de Rivas, the starting point of the trail into Chirripó National Park, depart from San Isidro at 5 AM from the central park and at 2 PM from a stop at the central market.

ESSENTIALS

Bank/ATM Banco Nacional (✉ *North side of park* ☎ *2771–3287*). **ATH Coopealianza** (✉ *South side of central park, beside Hotel Chirripó* ☞ *ATM only*).

Hospital Hospital Escalante Pradilla (✉ *North end of town* ☎ *2771–3122*).

Pharmacy Farmacia Santa Marta (✉ *Across from cultural center* ☎ *2771–4506*).

Internet Internet El Balcón (✉ *150 m east of Central Market, near Banco de Costa Rica* ☎ *2771–6300*).

Post Office Correo (✉ *200 m south of City Hall, south side of park*).

Visitor Information Ciprotur (✉ *Behind the MUSOC bus station, where San José buses arrive* ☎ *2771–6096*). **Selva Mar** (✉ *50 m south of central park* ☎ *2771–4582* ⊕ *www.exploringcostarica.com*).

8

EXPLORING

The **National Parks Service** (⊠ *Across from Cámara de Cañeros* ☎ *2771–3155*) has an office in town where you can get information on Chirripó National Park.

In a lush valley 7 km (4½ mi) northeast of San Isidro, the community-managed **Las Quebradas Biological Center** is a *centro biológico* (nature reserve) that protects 1,853 acres of dense forest in which elegant tree ferns grow in the shadows of massive trees, and colorful tanagers and euphonias flit about the foliage. A 3-km (2-mi) trail winds uphill through the forest and along the Río Quebradas, which supplies water to San Isidro and surrounding communities. There's also an easily accessible sensory garden, with plants to smell and taste. ✛ *At bottom of mountain as you approach San Isidro, take sharp left off Pan-American Hwy. at sign for Las Quebradas, go 7 km/4½ mi northeast; center is 2 km/1 mi north of town, along unpaved road* ☎ *2771–4131* 🖅 *$2* 🕙 *Tues.–Sun. 8–4.*

Los Cusingos Neotropical Bird Sanctuary was the home of the late Dr. Alexander Skutch, Central America's preeminent ornithologist/naturalist and a coauthor of *A Guide to the Birds of Costa Rica*, the birders' bible. His 190-acre estate, an island of forest amid a sea of new farms and housing developments, is now run by the nonprofit Tropical Science Center, which has improved the trails and restored the simple house where Dr. Skutch lived—without electricity—from 1941 until his death in 2004, just a week shy of his 100th birthday. Bird species you might see include fiery-billed araçaris—colorful, small members of the toucan family—and mixed tanager flocks. ✛ *12 km/7½ mi southeast of San Isidro, Quizarrá* ☎ *2200–5472* ⊕ *www.cct.or.cr* 🖅 *$10* 🕙 *Mon. to Sat. 7–4, Sun. 7 – 1, preferably by reservation.*

OUTDOOR ACTIVITIES

Selva Mar (⊠ *Half a block south of the cathedral* ☎ *2771–4582*) is the most experienced Southern Zone tour operator.

BIRD-WATCHING **Sunny Travel/Tropical Feathers** (☎ *2771–9686 or 2772–3275* ⊕ *www.costaricabirdingtours.com*), run by expert birder Noel Urena, has multiday bird-watching packages and arranges customized tours in the San Isidro and Dominical area and points south.

HIKING The major tourist draw is climbing Mount Chirripó (the highest peak is 3,820 meters or about 12,530 feet high) in Chirripó National Park. **Costa Rica Trekking Adventures** (☎ *2771–4582* ⊕ *www.chirripo.com*), run by Selva Mar, can arrange everything you need to climb the mountain, including transportation, guide, porters to carry your gear, meals, snacks, and beverages. But you still have to make the tough climb yourself, about eight hours uphill to the park lodge, and five hours to come down. The two-night, three-day packages are $440 per person, with at least two people. It's much cheaper to do it on your own, but you have to make all the advance arrangements yourself.

WHERE TO EAT AND STAY

¢–$

COSTA RICAN ✕ **El Trapiche de Nayo.** This rustic open-air restaurant with a panoramic valley view serves the kind of food Ticos eat at *turnos* (village fund-raising festivals), including hard-to-find *sopa de mondongo* (tripe soup). Easier to stomach are the *gallos* (do-it-yourself filled tortillas),

Valle De El
General Region

which you can stuff with hearts of palm, other root vegetables, and wood-fire-cooked chicken. On Saturdays, raw sugarcane is pressed in an antique mill and boiled in huge iron cauldrons to make smooth *sobado*, a molasses-flavored fudge. Service is leisurely, to say the least, and the restrooms—with seatless toilets—leave much to be desired. ⊠ *Pan-American Hwy.* ✢ *6 km/4 mi north of San Isidro* ☎ *2771–7267* ⊟ *AE, MC, V.*

$ ╳ **Taquería Mexico Lindo.** Locals, expats, and tourists crowd into this
MEXICAN casual cantina, famous for its authentic Mexican food cooked and served by an extended Mexican family. It's cheap and cheerful, with hearty servings of burritos (including veggie options), enchiladas, chiles rellenos, tuna-stuffed avocados, and daily specials served on terra-cotta dishes under a flutter of festive paper cutouts on the ceiling. Unusually for a Mexican place, the desserts are standouts and all homemade. ⊠ *Shopping arcade beside Hotel Chirripó, outside of Central Park in downtown San Isidro* ☎ *2771–8222* ⊟ *AE, MC, V* ☉ *Closed Sun.*

$ ▦ **Hotel Los Crestones.** Flowering hedges give this pleasant, two-story, motel-style building between the sometimes-noisy local stadium and a sedate funeral home a homey feel. Affordable rooms are large and comfortable, with tile floors, pretty floral linens, and some bathtubs. The quietest rooms are numbers 18 to 21. There's a small pool in a pleasant garden at the back where you can cool off. **Pros:** affordable, pleasant rooms; secure, covered parking for car. **Cons:** avoid rooms at the front, which can be noisy; a few rooms lack a/c. ⊠ *Southwest side of stadium, on road to Dominical* ☎ *2770–1200* ⊕ *www.hotelloscrestones.com* ⇥ *27 rooms* ♨ *In-room: no a/c (some), Wi-Fi. In-hotel: restaurant, pool* ⊟ *AE, MC, V* ⊙❘ *EP.*

¢ ⊞ **Hotel Zima.** Close to the main bus station and especially popular with backpackers heading up to Chirripó, this hotel's pleasant rooms are in bungalows arranged in a nicely landscaped row, reminiscent of a 1950s motel, complete with swimming pool. There are also rooms in a two-story building with porches. Some rooms have queen-size beds and air-conditioning; others have double or single beds and ceiling fans. Have breakfast at the small terrace restaurant or cross the highway and forage among the inexpensive eateries. **Pros:** handy to bus station and restaurants in town. **Cons:** not a scenic location, just off main highway; smallish rooms. ⊠ *Half a block east of main highway into San Isidro, across from MUSOC bus terminal* ☎ *2770–1114* ⇥ *28 rooms* ♨ *In-room: no a/c (some), no phone. In-hotel: restaurant, pool, laundry service, Internet terminal* ⊟ *AE, MC, V* ⊙❘ *EP.*

> ## HITTING THE TRAILS
>
> The hiking in the south is simply spectacular, so don't leave home without your boots. The most challenging hike in the country is Chirripó Mountain, a 6- to 10-hour haul up to the national-park hostel, a base camp for exploring surrounding peaks. Dramatic but less challenging hikes include the well-maintained, wide trails in the cool high-altitude forests of the Savegre Valley; the narrow Coastal Path south of Drake; and forest trails to waterfalls and swimming holes in the Golfo Dulce, Osa Peninsula, and around Dominical.

SAN GERARDO DE RIVAS

20 km/12½ mi northeast of San Isidro.

Chirripó National Park is the main reason to venture to San Gerardo de Rivas, but if you aren't up for this physically challenging adventure it's still a great place to spend a day or two. Spread over steep terrain at the end of the narrow valley of the boulder-strewn Río Chirripó, San Gerardo de Rivas has a cool climate, good bird-watching, spectacular views reminiscent of Nepal, and an outdoor menu that includes waterfall hikes.

GETTING HERE

More than half the one-hour drive from San Isidro is on a very rocky, very hilly, dirt road; 4WD is strongly recommended. There is a bus from San Isidro, and it is a slow, dusty ride up the mountain.

EXPLORING

☾ The **Hot Springs** (*Aguas Termales*), on a farm above the road to Herradura, are a favorite tourist stop. To get here, you must cross a river on a rickety bridge, then manage a steep climb on foot or by 4WD vehicle to a combination of natural rock and concrete pools in a forested area. It's nothing fancy and can be crowded with locals on weekends, so aim for a weekday soak. ⊠ *Above road to Herradura* ✛ *About 1½ km/1 mi past the ranger station, north of town* ☎ *2742–5210* ⊠ *$5* ⊙ *Daily 7–5:30.*

CLOSE UP

A Mosaic of Forests

Though the rain forest is the most famous region in Costa Rica, there are other types of forests here equally rich in life and well worth exploring. The **tropical dry forests** of the northwestern lowlands are similar to rain forests during the rainy season, but once the weather turns dry, most trees lose their leaves, and some burst simultaneously into full flower, notably the yellow-blossom buttercup tree and the pink tabebuia. Cacti, coyotes, and diamondback rattlesnakes can be found, in addition to typical rain-forest flora and fauna.

The **cloud forests** on the upper reaches of many Costa Rican mountains and volcanoes are so deeply lush that it can be hard to find the bark on a tree for all the growth on its trunk and branches. Vines, orchids, ferns, aroids, and bromeliads are everywhere. More light reaching the ground means plenty of undergrowth, too. Cloud forests are home to a multitude of animals, ranging from delicate glass frogs, whose undersides are so transparent that you can see many of their internal organs, to the legendary resplendent quetzal. The foliage and mist can make it hard to see wildlife.

Along both coasts are extensive **mangrove forests**, extremely productive ecosystems that play an important role as estuaries. Mangroves attract animals that feed on marine life, especially fish-eating birds such as cormorants, herons, pelicans, and ospreys. The forests that line Costa Rica's northeastern coast are dominated by the water-resistant *jolillo* palm or *palma real.* Mangroves are home to many of the same animals found in the rain forest—monkeys, parrots, iguanas—as well as river dwellers such as turtles and crocodiles.

8

☁ **Cloudbridge Private Nature Reserve,** a private nature reserve staffed by volunteers, has an easy trail to a waterfall, plus almost 20 km (12 mi) of river and ridge trails bordering Chirripó National Park. It's a pleasant alternative for hikers who aren't up to the challenge of Chirripó. ⊹ *2 km/1 mi northeast of San Gerardo de Rivas* ⊕ *www.cloudbridge. org* ✉ *By donation* ☉ *Daily sunrise–sunset.*

OUTDOOR ACTIVITIES

HIKING   **Ruta Urán.** Really fit hikers can undertake a five-day guided hike up a new alternative route to Chirripó led by experienced local guides. The hike eventually arrives at the Chirripo National Park hostel, and then descends by the usual national park route. The price of $575 for two hikers includes lodging, meals, and guide and park fees. ✉ *Comité de Turismo y Guias de Herradura, in National Park Office in San Gerardo de Rivas* ☎ 2742–5073

Selva Mar *(⇨ San Isidro, above)* also runs tours around San Gerardo de Rivas.

WHERE TO STAY

¢   🏠 **Albergue de Montaña El Pelícano.** On a precipitous ridge south of town, this wooden lodge is named for a chunk of wood that resembles a pelican—one of dozens of idiosyncratic wooden sculptures carved out of tree roots by owner Rafael Elizondo. Above the restaurant, which has a gorgeous view of the valley below San Gerardo, are economical small rooms with shared bath. More comfortable options are the two private wooden cabins with kitchenettes near the pool. The owners can help arrange everything for a climb up Chirripó. The climb to the hotel itself is quite steep and 4WD is advisable. **Pros:** proximity to Chirripó and a free ride to the trailhead; very cheap. **Cons:** shared bath; very tiny rooms, but most visitors are only here to sleep before setting off early to climb Chirripó. ⊠ *260 m south of national park office* ☎ *2742–5050* ⊕ *www.hotelpelicano.net* ↷ *10 rooms with shared bath, 4 cabins* ⚲ *In-room: no a/c, no phone, no TV. In-hotel: restaurant, tennis court, pool, Internet terminal* ▭ *MC, V* ⍟| *BP.*

$ 🍴 **Río Chirripó Retreat.** A popular place for yoga retreats, this lodge has clear mountain air, a rushing river, and a huge conical-roof adobe temple hung with a monastery bell and Tibetan prayer flags. You'll feel as though you have arrived in the Himalayas. The bougainvillea-bedecked bed-and-breakfast is a great place for bird-watching, clambering along the river rocks strewn with Druidic-looking stone seats and altars, or acclimatizing before climbing Chirripó. Or you can relax in the hot tub or the swimming pool overlooking the tumultuous river. Two-story wood cabins are cantilevered over a steep ravine, with twig-railing porches. The comfortable rooms have large bathrooms and walls stenciled with mysterious symbols. A new yoga platform with a view also doubles as a palatial guest room. **Pros:** dramatic scenic location; extravagant breakfasts with copious fresh fruits; meal package available. **Cons:** reserve well in advance to avoid group retreats; smallish rooms with two single beds each; shared balconies. ⊠ *Down a steep drive, just past cemetery* ☎ *2742–5109* ⊕ *www.riochirripo.com* ↷ *8 rooms, 2 cabins, 1 suite* ⚲ *In-room: no a/c, no phone, no TV. In-hotel: restaurant, pool, 1 suite with kitchen, Wi-Fi* ▭ *MC, V* ⍟| *BP.*

CHIRRIPÓ NATIONAL PARK

The park entrance is a 4-km/2-mi hike uphill from San Gerardo de Rivas.

The main attraction of this national park is Mount Chirripó, the highest mountain in Costa Rica and a mecca for both hikers and serious peak summiters. If you want to take up the challenge, be sure to make arrangements well in advance. The number of hikers in the park each day is limited to 35. Thirty-five reservations are booked by telephone often months ahead and usually snapped up by locals and tour companies, leaving only 10 spaces for hikers who show up at the park. Without reservations, you can try your luck and check in at the San Gerardo ranger station, which grants entrance on a first-come, first-served basis. Maximum stay is three days, two nights ($10 per person per night).

▌ DID YOU
KNOW?

Although it takes the fittest hikers at least four hours to get to the base camp of Chirripó, hundreds of competitors from around the world converge on tiny San Gerardo de Rivas every February to run a 34-km (22-mi) race up

and down Chirripó. A local family of hardy brothers shares the record time: three hours and 15 minutes!

GETTING HERE

You are required to report to the **San Gerardo de Rivas National Parks Service** (✉ *Main street* ☎ *2742–5083 reservation, 8 am–noon; 1-4 pm, Mon. to Fri.s*) before you start, either the day before, or the morning of your climb. The office is open 6:30–4, park admission is $15 per day, and they have trail maps. Don't try to sneak in: a park ranger will stop you at a checkpoint on the trail and ask to see your reservation voucher. You can reserve lodgings over the phone (maximum 4 people per reservation); ask for a copy of the wonderfully informative visitor's guide to be sent to you via e-mail (✉ *reservacioneschirripo@gmail.com*).

OUTDOOR ACTIVITIES

Hikes and other activities in the park are arranged by **Selva Mar** (⇨ *San Isidro, above*) and by the **Guides and Porters Association of San Gerardo** (☎ *2742–5073* ✉ *denisguiauran@hotmail.com*), who provide guides, porters, and provisions for Chirripó hikes, as well as an alternative hike up the Ruta Urán.

SAN VITO

110 km/68 mi southeast of San Isidro, 61 km/38 mi northeast of Golfito.

Except for the tropical greenery, the rolling hills around the bustling hilltop town of San Vito could be mistaken for a Tuscan landscape. The town actually owes its 1952 founding to 200 Italian families who converted forest into coffee, fruit, and cattle farms. The Italian flavor lingers in outdoor cafés serving ice cream and pastries and an abundance of shoe stores. A statue dedicated to the *pioneros* stands proudly in the middle of town. San Vito is also the center of the Coto Brus coffee region. Many coffee pickers are from the Guaymí tribe, who live in a large reserve nearby and also over the border in Panama. They're easy to recognize by the women's colorfully embroidered cotton dresses.

GETTING HERE AND AROUND

If you are driving south from San Isidro, your best route is along the wide, smooth Pan-American Highway via Buenos Aires to Paso Real, about 70 km (43 mi). Then take the scenic high road to San Vito, 40 km (25 mi) farther along. This road has recently been paved, and it's the most direct and the prettiest route. Another route, which many buses take, is via Ciudad Neily, about 35 km (22 mi) northeast of Golfito, and then 24 km (15 mi) of winding steep road up to San Vito, at almost 1,000 meters (3,280 feet) above sea level. At this writing, the road is potholed and in *mal estato* (bad shape). There are direct buses from San José four times a day, and buses from San Isidro seven times a day. You can also fly to Coto 47 and take a taxi to San Vito.

ESSENTIALS

Most of the banks in town have cash machines that accept foreign cards.

A ginger flower at the Wilson Botanical Garden in San Vito.

Bank/ATM Banco Nacional (⊠ *Across from central park* ☎ *2773–3601*).
ATH Coopealianza (⊠ *Center of town, north of hospital*).

Hospital Hospital San Vito (⊠ *South end of town on road to Wilson Botanical Garden* ☎ *2773–3103*).

Pharmacy Farmacia Coto Brus (⊠ *Center of town across from La Flor pastry shop* ☎ *2773–3076*).

Internet Cybershop (⊠ *1 block west of main street at north end of town* ☎ *2773–3521*).

Post Office Correo (⊠ *Far north end of town, beside police station*).

Taxis Taxi service (⊠ *Taxi stand beside park at center of town* ☎ *2773–3939*).

EXPLORING

Fodor'sChoice
★

The compelling tourist draw here is the world-renowned **Wilson Botanical Garden**, a must-see for gardeners and bird-watchers and enchanting even for those who are neither. Paths through the extensive grounds are lined with exotic plants and shaded by avenues of palm trees and 50-foot-high bamboo stalks. In 1961 U.S. landscapers Robert and Catherine Wilson bought 30 acres of coffee plantation and started planting tropical species, including palms, orchids, bromeliads, and heliconias. Today the property extends over 635 acres, and the gardens hold around 2,000 native and more than 3,000 exotic species. The palm collection—more than 700 species—is the second largest in the world. Fantastically shaped and colored bromeliads, which usually live in the tops of trees, have been brought down to the ground in impressive mass plantings, providing one of many photo opportunities. The property was transferred to the Organization for Tropical Studies in 1973, and in 1983 it became part of Amistad Biosphere Reserve. Under the name **Las Cruces Biological Station,** Wilson functions as a research and educational center, so there is a constant supply of expert botanists and biologists to take visitors on natural-history tours in the garden and the adjoining forest trails. If you spend a night at the garden lodge, you have the garden all to yourself in the late afternoon and early morning, when wildlife is most active. ✛ *6 km/4 mi south of San Vito on road to Ciudad Neily* ✎ *Apdo. 73–8257, San Vito* ☎ *2773–4004* ⊕ *www. esintro.co.cr* ✉ *$8* ⊗ *Daily 8–5.*

OUTDOOR ACTIVITIES

BIRD-
WATCHING
In addition to its plants, **Wilson Botanical Garden** (⇨ *Exploring, above*) is renowned for its birds. There are about 250 species of birds in the garden alone, including half of the country's hummingbird species, and 410 species total in the immediate area. Competing with the birds for your attention are more than 800 butterflies. Naturalist guides lead visitors on birding and natural-history tours through the garden ($22 per person). The Río Java trail, open only to overnight guests of Wilson, is also a great place to see birds.

WILDLIFE-
WATCHING
If you are an overnight guest at **Wilson Botanical Garden** (⇨ *Exploring, above*), you can walk the Río Java trail, through a forest thick with wildlife, particularly monkeys.

WHERE TO EAT AND STAY

$
ITALIAN
★
✕ **Pizzería Liliana.** Follow the locals' lead and treat yourself to authentic pizza at the classiest restaurant in town or dig into the macaroni *sanviteña*-style: with white sauce, ham, and mushrooms. The classics are here as well, and they're all homemade—lasagna, cannelloni, and ravioli. The authentically Italian vinaigrette salad dressing is a welcome change from more acidic Tico dressings. In true Italian fashion, the friendly, family-run restaurant can be noisy, but it's a happy buzz. For a more romantic dinner, ask for a table on the pretty garden terrace. ✉ *150 m west of central square* ☎ *2773–3080* ▭ *MC, V.*

$$$
La Amistad Ecolodge. Here's a rare opportunity to explore La Amistad Park, which borders this 25,000-acre family estate, most of which is primary forest studded with rivers and spectacular waterfalls. The alpine-style lodge offers comfortable quarters, great home-cooked food, and excellent cappuccino and espresso, made from the estate's own organic coffee beans. New junior suites are a little more luxurious, with queen beds. Daylong guided hikes or horseback rides traverse the property's 57 km (35 mi) of trails, excellent for bird-watching. The really adventurous can hike to two camps, take the Feel Green hiking tour, hiking to four camps. The staff, including a cook, carries all your gear and food in the truck and meets you at each camp. The cabins are as rustic as it gets; the shared baths have only (very) cold water. But the wildlife and walks are beyond exhilarating, and the food cooked in a wood-fire stove is simple but delicious. Bring along a really good sleeping bag for the cold mountain nights. You can also visit the camps on day tours. **Pros:** unequaled hiking trails; scenic waterfalls. **Cons:** rough access road; bring your own sleeping bag/pillow for camps. ✛ *32 km/20*

8

mi east of San Vito along a rough, rocky road ✍ *amistad@racsa.co.cr* ⊕ *www.laamistad.com* ⇝ *8 rooms, 4 junior suites in lodge, 6 cabins at each camp* ⚹ *In-room: no a/c, no phone, no TV. In-hotel: restaurant, bar, laundry service, Internet terminal* ⊟ *AE, MC, V* ⊺⚭⊺ *FAP.*

¢   ⊞ **Hotel El Ceibo.** The best deal in town, El Ceibo is tucked in a quiet cul-de-sac behind the main street, an Italian-style oasis with graceful

arcades and decorative balustrades overlooking potted palms. Rooms are compact but tidy, bright, and comfortable. Rooms 1 to 10 and 21 to 32 have small balconies opening onto a wooded ravine alive with birds. The restaurant, illuminated by a skylight, serves home-style Italian and Tico food at reasonable prices. **Pros:** central location; good price; relative quiet. **Cons:** some rooms are quite small; furnishings are nothing special. ⊠ *140 m east of San Vito's central park, behind Municipalidad* ☎ *2773–3025* ⇝ *40 rooms* ⚹ *In-room: no a/c, no phone. In-hotel: restaurant, bar* ⊟ *MC, V* ⊺⚭⊺ *EP.*

$–$$
Fodor's Choice
★

⊞ **Wilson Botanical Garden.** A highlight of any Costa Rican visit, this magical botanical garden has comfortable rooms in two modern buildings built of glass, steel, and wood that blend into a forested hillside. The smaller rooms have two single beds, and larger ones have three singles. Private balconies cantilevered over a ravine make bird-watching a snap even from your room. Each room is named after the exotic plant growing at the doorway. Room rates include three excellent home-style meals, a guided tour of the grounds, and 24-hour access to the garden. Staying overnight is the only way to see the garden at dusk and dawn or to walk the Sendero Río Java, a trail that follows a stream through a forest teeming with birds and monkeys. The staff here is cheerful and professional, and the youthful enthusiasm of visiting research students is contagious. **Pros:** unparalleled setting with 24-hour access to garden and nature trails; excellent birding and wildlife-viewing. **Cons:** rooms are becoming a little shabby; meals are served family-style, strictly on time. ⊹ *6 km/4 mi south of San Vito on road to Ciudad Neily* ⚭ *OTS, Apdo. 676–2050, San Pedro* ☎ *2524–0628 San José office, 2773–4004 lodge* ⊕ *www.esintro.co.cr* ⇝ *12 rooms* ⚹ *In-room: no a/c, no TV. In-hotel: restaurant, Wi-Fi* ⊟ *AE, MC, V* ⊺⚭⊺ *FAP.*

SHOPPING

In an old farmhouse on the east side of the road between San Vito and the botanical garden, **Finca Cántaros** (⊠ *Road to Ciudad Neily* ⊹ *3 km/2 mi south of San Vito* ☎ *2773–3760*) sells crafts by indigenous artisans from near and far, including Guaitil ceramic figures and *molas* (colorful appliqué work) made by Kuna women from the San Blas Islands in Panama. You can also find a great selection of colorful, high-glaze ceramics from San José artists. Profits help support the adjacent children's library. ■ TIP→ Along with shopping, you can walk bird-filled nature trails around a lake behind the shop.

EN ROUTE The 33-km (21-mi) road from **San Vito to Ciudad Neily** is twisting and spectacular, with views over the Coto Colorado plain to the Golfo Dulce and Osa Peninsula beyond. Watch out for killer potholes, though. The road from **San Vito to Paso Real** is equally scenic, traveling along a high ridge with sweeping valley views on either side. As you descend, the wide valley of the El General River opens up before you, planted with miles of spiky pineapples and tall sugarcane. The road has been repaved, and once again even drivers can enjoy the scenery without falling into potholes.

THE COAST

On the other side of a mountain ridge, just a scenic hour-long drive west of San Isidro, you reach the southern Pacific coast with its miles of beaches for sunning, surfing, kayaking, and snorkeling. Ballena National Marine Park alone encompasses almost 10 km (6 mi) of protected beaches. Scattered along the coast are small communities with increasing numbers of international residents and interesting restaurants and lodging options.

DOMINICAL

34 km/21 mi southwest of San Isidro, 40 km/25 mi south of Quepos.

Sleepy fishing village–turned–scruffy surfer town, Dominical is changing again as luxury villas pop up all over the hillsides above the beaches, bringing new wealth that is boosting the local economy. It's still a major surfing destination, attracting surfers of all ages, with a lively restaurant and nightlife scene. Bars and restaurants come and go with the waves of itinerant foreigners, so don't hesitate to try something new. Dominical's real magic lies beyond the town, in the surrounding terrestrial and marine wonders: the rain forest grows right up to the beach in some places, and the ocean offers world-class surfing.

GETTING HERE AND AROUND

The road west over the mountains and down to Dominical is scenic at its best and fog-shrouded and potholed at its worst. It has recently been repaved, but there are lots of curves, and potholes pop up unexpectedly, so take your time and enjoy the scenery along the hour-long drive from San Isidro. From Quepos, the road south is the only section of the Costanera still not paved, and it's a bumpy, dusty ride past palm-oil plantations. Buses from San Isidro leave four times a day, two times daily from Quepos. If you want to avoid driving altogether, Easy Ride (⇨ *Shuttle Van in Travel Smart Costa Rica)* has air-conditioned minibuses with room for six to eight passengers that make two trips to and from San José daily ($40).

ESSENTIALS

Bank/ATM Banco de Costa Rica (✉ *Plaza Pacífica* ☎ 2787–0381).

Hospital Clínica González Arellano (✉ *Next to pharmacy* ☎ 2787–0129).

Pharmacy Farmacia Dominical (✉ *Pueblo del Río Center at entrance to town* ☎ 2787–0454).

8

La Amistad National Park

By far the largest park in Costa Rica, at more than 1,980 square km (765 square mi), La Amistad is a mere portion of the vast La Amistad Biosphere Reserve that stretches into western Panama. Altitudes range from 1,000 meters (3,280 feet) to 3,500 meters (11,480 feet). There are miles of rugged, densely forested trails and plenty of wildlife (two-thirds of the country's vertebrate species live here), but because access is extremely difficult, it's not worth visiting the park unless you plan to spend several days, making this a trip only for experienced hikers. Unless you're comfortable being lost in the wilderness, hire a local guide for $20 a day from ASOPROLA, the local guide association (☎ 2743–1184, ⊕ www. actuarcostarica.com), which also organizes strenuous three-day guided trips, with two overnights at a mountain refuge ($143 per person with all meals). ASOPROLA also operates El Albergue La Amistad, at the Altamira park entrance, with both private and dormitory rooms with hot-water showers ($12), as well as an organic restaurant run by a local women's cooperative. The alternative is rustic campsites (bring your own tent) for $5 per person at the Potrero Grande park entrance. Reserve space about a week in advance. To get to the park entrance (4WD essential), drive 31 km (20 mi) west from San Vito along the road to Paso Real. Turn right at the park sign at Guacimo, near two small roadside restaurants. Then drive about 20 km (13 mi) uphill on a rough road. The last couple of kilometers are on foot. ☎ 2200–5355 ▤ $10 per day ⊙ Daily 8–4.

Internet Dominical Internet Cafe (⊠ *Above San Clemente Bar, main street* ☎ *2787–0191*). **Super Diuwak** (⊠ *Next to Hotel Diuwak on road to beach* ☎ *2787–0143*).

Post Office San Clemente Bar (⊠ *Main street, at bus stop, a mail drop-off only*).

Rental Cars Alamo (⊠ *Hotel Villas Río Mar, Dominical* ☎ *2787–0052* ⊕ *www.alamocostarica.com*).

Visitor Information Southern Expeditions (⊠ *On Main Street across from San Clemente Bar* ☎ *2787–0100*).

EXPLORING

Ⓒ ★ The **Hacienda Barú** nature reserve is a leader in both ecotourism and conservation, with a turtle protection project and nature education program in the local school. The bird-watching is spectacular, with excellent guides. You can stay at the cabins and poolside rooms or just come for the day to walk the forest and mangrove trails, zip through the canopy on cables, climb a tree, or stake out birds on an observation platform. ✛ *3 km/2 mi north of bridge into Dominical* ☎ *2787–0003* ⊕ *www.haciendabaru.com* ▤ *$6, tours $20–$60* ⊙ *Daily 7 AM–dusk.*

Ⓒ Five years in the making, **Parque Reptilandia** is an impressive reptile exhibit with more than 300 specimens of snakes, lizards, frogs, turtles, and other creatures in terrariums and large enclosures. You can see Central America's only Komodo dragon, Gila monsters, and a 150-

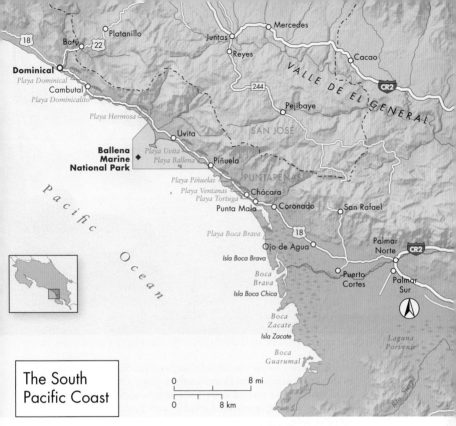

The South
Pacific Coast

0   8 mi

0   8 km

pound, African spur-thighed tortoise that likes to be petted. Kids love
the maternity ward showcasing newborn snakes. More mature snakes
live under a retractable roof that lets in sun and rain. Although snakes
are generally more active in sunlight, this is still a great rainy-day-at-the-
beach alternative activity. Guided night tours ($20) can also be arranged
to watch nocturnal animals at work. If you're not squeamish, feeding
day is Friday. ✛ *11 km/7 mi east of Dominical on road to San Isidro*
☎ *2787–8007* ⊕ *www.crreptiles.com* ✉ *$10* ⊙ *Daily 9–4:30.*

ℭ   The **Nauyaca Waterfalls** (Cataratas de Nauyaca), a massive double cascade
tumbling down 45 meters (150 feet) and 20 meters (65 feet), are one of
the most spectacular sights in Costa Rica. The waterfalls—also known as
Barú River Falls—are on private property, so the only way to reach them
is to take a hiking or horseback tour *(⇨ Outdoor Activities, below).*

Playa Dominical is long and flat, rarely crowded, and good for beach-
combing among all the flotsam and jetsam that the surf washes up onto
the brown sand. Swimmers should beware of fatally dangerous rip currents. In high season, flags mark off a relatively safe area for swimming,
under the watchful gaze of a professional lifeguard.

Playa Dominicalito, just 1 km (½ mi) south of Playa Dominical, is usually
calmer and more suited to boogie boarding.

"Nauyaca waterfall is a three-tiered waterfall. Well worth the visit." —Photo by Richard Bueno, Fodors.com member

A considerably smaller waterfall than Nauyaca Waterfalls, **Pozo Azul** is in the jungle about 5 km (3 mi) south of town. Off the main highway, head up the road toward Bella Vista lodge and take the first road to the right, past the new school and through a stream; follow the road straight uphill for about 300 meters (1,000 feet) to where the road widens. You can park here and climb down the steps to the river on the right, where there is a lovely swimming hole and waterfall, often populated by local kids when school is out. There sometimes is a guard on duty in the parking lot (tip him about 350 colones per hour), but be sure not to leave anything of value in your parked car.

OUTDOOR ACTIVITIES

Southern Expeditions (⊠ *On main street, across from San Clemente Bar & Grill* ☎ *2787–0100* ⊕ *southernexpeditionscr.com*), a major tour operator in the area, can arrange kayaking, white-water rafting, scuba diving, fishing, and nature tours in and around Ballena Marine National Park, Caños Island, and all the way down to Corcovado National Park.

Much of the lush forest that covers the steep hillsides above the beaches is protected within private nature reserves. Several of these reserves, such as Hacienda Barú and La Merced (⇨ *Ballena Marine National Park below*), are financing a biological corridor and preservation of the rain forest.

FISHING   Angling options range from expensive sportfishing charters to a trip in a small boat to catch red snapper and snook for supper. The five most common fish species here, in the order in which you are likely to catch them, are sailfish, dorado, yellowfin tuna, wahoo, and marlin. **Nick Fortney** (☎ *2786–5273* ⊕ *www.costaricahooksetters.com*), a

U.S. Coast Guard–licensed captain, comes down from Alaska every year to spend November to April in Dominical, offering inshore and offshore fishing trips on his custom 25-foot *El Hooksetter*. A half day for up to four fishers is $450; full day, with lunch included, is $650.

HORSEBACK RIDING **Don Lulo** (☎ *2787-0541, 2782-0542*) operates tours to Nauyaca Waterfalls that depart Monday to Saturday at 8 AM from the road to San Isidro, 10 km (6 mi) northeast of Dominical. The tour is $50 and includes breakfast and lunch at Don

> **PACK YOUR BOARD**
>
> The surfing is great in Dominical, thanks to the runoff from the Barú River mouth, which constantly changes the ocean bottom and creates well-shaped waves big enough to keep intermediate and advanced surfers challenged. The best surfing is near the river mouth, and the best time is two hours before or after high tide, to avoid the notorious riptides.

Lulo's family homestead near the falls. You can swim in the cool pool beneath the falls, so bring a bathing suit. There is a river to cross, but otherwise the ride is easy; horses proceed at a walk. Be sure to reserve a day in advance.

Friendly, well-trained horses at **Bella Vista Lodge** (✚ *5 km/3 mi southeast of Dominical* ☎ *2787–8069*) also take riders to the Nauyaca, via a scenic valley route, with lunch and a ride in an aerial tram included for $45. For the same price you can go for a gallop on the beach in the morning or afternoon, depending on tides. These tours include lunch. The three- to four-hour tours start at the lodge, then head down the steep Escaleras road 2 km (1 mi), passing Pozo Azul. Riders staying in hotels on the beach can also pick up the ride right on the beach.

SURFING **Green Iguana Surf Camp** (☎ *2787–0157* ⊕ *www.greeniguanasurfcamp.com*) gives two-hour individual lessons for $50 or $40 per person for small groups of two or more. They also have weeklong packages that include lodging at nearby Diuwak Resort, board rental, lessons, and transport to whichever nearby beach has the best waves each day (from $845). These longer packages include transportation to and from San José.

WHERE TO EAT

$–$$$
THAI
✕**Coconut Spice.** If you like rice with spice, you've come to the right place. This sophisticated restaurant has authentic Southeast Asian flavor in both food and furnishings. Try the hot-and-sour tom yan goong soup, tart with lemongrass and lime and heated up with chilies. The jumbo shrimp vary in price and can get quite expensive, but they're worth it: buttery, sweet, and cooked in spicy coconut sauce. There are also satays, curries, and other Indian standards. The restaurant recently moved to a larger location by the river, so bring along repellent. It's daily from 1 PM. ✉ *Pueblo del Río at entrance to Dominical* ☎ *2787–0073* ▤ *MC, V.*

$$
ITALIAN
✕**ConFusione.** The location—on a dead-end road at the southern end of the beach—may confound you on your first visit, but there's nothing confusing about the sophisticated Italian menu. Along with the usual dishes, the menu has some interesting tropical twists: fish sauces blending coconut with Cognac, and pineapple with cream. The most popular dish here is the *lomito*, local beef tenderloin expertly aged and cooked.

8

Appetizers are big enough to share, and pizzas are popular among the more budget-conscious surfers. The terrace dining room, though, is all grown up, glowing with gold light and warm earth tones. The wine list is varied and interesting, with a good selection of Italian wines at modest prices. BYOR—Bring Your Own Repellent. ⊠ *Domilocos Hotel, south end of Dominical Beach* ☎ *2787–0244* ▭ *MC, V* ⊗ *No lunch.*

$$–$$$ ╳ **La Parcela.** Picture a dream location: a high headland jutting out into
SEAFOOD   the sea with vistas up and down the coast. Throw in a breeze-swept terrace, polished service, and some fine seaside cuisine. This restaurant has had its ups and downs, often relying on its unmatched location, but the current management has got it right: a wide-ranging menu of pastas, salads, and seafood. Generous servings of perfectly cooked fish are topped with some interesting sauces, including a standout roasted red pepper sauce with almonds. Desserts here are rich—mud pie and a delectable chocolate cake—and substantial enough to share. If you're just passing through Dominical, this is a good place for a cold beer or a *naturale,* a tall glass of freshly whipped fruit juice. Sunsets here are spectacular. There is some controversy about this restaurant's eco-sensitive location, so call ahead to make sure it's still up and running. ✦ *4 km/2½ mi south of Dominical* ☎ *2787–0016* ▭ *AE, DC, MC, V.*

¢–$ ╳ **Restaurant Su Raza.** Among the handful of *sodas* (casual eateries) in
COSTARICAN   town serving typical Costa Rican food, this one is notable for its whole fish. Hearty portions of seafood are served on a wooden veranda that's a great bird-watching spot. Bring your binoculars, especially if you come just before sunset or for breakfast. Stick to the *desayuno típico* for breakfast, with traditional rice and beans and eggs. The omelets are great, but they come with limp frozen french fries, the bane of Tico restaurants. ⊠ *Across from San Clemente Grill, main road* ☎ *2787–0105* ▭ *No credit cards.*

$ ╳ **San Clemente Mexican-American Bar & Grill.** Signs you're in the local
TEX MEX   surfer hangout: dozens of broken surfboards affixed to the ceiling, photos of the sport's early years adorning the walls, and a big sound system and dance floor. Fresh seafood, sandwiches, and Tex-Mex standards like burritos and nachos make up the menu. The bargain "starving surfer's breakfast"—two eggs with *gallo pinto* (black beans and rice) or pancakes, plus coffee—is always popular. Owner Mike McGinnis is famous for making a blistering hot sauce and for being a super source of information about the area. ⊠ *Middle of main road* ☎ *2787–0055* ▭ *AE, MC, V.*

$ ╳ **Tortilla Flats.** Another perennially popular surfer hangout, this casual
MEXICAN   place has the advantage of being right across from the beach. Fresh-baked baguette sandwiches are stuffed with interesting combinations; the grilled chicken, avocado, tomato, and mozzarella California sandwich is the most popular. Light eaters can buy half a sandwich. Fresh-fish specials and typical Mexican fare round out the casual menu. The margaritas are excellent, and ladies are served free shots on Thursday night. ⊠ *On beach, Dominical* ☎ *2787–0033* ▭ *AE, MC, V.*

WHERE TO STAY

Lodgings in the lowlands of Dominical and the area a little to the north tend to be hot and muggy and not as comfortable as the more luxurious, private, and breezy places up in the hills above Dominicalito, to the south.

$–$$ **Coconut Grove Oceanfront Cottages.** Right on the beach, this well-maintained cluster of cabins and beach houses is ideal for couples or families who want to fend for themselves. The two bamboo-furnished beach houses sleep two to six and have full kitchens; the smaller cabins have kitchenettes and room for three. At night you can turn off the a/c, open the screened windows, and fall asleep to the sound of the sea. The largest cottage, No. 5, is also closest to the beach. There's a pretty pool, and yoga classes take place twice a week. The American owners have dogs, including one large but lazy Great Dane. **Pros:** best location in town: right on beach; close to cool ocean breezes; communal barbecue; friendly owner/hosts. **Cons:** furnishings are simple, not fancy; guests must love dogs. ⊠ *Turn off main highway at Km 147 ⊕ 3 km/2 mi south of Dominical* ☎ *2787–0130 ⊕ www.coconutgrovecr. com ⏎ 3 cabins, 2 beach houses ⚘ In-room: kitchen (some). In-hotel: pool, beachfront* ▭ *No credit cards* ⊙ *EP.*

$$–$$$ **Cuna del Angel Hotel and Spa.** Hosts of decorative angels abound at this made-in-heaven fantasyland for grown-ups. The over-the-top decor may not suit everyone, but this is a perfect spot for those who like to indulge themselves. The original 16 rooms are luxurious, chock-full of delightful touches, including luxurious linens and towels, stained-glass windows, and spectacular lamps. Nine new Jungle Rooms are smaller and darker, but cheaper and very comfortable, with pickled-wood walls, antiqued armoires, and balconies facing forest or garden. The spa is small and intimate, with a sensual Turkish bath, a selection of soothing massages, and a full-service hair salon. Once you feel rejuvenated, a lush garden, a terrace restaurant, and a pretty pool with an ocean view draw you outdoors. Dinner in the terrace restaurant is pleasant, with a sophisticated menu, and if your timing is right, there's entertainment by top national musicians at the hotel's once-a-month dinner concerts. **Pros:** endlessly amusing decor to keep you talking, admiring, and laughing; friendly service in hotel and spa, which is small and intimate. **Cons:** room balconies and terraces are quite close together, so not a lot of privacy; rooms that face the pool can be noisy if children are playing; steep steps to new Jungle Rooms. ⊠ *Puertocito ⊕ 9 km/5 m south of Dominical* ☎ *2787–8012* 📠 *2787–8015 Ext. 304 ⊕ www.cunadelangel. com ⏎ 25 rooms ⚘ In-room: Wi-Fi. In-hotel: restaurant, bar, pool, spa, no-smoking rooms* ⊙ *BP.*

$ ☾ ★   **Hacienda Barú National Wildlife Refuge and Ecolodge.** Base yourself in this model eco-lodge to explore vast tracts of surrounding forest, mangroves, and a Blue Flag beach with nesting turtles. The six original cabins have sitting rooms with wood furniture, kitchenettes, screened-in porches, and lush flower borders. Each cabin sleeps three or four people. Six handsome new guest rooms built with plantation teak have high ceilings, tiled showers, and small porches, looking onto a brand new swimming pool. A new solar system provides plenty of hot water for showers.

8

Linger for an hour or two atop a lofty bird observation platform in the hotel's rain-forest canopy, zip along the canopy tour, climb a 114-foot-high tree with ropes, or stay overnight at a shelter in the heart of the forest. Excellent local guides interpret the miles of trails, or you can follow the self-guided trail with the help of a handbook. There's a great gift shop here with lots of local crafts and nature books. **Pros:** prime wildlife viewing; excellent guides; trails and outdoor activities; spacious cabins with kitchens; comfortable new guest rooms; perfect for groups. **Cons:** older cabins are not fancy and have small, basic bathrooms. ⊕ *3 km/2 mi north of bridge into Dominical* ⌖ *Apdo. 215–8000, Pérez Zeledón 11901* ☎ *2787–0003* ⊕ *www.haciendabaru.com* ⤳ *6 cabinas, 6 guest rooms* ⚙ *In-room: no a/c, no phone, some kitchens, no TV. In-hotel: restaurant, beachfront* ☰ *AE, MC, V* ⏐◯⏐ *BP.*

$–$$ ⊡ **Necochea Inn.** The forest setting feels primeval, but the decor at this ★ handsome mountain retreat is a sophisticated mix of plush, contemporary furniture and wood, stone, and animal-print fabric. Downstairs living and dining rooms face a wall of sliding glass doors looking onto a stone-deck pool in the jungle and a slice of ocean for a view. Two streams run through the forested property, supplying a natural, burbling soundtrack. A curved stone stairway leads up to two luxurious, large rooms that share a spacious bath. The huge upstairs suite and a slightly smaller regular room have private porches, decadent bathrooms with deep tubs, antique armoires, and gleaming hardwood floors. A new creek-side suite has its own TV, a/c, and a romantic whirlpool tub on a private terrace. Host Yvonne de Necochea is full of energy and makes every guest feel at home. **Pros:** luxurious accommodation with a personal touch, including Yvonne's mural-size wildlife paintings; excellent breakfasts; and, if you ask, a rollicking night of karaoke. **Cons:** up a steep road that can be muddy; need your own car to get down hill to restaurants and beaches. ⊠ *South of Km 147, turn 2 km/1 mi up, past the Pozo Azul, Dominicalito* ☎ *2787–8072 or 8395–2984* ⊕ *www.thenecocheainn.com* ⤳ *3 rooms with shared bath, 2 suites, 1 room with private bath* ⚙ *In-room: a/c (in 1 room), no phone, TV (1 room). In-hotel: restaurant, pool* ☰ *MC, V* ⏐◯⏐ *BP.*

¢–$ ⊡ **Pacific Edge.** Unbeatable views and affordable prices set these styl- ★ ishly rustic cabins apart. The forest grows right up to the edge of the property, high on a mountain ridge south of town. Private, spacious wood cabins—one sleeps six; others sleep four—have kitchenettes, tiled bathrooms, hammocks strung on wide porches, and comfortable orthopedic mattresses covered with colorful Guatemalan bedspreads. Host Susie Atkinson serves great breakfasts in the lodge's bamboo-roof, pagoda-style dining room. Dinner—Thai-style shrimp, perhaps—is cooked on request. Two lookout towers at each end of the tiny pool catch the spectacular sunsets and passing whale pods. The road up to this lofty perch requires a 4WD vehicle, but a hotel shuttle can pick you up in town with advance notice. Be prepared for a barky welcome; Susie and her husband, George, love big (but gentle) dogs. The reception desk closes at 6 PM. **Pros:** fabulous views; bargain prices; serene setting; can make your own breakfast and simple snacks. **Cons:** very steep road that requires 4WD to get back and forth to town restaurants and

LIVING OFF THE GRID

Many hotels in remoter areas of the South Pacific generate their own electricity, so don't count on air-conditioning, using a hair dryer, calling home, checking your e-mail, or paying with a credit card (unless it's arranged in advance). Some lodges do have radio contact with the outside world and satellite phone systems you can use in emergencies, but bad weather can often block the satellite signal. On the positive side, you really can get away from it all in the Southern Zone. Pack as though you are a castaway from modern civilization. Be sure to bring the following:

■ Flashlight with extra batteries, or better still, one of the new kinetic flashlights that need no batteries

■ Insect repellent (lots of it)

■ Sunscreen (ditto)

■ After-sun lotion

■ All toiletries and medications you could conceivably need in small travel containers

■ Sturdy, breathable hiking shoes and lots of socks (your feet will get wet)

■ Waterproof walking sandals

■ Binoculars

■ Sun hat

■ Refillable water bottle

■ Portable, battery-operated reading light

■ Zip-lock baggies of all sizes to keep cameras, snacks, etc., dry and bug-free

beaches; must love dogs. ⊠ *Drive 4 km/2½ mi south of Dominical to Km 148, then turn up a rough road 1.2 km/1 mi* ☎ *2787–8010* ⊕ *www. pacificedge.info* ⤴ *4 cabinas* ⚷ *In-room: no a/c, no phone, refrigerator, no TV. In-hotel: restaurant, bar, pool* ☰ *AE, MC, V* ⑩ *EP*.

$ ☷ **Roca Verde.** This small, friendly hotel has the best beach access in the area. Rooms are sunny and stylish, with swirling flower murals, luxurious bathrooms, and cane-balustraded verandas looking onto a garden and a small pool. There's no TV reception in the rooms, but if you're lucky, you'll be here on a night when the local little theater group is performing in the hotel's open-air lobby. The fish-sculpture-festooned lobby is a gathering place for locals and also a gallery displaying work by local artists. The hotel arranges surfing lessons and fishing trips. Late-night dances on Saturdays, sometimes with live music, draw *bailarinas* (dancers) from surrounding towns. **Pros:** right on the beach; friendly bar; reasonably priced. **Cons:** can be very noisy Saturday night if you're not a party lover; restaurant is just average. ⊠ *1 km/½ mi south of Dominical* ☎ *2787–0036* ⊕ *www.hotelrocaverde.net* ⤴ *10 rooms* ⚷ *In-room: no phone, no TV. In-hotel: restaurant, pool, beachfront, laundry service* ☰ *AE, MC, V* ⑩ *EP*.

$$–$$$ ☷ **Villas Río Mar.** Upriver from the beach on exquisitely landscaped
★   grounds, this hotel is awash in clouds of terrestrial orchids and aflame with bright bougainvillea and hibiscus. Rooms are in adobe-style cabinas with cane ceilings, and have clean white-tile bathrooms. The newer junior suites have king-size beds, cable TV, and air-conditioning—a must, since the cabinas bake in the sun. Four suites also have whirlpool

tubs. Every room has a private porch screened with mosquito netting and furnished with bamboo chairs and hammocks. Plants and elegant table settings fill the huge thatch-roof restaurant with pool views. The breakfast buffet ($6.50 for nonguests) is a good deal here, as are theme-night buffets. A luxurious, large pool has a swim-up bar and handsome teak pool furniture. **Pros:** huge pool; lovely grounds; good restaurant. **Cons:** some rooms have no a/c, and it can get hot here; there are small beaches along the river, but it's a 15-minute walk along an alternately dusty/muddy road to town and the ocean beach. ⊕ *1 km/½ mi west of Dominical; turn right off highway into town and then right again under bridge and follow bumpy river road* ☎ *2787–0052* ⊕ *www.villasriomar. com* ⤳ *40 rooms, 12 junior suites* ♿ *In-room: no a/c (some), refrigerator, no TV (some). In-hotel: restaurant, bar, tennis court, pool, spa, mini-golf, Wi-Fi* ⊟ *AE, MC, V* ⧪ *BP.*

NIGHTLIFE

During the high season, Dominical hops at night, and when the surfers have fled to find bigger waves, there are enough locals around to keep some fun events afloat. At Friday night's **Movies in the Jungle** (⊠ *Marina Vista 3, high up on the Escaleras road at Cinema Escaleras in a private house with no sign; call for directions* ☎ *2787–8065*) , after a potluck dinner at 5, the movies start at 6, in dry season from December to April. Movie buff Harley "Toby" Toberman presents self-proclaimed weird shorts from his huge collection plus a full-length feature on a huge screen, with state-of-the-art equipment. Admission is $6, which goes into a projector-bulb fund. Saturday night the dance action is at the **Roca Verde** (⊕ *1 km/½ mi south of Dominical* ☎ *2787–0036*), with a mixed crowd that doesn't usually get warmed up until 11 PM. Friday night there's live music and dancing at **San Clemente Bar** (⊠ *On main road* ☎ *2787–0055*). At **Maracatu World Music Bar** (⊠ *Main street, across from San Clemente* ☎ *2787–0091*) the crowd is young and edgy, with an open mike on Tuesday, and salsa music on Wednesday, which is also ladies' night. An older crowd gathers at **Río Lindo Resort** (⊠ *At entrance to town* ☎ *2787–0028*) on Sunday from 4 to 9 PM for an alfresco fiesta by the pool, including barbecue, horseshoes, and calypso and bluesy music. Bring your swimsuit. There's live music and dancing in the hotel's Rum Bar on occasion.

SHOPPING

Banana Bay Gallery & Gifts (⊠ *Plaza Pacífica shopping center, highway just above Dominical* ☎ *2787–0106* ⊙ *Closed Sun.*) is not only air-conditioned, but also stocked with an always-intriguing and always-amusing mix of arts and crafts and unusual items, along with indigenous crafts such as tropical masks and lots of insect-theme toys for kids of all ages.

BALLENA MARINE NATIONAL PARK

20 km/12 mi southeast of Dominical.

Parque Nacional Marino Ballena (Whale Marine National Park) boasts four separate beaches, stretching for about 10 km (6 mi), and encompasses a mangrove estuary, a remnant coral reef, and more than 12,350 acres of ocean, home to tropical fish, dolphins, and humpback whales who use it as a nursery. ✉ *Park begins at Playa Uvita, about 20 km/20 mi south of Dominical* ☎ *2743–8236* 🎫 *$6* 🕐 *Daily 6–6.*

GETTING HERE AND AROUND
The park area includes the communities of Uvita, Bahía Ballena, and Ojochal, all easily accessible off the Costanera, a wide, paved highway. As soon as you get off the highway, however, the roads are bumpy and dusty. Alternatively, take a taxi or bus from Dominical. Buses leave Dominical at 10:30 AM and 5:30 PM daily, and there are longer-haul buses that pass along the Costanera and can drop you off in Uvita. Each of the park's four sectors has a small ranger station where you pay your admission.

ESSENTIALS
Uvita Information Center (☎ *8843–7142 or 2743–8889* ⊕ *www.uvita.info*).

EXPLORING
Playa Ventanas, just 1½ km (1 mi) south of Ballena Marine Park, is a beautiful beach that's popular for sea-kayaking, with some interesting tidal caves. The mountains that rise up behind these beaches hold rain forests, waterfalls, and wildlife. There is guarded, private parking here for 350 colones (about 75¢) an hour (except on Wednesday, when you park at your own risk).

At **La Merced National Wildlife Refuge,** owned by Selva Mar, you can ride the range or beach on horseback, explore the forest on a nature hike, or go bird-watching with an excellent guide. Tours include transportation from your hotel and a guide; the full-day tour includes lunch. For $6 you can explore the 10 kilometers (6 mi) of trails on your own with a trail map. ✉ *Reception center at Km 159 on the Costanera, north of Uvita* ☎ *8861–5147* ⊕ *www.rancholamerced.com* 🎫 *$35 half-day tour, $60 full-day tour* 🕐 *By reservation only.*

You'll find excellent bird-watching and hiking a little farther up the hill in the **Oro Verde Private Nature Reserve,** which offers daily two-hour birding tours at 6 AM and 2 PM ($35), as well as guided hikes through their primary forest reserve ($30) and a three-hour morning or afternoon horseback tour to a waterfall ($35). You can also have a hot lunch with a local family included in the tour. ✛ *3 km/2 mi uphill from Rancho La Merced, north of Uvita* ☎ *2743–8072* 🕐 *By reservation only.*

OUTDOOR ACTIVITIES
Outfitters in Dominical (⇨ *above*) run tours to the park and surrounding beaches. **La Merced National Wildlife Refuge** (⇨ *above*) has birding, forest hikes, and horseback riding. For local bookings and information, contact the Uvita Information Center (⇨ *above*).

DIVING AND
SNORKELING
Mystic Dive Center (☎ *2786–5217* ⊕ *www.mysticdivecenter.com*) specializes in dive and snorkel trips to Caño Island, about 50 km (31 mi), or an hour and 15 minutes, from Playa Ventanas ($95 full-day snorkeling; $145 full-day diving, including equipment, lunch, park fees, and guide).

The best spot for snorkeling in the park is at the north end of Playa Ballena, near the whale's tail. **Dolphin Tours of Bahía Ballena** (☎ *2743–8013,* 8825-4031 ⊕ *www.dolphintourcostarica.com*), with an office very close

8

CLOSE UP

Wildlife-Watching Tips

If you're accustomed to nature programs on TV, with visions of wildebeest and zebra swarming across African savanna, your first visit to a tropical forest can be a bewildering experience. If these forests are so diverse, where are all the animals? Web sites, brochures, and books are plastered with lovely descriptions and close-up images of wildlife that give travelers high hopes. Reality is much different but no less fascinating. Below are some tips to make your experience more enjoyable.

■ Don't expect to see rarely sighted animals. It might happen; it might not. Cats (especially jaguars), harpy eagles, and tapirs are a few rare sightings.

■ Monkeys can be the easiest animals to spot, but although they are as reliable as the tides in some locations, in others they are rare indeed.

■ Remember that nearly all animals spend most of their time avoiding detection.

■ Be quiet! Nothing is more unsettling to a wary animal than 20 *Homo sapiens* conversing as they hike. It's best to treat the forest like a house of worship—quiet reverence is in order.

■ Listen closely. Many visitors are surprised when a flock of parrots overhead is pointed out to them, despite the incredible volume of noise they produce. That low-pitched growl you hear is a howler monkey call, which is obvious if nearby, but easily missed over the din of conversation. Try stopping for a moment and closing your eyes.

■ Slowly observe different levels of the forest. An enormous caterpillar or an exquisitely camouflaged moth may be only a few inches from your face, and the silhouettes in the tree 100 meters (330 feet) away may be howler monkeys. Scan trunks and branches where a sleeping sloth or anteater might curl up. A quick glance farther down the trail may reveal an agouti or peccary crossing your path.

■ In any open area such as a clearing or river, use your binoculars and scan in the distance; scarlet macaws and toucans may be cruising above the treetops.

■ Cultivate some level of interest in the less charismatic denizens of the forest—the plants, insects, and spiders. On a good day in the forest you may see a resplendent quetzal or spider monkey, but should they fail to appear, focus on an intricate spiderweb, a column of marching army ants, mammal footprints in the mud, or colorful seeds and flowers fallen from high in the canopy.

to the beach, takes you on 2½-hour snorkeling tours ($60). Mystic Dive Center and Crocodive also offer snorkeling tours.

FISHING **Dolphin Tours of Bahía Ballena** (⇨ *Diving & Snorkeling, above*) offers half-day fishing trips for snook and red snapper that cost $500 for up to four anglers, $650 for a full day inshore or offshore.

ULTRALIGHT FLIGHTS For a bird's-eye view of Bahía Ballena and the park, take off in a two-seater ultralight flying machine with aeronautical engineer Georg Kiechle on a **Ultra Light Tours** (✉ ☎ *2743–8037* ⊕ *www.ultralighttours. com*). Tours cost $90 to $210 for trips lasting 30 to 60 minutes.

"Strolling across Playa Uvita, I saw this iguana; I think it was as interested in me as I was in him." —Photo by Justin Hubbell, Fodors.com

WHERE TO EAT

$$ ✕ **Citrus Restaurant.** This new incarnation of the tiny restaurant that once floated on a paddleboat nearby lives up to its name: it's tangy, tart, and refreshing. Now on dry land, in an exotic, Moroccan-inspired palace, Citrus has expanded to include a choice of elegant inside tables, or romantic, torch-lit terrace and riverside garden tables. The expanded menu offers very sophisticated "new-world cuisine," ranging from Mediterranean panini stuffed with roasted eggplant, peppers, and goat cheese; to fish and seafood with Asian accents of ginger, Szechuan, curry, and Thai. There's still plenty of French flavor, too, with escargots, steak frites, and duck breast coated with a mango-coconut sauce. Desserts are among the best in the country; if you like chocolate, don't pass up the simple but divine Choco-Choco flourless chocolate cake with vanilla ice cream. Service can be slow, so allow lots of time for lunch or dinner, from 11 AM to 10 PM. ⊠ *First left turn off main road into Ojochal* ✛ *15 km/9 mi south of Uvita* ☎ *2786–5175* ▤ *MC, V* ☉ *Closed Sun. and Mon.*

$$
FRENCH
★
✕ **Exotica Restaurant.** The tiny French-Canadian enclave of Ojochal is a gourmet's paradise, and this thatch-roof restaurant with only nine tables has been serving superb tropical fare with a French accent for more than a decade. For starters, there's a tangy refreshing avocado, pineapple, lime, and cilantro appetizer or an intriguing Tahitian fish carpaccio with bananas. Or try a hearty serving of fish or shrimp in a spicy banana-curry sauce. French favorites include Cognac liver pâté, and duck breast with an orange or pineapple sauce. Presentation is artistic, with flourishes of flowers and sprigs of exotic greenery. Desserts are all homemade and luscious. Chocoholics won't want to miss the chocolate chiffon cake with chocolate sauce and an accompanying

shot glass of cocoa liqueur. Breakfast and lunch customers can bring laptops to take advantage of the free Wi-Fi connection. Reservations are advised for dinner. ⊠ *Main road into Ojochal* ⊹ *15 km/9 mi south of Uvita* ☎ *2786–5050* ▭ *MC, V* ⊙ *Closed Sun.*

$–$$

PIZZA

✕ **Pizzeria El Jardín Tortuga.** Pizza is the claim to fame here, and it's served in a casual garden patio. The German pizza baker can make only six individual pizzas at a time in his wood-fired clay oven, but it's worth the wait for thin-crust pies heaped with toppings. There's also grilled fish on the menu, along with lasagna, roast pork, and curried chicken served in a new upstairs rancho. While you wait for your meal, you can enjoy the restaurant's bar, which is also popular with locals. ⊠ *Ojochal, past supermarket, left on bridge and first right* ☎ *2786–5059* ⊕ *www.theturtlesgarden.com* ▭ *No credit cards* ⊙ *Closed Tues.; Mon. and Tues. in low season.*

$

✕ **Tilapias El Pavón.** To enjoy an authentically Tico day in the country, follow a winding river road up to this family-run tilapia fish farm. You can work up an appetite on a short hike to a spectacular waterfall with a swimming hole (bring your suit and binoculars for bird-watching), then catch your own tilapia. The cooks at the open-air wooden restaurant overlooking the tidily kept fishponds will fry up your fish in 10 minutes, and present it whole or filleted, with rice, salad, yucca, and excellent *patacones* (fried, mashed plantains), plus a pitcher of fruit *naturale,* a feast for only $8. They also serve wine and beer. Open 9 AM to 8 PM every day (except Monday). ⊠ *Just before bridge in Punta Mala (2 km/1 mi south of Ojochal), follow a dirt road 4 km/2½ mi uphill to hamlet of Vergel* ☎ *8311-8213* ▭ *No credit cards* ⊙ *Closed Mon.*

WHERE TO STAY

$$–$$$

★

▥ **Cristal Ballena Hotel Resort.** High on a hillside with spectacular ocean views, this Austrian-owned hotel is the most luxurious base for exploring the area. The jewel in this blue-and-white Mediterranean-style hotel is a sparkling, 400-square-meter (4,400-square-foot) swimming pool that commands both mountain and sea views. If the setting doesn't relax you enough, a new spa offers holistic therapy and massages. Spacious, elegant rooms and suites set in carefully landscaped grounds have canopy beds, large tile bathrooms with sinks for two, and sliding-glass doors leading out to private terraces. If you tire of the view (not likely), there are large televisions on swivel bases. A pair of rustic cabins is set close together in a lush garden, but they get quite hot and don't have an ocean view (or TV). Breakfasts are hearty at the poolside Pura Vida restaurant, which also serves lunch. Dinner, featuring excellent fish (sushi on Thursday), along with some tasty Austrian specialties, is served in the upstairs, elegant, air-conditioned El Cristal restaurant, overlooking the pool. Service is on the slow side, but with an ocean vista and refreshing breezes, who cares? **Pros:** wonderful swimming pool for serious swimmers and loungers; great ocean, mountain, and sky views; luxurious rooms. **Cons:** restaurant service can be slow; steep walk to beach; bargain-price rustic garden cabins do not have a/c or TV. ⊹ *7 km/4 mi south of Uvita on the Costanera* ☎ *2786–5354* ⊕ *www.cristal-ballena. com* ⇥ *18 suites, 2 cabins* ⚹ *In-room: refrigerator. In-hotel: restaurant, bar, pool, spa, Wi-Fi* ▭ *AE, MC, V* ⏐⊙⏐*BP.*

¢–$ ⊞ **Diquis del Sur Resort.** An ideal—and affordable—tropical retreat for the winter-weary, this formerly run-down hotel in the hills above Ojochal has been given new life by a creative French-Canadian couple. Renée and Pierre Beaupré are just as delighted as their guests to be in this "earthly paradise," and their enthusiasm shows in the welcome you'll receive. The views look to mountains and the ocean and a garden full of mature fruit trees and flowering shrubs. Five bungalows with two units each are spread around the pretty grounds. Some have kitchens and air-conditioning; some have only a fan, but shady trees keep them cool. The full breakfast has a French accent—crepes, French toast, omelets—and is served in a thatch-roof dining room overlooking an inviting pool with a waterfall. There is a two-day minimum stay. **Pros:** bargain rates; great breakfasts; lots of privacy in well-spaced bungalows. **Cons:** some bungalows have no a/c; spare but adequate furnishings; rough road up from main highway. ⊹ *1 km/½ mi up dirt road signed* CALLE PAPAGAYO, *off Ojochal main road* ☎ *2786–5013* ⊕ *www.diquiscostarica.com* ➷ *5 bungalows (10 rooms), 1 cabin with kitchen* ⅆ *In-room: no a/c (some), no phone, kitchen (some), no TV. In-hotel: restaurant, bar, pool, Internet* ▭ *No credit cards* ⑂ *BP.*

$–$$ ⊞ **Villas Gaia.** Conveniently just off the highway, these spacious, tasteful villas owned by a sophisticated Dutch couple are spread around the jungle on a ridge behind Playa Tortuga, overlooking forest ravines. Most of the recently remodeled villas now have air-conditioning, plus handsome wood furniture and breezy terraces with ceiling fans. A luxurious house has air-conditioning and satellite TV. The restaurant, with chandeliers made of mangrove roots hanging from above, has an eclectic menu ranging from Mexican to Thai. There's also a new breakfast terrace under tall palms, and a lovely rancho/bar by the pool where you can enjoy ocean views and breezes. The pool also has comfortable, contoured teak lounges for sunbathing. A forest trail leads from the villas down to the beach, where you can swim safely. The hotel happily arranges horseback, mangrove, and sea-kayaking tours. **Pros:** easy access, right off the highway; serene setting; proximity to beaches and Ballena Park. **Cons:** you must climb some stairs to get to the villas; pool is small; beach is down a steep path; no a/c in some rooms. ⊹ *15 km/9 mi south of Uvita on coastal highway, Playa Tortuga* ☎ *2786–5044, 2244-0316 in San José* ⊕ *www.villasgaia.com* ➷ *14 cabinas, 1 house* ⅆ *In-room: no a/c (some), no phone, no TV. In-hotel: restaurant, bar, pool, laundry service* ▭ *AE, MC, V* ⑂ *CP.*

SHOPPING

★ Next door to Mystic Dive Center is **Green Leaf Arts & Artesania** (⊠ *Centro Comercial Ventanas, near Km 174* ⊹ *1 km/½ mi north of Ojochal* ☎ *2786–5233*), with a great selection of high-quality local art, indigenous crafts, and Asian home accessories, plus a wide selection of field guides and jewelry. Next door at the **Licorera Feliz** (same owner), you can pick up imported snacks, cheeses, and treats for a beach picnic, as well as imported beer and wine from the best selection available in the area. Both stores are open daily from 9 to 6. Brand new Super Comida (☎ *2786–5123*), next door, also stocks local and international groceries, open daily 7 to 6.

THE GOLFO DULCE

One of only three tropical fjords in the world, the Golfo Dulce has 180-meter-deep (600-foot-deep) waters in the center of a usually placid gulf that attracts humpback whales. At Chacarita, 33 km (20 mi) south of Palmar Sur, the southern coast assumes a split personality. Heading west, you reach the Osa Peninsula and, eventually, the Pacific Ocean and the wildest region of Costa Rica. Continuing due south is the Golfo Dulce, which means "Sweet Gulf" and suggests tranquil waters. This gulf creates two shorelines: an eastern shore that is accessible only by boat above Golfito, and a western shore, which is the eastern side of the Osa Peninsula. South of Golfito the coast fronts the Pacific Ocean once again (rather than the tranquil gulf), with wilder beaches that beckon surfers and nature lovers.

GOLFITO

339 km/212 mi southeast of San José.

Overlooking a small gulf (hence its name) and hemmed in by a steep bank of forest, Golfito has a great location. Lodges run world-class sportfishing trips and supply kayaks for paddling the gulf's warm, salty, and crystal-clear waters. When the sun sets behind the rolling silhouette of the Osa Peninsula, you can sometimes spot phosphorescent fish jumping. Golfito was a thriving banana port for several decades—United Fruit arrived in 1938—with elegant housing and lush landscaping for its plantation managers. After United Fruit pulled out in 1985, Golfito slipped into a state of poverty and neglect. The town itself consists of a pleasant older section and a long, scruffy strip of newer buildings. Visiting U.S. Navy ships dock here, and small cruise ships moor in the harbor. The Costa Rica Coast Guard Academy is also here.

NAVIGATING GOLFITO

Taxis and boats take you wherever you need to go in and around Golfito. You can hire taxi boats at the city dock in Golfito (about $75 round-trip [often negotiable] to go to area lodges or across to Puerto Jiménez). The only way to reach the remote Golfo Dulce lodges above Golfito is by boat. Early morning is the best time, when the water in the gulf is at its calmest. Most lodges include the boat transport in their rates.

GETTING HERE

From San José the trip is a long and often grueling eight-hour drive along paved roads crossing over often-foggy mountains. Your best bet, especially if you are visiting a lodge on the gulf, is to fly to Golfito, which takes only about an hour. Direct buses from San José leave twice daily.

ESSENTIALS

Bank/ATM ATH Coopealianza (⊠ *Across from hospital, north end of town*). **Banco Nacional** (⊠ *South of hospital* ☎ *2775–1101*).

Hospital Regional Hospital (⊠ *American Zone, near Deposito* ☎ *2775–1001*).

Pharmacy Farmacia Golfito (⊠ *Main street, across from city park* ☎ *2775–2442*).

The Golfo Dulce

Internet Wi-Fi is now widely available if you have your own laptop. Locals use computers at **CSI Internet** (⊠ *150 meters south of Banco Nacional near ship dock* ☎ *2775-0718*).

Post Office **Correo** (⊠ *Across from soccer field; climb flight of stairs off the main road, south of central park*).

Taxis **Taxi service** (☎ *2775–2020*).

Visitor Information **Land Sea Services** (⊠ *Next to Banana Bay Marina on left as you enter town* ☎ *2775-1614*) ; they also sell SANSA tickets. **Visitor Information Center** (⊠ *At municipal dock* ☎ *2775–1820* ⊙ *Mon.–Sat. 8–noon*).

EXPLORING

The northwestern end of town is the so-called **American Zone,** full of wooden houses on stilts, where the expatriate managers of United Fruit lived amid flowering trees imported from all over the world. Some of these vintage houses, built of durable Honduran hardwoods, are now being spruced up.

Golfito doesn't have a beach of its own, but **Playa Cacao** is a mere five-minute boat ride across the bay from town. Hire a boat at the city dock or from a mooring opposite the larger cruise-ship dock, north of Golfito's center. Playa Cacao has two casual restaurants and one collection of basic cabinas, but it makes a cooler, quieter option when the heat and noise in Golfito get unbearable.

Piedras Blancas National Park has some great birding. The park is verdant forest, home to many species of endemic plants and animals. It's also an important wildlife corridor because it connects to Corcovado National Park. Follow the main road northwest through the old American Zone, past the airstrip and a housing project: the place where a dirt road heads into the rain forest is ground zero for bird-watchers. ⊠ *Adjacent to Golfito National Wildlife Refuge* 🕾 *No phone* 🎫 *Free* ⊘ *Daily dawn–dusk.*

A Garden of Eden with mass plantings of ornamental palms, bromeliads, heliconias, cycads, orchids, flowering gingers, and spice trees,
★ **Casa Orquideas** has been tended with care for more than 25 years by American owners Ron and Trudy MacAllister. The 2½-hour tour, available Sunday and Thursday at 8:30 AM, includes touching, tasting, and smelling, plus spotting toucans and hummingbirds. Trudy is also a font of information on local lore and medicinal plants. Guided tours, given for a minimum of three people, are $8 per person. Self-guided visits cost $5. The garden is accessible only by boat; a water taxi from Golfito to the garden (about $60 to $75 round-trip for up to four people) is a tour in itself. ⊠ *North of Golfito on the Golfo Dulce* 🕾 *8829–1247* 🎫 *$5–$8* ⊘ *Tours Thurs. and Sun. only at 8:30* AM ⊘ *Closed Fri.*

OUTDOOR ACTIVITIES

FISHING The open ocean holds plenty of sailfish, marlin, and roosterfish during the dry months, as well as mahimahi, tuna, and wahoo during the rainy season; there's excellent bottom fishing any time of year. Captains are in constant radio contact with one another and tend to share fish finds.

Banana Bay Marina (🕾 *2775–0838 or 2775–1111* ⊕ *www.bananabaymarina. com*) has a fleet of five boats skippered by world-record-holding captains. A day's fishing for up to four averages $1,100. **C-Tales** (⊠ *Las Gaviotas Hotel* 🕾 *2775–0062, 2775–2156* ⊕ *www.c-tales.com*) operates fishing boats with English-speaking captains and mates. **Land Sea** (⊠ *Waterfront next to Banana Bay Marina* 🕾 *2775–1614* ⊕ *www.marinaservices-yachtdelivery. com*) can hook you up with independent captains in the area.

WHERE TO EAT

$–$$ ✕ **Banana Bay.** For consistently good American-style food, you can't
AMERICAN beat this breezy marina restaurant with a view of expensive yachts and fishing boats. Locals complain that the prices are high, but portions are hefty, and include generous salads, excellent chicken fajitas wrapped in homemade tortillas, and a delicious grilled dorado fish sandwich with a mountain of fries—a deal at $7.50. While you're waiting for your order, take advantage of the free Wi-Fi. It's open for breakfast, too. ⊠ *Golfito main street, south of town dock* 🕾 *2775–0838* 🍽 *MC, V.*

$ ✕ **Restaurante Mar y Luna.** This casual, affordable terrace restaurant jut-
COSTA RICAN ting out into Golfito Harbor has a pleasant harbor view. The seafood-heavy lineup includes shrimp and grilled whole fish. Chicken fillets smothered in a mushroom sauce and vegetarian dishes round out the menu. The quality varies, depending on who's in the kitchen, but during a recent visit the kitchen was in top form. ⊠ *South end of Golfito*

main street, just north of Hotel Las Gaviotas ✆ *2775–0192* ▭ *MC, V* ⊘ *Closed Mon.*

WHERE TO STAY

The atmosphere of the in-town hotels differs dramatically from that of the lodges in the delightfully remote east coast of the Golfo Dulce. The latter is a world of jungle and blue water, birds and fish, and desert-island beaches, with lodges accessible only by boat from either Golfito or Puerto Jiménez.

$$ 🏨 **Esquinas Rainforest Lodge.** This well-managed eco-lodge is a model conservation project run by Austrians who have tried to instill a sense of Teutonic order. (More than 80% of the guests here are from Germany and Austria.) But the tidy gravel paths winding past wooden cabins in manicured gardens are constantly being encroached upon by wild forest, with the garden looking wilder every year. A spring-fed pool is delightful, and fragrant white ginger and ylang-ylang encircle a pond that is home to contented, well-fed caimans. Another nearby pond has a new lookout for bird-watchers. Local guides lead visitors along thrilling trails that head to the waterfalls and primary forest of Piedras Blancas National Park. Rooms have tile floors, good reading lamps, and airy bathrooms with plenty of hot water. The dining room, romantically candlelit at night, serves excellent food. For families or foursomes, there is a new, fully equipped Jungle Villa with forest views (minimum stay four nights). **Pros:** excellent trails and wildlife-viewing opportunities in unique natural setting; hearty meals. **Cons:** no a/c and it can get hot here; some trails are challenging and you need to be steady on your feet; lodge is geared to nature lovers who aren't looking for luxury. ✉ *Near La Gamba* ✆ *5 km/3 mi west of Villa Briceño turnoff* ☎ *2741–8001, 2775–0140 in Golfito* ⊕ *www.esquinaslodge.com* ⤵ *14 rooms in 7 bungalows, 1 villa* ⚷ *In-room: no a/c, no phone, no TV. In-hotel: restaurant, bar, pool* ▭ *AE, MC, V* ⦿ *FAP.*

¢–$ 🏨 **Hotel Las Gaviotas.** Just south of town on the water's edge, this hotel has wonderful views over the inner gulf. Rooms have terra-cotta floors, teak furniture, and a veranda with chairs overlooking the well-tended tropical gardens and the shimmering gulf beyond. A pleasant open-air restaurant with fresh-tasting food looks onto the large pool, whose terrace is barely divided from the sea. The restaurant has an extensive wine and cocktail list, and the weekend barbecue buffets ($18) are the best deal in town. The hotel offers sportfishing trips from its own dock and has a good gift shop. **Pros:** great location and large pool; safe parking. **Cons:** fairly utilitarian furniture and spare decor; bathrooms are a little dreary. ✆ *3 km/2 mi south of Golfito town center* ✉ *Apdo. 12–8201, Golfito* ☎ *2775–0062* ⊕ *www.resortlasgaviotas.com* ⤵ *18 rooms, 3 cabinas* ⚷ *In-hotel: safe. In-hotel: restaurant, bar, pool* ▭ *AE, MC, V* ⦿ *EP.*

¢

COSTA RICAN

🏨 **Hotel Samoa del Sur.** Nautical kitsch at its best, this dockside hotel has a ship-shaped restaurant ($–$$$), complete with a billowy sail and a mermaid figurehead. This is definitely fisherman territory, with a pool table, loud music, and big TVs. Unexpectedly, the breakfast omelets may be the best in Costa Rica. The seaside theme carries through to spacious rooms, from shell-pattern bedspreads to shell-shaped hand soap. Rooms have two double beds, remote-control air-conditioning,

8

and tile bathrooms with hot water (a rarity in these parts). The mattresses are a little soft, and you are at the mercy of adjoining neighbors and the thumping music from the bar, but things usually quiet down by 11 PM. The eccentric French owner designed a swimming pool in the shape of butterfly wings, plus a kids' pool and play area. Guests who want to get out on the water can paddle complimentary kayaks. **Pros:** affordable and fun; lively restaurant. **Cons:** can be lots of rambunctious kids in pool; noisy bar in evenings; guard dogs at night may scare off some guests. ⊠ *Main street, 1 block north of town dock* ☎ *2775–0233* ⊕ *www.samoadelsur.com* ⇱ *14 rooms* ⌂ *In-room: no phone, Wi-Fi (some). In-hotel: restaurant, bar, pool, bicycles, laundry service, Wi-Fi in restaurant* ⊟ *AE, MC, V* ⦿*I EP.*

$$$ ⛱ **Playa Nicuesa Rainforest Lodge.** Hands down, this is the best lodge on
Fodor's Choice   the gulf, with an emphasis on adventure on both land and sea. Out the
★   front door of the lodge are beach, bay, and mangroves, with kayaks, snorkeling, fishing, sailing, and swimming; out the back door is a forested mountain with hiking trails, a waterfall, and plenty of wildlife and a resident naturalist to interpret the trails. For more contemplative types, there is a new yoga deck and a resident yoga instructor in high season. The two-story main lodge is a palatial tree house, crafted from 15 kinds of wood. Luxurious, hexagonal wooden cabins with open-air showers are scattered around a lush garden that ensures privacy. A stucco guesthouse with four large, comfortable rooms is shaded by mango trees. Solar power ensures a steady supply of electricity, and there's always lots of hot water. Imaginative meals are served in the second-story dining room–cum–lounge with an unbeatable tropical-garden view. The owners are active–New Yorkers devoted to running an eco-friendly operation and delivering top-level service. **Pros:** everything you need to have an active vacation; excellent food and service; idyllic setting; friendly, intelligent owners who interact with guests. **Cons:** no a/c; cabins are fairly open to nature, so there will be some insects outside the mosquito netting at night. ⊠ *Golfo Dulce, north of Golfito; accessible only by boat from Golfito or Puerto Jiménez* ⌂ *Apdo. 56, Golfito* ☎ *8824–6571, 2258–8250, 2222–0704 in San José, 866/504–8116 in U.S.* ⊕ *www.nicuesalodge.com* ⇱ *5 cabins, 4 rooms* ⌂ *In-room: no a/c, no phone, no TV. In-hotel: restaurant, bar, beachfront, water sports, no kids under 6* ⊟ *MC, V* ⦿ *Closed Oct.–Nov. 15* ⦿*I AI.*

SHOPPING

Ticos are drawn to Golfito's duty-free bargains on such imported items as TV sets, stereos, tires, wine, and liquor. To shop at the **Depósito Libre** you have to spend the night in Golfito, because you have to register in the afternoon with your passport to shop the next morning. Shopping is sheer madness in December. It's closed on Monday. **Tierra Mar** (⊠ *Waterfront next to Banana Bay Marina*) has an excellent selection of painted wood masks. It also has one-of-a-kind local crafts, such as woven straw hats, cotton purses, and painted gourds, and local paintings. In a class all its own, the **Mercado Artesania** (⊠ *Hotel Samoa Sur, main street, 1 block north of town dock*) is filled with every imaginable—and unimaginable—souvenir. Large paintings by local artists, huge painted fans from Thailand, hammocks, beach clothes, and life-size snake carvings are just a few of the offerings here. Even if you don't buy a thing, it's fun to look. Ask the hotel manager to unlock the door and visit the Shell Museum, the hotel owner's personal, lifelong collection of shells.

NIGHTLIFE

The bar at **Banana Bay Marina** (⊠ *Main street, south of town dock*) is usually full of English-speaking fishermen in the evening. Every night, **Bar Los Comales** (⊠ *Near the large dry dock at north end of town*) has dancing and karaoke until 2 AM. It's in a rougher section of town, so go with a group and leave in a taxi.

The bar at **Samoa del Sur** (⊠ *1 block north of town dock*) has a mix of Ticos and foreigners, mostly of the male persuasion, who gather for the loud music until 11 PM.

PLAYA ZANCUDO

51 km/32 mi south of Golfito.

For laid-back beaching involving hammocks strung between palms and nothing more demanding than watching the sun set, you can't beat breezy Playa Zancudo, with its miles of wide, flat beach and views of the Osa Peninsula. It isn't picture-perfect: the 10 km (6 mi) of dark brown sand is often strewn with flotsam and jetsam. But there's a constant breeze and a thick cushion of palm and almond trees between the beach and the dirt road running parallel. The standout feature is the magnificent view across the gulf to the tip of the Osa Peninsula. The beach runs almost due north–south, so you have center-stage seats for sunsets, too. Away from the beach breezes, be prepared for biting *zancudos* (no-see-ums).

There's a flurry of new construction here, with Canadians and Americans building substantial beachfront homes. Most hotels and restaurants are within sight of the beach. Life here is laid-back and very casual, centering on walking the beach, fishing, kayaking, swimming, and hanging out at the local bars and restaurants. Zancudo has a good surf break at the south end of the beach, but it's nothing compared with Playa Pavones a little to the south. Swimming is good two hours before or after high tide, especially at the calmer north end of the beach, and if you get tired of playing in the surf and sand, you can arrange a boat trip to the nearby mangrove estuary to see birds and crocodiles. Zancudo is also home to one of the area's best sportfishing operations, headquartered at the Zancudo Lodge.

GETTING HERE AND AROUND

The road from Golfito is paved for the first 11 km (7 mi), but after the turnoff at El Rodeo the trip entails almost two hours of bone shaking and a short ride on—but sometimes a long wait for—a cable river ferry (600 colones, about $1.10). You are much better off without a car here. You can hire a boat at the municipal dock in Golfito for the 25-minute ride ($30 for two) or take a $5 *collectivo* (communal) boat that leaves Zancudo Monday to Friday in high season at 7 AM, Saturday at 8 AM; the return boat leaves Golfito's Hotel Samoa del Sur at noon. (In low season, the shuttle runs Monday, Wednesday, and Friday only.) **Cabinas**

8

"Taken in the road to Puerto Jiménez. It was such a beautiful view of Gulfo Dulce." —Photo by jamie722, Fodors.com member

Los Cocos (✉ *Beach road* ☎ 2776–0012) has water-taxi service to Golfito ($20 per person; minimum $50) and service to Puerto Jiménez ($20 per person; minimum $60).

Getting around Playa Zancudo doesn't take much, since there's really only one long, dusty road parallel to the beach. You can rent a bike at Cabinas Sol y Mar or Tres Amigos Supermercado, both on the main road in Zancudo, for about $10 per day.

ESSENTIALS

Internet Oceano Internet Café (✉ *In Oceano Cabinas, 50 m south of Supermercado Bellavista* ☎ 2776–0921) has free Wi-Fi at the bar.

OUTDOOR ACTIVITIES

FISHING If you've got your own gear, you can do some good shore fishing from the beach or the mouth of the mangrove estuary, or hire a local boat to take you out into the gulf. The main edible catches are yellowfin tuna, snapper, and snook; catch-and-release fish include marlin, roosterfish, and swordfish.

The Zancudo Lodge (✉ *North end of town on main road* ☎ 2776–0008 ⊕ *www.zancudobeachresort.com*) runs the biggest charter operation in the area, with 12 boats ranging in length from 25 feet to 36 feet. A day's fishing includes gear, food, and drinks (about $750 for two fishers), and you can arrange to be picked up in Golfito or Puerto Jiménez. Captain John Olson at **Sportfishing Unlimited** (☎ 2776–0036, *web: www. SportFishingU.com*) offers 28-foot center-console boats with both fly and conventional tackle. The rate is $700 per day for two fishers, which includes lunch, drinks, and gear. Born and raised in Golfito, **Captain**

Ronny (☎ 2776–0201 ✉ golfitocr@ yahoo.com) has worked at all the area fishing lodges. The daily rate is an all-inclusive $800 for a maximum of four fishers.

KAYAKING The kayaking is great at the beach and along the nearby Río Colorado, lined with mangroves. **Cabinas Los Cocos** (✉ Beach road ☎ 2776–0012) has a popular tour ($50) that takes you for a 1½-hour motorboat ride up the river, then a 2-hour kayak tour along a jungly mangrove channel. The company also rents user-friendly sit-on-top kayaks with backrests for $5 per hour.

TO FLUSH OR NOT TO FLUSH?

Costa Rican toilets *do* flush, but in most of Costa Rica, septic systems weren't designed to accommodate toilet tissue (the pipes are too narrow). If you don't want to be the *gringo* who clogs up the works, watch for signs asking you not to put anything in the toilet. A wastebasket (*basurero*) is almost always provided to hold used tissue. Even upscale resorts and other places with modern septic systems have the basket, since the habit has been ingrained in locals.

WHERE TO EAT

$–$$ ✕ **Oceano Bar & Restaurant.** This pop-
ECLECTIC ular beachfront restaurant has a wide-ranging menu that gets raves from the locals. Choose from seafood, steaks, and creative salads, such as watermelon with feta bathed in a balsamic-mint dressing. The restaurant offers what is probably the country's only *poutine* (a Quebecois comfort food with french fries, gravy, and chunks of cheese). Fish sandwiches are also popular, along with enormous hamburgers. There's a lounge where you can sip martinis. Bring your laptop and surf on their Wi-Fi connection. ✉ Beach road, 50 m south of Supermercado Bellavista ☎ 2776–0921 ▭ MC, V ☉ Closed Oct.

$–$$ ✕ **Restaurant Sol y Mar.** On a breezy porch with a palm-fringed beach
ECLECTIC view, this restaurant has the most cosmopolitan food in Zancudo, with an eclectic menu of spicy *quesadillas* and super-stuffed burritos, savory chicken *cordon bleu,* and fresh fish with elegant French sauces. There's a touch of Thai here, too; one of the most popular dishes is mahimahi in a coconut-curry sauce. Desserts are decadent and delicious, including a standout carrot cake. As at a lot of restaurants catering to tourists, prices do not include tax and service, so be sure to factor in an extra 23% to the bill. ✉ Hotel Sol y Mar, main road ☎ 2776–0014 ▭ No credit cards.

WHERE TO STAY

$ ⌂ **Cabinas Los Cocos.** This cluster of castaway-island, self-catering cabins is designed for people who want to kick back and enjoy the beach. Artist Susan England and her husband, Andrew Robertson, are Zancudo fixtures and can organize any activity, including river safaris, kayaking tours, and visits to nature preserves. Two idyllic tropical cabins have thatch roofs and hammocks. The others are renovated 40-year-old banana-company houses moved here from Palmar Norte. These charming pastel wooden cottages give you the rare chance to share a little bit of Costa Rican history. Book early, because so many guests return the same time every year. **Pros:** like having your own beach house on a practically deserted, idyllic beach, with everything you need to live well; friendly, funny hosts who help you get the most out of your stay.

8

Cons: no a/c, but there are ceiling fans and ocean breezes. ⊠ *Beach road, about 200 m north of Sol y Mar* ☎ *2776–0012* ⊕ *www.loscocos. com* ⇥ *4 cabins* ⌂ *In-room: no a/c, no phone, kitchen, no TV. In-hotel: beachfront, laundry service* ▤ *No credit cards* ⏍ *EP.*

¢ ⌂ **Cabinas Sol y Mar.** As its name implies, Cabinas Sol y Mar has sun and sea, plus a beach fringed by coconut palms. Wooden cabinas painted leaf green have porches and high ceilings looking onto the gulf with spectacular views of the Osa Peninsula. Each breezy, roomy cabina sleeps four. Two of the sunny bathrooms feature pebble-lined showers. There's also an economy cabin for two, with its own fridge; and a three-story rental house. The alfresco restaurant *(⇨ above)* consistently serves the best food in town. The popular U-shaped bar is an easy place to meet new friends, including Laurie and Rick, the friendly Canadian-American owners. A well-stocked gift shop sells colorful sarongs and clothing from Thailand. **Pros:** beach location; affordable price; lively restaurant and bar. **Cons:** no a/c; simple cabins. ⊠ *Main road, south of Cabinas Los Cocos, Playa Zancudo* ☎ *2776–0014* ⊕ *www.zancudo.com* ⇥ *5 cabinas, 1 house* ⌂ *In-room: no a/c, no phone, no TV. In-hotel: restaurant, bar, beachfront, Wi-Fi in restaurant* ▤ *MC, V* ⏍ *EP.*

$$–$$$ ⌂ **The Zancudo Lodge.** Most people who stay here are anglers on all-inclusive sportfishing packages, taking advantage of the lodge's 12 fishing boats. But new owners are making the comfortable beachfront hotel a good choice even if you've never caught anything but a cold. Kayaks and surfboards are available for guests to enjoy the gulf without dropping a fishing line. The verdant grounds surround a newly renovated inviting pool and an open-air restaurant that serves both buffet and table-service meals. The rate includes all meals and drinks, including alcohol. The two-story hotel has been renovated and updated. Huge rooms have hardwood floors, firm queen beds, and ocean views. A new luxury suite with glass walls has been added and eight new rooms are in the works. **Pros:** fishers' delight with excellent boats and captains; most luxurious hotel in Zancudo, with a/c, a rarity in these parts. **Cons:** if you don't like a testosterone-charged fisherman atmosphere, this is not the place for you; evenings can get a little rowdy. ⊠ *Main road, north end of town, 200 m past police post, Playa Zancudo* ⌂ *Apdo. 41, Golfito* ☎ *2776–0008, 800/854–8791 in U.S.* ⊕ *www.zancudobeachresort.com* ⇥ *20 rooms, 1 suite* ⌂ *In-room: refrigerator. In-hotel: restaurant, bar, pool, beachfront, Wi-Fi* ▤ *AE, MC, V* ⏍ *FAP.*

PLAYA PAVONES

53 km/33 mi south of Golfito.

One of the most scenic beaches to drive past is remote Playa Pavones, on the southern edge of the mouth of Golfo Dulce. Through a fringe of palms you catch glimpses of brilliant blue water, white surf crashing against black rocks, and the soft silhouette of the Osa Peninsula across the gulf. The area attracts serious surfer purists, but also has pristine black-sand beaches and virgin rain forest. The coast is very rocky, so it's important to ask locals which beach to try. One of the best places to swim is in the Río Claro, under the bridge or at the river mouth (dry season only). The town of Pavones itself is an helter-skelter collection of *pensiones* (guest houses) and *sodas* (casual eateries) clustered around a soccer field.

GETTING HERE

There's no avoiding the bumpy road from Golfito to Conte, where the road forks north to Zancudo and south to Pavones. But the dirt road to Pavones is usually well graded. A public bus leaves from Golfito very early in the morning, and the drive takes about 2½ hours. A taxi from the airstrip in Golfito costs upwards of $90.

OUTDOOR ACTIVITIES

SURFING Pavones is famous for one of the longest waves in the world, thanks to the mouth of the Río Claro, which creates ideal sandbanks and well-shaped waves. The ocean bottom is cobblestone where the surfing waves break. The most consistent waves are from April to September, and that's when the surfing crowd heads down here from the Central Pacific coast beaches. But even at the crest of its surfing season Pavones is tranquility central compared with the surfing hot spots farther north.

Most surfers here are serious about their sport and bring their own boards. You can buy used surfboards and other surfing gear or sign up for a lesson ($35 plus $20 board rental) at **Sea Kings Surf Shop** (✉ *In town, by soccer field* ☎ *2776–2015* ⊕ *www.surfpavones.com*). **Cabinas La Ponderosa** (⇨ *Where to Stay and Eat, below*) rents surfboards ($20–$40) as well as bicycles ($20). **Clear Ricer Sports & Adventures** (☎ *2776–2016*) offers surf lessons ($50), including board rental; they also rent surfboards and snorkeling gear for $15 per half day, and bicycles for $5 per hour, and have an Internet café.

WHERE TO EAT

$ ✗ **Café de la Suerte.** Fortunately for food lovers, the "Good Luck Café"
VEGETARIAN serves truly astonishing vegetarian food from 7:30 to 5 that even a carnivore could love, along with intriguing exotic juice combinations and thick fruit smoothies. The homemade yogurt is a revelation: light, almost fluffy, and full of flavor. The Israeli owners serve it over a cornucopia of exotic fruits, sprinkled with their own granola, and mix it into refreshing fruit-flavor *lassis* (a yogurt-base drink from India). Healthful sandwiches are heavy on excellent hummus, and hot daily specials might include curried hearts of palm. Don't leave without buying a fudgy brownie or a brown-sugar oatmeal square for the road. Bring your laptop and use their Wi-Fi—the $1 an hour is donated to the local school. ✉ *Next to soccer field* ☎ *2776–2388* ⊕ *www.cafedelasuerte.com* ▭ *No credit cards* ⊗ *No dinner. Closed Sun. and Oct., Nov.*

WHERE TO STAY

$–$$ 🏨 **La Ponderosa Beach and Jungle Resort.** The world-famous Playa Pavones surfing break is just a 10-minute walk from this surfer-owned hotel, the only beach resort in the area. It's a cut above the usual surfer place, though, with a recent remodeling and a new swimming pool. Rooms have crisp white linens, new orthopedic mattresses, freshly tiled bathrooms, and a/c or screened windows to let in the sea breezes. Two of the three spacious suites have screened-in porches overlooking the lush garden and pool. A two-bedroom villa with fridge and a two-story house with full kitchen are available as weekly rentals. If you're not into surfing, there are nature trails winding through 14 acres of garden and forest, plus a yoga deck and massages. Everything is within walking distance, including a swimmable beach and restaurants, so you don't need a car. **Pros:** a surfer's haven, with gear for rent and lots of local knowledge, courtesy of surfing owners and other guests; affordable; close to beach and town; meal packages available for $25 per person. **Cons:** tends to attract a younger crowd; mosquitoes love the garden when there's no breeze. ⊠ *On beach* ☎ *2776–2076, 954/771–9166 in U.S.* ⊕ *www.laponderosapavones.com* ↘ *2 rooms, 3 suites, 2 houses* ♙ *In-room: no a/c (some), phone, refrigerator (some), DVD. In-hotel: restaurant, beachfront, bicycles* ▭ *No credit cards* ⍥ *EP.*

> **CAUTION**
>
> In the unlikely event that you are bitten by a snake, stay calm, move slowly, and try to remember what the snake looked like, to tell the clinic staff. Allow antivenom to be administered only by a trained person, in case of side effects. Five hours is the window before any tissue loss. To avoid snakebites, stay on trails and wear long, loose pants; in some areas high rubber boots are recommended.

$$ ☷ **Casa Siempre Domingo.** High on a breezy hill, this spacious bed-and-breakfast has the town's best view of the Golfo Dulce. Two of the four enormous rooms have 20-foot ceilings and double beds set high to catch the view out the large windows. The other two have pretty garden views. A new infinity swimming pool gives you yet another opportunity to enjoy the view poolside. The owners have a young son and welcome visiting playmates. Substantial breakfasts, prepared by owner Heidi, a food professional in her former life, are served at a large communal table in a screened-in great room, and there's a communal fridge for storing food and drinks. The steep driveway up to this lofty perch can be a little daunting. You'll need 4WD or else you can build up a set of steely muscles climbing up on foot. **Pros:** the view, the view, the view; spacious, well-appointed rooms; great breakfasts; kids welcome. **Cons:** a very steep drive uphill; a thigh-cramping walk up and down to the beach. ✛ *2 km/1 mi south of town; follow signs after Río Claro Bridge* ☎ *8820–4709* ⊕ *www.casa-domingo.com* ↘ *4 rooms* ♙ *In-room: no phone, no TV. In-hotel: pool* ▭ *No credit cards* ⍥ *BP.*

$$–$$$ ☷ **Tiskita Jungle Lodge.** This last outpost lodge is one of the premier attrac-
Fodor's Choice tions in the Southern Zone for nature lovers. Peter Aspinall, a passionate
★ farmer and conservationist, and his wife, Lisbeth, homesteaded here in 1977, and today the property includes a vast fruit orchard, with more than 100 varieties of trees that attract monkeys, coatis, birds, and other wildlife. Surrounding the orchard are 800 acres of primary and secondary forest, a habitat for the more than 275 species of birds and a 90-strong troop of squirrel monkeys. These are tours of the orchard, and a naturalist guide leads bird-watching and nature tours. Comfortable screened wooden cabins on stilts have rustic furniture and tiled bathrooms, some of them open-air. Trails invite you to explore the jungle and a cascading waterfall with freshwater pools. Healthy meals using local produce are served in an open-air dining room. Throughout the day you

can help yourself to freshly squeezed tropical juices in the fridge, and the cookie jar is always full. Cabins are spread out, with lots of steps to climb. Recently rebuilt No. 6 has the most privacy, with a huge porch looking onto a beautiful ocean view. The beach, with swimmable waters, is a steep 15-minute downhill walk. Many guests arrive by small plane at the hotel's private airstrip. **Pros:** unrivaled wildlife-viewing and birding; splendid natural isolation; excellent guides and opportunity to get to know the friendly, knowledgeable owners. **Cons:** some steep walks to cabins in forest; no a/c; expect some insect visitors in rustic cabins; not a lot of privacy in joined double and triple cabins, which share verandas. ⊕ *6 km/4 mi south of Playa Pavones* ✆ *Apdo. 13411–1000, San José* ☎ *2296–8125, 786–664–4443 in U.S.* ⊕ *www.tiskita.com* ⇥ *17 rooms arranged in 4 single cabins, 3 doubles, and 1 triple* ⌂ *In-room: no a/c, no phone, no TV. In-hotel: restaurant, bar, pool, beachfront, bicycles* ⊟ *No credit cards* ⊗ *Closed Sept. 15–Oct. 31* ⍾ *AI.*

NIGHTLIFE

The town's main watering hole is **Cantina Esquina del Mar** (⊠ *Beachfront, center of town*). It's nothing fancy, but it's lively.

THE OSA PENINSULA

If you came to Costa Rica seeking wilderness and adventure, this is it. You'll find the country's most breathtaking scenery and most abundant wildlife on the Osa Peninsula, a third of which is protected by Corcovado National Park. You can hike into the park on any of three routes or fly in on a charter plane. Corcovado also offers day trips from nearby luxury nature lodges, most of which lie within private preserves that are home for much of the same wildlife you might see in the park. And complementing the peninsula's lush forests and pristine beaches is the surrounding sea, with great fishing and some surfing.

There are two sides to the Osa: the gentler Golfo Dulce side, much of it accessible by car, albeit along rocky roads; and the much wilder and dramatic Pacific side, which is accessible only by boat, by charter plane, or by hiking a sublimely beautiful coastal trail.

PUERTO JIMÉNEZ

130 km/86 mi west of Golfito, 364 km/226 mi from San José.

You might not guess it from the rickety bicycles and ancient pickup trucks parked on the main street, but Puerto Jiménez is the largest town on the Osa Peninsula. This one-iguana town has a certain frontier charm, though. New restaurants, hotels, and "green" newcomers lend an interesting, funky edge. It's also the last civilized outpost on the peninsula. Heading south, you fall off the grid. That means no public electricity or telephones. So make your phone calls, send your e-mails, get cash, and stock up on supplies here. Be prepared for the humidity and mosquitoes—Puerto Jiménez has plenty of both. If you need a refreshing dip, head south of the airport to Playa Platanares, where there is a long stretch of beach with swimmable, warm water.

The main reason to come to Puerto Jiménez is to spend a night before or after visiting Corcovado National Park, since the town has the best access to the park's two main trailheads and an airport with flights from San José. It's also the base for the *collectivo* (public transport via pickup truck) to Carate.

GETTING HERE AND AROUND

Most visitors fly to the newly upgraded Puerto Jiménez airfield from San José, since the drive is grueling and long. Driving from Golfito is a little easier these days, with new bridges and the road newly paved all the way from Rincón to Puerto Jiménez. A better option from Golfito is the motorboat launch. A rickety old passenger launch ($1.50 each way) leaves Golfito at 11:30 AM every day and takes 1½ hours. Faster motorboat launches ($4) make the trip in 45 minutes, leaving Golfito six times a day starting at 5AM. The fast launches heading to Golfito leave Puerto Jiménez at 6 AM, noon, and 4 PM. You can also hire private taxi boats at the city dock. Prices are $50 to $65 between Golfito and Puerto Jiménez. Water taxis can also take you to beachfront lodges.

A *collectivo* ($8) leaves Puerto Jiménez twice daily for Cabo Matapalo and Carate. It's the cheapest way to travel, but the trip is along a very bumpy road—not recommended in rainy season (May–December). The collectivo leaves from a stop 200 meters west of the Super 96 at 6 AM and 1:30 PM.

Once you get to the main street in town, you can get around on foot or by bicycle.

ESSENTIALS

Bank/ATM Banco Nacional (⊠ *500 m south of Super 96, directly across from church* ☎ *2735–5020*).

Hospital Public Clinic and First Aid Station (⊠ *25 m west of post office* ☎ *2735–5063*).

Pharmacy Farmacia Hidalgo (⊠ *Main street, across from Carolina Restaurant* ☎ *2735–5564* �》 *Mon.–Sat. 8–8*).

Internet CaféNet El Sol (⊠ *Main street, next to Juanita's* ☎ *2735–5719, open 7 am -11 pm daily*). **Café Internet Osa Corcovado** (⊠ ☎ *2735–5230* ☽ *Closed Sun.*) has a more reliable high-speed connection, plus laptop data ports and, best of all, really strong air-conditioning.

The **National Parks Service Headquarters** (⊠ *Next to airport* ☎ *2735–5036*) has information about hiking trails in Corcovado National Park. The office is open weekdays 8 to 4.

Post Office Correo (⊠ *West side of soccer field*).

Rental Cars Solid Car Rental (⊠ *150 m north of airport, Puerto Jiménez* ☎ *2735–5777* ⊕ *www.solidcarrental.com*).

Visitor Information Osa Tropical (⊠ *Across from Banco Nacional on main street* ☎ *2735–5062* ✍ *osatropical@ice.co.cr*).

The Osa Peninsula

OUTDOOR ACTIVITIES

Escondido Trex (⊠ *Restaurante Carolina, 200 m south of soccer field* ☎ *2735–5210* ⊕ *www.escondidotrex.com*) arranges kayaking, charter-fishing, and small-boat outings for watching wildlife, and land-based outings, including a hike around Matapalo ($50). Isabel Esquivel at **Osa Tropical** (⊠ *Main road, across from Banco Nacional* ☎ *2735–5062*) runs the best general tour operation on the peninsula. Whatever travel question you ask the locals, they will usually say, "Ask Isabel." Along with arranging flights, ground transport, hotel bookings, tours, and car rentals, Osa Tropical is the radio communications center for many of the off-the-grid Osa lodges and tour operators.

BIRD-WATCHING The birding around the Osa Peninsula is world renowned, with more than 400 species. Endemic species include Baird's trogon, yellow-billed cotinga, whistling wren, black-cheeked ant tanager, and the glorious turquoise cotinga. There have even been sightings of the very rare harpy eagle in the last couple of years. One of the best spots on the peninsula to find a yellow-billed cotinga or a white-crested coquette is the bridge over the river at **Rincón** (⊕ *40 km/25 mi north of Puerto Jiménez*), if you get there before 7 AM.

Continued on page 498

Scuba Diving
and Snorkeling

by Gillian Gillers

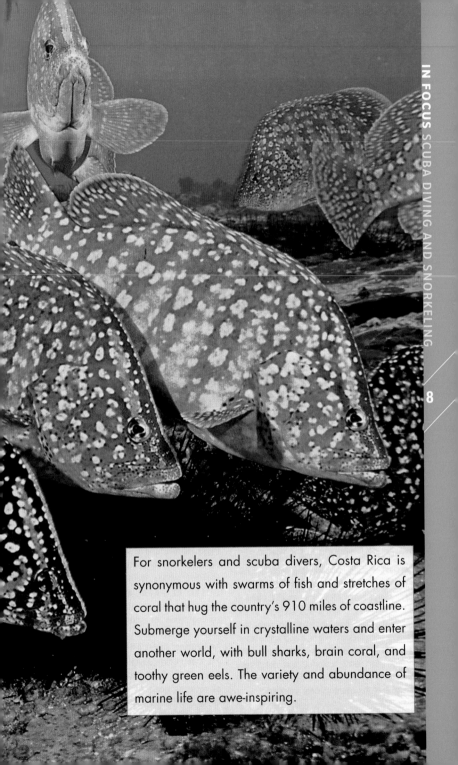

For snorkelers and scuba divers, Costa Rica is synonymous with swarms of fish and stretches of coral that hug the country's 910 miles of coastline. Submerge yourself in crystalline waters and enter another world, with bull sharks, brain coral, and toothy green eels. The variety and abundance of marine life are awe-inspiring.

WHEN AND WHERE TO GO

Swimming with the turtles on Cocos Island

The Pacific tends to be clearer than the Caribbean, and the fish are bigger and more abundant. Northern waters are generally best May through July, after winds die down and the water turns bluer and warmer. The southern Osa Peninsula is popular during the dry season, from January to April.

The Caribbean, known for its diverse coral and small fish, is good for beginners because it has less surge. The best months are September and October, when the ocean is as calm and flat as a swimming pool. April and May also offer decent conditions, but steer clear during the rest of the year, when rain and strong waves cloud the water.

CAHUIT Mounds of coral and a barrier reef (dubbed Long Shoal) run from Cahuita to Punta Mona, along 25 kilometers of Caribbean coastline. Arches, tunnels and canyons in the reef form a playground for small fish, crabs, and lobsters. Even though sediment and waste water have damaged much of the coral, the healthy sections are dense, colorful, and delightfully shaped. Gentle pools right off the beach allow for some of the country's best snorkeling.

ISLA DEL COCO (Cocos Island) Some 295 nautical miles and a 36-hour sail from Puntarenas, Cocos Island is one of the world's premier sites for advanced divers. Visibility is good all year, and hammerhead and white-tipped reef sharks are the main attractions.

ISLA DEL CAÑO (Caño Island) With clear water, big schools of fish, and healthy coral, this biological reserve is the second-best dive spot after Cocos. Stronger currents make Caño better suited for advanced divers, but novice snorkelers can frolic in the Garden, a shallow area to the north.

ISLA SANTA CATALINA (Santa Catalina Island) Known for sightings of golden cownose rays and giant mantas, these big rocks near Playa Flamingo have spots for beginner and advanced divers. Snorkelers should head to shallower waters near the beach.

GOLFO DE PAPAGAYO (Papagayo Gulf) This northern gulf has Costa Rica's highest concentration of snorkel and dive shops. Calm, protected waters make it the best place for beginner divers on the Pacific.

ISLA MURCIÉLAGO (Bat Island) Located inside Santa Rosa National Park, this cluster of rocks is good for advanced divers and famous for its fearsome bull sharks.

DIVING SCHOOLS

The beach towns on both coasts are riddled with diving schools and equipment rentals shops. If you're a first-timer and plan to go diving just once, taking a basic half-day class isn't difficult, and it will allow you to dive up to 40 feet with an instructor. A three- or four-day certification course gets you a lifetime license and allows you to dive up to 130 feet and without a guide. Outfitters can point snorkelers towards pristine spots. We list only the most reputable schools under the Outdoor Activity section throughout every chapter; look for the ones that are PADI (Professional Association of Diving Instructors) trained or give PADI certifications.

IN CASE OF AN EMERGENCY
DAN (Divers Alert Network) is an organization that provides emergency medical advice and assistance for underwater diving injuries. Doctors, emergency medical technicians, and nurses are available 24 hours a day to answer questions. If you would like to discuss a potential diving-related health problem, contact the non-emergency DAN switchboard (☎800/446–2671) or check out their website (⊕www.diversalertnetwork.org). Their emergency telephone line is 919/684–8111 or 919/684–9111 for international calls.

SNORKELING TIPS

Sea Star in Catalina Islands

■ Never turn your back on the ocean, especially if the waves are big.

■ Ask about rip tides before you go in.

■ Enter and exit from a sandy beach area.

■ Avoid snorkeling at dusk and never go in the water after dark.

■ Wear lots of sunscreen, especially on your back and butt cheeks.

■ Don't snorkel too close to the reef. You could get scratched if a wave pushes you.

■ Be mindful of boats.

DIVING TIPS

■ Make sure your instructor is certified by a known diving agency, such as PADI.

■ Stick to the instructor's guidelines on depth and timing.

■ Never hold your breath.

■ Never dive or snorkel (or swim or surf) alone. Also, never touch the coral or the fish—this is for your own good and the good of the marine life.

■ Don't drink alcohol before diving.

■ Never dive while taking medicine unless your doctor tells you it's safe.

■ Diving can be dangerous if you have certain medical problems. Ask your doctor how diving may affect your health.

■ If you don't feel good or if you are in pain after diving, go to the nearest emergency room immediately.

■ Don't fly for 12 hours after a no-decompression dive, even in a pressurized airplane.

CREATURES OF THE SEA

Underwater exploration is as close to visiting another world as you can come. Here you'll encounter some of the most bizarre creatures on this planet.

Pillar Coral

Calcareous skeleton of the coral

CORAL
Coral tends to cluster in colonies of identical individuals. The most diverse coral (at least 31 types) in Costa Rica can be found on the Caribbean coast, near Puerto Viejo. Like other plant-looking sea animals, many types of coral reproduce by spawning.

SEAHORSE
These magical little creatures are hard to spot because they are often camouflaged within black coral trees, with their tails curled around the branches. They are bottom feeders and usually found in 10 meter deep water.

FIREWORM
Look but don't touch! These stunning, slow-moving worms have poisonous bristles that flare out when disturbed. Getting stung is no fun; it will burn and itch for hours afterwards. Try taking the bristles out with adhesive tape and dabbing the infected area with alcohol.

GREEN EEL
Eels have a reputation for being vicious and ill-tempered, but they're really shy and secretive. Eels will only attack humans in self-defense. Though they may accidentally bite the hand that feeds them, it's just because they can't see or hear very well.

SPONGES
Common in the Caribbean, these strange animals don't have nervous, digestive, or circulatory systems. Instead, they rely on a constant water flow for food and oxygen, and to remove wastes. To reproduce, some sponges release both sperm and eggs into the water and hope the two collide.

Orange sponge

BOTTLENOSE DOLPHIN
Everybody loves dolphins. In some parts of the world they work with local fishermen, driving schools of fish into the nets and then eating the fish that escape. They've also been known to help injured divers to the surface.

GIANT MANTA RAY
Commonly spotted near Isla Santa Catalina, mantas often hang out at reef-side "cleaning stations" where small fish (like wrasses and angelfish) congregate. These cleaner fish feed in the manta's gills and over its skin, simultaneously scrubbing it free of parasites and dead skin.

BARRACUDA
Barracudas are not aggressive towards humans, but are vicious predators. Their diet consists of all sorts of fish. Large barracudas, when gorged, will even try to herd a school of fish into shallow water so that they can guard over them and eat them off when they're hungry again.

HAMMERHEAD SHARK
These sharks are distinctive not only for their strangely shaped, mallet-like head but also because they're one of the few creatures in the animal kingdom (besides humans and pigs) that can tan. If they spend too much time in shallow waters, they'll become noticeably darker. In 2007, scientists also discovered that hammerheads can reproduce asexually through a rare process called parthenogenesis: female hammerheads can actually develop an embryo without ever having been fertilized.

PARROTFISH
Parrotfish are named for their external set of tightly packed teeth that look just like a parrots beak. These strange looking teeth are used to rasp the algae off of coral and rock, thus feeding themselves and keeping the coral clean and healthy.

The best English-speaking birding guides are Liz Jones and
★ Abraham Gallo, who run **Bosque del Río Tigre Lodge** (⊠ *Dos Brazos del Tigre* ⊹ *12 km/7½ mi northwest of Puerto Jiménez* ⊕ *www.osaadventures.com*). They lead birding trips all around the peninsula, including visits to Corcovado National Park.

FISHING Along with Golfito across the water, Puerto Jiménez is a major fishing destination, with plenty of billfish and tuna, snapper and snook, almost all year, with the exception of June and July, when things slow down. The best offshore fishing is between December and April.

Southern Costa Rica Fishing (☎ *2735–5920* ⊕ *www.costaricasportsman.com*) in Puerto Jiménez is one of the most highly recommended fishing operations on the Osa Peninsula. Captain Mark Corn has 13 years of experience fishing these waters. A full day of fishing for up to six fishers, on a state-of-the-art 31-foot Bertram boat includes lunch and drinks ($1,350); half-day fishing is $850. Check out their Web site for multiday fishing packages that include lodging.

Taboga Aquatic Tours (☎ *2735–5265 or 8379–0705*), a more modest local fishing outfit, offers half-day inshore fishing for up to four for $300; a whole day offshore costs $500.

HIKING If you have 4WD, it's just a 30-minute ride west to the village of Dos Brazos and the **Tigre Sector** of Corcovado Park. Few hikers come to this pristine part of the park because it's difficult to access, which means you'll likely have it to yourself. You can take a taxi to Dos Brazos and hike from here, or use rustic but comfortable Bosque del Río Tigre Lodge as a base.

★ **Osa Aventura** (☎ *2735–5758* ⊕ *www.osaaventura.com*) specializes in multiday Corcovado hiking adventures led by Mike Boston, an ebullient tropical biologist who sounds like Sean Connery and looks like Crocodile Dundee. Hikers stay in way-off-the-beaten-track rustic lodges en route, and camp or stay in basic cabins in Corcovado. Mike also employs three young bilingual biologists to lead hikes and conduct scientific research projects, in which visitors can sometimes participate.

HORSEBACK The most popular horse trails in the area are at remote **Río Nuevo Lodge**
RIDING (⊠ *Office next to La Carolina Restaurant, main street* ☎ *2735–5411*),
↻ about 12 bumpy km (7½ mi) west of town. Rides along the river and up onto scenic forested ridges last from three to seven hours and include transportation there and back and a homesnack for $60 per person.

> **WORD OF MOUTH**
>
> "I love the Osa Peninsula in July. The local bus from San José will take nine hours or more—this is why most people fly. Once in Puerto Jiménez, there are several budget hotels in or near town. If you want to head down to the park, you can take the collectivo [communal truck] in the morning and then take it back to Puerto Jiménez in the afternoon: Very inexpensive but also uncomfortable. Think Indiana Jones. I didn't mind the back of a pickup at all but some people really hate it. In Puerto Jiménez, head to the Pearl of the Osa restaurant/bar and check out the beach there—it's one of the prettiest in the area."
>
> —Suzie2

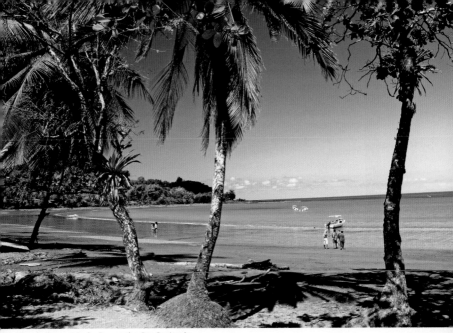
Beach views at Drake Bay on the Osa Peninsula.

KAYAKING

Puerto Jiménez is a good base for sea-kayaking trips on the calm Golfo Dulce and for exploring the nearby mangrove rivers and estuaries. Alberto Robleto, an enterprising local, has amassed an impressive fleet of kayaks with excellent safety equipment at **Aventuras Tropicales Golfo Dulce** (⊠ *South of airport on road to Playa Platanares* ☎ *2735–5195* ⊕ *www.aventurastropicales.com*). Tours include snorkeling, dolphin-watching, and bird-watching. The most popular is the three-hour mangrove tour ($30). A three- to five-day kayaking tour ($100 per day, four-person minimum) teaches survival skills in the tropical forest. Outrigger canoe trips ($70 for six hours) are also offered. A six-hour bike tour takes you through a local village, over hills, and across rivers ($50). All tours longer than three hours include a picnic lunch. **Escondido Trex** (⇨ *above*) has kayak fishing trips, mangrove tours, and popular sunset dolphin tours (all tours $40).

Finca Köbö Chocolate Tour (⊹ *18 km/11 mi west of Puerto Jiménez, near La Palma* ☎ *8398–7604* ⊕ *www.fincakobo.com* ✉ *$28, kids age 6–8, half price* ⊙ *Tours 9* AM *and 2* PM, *closed Oct., Nov.*) takes you right to the source to see how cacao grows and becomes chocolate at this organic cacao plantation. The two-hour tour includes a naturalist-guided walk around the roughly 50-acre property, which includes gardens, orchards, and both primary and secondary forest. The highlight of the tour is the tasting—dipping an array of tropical fruits grown on-site into a pot of homemade chocolate fondue.

CLOSE UP

Where Have All the Forests Gone?

The world gives high marks to Costa Rica for its environmental awareness, but accolades don't always match reality. In the last half century more than two-thirds of Costa Rica's original forests have been destroyed. Forests have traditionally been considered unproductive land, and their destruction was for a long time synonymous with development. In the 1970s and 1980s, international and domestic development policies fueled the destruction of large tracts of wilderness. Fortunately, in the 1970s alarmed Costa Rican conservationists began creating what is now the best national park system in Central America. The government has since made progress in curbing deforestation outside the national parks, too.

As you travel through Costa Rica, you see that its predominant landscapes are not cloud and rain forests but the coffee and banana plantations and cattle ranches that have replaced them. Deforestation not only spells disaster for endangered animals like the jaguar and the harpy eagle, but can also have grave consequences for human beings. Forests absorb rain and release water slowly, playing an important role in regulating the flow of rivers—which is why severely deforested regions often suffer twin plagues of floods during the rainy season and drought during the dry months. Tree covers also prevent topsoil erosion, thus keeping the land fertile and productive; in many parts of the country erosion has left once-productive farmland almost worthless.

WHERE TO EAT

¢–$
CAFÉ
× **Café la Onda.** The latest place for locals and visitors to meet and greet is this New Wave, college-style café, complete with easy chairs, magazines, a book exchange, and the added allure of air-conditioning. The casual fare runs from bagels—try their popular bagelwich, with ham, bacon, tomato, and jalapeño peppers—to stuffed sandwiches on homemade white or whole-wheat rolls, and salads. There are home-made cookies and cakes to accompany the excellent coffee, espresso, and refreshing fruit smoothies and shakes. You can also order box lunches here to take on hikes and fishing trips. ⊠ *Next door to Jagua Arts & Crafts near the airport* ☎ *2735–5853* ☉ *Weekdays 7:30–4:30; until 3* PM *on Sat. Closed Sun.*

¢–$$
SEAFOOD
× **Corcovado Marisquería, Restaurante y Bar.** If you're hungry for a bargain and enjoy a little local atmosphere, join the fishermen, local families, and young backpackers at this tiny restaurant that has spilled over into a large waterfront garden. Customers happily sit at a jumble of plastic and wood tables sheltered by makeshift tents and palm trees, ordering from a vast menu that offers more than 40 *bocas* (small bites) and *platos fuertes* (main courses) that run the gamut from seafood rice to whole lobster. You can make a meal of one or two bocas—say, clams in garlic butter and a cup of tangy ceviche or a shrimp omelet with salad—and walk away for less than $5. Wash it down with local or imported beer and sit as long as you like, looking out on the Golfo Dulce. It's open from 10 AM to 11 PM daily. ⊠ *100 m east of city dock, on the waterfront* ☎ *2735–5659 or 8898–2656* ▤ *MC, V.*

$–$$
ITALIAN
✕**Il Giardino.** Northern Italian cooking, in the form of tasty homemade pastas and excellent salads, is alive and well in Puerto Jiménez at this popular garden restaurant. Sadly, wood-oven pizzas are not the restaurant's forte, and service can be painfully slow. The owner is also a master carpenter, so the curvy blond-wood bar and hand-carved detailing in the casual restaurant are handsome indeed. Choose a table in the back garden if you're in the mood for a leisurely, romantic dinner. It's open from 5 to 10 PM. ✉ *25 m south of La Carolina, then 25 m west, downtown Puerto Jiménez* ☎ *2735–5129* ⊟ No credit cards.

¢–$
COSTA RICAN
✕**Restaurante Carolina.** This simple alfresco restaurant in the heart of Puerto Jiménez on the main drag is the central meetingplace for every foreigner in town, ergo a good place to pick up information. The place also serves decent *comida típica* (typical food) and reliably fresh seafood. Don't count on using a credit card, though, as phone lines are dodgy. ✉ *Main road, center of town* ☎ *2735–5185* ⊟ MC, V.

WHERE TO STAY

Playa Platanares is only about 6 km (4 mi) outside of Puerto Jiménez, but lodgings there have a very different feeling from those in town, since they are on a lovely and quiet beach. Bosque del Río Tigre is also outside of town, but inland, in a forested area beside a river.

$$$
★
🏠**Bosque del Río Tigre Lodge.** You can't get any closer to nature than this off-the-grid lodge, famous for its birding trails, wedged between the forest and the banks of the Río Tigre. Four second-story rooms have chest-high walls, and then are open to nature to the roof with no screens, just mosquito nets over the beds. You're at eye level with the trees and, despite the almost-alfresco rooms, you'll sleep comfortably with linens and pillows that always feel fresh. Electricity is solar-generated and limited, but on-demand gas heaters provide plenty of hot water in the garden showers. The gourmet food rivals that of the best luxury-lodge kitchens. Guests gather around a communal table at dinner with owners Liz Jones and Abraham Gallo, the best bird guides in the area. More than 360 species have been spotted on the property, including 250 species from the lodge porch. Abraham, a lifelong local, can show you hidden mountain trails into Corcovado National Park, less than a mile away. Miners still pan for gold in the nearby river, which has a great swimming hole. **Pros:** a birder's paradise; great hiking trails; fabulous food. **Cons:** shared bathroom (except in one separate cabin) and outdoor showers; limited electricity; must love the outdoors. ✉ *Dos Brazos del Tigre* ⊹ *12 km/7 mi west of Puerto Jiménez* ☎ *888/875–9543 in U.S.* ⊕ *www.bosquedelriotigre.com* ↪ *4 rooms with shared bath, 1 cabin with private bath* ⅄ In-room: no a/c, no phone, no TV. In-hotel: restaurant ⊟ MC, V ⊘ Closed Sept. and Oct. ⦿⫯ FAP.

¢–$
★
🏠**Cabinas Jiménez.** Overlooking the harbor, these creatively renovated rooms and bungalows set in a lush garden have the best water views in town. You can enjoy the sound of the surf from your own terrace or the new hammock hut, or jump right into the gulf when it laps up against the hotel garden at high tide; there's also a new plunge pool. Colorful wall murals, fresh tiled bathrooms, and air-conditioning make this affordable place a cut above the others in town. Coffeemakers and small fridges are another nice touch. The owner is a keen fisherman and offers

8

"Sweetie, a spider monkey, quickly found refuge from the rain underneath Alex's rain poncho!" —Photo by hipvirgochick, Fodors.com member

fishing trips and dolphin tours on his own boat. **Pros:** watery views; a/c; bungalows have pleasant, private terrace with hammock; helpful, knowledgeable manager Chris. **Cons:** rooms are on the small side; no food service. ✉ *200 m west of town dock* ☎ *2735–5090* ⊕ *www. cabinasjimenez.com* ⤳ *7 rooms, 3 bungalows* ⌂ *In-room: no phone, safe, refrigerator. In-hotel: beachfront, pool, water sports* ▭ *AE, D, MC, V* ⦿ *EP.*

¢ 🏠 **Cabinas Marcelina.** Two elderly Italian sisters run the best bargain hotel in town. Fresh, spotlessly clean rooms look out onto the pleasant garden and have homey, old-fashioned touches like lace shower curtains. All have private bathrooms and hot water, and half are air-conditioned. If you're traveling solo or need a break from your traveling companion, two single rooms with fans are $25 each. The lavish full breakfast, served in the garden, is an additional $6. **Pros:** affordable; some rooms have a/c; pleasant garden oasis in middle of town. **Cons:** rooms are quite small; fan-only rooms are very cheap but can be hot and sticky. ✉ *Main street, north side of Catholic church* ☎ *2735–5007, 2735–5286* ✍ *cabmarce@hotmail.com* ⤳ *8 rooms* ⌂ *In-room: no a/c (some), no phone, no TV* ▭ *No credit cards* ⦿ *EP.*

$–$$ 🏠 **Danta Corcovado Lodge.** This artistically rustic lodge within walking
ⵯ distance of the western edge of Corcovado National Park is reminiscent of an Adirondacks camp, with creatively designed twig chairs and headboards, twisted-branch windows, and furniture made of leftover tree stumps. Kids of all ages will like the cabin-in-the-woods atmosphere. An ideal place to start a hike into Corcovado, the 100% locally run lodge offers accommodations to suit all budgets, from bunk-bed rooms with shared bath to spacious forest cabins, to a wheelchair-accessible master

suite with a spacious, semi-alfresco bathroom, paved with smooth river stones. Breakfast is included and traditional Costa Rican meals are served in an alfresco restaurant, joined to the lodge by a covered breezeway. The Los Patos entrance to the park is 8 km (5 mi) away; if you'd rather not walk, the lodge offers a horseback tour to the park entrance, with lunch by a waterfall. You can enjoy much of the same national park wildlife by walking the trails of this 86-acre, reforested property. **Pros:** proximity to Corcovado National Park; comfortable rusticity; affordable. **Cons:** no a/c; close encounters of the insect kind in cabins. ⊠ *Guadalupe ✛ 3 km/2 mi northwest of La Palma* ☎ *2735–1111* ⊕ *www.dantalodge.com* ⌨ *3 rooms, 1 suite, 5 cabins sleeping 3–8 people* ⌂ *In-room: no a/c, some shared bath. In-hotel: restaurant* ⊟ *MC, V* ⦿ *BP.*

$$–$$$$
Fodor's Choice
★

▦ **Iguana Lodge.** If a long stretch of deserted beach is your idea of heaven, this luxury lodge with breezy, screened-in, two-story cabins set among mature trees is for you. The gentle Golfo Dulce waters are perfect for swimming, sea-kayaking, and boogie boarding. Cabins are furnished elegantly in bamboo, with thoughtful touches like Egyptian cotton sheets and a raft of candles for romantic evenings. The upper-level cabins have the nicest views and catch the best breezes. Pebble-lined showers have plenty of solar-heated hot water and excellent water pressure. Eight new rooms in the former Pearl of the Osa Hotel, adjoining Iguana Lodge, have been upgraded, with marble bathrooms and upscale detailing. Extravagant buffet-style dinners, with exotic foods reflecting the owners' worldwide travels, are served in a thatch-roof dining room with a huge table that can accommodate up to 32 diners. The lavish breakfasts are worth getting up for. You can opt for lunch or dinner in the Pearl of the Osa restaurant, on the beach. A yoga platform and a Japanese soaking tub add a contemplative touch. Birds are plentiful in the Playa Preciosa Platanares Mixed Refuge, which borders the lodge. **Pros:** top-of-the-line accommodation and food in tranquil tropical setting; complimentary kayaks; interesting turtle conservation program. **Cons:** no a/c, so can be hot; new club rooms are small and can be noisy; leave your hair dryer at home and be prepared to get friendly with an insect or two. ⊠ *Playa Platanares ✛ 5 km/3 mi south of Puerto Jiménez airport* ☎ *8848–0752* 🖷 *2735–5436* ⊕ *www.iguanalodge.com* ⌨ *4 duplex cabins with 2 rooms each, 8 rooms in hotel, 1 house* ⌂ *In-room: no a/c, no phone, no TV. In-hotel: restaurant, beachfront, water sports* ⊟ *MC, V* ⦿ *MAP*

8

NIGHTLIFE

With live salsa music, **Pearl of the Osa** (✉ *Next door to Iguana Lodge on Playa Platanares*) attracts a big crowd Friday night. The crowd is a mix of ages, and the music is loud and a lot of fun.

SHOPPING

★ Jewelry maker Karen Herrera (✉ *Beside airport*) has collected the finest arts and crafts in the area and displayed them in an impressive shop. **Jagua Arts & Crafts** has some rare items, including colorful cotton dresses and woven Panama hats made by the Guaymí people. Other interesting items are exquisitely detailed bird carvings made by a family in Rincón; stained-glass mosaic boxes, mirrors, and trivets made by a San José artist; local paintings; and serious art ceramics. There's also a selection of natural-history field guides and books.

CORCOVADO NATIONAL PARK

Fodor'sChoice Corcovado National Park is the last and largest outpost of virgin low-
★ land rain forest in Central America and teeming with wildlife. Visitors who tread softly along the park's trails may glimpse howler, spider, and squirrel monkeys, peccaries (wild pigs), poison-arrow frogs, scarlet macaws, and, very rarely, jaguars and tapirs.

Most first-time visitors to Corcovado come on a daylong boat tour or hike. But to get to the most pristine, wildlife-rich areas, you need to walk, and that means a minimum of three days: one day to walk in, one day to walk out, and one day inside.

GETTING HERE AND AROUND

The easiest way to visit remote Corcovado is on a day trip via boat from a Drake Bay lodge or on foot from Carate. The 20-minute boat trip from Drake Bay gets you to the San Pedrillo entrance in the dry season (January–April). The boat trip from Drake to Sirena takes 45 minutes to 1 hour. From Carate airfield, where the collective taxi from Puerto Jiménez stops, it's about a 45-minute walk along the beach to the La Leona park entrance.

For getting to Corcovado from elsewhere, the most expensive option—but also the easiest way to get right to the heart of the park—is flying in on a small charter plane ($275) to the tiny La Sirena airstrip in the park. **Alfa Romeo Aero Taxi** (E *Puerto Jiménez airport* ☎ *735–5178*).

Less expensive is hiring a taxi in Puerto Jiménez ($45) to the Los Patos trailhead, or at least to the first crossing of the Río Rincón (from which you hike a few miles upriver to the trailhead). The cheapest, and least convenient, option is to take a morning bus for less than $1 from Puerto Jiménez at 8 AM to La Palma and then hike or take a taxi 14 km (9 mi) to the Los Patos entrance.

ESSENTIALS

Hours of Operation Ranger stations are officially open from 8 AM to 4 PM daily, but you can walk in almost anytime as long as you pay in advance.

Contacts National Parks Service in Puerto Jiménez (☎ *2735–5580* ✉ *pncorcovado@gmail.com* 🛄 *$10 per day* ☉ *Daily 8–4*).

Corcovado
National Park

0   5 mi
0   5 km

OUTDOOR ACTIVITIES

If your reason for coming to the Osa is Corcovado, choose a lodge that has resident naturalist guides. On the Drake Bay and gulf sides of the park, all the lodges arrange guided trips into Corcovado, most with their own guides, but some with freelance guides. Tour operators in Puerto Jiménez and Drake Bay also run guided trips in the park.

HIKING   There are two main hiking routes to Corcovado. One begins near La Palma, at the Los Patos entrance. There is one beach trail to the park, an easy 45-minute beach walk from Carate to the La Leona entrance. The former beach trail from San Pedrillo to La Sirena has been closed. You can still enter the park at the San Pedrillo station, though, and hike the trails there.

Hiking is always tough in the tropical heat, but the forest route (Los Patos) is cooler than the beach hike to La Leona and San Pedrillo. Although it is possible to hike La Leona at high tide, it's more difficult since you have to walk on a slope rather than the flat part of the beach. The hike between any two stations takes all day.

The hike from La Leona to Sirena is about 16 km (10 mi) and requires crossing one big river mouth and a stretch of beach that can be crossed only at low tide. Some guides do it very early in the morning, just before sunrise, to avoid the blistering heat along the beach.

The 20-km (12.5-mi) trail from Los Patos to Sirena is lovely and forested, including an 8 km walk (5 mi) along the verdant Río Rincón valley. The Sirena ranger station has great trails around it that can easily fill a couple of days.

Osa Aventura (⇨ *see Outdoor Activities in Puerto Jiménez, above*) specializes in wildlife tours.

> **WARNING**
>
> Swimming on the beach near Sirena is not advised because of rip currents and bull sharks. Also steer clear of the brackish Río Sirena, home to crocs, bull sharks, and snakes. The only advisable swimming area is the Río Claro.

WHERE TO EAT

Basic meals can be arranged at Sirena if you reserve in advance with the National Parks Service office in Puerto Jiménez. It's always a good idea to ask about what meals are available for sale when you make your reservation.

WHERE TO STAY

Camping or sleeping in the ranger's stations are your only lodging options inside the park, and both take planning and preparation. You must reserve in advance, during peak visitor times, at least 30 days ahead. Bunks at the Sirena ranger station (which is in a lamentable state of disrepair) are limited to 20 people a day, as are meals, which are very basic. Bring your own sheets, a pillow, and a good mosquito net. Campers planning to camp at La Leona, San Pedrillo, Los Patos or La Sirena need to bring their own tents, gear, and food (although meals are sometimes available at La Leona). There is a maximum stay of four nights and five days. To make reservations you must fill out a request, via e-mail or in person at the park office in Puerto Jiménez, then make a deposit in the park's Banco Nacional account, then e-mail, fax, or present the receipt in person to the park office. Lodging is $8 per night, not including meals; camping costs $4 per person per night.

DID YOU KNOW?

Corcovado has 13 ecosystems within its boundaries, ranging from mangroves and swamps to lowland rain forest. The park also has more forest giants—trees that stand 50 to 80 meters (165 to 264 feet) high—than anywhere in Central America.

CABO MATAPALO

21 km/14 mi south of Puerto Jiménez.

The southern tip of the Osa Peninsula, where virgin rain forest meets the sea at a rocky point, retains the kind of natural beauty that people travel halfway across the world to experience. From its ridges you can look out on the blue Golfo Dulce and the Pacific Ocean, sometimes spotting whales in the distance. The forest is tall and dense, with the highest and most diverse tree species in the country, usually draped with thick lianas. The name Matapalo refers to the strangler fig, which germinates in the branches of other trees and extends its roots downward, eventually smothering the supporting tree by blocking the sun-

"This is the view from the deck of the Tucan cabina at Bosque del Cabo." —Photo by Monica Richards, Fodors.com member

light. Flocks of brilliant scarlet macaws and troops of monkeys are the other draws here.

GETTING HERE AND AROUND

If you drive one hour south from Puerto Jiménez, be prepared for a bumpy ride and a lot of river crossings. In rainy season cars are sometimes washed out along rivers to the ocean. Most hotels arrange transportation in 4WD taxis or their own trucks. The cheapest—and the roughest—way to travel is by *collectivo,* an open-air communal truck ($8), that leaves Puerto Jiménez twice a day (at 6 AM and 1:30 PM). Buses do not serve Cabo Matapalo.

OUTDOOR ACTIVITIES

Outfitters in Puerto Jiménez run tours in this area. Each of the lodges listed has resident guides who can take guests on nature hikes. For extreme forest sports, **Everyday Adventures** (☎ *8353–8619* ⊕ *www. psychotours.com*) takes you on not-so-everyday adventures: rappelling down waterfalls ($85), climbing up a 43-meter (140-foot) strangler fig tree ($55), and rain-forest hiking ($45). Or you can go all out with a combination rappelling/climbing tour for $120.

SURFING On the eastern side of Cabo Matapalo, waves break over a platform that creates a perfect right, drawing surfers from far and wide, especially beginners. Local surf expert Oldemar (aka Pollo) Fernandez offers daily lessons at Pan Dulce Beach at his Pollo Surf School (☎ *8366–6559,* ⊕ *www.pollosurfschool.com*). For $55 per person in a group lesson; $110 for private lessons.

WHERE TO STAY

$$$$ ⊞ **Bosque del Cabo.** Atop a cliff at the tip of Cabo Matapalo, this lodge
Fodor's Choice   has unparalleled views of the Golfo Dulce merging with the endless
★   blue of the Pacific. The property, with hundreds of acres of animal-
rich primary forest, also has the most beautiful landscaping on the
peninsula. Deluxe thatch-roof cabins have king-size beds, with private, outdoor garden showers with hot water. Private decks are perfect for sunning by day and stargazing at night. A suspension bridge
through the forest links the main lodge with three more rustic cabins
set in a tropical garden that is great for bird-watching. Excellent meals
are served in a rancho restaurant overlooking a garden alive with
hummingbirds by day and serenaded by a chorus of frogs at night.
Solar- and hydro-powered generators provide enough light to read by,
and with the ocean breezes, you won't miss air-conditioning. Resident
guides are on hand to lead you along forest trails—on foot or along a
canopy zip line—and down to the beach with its natural warm tidal
whirlpools and river waterfalls. The owners work hard to make their
lodge as environmentally responsible as possible. **Pros:** luxurious, artistic bungalows; fabulous trails and guides; congenial atmosphere among
guests at cocktail hour and dinner. **Cons:** steep trail to beach and back;
very small pool; limited electricity supply. ⊹ *22 km/14 mi south of
Puerto Jiménez on road to Carate* ⬡ *Box 02-5635, Miami, FL 33102*
☏ *2735–5206, 8389–2846 at lodge* ⊕ *www.bosquedelcabo.com* ⇆ *10
ocean-view cabins; 2 garden cabins; 3 houses, 1 with pool* ⬡ *In-room:
no a/c, no phone, kitchen (some), no TV. In-hotel: restaurant, bar, pool,
beachfront* ⊟ *MC, V* ⏀ *FAP.*

$$$$ ⊞ **El Remanso.** You'll find tranquility and elegant simplicity at this almost
★   spiritual retreat in a forest brimming with birds and wildlife, 122 meters
(400 feet) above a beach studded with tide pools. Luxurious two-person
cabinas have screened windows, large verandas, and showers behind
curving Gaudí-like walls. A new deluxe cabin, on the path to the beach,
has stunning ocean views and lots of privacy. There's also a large family
cabin and a very private, deluxe two-story cabin, perfect for honeymoons. Four spacious rooms and two suites in a new two-story building
have king-size beds, bathtubs, and verandas overlooking a swimming
pool. Meals using local produce are served on a newly expanded deck
restaurant. Waterfall rappelling, zip-line access to a canopy platform,
and biologist-guided nature walks are the highlights, apart from soaking in the serenity. This is the most relaxed lodge in the area. **Pros:** gorgeous natural setting; privacy in cabins; jungle views; access to beach.
Cons: no a/c; no hair dryers; food is often good but not spectacular. ⊠
South of entrance to Bosque del Cabo on road to Carate ☏ *2735–5569
office, 2735–5938 lodge* ⊕ *www.elremanso.com* ⇆ *4 rooms, 2 suites, 5
cabinas* ⬡ *In-room: no a/c, no phone, no TV. In-hotel: restaurant, bar,
beachfront, Internet terminal* ⊟ *MC, V* ⏀ *FAP.*

$$$$ ⊞ **Lapa Ríos.** The most spectacular eco-resort in Costa Rica, Lapa Ríos
Fodor's Choice   has won numerous awards for its mix of conservation and comfort
★   at the edge of civilization. After catching your breath when you see
the view from the high, breezy jungle ridge rife with wildlife, your
next sharp intake may be when you see the bill. But in this case the

price is not inflated. Spacious, airy cabins built of gleaming hardwoods have four-poster queen beds, stylish bathrooms, and showers with one screened wall open to nature. Private teak-decked garden terraces allow you to view passing monkeys and toucans from a lounge chair. There's an infinity pool, a spa, and a yoga deck. Inspired meals, served under a soaring thatch roof, include lots of seafood, exotic local fruits and vegetables, and mouthwatering desserts. You can eat whenever—and as much as—you want. Resident naturalist guides lead tours through pristine wilderness and to nearby beaches on foot or on horseback. Along with the high cost of transporting and providing all these luxuries in a remote location, it's the exceptional service that justifies the high price tag, which includes transfers from Puerto Jiménez in new 4WD vehicles. Don't miss their free sustainability tour called Pigs, Twigs and Garbage, which highlights the resort's ingenious eco-friendly infrastructure, including pigs' contribution to energy fuels. ■TIP➔ If you don't like to climb stairs, request a cabin close to the main lodge. **Pros:** excellent, professional service; Tico-flavor atmosphere with local employees; delicious typical and international dishes. **Cons:** steep price, but this is a once-in-a-lifetime experience; some steps to climb to farther cabins; steep trail to beach, but there is a shuttle service. ✚ *20 km/12 mi south of Puerto Jiménez* ✑ *Apdo. 100–8203, Puerto Jiménez* ☎ *2735–5130* ⊕ *www.laparios.com* ⤴ *16 cabinas* ⌂ *In-room: no a/c, no phone, no TV. In-hotel: restaurant, bar, pool, spa, beachfront, laundry service* ▭ *AE, MC, V* ⦿ *AI.*

CARATE

60 km/37 mi west of Puerto Jiménez.

Carate is literally the end of the road. The black volcanic-sand beach stretches for more than 3 km (2 mi), with surf that's perfect for boogie boarding and body surfing but not for serious board surfing or safe swimming. The main entertainment at the beach is watching the noisy but magnificent scarlet macaws feasting on almonds in the beach almond trees that edge the shore. Carate has no phone service; a couple of lodges have satellite phones and iffy Wi-Fi and cell-phone connections.

GETTING HERE AND AROUND

The road from Matapalo to Carate covers 40 suspension-testing km (25 mi); at this writing, there is a new bridge over the Agua Buena River and the road is graded and relatively smooth, but that can all change with one drenching wet season. You're better off taking the *collectivo* from Puerto Jiménez (➪ *Getting Here and Around in Puerto Jiménez, above*). Or give yourself a break and fly via charter plane to Carate's small airport, which has been upgraded recently; arrange flights through your lodge. From here it's just 3 km (2 mi), roughly a 40-minute walk along the beach to the La Leona ranger station entrance to Corcovado National Park. In rainy season (May to December) it is sometimes impossible to cross the raging Río Carate that separates the landing strip from the beach path to the park, and you may end up stranded on either side. Parking at the store in Carate is $5 per day.

8

OUTDOOR ACTIVITIES

Activities here revolve around Corcovado National Park and its environs. Hiking, horseback riding, canopy tours, and other adventures must be organized through your hotel.

WHERE TO STAY

$$–$$$ ☷ **Lookout Inn.** The only hotel on Carate's beach, this barefoot inn—shoes come off at the bottom step—is set on a precipitous hillside (steep stairs are plentiful here, including a 500-step "Stairway to Heaven" up to a lofty lookout). Luxurious rooms in the lodge have huge ceramic bathrooms. Two screened-in wooden cabins are perfect for those craving privacy, and one new cabin, the Monkey House, is great for families, with a queen bed and two singles in a loft. It's also under the monkeys' favorite treetop freeway. Cheaper tentlike "tiki" cabinas sit on 10-foot platforms and share a bathhouse. This place is full of quirky artistic touches, including a swinging bed in another new cabin, the Swing Inn Spa. But the quirkiest element is owner Terry Conroy, an energetic host who makes sure everyone joins in on activities. His serene Tica wife, Katya, balances her husband and makes a mean margarita. Inventive meals with lots of fresh fish and Asian flavors are served on two breezy terraces with spectacular views of the coastline. Dozens of scarlet macaws frequent the garden, and monkeys come to feast on bananas. There's also a spring-fed plunge pool with a hammock rancho, a yoga deck, a new spa, a shaded pavilion on the beach, and a bird-watching trail through primary forest. The hotel organizes beach and trail rides on horseback. **Pros:** proximity to beach and access on foot to Corcovado Park; excellent food; party atmosphere; guaranteed scarlet macaw sightings (or your money back!). **Cons:** very steep drive/stair climb up to lodge and down to beach; very limited communication with outside world; cabins have more privacy than main lodge rooms. ⊠ *300 m east of Carate landing strip* ☎ *2735–5431, 757–644–5967 in U.S.* ⊕ *www.lookout-inn.com* ➫ *3 rooms, 4 cabins, 2 tiki cabins with shared bath* △ *In-room: no a/c, no phone, no TV. In-hotel: restaurant, bars, pool, spa, beachfront, laundry service, some pets allowed* ▭ *MC, V* ⑩ *FAP.*

$$–$$$ ☷ **Luna Lodge.** Luna Lodge's ultimate charm lies in its remoteness and
★ tranquility. On a mountaintop overlooking the ocean and the rain forest, it's a true retreat, with a huge hardwood pavilion for practicing yoga or contemplating magnificent sunsets. Just below the yoga platform there's an elegant massage hut with ethereal views. Round bungalows in the garden, spaced apart for privacy, have thatch roofs, garden showers, and decks for bird-watching or relaxing in wood-and-leather rocking chairs. Three deluxe rooms near the main lodge have private baths and share a spacious deck. For real adventure, bed down in one of the lodge's comfortable new platform tents, set on a hilltop with ocean view and private bathrooms. Guided hikes to nearby waterfalls and swimming holes are precipitous and thrilling, and lounging around the beautiful new pebble-deck pool is pure nirvana. Healthful meals have an imaginative vegetarian flair, tempered with servings of fish and chicken spiced with herbs from a hilltop organic garden. Host Lana Wedmore is a model of amiable helpfulness. **Pros:** scenic setting for peace, yoga, and

therapeutic massage; comfortable lodging and healthful food; excellent birding. **Cons:** extremely steep road up to lodge; beach is quite a hike back down (and up!); no a/c; open cabins mean there may be some encounters of the small wildlife kind. ⊕ *2 km/1 mi up a steep, partially paved road from Carate* ☎ *8380–5036 or 2206–5859, 888/409–8448 in U.S.* ⊕ *www.lunalodge.com* ⇨ *8 bungalows, 3 rooms, 5 tents* ⚒ *In-room: no a/c, no phone, no TV. In-hotel: restaurant, bar, pool, spa* ▭ *MC, V* ⎸⦿⎸ *FAP.*

DRAKE BAY

18 km/11 mi north of Corcovado, 40 km/25 mi southwest of Palmar Sur, 310 km/193 mi south of San José.

This is castaway country, a real tropical adventure, with plenty of hiking and some rough but thrilling boat rides. The rugged coast that stretches south from the mouth of the Río Sierpe to Corcovado probably doesn't look much different from what it did in Sir Francis Drake's day (1540–96), when, as legend has it, the British explorer anchored here. Small, picture-perfect beaches with surf crashing against dark volcanic rocks are backed by steaming, thick jungle. Nature lodges scattered along the coast are hemmed in by the rain forest, which is home to troops of monkeys, sloths, scarlet macaws, and hundreds of other bird species.

GETTING HERE AND AROUND

The fastest way to get to Drake Bay is to fly directly to the airstrip. You can also fly to Palmar Sur and take a taxi to Sierpe and then a boat to Drake Bay. From the airport, it's a 25-minute taxi ride to Sierpe; small, open boats leave at low tide, usually 11 to 11:30 AM for the one-hour trip to Drake. There is also a new late-afternoon boat service. Captains will often stop along the way to view wildlife in the river mangroves. Many lodges arrange boat transportation from Drake Bay or Sierpe. From Rincón you can drive to Drake on a 20-km (12-mi) graded dirt road. Buses leave Puerto Jiménez for La Palma every two hours from 6 AM to 8 PM, connecting in La Palma with buses to Drake Bay at 10:30 AM and 4 PM. Buses leave Drake at 4 AM and 1 PM for La Palma, to connect with buses to either Puerto Jiménez or San José. The drive from San José to Drake is scenic, but an exhausting seven hours long.

Exceptionally fit backpackers can hike to the northern entrance of Corcovado along an 18-km (11-mi) coastal path that follows the shoreline, cutting through shady forest when the coast gets too rocky. But it is impossible to walk during rainy season (September to December), when rivers flood and tides are too high.

ESSENTIALS

Drake just got electricity in 2004, so there are still very few services.

Internet Internet Cafe (✉ *Drake village, 25 meters west of elementary school*).

Visitor Information Corcovado Expeditions (✉ *Drake* ☎ *8818–9962* ⊕ *www.corcovadoexpeditions.net*).

8

One of Punta Marenco Lodge's boat excursions.

The cheapest accommodations in the area can be found in the town of **Drake**, which is spread out along the bay. A trio of upscale nature lodges—Drake Bay Wilderness Resort, Aguila de Osa Inn, and La Paloma Lodge—are also clumped near the Río Agujitas on the bay's southern end. They all offer comprehensive packages, including trips to Corcovado and Caño Island. Lodges farther south, such as Punta Marenco Lodge and Casa Corcovado, run excursions from even wilder settings. During the dry season you can reach the town of Drake via a graded dirt road from Rincón.

OUTDOOR ACTIVITIES

Jinetes de Osa (⊠ *Drake village, west side of bay* ☎ *2231–5806* ⊕ *www. jinetesdeosa.com*) has diving ($105 plus $20 for gear) and snorkeling ($75) and dolphin-watching tours ($105), as well as a canopy tour ($55) with some interesting bridge, ladder, and rope transitions between platforms.

WHERE TO STAY

$$$$ 🍴 **Aguila de Osa Inn.** A sportfisher's dream lodge, Aguila de Osa has spacious rooms with hardwood interiors, oversize bamboo beds, and luxurious tile-and-glass-brick bathrooms. Stained-glass lamps with tropical themes and hand-carved doors add artistic flair. Be prepared for a steep climb up stone stairs to your room with a view of Drake Bay. Morning coffee arrives outside your room before 6 AM. Dinner here is a real event, with huge platters of perfectly cooked fish—sometimes guests' own catches—and meats, served family-style. The lodge has two 31-foot, high-tech sportfishing boats, as well as dive trips and excursions into Corcovado Park. Two-night packages include transfers from

Snorkelers Paradise

Most of uninhabited 2½-square-km (1-square-mi) **Caño Island Biological Reserve** is covered in evergreen forest that includes fig, locust, and rubber trees. Coastal Indians used it as a burial ground, and the numerous bits and pieces unearthed here have prompted archaeologists to speculate about pre-Columbian long-distance maritime trade. Occasionally, mysterious stones that have been carved into perfect spheres of varying sizes are discovered. The uninhabited island's main attraction now is the ocean around it, superb for scuba diving and snorkeling. The snorkeling is best around the rocky points flanking the island's main beach; if you're a certified diver, you'll probably want to explore Bajo del Diablo and Paraíso, where you're guaranteed to encounter thousands of good-size fish, including white-tip, nurse, and trigger sharks.

The only way to get to the island, 19 km (12 mi) due west of the Osa Peninsula, is by boat arranged by your lodge or a tour company. Lodges and the Jinetes de Osa tour company in Drake Bay run day trips here, as do tour companies in Dominical, Uvita, and Sierpe.

Drake Bay or Palmar Sur airports. **Pros:** great for fishing enthusiasts; elegant lodge and rooms; convivial, communal dining. **Cons:** no ocean views or breezes, and heat and humidity can be stifling; steep climb to some rooms, on sometimes slippery stone stairs; some rooms have little privacy, notably No. 10. ⊠ *South end of Drake at mouth of Río Agujitas* ☎ *2296–2190 in San José,* 8840–2929 lodge, 866/924–8452 toll-free in U.S. ⊕ *www.aguiladeosa.com* ⤳ *11 rooms, 2 suites* ⚠ *In-room: no a/c, no phone, refrigerator (some), no TV. In-hotel: restaurant, bar, water sports, laundry service, Internet terminal, Wi-Fi* ⊟ *AE, MC, V* ⦿ *FAP.*

$$$–$$$$
★ 🖼 **Casa Corcovado Jungle Lodge.** This hilltop jungle lodge has it all: a prime location on the edge of Corcovado National Park, luxury accommodations, and first-class service. Spanish colonial–style bungalows are spread out, each with its own garden for maximum privacy. The bungalows have elegant furniture, four-poster beds, and huge tile bathrooms, some with open-air garden showers. Laundry service is extra, but each room has clotheslines for drying your sure-to-be-damp clothes. Two swimming pools and self-guided nature trails on the property keep you busy outdoors, and the games room has books and board games to occupy evenings and rainy afternoons. The hilltop sunset margarita bar has excellent views of the sun setting behind Caño Island. The vast restaurant, studded with art deco stained glass, serves excellent breakfasts and packs hearty picnic lunches. At this writing, dinners are less successful, but new chefs are revising the menu. The minimum stay is two nights, but the best deal is a three-night package that includes transportation from San José, all meals, and a trip to Caño Island and Corcovado National Park. **Pros:** unrivaled location adjoining national park and close to Caño Island; excellent tours, service, and facilities. **Cons:** an adventure to get here: be prepared for a hair-raising, wet landing; steep climb to lodge from beach, but there is a tractor-pulled cart

8

Understanding Costa Rica's Climate

Although you may associate the tropics with rain, precipitation in Costa Rica varies considerably, depending on where you are and when you're here. This is a result of the mountainous terrain and regional weather patterns. A phenomenon called rain shadow—when one side of a mountain range receives much more than the other—plays an important ecological role in Costa Rica. Four mountain ranges combine to create an intercontinental divide that separates the country into Atlantic and Pacific slopes; because of the trade winds, the Atlantic slope receives much more rain than the Pacific. The trade winds steadily pump moisture-laden clouds southwest over the isthmus, where they encounter warm air or mountains, which make them rise. As the clouds rise, they cool, lose their ability to hold moisture, and eventually dump most of their liquid luggage on the Caribbean side.

During the rainy season—mid-May to December—the role of the trade winds is diminished, as regular storms roll off the Pacific Ocean and soak the western side of the isthmus. Though it rains all over Costa Rica during these months, it often rains more on the Pacific side of the mountains than on the Atlantic. Come December, the trade winds take over again, and while the Caribbean prepares for its wettest time of the year, hardly a drop falls on the western side until May.

Climate variation within the country results in a mosaic of forests. The combination of humidity and temperature helps determine what grows where; but whereas some species have very restricted ranges, others seem to thrive just about anywhere. Plants such as strangler figs and bromeliads grow all over Costa Rica, and animals such as the collared peccary and coati—a long-nose cousin of the raccoon—can pretty much live wherever human beings let them. Other species have extremely limited ranges, such as the mangrove hummingbird, restricted to the mangrove forests of the Pacific coast, and the volcano junco, a gray sparrow that lives only around the highest peaks of the Cordillera de Talamanca.

---

to transport guests and luggage; no a/c; limited electricity. ⊠ *Northern border of Corcovado* ☎ *2256–3181, 888/896–6097 toll-free in U.S.* ⊕ *www.casacorcovado.com* 🔊 *14 bungalows* ⅃ *In-room: no a/c, no phone, no TV. In-hotel: restaurant, bars, pools, beachfront, water sports* ▤ *AE, MC, V* ⊘ *Closed mid-Sept.–mid-Nov.* ⏀ *AI.*

$$–$$$ 🖫 **Drake Bay Wilderness Resort.** On a grassy point between Río Agujitas and the ocean, this breezy resort has the best views of Drake Bay. It's also kid-friendly, with a pool, open ground for romping, and tidal pools to explore. Keep an eye out for precocious squirrel monkeys. The wooden cabins are camp-style, three rooms to a building. But with hot water, tile bathrooms, and carved animal bedposts supporting firm queen-size beds, this is very comfortable camping. There's no air-conditioning, but ocean breezes make for cool evenings. There are also five less expensive, tentlike cabanas on platforms with shared baths, right at the water's edge. Kayaks are at your disposal for exploring the river. Most guests come to see the rain forest, but you

can also opt for mangrove, scuba diving, sportfishing, and dolphin- and whale-watching tours. **Pros:** great location; family-friendly and affordable; good food; free laundry service. **Cons:** not a lot of privacy; no a/c. ⊠ *On peninsula at mouth of Río Agujitas, on southern end of bay* ✆ *Apdo. 1370010–1000, San José* ☎ *8337–8004, 561/371-3437 in U.S.* ⊕ *www.drakebay.com* ⤵ *20 rooms, 5 economy cabins* ⚥ *In-room: no a/c, no phone, no TV. In-hotel: restaurant, bar, pool, laundry facilities, Wi-Fi* ▭ *AE, MC, V* ⦿| *FAP.*

$$–$$$ ⌂ **Jinetes de Osa.** The most comfortable and reasonably priced place to stay right in the village of Drake, this small bay-side hotel with a casual open-air restaurant has simple rooms, all with tile floors and hot-water showers. Rooms open out onto a pleasant terrace with a view of the town and the bay. Guests get to leave their artistic signatures on painted driftwood mobiles that decorate the restaurant. The on-site diving operation is well run, so the lodge is often filled with groups of divers. **Pros:** convenient location; affordable; adventuresome, active clientele. **Cons:** standard rooms are smallish, so opt for the larger deluxe room if you can; no a/c. ⊠ *Drake village, west side of bay* ☎ *2231–5806 in San José* ⊕ *www.costaricadiving.com* ⤵ *9 rooms* ⚥ *In-room: no a/c, no phone, no TV. In-hotel: restaurant, beachfront* ▭ *MC, V* ⦿| *FAP.*

$$$$ ⌂ **La Paloma Lodge.** Sweeping ocean views and lots of tropical-foliage
★ privacy make this villa lodge the area's most romantic. Planted in a jungle garden on a ridge jutting into Drake Bay, elegant, spacious wooden villas have bedroom lofts, spiffy bathrooms, and large porches with summery green wicker furniture. Numbers 1 and 3 have the best sea views. Four standard rooms lined up in a shared building are anything but standard: they're spacious and luxurious with jungle and garden views. Room D has a wraparound deck overlooking an expanse of jungle that will delight bird-watchers. A small pool overlooks forest and ocean, or you can head down the hill to Playa Cocolito, the hotel's gem of a beach at the edge of the coastal path to Corcovado. The hotel runs a diving school and offers river kayaking. The flower-filled restaurant serves tropical fare, and there's always afternoon tea and baked treats when you can mingle with the other guests. The lodge now has the added luxury of public electricity with a generator backup. Manager Nichole Dupont maintains a high standard of service. There's a three-night minimum stay; packages are the best bet, as they include transportation from San José, all meals, and some tours. **Pros:** idyllic setting with ocean views and easy access to Coastal Footpath; great service; interesting guests from all over the world.

8

Cons: expensive; no a/c; open cabins mean you will have to contend with some insect visitors. ⊠ *Drake Bay, 300 m past Drake Bay Wilderness Resort* ☎ *2293–7502* ⊕ *www.lapalomalodge.com* ⇆ *4 rooms, 7 cabinas* ⚴ *In-room: no a/c, no phone, no TV. In-hotel: restaurant, bar, pool, beachfront, diving, water sports, Wi-Fi in restaurant* ▭ *MC, V* ⊙ *Closed Sept.–Oct.* ⏲ *FAP.*

$$ ⚟ **Punta Marenco Lodge.** This rustic lodge has the best location on the Pacific side of the Osa, and it's the best deal on the coast. After a bumpy period when the lodge was leased out, the owners have returned to upgrade and run it themselves. South Seas island–style cabins with thatch roofs perch on the spine of a ridge overlooking the sea. Private porches are perfect for siestas, sunsets, and stargazing. Four new, spacious cabins have garden and sea views, ideal for bird-watchers; No. 4 has a huge bed with a frog headboard. Toucans and scarlet macaws visit every morning, and paths lead to the scenic coastal trail and deep into the Río Claro National Wildlife Refuge. A resident guide is on hand for nature walks, and the lodge can arrange oceangoing tours, including diving and dolphin-watching excursions. The rancho restaurant has a family feel, with communal tables and typical Tico food. There is electricity for only a few hours in the evening, and no hot water. Insects frequent the thatch roofs, but so do tiny lizards that eat them up. You can hike here from Drake or take a boat from Drake or Sierpe (included in packages). **Pros:** castaway-island remoteness; trails are as good as those in Corcovado National Park; very reasonable price. **Cons:** very rustic; steep climb uphill to lodge after thrilling wet landing on beach; simple food; very limited electricity and contact with outside world. ⊠ *Beachfront, directly east of Caño Island and north of Casa Corcovado* ☎ *2292–2775 for reservations, 2294–8947;* ⊕ *www. corcovadozone.com* ⇆ *18 cabinas* ⚴ *In-room: no a/c, no phone, no TV. In-hotel: restaurant, beachfront* ▭ *MC, V* ⏲ *AI.*

NIGHTLIFE

When you're on the Osa Peninsula, the wildest nightlife is outdoors. ★ Join entomologist Tracie Stice, also known as the Bug Lady, on the ⟳ **Night Tour** (☎ *8812–6673 or 8867–6143* ⊕ *www.thenighttour.com*) of insects, bats, reptiles, and anything else moving around at night. Tracie is a wealth of bug lore, with riveting stories from around the world. Headlamps and infrared flashlights help you see in the dark. Tours are $35 per person.

Caribbean

WORD OF MOUTH

"We continued walking and all of a sudden there were many small, dark shapes scurrying across the sand towards the water in front of us. It was a whole nest of turtle hatchlings that were making their way to the ocean. It was one of the most amazing things I've ever seen!"

—cmerrell

WELCOME TO CARIBBEAN

TOP REASONS TO GO

★ **Turtles:** People from around the world flock to the northern Caribbean for the annual nesting of four species.

★ **Food and flavors:** Leave gallo pinto behind in favor of mouthwatering *rondón* (meat or fish stew), or *caribeno* (Caribbean) rice and beans, stewed in coconut milk.

★ **Dolphin-watching:** Bottle-nosed, tucuxi, and Atlantic spotted dolphins ply the southern Caribbean coast.

★ **Music:** Mix reggae and calypso with your salsa. Rhythms waft in from the far-off Caribbean Islands; and homegrown musicians are making names for themselves, too.

★ **Sportfishing:** World-class tarpon and snook attract serious anglers to the shores off Barra del Colorado and Tortuguero national parks.

1 Northern Lowlands. The Northern Lowlands have little to offer tourists in their own right, but are close to Braulio Carrillo Park and rafting-trip put-in points.

2 Northern Caribbean Coast. The Northern Caribbean Coast encompasses the coastal jungles and canals of Tortuguero National Park and Barra del Colorado Wildlife Refuge. Boat and air travel are the only ways to reach this roadless region.

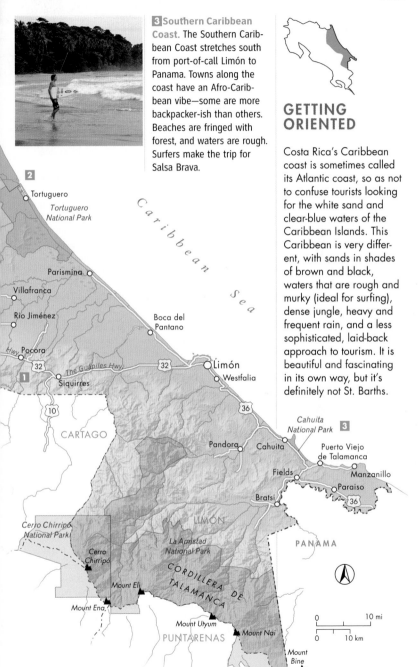

3 Southern Caribbean Coast. The Southern Caribbean Coast stretches south from port-of-call Limón to Panama. Towns along the coast have an Afro-Caribbean vibe—some are more backpacker-ish than others. Beaches are fringed with forest, and waters are rough. Surfers make the trip for Salsa Brava.

GETTING ORIENTED

Costa Rica's Caribbean coast is sometimes called its Atlantic coast, so as not to confuse tourists looking for the white sand and clear-blue waters of the Caribbean Islands. This Caribbean is very different, with sands in shades of brown and black, waters that are rough and murky (ideal for surfing), dense jungle, heavy and frequent rain, and a less sophisticated, laid-back approach to tourism. It is beautiful and fascinating in its own way, but it's definitely not St. Barths.

CARIBBEAN PLANNER

When to Go

Climate is the Caribbean's bugaboo and will forever prevent it from becoming the same high-powered tourist destination that the North Pacific is. (Frankly, we consider that to be a blessing.) The Caribbean lacks a true dry season, though February to April and September to October could be called drier seasons, with many sunny days and intermittent showers. The heaviest rains (and periodic road closures) come in December and January, high season elsewhere. During the rainiest months prices are lower and visitors fewer.

Temperatures remain constant year-round, with daily highs of 29°C to 31°C (84°F to 88°F) and lows of 21°C to 23°C (69°F to 73°F). Yet, despite weather patterns that differ from the rest of Costa Rica, places here charge high-season rates from December to April, and again in July and August. (Tortuguero sets its own high and low seasons, with higher prices the norm during prime turtle-watching months of July through September.) Not to fear though: prices skew a bit lower in the Caribbean than elsewhere in the country.

Getting There

Old-timers still remember the days when the only access to this region was the railroad that once connected San José with Limón. From there, boats would take them up and down the coast. Today, this historically isolated area is one of the country's most accessible. The southern coast is a three- to four-hour drive from San José, over mostly decent roads (by Costa Rican standards), and public transportation is frequent and reliable. Gas stations are plentiful between Guápiles and Limón, but their numbers dwindle to one between Limón and Puerto Viejo de Talamanca. The northern Caribbean coast is another story: the total absence of roads means you have to arrive by plane or boat. Most travelers go with a tour booked through one of the large lodges.

If you're driving here, remember that fog often covers the mountains in Braulio Carrillo National Park, north of San José, by early afternoon. Cross this area in the morning if you can. Always exercise utmost caution on the portion of highway that twists and turns through the park. Check road conditions before you set out; occasional closures through Braulio Carrillo necessitate leaving San José from the southeast, passing through Cartago, Paraíso, and Turrialba, then rejoining the Caribbean highway at Siquirres.

The Complete Package

One of Costa Rica's most remote regions is also one of its prime tourist destinations. No roads lead to Tortuguero on the northeast coast, so plane or boat is your only option. If you don't want to bother with logistics, consider booking a package tour with one of the lodges we list. It will include all transport from San José, overnights, meals, and guided tours. Prices look high at first, but considering all you get, they are quite reasonable. Other types of regional tours are also available: **Horizontes** (☎ 2222–2022 ⊕ www.horizontes.com) tours include naturalist guides and transport by 4WD vehicle.

What to Do

ACTIVITY	WHERE TO DO IT
Biking	Cahuita, Puerto Viejo de Talamanca
Bird-watching	EARTH, Tortuguero, Gandoca-Manzanillo Wildlife Refuge
Butterfly-viewing	Cahuita, Puerto Viejo de Talamanca, Limón
Diving	Gandoca-Manzanillo Wildlife Refuge
Dolphin-watching	Gandoca-Manzanillo Wildlife Refuge
Fishing	Barra del Colorado, San Juan River, Tortuguero
Kayaking	Gandoca-Manzanillo Wildlife Refuge, Tortuguero
Snorkeling	Cahuita National Park, Gandoca-Manzanillo Wildlife Refuge
Surfing	Cahuita, Puerto Viejo de Talamanca, Limón
Turtle-watching	Gandoca-Manzanillo Wildlife Refuge, Tortuguero
White-water rafting	Siquirres
Wildlife-viewing	Tortuguero, Barra del Colorado, Gandoca-Manzanillo Wildlife Refuge, Guápiles
Zip-lining	Gandoca-Manzanillo Wildlife Refuge, Limón

Dining and Lodging Prices

WHAT IT COSTS IN DOLLARS

	¢	$	$$	$$$	$$$$
Restaurants	under $5	$5–$10	$10–$15	$15–$25	over $25
Hotels	under $50	$50–$75	$75–$150	$150–$250	over $250

Restaurant prices are per person for a main course at dinner. Hotel prices are for two people in a standard double room in high season, excluding service and tax (16.4%).

How Much Time?

Attractions near Guápiles and Siquirres lend themselves to long day trips from San José. Tour operators also have whirlwind daylong Tortuguero trips from San José. We recommend you avoid these—the area really deserves two or, ideally, three days. Choose a single Caribbean destination and stay put if you have just a few days. (Cahuita and Puerto Viejo de Talamanca are ideal for that purpose.) If you have a week, you can tackle the north and south coasts.

Choosing a Place to Stay

The high-rise, glitzy resorts of the Pacific coast are nowhere to be found in the Caribbean. The norm here is small, independent lodgings, usually family owned and operated. Fewer visitors in this region mean plenty of decent lodging at affordable prices most of the year. But tourism *is* growing, so it's risky to show up without reservations. Surprisingly few places here have air-conditioning, but sea breezes and ceiling fans usually provide sufficient ventilation. Smaller places frequently don't take credit cards; those that do may give discounts if you pay with cash.

9

TORTUGUERO NATIONAL PARK

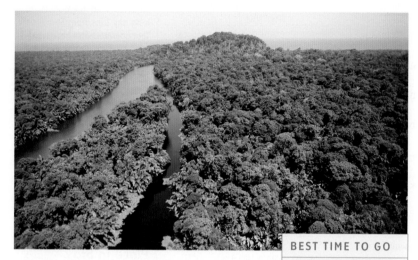

At various times of the year, four species of sea turtles—green, hawksbill, loggerhead, and giant leatherback—lumber up the 35 km (22 mi) of beach to deposit their eggs for safekeeping.

In 1975 the Costa Rican government established Tortuguero National Park to protect the sea turtle population, which had been decimated after centuries of being aggressively hunted for its eggs and carapaces. This is the best place in Costa Rica to observe these magnificent creatures' nesting and hatching rituals. Still, despite preservation efforts, less than 1% of the hatchlings will make it to adulthood.

Turtles may be the name of the game here, but keep your eyes peeled for non–turtle species, too: tapirs, jaguars, anteaters, ocelots, howler monkeys, white-faced capuchin monkeys, three-toed sloths, collared and white-lipped peccaries, coatis, and blue morpho butterflies also populate the park. The palm-lined beaches of the park stretch off as far as the eye can see. You can wander the beach independently when the turtles aren't nesting, but riptides make swimming dangerous, and shark rumors persist.

BEST TIME TO GO

The July–October nesting season for the green turtle is Tortuguero's most popular time to visit. It rains here (a lot!) year-round, so expect to get wet no matter when you go. February through April and September and October are a tad drier.

FUN FACT

One of nature's mysteries is how turtles find their way back to the same beach years later. It's thought that the sand leaves a biological imprint on the turtle hatchlings during their scurry to the sea, which directs females to return here years later to nest.

BEST WAY TO EXPLORE

TOURS

Most visitors opt for a fully escorted tour with one of the big lodges, because you're looked after from the moment you're picked up at your San José hotel until you're dropped off a day or two or seven later. All include a couple of standard tours of the park in their package prices. It's entirely possible to stay at a smaller in-town place and make à la carte arrangements yourself. No matter which way you go, your park tour will be on foot or by boat. Remember: no four-wheeled vehicles up here.

BOAT RIDES

It's not quite "The African Queen," but a boat ride along the narrow vine-draped canals here is pretty close. Once you're off the main canal, the specially designed, narrow tour boats glide relatively quietly—using mandated electric motors—and very slowly, which makes for better wildlife spotting and less waves that erode the lagoon banks. Another alternative is to rent a kayak and go at your own speed along the canals.

BIRD-WATCHING AND WILDLIFE

This is a birder's dream destination. Some of the rarer species you'll find here include the snowy cotinga, palm warbler, and yellow-tailed oriole. Waterbirds and herons abound. On a recent foray, members of the Birding Club of Costa Rica were treated to a close-up view of a wide-eyed rufescent tiger-heron chick sitting in his nest, squawking impatiently for food. You'll also see iguanas, caimans, and sloths. Bird-watching and wildlife-spotting sometimes collide: while watching two beautiful agami herons feeding on a muddy bank, birders were shaken up by the sudden splash of a crocodile attacking the herons. Happily, the herons were quicker off the mark than the birders were!

TOP REASONS TO GO

TURTLES

Tortuguero takes its name from the Spanish word for turtle (*tortuga*) and here you'll get the chance to observe the nesting and hatching of four species of sea turtle, and to ponder one of nature's amazing rituals.

PLANE OR BOAT ONLY

Whoever coined the old adage "Getting there is half the fun" might have had Tortuguero in mind. Plane and boat are the only ways to get to this no-road sector of Costa Rica. If you have the time, the fully escorted boat trips to and from the jungle give you a real Indiana Jones experience.

LUXURY IN THE JUNGLE

Don't let tales of Tortuguero's isolation dissuade you from making a trip. No question: the place is remote. But the lodges up here package everything (overnight lodging, meals, tours, and, best of all, guided round-trip transport) into one price in true "leave the driving to them" fashion. You won't lift a finger.

9

CAHUITA NATIONAL PARK

In a land known for its dark-sand beaches, the coral-based white sand of Cahuita National Park (Parque Nacional Cahuita) is a real standout.

The only Costa Rican park jointly administered by the National Parks Service and a community, it starts at the southern edge of the village of Cahuita and runs pristine mile after pristine milesouthward. Whereas most of the country's protected areas tender only land-based activities, this park entices you offshore as well.

Roughly parallel to the coastline, a 7-km (4-mi) trail passes through the forest to Cahuita Point. A hike of a few hours along the trail—always easiest in the dry season—lets you spot howler and white-faced capuchin monkeys, coatimundis, armadillos, and raccoons. The coastline is encircled by a 2½-square-km (1-square-mi) coral reef, protection of which was the reason for the park's creation. You'll find superb snorkeling off Cahuita Point, but sadly, the coral reef is slowly being killed by sediment, intensified by deforestation and the erosive effects of the 1991 earthquake that hit the coast.

BEST TIME TO GO

As is the case on this coast, you can expect rain here no matter what the time of year. February through April and September and October are drier months, and offer the best visibility for snorkeling. (Those are the least desirable months if you're here to surf.)

FUN FACT

When Costa Rica began charging admission to national parks, residents successfully requested an exemption, fearing that such charges would harm the local economy. Your admission fee to this park is voluntary.

BEST WAY TO EXPLORE

CYCLING

Cycling makes a pleasant way to see the park in the dry season. Seemingly everybody in Cahuita and Puerto Viejo de Talamanca rents bicycles. (The southern entrance to the park is close enough to Puerto Viejo that it could be your starting point, too.) The park trail gets pretty muddy at times, and you run into logs, river estuaries, and other obstacles.

HIKING

A serious 7-km (4-mi) hiking trail runs from the park entrance at Kelly Creek all the way to Puerto Vargas. Take a bus or catch a ride to Puerto Vargas and hike back around the point in the course of a day. Remember to bring plenty of water, food, and sunscreen.

SNORKELING

Tour operators in Cahuita will bring you to a selection of prime snorkeling spots offshore. If you want to swim out on your own, the best snorkeling spot is off Punta Vargas at the south end of the park. Along with the chance to see some of the 500 or so species of tropical fish that live here, you'll see some amazing coral formations, including impressive elk horn, majestic blue stag horn, and eerie yellow brain corals. When the water is clear and warm, the snorkeling is great. But that warm water also appeals to jelly fish—if you start to feel a tingling sensation on your arms or legs, make a beeline for the shore. Each little sting doesn't hurt much, but accumulated stings can result in a major allergic reaction in some people.

BEACHING IT

The waves here are fabulous for body surfing along the section of beach at the Puerto Vargas entrance. This wide swath of shoreline is also great for strolling, jogging, or just basking in the Caribbean sun—be careful of riptides along this stretch of coast. The safest swimming is in front of the camping area.

TOP REASONS TO GO

SNORKELING

Costa Rica's largest living coral reef just offshore means the snorkeling is phenomenal here. Watch for blue parrot fish and angelfish as they weave their way among equally colorful species of coral, sponges, and seaweeds. Visit during the Caribbean coast's two mini-dry seasons for the best visibility.

EASY ACCESS

With one of its two entrances sitting in "downtown" Cahuita, access to the park is a snap. But ease of access does not mean the place is overrun with visitors. Fortunately, this is no Manuel Antonio.

LOTS OF LODGING

Closeness to Cahuita and Puerto Viejo de Talamanca and their spectrum of lodging options means you'll have no trouble finding a place to stay that fits your budget. You can even camp in the park if you're up to roughing it.

9

ECO-LODGES IN THE CARIBBEAN

GOOD PRACTICES

Year-round rainfall begets year-round greenery on the Caribbean coast. You can count on lushness here when the rest of Costa Rica's landscape turns dusty during its dry season.

Not only does Costa Rica's Caribbean region host a different culture than the rest of the country, but its landscape is entirely different, too. Things are verdant all year, and that gives the eastern portion of the country a more tropical feel than the rest of Costa Rica. Development has been slow to come to the coast—anyone over the age of 20 well remembers the days of few roads, no phones, and no television. For you, that means far fewer visitors than along north and central Pacific coasts and a far more authentic experience since the environment is better preserved and the local culture respected. *Small* is the watchword for tourism around here—always has been and always will be. Developers do float occasional trial balloons about international megatourism projects in this region, but they get shot down quickly by the folks here who do not want their Caribbean coast to turn into the Pacific coast, thank you very much.

Stay at locally owned lodgings. That's easy in the Caribbean, since the international chains are nowhere to be found here. Smaller lodgings that support the local economy are the universal norm. A stay here means that you are supporting those communities, too.

Consider taking public or semipublic transportation when visiting the Caribbean. Cahuita and Puerto Viejo de Talamanca have good bus and shuttle service; your own two feet, bicycles, and taxis make it easy to get around once you arrive. Of course, a Tortuguero visit means you leave the transportation to someone else. There's no other choice.

TOP ECO-LODGES IN THE CARIBBEAN

CASA MARBELLA, TORTUGUERO

Most visitors to Tortuguero opt for a stay at one of the big all-inclusive lodges lining the canals outside the village. Yet our favorite in-town lodging provides a far more intimate Tortuguero experience with one-on-one nature tours, rather than big groups, for just a fraction of the cost. Canadian owner and naturalist Daryl Loth is a knowledgeable and well-respected figure in the area. Though onetime outsiders, the folks at Casa Marbella have become arguably the town's biggest boosters, working closely with people here to develop sustainable, non-intrusive tourism that will benefit the entire community. We like and appreciate this "transplanted foreigner" model.

BIOGEM

In 2009, the nonprofit Natural Resources Defense Council (NRDC) named the entire country one of its BioGems, a designation the New York–based environmental crusader usually reserves for a single site or species. In doing so, NRDC recognizes the country's wealth of biodiversity and its fragile status. The organization has pledged to work with the Costa Rican government in areas of reforestation and development of renewable energy technology. (With approximately 99% of Costa Rica's energy coming from hydroelectric and wind power, the country already does an impressive job in that latter regard.) Caribbean residents know NRDC well. The organization worked closely with people in the region at the grassroots level to block attempts to turn the southern Caribbean coast over to offshore oil exploration. Such drilling would have damaged the coast's fragile mangroves, sand beaches, and coral reefs. After many years, the oil companies' proposals have, thankfully, been put to rest for good.

ALMONDS & CORALS, GANDOCA-MANZANILLO WILDLIFE REFUGE

Almonds & Corals scatters its comfortable platformed bungalows unobtrusively throughout its forest property along the coast and connects them with each other and to its restaurant, reception, and the beach by softly lighted paths. That and the myriad of environmentally themed activities conducted by local guides really do give that "get away from it all" experience with a bit of rustic luxury.

RAIN FOREST AERIAL TRAM, BRAULIO CARRILLO NATIONAL PARK

Yes. Despite the name, there is accommodation here. The park is one of the Caribbean region's premier attractions, and staying here lets you enjoy the place after the day-trippers have left. The unobtrusive cabins are so inconspicuously tucked away that few people even know they exist. In an effort to minimize impact, cabins are not available for stays unless at least two can be rented at a time. Food is locally grown, and electricity shuts off after 9 PM. Of course, the rates include the full complement of the site's eco-theme activities.

9

By Jeffrey Van Fleet

Everything about Costa Rica's Caribbean coast seems different: different culture, different history, different climate, and different activities. It is rainier here than in other parts of Costa Rica, so the region will never draw the typical fun-in-the-sun crowd that frequents the drier Pacific coast.

Never fear though: you'll find a year-round forested lushness and just as many activities at a more reasonable price. This region was long ago discovered by European adventure seekers but is much less known in North American circles.

GETTING HERE AND AROUND

You can fly daily from San José to the airstrip in Tortuguero (TTQ) or five times weekly to Barra del Colorado (BCL) via SANSA. Nature Air flies daily to Tortuguero. Nature Air also flies five times weekly to the small airport in Bocas del Toro, Panama (BOC).

Autotransportes MEPE, which has a lock on bus service to the south Caribbean coast, has a reputation for being lackadaisical, but is really quite dependable. Drivers and ticket sellers are accustomed to dealing with foreigners; even if their English is limited, they'll figure out what you want. Bus fares to this region are reasonable. From San José, expect to pay $2.50 to Guápiles, $5 to Limón, $8 to Cahuita, $9 to Puerto Viejo de Talamanca, and $12 to Sixaola and the Panamanian border.

If you prefer a more private form of travel, consider taking a shuttle. Gray Line Tourist Bus has daily service that departs from many San José hotels for Cahuita and Puerto Viejo de Talamanca. Tickets are $35 and must be reserved at least a day in advance. Comfortable air-conditioned Interbus vans depart from San José hotels daily for Guápiles, Siquirres, Limón, Cahuita, Puerto Viejo de Talamanca and the Gandoca-Manzanillo Wildlife Refuge. Reserve tickets ($39) a day in advance.

ESSENTIALS

Bus Contacts Gray Line Tourist Bus (☏ 2220–2126 ⊕ www.graylinecostarica.com) **Interbus** (☏ 2283–5573 ⊕ www.interbusonline.com)

THE NORTHERN LOWLANDS

That proverbial fork in the road presents you with a choice just beyond the immense Braulio Carrillo National Park north of San José. The highway branches at Santa Clara, having completed its descent onto the Caribbean plain. A left turn takes you north to Puerto Viejo de Sarapiquí and the forest-clad hills of the eastern slope of the Cordillera Central *(⇨ Chapter 3)*. If you stay on the well-maintained main Guápiles Highway, you head southeast toward Limón and the Caribbean coast. The highway passes through sultry agricultural lowlands, home to large banana and cacao plantations, but bypasses the region's three main communities: burgeoning Guápiles and the smaller towns of Guácimo and Siquirres. You may not see any reason to stop when driving through the region—the Caribbean coast beckons, after all—but a couple of lesser-known sights might be an incentive to take a break.

GUÁPILES

60 km/38 mi northeast of San José.

Guápiles, one of the country's fastest-growing cities, is the hub of northeastern Costa Rica, and with all the facilities in town, residents of the region barely need to trek to San José anymore. The smaller town of Guácimo lies 12 km (7 mi) east on the Guápiles Highway.

GETTING HERE AND AROUND

Guápiles lies just north of Braulio Carrillo National Park and straddles the highway to the Caribbean. It's an easy one-hour drive from San José just 60 km (38 mi) to the southwest, or Limón 84 km (50 mi) to the east. Empresarios Guapileños buses connect San José's Gran Terminal del Caribe with Guápiles every hour from early morning until late evening, and provide service seven times daily to Guácimo.

ESSENTIALS

Bank/ATM BAC San José (⊠ *Across from AyA* ☎ *2710–7434*) **Banco Nacional** (⊠ *400 m east of Palí supermarket* ☎ *2713–2000*)

Hospital Hospital de Guápiles (⊠ *90 m south of fire station* ☎ *2710–6801*)

Pharmacy Farmacia San Martín (⊠ *Across from Palí* ☎ *2710–1115*) **Farmacia Santa Marta** (⊠ *Across from Banco Nacional* ☎ *2710–6253*)

Post Office Correos (⊠ *North of MUCAP*)

EXPLORING

Curious about how those tropical houseplants you have at home started out? Ornamental plant farm **Costa Flores** conducts 1½-hour English-language tours—advance reservations are required—through its gardens and facilities. (Riotously colored heliconias are a specialty here.) The tour ends at the packinghouse, where you see how plants are prepared for export. You get to create your own floral bouquet to take with you as a souvenir. ⊠ *3½km/2 mi north of Guácimo on road to Río Jiménez* ☎ *2716–7645* ⊘ *$18* ⊙ *Daily 6–4.*

The nonprofit university called **EARTH** (Escuela de Agricultura de la Región Tropical Húmeda, or Agricultural School of the Humid Tropical

Rain Forest Aerial Tram

Just 15 km (9 mi) beyond the north-eastern boundary of Braulio Carrillo, a 1,200-acre reserve houses a privately owned and operated engineering marvel: a series of gondolas strung together in a modified ski-lift pulley system. (To lessen the impact on the jungle, the support pylons were lowered into place by helicopter.) The tram gives you a way of seeing the rain forest canopy and its spectacular array of epiphyte plant life and birds from just above, a feat you could otherwise accomplish only by climbing the trees yourself. Though purists complain that it treats the rain forest like an amusement park, it's an entertaining way to learn the value and beauty of rain forest ecology.

The 21 gondolas hold five people each, plus a bilingual biologist-guide equipped with a walkie-talkie to request brief stops for gaping or snapping pictures. The ride covers 2½ km (1½ mi) in 80 minutes. The price includes a biologist-guided walk through the area for ground-level orientation before or after the tram ride. Several add-ons are possible, too, with frog, snake, and butterfly exhibits, a medicinal-plant garden, and a zip-line canopy tour on-site ($45), as well as a half-day birding tour ($83). You can arrange a personal pickup in San José for a fee; alternatively, there are public buses (on the Guápiles line) every half hour from the Gran Terminal del Caribe in San José. Drivers know the tram as the tele-férico. Many San José tour operators make a daylong tour combining the tram with another half-day option; combos with the Britt Coffee Tour or INBioparque in Santo Domingo, both near Heredia, are especially popular. Ten rustic (no a/c or TV) but cozy *cabinas* (cottages) are available on-site for $94 per person. The facility operates the lodging only if at least two cabins are being rented at the same time. (Reservations are required.) Electricity shuts off after 9 PM. Cabin rates include meals, tram tours, and guided walks. A café is open to all for breakfast, lunch, and dinner. If you're traveling the Central Pacific coast, you'll find similar installations near the town of Jacó (⇨ Chapter 7) 3 km (2 mi) north of Supermercado Maxi Bodega, although without the accommodation, and a restaurant open for breakfast and lunch only. The admission price at the Pacific facility includes the tram ride, nature walk, snake exhibit, heli-conia and medicinal plant gardens, and transport from Jacó-area hotels, as opposed to the à la carte pricing used at the Braulio Carrillo tram. The company also operates trams in the Caribbean-island nations of Jamaica, Dominica, and St. Lucia, all outside the scope of this book.

Reservations: ⊠ *Teleférico del Bosque Lluvioso, Avda. 7 at C. 7, San José* *P2257–5961, 866/759–8726 in North America* ⊕ *www.rainforestrams.com* 🖂 *$55, $27.50 for children under 12; $100, $72.50 for children under 12, includes round-trip transporta-tion to the site from San José hotels* ⊙ *Tours: Mon. 9–4, Tues.–Sun. 6:30–4. Call for reservations 6 am–9:30 pm* ⊟ *AE, D, DC, MC, V.*

Region) researches the production of less pesticide–dependent bananas and other forms of sustainable tropical agriculture, as well as medicinal plants. The university graduates some 100 students from Latin America and Africa each year. EARTH's elegant stationery, calendars, and other paper products are made from banana stems, tobacco leaves, and coffee leaves and grounds, and are sold at the on-site Oropéndola store and in many tourist shops around the country. The property encompasses a banana plantation and a forest reserve with nature trails. Half-day tours are $15; full-day, $25; and lunch is $12 for day visitors. Though priority is given to researchers and conference groups, you're welcome to stay in the school's 50-person lodging facility, with private bathrooms, hot water, and ceiling fans, for $65 a night, which includes the use of a swimming pool and exercise equipment. The site is a birdwatchers' favorite; some 250 species have been spotted here. Reservations are required. ⊠ *Pocora de Guácimo, 15 km/9 mi east of Guápiles on Guápiles Hwy.* ☎ *2713–0000* ⊕ *www.earth.ac.cr.*

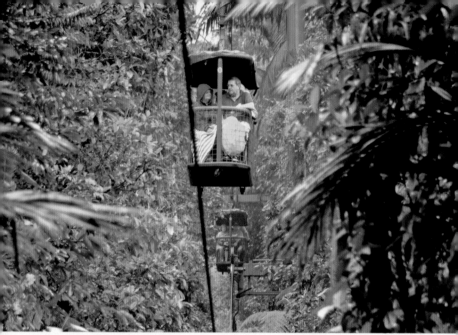

Rain forest trams are a great way to experience the Braulio Carrillo National Park.

SIQUIRRES

28km/17mi east of Guápiles.

Its name is a corruption of the words *Si quieres* (if you want), fittingly impassive for this lackluster town. It anchors a fertile banana- and pineapple-growing region, and marks the transition point between the agricultural lowlands and the tropical, palm-laden coast. Siquirres has the unfortunate historical distinction of having once been the western-most point to which Afro-Caribbean people could migrate. Costa Rica implemented the law in the late 1880s—when large numbers of Afro-Caribbeans immigrated (mainly from Jamaica) to construct the Atlantic Railroad—but abolished it in the 1949 constitution.

GETTING HERE

Siquirres lies just off the main highway and is easily accessible from the east, west, or south (if you're arriving from Turrialba). Autotransportes Caribeños buses connect San José's Gran Terminal del Caribe with Siquirres several times daily.

ESSENTIALS

Bank/ATM Banco Nacional (✉ *50 m south of Acon gas station* ☎ *2768–8128*)

Medical Clinic Centro de Salud de Siquirres (✉ *East side of soccer field* ☎ *2768–6138*)

Pharmacy Farmacia Santa Lucía (✉ *50 m west of fire station* ☎ *2768–9304*)

Post Office Correos (✉ *Next to Guardia Rural*)

EXPLORING

Pineapples don't get the same attention in world circles as Costa Rican coffee and bananas, but the **Agri Tours Pineapple Tour** (⊠ *On highway 7 km/4 mi east of Siquirres* ☎ *2765–8189, 2282–1316 in San José* ⊕ *www. agritourscr.com*), affiliated with Del Monte Foods, can acquaint you with the life and times of this lesser-known crop, from cultivation to drying and packing at a farm just east of town. The two-hour tour is $20, samples included. Call to make a reservation.

OUTDOOR ACTIVITIES

★ Siquirres's proximity to the put-in sites of several classic rafting excursions makes it an ideal place to begin a trip. Old standby **Ríos Tropicales** (⊠ *On the highway in Siquirres* ☎ *2233–6455; 866/722–8273 in North America* ⊕ *www.riostropicales.com*) has tours on a Class III to IV section of the Pacuare River between Siquirres and San Martín, as well as the equally difficult section between Tres Equis and Siquirres. Not quite so wild, but still with Class III rapids, is the nearby Florida section of the Reventazón. Day excursions normally begin in San José, but if you're out in this part of the country, you can kick off your excursion here at the company's operations center in Siquirres.

THE NORTHERN CARIBBEAN COAST

Some compare these dense layers of green set off by brilliantly colored flowers—a vision doubled by the jungle's reflection in mirror-smooth canals—to the Amazon. That might be stretching it, but there's still an Indiana Jones mystique to the journey up here, especially when you get off the main canals and into the narrower lagoons. The region remains one of those Costa Rican anomalies: roadless and remote, it's nevertheless one of the country's most-visited places. The tourism seasons here are defined not by the rains or lack thereof (it's wet most of the year) but by the months of prime turtle hatching in Tortuguero, or by what's biting in sportfishing paradise Barra del Colorado.

In 1970 a system of canals running parallel to the shoreline was constructed to provide safer access to the region than the dangerous journey up the seacoast. You can continue up the canals, natural and man-made, that begin in Moín, near Limón, and run all the way to Tortuguero and beyond to the less-visited Barra del Colorado Wildlife Refuge. Or you can embark at various points north of Guápiles and Siquirres, as do public transportation and most of the package tours. (The lodges' minivans bring you from San José to the put-in point, where you continue your journey by boat.)

TORTUGUERO

North of the national park of the same name, the hamlet of Tortuguero is a pleasant little place with 600 inhabitants, two churches, three bars, a handful of souvenir shops, and a growing selection of inexpensive lodgings. (And one more plus: there are no motor vehicles here, a refreshing change from the traffic woes that plague the rest of Costa Rica.) You can also take a stroll on the 32-km (20-mi) beach,

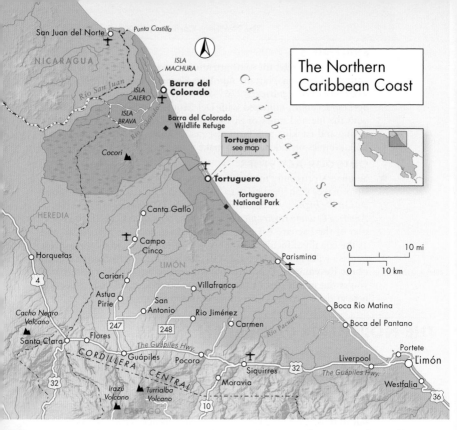

The Northern Caribbean Coast

but swimming is not recommended because of strong riptides and large numbers of bull sharks and barracuda.

The stretch of beach between the Colorado and Matina rivers was first mentioned as a nesting ground for sea turtles in a 1592 Dutch chronicle. Nearly a century earlier, Christopher Columbus compared traversing the north Caribbean coast and its swimming turtles to navigating through rocks. Because the area is so isolated—there's no road here to this day—the turtles nested undisturbed for centuries. By the mid-1900s, however, the harvesting of eggs and poaching of turtles had reached such a level that these creatures faced extinction. In 1963 an executive decree regulated the hunting of turtles and the gathering of eggs, and in 1970 the government established Tortuguero National Park; modern Tortuguero bases its economy on tourism.

GETTING HERE AND AROUND

It's easier than you'd think to get to remote Tortuguero. Flying is the quickest (and most expensive) option. SANSA and Nature Air provide early-morning flights to and from San José. SANSA agent **Victor Barrantes** (☏ 2709–8055 or 8838–6330) meets both planes—they arrive and depart within 15 minutes of each other—and offers boat-taxi service to and from town for $3. Call and confirm with him the day before if you need a ride. If you're staying at one of the lodges, its boat will meet you at the airstrip.

The big lodges all have packages that include transportation to and from San José along with lodging, meals, and tours. Guide-staffed minivans pick you up at your San José hotel and drive you to the put-in site, usually somewhere north of Siquirres, where you board a covered boat for the final leg on the canals to Tortuguero. The trip up entails sightseeing and animal-viewing. The trip back to San José stops only for a lunch break. This is the classic "leave the driving to them" way to get to Tortuguero.

A boat from the port of Moín, near Limón, is the traditional budget method of getting to Tortuguero if you are already on the Caribbean coast. Arrive at the docks by 9 AM and you should be able to find someone to take you there. The going price is $30 per person one way, $50 round-trip, and travel time is about three hours. **Alexis Soto and Sebastián Torres** (☎ 900/296–2626 beeper) partner to provide a reliable boat service between Moín and Tortuguero for about $50 round-trip. Arrange in advance. If you arrive in Moín in your own vehicle, JAPDEVA, Costa Rica's Atlantic port authority, operates a secure, guarded parking facility for your car while you are in Tortuguero.

It's entirely possible to make the trip independently from San José, a good option if you are staying in the village rather than at a lodge. A direct bus departs from San José's Gran Terminal del Caribe to Cariari, north of Guápiles, at 9 AM. At Cariari, disembark and walk five blocks to the local terminal, where you can board a noon bus for the small crossroads of La Pavona. From here, boats leave at 1:30 PM to take you to Tortuguero, arriving around 3 PM. The **Cariari–La Pavona–Tortuguero** bus-boat service is provided by **COOPETRACA** (☎2767–7137) or **Viajes Clic-Clic** (☎2709–8155, 8844–0463, or 8308–2006) for $10 one way. La Pavona has secure parking facilities. ■**TIP→** Avoid Rubén Bananero, a company that provides bus-boat transport from Cariari via an inconvenient route through the Geest banana plantation. They begin to hustle you the minute you get off the bus in Cariari, insisting the La Pavona route does not exist. They also require that you buy a round-trip ticket, limiting your return options, and do everything they can to steer you toward hotels that pay them a commission. Others will also try to take you to their own dedicated "information dock" in the village, steering you toward their own guides. If you've made advance reservations for guides or hotels, stand your ground and say, *"No, gracias."*

9

Water taxis provide transport from multiple points in the village to the lodges. Expect to pay about $2 to $3 per trip.

ESSENTIALS

Internet La Casona (⊠ *North side of soccer field* ☏ *2709–8092*)

> **CAUTION**
>
> Wear mosquito repellent in low-lying coastal areas, where a few cases of dengue have been reported.

Visitor Information Kiosk (⊠ *Town center ☞ Information on the town's history, the park, turtles, and other wildlife; unstaffed booth with free brochures*) **Tortuguero Information Center** (⊠ *Across from Catholic church* ☏ *2709–8011 or 8833–0827* ⊕ *www.tortuguerovillage.com*)

EXPLORING

Fodor's Choice
★
🄲

Tortuguero National Park. The name Tortuguero means "turtle region," and what better place to see sea turtles and observe the age-old cycle of these magnificent animals nesting, hatching and scurrying to the ocean? ☏ *2710–2929 or 2710–2939* 🎫 *$10* ⊗ *Daily 6–6.*

▌**DID YOU KNOW?**

Some people still believe turtle eggs to be an aphrodisiacal delicacy, and some bars (illegally) serve them as snacks. It's a big part of the human contribution to turtles' disappearance.

The **Caribbean Conservation Corporation** *(CCC)* runs a visitor center and a museum with excellent animal photos, a video narrating local and natural history, and detailed discussions of the latest ecological goings-on and what you can do to help. There's a souvenir shop next door. For the committed ecotourist, the **John H. Phipps Biological Field Station,** affiliated with the CCC, has camping areas and dorm-style quarters with a communal kitchen. If you want to get involved in the life of the turtles, helping researchers to track turtle migration (current research, using satellite technology, has tracked turtles as far as the Florida Keys), or helping to catalog the population of neotropical migrant birds, arrange a stay in advance through the center. ⊠ *From beach, walk north along path and watch for sign* ☏ *2709–8091; 800/678–7853 in North America* ⊕ *www.cccturtle.org* 🎫 *$1* ⊗ *Mon.–Sat. 8–4, Sun. 9–5.*

OUTDOOR ACTIVITIES

Tortuguero is one of those "everybody's a guide" places. Quality varies, but most guides are quite knowledgeable. If you stay at one of the lodges, guided tours are *usually* included in your package price (check when you book). If you hire a private guide, $5 per person per hour is the going rate, with most excursions lasting three hours.

TOUR
GUIDES AND
OPERATORS

Call or stop by the visitor center at the **Caribbean Conservation Corporation** (☏ *2709–8091; 2297–5510 in San José* ⊕ *www.cccturtle.org*) to get a recommendation for good local guides.

★ **Daryl Loth** (☏ *8833–0827 or 2709–8011* ✉ *safari@racsa.co.cr*) has a wealth of information about the area and conducts boat excursions on the canals and responsible turtle-watching tours in season with advance notice. **Victor Barrantes** (☏ *2709–8055 or 8838–6330* ✉ *tortuguero_info@racsa.co.cr*) is the local SANSA agent who conducts hiking

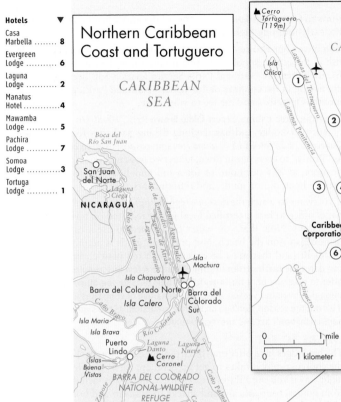

Northern Caribbean Coast and Tortuguero

▲ Cerro
Tortuguero
(119m)

CARIBBEAN
SEA

Isla
Chica

① ✈

②

③ ④

⑤

**Caribbean Conservation
Corporation/Visitor Center**

⑦ Tortuguero
Village

⑥

⑧

Park Entrance

Isla Cuatro
Esquinas

Parque
Nacional
Tortuguero

0 ————— 1 mile
0 ————— 1 kilometer

CARIBBEAN
SEA

Boca del
Río San Juan

San Juan
del Norte

Laguna
Ciega

NICARAGUA

Las. de Esmedio Dulce

Laguna Perértorio

Laguna de Arcas

Isla
Machura

Isla Chapudero ✈

Barra del Colorado Norte ○○ Barra del
Colorado
Sur

Isla Calero

Caño Bravo

Río Colorado

Isla Maria

Isla Brava

Puerto
Lindo

Laguna
Danto

Laguna
Nueve

▲ Cerro
Coronel

Islas
Buena
Vistas

**BARRA DEL COLORADO
NATIONAL WILDLIFE
REFUGE**

Río Zapote

Caño Palma

Caño Moreno

Río Penitencia

Caño Suerte

Canal

Río Swerk

Caño Chiquero

**TORTUGUERO
NATIONAL PARK**

Chiquero

Parismina ○

0 ————— 5 miles
0 ————— 5 kilometers

tours to Cerro Tortuguero and around the area when he's not meeting the early-morning flights.

FISHING You have your choice of mackerel, tarpon, snook, and snapper if you fish in the ocean; snook and calba if you fish in the canals. If you opt for the latter, the National Parks Service levies a $30 license fee (you are fishing in the confines of Tortuguero National Park), good for one month. Operators add the fee to your price.

Longtime area fishing expert **Eddie Brown** (☎ *2710–8016*) is based out of Tortuga Lodge and has daylong fishing packages for $500. **Elvin Gutiérrez** (☎ *2709–8115* ⊕ *www.tortugerosportsfishing.com*), known as "Primo" to everyone in town, takes two passengers out for two hours or more, at $75 per hour, or for a full nine-hour day ($500). Prices include boat, motor, guide, and refreshments.

TURTLE-WATCHING If you want to watch the *deshove* (egg laying), contact your hotel or the parks office to hire a certified local guide, required on turtle-watching excursions. Note that you won't be allowed to use a camera—flash or nonflash—on the beach, and only your guide is permitted to use a flashlight (and that must be covered with red plastic), because lights can deter the turtles from nesting. ■TIP→ A few unscrupulous locals will offer to take you on a turtle-watching tour outside the allowed February-through-November season, disturbing sensitive nesting sites in the process. If it's not the season, don't go on a turtle excursion. As the signs around town admonish: DON'T BECOME ANOTHER PREDATOR.

WHERE TO EAT

The big lodges here offer one- or two-night excursion packages. (Given the choreography it takes to get up here, opt for a more leisurely two-night stay if you can.) Rates are expensive, but prices include everything from guides, tours, meals, and snacks to minivan and boat transport, and in some cases air transport to and from San José. If you stop and calculate what you get, the price may not be as bad as it first seems, and the tours are undeniably great fun. Usually *not* included in package prices? Alcoholic beverages, soda, bottled water, and the $10 entrance to Tortuguero National Park. Ask to be sure. Few of the lodges have phones, although all have radio contact with the outside world. All reservations must be made with their offices in San José. Be sure to travel light; you get a baggage allowance of 25 pounds, usually strictly enforced. There's just no space in the boats for you to bring more.

$ ✕ **Budda Café.** Hip was never a word that went hand in hand with Tor-
ITALIAN tuguero, but this place has changed the rules. Pizza, crepes, pastas, and fresh fish are on the menu at this small, canal-side café in the center of town. Lattice wood over the windows, a thatched roof, and of course, a Buddha statue make up the furnishings. Jazzy cha-cha or a Dean Martin ballad might be playing in the background. ⊠ *Next to police station, Tortuguero village* ☎ *2709–8084* ▭ *AE, MC, V* ⊗ *Closed Mon.*

$ ✕ **Miss Junie.** Longtime Tortuguero doyenne Miss Junie has suppos-
COSTA RICAN edly retired as the village's best-known cook, a tradition she learned at her mother's knee more than a half century ago, but still can be seen in the kitchen of the open-air restaurant adjoining her home. (Fidel Castro and Che Guevara were among the early diners here.)

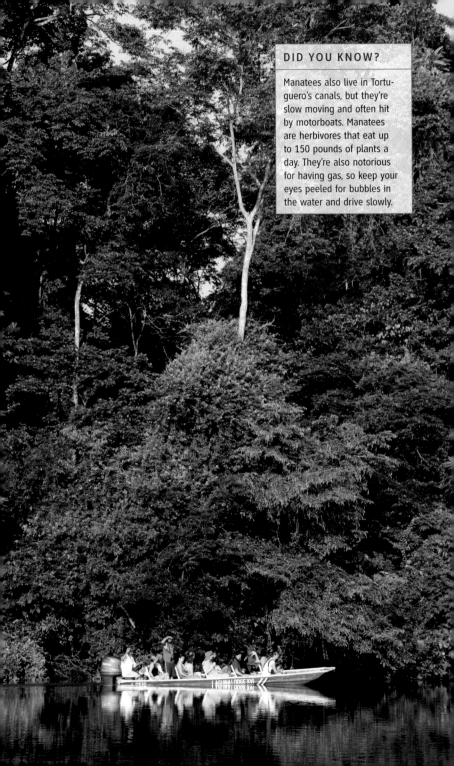

Selection is limited, and reservations are required, but you can usually count on a chicken, beef, or fish platter with rice and beans simmered in coconut milk. Your meal includes a beverage and dessert. ⊠ *150 m north of Paraso Tropical, Tortuguero village* ☎ *2709–8102* ⚑ *Reservations essential* ⊟ *No credit cards.*

¢   ✕ **The Vine Bakery.** Pastas, pizzas, and sandwiches are on the menu, but
CAFÉ this small bakery and coffee shop is also a great place to stop for breads made with banana, carrot, and *natilla* (cream), for example. ⊠ *25 m north of Catholic church, Tortuguero village* ☎ *2709–8132* ⊟ *No credit cards* ☙ *No dinner.*

WHERE TO STAY

¢–$ 🛏 **Casa Marbella.** This bed-and-breakfast, the best of the in-town lodg-
Fodor'sChoice ings, is a real find. Canadian owner and naturalist Daryl Loth is a
★ respected authority on all things Tortuguero, and one of the community's biggest boosters. If he's unable to take you out in his boat himself, he'll find someone who can. Immaculate rooms have tile floors and varnished-wood finishing with vaulted ceilings and skylights in the bathrooms. Ample breakfasts are served on the covered back patio facing the lodging's own private canal dock. The terrace is also a relaxing place for a coffee break on a rainy afternoon. There's a small kitchenette for your use. **Pros:** knowledgeable owner; immaculate rooms. **Cons:** some street noise; no access to lodge-package amenities of big lodges. ⊠ *Across from Catholic church, Tortuguero village* ☎ *2709–8011* ⊕ *casamarbella.tripod.com* ➫ *8 rooms* ⚒ *In-room: no a/c, no phone, no TV* ⊟ *No credit cards* ⍥ *BP.*

$$$$ 🛏 **Evergreen Lodge.** Owned by the Pachira Lodge people, the Evergreen
Fodor'sChoice offers an entirely different (and intimate) concept in Tortuguero lodg-
★ ing: whereas other lodges have cabins arranged around a clearing, at Evergreen they penetrate deep into the forest. A network of walking trails extends to Canal Chiquerito, the third waterway inland. Cabins are made from deep-red almond wood or gypsum wood. All have one double and one single, as well as venetian blinds for privacy. Honeymooners make up a substantial portion of the clientele here. Watch for the whimsical ANT CROSSING signs as you walk around the grounds. **Pros:** seclusion from other lodges; lush wooded setting. **Cons:** rustic rooms; farther from town than other lodges. ⊠ *2 km/1 mi from Tortuguero village on Canal Penitencia* ☎ *2257–7742; 800/644–7438 in North America* ⊕ *www.evergreentortuguero.com* ➫ *26 cabins* ⚒ *In-room: no a/c, no phone, no TV. In-hotel: restaurant, bar* ⊟ *AE, D, DC, MC, V* ⍥ *AI.*

$$$$ 🛏 **Laguna Lodge.** Laguna is the largest of the Tortuguero lodges, and it hums with activity. Jam-packed package tours begin in San José and embark from boats at Caño Blanco, north of Siquirres. A mix of concrete and wood buildings spread out over 12 acres of grounds on a thin sliver of land between the ocean and the first canal inland. Rooms have wood paneling and floors, and tiled bathrooms. The property includes a

butterfly garden and a small network of trails through secondary forest. Meals are served buffet-style at the open-air restaurant that extends out over the canal. The snazzy combo reception–gift shop–meeting room building seems to have sprung straight from the mind of Gaudí. **Pros:** many activities; unique architecture. **Cons:** large numbers of guests; not for those who crave anonymity. ☎ *2709–8082; 2272–4943 in San José ⊕ www.lagunatortuguero.com ↬ 80 rooms ⌂ In-room: no a/c, no phone, no TV. In-hotel: 2 restaurants, bars, pool, laundry service, Internet terminal ▭ AE, D, DC, MC, V ⏷⊙⏸ AI.*

$$$$ ⊡ **Manatus Hotel.** Take one longtime budget lodging, give it a makeover worthy of a television reality show, reincarnate it as Tortuguero's luxurious hotel, and you've got yourself Manatus Hotel. Amenities such as air-conditioning, massage, and television are simply not found up here, but Manatus has them. Bright rooms with large windows each have two four-post queen-size beds with flowered quilted spreads, all under vaulted ceilings. Packages include round-trip van and boat transportation from San José, as well as all meals in the snazzy riverside restaurant. **Pros:** intimate surroundings; numerous creature comforts. **Cons:** fills up quickly in high season; degree of luxury may feel out of place in Tortuguero. ⊠ *Across river, about 1 km/½mi north of Tortuguero* ☎ *2709–8197; 2239–4854 in San José ⊕ www.manatuscostarica.com ↬ 12 rooms ⌂ In-room: no phone, refrigerator. In-hotel: restaurant, room service, bar, pool, gym, spa, laundry service, Internet terminal ▭ AE, D, DC, MC, V ⏷⊙⏸ AI.*

$$$$ ⊡ **Mawamba Lodge.** Nestled between the river and the ocean, Mawamba
★ is the perfect place to kick back and relax. It is also the only jungle lodge within walking distance (about 10 minutes) of town. Packages include transport from San José; when you arrive at the river town of Matina, you're whisked into a launch for a 2½-hour ride to a 15-acre site with comfortable (hot water!) rustic cabinas with bright colors and garden views. Meals are taken in the spacious dining room, and are included in the price, along with transfers and guided tours of the jungle and canals; trips to turtle-heavy beaches cost $10 extra. Packages begin at $263 per person. **Pros:** many activities; walking distance to village. **Cons:** rustic rooms; not for those who crave anonymity. ⊠ *½km/¼mi north of Tortuguero on ocean side of canal* ☎ *2709–8181, 2293–8181 in San José ⊕ www.grupomawamba.com ↬ 58 cabinas ⌂ In-room: no a/c, no phone, safe, no TV. In-hotel: restaurant, bar, pool, beachfront, laundry service, Internet terminal ▭ AE, D, DC, MC, V ⏷⊙⏸ AI.*

$$$$ ⊡ **Pachira Lodge.** This is the prettiest of Tortuguero's lodges, but not the
Fodor'sChoice costliest. Each almond-wood cabina in the lush, well-manicured gar-
★ dens contains four guest rooms with high ceilings, king-size beds, and bamboo furniture. The stunning pool is shaped like a giant sea turtle: the head is a whirlpool tub, the left paw is a wading pool, and the right paw is equipped for swimmers with disabilities. There is no cross-river transportation into town. Package deals include transport from San José, a jungle tour, and all meals; rates begin at $209 per person. Pachira is known for being the most competitive marketer of the lodges here, and the place is often full. **Pros:** many activities; good value. **Cons:** large numbers of guests; can be difficult to find space; not for those who crave

9

"Cruising down the canal in Tortuguero Park, we discovered this emerald baselisk, a magnificient looking creature."—Photo by Liz Stuart, Fodors.com member

anonymity. ⊠ *Across river from Mawamba Lodge* 🕾 *2257–4242 in San José; 800/644–7438 in North America* ⊕ *www.pachiralodge.com* ⤸ *88 rooms* ⚄ *In-room: no a/c, no phone, no TV. In-hotel: restaurant, bar, pool, laundry service* ▭ *AE, MC, V* ⦿ *AI.*

$$$$ 🏨 **Samoa Lodge.** A location on the inland side of the second canal in from the ocean gives this place plenty of room to spread out, and indeed, a network of hiking trails on the lodge's grounds is one of the attractions here. Buildings are scattered around manicured gardens and contain rooms with vaulted ceilings, all with either one double and one single bed or three single beds. **Pros:** seclusion from other lodges; ample grounds; network of hiking trails. **Cons:** rustic rooms; farther from town than other lodges. ⊠ *2 km/1 mi from Tortuguero village on Canal Penitencia* 🕾 *2258–6244 in San José* ⊕ *www.samoalodge.com* ⚄ *In-room: no a/c, no phone, no TV. In-hotel: restaurant, bar, pool, no-smoking rooms* ▭ *AE, D, DC, MC, V* ⦿ *AI.*

$$$$ 🏨 **Tortuga Lodge.** Lush lawns, orchids, and tropical trees surround
★ this thatched riverside lodge owned by Costa Rica Expeditions and renowned for its nature packages and top-notch, personalized service. Tortuga sets itself apart with its smaller size, and markets itself to a higher-budget clientele than do its major competitors here (Laguna, Mawamba, and Pachira). Tortuga's packages all include its own charter flights to Tortuguero rather than the land/boat combos from San José used by the other lodges. Guest rooms are comfortable, with much-appreciated mosquito blinds. The penthouse suite, with two king-size beds and an extra smaller bed, has ample room for a family. The chefs do an excellent job preparing hearty food, which is served family-style

rather than in a buffet line as at other lodges. Tortuguero National Park is 20 minutes south by boat. **Pros:** many activities; seclusion from other lodges. **Cons:** rustic rooms; farther from park than most lodges here. ✉ *Across the river from airstrip 2 km/1 mi from Tortuguero* ☎ *2710–8016; 2257–0766 in San José* ⊕ *www.costaricaexpeditions.com* ⤴ *26 rooms* ♿ *In-room: no a/c, no phone, no TV. In-hotel: restaurant, bar, pool, laundry service* ▭ *AE, MC, V* ¦◎¦ *AI.*

BARRA DEL COLORADO

Up the coast from Tortuguero is the ramshackle hamlet of Barra del Colorado, a popular sportfishing hub characterized by plain stilted wooden houses, dirt paths, and a complete absence of motorized land vehicles (though some locals have added motors to their hand-hewn canoes).

EXPLORING

Bordered to the north by the Río San Juan and the frontier with Nicaragua is the vast, 905-square-km (350-square-mi) **Barra del Colorado Wildlife Refuge** *(Refugio Nacional de Vida Silvestre Barra del Colorado)*, Costa Rica's largest reserve, and really the only local attraction for nonanglers. Most people arrange trips here through their lodge. Transportation once you get here is almost exclusively waterborne, as there are virtually no paths in this swampy terrain. The list of species that you're likely to see from your boat is almost the same as that for Tortuguero; the main difference here is the feeling of being farther off the beaten track. You can realistically get as far as the 640,000-acre **Río Indio-Maíz Biological Reserve** when crossing the border here. The reserve is a continuation of the Barra del Colorado Wildlife Refuge, but in Nicaraguan territory. ✉ *30 km/18 mi north of Tortuguero* ☎ *No phone* ▱ *Free* ◷ *24 hrs.*

TO AND FROM BARRA DEL COLORADO
25 km/16 mi northwest of Tortuguero.

SANSA has very early morning flights from San José. You're likely staying at a fishing lodge if you come this far, and a representative will meet your flight and escort you to your lodge and back.

THE SOUTHERN CARIBBEAN COAST

The landscape along the Guápiles Highway changes from farmland to tropics as you approach the port city of Limón. Place names change, too. You'll see signs to towns called Bristol, Stratford, and Liverpool, reflecting the region's British Caribbean heritage. European backpackers discovered tourist towns par excellence Cahuita and Puerto Viejo de Talamanca; now visitors of all nationalities and budgets flock there.

LIMÓN

100 km/62 mi southeast of Guápiles, 160 km/100 mi north and east of San José.

The colorful Afro-Caribbean flavor of one of Costa Rica's most important ports (population 90,000) is the first sign of life for seafaring visitors to Costa Rica's east coast. Christopher Columbus was the first tourist here: he dropped anchor on his final voyage to the New World in 1502. Limón (sometimes called "Puerto Limón") is a lively, if shabby, town with a 24-hour street life. The wooden houses are brightly painted, but the grid-plan streets look rather worn, partly because of the damage caused by a 1991 earthquake. Street crime, including pickpocketing and nighttime mugging, is not uncommon here. Long charged with neglecting the city, the national government has now turned attention to Limón. New businesses are coming in, a positive sign of urban renewal, and the town has beefed up security with a more visible police presence.

Limón receives thousands of visitors every year, owing in large part to its newest incarnation as a port of call. Carnival, Celebrity, Holland America, Princess, and Royal Caribbean cruise ships all dock here on certain of their Panama Canal or Western Caribbean itineraries. The downtown Terminal de Cruceros hums with activity between October and May, with one or two boats each day December through March, but many fewer outside those peak months. This is the place to find telephones, Internet cafés, manicurists (they do quite a brisk business), a tourist-information booth, and tour-operator stands, too. Downtown shopkeepers have all learned how to convert their colón prices to dollars, and post the day's exchange rate. St. Thomas or Puerto Vallarta it is not—perhaps someday, residents hope—but Limón has a tourist vibe these days that the city has never before experienced. The terminal contains souvenir stands staffed by low-key vendors who invite you to look, but don't pester you if your answer is "*No, gracias.*"

NAVIGATING LIMÓN *Avenidas* (avenues) run east and west, and *calles* (streets) north and south, but Limón's street-numbering system differs from that of other Costa Rican cities. "Number one" of each avenida and calle begins at the water and numbers increase sequentially as you move inland, unlike the evens-on-one-side, odds-on-the-other scheme used in San José. But the scarcity of street signs means everyone uses landmarks anyway. Official red taxis ply the streets, or wait at designated taxi stands near Parque Vargas, the Mercado Municipal, and the cruise-ship terminal.

GETTING HERE AND AROUND

If you're coming to the Caribbean coast, you'll pass through Limón. The Guápiles Highway that began in San José ends here at the ocean, but bypasses the heart of downtown by a couple of blocks. Budget about 3½ hours for the trip. Just after the sign to SIXAOLA and the coastal highway south to Cahuita and Puerto Viejo de Talamanca is the city center. The main bus terminal lies at Avenida 2 and Calle 8, across from the soccer stadium, and serves routes from San José, Guápiles, and Siquirres, with buses arriving several times daily from each. Opt for the *directo* (express) service from San José rather than the *corriente* buses, which make many stops along the route. Buses to Cahuita and Puerto Viejo de

Continued on page 549

It was so awesome to see this huge dorado (mahi-mahi) my husband boated with help from a great first mate. – janenicole, Fodors.com member

SPORTFISHING

by Elizabeth Goodwin

Adventurous anglers flock to Costa Rica to test their will—and patience—against an assortment of feisty fresh- and saltwater fish. Just remember: catch-and-release is sometimes expected, so the pleasure's all in the pursuit.

With so many options the hardest decision is where to go. Inshore fishing in the country's rivers and lakes yields roosterfish, snapper, barracuda, jacks, and snook. Fly-fishing afficiondas love the extra-large tarpon and snook because of their sheer size and fight. The country's coasts swarm with a multitude of bigger game, including the majestic billfish that Hemingway made famous—the marlin and the sailfish.

There are a multitude of top-notch fishing outfitters up and down both coasts and around rivers and lakes, so planning a fishing trip is easy. We list our favorites throughout the book under Outdoor Activities. Charter boats range from 22 feet to 60 feet in length. With a good captain, a boat in the 22- to 26-foot range for up to three anglers can cost from $500 to $750 a day. A 28- to 32-foot boat fits four and costs from $800 to $1,200 per day. A boat for six people costs $1,400 to $1,800 and measures between 36 and 47 feet. A 60-foot boat for up to ten anglers costs about $3,000 a day. A good charter boat company employs experienced captains and offers good equipment, bait, and food and beverages.

CHOOSING A DESTINATION

Costa Rica teems with a constant supply of *pescado* (fish), some of which might seem unique to North Americans. Below are some local catches and where you'll find them.

A local fisherman in Puerto Viejo.
xelas, fodors.com member.

Barra del Colorado (See Chapter 9) is a popular sportfishing hub and a great departure point for freshwater fishing on the Caribbean side of the country. Fly fishers looking for the ultimate challenge head to **San Juan River** for its legendary tarpon. The **Colorado River** lures anglers with jack, tuna, snook, tarpon, and dorado. Transportation and tours can be arranged by the hotels listed in **Puerto Viejo de Sarapiquí** and **Las Horquetas** (See Chapter 4).

Lake Arenal and **Caño Negro Lagoon** are also great freshwater spots to snag extra-large tarpon, snook, and the ugly-but-fascinating guapote bass. Start your fishing journey in nearby **La Fortuna** (See Chapter 5).

On the Pacific side, **Tamarindo** is the main departure point for anglers looking to find big game, including tuna, roosterfish, and marlin. Boats also leave from **Playas del Coco, Ocotal, Tambor,** and **Flamingo Beach,** which are best fished May through August. All are close to the well-stocked northern Papagayo Gulf. If you're hunting sailfish and marlin between December and April, head to the Central Pacific coast around **Los Sueños** and **Quepos,** where up to 10 sailfish are caught per boat *(See Chapters 6 and 7).* The southern Pacific towns, like **Puerto Jimenez, Golfito,** and **Zancudo,** are less developed than the other Pacific regions and are famous for their excellent inshore fishing for snapper and roosterfish, though offshore big game is also good in the area, especially November through January *(See Chapter 8).*

FISHING LICENSE

Costa Rica requires that all anglers have a valid Costa Rica fishing license. You can usually pick one up at the dock entrance on the morning of your first day of fishing for $24.00. It's good for one year from the date of purchase. Keep in mind that, many charters do not fold this into their costs because license enforcement is lax and it is occasionally difficult to track down people who sell fishing licenses. You may want to ask about this before you head out.

(top) Osa Peninsula, (bottom left) *Plat de jour* is Wahoo, (bottom right) School of Tarpon

THE FISH YOU'LL FIND

By law billfish are catch-and-release only.

GASPAR (alligator gar), found in Barra del Colorado River and Lake Arenal, looks like a holdover from prehistoric times and has a long narrow snout full of sharp teeth; they make great sport on light tackle. Gar meat is firm and sweet (some say shrimplike), but the eggs are toxic to humans.

Snook

MARLIN AND SAILFISH migrate northward through the year, beginning about November, when they are plentiful in the Golfito region. From December into April they spread north to Quepos, which has some of the country's best deep-sea fishing, and are present in large numbers along the Nicoya Peninsula at Carrillo and Sámara from February to April, and near Tamarindo and Flamingo from May to September. Pacific sailfish average more than 45 kilos (100 pounds), and are usually fought on a 15-pound line or less. Costa Rican laws require that all sails be released and bans sportsfishers from bringing them on board for photo ops.

Sailfish

GUAPOTE (rainbow bass) make their home in Lake Arenal. It's a hard-hitting catch: 5- to 6-pounders are common. Taxonomically, guapote are not related to bass, but are caught similarly, by casting or flipping plugs or spinner bait. Streams near the Cerro de la Muerte, off the Pan-American Highway leading south from San José, are stocked with guapote. The fish tend to be small, but the scenery makes a day here worthwhile.

TARPON AND SNOOK fishing are big on the Caribbean coast, centered at the mouth of the Barra del Colorado River. The acrobatic tarpon, which averages about 38 kilos (85 pounds) here, is able to swim freely between salt water and freshwater and is considered by many to be the most exciting catch on earth. Tarpon sometimes strike like a rocket, hurtling 5 meters (16 feet) into the air, flipping, and twisting left and right. Anglers say the success rate of experts is to land about 1 out of every 10 tarpon hooked. In the Colorado, schools of up to 100 tarpon following and feeding on schools of titi (small, sardinelike fish) travel for more than 160 km (100 mi) to Lake Nicaragua. The long-standing International Game Fishing Association all-tackle record was taken in this area.

WHEN TO GO

In Costa Rica, you're guaranteed a few good catches no matter what the season, as demonstrated by the cadre of sportsmen who circle the coasts year-round chasing that perfect catch. If your heart is set on an area or a type of fish, do your research ahead of time and plan accordingly.

The Nicas

Immigration issues generate intense debate in the United States and Western Europe. Who would guess that it has become a contentious matter here in Costa Rica, too? Over the past four decades, war, poverty, dictatorship, revolution, earthquakes, and hurricanes have beset Nicaragua, Costa Rica's northern neighbor. Each new calamity has brought a wave of refugees fleeing south. Approximations vary—no one can know for sure—but high-end estimates guess that 20% of Costa Rica's population today is Nicaraguan. Speaking with a faster, more clipped accent than Costa Ricans, they do not fade into the scenery.

The refrain among Ticos is a familiar one: "They're taking our jobs!" Yet, truth be told, Nicaraguans are performing the low-end labor that Costa Ricans just won't do anymore: your hotel chambermaid may likely be Nicaraguan; the glitzy resort where you're staying was probably built with the sweat of many Nicaraguan construction workers; and the beans that went into that delicious morning cup of Costa Rican java were likely harvested by Nicaraguan coffee pickers.

Talamanca and all points on the south coast arrive and depart from a stop across from Radio Casino on Avenida 4 between calles 3 and 4.

ESSENTIALS

Bank/ATM BAC San José (✉ *Avda. 3, Cs. 2–3* ☎ *2798–0155*). **Banco Nacional** (✉ *Avda. 2, Cs. 3–4* ☎ *2758–0094*). **Scotiabank** (✉ *Avda. 3 and C. 2* ☎ *2798–0009*).

Hospital Hospital Dr. Tony Facio (✉ *Highway to Portete* ☎ *2758–2222*)

Internet Café Internet (✉ *Gran Terminal del Caribe, Avda. 2 and C. 8, across from the soccer stadium* ☎ *2798–0128*). **Internet Cinco Estrellas** (✉ *50 m north of Terminal de Cruceros* ☎ *2758–5752*).

Pharmacy Farmacia Buenos Aires (✉ *25 m east of Mercado Municipal* ☎ *2798–4732*). **Farmacia Limonense** (✉ *1st fl., Radio Casino* ☎ *2758–0654*).

Post Office Correos (✉ *Avda. 2 and C. 4*). **DHL** (✉ *Across from Terminal de Cruceros* ☎ *2758–1256*). **UPS** (✉ *West side of Parque Vargas* ☎ *2798–3637*).

Visitor Information JAPDEVA (Atlantic Port Authority) (✉ *Terminal de Cruceros* ☞ *Accessible to cruise-ship passengers only*).

EXPLORING

The aquamarine wooden port building faces the cruise terminal, and just to the east lies the city's palm-lined central park, **Parque Vargas**. From the promenade facing the ocean you can see the raised dead coral left stranded by the 1991 earthquake. Nine or so Hoffman's two-toed sloths live in the trees of Parque Vargas; ask a passerby to point them out, as spotting them requires a trained eye.

A couple of blocks west of the north side of Parque Vargas is the lively enclosed **Municipal Market** (*Mercado Municipal*) ✉ *Pedestrian mall, Avda.*

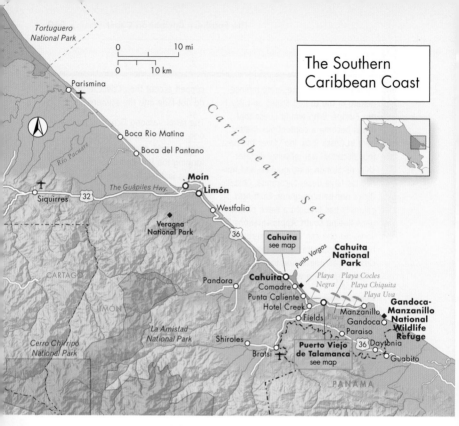

The Southern Caribbean Coast

2, Cs. 3–4), where you can buy fruit for the road ahead and experience the sights, sounds, and smells of a Central American market.

On the left side of the highway as you enter Limón is a large **cemetery**. Notice the COLONIA CHINA ("Chinese colony") and corresponding sign in Chinese on the hill in the cemetery: Chinese workers made up a large part of the 1880s railroad-construction team that worked here. Thousands died of malaria and yellow fever.

OUTDOOR ACTIVITIES

Limón's growing crop of tour operators serves cruise-ship passengers almost exclusively. **Laura Tropical Tours** (✉ *Terminal de Cruceros* ☎ *2758–1240*) has excursions to banana plantations, Tortuguero, and Cahuita National Park. **Mambo Tours** (✉ *Terminal de Cruceros* ☎ *2798–1542*) can take you on three- to eight-hour excursions around the region, and even on an all-day trip to the Rain Forest Aerial Tram or San José.

The region's newest attraction, **Veragua Rainforest Adventure Park**, is a 4,000-acre nature theme park, about 30 minutes west of Limón. It's popular with cruise-ship passengers in port for the day, but if you're in the area, it's well worth a stop. Veragua's great strength is its small army of enthusiastic, super-informed guides who take you through a network of nature trails and exhibits of hummingbirds, snakes, frogs, and butterflies and other insects. A gondola ride overlooks the complex and transports you through the rain forest canopy. ✉ *Veragua de Liverpool 15 km/9 mi west of Limón* ☎ *2296–5056 in San José* ⊕ *www.veraguarainforest.com* ✆ *Half-day tour 65, children under 12, 45; full-day tour 99, children under 12, 70; full-day tour with transportation from San José, $139, children under 12, $99* ☉ *Tues.–Sun. 8–4.*

WHERE TO EAT AND STAY

$ ✕ **Brisas del Caribe.** Here's a case

SEAFOOD study in what happens when cruise ships come to town. This old downtown standby, once as charmingly off-kilter as the crooked umbrellas on its front tables, got rid of its video poker machines (and the locals who always hoped to get lucky playing them), tiled the floors, and remodeled. The food is still good—seafood and surprisingly decent hamburgers, a real rarity in Costa Rica, are the fare here—but a bit of the local color has faded. Passenger or not, you can partake of the lunch buffet on cruise days. ✉ *North side of Parque Vargas* ☎ *2758–0138* 🖃 *AE, D, DC, MC, V.*

$ 🏨 **Hotel Maribú Caribe.** Perched on a cliff overlooking the Caribbean Sea between Limón and Portete, these white conical thatch huts have great views, but you're a long way from the ocean itself. The lovely grounds have green lawns, shrubs, palm trees, and a large, kidney-shaped pool. The poolside bar discourages exertion. The hotel is immensely popular on weekends, but during the week you'll likely have the place to yourself. **Pros:** good moderate value; secluded location. **Cons:** no access to beach; far from center of town. ✉ *4 km/2½ mi north on road to Portete* ☎ *2795–2543* ✉ *maribucaribe@hotmail.com* ➦ *50 rooms* ⌂ *In-room: Wi-Fi. In-hotel: restaurant, bar, laundry service* 🖃 *AE, D, DC, MC, V* ⊙| *EP.*

¢ 🏨 **Park Hotel.** The prices at this pastel-and-pink business-class hotel in central Limón can't be beat. All rooms have modern furnishings and private balconies, so opt for one fronting the ocean. The air-conditioned dining room is a pleasant respite from the heat of the port city. **Pros:** good budget value; great ocean views. **Cons:** small rooms; air-conditioning too icy at times. ✉ *Avda. 3, Cs. 2–3* ☎ *2798–0555* ✉ *parkhotellimon@ice.co.cr* ➦ *32 rooms* ⌂ *In-hotel: restaurant* 🖃 *AE, D, DC, MC, V* ⊙| *EP.*

SHOPPING

The cruise-ship terminal contains an orderly maze of souvenir stands. Vendors are friendly; there's no pressure to buy. Many shops populate the restored port building across the street as well. Spelling is not its forte, but the **Caribean Banana** (✉ *50 m north Terminal de Cruceros,*

SHIP AHOY!

If you arrive in Limón on a cruise ship, a day in the Caribbean is yours for the taking. The Tortuguero canals, the beaches at Puerto Viejo de Talamanca, the sloth rescue center at Aviarios Sloth Sanctuary near Cahuita, or the Veragua Rainforest Adventure Park, just a few miles away, are four popular excursions. A few hardy souls venture as far away as the Rain Forest Aerial Tram or San José. A legion of taxi drivers waits at the terminal exit if you have not arranged an organized shore excursion through your cruise company.

9

A carnival in Limón.

west side of Parque Vargas) stands out from the other shops in the cruise-terminal area with a terrific selection of wood carvings.

MOÍN

5 km/3 mi north of Limón.

The docks at Moín are a logical next stop after visiting neighboring Limón, especially if you want to take a boat north to explore the Caribbean coast.

GETTING HERE

Moín is a quick taxi ride from the center of Limón.

You'll probably be able to negotiate a waterway and national-park tour with a local guide, and if you call in advance, you can arrange a tour with the man considered the best guide on the Caribbean coast:

★ **Modesto Watson** (☎ 2226–0986 ⊕ *www.tortuguerocanals.com*), a local Miskito Indian guide. He's legendary for his bird- and animal-spotting skills as well as his howler monkey imitations. The family's *Riverboat Francesca* can take you up the canals for two-day–one-night excursions to Tortuguero for $165 to $220 per person, depending on the lodge used.

CAHUITA

44 km/26 mi southeast of Limón.

Dusty Cahuita, its main dirt street flanked by wooden-slat cabins, is a backpackers' vacation town—a hippie hangout with a dash of Afro-

The Old Atlantic Railroad

Christopher Columbus became the Caribbean's (and the country's) first tourist when he landed at Uvita Island near Limón during his fourth voyage to the New World in 1502. But the region was already home to thriving, if small, communities of Kekoldi, Bribrí, and Cabécar indigenous peoples. If Costa Rica was an isolated backwater, its Caribbean coastal region remained even more remote from colonial times through most of the 19th century.

New York industrialist Minor Keith changed all that in 1871 with his plan to launch the British-funded Atlantic Railroad, a mode of transportation that would permit easier export of coffee and bananas to Europe. Such a project required a massive labor force, and thousands of West Indians, Asians, and Italians were brought to Costa Rica to construct the 522-km (335-mi) railroad from Limón to San José. Thousands are reputed to have died of yellow fever, malaria, and snakebite during construction of the project. Those who survived were paid relatively well, however, and by the 1930s many Afro-Caribbean residents owned their own small plots of land. When the price of cacao rose in the 1950s, they emerged as comfortable landowners. Not that they had much choice about

going elsewhere: until the Civil War of 1948, black Costa Ricans were forbidden from crossing into the Central Valley lest they upset the country's racial balance, and they were thus prevented from moving when United Fruit abandoned many of its blight-ridden northern Caribbean plantations in the 1930s for green-field sites on the Pacific plain.

Costly upkeep of rail service, construction of the Braulio Carrillo Highway to the coast, declining banana production, and an earthquake that rocked the region in 1991 all sounded the death knell for the railroad. The earthquake was also a wake-up call for many here. The long lag time for aid to reach stricken areas symbolized the central government's historic neglect of the region. Development has been slow to reach this part of the country. (Telephones and electricity are still newfangled inventions in some smaller communities here.) As elsewhere in the country, communities now look to tourism to put colones in the coffers. San José has resurrected commuter-rail service, and a few folks here hold out faint hopes that Caribbean train service will start up once again, but that's likely a long way off.

9

Caribbean spice tossed in. And after years of negative crime-related publicity, Cahuita has beefed up security—this is one of the few places in the country where you will be conscious of a visible and reassuring, though not oppressive, police presence—and has made a well-deserved comeback on the tourist circuit. Tucked in among the backpackers' digs are a few surprisingly nice get-away-from-it-all lodgings, and restaurants with some tasty cuisine at decent prices. No question that nearby Puerto Viejo de Talamanca has overtaken Cahuita and become the hottest spot on the southern Caribbean coast. But as Puerto Viejo grows exponentially, Cahuita's appeal is that it remains small and manageable. It's well worth a look.

Cahuita's tiny center is quite walkable, if dusty in the dry season and muddy in the wet season. It's about a 30-minute walk to the end of the Playa Negra road to Hotel La Diosa. Take a taxi to or from Playa Negra after dark. Cahuita has no officially licensed red taxis; transportation is provided informally by private individuals. To be on the safe side, have your hotel or restaurant call a driver for you.

> **RECYCLE!**
>
> Unfortunately it's difficult to recycle in most places in Costa Rica, but Cahuita and Puerto Viejo de Talamanca have made it a breeze. Deposit your aluminum cans and glass and plastic beverage bottles in the *Recicaribe* barrels you'll see in either community.

Bicycles are a popular means of utilitarian transport in Cahuita. Seemingly everyone rents basic touring bikes for $5 to $10 per day, but quality varies widely. **Cabinas Brigitte** (⊠ *Playa Negra road 1½ km/1 mi from town* ☎ *2755–0053*) rents good bikes for $6 per day. **Cahuita Tours** (⇨ *below*) also has bike rentals.

GETTING HERE AND AROUND

Autotransportes MEPE buses travel from San José five times a day, and approximately hourly throughout the day from Limón and Puerto Viejo de Talamanca. Car travel is straightforward: watch for signs in Limón and head 45 minutes south on the coastal highway. Road conditions wax and wane with the severity of the previous year's rains and with the speed at which highway crews patch the potholes. Cahuita has three entrances from the highway: the first takes you to the far north end of the Playa Negra road, near the Magellan Inn; the second, to the middle section of Playa Negra, near the Atlántida; and the third, to the tiny downtown.

The proximity of the Panamanian border means added police vigilance on the coastal highway. No matter what your mode of transport, expect a passport inspection and cursory vehicle search at a police checkpoint just north of Cahuita. If you're on public transportation, you'll disembark from the bus while it is searched.

ESSENTIALS

Bank/ATM Banco de Costa Rica (⊠ *Entrance to town* ☎ *2755–0401* ☞ *Visa only*).

Internet Cabinas Palmer Internet (⊠ *50 m east of Coco's* ☎ *2755–0435*).

EXPLORING

A full-fledged nature center a few miles northwest of Cahuita and well worth a stop,

Fodor'sChoice
★
ⓒ
Aviarios Sloth Sanctuary has dense gardens that have attracted more than 300 bird species. Proceeds go to good-hearted owners Judy and Luis Arroyo's sloth-rescue center on the premises. Buttercup, the very first of their charges, holds court in the nature-focused gift shop. ⊠ *9 km/5 mi northwest of Cahuita, follow signs on Río Estrella delta* ☎ *2750–0775* ⊕ *www.slothrescue.org* ⊴ *$25 for tours* ☉ *Daily 7–2:30.*

At most butterfly gardens around Costa Rica you get wet during the rainy season. (The mesh enclosures don't offer much protection from

Cahuita

Caribbean Sea

Punta Cahuita

Post Office ❶

Police

School

TO PLAYA NEGRA

Cahuita Tours

Phones

KEY

① Hotels

❶ Restaurants

Bus Terminal

Parque Nacional Cahuita

⑧ ⑥ ⑦

0   100 yards

0   150 meters

TO RTE. 36
(LIMÓN & PUERTO VIEJO),
CAHUITA BUTTERFLY GARDEN,
AVIARIOS DEL CARIBE, COCAO TRAILS

the moisture.) But that's not the case at the **Cahuita Butterfly Garden**, where a wood roof covers the perimeter of the 1,100-square-meter (11,800-square-foot) facility. The friendly owners conduct tours in English, French, and Spanish. There's a souvenir shop and small café that serves refreshments, as well as a lounge area outfitted with whimsical wooden chairs. (The owner is a sculptor.) ✉ *Coastal highway, 200 m before main entrance to Cahuita* ☎ *2755–0361* 💰 *$8* 🕙 *Sun.–Fri. 8:30–3:30, Sat. 8:30–noon.*

OUTDOOR ACTIVITIES

Cahuita is small enough that its tour operators don't focus simply on the town and nearby national park, but instead line up excursions around the region, even as far away as the Tortuguero canals to the north and Bocas del Toro, Panama, to the south. **Cahuita Tours** (✉ *Main street, 180 m north of Coco's* ☎ *2755–0000* ⊕ *www.cahuitatours.com*) is the town's largest and most established tour operator. They can set you up with any of a variety of adventures, including river rafting, kayaking, and visiting indigenous reserves (for a glimpse into traditional life). They can also reconfirm flights and make lodging reservations. We recommend them over their competitors.

WHERE TO EAT

$ ✕ **Miss Edith.** Miss Edith is revered
CARIBBEAN   for her flavorful Caribbean cooking, vegetarian meals, and herbal
teas for whatever ails you. Back
in the old days, she served on her
own front porch; she's since moved
to more ample surroundings on an
easy-to-miss side street at the north
end of town. A bit of the mystique
disappeared with the move, but
her made-to-order dishes—*rondón*

(stew of vegetables and beef or fish) and spicy jerk chicken—are good
no matter where they are served. You can get breakfast here (except on
Sunday). ⊠ *East of police station* ☎ *2755–0248* ▭ *No credit cards.*

WHERE TO STAY

$ ⊡ **Alby Lodge.** You're right in town, but you'd never know it at this
friendly lodging. Cabins with hardwood floors are propped up on stilts
and have hot-water baths, log tables, mosquito nets, and a hammock
on the front porch. Make use of the shared kitchen facilities and outdoor barbecue. The forested grounds and high thatch roof keep the
temperature pleasantly bearable in otherwise balmy Cahuita. It's next
to the park, so the howler monkeys are your morning alarm clock. **Pros:**
central location; friendly staff. **Cons:** sometimes a bit noisy; spartan
rooms. ⊠ *180 m west of national park entrance* ☎ *2755–0031* ⊕ *www.
albylodge.com* ⌦ *4 cabins* ⚴ *In-room: no a/c, no phone, no TV, Wi-Fi*
▭ *No credit cards* ⦿ *EP.*

$ ⊡ **Atlántida Lodge.** Attractively landscaped grounds, the beach across the
road, and a large pool are Atlántida's main assets. You're welcomed to
your room by a lovely assortment of fresh and dried flowers; the rooms
themselves are a little on the rustic side, but have tile floors and pretty
terraces. Two rooms have hot tubs. All the coffee and bananas you can
drink and eat are yours as well. **Pros:** good value; decent pool. **Cons:**
some dark rooms; lackluster staff. ⊠ *Next to soccer field at Playa Negra*
☎ *2755–0115* ✉ *atlantis@racsa.co.cr* ⌦ *32 rooms, 2 suites* ⚴ *In-room:*
no a/c, no phone, no TV. In-hotel: restaurant, bar, pool, gym, laundry
service ▭ *AE, D, DC, MC, V* ⦿ *EP.*

¢–$ ⊡ **Bungalows Aché.** Like Alby Lodge next door, Aché scatters wooden
bungalows—three octagonal structures in this case—around wooded
grounds that make the close-by town center seem far away. The buildings come with a rocking chair and porch hammock. The largest
bungalow sleeps four. The Swiss owner accepts euros, dollars, and colones. **Pros:** central location; friendly staff. **Cons:** small rooms; spartan
rooms. ⊠ *180 m west of national park entrance* ☎ *2755–0119* ⊕ *www.
bungalowsache.com* ⌦ *3 bungalows* ⚴ *In-room: no a/c, no phone,
refrigerator, safe, no TV* ▭ *No credit cards* ⦿ *EP.*

$ ⊡ **Bungalows Malú.** This is one of the rare places with air-conditioning
on the coast, but it doesn't need it: the octagonal stone-and-wood bungalows spread out on the grounds here get plenty of cool breezes from
the beach across the road. Each unit has shuttered screened windows,

hardwood floors, and a private porch with a hammock. **Pros:** good value; air-conditioning. **Cons:** far from sights; bungalows are dark inside. ⊠ *Playa Negra road, 2 km/1 mi north of Cahuita* ☎ *2755–0114* ✎ *bungalowmalu@gmail.com* ⌧ *6 bungalows* ♿ *In-room: no phone, refrigerator, no TV. In-hotel: restaurant, bar, pool, Internet terminal* ▤ *MC, V* ⚇ *BP.*

$–$$ 🏨 **El Encanto Bed & Breakfast Inn.** Zen

Fodor's Choice Buddhist owners have cultivated a
★   serene and beautiful environment
here, ideal for physical and spiritual relaxation. Lodgings are in a garden with an extensive bromeliad collection and Buddha figures. Choose between comfortable rooms or bungalows, all decorated with art from around the globe; some rooms have a double vaulted ceiling with strategically placed screens that keep the place wonderfully ventilated. Amenities include queen-size beds, hot water, and secure parking. Breakfast comes complete with homemade breads and cakes. The beach is across the street, and massage and yoga classes are available on weekends. **Pros:** friendly owners; good value; central location. **Cons:** not for young travelers looking for a scene. ⊠ *200 m west of police station on Playa Negra road* ☎ *2755–0113* ⊕ *www.elencantocahuita.com* ⌧ *3 rooms, 3 bungalows, 1 apartment* ♿ *In-room: no a/c, no phone, kitchen (some), no TV (some). In-hotel: pool* ▤ *AE, MC, V* ⚇ *BP.*

$$ 🏨 **Hotel La Diosa.** The owners' interest in Eastern religions is evidenced in the hotel's name (La Diosa means "goddess") and by the sign depicting a Hindu goddess. They have also opted for little touches such as the rounding of corners and cachá-wood rails to "enhance feminine energy." The place hosts occasional yoga workshops, too, but that's as New Age as it gets. Brightly painted stone or wood cabins—a few have air-conditioning, a rarity here—are scattered around the grounds. All have bright furnishings and art posters hang on the walls, and one room even comes with a whirlpool tub. A bridge leads from the pool to the beach. **Pros:** seclusion; air-conditioning available. **Cons:** far from sights; small rooms. ⊠ *2 km/1 mi north of town at end of Playa Negra road* ☎ *2755–0055; 800/623–3198 in North America* ⊕ *www.hotelladiosa. net* ⌧ *13 cabins* ♿ *In-room: no a/c (some), no phone, no TV, Wi-Fi. In-hotel: restaurant, bar, pool,* ▤ *AE, D, DC, MC, V* ⚇ *BP.*

$ 🏨 **Kelly Creek Hotel & Restaurante.** Owners from Madrid have created a wonderful budget option in a handsome wooden hotel on the creek bank across a short pedestrian bridge from the park entrance. Each of the four hardwood-finished guest rooms is big enough to sleep a small army and has two double beds. Owner Andrés de Alcalá barbecues meat and fresh fish on an open-air grill and also cooks paella and other Spanish specialties. Stop by the restaurant ($–$$) for dinner, even if you're not staying here, but order the paella by 2 PM. Caimans come to the creek bank in search of snacks, and the monkeys and parrots

A TOWN THAT WON'T LET YOU DOWN

Cahuita's first tourist of note was Costa Rican president Alfredo González, whose boat shipwrecked on this stretch of coast in 1915. The president was so grateful for the aid settlers gave him that he purchased a tract of land here and donated it to them to construct a town.

9

Wildlife watching in Cahuita National Park.

who live in the national park are just yards away, as is the lively center of Cahuita. You'll get a small discount if you pay in cash. **Pros:** good value; terrific Spanish restaurant; friendly owners. **Cons:** dark rooms; occasional, but rare, street noise. ✉ *Next to park entrance* ☎ *2755–0007* ⊕ *www.hotelkellycreek.com* ⏏ *4 rooms* ⚴ *In-room: no a/c, no phone, no TV, Wi-Fi. In-hotel: restaurant* ⊟ *AE, MC, V* ⊚ *EP.*

$ $$ 🏨 **Magellan Inn.** Arguably Cahuita's most elegant lodging, this group of
★ bungalows is graced with tile-floor terraces facing a pool and gardens growing on an ancient coral reef. Carpeted rooms have original paintings and custom-made wooden furniture. Feast on intensely flavored French and creole seafood specialties at the Casa Creole ($–$$), open for dinner each evening on the hotel's patio; don't miss the house pâté or the homemade ice cream. The open-air bar rocks to great blues and jazz recordings in the evening and mellows with classical music at breakfast. **Pros:** seclusion; good value; scrumptious dinners. **Cons:** far from sights; staff can be too businesslike. ✉ *2 km/1 mi north of town at end of Playa Negra road* ☎ *2755–0035* ⊕ *www.magellaninn.com* ⏏ *6 rooms* ⚴ *In-room: no a/c (some), no phone, no TV (some). In-hotel: restaurant, bar, pool, laundry service, Wi-Fi hotspote* ⊟ *AE, D, DC, MC, V* ⊚ *BP.*

NIGHTLIFE

Aside from a local bar or two, Cahuita's nightlife centers on restaurants, all pleasant places to linger over dinner for the evening. Lively reggae, soca, and samba blast weekend evenings from the turquoise **Coco's Bar** (✉ *Main road* ☎ *No phone*). The assemblage of dogs dozing on its veranda illustrates the rhythm of local life.

CAHUITA NATIONAL PARK

Just south of Cahuita.

Parque Nacional Cahuita begins at the southern edge of the town of the same name. Its rain forest extends right to the edge of its curving, utterly undeveloped 3-km (2-mi) white-sand beach. ☎ *2755–0461 Cahuita entrance; 2755–0302 Puerto Vargas entrance* ✉ *By donation at Cahuita entrance, $10 at Puerto Vargas entrance* ⊗ *Daily 6–5 Cahuita entrance, daily 7–4 Puerto Vargas entrance.*

GETTING HERE AND AROUND

Choose from two park entrances: one is at the southern end of the village of Cahuita; the other is at Puerto Vargas, just off the main road, 5 km (3 mi) south of town. If you don't have a car, you can get here easily via bike or taxi.

OUTDOOR ADVENTURES

Operators in Cahuita or Puerto Viejo de Talamanca can hook you up with excursions to and in the park, or you can go on your own, especially if you use the entrance at the south edge of the village.

SNORKELING
Cahuita's reefs are just one of several high-quality snorkeling spots in the region. Rent snorkeling gear in Cahuita or Puerto Viejo de Talamanca or through your hotel; most hotels also organize trips. It's wise to work with a guide, as the number of good snorkeling spots is limited and they're not always easily accessible. Cahuita established a community lifeguard team in 2002, unusual in Costa Rica. ■TIP➔ As elsewhere up and down the Caribbean coast, the undertow poses risks for even experienced swimmers. Use extreme caution and never swim alone.

PUERTO VIEJO DE TALAMANCA

16 km/10 mi south of Cahuita.

This muddy, colorful little town is one of the hottest spots on the international budget-travel circuit, and swarms with surfers, New Age hippies, beaded and spangled punks, would-be Rastafarians of all colors and descriptions, and wheelers and dealers—both pleasant and otherwise. Time was when most kids came here with only one thing on their mind: surfing. Today many seem to be looking for a party, with or without the surf.

But if alternative lifestyles aren't your bag, there are plenty of more "grown-up" offerings on the road heading southeast and northwest out of town. At last count, some 50 nationalities were represented in this tiny community, and most are united in concern for the environment and orderly development of tourism. (Few want to see the place become just another Costa Rican resort community.) Some locals bemoan the loss of their town's innocence, as drugs and other evils have surfaced, but only in small doses: this is still a fun town to visit, with a great variety of hotels, cabinas, and restaurants in every price range. Unlike some other parts of Costa Rica, no one has been priced out of the market here.

Locals use "Puerto Viejo" to refer to the village. They drop the "de Talamanca" part; we use the complete name to avoid confusion with the other Puerto Viejo: Puerto Viejo de Sarapiquí in the Northern Plains. You have access to the beach right in town, and the Salsa Brava, famed in surfers' circles for its pounding waves, is here off the coast, too. The best strands of Caribbean sand are outside the village: Playa Cocles, Playa Chiq-

uita (technically a series of beaches), and Punta Uva, all dark-sand beaches, line the road heading southeast from town. Playa Negra—not the Playa Negra near Cahuita—is the black-sand beach northwest of town. Punta Uva, with fewer hotels and the farthest from the village, sees fewer crowds and more tranquility. Playa Negra shares that distinction, too—for now—but developers have eyed the beach as the next area for expansion.

NAVIGATING PUERTO VIEJO DE TALAMANCA You can manage the town center quite easily on foot, though it is dusty in the dry season and muddy when it rains. (The main street is, thankfully, paved.) Everyone gets around by bike here, and seemingly everyone has one for rent. Quality varies widely. Expect to pay $10 per day for a good bike. **Cabinas Grant** (⌧ *100 m south of bus stop* ☎ *2750–0292*) has the best selection of quality bikes in town. Priority is given to guests at **Casa Verde Lodge** (⌧ *200 m south and 200 m east of bus stop* ☎ *2750–0015*), but they usually have extra bikes you can rent for a half or full day even if you don't stay here. There are a couple of official red licensed cabs, but most taxi service here is informal, with private individuals providing rides. To be on the safe side, have your hotel or restaurant call one for you.

GETTING HERE AND AROUND

The turnoff to Puerto Viejo de Talamanca is 10 km (6 mi) down the coastal highway south of Cahuita. (The highway itself continues south to Bribrí and Sixaola at the Panamanian border.) The village lies another 5 km (3 mi) beyond the turnoff. The paved road passes through town and continues to Playas Cocles and Chiquita and Punta Uva before the pavement peters out at the entrance to the village of Manzanillo. "Badly potholed" describes the condition of the road from the highway into town, and as far as Playa Cocles. The newer paved sections beyond Cocles haven't disintegrated . . . yet. Autotransportes MEPE buses travel from San José five times a day, and approximately hourly throughout the day from Limón and Cahuita. All buses from San José go into Puerto Viejo de Talamanca; most, though not all, Limón-originating buses do as well, but a couple drop you off on the highway. Check if you board in Limón.

A scant four buses per day ply the 15-km (9-mi) paved road between Puerto Viejo and Manzanillo, so unless your schedule meshes exactly with theirs, you're better off biking or taking a taxi to and from the

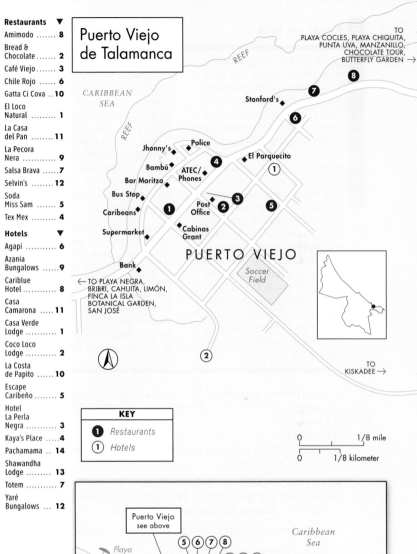

Puerto Viejo de Talamanca

Jhonny's

Police

Bambú

Bar Maritza

Bus Stop

Caribeans

Supermarket

ATEC/ Phones

El Parquecito

Stanford's

Post Office

Cabinas Grant

Bank

PUERTO VIEJO

Soccer Field

CARIBBEAN SEA

REEF

REEF

TO PLAYA COCLES, PLAYA CHIQUITA, PUNTA UVA, MANZANILLO, CHOCOLATE TOUR, BUTTERFLY GARDEN →

← TO PLAYA NEGRA, BRIBRÍ, CAHUITA, LIMÓN, FINCA LA ISLA BOTANICAL GARDEN, SAN JOSÉ

TO KISKADEE →

KEY

❶ *Restaurants*

① *Hotels*

0 _____ 1/8 mile

0 _____ 1/8 kilometer

Puerto Viejo see above

Playa Negra

Finca La Isla Botanical Garden

← TO LIMON

Caribbean Sea

Playa Cocles

Playa Chiquita

Punta Uva

Butterfly Garden

Chocolate Tour

Café Internet Río Negro

Río Cocles

Río Caño Negro

Gandaca-Manzanillo National Wildlife Refuge

TO MANZANILLO →

CLOSE UP

Reefs at Risk

One of the most complex organisms in the marine world, a coral reef is an extraordinary and extraordinarily delicate habitat. Coral reefs are the result of the symbiotic relationship between single-cell organisms called zooxanthellae and coral polyps. The zooxanthellae grow inside the cells of the polyps, producing oxygen and nutrients that are released into the coral tissues. Corals secrete calcium carbonate (limestone) that, over time, forms the vast coral reef "superstructure." Zooxanthellae require exposure to sunlight to thrive. The healthiest coral reefs are in clear, clean, tropical seawater at a temperature of 20°C to 25°C (70°F to 80°F). Healthy coral reefs are biologically rich gardens occupied by a diverse selection of life forms, from microscopic unicellular algae and phytoplankton to a wide range of fish.

Unfortunately, coral reefs in Costa Rica are in danger. Dirt and sediment from banana plantations and logging areas, as well as runoff from pesticide use, are killing them. The dirty runoff literally clogs the pores of the zooxanthellae and smothers them. In the Golfo Dulce, 98% of one of the oldest reefs in Costa Rica has been destroyed by this sedimentation. The once-enormous reefs of Cahuita are almost entirely gone.

Human visitors, including careless snorkelers, have also damaged reefs. Just touching a reef damages it. When exploring a coral reef, look but don't touch, and snorkel only on its outer side, preferably in calm weather. Can the reefs be saved? With commitment and time, yes. Coral is resilient, and will grow back—if the Costa Rican government makes it a priority.

---

far-flung beaches along the way. Taxis charge $8 to Playas Cocles and Chiquita (as well as north to Playa Negra), $9 to Punta Uva, and $14 to Manzanillo.

ESSENTIALS

Bank/ATM Banco de Costa Rica (⊠ 50 m south of bridge at entrance to town ☎ 2750–0707 ⌕ Visa only).

Internet ATEC (⊠ Across from Restaurant Tamara ☎ 2750–0398).
Café Internet Río Negro (⊠ Playa Cocles 4 km/2½ mi southeast of town ☎ 2750–0801). **El Tesoro** (⊠ Playa Cocles ☎ 2750–0128).

Pharmacy Farmacia Amiga (⊠ Next to Banco de Costa Rica ☎ 2750–0698).

Post Office Correos (⊠ 50 m west of ATEC).

Visitor Information ATEC (⊠ Across from Restaurant Tamara ☎ 2750–0191 ⊕ www.ateccr.org).

EXPLORING

At the **Finca la Isla Botanical Garden** you can explore a working tropical fruit, spice, and ornamental plant farm. Sloths abound, and you might see a few poison dart frogs. A $10 guided tour includes admission and a glass of the farm's homemade fruit juice. You get the fruit juice if you wander around on your own, too—a $1 self-guided-tour book is available in English, Spanish, French, or German. Watch the demonstration showing how cacao beans are turned into chocolate, and sample some of the product at the end of the tour. ⊠ *½ km/¼ mi west of town at Playa Negra* ☎ *2750–0046* ⊕ *www.greencoast.com/garden.htm* ✉ *$5, guided tour $10* ⊗ *Fri.–Mon. 10–4.*

☙ Cacao once ruled the Talamanca region, but few plantations are left these days. One friendly Swiss couple continues the tradition and shows you the workings of their chocolate plantation on their **Chocorart** chocolate tour. Follow the little-known life cycle of this crop from cultivation to processing. There's sampling at the tour's conclusion. Call or e-mail to reserve a tour (you need a minimum of four people) and to be picked up from the Playa Chiquita School. Since these folks are Swiss, they can tailor the commentary in German, French, or Italian, in addition to English or Spanish. ⊠ *6 km/4 mi southeast of town at Playa Chiquita* ☎ *2750–0075* ✉ *chocorart@racsa.co.cr* ✉ *15 per person* ⊗ *By appointment.*

☙ Unlike most such establishments in Costa Rica, which are for show only, the working **Butterfly Garden** cultivates 60 to 80 species of butterflies, three of which are unique to the area, for shipment to similar facilities around the world. The knowledgeable staff provides guided tours with bilingual commentary. ⊠ *7 km/4½ mi southeast of town at Punta Uva* ☎ *2750–0086* ✉ *5, free for kids under 6* ⊗ *Daily 8–4.*

OUTDOOR ACTIVITIES

As in Cahuita, tour operators and outfitters here can set up tours and activities anywhere on the south Caribbean coast.

Tours with **ATEC** (*Talamancan Association of Ecotourism and Conservation*)(⊠ *Across from Restaurant Tamara* ☎ *2750–0191* ⊕ *www.ateccr. org*) have an environmental or cultural bent, such as Afro-Caribbean or indigenous-culture walks—tours to the nearby Kekoldi indigenous reserve are especially popular—rain forest hikes, coral-reef snorkeling trips, fishing trips, bird-watching tours, night walks, and adventure treks. Local organizations and wildlife refuges receive 15% to 20% of ATEC's proceeds. Well-established operator **Terra Aventuras** (⊠ *100 m south of bus stop* ☎ *2750–0750* ⊕ *www.terraventuras.com*) can lead you around Puerto Viejo de Talamanca and Cahuita, or take you on excursions to Tortuguero, the Gandoca-Manzanillo Wildlife Refuge, and Bocas del Toro in Panama. It also rents good-quality surfboards, bicycles, boogie boards, and snorkeling gear.

★ Rafting excursions lie about two hours away, but one San José–based outfitter has an office here. **Exploradores Outdoors** (⊠ *Across from ATEC* ☎ *2750–2020; 2222–6262 in San José* ⊕ *www.exploradoresoutdoors. com*) is highly regarded and has day excursions on the Pacuare river, with a pickup point here or in San José, and the option to start in one place and be dropped off at the other. The outfitter also offers sea-kayaking excursions off the coast of the Gandoca-Manzanillo Wildlife Refuge.

SURFING Surfing is the name of the game in Puerto Viejo, for everyone from newbies to Kelly Slaters. The best conditions are late December through March, but there's action all year. Longtime surfers compare the south Caribbean to Hawaii, but without the "who-do-you-think-you-are?" attitude. There are a number of breaks here, most famously **Salsa Brava,**

9

which translates to "wild sauce." It breaks fairly far offshore and requires maneuvering past some tricky currents and a shallow reef. Hollow and primarily right breaking, Salsa Brava is one gnarly wave when it gets big. If it gets *too* big, or not big enough, check out the breaks at Punta Uva, Punta Cocles, or Playa Chiquita. Boogie boarders and bodysurfers can also dig the beach-break waves at various points along this tantalizingly beautiful coast.

> **CAUTION**
>
> The conditions that make the Caribbean so popular among surfers spell danger for swimmers. Drownings occur each year. Strong riptides can pull you out to sea, even in waist-deep water, before you realize what's happening. Never swim alone in these parts—good advice anywhere.

If you're, say, over 30, but have always wanted to try surfing, consider the friendly, two-hour $50 surf school at **Aventuras Bravas** (⊠ *Across from Stanford's* ☎ *8849–7600* ⊕ *www.braveadventure.net*). You start out with a small wave near the bus stop, and get a money-back guarantee that you'll be standing by the end of the lesson. You can also rent equipment here.

WHERE TO EAT

$$
ITALIAN
★

✕ **Amimodo.** The name translates to "my way," and the exuberant Italian owners really do it their way, combining the cuisine of their native northern Italy with Caribbean flavors. Your antipasto might be classic bruschetta or *jamón de tiburón* (shark ham with avocado dressing), and your ravioli might be stuffed with tropical shrimp, pineapple, and curry, with avocado sauce on the side. The tropical veranda with gingerbread trim spills over onto the beach with abundant greenery, and the restaurant is a popular gathering place for Puerto Viejo's Italian community. ⊠ *200 m east of Stanford's* ☎ *2750–0257* ⊟ *MC, V* ☻ *Closed Thurs.*

¢
COSTA RICAN
★

✕ **Bread & Chocolate.** The take-away line for brownies forms at the gate before this place opens at 6:30 AM, but stick around and fortify yourself with a hearty breakfast of cinnamon-oatmeal pancakes, French toast, or creamy scrambled eggs, washed down with a cup of French-press coffee. Lunch brings jerk chicken, roasted red peppers, and chocolate truffles. Everything is homemade, right down to the mayonnaise. Make your dinner early; the place closes at 6 PM. This is one of several bakery-slash-breakfast-and-lunch cafés open in town; the friendly owner gives this place the edge. ⊠ *50 m south of post office* ☎ *2750–0723* ⊟ *No credit cards* ☻ *Closed Mon. Closed Tues, Apr.–Nov. No dinner Sun.*

$
ITALIAN

✕ **Café Viejo.** This has fast become the hot place to see and be seen on Puerto Viejo's main drag. The owners, four brothers who learned to cook at the knee of their Italian grandmother back in Rimini, have concocted a menu, several pages long, of pizzas and handmade pastas. Recorded reggae and mambo music bops in the background. ⊠ *Across from ATEC* ☎ *2750–0817* ⊟ *MC, V* ☻ *Closed Tues. No lunch.*

$
THAI

✕ **Chile Rojo.** There's not a thing about the name or furnishings to reflect its Thai and Middle-Eastern offerings, but business is brisk here. Choose from Thai grilled tuna, falafel, hummus, and samosas. Sushi is available on Saturday. In deference to the town's European tourist trade, the restaurant accepts euros as payment, too. ⊠ *Across from Stanford's* ☎ *2750–0319* ▭ *No credit cards* ◷ *Closed Mon.*

$

ECLECTIC

Fodor's Choice

★

✕ **El Loco Natural.** El Loco Natural epitomizes Puerto Viejo: lively, organic, all the rage, but confident enough not to seek trendiness. Ordering is by sauces: Thai peanut, Indonesian-Caribbean curry, Mexican chipotle, Jamaican jerk-style, or Malaysian-guayaba curry. Then select vegetables, chicken, shrimp, or fish (marlin or tuna). You'll be better able to converse with your fellow diners if you sit at the tables inside. Live music gets going late on Thursday and Sunday evenings. ⊠ *200 m south of Stanford's* ☎ *2750–0530* ▭ *No credit cards* ◷ *Closed Wed., no lunch.*

$

ITALIAN

✕ **Gatta Ci Cova.** Chef-owner Ilario Giannoni strolls the 100 meters over from his La Pecora Nera restaurant to watch over his new baby these days. The restaurant, whose name comes from an Italian expression meaning "things kept secret," provides a less formal, less expensive alternative to the original, but still has all the flair and all the fun. Lunch offerings focus on the $10 plato del día, a bargain with appetizer, salad, a rotating selection of pastas, dessert, and a glass of wine. ⊠ *3 km/2 mi southeast of town at Playa Cocles* ☎ *2750–0730* ▭ *AE, D, DC, MC, V* ◷ *Closed Mon.*

¢

CAFÉ

✕ **La Casa del Pan.** The young owners at this tiny bakery whip up German-style breads. It's worth a stop if you're on the road between Puerto Viejo and the beaches. ⊠ *5 km (3 mi) southeast of town at Playa Chiquita* ☎ *8843–4552* ▭ *No credit cards* ◷ *Closed. Tues., no dinner. Breakfast served.*

$$$

ITALIAN

Fodor's Choice

★

✕ **La Pecora Nera.** Though the name means "black sheep" in Italian, there's nothing shameful about this thatch-roof roadside restaurant. There's always a lot more to choose from than you'll see on the sparse-looking menu. Wait for owner/chef Ilario Giannoni to come out of the kitchen and triumphantly announce—with flair worthy of an Italian opera—which additional light Tuscan entrées, appetizers, and desserts they've concocted that day. Be prepared for a long, leisurely dining experience with attentive service. It's worth the wait; this is one of the country's top Italian restaurants. ⊠ *3 km/2 mi southeast of town at Playa Cocles* ☎ *2750–0490* ▭ *AE, D, DC, MC, V* ◷ *Closed Mon. No lunch.*

$

SEAFOOD

✕ **Salsa Brava.** The restaurant overlooking the Salsa Brava break—with sublime surf vistas—has taken the name of this famed surfing spot. Opt for casual counter service or grab a seat at one of the colorful roadside tables. Lunch and dinner center on grilled fish and meat, with red snapper prepared in olive oil, garlic, and cayenne pepper a specialty. ⊠ *100 m east of Stanford's* ☎ *2750–0241* ▭ *AE, D, DC, MC, V* ◷ *Closed Mon.*

¢–$

CARIBBEAN

✕ **Selvin's.** An old standby at Punta Uva, Selvin's keeps limited hours, especially in the off-season, so head out here if you're fortunate enough to be in town when it's open. The owner, known to everyone in town as "Blanca," cooks up a menu of rondón, rice and beans, lobster, shrimp, and chicken with sweet mole sauce. This is one of the few places around that accepts traveler's checks as payment. ⊠ *7 km (4½ mi) southeast of town at Punta Uva* ☎ *2750–0664* ▭ *No credit cards* ◷ *Closed Mon. and Tues. Dec.–May and Mon.–Thurs. June–Nov.*

9

¢ ✕ **Soda Miss Sam.** Longtime restaurateur Miss Sam still dishes up hearty

CARIBBEAN Caribbean cuisine at this small restaurant, a Puerto Viejo institution—she prefers not to divulge how many years she's been doing so—and the front porch is still full of diners. Rice and beans are usually going, or you can get a *casado* (plate with rice, beans, and fried plantains) with chicken, beef, pork, or fish and freshly squeezed fruit juices as accompaniment. It's open for breakfast, too. ⊠ *300 m south, 200 m east of bus stop* ☎ *2750–0108* ▭ *No credit cards* ⊘ *Closed Tues.*

$ ✕ **Tex Mex.** Begin the day here with a hearty Gringo- or Tico-style break-

MEXICAN fast. (Expect *gallo pinto* [rice and beans] or an ample fruit plate if you opt for the latter.) Lunch and dinner give way to standard nachos, burritos, tacos, and enchiladas. Tex Mex screens free DVD movies, yours for the price of a drink, each evening except Thursday. ⊠ *50 m east of ATEC* ☎ *2750–0525* ▭ *No credit cards* ⊘ *Closed Thurs.*

WHERE TO STAY

¢–$$ ▦ **Agapi.** Agapi means "love" in Greek, and Costa Rican–Greek owners Cecilia and Tasso lovingly watch over their guests with some of the most attentive service around. Seven furnished apartments overlook the beach and come complete with fully equipped kitchen, hot-water bath, hammock, mosquito nets over the beds, and private balcony. An additional six rooms have two full-size beds each, and all have an ocean view. A common area in the back contains a beachside barbecue. **Pros:** kitchens; central location. **Cons:** not for travelers who want anonymity; first-floor rooms are dark. ⊠ *1 km/½ mi southeast of Stanford's* ☎ *2750–0446* ⊕ *www.agapisite.com* ⤳ *5 rooms, 12 apartments* ⌂ *In-room: no a/c (some), no phone, kitchen (some), refrigerator, no TV (some). In-hotel: laundry service, Wi-Fi hotspot* ▭ *AE, D, DC, MC, V* ¶◎¶ *EP.*

$$ ▦ **Azania Bungalows.** Eight thatch-roof, A-frame bungalows spread around Azania's ample gardens, and sleep four. The first floor contains a queen-size bed, and a ladder leads to the second floor with a pair of single beds. Much-appreciated mosquito netting covers all of them. You'll luxuriate in the semi-open shower in the blue-tile bathrooms. Meals are served in the hotel's Argentine restaurant next to the free-form pool. **Pros:** good value; good Argentine restaurant. **Cons:** difficult to make reservations; bungalows are dark inside. ⊠ *1½ km/1 mi southeast of town at Playa Cocles* ☎ *2750–0540* ⊕ *www.azania-costarica.com* ⤳ *8 bungalows* ⌂ *In-room: no a/c, no phone, refrigerator, no TV, Wi-Fi. In-hotel: restaurant, bar, pool, laundry service, Internet terminal* ▭ *AE, D, DC, MC, V* ¶◎¶ *BP.*

$$ ▦ **Cariblue Hotel.** The youthful Italian owners who came here to surf

Fodor'sChoice years ago stayed on and built a lodging that combines refinement with

★ that hip Puerto Viejo vibe in exactly the right proportions. Cariblue's finely crafted all-wooden bungalows are spaciously arrayed on the edge of the jungle, across the road from the splendid white-sand beaches of Punta Cocles. Cabinas are linked to the main ranch-style building by paths that meander across a gently sloping lawn shaded by enormous trees. Expansive verandas and beautiful tile mosaics in the bathrooms add an air of refinement; hammocks add an air of relaxation. Breakfasts are huge. Italian cuisine dominates for lunch, and dinner is served at the lively Soleluna restaurant ($–$$) on-site. **Pros:** friendly owners; good

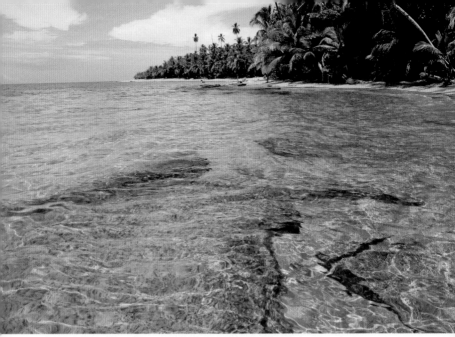
Calm waters over the reef just off Punta Uva Beach near Puerto Viejo de Talamanca.

restaurant. **Cons:** need car to stay here; a few reports of lackluster staff. ⊠ *2 km/1 mi southeast of town at Playa Cocles* ☎ *2750–0035* ⊕ *www.cariblue.com* ↰ *21 bungalows* ⬙ *In-room: no a/c (some), no phone, safe (some), no TV (some). In-hotel: restaurant, bars, pool, laundry service, Wi-Fi hotspot* ⊟ *AE, D, DC, MC, V* ⦿ *BP.*

$ 🏨 **Casa Camarona.** Though half the rooms have air-conditioning at this secluded lodging, you hardly need it. The abundant shade and sea breezes keep the rooms delightfully cool. All the spacious, wooden, rustic rooms front the ocean—the second-story rooms have the best view—and have two double beds. Meals are served at the seaside Caribbean restaurant. **Pros:** good value; air-conditioning. **Cons:** need a car to stay here; some dark rooms. ⊠ *3 km/2 mi south of town at Playa Cocles* ☎ *2750–0151; 283–6711 in San José* ⊕ *www.casacamarona.co.cr* ↰ *17 rooms* ⬙ *In-room: no a/c (some), no phone, no TV. In-hotel: restaurant, bar, laundry service, no-smoking rooms* ⊟ *AE, D, DC, MC, V* ⦿ *CP.*

¢–$ 🏨 **Casa Verde Lodge.** If you've graduated from your backpacker days and
Fodor's Choice are a bit more flush with cash but still want to be near the action, this old
★ standby on a quiet street a couple of blocks from the center of town is ideal. The comfortable cabinas are decorated with an interesting variety of touches such as shell mobiles, watercolor frescoes, and indigenous tapestries. Overall, rooms at this Swiss-run lodging have a neat-as-a-pin quality. Exotic birds flutter constantly through the lush plantings that screen the cabinas from the street. The place is immensely popular, since the price is low and it's clean and well run; reserve well in advance. You'll receive a small discount if you pay in cash. **Pros:** good value; immaculate. **Cons:** difficult to find space; businesslike staff. ⊠ *200 m south and 200 m east of bus stop* ☎ *2750–0015* ⊕ *www.cabinascasaverde.com* ↰ *17*

rooms, 9 with bath; 2 apartments △ In-room: no a/c (some), no phone, refrigerator (some), no TV. In-hotel: restaurant, pool, bicycles, laundry service ☰ AE, MC, V ᑌOᗑ EP.

¢–$ ☷ **Coco Loco Lodge.** The cool, forested grounds here lie close to the center of town but seem far away. The Austrian owners lavish you with lots of personal attention. The bungalows on stilts are simply furnished but contain hot-water baths, mosquito nets over the beds (you'll need them), and hammocks on the porch. There are also two fully furnished houses available for short- or long-term rental. Great coffee is included in the room rate; a huge buffet breakfast is extra. You'll receive a discount if you pay with cash. **Pros:** good budget value; central location. **Cons:** rustic rooms; dark road at night. ⊠ *180 m south of bridge at entrance to town* ☎ *2750–0281* ⊕ *www.cocolocolodge.com* ⇗ *8 cabins, 2 houses* △ *In-room: no a/c, no phone, kitchen (some), refrigerator (some). In-hotel: Internet terminal, Wi-Fi hotspot ☰ MC, V ᑌOᗑ EP.*

$–$$ ☷ **Escape Caribeño.** Wonderfully friendly Italian owners Gloria and Mauro Marchiori are what make this place: they treat you like family. A dozen immaculate hardwood bungalows line a pleasant garden amply populated with hummingbirds, just outside town. All cabins have hammocks, mosquito nets, double beds, and even a bunk bed or two for larger groups. Across the road lie two stucco cabins in a wooded spot on the beach. Breakfast is served in a thatch-roof dining area in the center of the garden. You'll receive a small discount if you pay with cash. **Pros:** central location; gregarious owners. **Cons:** some small rooms; some spartan rooms. ⊠ *400 m southeast of Stanford's* ☎ *2750–0103* ⊕ *www.escapecaribeno.com* ⇗ *14 cabins* △ *In-room: no phone, safe, refrigerator, Wi-Fi ☰ AE, D, DC, MC, V ᑌOᗑ EP.*

$$ ☷ **Hotel La Perla Negra.** Fine design is evident in the construction of this handsome, two-story dark-wood structure across a tiny dirt road near the end of Playa Negra. All rooms have balconies, half with ocean views, half with jungle views. The three-meal restaurant features grilled meats and fish. Between the building and the beach is a spacious, inviting pool. Though the hotel does not accept credit cards, you can make your payment through PayPal. **Pros:** secluded; quality construction of buildings. **Cons:** far from sights; situated on lesser-known Playa Negra. ⊠ *Playa Negra, 1 km/½ mi north of Puerto Viejo* ☎ *2750–0111* ⊕ *www.perlanegra-beachresort.com* ⇗ *24 rooms, 7 houses* △ *In-room: no a/c (some), no phone, no TV. In-hotel: restaurant, bar, tennis court, pool, laundry service, Wi-Fi hotspot ☰ AE, D, DC, MC, V ᑌOᗑ CP.*

¢–$ ☷ **Kaya's Place.** Rooms range from the upper-level half-dozen with shared cold-water bath to the sumptuous garden-view rooms at the back at this place at Playa Negra just outside town. The friendly, environmentally conscious owners also have a meditation room in the back. All rooms make maximum use of ironwood, nispero, and blackwood construction and furnishings. The irregular shapes take advantage of every inch of wood, to keep things in as natural a state as possible. Few of the railings and room corners follow straight lines or 90-degree angles. ⊠ *200 m north of town at Playa Negra* ☎ *2750–0690* ⊕ *www.kayasplace.com* ⇗ *25 rooms, 14 with bath* △ *In-room: no a/c, no phone, no TV. In-hotel: restaurant, bar, bicycles, laundry service ☰ AE, DC, V.*

$–$$ 🏠 **La Costa de Papito**. Papito's raised cabins are deep in the property's wooded grounds and furnished with whimsical bright tropical-blue and zebra-stripe prints. Breakfast, with an extra cost of $6, is served at the table and chairs on your porch, which has a hammock or swing chair. You'll get a 15% discount if you pay in cash. **Pros:** good value; friendly owner. **Cons:** need car to stay here; some noise from bar area. ✉ *2 km/1 mi southeast of town at Playa Cocles* ☎ *2750–0080* ⊕ *www. lacostadepapito.com* ⤵ *13 cabins* ♿ *In-room: no phone, no TV, Wi-Fi. In-hotel: restaurant, spa, bicycles, Internet terminal* ⊟ *AE, D, DC, MC, V* 🍴 *EP.*

$ 🏠 **Pachamama**. So cool and shady is this place set within the confines of the Gandoca-Manzanillo Wildlife Refuge that the owners took out the ceiling fans. No one ever needed them. Though still within sight of the Puerto Viejo–Manzanillo road, Pachamama delivers a get-away-from-it-all nature experience at a fraction of the cost of other Costa Rican eco-lodges. Cozy wood cabins are simply furnished with two beds and mosquito netting and have colorful spreads and drapes. A house can be rented by the week or month. Personal touches such as breakfast (included in the rates of the bungalows, but not the kitchen-equipped house) brought to the porch of your cabin are standard. The bungalows are joined by a kitchen and are ideal for renting by a group or family. **Pros:** seclusion; friendly owners. **Cons:** far from sights; need car to stay here. ✉ *9 km/5½ mi southeast of town at Punta Uva* ☎ *2759–9196* ⊕ *www.pachamamacaribe.com* ⤵ *2 bungalows, 3 houses* ♿ *In-room: no a/c, no phone, kitchen (some), no TV. In-hotel: bicycles, laundry service* ⊟ *MC, V* 🍴 *BP, EP.*

$$ 🏠 **Shawandha Lodge**. The service is personalized and friendly at Sha-
★ wandha, whose spacious, beautifully designed bungalows are well back from the road at Playa Chiquita. The thatch-roof bungalows have elegant hardwoods, four-poster beds, and verandas with hammocks. Each bathroom has a unique and beautiful tile mosaic. The hearty breakfast starts off with an impressive fruit plate. A white-sand beach lies 180 meters (600 feet) away, across the road. Even if you don't stay here, stop by and enjoy a distinctive French-Caribbean dinner in the open-air restaurant. **Pros:** elegant bungalows; sumptuous restaurant. **Cons:** far from sights. ✉ *6 km/4 mi southeast of town at Playa Chiquita* ☎ *2750–0018* ⊕ *www.shawandhalodge.com* ⤵ *13 bungalows* ♿ *In-room: no a/c, no phone, safe, no TV. In-hotel: restaurant, bar, laundry service* ⊟ *AE, MC, V* 🍴 *BP.*

$$ 🏠 **Totem**. Each of the tropical-blue units here contains a living room and bedroom with bamboo furnishings, a queen bed, and bunks. We like the two rooms on the upper balcony with stupendous ocean views and overlooking the gurgling, fountain-fed pool. The restaurant serves superb pizza. **Pros:** good value; terrific restaurant. **Cons:** need car to stay here; some reports of lackluster staff. ✉ *1½ km/1 mi southeast of town at Playa Cocles* ☎ *2750–0758* ⊕ *www.totemsite.com* ⤵ *12 rooms, 6 suites* ♿ *In-room: no a/c (some), refrigerator. In-hotel: restaurant, bar, pool, Internet terminal, Wi-Fi hotspot* ⊟ *AE, D, DC, MC, V* 🍴 *BP.*

9

$–$$ 🛏 **Yaré Bungalows.** The sound of the jungle is overpowering, especially at night, as you relax in your brightly pastel-painted Yaré cabina. All rooms have hot water and verandas with hammocks. The restaurant is open for breakfast, lunch, and dinner. **Pros:** good value, whimsical bungalows. **Cons:** sound travels far; far from sights. ⊠ *3½ km/2 mi southeast of town at Playa Cocles* 🏤 *Apdo. 117–1007, San José* ☎ *2750–0106; 888/250–6472 in North America* ⊕ *www.bungalowsyare.com* 🛏 *22 rooms* ⌂ *In-room: no a/c (some), no phone, safe (some), kitchen (some), safe, no TV. In-hotel: restaurant, bar, laundry service* ⊟ *AE, D, DC, MC, V* ⊚| *BP.*

A BAD RAP

The Caribbean has a reputation among Costa Ricans for being crime-ridden, mainly because of a few high-profile cases here years ago, the nearness of the Panamanian border, and the fact that this is an impoverished region compared with other parts of the country. In actuality, the problem is no better or worse here than elsewhere. Just take the standard precautions you would when you travel anywhere and stick to well-traveled tourist paths.

NEED A BREAK? At first glance, this small café could use a spelling lesson, but since **Caribeans** deals in coffee, the play on words is apt. Treat yourself to a latté, mocha, or coconut cappuccino, all made from organic, fair-trade coffee from the Turrialba region in the far-eastern Central Valley, and roasted here. The place is open daily except Tuesday. ⊠ *50 m west of bus stop* ☎ *8836–8930.*

NIGHTLIFE

The distinction between dining spot and nightspot blurs as the evening progresses, as many restaurants become pleasant places to linger over dinner. Bars each have their special nights for live music. The town's main drag between El Loco Natural and Salsa Brava is packed with pedestrians, bicycles, and a few cars most evenings, the block between Café Viejo and El Parquecito getting the most action. Wander around; something is bound to entice you in. ■TIP→ When out after dark, ask a staff member at the restaurant, bar, or club to call you a taxi at the end of the night.

BARS **Bar Maritza** (⊠ *50 m east of bus stop*) is frequented by locals, and has live music on Sunday night. Grab a beer, and chow down on pizza or sandwiches at **El Dorado** (⊠ *Across from ATEC*), a much quieter alternative to the noisier bars. **Tex Mex** (⊠ *50 m east of ATEC*) serves drinks and two big-screen movies every evening except Thursday.

DANCE CLUBS Ticos come from miles around for the Friday and Monday reggae nights at **Bambú** (⊠ *Next to Jhonny's*), but the place is closed most other evenings. **Jhonny's Place** (⊠ *230 m east of bus stop*) has nights variously devoted to reggae, jazz, R&B, and hip-hop. **Stanford's** (⊠ *100 m from the town center on the road to Manzanillo*) is the place to merengue or salsa the weekend nights away. Partake of light meals on the new second-floor patio dining room if dancing isn't your thing.

LIVE MUSIC   Caribbean restaurant **El Parquecito** (✉ *50 m east of ATEC*) pulls live-music duty Tuesday, Friday, and Saturday evenings. You're bound to hear "No Woman No Cry" and all the other reggae anthems. Organic-food restaurant **El Loco Natural** (✉ *150 m west of ATEC* ☎ *2750–0263*) has live music Thursday and Sunday evenings.

SHOPPING

Vendors set up stands at night on the beach road near El Parquecito, jewelry being the prime fare. But the town counts a few honest-to-goodness souvenir stores, too.

Buy your semi-official Puerto Viejo T-shirt at **Color Caribe** (✉ *100 m south of bus stop*), and check out the huge selection of Rastafarian clothing, plus hammocks, wood carvings, and whimsical mobiles.

★   Puerto Viejo's best shop, **Luluberlu** (✉ *200 m south and 50 m east of bus stop*), sells a wonderful selection of local indigenous carvings—balsa and *chonta* wood are especially popular—and jewelry, paintings, and ceramics by 30 artists from the region.

GANDOCA-MANZANILLO NATIONAL WILDLIFE REFUGE

15 km/9 mi southeast of Puerto Viejo.

GETTING HERE

The road from Puerto Viejo de Talamanca ends at the entrance to the village of Manzanillo. Just three buses each day—morning, midday, and late afternoon—connect the two. All taxi drivers in Puerto Viejo charge $10 for the trip here.

EXPLORING

Gandoca-Manzanillo National Wildlife Refuge. The Refugio Nacional de Vida Silvestre Gandoca-Manzanillo stretches along the southeastern coast beginning southeast of Puerto Viejo de Talamanca to the town of Manzanillo and on to the Panamanian border. Its limits are not clearly defined. Because of weak laws governing the conservation of refuges and the rising value of coastal land in this area, Gandoca-Manzanillo is less pristine than Cahuita National Park and continues to be developed. However, the refuge still has plenty of rain forest, *orey* (a dark tropical wood) and jolillo swamps, 10 km (6 mi) of beach where four species of turtles lay their eggs, and almost 3 square km (1 square mi) of *cativo* (a tropical hardwood) forest and coral reef. The Gandoca estuary is a nursery for tarpon and a wallowing spot for crocodiles and caimans.

The easiest way to explore the refuge is to hike along the coast south of Manzanillo. You can hike back out the way you came in or arrange (in Puerto Viejo de Talamanca) to have a boat pick you up at Punta Mono (Monkey Point), a three- to four-hour walk from Manzanillo, where you find secluded beaches hidden by tall cliffs of fossilized coral. The mangroves of Gandoca, with abundant caimans, iguanas, and water-fowl, lie six to eight hours away. Park administrators can tell you more and recommend a local guide; inquire when you enter Manzanillo village and the locals will point you toward them. ✉ *15 km/9 mi southeast of Puerto Viejo de Talamanca* ☎ *2750–0398 for ATEC* ⊙ *Daily 7–4.*

The nearby village of **Manzanillo** maintains that "end of the world" feel. Tourism is still in its infancy this far down the coast, though with the road paved all the way here, the town is now a popular destination among people in Limón for weekend day trips. The rest of the week, you'll likely have the place to yourself.

OUTDOOR ACTIVITIES

A guide can help you get the most out of this relatively unexplored corner of the country. The **Association of Indigenous Naturalist Guides of Manzanillo** (⊠ *Main road* ☎ *2759–9064 or 8843–9122* ✐ *guiasmant@ yahoo.com.mx*) is a consortium of high-quality, knowledgeable local guides who know the area well and lead a variety of half- and full-day tours. (The U.S. Agency for International Development planted the seed money to get the project going.) They can take you for a hike in the reserve or out to Monkey Point, with a return trip by boat. They also have horseback riding; bird-, dolphin-, and turtle-watching; and traditional fishing excursions.

DIVING AND SNORKELING   The friendly staff at **Aquamor Talamanca Adventures** (⊠ *Main road* ☎ *2759– 9012* ⊕ *www.greencoast.com/aquamor2.htm*) specializes in land- and ocean-focused tours of the Gandoca-Manzanillo Wildlife Refuge, and can tend to all your water-sporting needs in these parts, with guided kayaking, snorkeling, and scuba-diving tours, as well as equipment rental. They also offer the complete sequence of PADI-certified diving courses. Companies in Puerto Viejo de Talamanca (⇨ *above*) can arrange boat trips to dive spots and beaches in the refuge as well.

DOLPHIN-WATCHING   The **Talamanca Dolphin Foundation** (⊠ *Main road, Manzanillo* ☎ *2759– 9188* ⊕ *www.dolphinlink.org*) has 2½-hour dolphin observation tours— excellent opportunities to see bottle-nosed, *tucuxi* (gray), and Atlantic spotted dolphins swimming this section of the coast.

WHERE TO EAT AND STAY

$ ✕ **Restaurant Maxi's.** Cooled by sea breezes and shaded by tall, stately
SEAFOOD   palms, this two-story, brightly painted wooden building offers weary travelers cold beer, potent cocktails, and great seafood at unbeatable prices after a day's hike in the refuge. Locals and expatriates alike—and even chefs from Puerto Viejo's fancier restaurants—come here for their lobster fix, and the fresh fish is wonderful, too. At one time, perhaps before tourism became big in this area, Costa Ricans made Maxi's into an entire day trip. Now that the road is paved all the way to Manzanillo, the weekend crowds are getting ever larger. Locals tend to congregate in the rowdy but pleasant downstairs bar, where reggae beats into the wee hours. ⊠ *Main road, Manzanillo* ☎ *2759–9073* ▭ *No credit cards.*

$$$$ ⊡ **Almonds & Corals.** Buried in a dark, densely atmospheric beachfront jungle within the Gandoca-Manzanillo Wildlife Refuge, Almonds & Corals takes scatters bungalows throughout its site on freestanding platforms raised on stilts and linked by boardwalks lighted by kerosene lamps. Each safari-style unit is protected by a peaked roof and enclosed in mosquito netting, and has beds, electric lamps, hammocks, and hot water. A fine three-meal restaurant is tucked into the greenery halfway down to the property's exquisite, secluded beach. The concept is quite luxurious for the Caribbean coast, but the locale does provide that close-

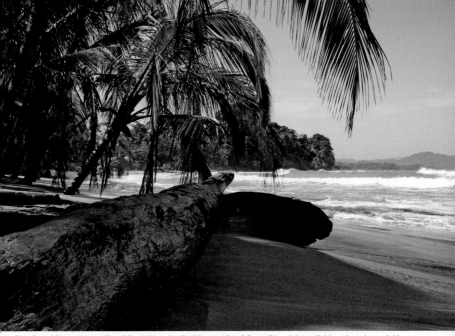

"We found Playa Manzanillo while visiting the Caribbean side of Costa Rica. A beautiful beach and very laid-back atmosphere." —Photo by dgray, Fodors.com member

to-nature experience. Your wake-up call is provided by howler monkeys and chatty parrots. These folks also offer multiday packages that include round-trip transportation from San José. **Pros:** rustic comfort; lots of activities. **Cons:** far from sights; need car to stay here. ⊠ *Near end of road to Manzanillo* ✍ *Apdo. 681–2300, San José* ☎ *2759–9056; 2272–2024 in San José* ⊕ *www.almondsandcorals.com* ↴ *24 bungalows* ☖ *In-room: no a/c, refrigeratorno TV. In-hotel: restaurant, bar, laundry service, Internet terminal* ▭ *AE, D, DC, MC, V* ⦿ *MAP.*

¢ ▦ **Cabinas Something Different.** On a quiet street, these shiny, spic-and-span motel-style cabinas are the nicest option in the village of Manzanillo. Each bright tile-floor unit comes with a TV—quite a rarity in these parts—a table, and a small porch. Several sleep up to four people. **Pros:** good budget value; television. **Cons:** small rooms; spartan rooms. ⊠ *180 m south of Aquamor, Manzanillo* ☎ *2759–9014* ↴ *18 cabinas* ☖ *In-room: no a/c (some), no phone, refrigerator* ▭ *No credit cards* ⦿ *EP.*

CROSSING INTO PANAMA VIA SIXAOLA

Costa Rica's sleepy border post at Sixaola fronts Guabito, Panama's equally quiet border crossing, 44 km (26 mi) south of the turnoff to Puerto Viejo de Talamanca. Both are merely collections of banana-plantation stilt houses and a few stores and bars; neither has any lodging or dining options, but this is a much more low-key crossing into Panama than the busy border post at Paso Canoas on the Pan-American Highway near the Pacific coast. If you've come this far, you're likely headed to **Bocas del Toro**, the real attraction in the northwestern part of Panama. This archipelago of 68 islands continues the Afro-Caribbean and indigenous themes seen on Costa Rica's Atlantic coast, and offers diving, snorkeling, swimming, and wildlife-viewing. The larger islands are home to a growing selection of hotels and restaurants, everything from funky to fabulous. "Bocas" has acquired a cult following among long-term foreign visitors to Costa Rica, who find it a convenient

> **ANOTHER GOOD BOOK**
>
> If you're headed to Panama, we'd be remiss in not recommending that you pick up a copy of *Fodor's Panama* for far more detail about Bocas del Toro and the rest of the country than we can provide here.

place to travel when their permitted three-month status as a tourist has expired, since a quick 72-hour jaunt out of the country gets you another three months in Costa Rica.

■TIP➔ Whatever your destination in Panama, come armed with dollars. Panama uses U.S. currency, but refers to the dollar as the *balboa*. (It does mint its own coins, all the same size as their U.S. counterparts.) No one anywhere will accept or exchange your Costa Rican colones.

Costa Rican rental vehicles may not leave the country, so crossing into Panama as a tourist is an option only via public transportation. The public bus route from San José to Cahuita and Puerto Viejo de Talamanca terminates here at the border approximately six hours after leaving the capital. Taxis in Puerto Viejo de Talamanca charge about $50 for the jaunt to the border, a much quicker and reasonable option if you can split the fare among a group. Disembark and head for the Costa Rican immigration office (☎2754–2044) down a flight of stairs from the west end of a former railroad bridge. Officials place an exit stamp in your passport, after which you walk across the bridge and present your passport to Panamanian immigration. U.S., U.K., and Canadian visitors must also purchase a $5 tourist card for entry into the country; Australian and New Zealand citizens need only their passports.

The **Consulate of Panama** (☎2280–1570) in San José can provide more information. The border crossings are open 7 AM–5 PM (8 AM–6 PM Panamanian time) daily. Set your watch one hour ahead when you enter Panama.

Taxis wait on the Panamanian side to transport you to the small city of Changuinola, the first community of any size inside the country, from which there are bus and air connections for travel farther into Panama. Taxis can also take you to Almirante, where you'll find boat launches to Bocas del Toro.

UNDERSTANDING COSTA RICA

COSTA RICA AT A GLANCE

FAST FACTS

Capital: San José

Type of government: Democratic republic

Independence: September 15, 1821 (from Spain)

Population: 4,248,508

Population density: 82 persons per square km (204 persons per square mi)

Literacy: 95%

Language: Spanish (official); English spoken by most in the tourism industry

Ethnic groups: White (including mestizo) 94%, black 3%, Amerindian 1%, Asian 1%, other 1%

Religion: Roman Catholic 76%, Evangelical Protestant 15%, other 6%, none 3%

GEOGRAPHY AND ENVIRONMENT

Land area: 51,100 square km (19,730 square mi); slightly smaller than the U.S. state of West Virginia

Coastline: 1,290 km (802 mi)

Terrain: Rugged central range with 112 volcanic craters that separates the eastern and western coastal plains

Natural resources: Hydroelectric power, forest products, fisheries products

Natural hazards: Droughts, flash floods, thunderstorms, earthquakes, hurricanes, active volcanoes, landslides

Flora: 9,000 species, including 1,200 orchid species and 800 fern species; tidal mangrove swamps, tropical rain forest, subalpine forest

Fauna: 36,518 species, including 34,000 species of insects and 2,000 species of butterflies

Environmental issues: Deforestation, rapid industrialization and urbanization, air and water pollution, soil degradation, plastic waste, fisheries protection

ECONOMY

Currency: Colón, *(pl.)* colones

GDP: $37.97 billion

Per capita income: $4,670

Unemployment: 6.6%

Major industries: Tourism, microprocessors, food processing, textiles and clothing, construction materials, fertilizer, plastic products

Agricultural products: Bananas, coffee, pineapples, sugarcane, corn, rice, beans, potatoes, beef

Exports: $6.2 billion

Major export products: Bananas, coffee, pineapples, electronic components, fertilizers, sugar, textiles, electricity

Export partners: (in order of volume) U.S., Hong Kong, Holland, Guatemala, Canada, Malaysia, Nicaragua, Germany

Imports: $7.84 billion

Major import products: Chemicals, consumer goods, electronic components, machinery, petroleum products, vehicles

Import partners: U.S. (41%), Japan (5.6%), Venezuela (4.8), Mexico (4.8%), Ireland (4.2%), China (4.2%), Brazil (4.2%)

DID YOU KNOW?

- Tourism earns more foreign exchange than bananas and coffee combined.

- Costa Rica did away with its military in 1949.

- Five percent of the world's identified plant and animal species are found in this country.

- Costa Rica is the home of five active volcanoes—including Volcán Arenal, the second-largest active volcano in the world.

WILDLIFE AND PLANT GLOSSARY

Here is a rundown of some of the most common and attention-grabbing mammals, birds, reptiles, amphibians, plants, and even a few insects that you might encounter. We give the common Costa Rican names, so you can understand the local lingo, followed by the latest scientific terms.

Fauna

Agouti (*guatusa*; *Dasyprocta punctata*): A 20-inch, tail-less rodent with small ears and a large muzzle, the agouti is reddish brown on the Pacific side, more of a tawny orange on the Caribbean slope. It sits on its haunches to eat large seeds and fruit and resembles a large rabbit without the long ears.

Anteater (*oso hormiguero*): Three species of anteater inhabit Costa Rica—the very rare giant (*Myrmecophaga tridactyla*), the nocturnal silky (*Cyclopes didactylus*), and the Collared, or Vested (*Tamandua mexicana*). Only the last is commonly seen, and too often as roadkill. This medium-size anteater, 30 inches long with an 18-inch tail, laps up ants and termites with its long, sticky tongue and has long, sharp claws for ripping into insect nests.

Armadillo (*cusuco*; *Dasypus novemcinctus*): The nine-banded armadillo is widespread in Costa Rica and also found in the southern United States. This nocturnal and solitary edentate roots in soil with a long muzzle for a varied diet of insects, small animals, and plant material.

Baird's Tapir (*danta*; *Tapirus bairdii*): The largest land mammal in Costa Rica (to 6½ feet), Baird's tapir is something like a small rhinoceros without armor. Adapted to a wide range of habitats, it's nocturnal, seldom seen, but said to defecate and sometimes sleep in water. Tapirs are herbivorous and use their prehensile snouts to harvest vegetation. The best opportunities for viewing wild tapirs are in Corcovado National Park.

Bat (*murciélogo*): With more than 100 species, Costa Rica's bats can be found eating fruit, insects, fish, small vertebrates, nectar, and even blood, in the case of the infamous vampire bat (*vampiro, Desmodus rotundus*), which far prefers cattle blood to that of any tourist. As a group, bats are extremely important ecologically, and are essential to seed dispersal, pollination, and controlling insect populations.

Butterfly (*mariposa*): Estimates of the number of butterfly species in Costa Rica vary, but all range in the thousands. The growing number of butterfly gardens popping up around the country is testament to their popularity among visitors. Three Costa Rican Morpho species—spectacular, large butterflies—have a brilliant-blue upper wing surface, giving them their local nickname of *pedazos de ciel* (pieces of sky). The blue morpho (*Morpho peleides*), arguably the most distinctive, is common in moister areas and has an intense ultraviolet upper surface. Adults feed on fermenting fruit; they never visit flowers.

Caiman (*caiman*): The spectacled caiman (*Caiman crocodilus*) is a small crocodilian (to 7 feet) inhabiting freshwater, subsisting mainly on fish. Most active at night (it has bright-red eye shine), it basks by day. It is distinguished from the American crocodile by a sloping brow and smooth back scales.

Coati (*pizote*; *Nasua narica*): This is a long-nose relative of the raccoon, its long tail often held straight up. Lone males or groups of females with young are active during the day, on the ground, or in trees. Omnivorous coatis feed on fruit, invertebrates, and small vertebrates. Unfortunately, many have learned to beg from tourists, especially in Monteverde and on the roads around Arenal.

Cougar (*puma*; *Felis concolor*): Mountain lions are the largest unspotted cats (to 8 feet, including the tail) in Costa Rica. Widespread but rare, they live in essentially all-wild habitats and feed on vertebrates ranging from snakes to deer.

Crocodile (*lagarto*; *Crocodylus acutus*): The American crocodile, up to 16 feet in length, is found in most major river systems, particularly the Tempisque and Tárcoles estuaries. It seldom attacks humans, preferring fish and birds. It's distinguished from the caiman by size, a flat head, narrow snout, and spiky scales.

Ctenosaur (*garrobo; Ctenosaura similis*): Also known as the black, or spiny-tailed, iguana, this is a large (up to 18 inches long with an 18-inch tail) tan lizard with four dark bands on its body and a tail ringed with sharp, curved spines, reminiscent of a dinosaur. Terrestrial and arboreal, it sleeps in burrows or tree hollows. It lives along the coast in the dry northwest and in wetter areas farther south. The fastest known reptile (clocked on land), the ctenosaur has been recorded moving at 21.7 mi per hour.

Dolphin (*delfín*): Several species, including bottlenose dolphins (*Tursiops truncatus*), frolic in Costa Rican waters. Often seen off Pacific shores are spotted dolphins (*Stenella attenuata*), which are small (up to 6 feet), with pale spots on the posterior half of the body; they commonly travel in groups of 20 or more and play around vessels and in bow wakes. Tucuxi dolphins (*Sotalia fluviatilis*) have also been spotted in small groups off the southern Caribbean coast, frequently with bottlenose dolphins.

Frog and Toad (*rana*, frog; *sapo*, toad): Some 120 species of frog exist in Costa Rica; many are nocturnal. The most colorful daytime amphibians are the tiny strawberry poison dart frog (*Dendrobates pumilio*) and green-and-black poison dart frog. The bright coloration of these two species, either red with blue or green hind legs or charcoal black with fluorescent green markings, warns potential predators of their toxicity. The red-eyed leaf frog (*Agalychnis callidryas*) is among the showiest of nocturnal species. The large, brown marine toad (*Bufo marinus*), also called cane toad or giant toad, comes out at night.

Howler Monkey (*mono congo; Alouatta palliata*): These dark, chunky-bodied monkeys (to 22 inches long with a 24-inch tail) with black faces travel in troops of up to 20. Lethargic mammals, they eat leaves, fruits, and flowers. The males' deep, resounding howls sound like lions roaring, but actually serve as communication among and between troops.

Hummingbird (*Trochilidae*): Weighing just a fraction of an ounce, hummingbirds are nonetheless some of the most notable residents of tropical forests. At least 50 varieties can be found in Costa Rica, visiting typically red, tubular flowers in their seemingly endless search for energy-rich nectar. Because of their assortment of iridescent colors and bizarre bills and tail shapes, watching them can be a spectator sport. Best bets are hummingbird feeders and anywhere with great numbers of flowers.

Iguana (*iguana*): Mostly arboreal but good at swimming, the iguana is Costa Rica's largest lizard: males can grow to 10 feet, including tail. Only young green iguanas (*Iguana iguana*) are bright green; adults are much duller, females dark grayish, and males olive (with orangish heads in breeding season). All have round cheek scales and smooth tails.

Jaguar (*tigre; Panthera onca*): The largest New World feline (to 6 feet, with a 2-foot tail), this top-of-the-line predator is exceedingly rare but lives in a wide variety of habitats, from dry forest to cloud forest. It's most common in the vast Amistad Biosphere Reserve, but it is almost never seen in the wild.

Jesus Christ Lizard (*gallego*): Flaps of skin on long toes enable this spectacular lizard to run across water. Costa Rica has three species of this lizard, which is more properly called the basilisk: lineated (*Basiliscus basiliscus*) on the Pacific side is brown with pale lateral stripes; in the Caribbean, emerald (*Basiliscus plumifrons*) is marked with turquoise and black on a green body; and striped (*Basiliscus vittatus*), also on the Caribbean side, resembling the lineated basilisk. Adult males grow to 3 feet (mostly tail), with crests on the head, back, and base of the tail.

Leaf-Cutter Ant (*zompopas*; *Atta spp.*): Found in all lowland habitats, these are the most commonly noticed neotropical ants, and one of the country's most fascinating animal phenomena. Columns of ants carrying bits of leaves twice their size sometimes extend for several hundred yards from an underground nest to plants being harvested. The ants don't eat the leaves; their food is a fungus they cultivate on the leaves.

Macaw (*lapas*): Costa Rica's two species are the scarlet macaw (*Ara macao*), on the Pacific side (Osa Peninsula and Carara Biological Reserve), and the severely threatened great green macaw (*Ara ambigua*), on the Caribbean side. These are huge, raucous parrots with long tails; their immense bills are used to rip fruit apart to reach the seeds. They nest in hollow trees and are victimized by pet-trade poachers and deforestation.

Magnificent Frigatebird (*tijereta del mar*; *Fregata magnificens*): A large, black soaring bird with slender wings and forked tail, this is one of the most effortless and agile flyers in the avian world. More common on the Pacific coast, it doesn't dive or swim but swoops to pluck its food, often from the mouths of other birds.

Manatee (*manatí*; *Trichechus manatus*): Although endangered throughout its range, the West Indian manatee can be spotted in Tortuguero, meandering along in shallow water, browsing on submerged vegetation. The moniker "sea cow" is apt, as they spend nearly all their time resting or feeding. Their large, somewhat amorphous bodies won't win any beauty contests, but they do appear quite graceful.

Margay (*caucel*; *Felis wiedii*): Fairly small, this spotted nocturnal cat (22 inches long, with an 18-inch tail) is similar to the ocelot but has a longer tail and is far more arboreal: mobile ankle joints allow it to climb down trunks head first. It eats small vertebrates.

Motmot (*pájaro bobo*): These handsome, turquoise-and-rufous birds of the understory have racket-shaped tails. Nesting in burrows, they sit patiently while scanning for large insect prey or small vertebrates. Costa Rica has six species.

Northern Jacana (*gallito de agua*; *Jacana spinosa*): These birds are sometimes called "lily trotters" because their long toes allow them to walk on floating vegetation. Feeding on aquatic organisms and plants, they're found in almost any body of water. They expose yellow wing feathers in flight. Sex roles are reversed; "liberated" females are larger and compete for mates (often more than one), whereas the males tend to the nest and care for the young.

Ocelot (*manigordo*; *Felis pardalis*): Mostly terrestrial, this medium-size spotted cat (33 inches long, with a 16-inch tail) is active night and day, and feeds on rodents and other vertebrates. Forepaws are rather large in relation to the body, hence the local name, *manigordo,* which means "fat hand."

Opossum (*zorro pelón*; *Didelphis marsupialis*): Like the kangaroo, the common opossum belongs to that rare breed of mammals known as marsupials, distinguished by their brief gestation period and completion of development and nourishment following birth in the mother's pouch. The Costa Rican incarnation does not "play possum," and will bite if cornered rather than pretend to be dead.

Oropendola (*oropéndola*; *Psarocolius spp.*): These crow-size birds in the oriole family have a bright-yellow tail and nest in colonies, in pendulous nests (up to 6 feet long) built by females in isolated trees. The Montezuma species has an orange beak and blue cheeks, the chestnut-headed has a yellow beak. Males make an unmistakable, loud, gurgling liquid call. The bird is far more numerous on the Caribbean side.

Parakeet and Parrot (*pericos*, parakeets; *loros*, parrots): There are 15 species in Costa Rica (plus two macaws), all clad in green, most with a splash of a primary color or two on the head or wings. They travel in boisterous flocks, prey on immature seeds, and nest in cavities.

Peccary: Piglike animals with thin legs and thick necks, peccaries travel in small groups (larger where the population is still numerous); root in soil for fruit, seeds, and small creatures; and have a strong musk odor. You'll usually smell them before you see them. Costa Rica has two species: the collared peccary (*saíno, Tayassu tajacu*) and the white-lipped peccary (*chancho de monte, Tayassu pecari*). The latter is now nearly extinct.

Pelican (*pelícano*): Large size, a big bill, and a throat pouch make the brown pelican (*Pelecanus occidentalis*) unmistakable in coastal areas (it's far more abundant on the Pacific side). Pelicans often fly in V formations and dive for fish.

Quetzal One of the world's most exquisite birds, the resplendent quetzal (*Pharomachrus mocinno*) was revered by the Maya. Glittering green plumage and the male's long tail coverts draw thousands of people to highland cloud forests for sightings from February to April.

Roseate Spoonbill (*garza rosada; Ajaja ajaja*): Pink plumage and a spatulate bill set this wader apart from all other wetland birds; it feeds by swishing its bill back and forth in water while using its feet to stir up bottom-dwelling creatures. Spoonbills are most common around Palo Verde and Caño Negro.

Sloth (*perezoso*): Costa Rica is home to the brown-throated, three-toed sloth (*Bradypus variegatus*) and Hoffmann's two-toed sloth (*Choloepus hoffmanni*). Both grow to 2 feet, but two-toed (check forelegs) sloths often look bigger because of longer fur and are the only species in the highlands. Sloths are herbivorous, accustomed to a low-energy diet, and well camouflaged.

Snake (*culebra*): Costa Rica's serpents can be found in trees, above and below ground, and even in the sea on the Pacific coast. Most of the more than 125 species are harmless, but are best appreciated from a distance. Notable members of this group include Costa Rica's largest snake, the boa constrictor (*Boa constrictor*), reaching up to 15 feet, and the fer-de-lance (*terciopelo, Bothrops asper*), which is a much smaller (up to 6 feet) but far more dangerous viper.

Spider Monkey (*mono colorado, mono araña*): Lanky and long-tailed, the black-handed spider monkey (*Ateles geoffroyi*) is the largest monkey in Costa Rica (to 24 inches, with a 32-inch tail). Moving in groups of two to four, they eat ripe fruit, leaves, and flowers. Incredible aerialists, they can swing effortlessly through branches using long arms and legs and prehensile tails. They are quite aggressive and will challenge onlookers and often throw down branches. Caribbean and southern Pacific populations are dark reddish brown; northwesterners are blond.

Squirrel Monkey (*mono tití*): The smallest of four Costa Rican monkeys (11 inches, with a 15-inch tail), the red-backed squirrel monkey (*Saimiri oerstedii*) has a distinctive facial pattern (black cap and muzzle, white mask) and gold-orange coloration on its back. It is the only Costa Rican monkey without a prehensile tail. The species travels in noisy, active groups of 20 or more, feeding on fruit and insects. Numbers of this endangered species have been estimated between 2,000 and 4,000 individuals. Most squirrel monkeys in Costa Rica are found in Manuel Antonio National Park, in parts of the Osa Peninsula, and around the Golfo Dulce.

Three-Wattled Bellbird (*pájaro campana; Procnias tricarunculata*): Although endangered, the bellbird can be readily identified in cloud forests (around Monteverde, for example), where it breeds by its extraordinary call, a bold and aggressive "bonk," unlike any other creature in the forest. If you spot a male calling, look for the three pendulous wattles at the base of its beak.

Toucan (*tucán, tucancillo*): The keel-billed toucan (*Ramphastos sulfuratus*) with the rainbow-colored beak is familiar to anyone who's seen a box of Froot Loops cereal. Chestnut-mandibled toucans (*Ramphastos swainsonii*) are the largest (18 inches and 22 inches); as the name implies, their lower beaks are brown. The smaller, stouter emerald toucanet (*Aulacorhynchus prasinus*) and yellow-eared toucanet (*Selenidera spectabilis*) are aptly named. Aracaris (*Pteroglossus Spp.*) are similar to toucans, but colored orange-and-yellow with the trademark toucan bill.

Turtles (*tortuga*): Observing the nesting rituals of the five species of marine turtles here is one of those truly memorable Costa Rican experiences. Each species has its own nesting season and locale. The olive ridley (*lora; Lepidochelys olivacea*) is the smallest of the sea turtles (average carapace, or hardback shell, is 21–29 inches) and the least shy. Thousands engage in nighttime group nesting rituals on the North Pacific's Ostional. At the other extreme, but only slightly farther north on Playa Grande, nests the leatherback (*baula; Dermochelys coriacea*) with its five-foot-long shell. On the north Caribbean coast, Tortuguero hosts four of them: the leatherback, the hawksbill (*carey; Eretmochelys imbricata*), the loggerhead (*caguama; Caretta caretta*), and the green (*tortuga verde; Chelonia mydas*), with its long nesting season (June–October) that draws the most visitors and researchers.

Whales (*ballena*): Humpback whales (*Megaptera novaeanglia*) appear off the Pacific coast between November and February; they migrate from California and as far as Hawaii. You can also spot Sey whales, Bryde's whales, and farther out to sea, blue whales and sperm whales. On the Caribbean side, there are smaller (12 to 14 feet) Koiga whales.

White-Faced Capuchin Monkey (*mono cara blanca; Cebus capuchinus*): Medium-size and omnivorous, this monkey (to 18 inches, with a 20-inch tail) has black fur and a pink face surrounded by a whitish bib. Extremely active foragers, they move singly or in groups of up to 20, examining the environment closely and even coming to the ground. It's the most commonly seen monkey in Costa Rica. It's also the most often fed by visitors, to the point where some monkey populations now have elevated cholesterol levels.

White-Tailed Deer (*venado; Odocoileus virginianus*): Bambi would feel at home in Costa Rica, although his counterparts here are slightly smaller. As befits the name, these animals possess the distinctive white underside to their tail (and to their bellies). They are seen in drier parts of the country, especially in the northwest province of Guanacaste.

White-Throated Magpie-jay (*urraca; Calocitta formosa*): This southern relative of the blue jay, with a long tail and distinctive topknot (crest of forward-curved feathers), is found in the dry northwest. Bold and inquisitive, with amazingly varied vocalizations, these birds travel in noisy groups of four or more.

Flora

Ant-acacia (*acacia; Acacia* spp.): If you'll be in the tropical dry forest of Guanacaste, learn to avoid this plant. As if its sharp thorns weren't enough, acacias exhibit an intense symbiosis with various ant species (*Pseudomyrmex* spp.) that will attack anything—herbivores, other plants, and unaware human visitors that come in contact with the tree. The ants and the acacias have an intriguing relationship, though, so do look, but don't touch.

Bromeliad (*piña silvestre*): Members of the family Bromeliaceae are *epiphytes,* living on the trunk and branches of trees. They are not parasitic, however, and so have adapted to acquire all the necessary water and nutrients from what falls into the central "tank" formed by the leaf structure. Amphibians and insects also use the water held in bromeliads to reproduce, forming small aquatic communities perched atop tree branches. In especially wet areas, small bromeliads can even be found on power lines. Their spectacular, colorful efflorescences make popular—and expensive—houseplants in northern climes.

Heliconia (*heliconia; Heliconia* spp.): It's hard to miss these stunning plants, many of which have huge inflorescences of red, orange, and yellow, sometimes shaped like lobster claws, and leaves very much the size and shape of a banana plant. With luck, you'll catch a visiting hummingbird with a beak specially designed to delve into a heliconia flower—truly a visual treat.

Mangroves (*manglares*): Taken together, this handful of salt-tolerant trees with tangled, above-ground roots make up their own distinct ecosystem. Buttressing the land against the sea, they serve as nurseries for countless species of fish, crabs, and other marine animals and provide roosting habitat for marine birds. Mangroves are found on the coast in protected areas such as bays and estuaries.

Naked Indian Tree (*indio desnudo; Bursera simaruba*): This tree can be found in forests throughout Costa Rica, often forming living fences, and is instantly identifiable by its orange bark that continually sloughs off, giving rise to another common name, the sunburnt tourist tree. One theory suggests that the shedding of its bark aids in removing parasites from the tree's exterior.

Orchid (*orquídea*): The huge Orchidaceae family has more than 1,200 representatives in Costa Rica alone, with nearly 90% percent living as epiphytes on other plants. The great diversity of the group includes not only examples of great beauty but exquisite adaptations between flowers and their insect pollinators. With a combination of rewards (nectar) and trickery (visual and chemical cues), orchids exhibit myriad ways of enticing insects to cooperate.

Strangler Fig (*Matapalo; Ficus spp.*): Starting as seedlings high in the canopy, these aggressive plants grow both up toward the light, and down to the soil, slowly taking over the host tree. Eventually they encircle and appear to "strangle" the host, actually killing it by hogging all the available sunlight, leaving a ring of fig trunk around an empty interior. Figs with ripe fruit are excellent places for wildlife-spotting, as they attract monkeys, birds, and an assortment of other creatures.

MENU GUIDE

Rice and beans are the heart of Costa Rica's *comida típica* (typical food). It's possible to order everything from sushi to crepes in and around San José, but most Ticos have a simple diet built around rice, beans, and the myriad fruits and vegetables that flourish here. Costa Rican food isn't spicy, and many dishes are seasoned with the same five ingredients—onion, salt, garlic, cilantro, and red bell pepper.

SPANISH	ENGLISH
GENERAL DINING	
Almuerzo	Lunch
Bocas	Appetizers or snacks (literally "mouthfuls") served with drinks in the tradition of Spanish tapas
Casado	Heaping plate of rice, beans, fried plantains, cabbage salad, tomatoes, macarrones (noodles), and fish, chicken, or meat—or any variation thereof; casado and plato del día are often used interchangeably.
Cena	Dinner
Desayuno	Breakfast
Plato del día	Plate of the day
Soda	An inexpensive café; casados are always found at sodas.
ESPECIALIDADES (SPECIALTIES)	
Arreglados	Sandwiches or meat and vegetable puff pastry
Arroz con mariscos	Fried rice with fish, shrimp, octopus, and clams, or whatever's fresh that day
Arroz con pollo	Chicken with rice
Camarones	Shrimp
Ceviche	Chilled, raw seafood marinated in lime juice, served with chopped onion and garlic
Chilaquiles	Meat-stuffed tortillas
Chorreados	Corn pancakes, served with natilla (sour cream)
Corvina	Sea bass

SPANISH	ENGLISH
Empanadas	Savory or sweet pastry turnover filled with fruit or meat and vegetables
Empanaditas	Small empanadas
Gallo pinto	Rice sautéed with black beans (literally, "spotted rooster"), often served for breakfast
Langosta	Lobster
Langostino	Prawns
Olla de carne	Soup of beef, chayote squash, corn, yuca (a tuber), and potatoes
Palmitos	Hearts of palm, served in salads or as a side dish.
Pejibaye	A nutty, orange-colored palm fruit eaten in salads, soups, and as a snack
Pescado ahumado	Smoked marlin
Picadillo	Chayote squash, potatoes, carrots, or other vegetables chopped into small cubes and combined with onions, garlic, and ground beef
Pozol	Corn soup
Salsa caribeño	A combination of tomatoes, onions, and spices that accompanies most fish dishes on the Caribbean coast

POSTRES (DESSERTS) & DULCES (SWEETS)

Cajeta de coco	Fudge made with coconut and orange peel
Cajeta	Molasses-flavored fudge
Dulce de leche	Thick syrup of boiled milk and sugar
Flan	Caramel-topped egg custard
Mazamorra	Cornstarch pudding
Pan de maiz	Sweet corn bread
Torta chilena	Flaky, multilayered cake with dulce de leche filling
Tres leches cake	"Three milks" cake, made with condensed and evaporated milk and cream

SPANISH	ENGLISH

FRUTAS (FRUITS)

Aguacate	Avocado
Anon	Sugar apple; sweet white flesh; resembles an artichoke with a thick rind
Banano	Banana
Bilimbi	Looks like a miniature cucumber crossed with a star fruit; ground into a savory relish
Fresa	Strawberry
Cas	A smaller guava
Granadilla	Passion fruit
Guanábana	Soursop; large, spiky yellow fruit with white flesh and a musky taste
Guayaba	Guava
Mamon chino	Rambutan; red spiky ball protecting a white fruit similar to a lychee
Mango	Many varieties, from sour green to succulently sweet Oro (golden); March is the height of mango season.
Manzana de agua	Water apple, shaped like a pear; juicy but not very sweet
Marañon	Cashew fruit; used in juices
Melon	Cantaloupe
Mora	Blackberry
Palmito	Heart of palm
Piña	Pineapple
Papaya	One of the most popular and ubiquitous fruits
Pipa	Green coconut; sold at roadside stands with ends chopped off and straws stuck inside
Sandia	Watermelon
Carambola	Star fruit

SPANISH	ENGLISH
BEBIDAS (BEVERAGES)	
Agua dulce	Hot water sweetened with raw sugarcane
Batido	Fruit shake made with milk (con leche) or water (con agua)
Café con leche	Coffee with hot milk
Café negro	Black coffee
Fresco natural	Fresh-squeezed juice
Guaro	Harsh, clear spirit distilled from fermented sugarcane
Horchata	Cinnamon-flavored rice drink.
Refrescos	Tropical fruit smoothie with ice and sugar

VOCABULARY

ENGLISH	SPANISH	PRONUNCIATION

BASICS

ENGLISH	SPANISH	PRONUNCIATION
Yes/no	Sí/no	see/no
OK.	De acuerdo.	de a-**kwer**-doe
Please.	Por favor.	pore fah-**vore**
May I?	¿Me permite?	may pair-**mee**-tay
Thank you (very much).	(Muchas) gracias.	(**moo**-chas) **grah**-see-as
You're welcome.	Con mucho gusto.	con **moo**-cho **goose**-toe
Excuse me.	Con permiso.	con pair-**mee**-so
Pardon me.	¿Perdón?	pair-**dohn**
Could you tell me?	¿Podría decirme?	po-dree-ah deh-**seer**-meh
I'm sorry.	Disculpe	Dee-**skool**-peh
Good morning!	¡Buenos días!	**bway**-nohs **dee**-ahs
Good afternoon!	¡Buenas tardes!	**bway**-nahs **tar**-dess
Good evening!	¡Buenas noches!	**bway**-nahs **no**-chess
Goodbye!	¡Adiós!/¡Hasta luego!	ah-dee-**ohss**/**ah**-stah-lwe-go
Mr./Mrs.	Señor/Señora	sen-**yor**/sen-**yohr**-ah
Miss	Señorita	sen-yo-**ree**-tah
Pleased to meet you.	Mucho gusto.	**moo**-cho **goose**-toe
How are you?	¿Cómo está usted?	**ko**-mo es-**tah** oo-**sted**
Very well, thank you.	Muy bien, gracias.	**moo**-ee bee-**en**, **grah**-see-as
And you?	¿Y usted?	ee oos-**ted**

DAYS OF THE WEEK

ENGLISH	SPANISH	PRONUNCIATION
Sunday	domingo	doe-**meen**-goh
Monday	lunes	**loo**-ness
Tuesday	martes	**mahr**-tess
Wednesday	miércoles	me-**air**-koh-less

ENGLISH	SPANISH	PRONUNCIATION
Thursday	jueves	hoo-**ev**-ess
Friday	viernes	vee-**air**-ness
Saturday	sábado	**sah**-bah-doh

MONTHS

January	enero	eh-**neh**-roh
February	febrero	feh-**breh**-roh
March	marzo	**mahr**-soh
April	abril	ah-**breel**
May	mayo	**my**-oh
June	junio	**hoo**-nee-oh
July	julio	**hoo**-lee-yoh
August	agosto	ah-**ghost**-toh
September	septiembre	sep-tee-**em**-breh
October	octubre	oak-**too**-breh
November	noviembre	no-vee-**em**-breh
December	diciembre	dee-see-**em**-breh

USEFUL PHRASES

Do you speak English?	¿Habla usted inglés?	**ah**-blah oos-**ted** in-**glehs**
I don't speak Spanish.	No hablo español.	no **ah**-bloh es-pahn-**yol**
I don't under-stand (you).	No entiendo.	no en-tee-**en**-doh
I understand (you).	Entiendo.	en-tee-**en**-doh
I don't know.	No sé.	no seh
I am American/ British.	Soy americano (americana) / inglés(a).	soy ah-meh-ree- **kah**-no (ah-meh-ree- **kah**-nah) / in-**glehs (ah)**
What's your name?	¿Cómo se llama usted?	koh-mo seh **yah**-mah **oos**-ted
My name is . . .	Me llamo . . .	may **yah**-moh

ENGLISH	SPANISH	PRONUNCIATION
What time is it?	¿Qué hora es?	keh **o**-rah es
It is one, two, three . . . o'clock.	Es la una. . . . Son las dos, tres.	es la **oo**-nah/sohn lahs dohs, tress
How?	¿Cómo?	**koh**-mo
When?	¿Cuándo?	**kwahn**-doh
This/Next week	Esta semana / la semana que entra	**es**-teh seh-**mah**- nah / lah seh-**mah**- nah keh **en**-trah
This/Next month	Este mes/el próximo mes	**es**-teh mehs/el **proke**-see-mo mehs
This/Next year	Este año/el año que viene	**es**-teh **ahn**-yo/el **ahn**-yo keh vee-**yen**-ay
Yesterday/today/ tomorrow	Ayer/hoy/mañana	ah-**yehr**/oy/mahn- **yah**-nah
This morning/ afternoon	Esta mañana/ tarde	**es**-tah mahn-**yah**- nah/ **tar**-deh
Tonight	Esta noche	**es**-tah **no**-cheh
What?	¿Qué?	keh
What is it?	¿Qué es esto?	keh es **es**-toh
Why?	¿Por qué?	pore **keh**
Who?	¿Quién?	kee-**yen**
Where is . . . ?	¿Dónde está . . . ?	**dohn**-deh es-**tah**
the bus stop?	la parada del autobus?	la pah-**rah**-dah del oh-toh-**boos**
the post office?	la oficina de correos?	la oh-fee-**see**-nah deh koh-**reh**-os
the museum?	el museo?	el moo-**seh**-oh
the hospital?	el hospital?	el ohss-pee-**tal**
the bathroom?	el baño?	el **bahn**-yoh
Here/there	Aquí/allá	ah-**key**/ah-**yah**
Open/closed	Abierto/cerrado	ah-bee-**er**-toh/ ser-**ah**-doh
Left/right	Izquierda/derecha	iss-key-**er**-dah/ dare-**eh**-chah
Straight ahead	Derecho	dare-**eh**-choh
Is it near/far?	¿Está cerca/lejos?	es-**tah** **sehr**-kah/ **leh**-hoss

ENGLISH	SPANISH	PRONUNCIATION
I'd like . . .	Quisiera . . .	kee-see-ehr-ah
a room.	un cuarto/una habitación.	oon **kwahr**-toh/ **oo**-nah ah-bee- tah-see-**on**
the key.	la llave.	lah **yah**-veh
a newspaper.	un periódico.	oon pehr-ee-**oh**- dee-koh
a stamp.	la estampilla.	lah es-stahm-**pee**-yah
I'd like to buy . . .	Quisiera comprar . . .	kee-see-**ehr**-ah kohm-**prahr**
a dictionary.	un diccionario.	oon deek-see-oh- **nah**-ree-oh
soap.	jabón.	hah-**bohn**
suntan lotion.	loción bronceadora.	loh-see-**ohn** brohn- seh-ah-**do**-rah
a map.	un mapa.	oon **mah**-pah
a magazine.	una revista.	**oon**-ah reh-**veess**-tah
a postcard.	una tarjeta postal.	**oon**-ah tar-**het**-ah post-**ahl**
How much is it?	¿Cuánto cuesta?	**kwahn**-toh **kwes**-tah
Telephone	Teléfono	tel-**ef**-oh-no
Help!	¡Auxilio!	owk-**see**-lee-oh
	¡Ayuda!	ah-**yoo**-dah
	¡Socorro!	soh-**kohr**-roh
Fire!	¡Incendio!	en-**sen**-dee-oo
Caution!/Look out!	¡Cuidado!	kwee-**dah**-doh

ENGLISH	SPANISH	PRONUNCIATION

SALUD (HEALTH)

ENGLISH	SPANISH	PRONUNCIATION
I am ill.	Estoy enfermo(a).	es-**toy** en-**fehr**- moh(mah)
Please call a doctor.	Por favor llame a un médico.	pohr fah-**vor ya**-meh ah oon **med**-ee-koh
acetaminophen	acetaminofen	a-say-ta-**mee**-no-fen
ambulance	ambulancia	ahm-boo-**lahn**-see-a
antibiotic	antibiótico	ahn-tee-bee-**oh**-tee-co
aspirin	aspirina	ah-spi-**ree**-na
capsule	cápsula	**cahp**-soo-la
clinic	clínica	**clee**-nee-ca
cold	resfriado	rays-free-**ah**-do
cough	tos	toess
diarrhea	diarrea	dee-ah-**ray**-a
fever	fiebre	fee-**ay**-bray
flu	Gripe	**gree**-pay
headache	dolor de cabeza	doh-**lor** day cah- **bay**-sa
hospital	hospital	oh-spee-**tahl**
medication	medicamento	meh-dee-cah-**men**-to
pain	dolor	doh-**lor**
pharmacy	farmacia	fahr-**mah**-see-a
physician	médico	**meh**-dee-co
prescription	receta	ray-**say**-ta
stomachache	dolor de estómago	doh-**lor** day eh-**sto**-mah-go

Travel Smart
Costa Rica

WORD OF MOUTH

"What we did find confounding in CR that we have never experienced before was that as soon as you park your car, there is a certain local interest in it. This happened in both business and rural centers. At the grocery store and at the gas station, an adult stayed with the car and a few kids and the other adult went and shopped or made the potty run. We then switched off."

—mom23rugrats

www.fodors.com/community

GETTING HERE AND AROUND

■ AIR TRAVEL

If you are visiting several regions of the country, flying into San José's Aeropuerto Internacional Juan Santamaría, in the center of the country, is the best option. Flying into Liberia's Daniel Oduber Quirós International Airport makes sense if you are planning to spend your vacation in Guanacaste. Bus travel time between the Liberia airport and most of the resorts is less than two hours.

Most travelers fly into the larger San José airport, the transportation hub to nearly every point in the country. Rarely does an international flight get into San José early enough to make a domestic connection, particularly in the rainy season, as the weather is typically unsuitable for flying in the afternoon. So you'll likely end up spending your first night in or near the city, and leave for your domestic destination the next morning out of the SANSA terminal next to the international airport or via Nature Air out of tiny Tobias Bolaños Airport.

Heavy rains in the afternoon and evening during the May-to-November rainy season occasionally cause flights coming into San José to be rerouted to Panama City, where you may be forced to spend the night. October tends to be the worst month for reroutes. ■TIP→ In the rainy season, always book a flight with the earliest arrival time available.

Once you're in Costa Rica, some airlines recommend that you call the San José office about three days before your return flight to reconfirm; others, such as TACA, explicitly say it's not necessary. It's always a good idea to call the local office the day before you are scheduled to return home to make sure your flight time hasn't changed.

The tiny, domestic passenger planes in Costa Rica require that you pack light. A luggage weight limit of 12 kilograms (27 pounds) is imposed by SANSA; Nature Air allows 13.6 kilograms (30 pounds). On some flights extra luggage is allowed, but is charged about $0.55 to $1 per pound. Heavy packers can leave their surplus for free in a locked area at Nature Air's terminal. SANSA does not store extra baggage.

If you arrive in Costa Rica and your baggage doesn't, the first thing you should do is go to the baggage claims counter and file an official report with your specific contact information. Then call your airline to find out if they can track it and how long you have to wait—generally bags are located within two days. Continue on your trip as you can; bags can be sent to you just about anywhere in the country. Don't expect too much from local officials; try to get updates from the airline directly.

If your bag has been searched and contents are missing or damaged, file a claim with the TSA Consumer Response Center as soon as possible. If your bags arrive damaged or fail to arrive at all, file a written report with the airline before leaving the airport.

When you fly out of Costa Rica, you'll have to pay a $26 airport departure tax in colones or with a Visa credit card. You can pay the tax upon arrival or departure at the Bancrédito counter in the airport, or at any Bancrédito or Banco de Costa Rica branch in Costa Rica during your trip. Lines can be long, so don't leave it until the last minute. A few Guanacaste hotels will collect the tax for you if you are flying out of Liberia.

Airline Security Issues Transportation Security Administration (⊕ www.tsa.gov) has answers for almost every question that might come up.

AIRPORTS

Costa Rica has two international airports. Aeropuerto Internacional Juan Santamaría (SJO) is the country's main airport. It's about 17 km (10 mi), or 30 minutes by car, northwest of downtown San José, just outside the city of Alajuela. The SANSA terminal for domestic flights is here. The country's other international airport is Daniel Oduber Quirós International Airport (LIR), a small airport near Liberia, in the North Pacific, the hub for domestic charter airline Macaw Air. Four commercial airlines fly to Liberia: American Airlines, from Dallas and Miami; Delta, from Atlanta; Continental, from Houston; and US Airways from Charlotte, North Carolina; regularly scheduled charter flights from the United States are few. The tiny Tobias Bolaños airport (SYQ), in the San José suburb of Pavas (west of the city), serves domestic airline Nature Air, domestic charter companies, and a handful of private planes.

Other places where planes land in Costa Rica aren't exactly airports. They're more like a carport with a landing strip, at which an airline representative arrives just minutes before a plane is due to land or take off.

Most North American flights arrive at this airport in the evening and depart early in the morning, which are the busiest times. Prepare yourself for long waits at immigration and customs, and for check-in and security checkpoints at both airports. Enhanced security measures took effect in 2010. Liquids (over three ounces) and powders are not permitted through security checkpoints or the gates. Carry-on bags are searched again at the gates and you will be patted down. Get to the airport three hours before your flight—Juan Santamaría is a full-service airport with many arrivals and departures each day, so if you miss your flight or have some other unexpected mishap, you're better off here. Fares are usually lower to San José than to Liberia.

Airport Information Aeropuerto Internacional Daniel Oduber Quirós (*LIR* ✢ *13 km/8 mi west of Liberia* ☎ *2668–1010 in Costa Rica*). **Aeropuerto Internacional Juan Santamaría** (*SJO* ✢ *17 km/10 mi northwest of downtown San José, just outside Alajuela* ☎ *2437–2400, 2437–2626 in Costa Rica for departure and arrival info*). **Aeropuerto Internacional Tobías Bolaños** (*SYQ* ✢ *6 km/4 mi west of San José, Pavas* ☎ *2232–2820 in Costa Rica*).

GROUND TRANSPORTATION

At Aeropuerto Internacional Juan Santamaría, you exit the terminal into a fume-filled parking area flanked by hordes of taxis and tour vans. If you're with a tour, you need only look for a representative of your tour company with a sign that bears your name. If you need a taxi, first buy a voucher at a counter just to the left of the arrivals exit, then present it to the driver of one of the orange Taxis Unidos cabs (no other taxis are allowed in the arrivals area). Rates are standardized to the various parts of town; most areas of San José are $20 to $22. Avoid the shuttle companies' *collectivos,* or minivans—they're almost the same price as a taxi (for two or fewer people), but the van is often crammed with other passengers, and you'll have to make stops at their hotels, making your transfer another journey in itself.

FLIGHTS

From the United States: American flies from Miami and Dallas; Continental flies from Houston and Newark; Delta flies from Atlanta; US Airways flies from Charlotte; Spirit Air flies from Fort Lauderdale; Jet Blue flies from Orlando; Frontier flies from Denver; Central American airline TACA flies from Miami, New York, and Los Angeles; and Dutch airline Martinair flies from Miami and Orlando. From New York, flights to San José are 5½ hours nonstop or 7 to 8 hours via Miami. From Los Angeles, flights are about 5½ hours nonstop or 8½ hours via Houston; from Houston, 3½ hours nonstop; from Miami, 3 hours; from Charlotte, 4 hours; and from Chicago, 7 hours, through Houston or Charlotte. In general, nonstop flights aren't that much more expensive. Median ticket prices from hubs such as New York, Los Angeles, and Seattle hover between $400 and $600, although the range can vary widely up or down.

Other than obvious considerations such as price and scheduling, a regional airline like TACA (a Central American airline) is a good choice if you're visiting more than one Central American country; U.S. airlines don't serve routes such as Costa Rica–Honduras.

From elsewhere in Central America: international flights to Costa Rica tend to be cheaper than those to Nicaragua or Panama, so if you're doing two or three countries, it makes sense, budget-wise, to start in Costa Rica. Copa and TACA fly between Panama City and San José and between Managua, Nicaragua, and San José. Nature Air flies between Bocas del Toro, Panama, and San José. At this writing, Nature Air flights into Limón were still on offer, but the fate of the route was uncertain because of infrastructure problems. Given Costa Rica's often-difficult driving conditions, distances that appear short on a map can represent hours of driving on dirt roads pocked with craters; buses can be a slow and uncomfortable way to travel. Domestic flights are a desirable and practical option. And because 4WD rental rates can be steep, flying is often cheaper than driving. Most major destinations are served by daily domestic flights.

The informality of domestic air service—"airports" other than Liberia and San José usually consist of only an airstrip with no central building at which to buy tickets—means you might want to purchase your domestic airplane tickets in advance (by phone or online), although you can buy them at the San José or Liberia airports or at travel agencies once you're in the country. In theory, you can purchase tickets up to two hours before the flight departs. This is a potentially viable option in the May-through-November low season, but we recommend grabbing a seat as soon as you know your itinerary.

There are two major domestic commercial airlines: SANSA and Nature Air. Most Nature Air and SANSA flights leave from the San José area (⇨ *Airports*). Commercial planes are small—holding between 6 and 19 passengers. Charter company Macaw Air flies its five-passenger Cessna 206 out of Liberia, allowing you to bypass San José altogether. Domestic flights originating in San José are generally nonstop, with the exception of some flights to the far south, where you might stop in Drake Bay first, then continue on to Puerto Jiménez, for example. SANSA and Nature Air both have a few nonstop interdestinational flights, such as Tamarindo–Liberia, and a number of flights with quick connections or stops. You can buy SANSA and Nature Air tickets online, over the phone, and at most travel agencies in Costa Rica. Reserve Macaw Air tickets by e-mail or by phone.

Charter flights within Costa Rica are not as expensive as one might think, and can be an especially good deal if you are traveling in a group. If a group this size charters a small plane, the price per person will be only slightly more than taking a regularly scheduled domestic flight, and you can set your own departure time. The country has dozens of airstrips that are accessible only by charter planes. Charter planes are most often booked through tour operators, travel agents, or remote lodges. Most charter planes are smaller than domestic commercial planes.

■TIP➔ **Don't book a domestic flight for the day you arrive in or leave Costa Rica; connections will be extremely tight, if possible at all, and you'll be at the mercy of temperamental weather and delays.**

Airline Contacts American Airlines (☎ *800/433–7300, 2257–1266 in Costa Rica* ⊕ *www.aa.com*). **Continental Airlines** (☎ *800/231–0856 for international reservations, 0800/2044–0005 in Costa Rica* ⊕ *www.continental.com*). **Delta Airlines** (☎ *800/241–4141 for international reservations, 0800/2056–2002 in Costa Rica* ⊕ *www.delta.com*). **Frontier Airlines** (☎ *800/432–1359 for international reservations* ⊕ *www.frontierairlines.com*). **Jet Blue** (☎ *800/538–2583 for international reservations* ⊕ *www.jetblue.com*). **Martinair** (☎ *800/627–8462 for international*

NICARAGUA

Los Chiles
Upala
Barra del Colorado
CARIBBEAN SEA
Tortuguero

Liberia
Bagaces
Parismina
Gulf of Papagayo
La Fortuna
Guápiles
Limón
Filadelfia (Four Seasons)

Tamárindo
Nicoya
Gulf of Nicoya
Cahuita
Nosara
Chacarita
San José
Atirro

Sámara
Punta Islita
Playa Coyote
Tambor
Parrita
San Isidro

PACIFIC OCEAN
Quepos
Buenos Aires

San Vito

Palmar Sur
Río Claro
Coto 47
Drake
Golfito

Domestic Flights

0 — 30 miles
0 — 45 km

Puerto Jiménez
Carate
La Sirena

PANAMA

reservations ⊕ www.martinair.com). **US Airways** (☎ 800/622–1015 for international reservations, 0800/2011–0793 in Costa Rica ⊕ www.usairways.com).

Domestic and Charter Airlines Aerobell Air Charter (☎ 2290–0000 in Costa Rica ⊕ www.aerobell.com). **Copa** (☎ 800/359–2672 in U.S. and Canada, 2223–2672 in Costa Rica ⊕ www.copaair.com). **Macaw Air** (☎ 8364–1223 in Costa Rica ⊕ www.macawair. com). **Nature Air** (☎ 800/235–9272 in North America, 2299–6000 in Costa Rica ⊕ www. natureair.com). **SANSA** (☎ 2290–4100 in Costa Rica ⊕ www.flysansa.com). **TACA** (☎ 400–8222 in U.S., 2299–8222 in Costa Rica ⊕ www.taca.com) .

▌BUS TRAVEL

Tica Bus has daily runs between Costa Rica and Panama or Nicaragua; Transnica has daily service between Costa Rica and Granada and Managua. We recommend choosing Tica Bus if at all possible, but Transnica is acceptable in a pinch. Both companies have comfortable, air-conditioned coaches with videos and onboard toilets, and help with border procedures.

All Costa Rican towns are connected by regular bus service. Bus service in Costa Rica is reliable, comprehensive, and inexpensive. Buses between major cities are modern and air-conditioned, but once you get into the rural areas, you may get a converted school bus without air-conditioning. The kind of bus you get is the luck of the draw (no upgrades here). Bus travel in Costa Rica is formal, meaning no pigs or chickens inside and no people or luggage on the roof. On longer routes, buses stop midway at modest restaurants. Near the ends of their runs many nonexpress buses turn into large taxis, dropping passengers off one by one at their destinations; to save time, take a *directo* (express) bus. Be prepared for bus-company employees and bus drivers to speak Spanish only.

The main inconvenience of long-distance buses, aside from being much slower than flying, is that you usually have to return to San José to travel between outlying regions. For example, a bus from San José to the Osa Peninsula is nine hours or more, whereas the flight is one hour. Shorter distances reduce the difference—the bus to Quepos is 3½ hours and the flight 30 minutes—and in those cases the huge price difference might be worth the extra hours of travel. There is no main bus station in San José; buses leave from a variety of departure points, depending on the region they serve.

■ TIP→ Don't put your belongings in the overhead bin unless you have to, and if you do, keep your eye on them. If anyone—even someone who looks like a bus employee—offers to put your luggage on the bus or in the luggage compartment underneath for you, politely decline. If you must put your luggage underneath the bus, get off quickly when you arrive to retrieve it.

Most bus companies don't have printed bus schedules to give out, although departure times may be printed on a sign at the bus company's office and ticket window. Bus-line phones are usually busy or go unanswered. The schedules and prices we list are accurate at this writing, but change frequently. ■ TIP→ For the most-reliable schedule information, go to the bus station a day before your departure. The ICT tourist office (⇨ *Visitor Information below*) hands out bus schedules and provides a PDF version on its Web site, but this should be used as only a rough guide, as it is updated infrequently. Hotel employees can usually give you the information you need.

Buses usually depart and arrive on time; they may even leave a few minutes before the scheduled departure time if full.

Tickets are sold at bus stations and on the buses themselves; reservations aren't accepted, and you must pay in person with cash. If you pay on the bus, be sure to have loose change and small bills handy; avoid paying with a 10,000 colón bill. Buses to popular beach and mountain destinations often sell out on weekends and the days before and after a holiday. It's also difficult to get tickets back to San José on Sunday afternoon. Some companies won't sell you a round-trip ticket from the departure point; especially during the peak season, make sure the first thing you do upon arrival in your destination is to buy a return ticket. Sometimes tickets include seat numbers, which are usually printed on the tops of the chairs. Smoking is not permitted on buses.

Two private bus companies, Gray Line and Interbus, travel to the most popular tourist destinations in modern, air-conditioned vans. Interbus vans usually seat seven people, and coaches can also be reserved for large groups; Gray Line vans seat 14 to 20 people. Be sure to double-check information that is listed on the Web site—published prices may not be accurate and routes are not always running. This service costs about $25 to $50 one way, but can take hours off your trip. Gray Line has a weekly pass (around $132, depending on route) good for unlimited travel for one week on a specific route of your choice; reservations need to be made 24 hours in advance. Interbus offers three- to seven-trip Flexipasses; prices range from $120 to $265 and the passes are good for one month. Hotel-to-hotel service is offered as long as your lodging is on the route; if you're heading off the beaten track, it's a hotel-to-nearest-hotel service.

Bus Information Tica Bus (✉ *200 m north and 100 m west of Torre Mercedes, Paseo Colón, San José* ☏ *2223–8680* ⊕ *www.ticabus. com*). **Transnica** (✉ *C. 22, Avdas. 3–5, San José* ☏ *2223–4123* ⊕ *www.transnica.com*).

Shuttle-Van Services **Costa Rica Shuttle**
(☎ *2289–9509* ⊕ *www.costaricashuttle.com*).
Gray Line (☎ *2220–2126, 800/719–3905 in
North America* ⊕ *www.graylinecostarica.com*).
Interbus (☎ *2283–5573*
⊕ *www.interbusonline.com*).

▌CAR TRAVEL

Hiring a car with a driver makes the most
sense for sightseeing in and around San
José. You can also usually hire a taxi
driver to ferry you around; most will
stick to the meter, which at this writing
will tick at a rate of about $5 per hour
for the time the driver is waiting for you.
At $75 to $120 per day plus the driver's
food, hiring a driver for areas outside the
San José area costs almost the same as
renting a 4WD, but is more expensive
for multiday trips, when you'll also have
to pay for the driver's room. Some drivers are also knowledgeable guides; others just drive. Unless they're driving large
passenger vans for established companies,
it's doubtful that drivers have any special
training or licensing. Hotels can usually
direct you to trusted drivers; you can also
find recommendations on www.fodors.
com. Alternatively, Alamo (⇨ *below*) provides professional car-and-driver services
for minimum three-day rentals (available
May to November only). You pay $75 on
top of the rental fee, plus the driver's food
and lodging. Costa Rica Shuttle (⇨ *By
Bus*) provides drivers on similar terms
for $130 per day.

Most rental companies have an office close
to Aeropuerto Internacional Juan Santamaría where you can drop off your car
(even if you picked up the car at another
San José branch) and provide transport
to get you to your flight. Leave yourself a
half hour for the return time and shuttle.

GASOLINE

There is no self-service gas in Costa Rica;
24-hour stations are generally available
only in San José or on the Pan-American
Highway. Most other stations are open

from about 7 to 7, some until midnight. It
is not customary to tip attendants.

Gas prices are fixed by the government,
and gas stations around the country are
legally bound to stick to the determined
prices. Ten-percent-ethanol gas is gradu-
ally being introduced. Try to fill your tank
in cities—gas is more expensive (and more
likely to be dirty) at informal fill-up places
in rural areas, where gas stations can be
few and far between. Major credit cards
are widely accepted. Ask the attendant
if you want a *factura* (receipt). Regular
unleaded gasoline is called *regular* and
high-octane unleaded is called *súper*. Gas
is sold by the liter.

PARKING

On-street parking is scarce in downtown San José; where you find it, you'll
also find *guachimanes* (informal, usually
self-appointed guards). They freely admit
they don't get paid enough to actually get
involved if someone tries something with
your car, but it's best to give them a couple of hundred colones per hour anyway.
In centers such as San José, Alajuela, and
Heredia, you'll find several signs with a
large E in a red circle, and the words *con
boleto* (with a ticket). These tickets can be
bought for ½ hour (200 colones), 1 hour
(400 colones) or 2 hours (800 colones) at
the respective municipal hall. *It's a 4,000-
colón fine (about $7) if you're caught in
one of these spaces without a ticket.*

Safer and ubiquitous are the public lots
(*parqueos*), which average flat rates of
approximately $1.25 per hour. Most are
open late, especially near hopping nightspots or theaters, but check beforehand.
Never leave anything inside the car. It is illegal to park in the zones marked by yellow
curb paint, or in front of garage doors or
driveways, usually marked with signs reading *No Estacionar* (No Parking). Downtown parking laws are strictly enforced;
the fine for illegal parking is 5,000 colones
(about $9). However, the city center's nar-
row throughways are often bottlenecked
by "waiting" cars and taxis—double-
parked with someone in the car. Despite

the cacophonic honking, this is largely tolerated. Outside of the main hubs of the Central Valley, parking rules are far more lax, and *guachimanes,* private walled, and guarded hotel or restaurant parking are the rule, with few public lots.

RENTAL CARS

When you reserve a car, ask about cancellation penalties, taxes, drop-off charges (if you're planning to pick up the car in one city and leave it in another), and surcharges (for being under or over a certain age, for additional drivers, or for driving across state or country borders or beyond a specific distance from your point of rental). All these things can add substantially to your costs. Request such extras as car seats and GPS devices when you book.

Rates are sometimes—but not always—better if you book in advance or reserve through a rental agency's Web site. There are other reasons to book ahead, though: for popular destinations, during busy times of the year, or to ensure that you get certain types of cars (vans, SUVs, exotic sports cars).

■ TIP→ If you're planning to go to only one or two major areas, taking a shuttle van or a domestic flight is usually a better and cheaper option than driving. Renting is a good choice if you're destination hopping, staying at a hotel that's a trek to town, or going well off the beaten path. Car trips to northern Guanacaste from San José can take an entire day, so flying is probably better if you don't have long to spend in the country. Flying is definitely better than driving for visiting the South Pacific.

A standard vehicle is fine for most destinations, but a *doble-tracción* (4WD) is often essential to reach the remoter parts of the country, especially during the rainy season. Even in the dry season, you must have a 4WD vehicle to reach Monteverde and some destinations in Guanacaste. The big 4WD vehicles, such as a Suzuki Grand Vitara, can cost roughly twice as much as an economy car, but compact 4WDs, such as the Daihatsu Terios, are more

reasonable, and should be booked well in advance. Most cars in Costa Rica have manual transmissions. ■ TIP→ Specify when making the reservation if you want an automatic transmission; it usually costs about $5 more per day, but some companies, such as Alamo and Hertz, don't charge extra. Larger, more expensive automatic Montero and Sorento models are also available.

If you plan to rent any kind of vehicle between December 15 and January 3, or during Holy Week (the week leading up to Easter)—when most Costa Ricans are on vacation—reserve several months ahead of time.

Costa Rica has around 30 car-rental firms. Most local firms are affiliated with international car-rental chains and offer the same guarantees and services as their branches abroad; local company Tricolor gets high marks from travelers on our Fodor's Forum. At least a dozen rental offices line San José's Paseo Colón; most large hotels and Aeropuerto Internacional Juan Santamaría have representatives. Renting in or near San José is by far the easiest way to go. It's getting easier to rent outside of San José, particularly on the Pacific coast. Several rental companies have set up branches in Liberia, Quepos, Jacó, Tamarindo, and La Fortuna. In most other places across the country it's either impossible or very difficult and expensive to rent a car.

Car seats are compulsory for children under four years old, and can be rented for about $5 per day; reserve in advance. Rental cars may not be driven across borders to Nicaragua and Panama. For a $50 fee, National and Alamo will let you drop off a Costa Rican rental car at the Nicaragua border and provide you with a Nicaraguan rental on the other side. Seat-belt use is compulsory in the front seat. Fuel-efficiency measures restrict certain cars from San José's city center during rush hours once a week, according to the final license-plate number (e.g., plates that end in 9 are restricted on Friday). This also applies to rental cars; if you are stopped, do not pay a bribe. To rent a car, you need a driver's license, a valid passport, and a credit card. The minimum renter age varies; agencies such as Economy, Budget, and Alamo rent to anyone over 21; Avis sets the limit at 23, Hertz at 25. Though it's rare, some agencies have a maximum age limit.

High-season rates in San José begin at $45 a day and $300 a week for an economy car with air-conditioning, manual transmission, unlimited mileage, plus obligatory insurance; but rates fluctuate considerably according to demand, season, and company. Rates for a 4WD vehicle during high season are $70 to $90 a day and $450 to $550 per week. Often companies will also require a $1,000 deposit, payable by credit card.

Cars picked up at or returned to Aeropuerto Internacional Juan Santamaría incur a 12% surcharge. Arrangements can be made to pick up cars directly at the Liberia airport, but a range of firms have offices nearby and transport you from the airport free of charge—and with no surcharge for an airport pickup. Check cars thoroughly for damage before you sign the rental contract. Even tough-looking 4WD vehicles should be coddled. ■ TIP→ The charges levied by rental companies for damage—no matter how minor—are outrageous even by U.S. or European standards. It's very wise to opt for full-coverage insurance. One-way service surcharges are $50 to $150, depending on the drop-off point; National allows travelers free car drop-off at any of its offices with a minimum three-day rental. To avoid a hefty refueling fee, fill the tank just before you turn in the car. It's almost never a deal to buy the tank of gas that's in the car when you rent it; the understanding is that you'll return it empty, but some fuel usually remains. Additional drivers are about $5 to $10 per day if there is any charge at all. Almost all agencies, with the exception of Budget Rent-a-Car, have cellphone rental; prices range between $2 and $6 per day, with national per-minute costs between 50¢ and $2.

International driving permits (IDPs), which are used only in conjunction with a valid driver's license and translate your license into 10 languages, are not necessary in Costa Rica. Your own driver's license is good for the length of your initial tourist visa. You must carry your passport, or a copy of it with the entry stamp, to prove when you entered the country.

Major Agencies Alamo (☎ 2242-7733 in Costa Rica ⊕ www.alamocostarica.com). **Avis** (☎ 2293-2222 in Costa Rica ⊕ www.avis.co.cr). **Budget** (☎ 2436-2000 in Costa Rica ⊕ www.budget.co.cr). **Dollar** (☎ 877/767-8651 or 866/746-7765 in North America, 2443-2950 in Costa Rica ⊕ www.dollarcostarica.com). **Hertz** (☎ 888/437-8927 in North America, 2221-1818 in Costa Rica ⊕ www.costaricarentacar.net). **National Car Rental** (☎ 877/862-8227 in North America, 2242-7878 in Costa Rica ⊕ www.natcar.com).

Local Agencies Economy (☎ 877/326-7368 in North America, 2299-2000 in Costa Rica ⊕ www.economyrentacar.com). **Tricolor** (☎ 800/949-0234 in North America, 2440-3333 in Costa Rica ⊕ www.tricolorcarrental.com).

ROAD CONDITIONS

Many travelers shy away from renting a car in Costa Rica, if only for fear of the road conditions. Indeed, this is not an ideal place to drive: in San José traffic is bad and car theft is rampant (look for guarded parking lots or hotels with lots); in rural areas roads are often unpaved or potholed—and tires aren't usually covered by the basic insurance. And Ticos are reckless drivers—with one of the highest accident rates in the world. But though driving can be a challenge, it's a great way to explore certain regions, especially Guanacaste, the Northern Plains, and the Caribbean coast (apart from Tortuguero and Barra del Colorado). Keep in mind that mountains and poor road conditions make most trips longer than you'd normally expect.

San José is terribly congested during weekday morning and afternoon rush hours

(7 to 9 AM and 4 to 6 PM). Avoid returning to the city on Sunday evening, when traffic to San José from the Pacific coast beaches backs up for hours. The winding Pan-American Highway south of the capital is notorious for long snakes of traffic stuck behind slow-moving trucks. Look out for potholes, even in the smoothest sections of the best roads. Also watch for unmarked speed bumps where you'd least expect them, particularly on rural main thoroughfares. During the rainy season roads are in much worse shape. Check with your destination before setting out; roads, especially in Limón Province, are prone to washouts and landslides.

San José has many one-way streets and traffic circles. Streets in the capital are narrow. Pedestrians are supposed to have the right-of-way but do not in reality, so be alert when walking. The local driving style is erratic and aggressive but not fast, because road conditions don't permit too much speed. Frequent fender benders tie up traffic. Keep your windows rolled up in the center of the city, because thieves may reach into your car at stoplights and snatch your purse, jewelry, and so on.

Signage is notoriously bad, but improving. Watch carefully for *No Hay Paso* (Do Not Enter) signs; one-way streets are common, and it's not unusual for a street to transform from a two-way to a one-way. Streetlights are often out of service and key signs missing or knocked down because of accidents.

Outside of San José you'll run into long stretches of unpaved road. Frequent hazards in the countryside are potholes, landslides during the rainy season, and cattle on the roads. Drunk drivers are a hazard throughout the country on weekend nights. Driving at night is not recommended anyway, since roads are poorly lighted and many don't have painted center lines or shoulder lines.

ROADSIDE EMERGENCIES

Costa Rica has no highway emergency service organization. In Costa Rica 911 is the nationwide number for accidents. Traffic police are scattered around the country, but Costa Ricans are very good about stopping for people with car trouble. Whatever happens, don't move the car after an accident, even if a monstrous traffic jam ensues. Call 911 first if the accident is serious (nearly everyone has a cell phone here and it's almost a given that someone will offer to help). Also be sure to call the emergency number your car-rental agency has given you. For fender benders, contact the Traffic Police, who will try to locate a person to assist you in English—but don't count on it. If you don't speak Spanish, you may want to contact the rental agency before trying the police. If your own car is stolen, call the Judicial Investigative Police (OIJ, pronounced oh-ee-hota), which will find an English-speaking representative to assist you.

Emergency Services Ambulance and Police (☎ *911*).

RULES OF THE ROAD

Driving is on the right side of the road in Costa Rica. The highway speed limit is usually 90 KPH (54 MPH), which drops to 60 KPH (36 MPH) in residential areas. In towns, limits range from 30 to 50 kph (18 to 31 MPH). Speed limits are enforced in all regions of the country. Seat belts are required, and an awareness campaign has increased enforcement. ALTO means "stop" and CEDA means "yield." Right turns on red are permitted except where signs indicate otherwise, but in San José this is usually not possible because of one-way streets and pedestrian crossings.

Local drunk driving laws are strict. You'll get nailed with a 10,000-colón fine if you're caught driving in a "pre-drunk" state (blood alcohol levels of 0.049% to 0.099%). If your level is higher than that, you'll pay 20,000 colones, the car will be confiscated, and your license will be taken away. Policemen who stop drivers for speeding and drunk driving are often looking for payment on the spot—essentially a bribe. Whether you're guilty or not, you'll get a ticket if you don't give in. Asking for a ticket instead of paying the bribe discourages corruption and does not compromise your safety. You can generally pay the ticket at your car-rental company, which will remit it on your behalf.

Car seats are required for children ages four and under, but car-seat laws are not rigorously enforced. Children over 12 are allowed in the front seat. Drivers are prohibited from using handheld cell phones, but this is almost never enforced, and distracted chatters are the norm.

■ CRUISE SHIP TRAVEL

The quality of shore excursions at Costa Rica's Pacific ports (Caldera, Quepos, Golfito) and Limón, on the Caribbean, has skyrocketed in past years, as operators scramble to serve the influx of cruisers who stop in, usually on their way to or from the Panama Canal. Most large cruises stop in the country only once, although some make stops on both coasts. Small-scale ships, including Windstar Cruises (capacity for 145), Seabourn (60 guests), and highly recommended, conservation-minded Lindblad (62 guests) offer Costa Rica–focused cruises along the Pacific coast.

Cruise Lines Carnival (☎ 888/227–6482 in North America ⊕ www.carnival.com). **Celebrity** (☎ 800/647–2251 in North America ⊕ www.celebritycruises.com). **Crystal** (☎ 800/722–0021 in North America ⊕ www.crystalcruises.com). **Cunard** (☎ 800/728–6273 in North America ⊕ www.cunard.com). **Disney** (☎ 800/951–3532 in North America ⊕ disneycruise.disney.go.com). **Holland America** (☎ 800/932–4259 in North America ⊕ www.hollandamerica.com). **Lindblad** (☎ 800/397–3348 in North America ⊕ www.expeditions.com). **Norwegian** (☎ 800/327–7030 in North America ⊕ www.ncl.com). **Princess** (☎ 800/774–6237 in North America ⊕ www.princess.com). **Regent Seven Seas** (☎ 877/505–5370 in North America ⊕ www.rssc.com). **Royal Caribbean** (☎ 800/521–8611 in North America ⊕ www.royalcaribbean.com). **Seabourn Cruise Line** (☎ 800/929–9391 ⊕ www.seabourn.com). **Silversea** (☎ 800/722–9955 in North America ⊕ www.silversea.com). **Windstar Cruises** (☎ 206/292–9606 or 800/258–7245 ⊕ www.windstarcruises.com).

■ TAXI TRAVEL

Taxis are cheap and your best bet for getting around San José. Just about every driver is friendly and eager to use a few English words to tell you about a cousin or sister in New Jersey; however, cabbies truly conversant in English are scarce. Most are knowledgeable, but given the haphazard address system, may cheerfully engage passersby or other taxi drivers to find your destination. Tipping is not expected, but a good idea when you've had some extra help.

Cabs are red, usually with a yellow light on top. To hail one, extend your hand and wave it at about hip height. If it's available, the driver will often flick his headlights before pulling over. Cabs can be scarce when it's raining or during rush hour. The city is dotted with *paradas de taxi*, taxi lineups where you stand the best chance of grabbing one. Your hotel can usually call you a reputable taxi or private car service, and when you're out to dinner or on the town, the restaurant or disco can just as easily call you a cab—it's much easier than trying to hail one on the street in the wee hours, and safer, too.

■TIP→ Taxi drivers are infamous for "not having change." If it's just a few hundred colones, you may as well round up. If it's a lot, ask them to drive to a store or gas station where you can make change. They'll often miraculously come up with the difference, or wait patiently while you get it. To avoid this situation, never use a 10,000-colón bill in a taxi, and avoid paying with 5,000-colón bills unless you've run up almost that much in fares.

Technically this system applies throughout the country, but rural and unofficial cabs often use their odometers to creatively calculate fares. Manuel Antonio drivers are notorious for overcharging. It's illegal, but taxis charge up to double for hotel pickups or fares that take them out of the province (such as San José to Alajuela or vice versa). Ask the manager at your hotel about the going rate for the destination to which you're heading. Drivers have a fairly standard list of off-the-meter illegal fares.

In the capital there's usually no reason to take the risk with an unofficial taxi (*pirata*), but they are often the only option outside main hubs. See the regional chapters for recommended drivers, or check with your hotel or restaurant for reliable service.

It's always a good idea to make a note of the cab number (painted in a yellow triangle on the door), and sit in the backseat for safety.

▮ TRAIN TRAVEL

An earthquake in 1991 wreaked havoc on the country's century-old rail links, and service was completely suspended in 1995. An east-west commuter-rail route now plies San José, and another route connects the capital with Heredia, but these are geared to the needs of workaday commuters.

More popular is the Tico Train, a tourist day trip that leaves from the Pacific station in southern San José to the Pacific port of Caldera. Trains leave Saturday and Sunday at 7 AM, returning by 8:30 PM ($39 per passenger over four years old). Fueled as much by nostalgia as hydrocarbons, the scenic trip (four hours each way) follows a historic route; passengers are serenaded by a strolling guitar player, given traditional snacks, and free to wander about on a five-hour beach stop.

Information Tico Train Tour to Caldera (☎ *2233–3300 in Costa Rica* ⊕ *www.ticotraintour.com*).

ESSENTIALS

▋ ACCOMMODATIONS

Low-end alternatives are often referred to as *cabinas* whether they offer concrete-block motels or freestanding cottages. Most have private rooms, cold-water concrete showers, fans instead of air-conditioning, and limited—if any—secure parking or storage, and may share bathrooms. Owners tend to be Costa Rican. Often without Web sites, e-mail, or links to major agencies, these hotels tend to follow a first-come, first-served booking policy. They may have room during peak seasons when mid- or upper-end options are booked solid.

Midrange options include boutique hotels, tasteful bungalows, bed-and-breakfasts, and downtown casino hotels. Those in the hotter beach areas may not have hot-water showers. Many have pools, Internet access, and meal options. They tend to be foreign-owned and, with the exception of the casinos, have personalized service. Because they're generally small, you may have to book one or two months ahead, and up to six months in the high season. Booking through an association or agency can significantly reduce the time you spend scanning the Internet, but you can often get a better deal and negotiate longer-stay or low-season discounts. The Costa Rican Hotel Association has online search and booking capabilities. ICT provides hotel lists searchable by star category. Costa Rica Travel Review lists and rates properties and provides a number of links.

High-end accommodations can be found almost everywhere. They range from luxury tents to exquisite hotels and villa rentals, and are often more secluded. You'll find all the amenities you expect at such areas, with one notable exception: the roads and routes to even five-star villas can be atrocious. This category is sometimes booked up to a year in advance for Christmas, and during this season you

may be able to book only through agents or central reservations offices. Resorts are generally one of two kinds: luxurious privileged gateways to the best of the country (such as Punta Islita) or generic budget all-inclusives (such as the Barceló) that probably run counter to what you're coming to Costa Rica for. Several chain hotels have franchises in Costa Rica, leaning toward the generic and all-inclusive. The upside is that they are rarely booked solid, so you can always fall back on one in a worst-case scenario, and they often have member discounts.

Nature lodges and hotels in the South Pacific (where restaurants aren't an option) may be less expensive than they initially appear, as the price of a room usually includes three hearty meals a day, and sometimes guided hikes. These, and other remote accommodations, may not have daily Internet access even though they have a Web site: be patient if you're attempting to book directly. Since many of the hotels are remote and have an eco-friendly approach (even to luxury), air-conditioning, in-room telephones, and TVs are exceptions to the rule. Consider how isolated you want to be; some rural and eco-lodges are miles from neighbors and other services and have few rainy-day diversions.

The ICT's voluntary "green leaf" rating system evaluates establishments in terms of sustainable-tourism criteria; a detailed description of the program and a search function to find lodging by sustainability level can be found at ⊕ *www.turismo-sostenible.co.cr.*

The lodgings we list are Costa Rica's cream of the crop in each price category. We always list the facilities that are available, but we don't specify whether they cost extra; when pricing accommodations, always ask what's included and what costs extra. Properties are assigned price categories based on the range from the least-expensive standard double room at high season (excluding holidays) to the most expensive. Keep in mind that hotel prices we list exclude 16.4% service and tax.

For Costa Rica's popular beach and mountain resorts, be sure to reserve well in advance for the dry season (mid-December–April everywhere except the Caribbean coast, which has a short September–October "dry" season). During the rainy season (May–mid-November except on the Caribbean coast, where it's almost always rainy) most hotels drop their rates considerably, which sometimes sends them into a lower price category than the one we indicate.

■TIP→ If you're having trouble finding a hotel that isn't completely booked, consider contacting a tour operator who can arrange your entire trip. Because they reserve blocks of rooms far in advance, you might have better luck.

Most hotels and other lodgings require you to give your credit-card details before they will confirm your reservation. If you don't feel comfortable e-mailing this information, ask if you can fax it (some places even prefer faxes). However you book, get confirmation in writing and have a copy of it handy when you check in.

Be sure you understand the hotel's cancellation policy. Some places allow you to cancel without any kind of penalty—even if you prepaid to secure a discounted rate—if you cancel at least 24 hours in advance. Others require you to cancel a week in advance or penalize you the cost of one night. Small inns and bed-and-breakfasts are most likely to require you to cancel far in advance. Most hotels allow children under a certain age to stay in their parents' room at no extra charge, but others charge for them as extra adults; find out the cutoff age for discounts.

Hotels operate on the European Plan (EP, no meals) unless we specify that they use the Breakfast Plan (BP, with full breakfast), Continental Plan (CP, Continental breakfast), Full American Plan (FAP, all meals), or Modified American Plan (MAP, breakfast and dinner), or are all-inclusive (AI, all meals and most activities).

Lodging Resources Costa Rica Travel Review (⊕ www.costaricatravelreview.com). **Costa Rican Hotels Association** (☎ 2248–0990 in Costa Rica ⊕ www.costaricanhotels.com).**Instituto Costarricense de Turismo** (ICT ☎ 866/267–8274 in North America, 2299–5800 in Costa Rica ⊕ www.visitcostarica.com).

APARTMENT AND HOUSE RENTALS

Rental houses are now common all over Costa Rica, and are particularly popular in the Pacific coast destinations of Manuel Antonio, Tamarindo, Ocotal, and Jacó. Furnished rentals accommodate a crowd or a family, often for less and at a higher comfort level. Generally, properties are owned by individual owners or consortiums, most of them based in the United States, with house managers in Costa Rica. Resort communities with villa-style lodgings are also growing. Nosara Home Page lists apartments and villas on the Nicoya Peninsula; Villas International has an extensive list of properties in Quepos and Tamarindo. For the southern Nicoya Peninsula check Costa Rica Beach Rentals. The House of Rentals, a Century 21 affiliate, arranges houses and condos in the Flamingo and Potrero areas.

Contacts Century 21 (☎ 2654–4004 in Costa Rica, 877/661–2060 from U.S. ⊕ www.century21costarica.net). **Costa Rica Beach Rentals** (☎ 2640–0065 ⊕ www.costarica-beachrentals.com). **Nosara Beach Rentals** (☎ 2682–0153 ⊕ www.nosarabeachrentals.com).

Villas & Apartments Abroad (☎ 212/213–6435 in U.S., 800/433–3020 ⊕ www.vaanyc.com). **Villas Caribe** (☎ 800/645–7498 ⊕ www.villascaribe.com).

Villas International (☎ 415/499–9490 in U.S., 800/221–2260 ⊕ www.villasintl.com).

BED-AND-BREAKFASTS

A number of quintessential bed-and-breakfasts—small and homey—are clustered in the Central Valley, generally offering hearty breakfasts and friendly inside information for $50 to $70 per night. You'll also find them scattered through the rest of the country, mixed in with other self-titled bed-and-breakfasts that range from small cabins in the mountains to luxurious boutique hotel–style digs in northern Guanacaste.

Reservation Services Bed & Breakfast.com
(☎ 512/322–2710 or 800/462–2632
⊕ www.bedandbreakfast.com) also sends out an online newsletter. **Bed & Breakfast Inns Online** (☎ 615/868–1946 or 800/215–7365 ⊕ www.bbonline.com). **Pamela Lanier's Bed and Breakfasts, Inns and Guesthouses International** (⊕ www.lanierbb.com/Costa_Rica).

HOME EXCHANGES

With a direct home exchange you stay in someone else's home while they stay in yours. Some outfits also deal with vacation homes, so you're not actually staying in someone's full-time residence, just their vacant weekend place.

A handful of home exchanges are available; this involves an initial small registration fee, and you'll have to plan ahead. It's an excellent way to immerse yourself in the true Costa Rica, particularly if you've been here before and aren't relying so heavily on the tourism support that hotels can offer. Drawbacks include restricted options and dates. Many companies list home exchanges, but we've found HomeLink International, which lists a handful of jazzy houses in Costa Rica, and Intervac to be the most reliable.

Exchange Clubs Home Exchange
(☎ 800/877–8723 ⊕ www.homeexchange.com); $59.95 for a one-year online listing. **Intervac U.S.** (☎ 800/756–4663 ⊕ www.intervacus.com); $95 for Web-only membership; $195 includes Web access and a catalog.

HOSTELS

Hostels offer bare-bones lodging at low, low prices—often in shared dorm rooms with shared baths—to people of all ages, though the primary market is young travelers, especially students. Most hostels serve breakfast; dinner and/or shared cooking facilities may also be available. In some hostels you aren't allowed to be in your room during the day, and there may be a curfew at night. Nevertheless, hostels provide a sense of community, with public rooms where travelers often gather to share stories. Many hostels are affiliated with Hostelling International (HI), an umbrella group of hostel associations with some 4,500 member properties in more than 70 countries. Other hostels are completely independent and may be nothing more than a really cheap hotel.

Costa Rica has a sprinkling of youth hostels and hotels affiliated with Hostelling International; most are tantamount to inexpensive hotels, appropriate for families. Youth-oriented Hostal Toruma in San José, part of the Costarrican [sic] Hostel Network, is an exception, as is Hostel Playa Tamarindo; the former offers private rooms as well as dorms, and the latter has surf racks. Tranquilo Backpackers, Gaudy's Backpackers, and Hostel Costa Linda also lean toward boisterous, younger guests.

ADDRESSES

In Costa Rica addresses are usually given in terms of how many meters the place is from a landmark. Street names and building numbers are not commonly used. Churches, stores, even large trees that no longer exist—almost anything can be a landmark, as long as everyone knows where it is, or where it used to be. A typical address in San José is *100 metros este y 100 metros sur del Más X Menos* (100 meters east and 100 meters south from the Más X Menos supermarket). ■TIP➔ In towns and cities in Costa Rica, each block is assumed to be 100 meters, although some blocks may be much longer and some may be shorter. So if someone tells you to head down the road 500 meters, they mean five blocks. Ticos, as Costa Ricans call themselves, are generally happy to help lost visitors, and they spend a lot of time describing where things are. But be warned—even if they don't know where something is, Ticos will often give uncertain or even wrong information rather than seem unhelpful; triangulated direction-asking is a must. Ask at least two, if not three, people in quick succession to avoid getting hopelessly lost. Key direction terms are *lugar* (place), *calle* (street), *avenida* (avenue), *puente* (bridge), *piso* (floor), *edificio* (building), *cruce* (intersection), *semáforo* (traffic light), *rotonda* (traffic circle), and *cuadra* (block).

COMMUNICATIONS

INTERNET

Downtown San José is full of Internet cafés with high-speed connections; prices are usually less than $1 per hour. As you move away from the capital, prices rise to $2 to $4 per hour and connections become slower and more unreliable. Wildly expensive satellite Internet is available at some remote, exclusive hotels. Cafés are generally good places to make international Internet calls, but expect echoes and a mediocre connection. Most major hotels have free wireless access or use of a guest Internet computer. Eateries such as Denny's, Bagelmen's, and a number of upscale cafés are also Wi-Fi–friendly, although a few travelers have been robbed of their laptops in public restaurants. Dial-up access is spotty and frustrating, but if you're desperate and have both a computer and access to a telephone line, you can buy one of RACSA's (the state Internet service provider) prepaid Internet cards in three amounts: 1,800 colones (5 hours), 3,550 colones (10 hours), and 5,300 colones (15 hours). Cards are sold at Kodak stores, Perimercado supermarkets, and some branches of the Banco Nacional. The cards come with the access numbers, and a help line with English-speaking operators.

Contacts Cybercafes (⊕ *www.cybercafes. com*) lists more than 4,000 Internet cafés worldwide.

PHONES

The good news is that you can now make a direct-dial telephone call from virtually any point on earth. The bad news? You can't always do so cheaply. Calling from a hotel is almost always the most expensive option; hotels usually add huge surcharges to all calls, particularly international ones. In some countries you can phone from call centers or even the post office. Calling cards usually keep costs to a minimum, but only if you purchase them locally. And then there are mobile phones (⇨ *below*), which are sometimes more prevalent—particularly in the developing world—than landlines; as expensive as mobile phone calls can be, they are still usually a much cheaper option than calling from your hotel.

CALLING WITHIN COSTA RICA

In 2008, all phone numbers in Costa Rica were assigned an extra number. A 2 was tacked on to the front of all landline numbers and an 8 was added to the front of all mobile phone numbers. In-country 800 numbers were not affected by the change. Many signs and business cards still show the old seven-digit number.

The Costa Rican phone system is very good by the standards of other developing countries. However, phone numbers do change often. Some phones have a card reader on the right-hand side, but the readers are hit-and-miss. There are no area codes in Costa Rica, so you only need dial the eight-digit number, without the 506 country code. Fewer and farther between are the gray coin-operated phones; posted on each are the coins accepted (it varies from phone to phone).

CALLING OUTSIDE COSTA RICA

The country code for the United States is 1.

Internet telephony is by far the cheapest way to call home; it is a viable option in the Central Valley and major tourist hubs. For other regions or for more privacy, a pay phone using an international phone card (⇨ *Calling Cards, below*) is the next step up; you can also call from a pay phone using your own long-distance calling card. Dialing directly from a hotel room is very expensive, as is recruiting an international operator to connect you.

■ TIP➔ Watch out for pay phones marked CALL USA/CANADA WITH A CREDIT CARD. They are *wildly* expensive.

To call overseas directly, dial 00, then the country code (dial 1 for the U.S. and Canada), the area code, and the number. You can make international calls from almost any phone with an international calling card purchased in Costa Rica. First dial 199, then the PIN on the back of your card (revealed after scratching off a protective coating), then dial the phone number as you would a direct long-distance call.

When requesting a calling card from your phone provider, ask specifically about calls from Costa Rica. Most 800-number cards don't work in Costa Rica. Callingcards.com is a great resource for prepaid international calling cards. At this writing, it lists at least two calling-card companies with rates of 29¢ and 56¢ per minute for calls from Costa Rica to the United States.

You may find the local access number blocked in many hotel rooms. First ask the hotel operator to connect you. If the hotel operator balks, ask for an international operator, or dial the international operator yourself. For service in English, you'll have more luck dialing the international operator (☎ 175 or 116). One way to improve your odds of getting connected to your long-distance carrier is to sign up with more than one company: a hotel may block Sprint, for example, but not MCI. If all else fails, call from a pay phone.

AT&T, MCI, and Sprint access codes make calling long distance relatively convenient but can be very expensive.

To make a person-to-person direct-dial call from any phone, dial 09 (instead of 00 for a regular call), the country code for the country you're calling, and then the number. The operator will ask for the name of the person you're contacting, and billing at direct-dial rates begins only once that person comes to the phone.

Direct-dial calls to the United States and Canada are 27¢ per minute.

Phone Resources Callingcards.com (⊕ *www.callingcards.com*). **International information** (☎ *124*). **International operator** (☎ *175 or 116*).

CALLING CARDS

Most public phones require phone cards (for local or international calls), but phone cards can also be used from any non-rotary telephone in Costa Rica, including residential phones, cell phones, and hotel phones. It's rare to be charged a per-minute rate for the mere use of the phone in a hotel.

Phone cards are sold in an array of shops, including Más X Menos supermarkets, post offices, offices of the Costa Rican Electricity Institute (ICE), and at any business displaying the gold-and-blue TARJETAS TELEFÓNICAS sign. International cards tend to be easier to find in downtown San José and in tourism areas.

Tarjetas para llamadas nacionales (domestic calling cards) are available in denominations of 500 colones and 1,000 colones. Phone-card rates are standard throughout the country, about 1¢ per minute, half that at night; a 500-colón card provides about 125 minutes of daytime landline calls. This decreases sharply if calling a cell phone; rates vary. *Tarjetas para llamadas internacionales* (international calling cards) are sold in $10, $20, 3,000-colón, and 10,000-colón amounts (denominations are inexplicably split between dollars and colones). It's harder to find the 10,000-colón cards; your best bet is to try a Fischel pharmacy or an ICE office. In busy spots, roaming card-hawkers abound; feel free to take advantage of the convenience—they're legit.

Some public phones accept *tarjetas chip* ("chip" cards), which record what you spend. ■TIP➔ Avoid buying chip cards: they malfunction, you can use them only at the few-and-far-between chip phones, and they are sold in small denominations that are not sufficient for international calls.

MOBILE PHONES

If you have an unblocked phone (some countries use different frequencies than what's used in the United States) and your service provider uses the world-standard GSM network (as do T-Mobile, Cingular, and Verizon), you can probably use your phone abroad. ■TIP➔ If you travel internationally frequently, save one of your old mobile phones or buy a cheap one on the Internet; ask your cell phone company to unlock it for you, and take it with you as a travel phone, buying a new SIM card with pay-as-you-go service in each destination.

If your cell phone company has service to Costa Rica, you theoretically can use it here, but expect reception to be impossibly bad in many areas of this mountainous country. Costa Rica works on a 1,800 MHz system—a tri- or quad-band cell phone is your best bet. Note that roaming fees can be steep.

Most car-rental agencies have good deals on cell phones, often better than the companies that specialize in cell-phone rental. If you're not renting a car, a number of companies will rent TDMA or GSM phones; remember, coverage can be spotty. Although service is evening out, TDMA phones have tended to work best in the Central Valley and Guanacaste; GSM is better for remote areas such as Dominical, Sámara, and Tortuguero. Specify your destination when renting. Rates range from $5 to $15 per day, plus varying rates for local or international coverage and minimum usage charges. Local calls average 70¢ per minute, international $1.25 to $1.50. You'll need your ID, a credit card, and a deposit, which varies per phone and service but averages $300 to $400; some rent only to those over 21. The deposit drops significantly with companies that can hook you up with a rented local chip for your own phone.

Friendly and professional, Cell Service Costa Rica will get you hooked up and provides door-to-door service; it doesn't rent SIM cards. Cellular Telephone Rentals Costa Rica has higher daily rates but free local calls, and will set you up with a card for your phone. Most rental companies in Costa Rica do not charge for text messages.

Contacts **Cell Service Costa Rica** (☎ 2296–5553 *in Costa Rica* ⊕ *www.cellservicecr.com*). **Cellular Telephone Rentals Costa Rica** (☎ 800/769–7137 *in U.S., 2290–7534 in Costa Rica* ⊕ *www.cellulartelephonerentals.com*).

▌ CUSTOMS AND DUTIES

You're always allowed to bring goods of a certain value back home without having to pay any duty or import tax. But there's a limit on the amount of tobacco and liquor you can bring back duty free, and some countries have separate limits for perfumes; for exact figures, check with your customs department. The values of so-called duty-free goods are included in these amounts. When you shop abroad, save all your receipts, as customs inspectors may ask to see them as well as the items you purchased. If the total value of your goods is more than the duty-free limit, you'll have to pay a tax (most often a flat percentage) on the value of everything beyond that limit.

When shopping in Costa Rica, keep receipts for all purchases. Be ready to show customs (*aduanas*) officials what you've bought. Pack purchases together in an easily accessible place. The Patrimony Protection Department recommends obtaining a letter (free) from its office in the National Museum attesting that high-quality replicas of pre-Columbian artifacts are in fact copies, to avoid customs hassles. In practice, few people request such a letter, and problems with such souvenirs are infrequent. The only orchids you can take home are packaged in a tube and come with an export permit.

If you think a duty is incorrect, appeal the assessment. If you object to the way your clearance was handled, note the inspector's badge number. In either case, first ask to see a supervisor. If the problem isn't resolved, write to the appropriate authorities, beginning with the port director at your point of entry.

It usually takes about 10 to 30 minutes to clear customs when arriving in Costa Rica.

Visitors entering Costa Rica may bring in 500 grams of tobacco, 5 liters of wine or spirits, 2 kilograms of sweets and chocolates, and the equivalent of $500 worth of merchandise. One camera and one video camera, six rolls of film, binoculars, and electrical items for personal use only are also allowed. Make sure you have personalized prescriptions for any medication you are taking. Customs officials at San José's international airport rarely examine tourists' luggage, but if you enter by land, they'll probably look through your bags. Officers at the airport generally speak English and are usually your best (only, really) option for resolving any problem.

You can try calling the Customs office, but if you get through and get results, let us know!

Pets (cats or dogs) with updated health and vaccination certificates are welcome in Costa Rica; no prior authorization is required if bringing a dog or cat that has up-to-date health and vaccination cards. The Servicio Nacional de Salud Animal can provide more info.

Information in Costa Rica

Customs (☎ 2441–6069 in Costa Rica ⊕ www.hacienda.go.cr). **Patrimony Protection Office** (☎ 2291–3517 in Costa Rica). **Servicio Nacional de Salud Animal** (☎ 2260–8300 in Costa Rica ⊕ www.senasa.go.cr).

U.S. Information **U.S. Customs and Border Protection** (⊕ www.cbp.gov).

∎ EATING OUT

The cilantro-and-onion-flavored pot of rice and beans known as *gallo pinto* is synonymous with all things Tico, as evidenced by the expression "As Tico as *gallo pinto*." Nonetheless, Nicaraguans fiercely beg to differ, claiming the dish as their own and spurring a back-and-forth competition for the world's largest batch of the dish.

Mounds of this hearty breakfast can be found at the quintessential Costa Rican informal eatery—the *soda*. For lunch the dish is called *casados:* the beans and rice are served separately, accompanied by meat, coleslaw, and fried plantains. Increasingly common as you move away from San José are the thatched conical roofs of the round, open *rancho* restaurants that serve a combination of traditional staples with simple international fare. Kitchens cooking up sophisticated cuisine from Thailand, India, Italy, Lebanon, and more dot the capital and popular tourist centers. Vegetarians sticking to lower-budget establishments won't go hungry, but may develop a love-hate relationship with rice, beans, and fried cheese. A simple *sin carne* (no meat) request is often interpreted as

LOCAL DOS AND TABOOS

CUSTOMS OF THE COUNTRY

Ticos tend to use formal Spanish, preferring, for example, *con mucho gusto* (with much pleasure) instead of *de nada* for "you're welcome." Family is very important in Costa Rica. It is considered polite to ask about your marital status and family.

Ticos can be disarmingly direct; don't be surprised (or offended) if locals pick up on a physical trait and give you a nickname: *Chino* for anyone of Asian ethnicity, or *Gordita* if you have even an extra ounce around your hips. It's meant affectionately. In almost every other situation, a circumspect approach is advised; North American straightforwardness often comes across as abrupt here. Preceding requests with a bit of small talk (even if it's a hotel employee) goes a long way. Also, be very aware of body language and other cues—Costa Ricans don't like to say no, and will often avoid answering a question or simply say *gracias* when they really mean no.

A large number of Costa Rican men make a habit of ogling or making gratuitous comments when young women pass on the street. Women should take care not to dress in skimpy clothing.

The expression "Tico time" was coined for a reason. Transportation, theaters, government, and major businesses tend to stick to official schedules. Anything else is flexible, and best handled by building in a little buffer time and sliding into the tropical groove.

GREETINGS

Costa Ricans are extremely polite, quick to shake hands (light squeezes are the norm) and place a kiss on the right cheek (meaning you need to bear left when going in for the peck). The formal pronoun *usted* (you) is used almost exclusively; the slangier *vos* is thrown about in informal settings and among close or young friends and relatives.

SIGHTSEEING

As you would anywhere, dress and behave respectfully when visiting churches. In churches men and women should not wear shorts, sleeveless shirts, or sandals; women should wear pants or skirts below the knee. Bathing suits, short shorts, and other skimpy attire are inappropriate city wear, but tend to be the uniform in beach towns; even here, however, cover up for all but the most informal restaurants. Locals tend to dress somewhat formally, with women favoring clothes that show off their curves.

Beggars are not a major problem, but if you're in San José, you'll come across a few. It's always better to give to an established organization, but the safety net for Costa Ricans with disabilities is riddled with holes, so even a couple of hundred colones will be appreciated. Simply keep walking past the addicts—they will almost always just move on to the next person. A couple of savvy panhandlers speak excellent English and will try to draw you into conversation with a sob story about a lost passport. Keep walking.

Banks and other offices allow pregnant women and the elderly to move immediately to the front of the line, and this respect is carried over to other establishments and crowded buses. If you're in a crowd and need to step in front of them, murmur, *"Con permiso"* ("Excuse me").

OUT ON THE TOWN

To catch a waiter's attention, wave discreetly or say, *"Disculpe, señor"* (or *señora* for women); best to leave the finger snapping to the locals. For the bill, ask for *"La cuenta, por favor."* (No one will bring the check to you until you ask.) Pockets of no-smoking sections are growing, especially in the swankier restaurants, but smoking is still tolerated in many public spaces. It's prohibited in government buildings, cinemas, theaters, other public entertainment venues, and public transport. Excessive displays of affection

LOCAL DOS AND TABOOS

draw frowns, clearly lost on the gaggles of lip-locked couples. Locals tend to dress up to go out, whatever the activity: a snazzy (but not too dressy) outfit will serve you well in San José. If invited to someone's home, bring a gift such as flowers or a bottle of wine or some trinket from your home country. If offered food at someone's home, it's polite to accept it and eat it (even if you aren't hungry).

LANGUAGE

One of the best ways to avoid being an Ugly American is to learn a little of the local language. You need not strive for fluency; even just mastering a few basic words and terms is bound to make chatting with the locals more rewarding.

Spanish is the official language, although many tour guides and locals in heavily touristed areas speak English. You'll have a better time if you learn some basic Spanish before you go and if you bring a phrase book with you. At the very least, learn the rudiments of polite conversation—niceties such as *por favor* (please) and *gracias* (thank you) will be warmly appreciated. *For more words and phrases, see the Spanish glossary in the "Understanding Costa Rica" chapter.* In the Caribbean province of Limón a creole English called Mekatelyu is widely spoken by older generations. English is understood by most everyone in these parts.

An open-ended *"Dónde está . . . ? "* ("Where is . . . ? ") may result in a wall of rapid-fire Spanish. Better to avoid language as much as possible when asking for directions. You're going to have to stop often anyway, so it can be helpful to make the journey in segments: in the city, say the name of the place you want to go, and point [adding a questioning *izquierda* (left), *derecha* (right), or *directo* (straight)]; do this frequently, and you'll get there. On longer journeys, keep a good map handy, and use the same strategy, asking for a nearby town on your journey rather than the final destination—you're more likely to get accurate directions.

And of course, you can't go wrong with an amiable *Pura vida,* which serves as "hello," "good-bye," "thanks," "cool," "how's it going," and all things amiable.

A phrase book and language-tape set can help get you started. *Fodor's Spanish for Travelers* (available at bookstores everywhere) is excellent.

"no beef," and you may get a plate of pork, chicken, or fish, so don't be afraid to sound high-maintenance. Specify *solo vegetales* (only vegetables), and for good measure, *nada de cerdo, pollo o pescado* (no pork, chicken, or fish). More cosmopolitan restaurants are more conscious of vegetarians—upscale Asian restaurants often offer a vegetarian section on the menu. In a pinch, the vegetarian fast-food chain Vishnu is always good for a quick meal. If your kids balk at the choices on the menu, ask for plain grilled chicken, fish, or beef: "*Pollo/pescado/carne sencillo para niños*" ("Grilled chicken/fish/ meat for children"). Most restaurants are willing to accommodate with options and portion size.

Natural juices, called *frescos,* come with teeth-shattering amounts of sugar. If you're watching your child's intake, request one with only a little sugar (*con poco azúcar*); chances are it will be sweet enough, but you can always top it off if need be. Water is generally safe to drink (especially around San José), but quality can vary; to be safe, drink bottled water.

MEALS AND MEALTIMES

In San José and surrounding cities, *sodas* are usually open daily 7 AM to 7 or 9 PM, though some close on Sunday. Other restaurants are usually open 11 AM to 9 PM. In rural areas restaurants are usually closed on Sunday, except around resorts. In resort areas some restaurants may be open late. Most all-night restaurants are in downtown San José casinos. However, Nuestra Tierra and Manolos are both good 24-hour options, and for late-night cravings the doors at Denny's at the Best Western Irazú just north of San José are always open. Normal dining hours in Costa Rica are noon to 3 and 6 to 9. *Desayuno* (breakfast) is served at most sodas and hotels. The traditional breakfast is *gallo pinto,* eggs, plantains, and fried cheese; hotel breakfasts vary widely and generally offer fruit and lighter international options in addition to the local stick-to-your-ribs plate. *Almuerzo* (lunch) is *casado* time,

and *cena* (supper) runs the gamut of just about anything you choose.

Except for those in hotels, many restaurants close between Christmas and New Year's Day and during Holy Week (Palm Sunday to Easter Sunday). Call before heading out. Those that do stay open may not sell alcohol between Holy Thursday and Easter Sunday. Even if you keep your base in San José, consider venturing to the Central Valley towns for a meal or two.

Unless otherwise noted, the restaurants listed in this guide are open daily for lunch and dinner.

Credit cards are not accepted at many restaurants in rural areas. Always ask before you order to find out if your credit card will be accepted. Visa and MasterCard are the most commonly accepted cards; American Express and Diners Club are less widely accepted. The Discover card is increasingly accepted. ■ TIP➔ Remember that 23% is added to all menu prices: 13% for tax and 10% for service. Because a gratuity (propina) is included, there's no need to tip, but if your service is good, it's nice to add a little money to the obligatory 10%.

RESERVATIONS AND DRESS

Costa Ricans generally dress more formally than North Americans. For dinner, long pants and closed-toe shoes are standard for men except for beach locations, and women tend to wear dressy clothes that show off their figures, with high heels. Shorts, flip-flops, and tank tops are not acceptable, except at inexpensive restaurants in beach towns.

WINES, BEER, AND SPIRITS

The ubiquitous sodas generally don't have liquor licenses, but getting a drink in any other eatery isn't usually a problem. Don't let Holy Thursday and Good Friday catch you off guard when the country's dry laws are strictly in effect. Bars close, and coolers and alcohol shelves in restaurants and stores are sealed off with plastic and police tape. In general, restaurant prices for imported alcohol—which includes just about everything except beer, rum, and *guaro*, the local sugarcane firewater—may be more than what you'd like to pay.

House wines are typically a low-end Chilean choice (this simply isn't wine-drinking country), so unless you see a familiar wine on the list, you might want to take a pass. Our advice? Go tropical! The country's abundant tropical fruit juices mix refreshingly well with rum, and to a lesser extent, *guaro*. You may also want to make a trip to the local supermarket to pick up something for an aperitif in your room—the selection will often be larger, and the prices much lower.

Costa Rica's brewery—run by Florida Ice & Farms—has a virtual monopoly on beer production, but produces some respectable lagers that pair well with beach lounging. Emblematic Imperial (known by the red, black, and yellow eagle logo that adorns bar signs and tourist T-shirts) is the favorite. The slightly more bitter Pilsen is a close runner-up, followed by the gold, dark, and light variations of Bavaria. Rock Ice is a relatively new product marketed to the younger crowd, with a higher alcohol content. The brewery also produces Heineken, and distributes imported brands such as Mexico's Corona. Those with exotic tastes (and deep pockets) can also find beers from as far away as Italy.

▍ELECTRICITY

North American appliances are compatible with Costa Rica's electrical system (110 volts) and outlets (parallel two-prong). Australian and European appliances require a two-prong adapter and a 220-volt to 110-volt transformer. Never use an outlet that specifically warns against using higher-voltage appliances without a transformer. Dual-voltage appliances (i.e., they operate equally well on 110 and 220 volts) such as most laptops, phone chargers, and hair dryers need only a two-prong adapter, but you should bring a surge protector for your computer.

Consider making a small investment in a universal adapter, which has several types of plugs in one lightweight, compact unit. Always check labels and manufacturer instructions to be sure. Don't use 110-volt outlets marked FOR SHAVERS ONLY for high-wattage appliances such as hair dryers.

Contacts Steve Kropla's Help for World Travelers (⊕ *www.kropla.com*) has information on electrical and telephone plugs around the world. **Walkabout Travel Gear** (⊕ *www.walkabouttravelgear.com*) has a good coverage of electricity under "adapters."

▍EMERGENCIES

Dial 911 for an ambulance, the fire department, or the police. Costa Ricans are usually quick to respond to emergencies. In a hotel or restaurant, the staff will usually offer immediate assistance, and in a public area passersby can be counted on to stop and help.

For emergencies ranging from health problems to lost passports, contact your embassy.

U.S. Embassy United States Embassy (*Embajada de los Estados Unidos* ⊠ *C. 120 and Avda. 0, Pavas, San José* ☎ *2519–2000, 2519–2280 in Costa Rica for after-hours emergencies* ⊕ *www.usembassy.or.cr*).

General Emergency Contacts Ambulance (Cruz Roja), Fire, Police (☎ *911*). **Traffic Police** (☎ *2222–9330*).

▌ HEALTH

Most travelers to Costa Rica do not get any vaccinations or take any special medications. However, according to the U.S. Centers for Disease Control, travel to Costa Rica poses some risk of malaria, hepatitis A and B, dengue fever, typhoid fever, and rabies. The CDC recommends getting vaccines for hepatitis A and B and typhoid fever, especially if you are going to be in remote areas or plan to stay for more than six weeks.

Check with the CDC for detailed health advisories and recommended vaccinations. In areas with malaria and dengue, both of which are carried by mosquitoes, bring mosquito nets, wear clothing that covers your whole body, and apply repellent containing DEET in living and sleeping areas. There are some pockets of malaria near the Nicaraguan border on the Caribbean coast. You probably won't need to take malaria pills before your trip unless you are staying for a prolonged period in the north, camping on northern coasts, or crossing the border into Nicaragua or Panama. You should discuss the option with your doctor. Children traveling to Central America should have current inoculations against measles, mumps, rubella, and polio.

SPECIFIC ISSUES IN COSTA RICA

Malaria is not a problem in Costa Rica except in some remote northern Caribbean areas near the Nicaraguan border. Poisonous snakes, scorpions, and other pests pose a small (often overrated) threat. The CDC marks Costa Rica as an area infested by the *Aedes aegypti* (dengue-carrier) mosquito, but not as an epidemic region. A few thousand cases in locals are recorded each year; the numbers had been dropping, but dramatic spikes in 2005 and 2007 have spurred major eradication efforts. Cases of fatal hemorrhagic dengue are rare. The highest-risk area is the Caribbean, and the rainy season is peak dengue season elsewhere. You're unlikely to be felled by this disease, but you can't

take its prevention too seriously: *repelente* (insect repellent spray) and *espirales* (mosquito coils) are sold in supermarkets and small country stores. U.S. insect repellent brands with DEET are sold in pharmacies and supermarkets. Mosquito nets are available in some remote lodges; you can buy them in camping stores in San José.

▌TIP→ Mild insect repellents, like the ones in some skin softeners, are no match for the intense mosquito activity in the hot, humid regions of the Caribbean, Osa Peninsula, and Southern Pacific. Repellants made with DEET or picaridin are the most effective. Perfume, aftershave, and other lotions and potions can actually attract mosquitoes.

It's unlikely that you will contract malaria or dengue, but if you start suffering from high fever, the shakes, or joint pain, make sure you ask to be tested for these diseases when you go to the local clinic. Your embassy can provide you with a list of recommended doctors and dentists.

Costa Rica has experienced cases of H1N1 influenza, the so-called "swine flu." Even its president was laid low by a week of the illness, to date, the world's only head of state to be affected. Standard precautions, such as washing hands regularly and getting vaccinated yourself, can minimize the risk.

Government facilities—the so-called Caja hospitals (short for Caja Costarricense de Seguro Social, or Costa Rican Social Security System)—and clinics are of acceptable quality, but notoriously overburdened, a common complaint in socialized-medicine systems anywhere. Private hospitals are more accustomed to serving foreigners. They include Hospital CIMA, Clínica Bíblica, and Clínica Católica, which all have 24-hour pharmacies. Outside of San José most major towns have pharmacies that are open until at least 8 or 9 PM, but usually the nearest hospital emergency room is the only after-hours option. The long-established and ubiquitous Fischel pharmacies are great places for your prescription needs, and usually staff a doctor who can help with minor ailments.

Antibiotics and psychotropic medications (for sleep, anxiety, or pain) require prescriptions in Costa Rica. Little else does. But plan ahead and bring an adequate supply with you from home; matches may not be exact.

For specific clinic, hospital, and pharmacy listings, see Chapters 3 through 9. Most food and water is sanitary in Costa Rica. In rural areas you run a mild risk of encountering drinking water, fresh fruit, and vegetables contaminated by fecal matter, which in most cases causes a bit of *turista* (traveler's diarrhea) but can cause leptospirosis (which can be treated by antibiotics if detected early). You can stay on the safe side by avoiding uncooked food, unpasteurized milk (including milk products), and ice—ask for drinks *sin hielo* (without ice)—and by drinking bottled water. Mild cases of turista may respond to Imodium (known generically as loperamide) or Pepto-Bismol (not as strong), both of which can be purchased over the counter. Drink plenty of purified water or tea; chamomile (*manzanilla* in Spanish) is a good folk remedy. In severe cases, rehydrate yourself with a salt-sugar solution (½ teaspoon salt and 4 tablespoons sugar per quart of water).

Ceviche, raw fish cured in lemon juice—a favorite appetizer, especially at seaside resorts—is generally safe to eat. ■TIP→ Buy organic foods whenever possible; chemicals, many of which have been banned elsewhere, are sprayed freely here without regulation.

Heatstroke and dehydration are real dangers, especially for hikers, so drink lots of water. Take at least 1 liter per person for every hour you plan to be on the trail. Sunburn is the most common traveler's health problem. Use sunscreen with SPF 30 or higher. Most pharmacies and supermarkets carry sunscreen in a wide range of SPFs, though it is relatively pricey.

The greatest danger to your person actually lies off Costa Rica's popular beaches—riptides are common wherever there are waves, and tourists run into serious difficulties in them every year. If you see waves, ask the locals where it's safe to swim; and if you're uncertain, don't go in deeper than your waist. If you get caught in a rip current, swim parallel to the beach until you're free of it, and then swim back to shore. ■TIP→ Avoid swimming where a town's main river opens up to the sea. Septic tanks aren't common. Do not fly within 24 hours of scuba diving.

OVER-THE-COUNTER REMEDIES
Farmacia is Spanish for "pharmacy," and the names for common drugs *aspirina*, Tylenol, and *ibuprofen* are basically the same as they are in English. Pepto-Bismol is widely available. Many drugs for which you need a prescription back home are sold over the counter in Costa Rica. Pharmacies throughout the country are generally open from 8 to 8, though it's best to consult with your hotel's staff to be sure. Some pharmacies in San José affiliated with clinics stay open 24 hours.

■ HOURS OF OPERATION

Like the rest of the world, Costa Rica's business hours have been expanding. Megamalls are usually open seven days a week, opening around 10 AM and closing around 9 PM; tourism-based businesses and museums also usually keep a Monday-to-Sunday schedule but open an hour earlier. Many smaller or rural museums are open Monday to Friday. National parks often close one day for maintenance; for example, Manuel Antonio is closed Monday. Restaurants in the city often close on Sunday, and sometimes Monday. Eateries in beach towns and other tourism-oriented areas are more likely to open seven days a week. Bars and nightclubs are generally open until 1 or 2 AM, at which time night owls flock to places like the El Pueblo center in San José to keep partying until 4 AM. Last calls vary from place to place, but it's not hard to find bartenders happy to sell you a drink for the road at closing time.

Some government offices and smaller businesses close for lunch, but *jornada continua* (without the lunch break) is becoming more common, and most commercial establishments follow an 8 AM to 5 PM schedule.

Three public holidays (April 11, July 25, and October 12) are bumped to the following Monday when they fall on a weekend or midweek. Government offices and commercial establishments observe all the holidays. The only days the country truly shuts down are Easter Thursday and Friday; some buses still run, but no alcohol can be purchased, and most restaurants and all stores are closed.

HOLIDAYS

January 1: New Year (Año Nuevo)

April 11: Juan Santamaría Day, a national hero

Easter Week: Thursday and Good Friday, religious activities (Semana Santa)

May 1: International Labor Day (Día del Trabajador)

July 25: Annexation of Guanacaste Province (Anexión de Guanacaste)

August 2: Day of the Virgin of Los Angeles, patron saint of Costa Rica (Virgen de los Ángeles)

August 15: Mother's Day (Día de la Madre)

September 15: Independence Day (Día de Independencia)

October 12: Culture Day (*Día de la Cultura,* or *Día de la Raza*)

December 25: Christmas (Navidad)

▌ MAIL

The Spanish word for post office is *correo.* Mail from the United States can take up to two to three weeks to arrive in Costa Rica (occasionally it never arrives at all). Within the country, mail service is even less reliable. Outgoing mail is marginally quicker, with delivery to North America in 5 to 10 days, especially when sent from San José. It's worth registering mail; prices

are only slightly higher. All overseas cards and letters will automatically be sent airmail. Mail theft is a chronic problem, so do not mail checks, cash, or anything else of value.

Minimum postage for postcards and letters from Costa Rica to the United States and Canada costs the equivalent of U.S. 50¢.

You can have mail sent poste restante (*lista de correos*) to any Costa Rican post office (specify Correo Central to make sure it goes to the main downtown office). In written addresses, *apartado,* abbreviated *apdo.,* indicates a post office box.

Post offices are generally open weekdays 7:30 to 5:30, and on Saturday 8 to noon. Stamps can be purchased at post offices and some hotels and souvenir shops. These vendors will also accept the mail you wish to send; don't bother looking for a mailbox, as only a handful (usually in rural areas with no post office) have been authorized. Always check with your hotel, which may sell stamps and post your letters for you.

SHIPPING PACKAGES

Shipping parcels through the post office is not for those in a hurry, because packages to the United States and Canada can take weeks. Also, packages may be pilfered. However, post-office shipping is the cheapest way to go, with rates at $6 to $13 per kilogram.

Some stores offer shipping, but it is usually quite expensive. If you can, carry your packages home with you.

UPS has offices in San José, Tamarindo, Jacó, Manuel Antonio, Sarchí, Nuevo Arenal, La Fortuna, and Limón. DHL has drop-offs in San José (Rohrmoser, Paseo Colón), Curridabat, Escazú, Heredia, Liberia, Limón, Ciudad Quesada, Jacó, Quepos, and San Isidro. Both have central information numbers with English-speaking staff to direct you to the nearest office. FedEx has offices in San José; it offers package pickup service in San José and other centers, such as Limón; call for availability. Prices are about 10 times what you'd pay at the post office, but packages arrive in a matter of days. ("Overnight" is usually a misnomer—shipments to most North American cities take two business days.)

Express Services Main Offices DHL
(✉ *600 m northwest of the Real Cariari Mall, La Aurora, Heredia* ☎ *2209–6000 in Costa Rica* ☞ *Call for other locations*). **FedEx** (✉ *Zona Franca Metropolitana, Barreal de Heredia, Local 1B, Heredia* ✉ *Centro de Servicio Mundial, Paseo Colón, 100 m east of León Cortés statue, San José* ☎ *800/463–3339 in North America*). **UPS** (UPS ✉ *50 m east of Pizza Hut, Pavas, San José* ☎ *2290–2828 in Costa Rica* ☞ *Call for other locations*).

■ MONEY

In general, Costa Rica is cheaper than North America or Europe, but travelers looking for dirt-cheap developing-nation deals may find it's more expensive than they bargained for—and prices are rising as more foreigners visit and relocate here.

Food in modest restaurants and public transportation are inexpensive. A one-mile taxi ride costs about $1. Here are some sample prices to give you an idea of the cost of living in Costa Rica: the local currency is the colón (plural: colones).

Prices throughout this guide are given for adults. Substantially reduced fees are almost always available for children, students, and senior citizens.

ATMS AND BANKS

Lines at San José banks would try the patience of a saint; instead, get your spending money at a *cajero automático* (automatic teller machine). If you do use the bank, remember that Monday, Friday, and the first and last days of the month are the busiest days.

Although they are springing up at a healthy rate, don't count on using an ATM outside of San José. Though not exhaustive, the A Toda Hora (ATH) company Web site lists locations of its ATH cash machines, and notes which ones offer colones (usually in increments of 1,000 colones), dollars (in increments of $20), or both; choose your region or city in the box on the homepage called *Busqueda de Cajeros*.

All ATMs are 24-hour; you'll find them in major grocery stores, some hotels, gas stations, and even a few McDonald's, in addition to banks. ATH, Red Total, and Scotiabank machines supposedly accept both Cirrus (a partner with MasterCard) and Plus (a partner with Visa) cards, but often don't. If you'll be spending time away from major tourist centers, particularly in the Caribbean, get most or all of the cash you need in San José and carry a few U.S. dollars in case you run out of colones. It's helpful to have both a Visa and a MasterCard—even in San José—as many machines accept only one or the other. Both companies have sites with fairly comprehensive lists of accessible ATMs around the world *(⇨ below)*.

ATMs are sometimes out of order and sometimes run out of cash on weekends. ■ TIP➔ PIN codes with more than four digits are not recognized at Costa Rican ATMs. If you have a five-digit PIN, change it with your bank before you travel.

The Credomatic office, housed in the BAC San José central offices on C. Central between Avdas. 3 and 5, is the local representative for most major credit cards; get cash advances here, or at any bank (Banco Nacional and BAC San José are good for both MasterCard and Visa; Banco Popular, and Banco de Costa Rica always accept Visa).

State banks have branches with slightly staggered hours; core times are weekdays 9 to 4, and some are open Saturday morning. Several branches of Banco Nacional are open until 6, or occasionally 7. Private banks—Scotiabank and BAC San José—tend to keep longer hours and are usually the best places to change U.S. dollars and traveler's checks; rates may be marginally better in state banks, but the long waits usually cancel out any benefit. The BAC San José in

Aeropuerto Internacional Juan Santamaría is open every day 5 AM to 10 PM.

Although it seems counterintuitive, ■ TIP→ whenever possible use ATMs only during bank business hours. ATMs here have been known to "eat" cards, and are frequently out of cash. When the bank is open, you can go in to retrieve your card or get cash from a teller. As a safety precaution, look for a machine in a bank with a guard nearby.

Resources A Toda Hora (*ATH* ⊕ *www.ath. fi.cr*). **MasterCard** (⊕ *www.mastercard.com/ atmlocator/index.jsp*). **Visa** (⊕ *www.visalatam. com/e_index.jsp*).

CREDIT CARDS

Throughout this guide, the following abbreviations are used: **AE**, American Express; **D**, Discover; **DC**, Diners Club; **MC**, MasterCard; and **V**, Visa.

It's a good idea to inform your credit-card company before you travel, especially if you're going abroad and don't travel internationally very often. Record all your credit-card numbers—as well as the phone numbers to call if your cards are lost or stolen—in a safe place. Both MasterCard and Visa have general numbers you can call (collect if you're abroad) if your card is lost, but you're better off calling the number of your issuing bank, since MasterCard and Visa usually just transfer you to your bank; your bank's number is generally printed on your card.

All major credit cards are accepted at most major hotels and restaurants in this book; establishments affiliated with Credomatic also accept the Discover card, although many businesses don't know what it is. As the phone system improves and expands, many budget hotels, restaurants, and other properties have begun to accept plastic; but plenty of properties still require payment in cash. Don't count on using your credit card outside of San José. ■ TIP→ Carry enough cash to patronize the many businesses without credit-card capability. Note that some hotels, restaurants, tour companies, and other businesses add

a surcharge (around 5%) to the bill if you pay with a credit card, or give you a 5% to 10% discount if you pay in cash. It's always a good idea to pay for large purchases with a major credit card if possible, so you can cancel payment or get reimbursed if there's a problem.

CURRENCY AND EXCHANGE

At this writing, the colón is 570 to the U.S. dollar and 825 to the euro. Coins come in denominations of 5, 10, 25, 50, 100, and 500 colones. Be careful not to mix up the very similar 100- and 500-colón coins. Bills are undergoing a design change at this writing. Motifs and sizes of old denominations of 1,000, 2,000, 5,000, and 10,000 colones are changing, with new denominations of 20,000 and 50,000 colones being added. For the time being, both designs are legal tender. Avoid using larger denomination bills in taxis and small stores. Many businesses accept U.S. dollars, although will use a less favorable exchange rate in their calculations.

Costa Rican colones are sold abroad at terrible rates, so you should wait until you arrive in Costa Rica to get local currency. U.S. dollars are still the easiest to exchange, but euros can be exchanged for colones at just about any Banco Nacional branch and San José and Escazú branches of other banks, such as BAC San José. Private banks—Scotiabank and BAC San José—are the best places to change U.S. dollars and traveler's checks. There is a branch of the BAC San José in the airport (open daily 5 AM to 10 PM) where you can exchange money when you arrive—it's a much better deal than the Global Exchange counter. Taxi and van drivers who pick up at the airport accept U.S. dollars.

Outdoor money changers are rarely seen on the street, but avoid them if they approach; you will most certainly get a bad deal.

■ TIP→ Even if a currency-exchange booth has a sign promising no commission, rest assured that there's some kind of huge, hidden fee. (Oh . . . that's right. The sign didn't say no fee.) And as for rates, you're almost always better off getting foreign currency at an ATM or exchanging money at a bank.

▌ PACKING

Travel light, and make sure you can carry your luggage without assistance. Even if you're planning to stay only in luxury resorts, odds are that at least once you'll have to haul your stuff a distance from bus stops, the shuttle drop-off, or the airport. Another incentive to pack light: domestic airlines have tight weight restrictions (at this writing 11.3 to 13 kilograms [25 to 30 pounds]) and not all buses have luggage compartments. Frameless backpacks and duffel bags can be squeezed into tight spaces and are less conspicuous than fancier luggage.

Bring comfortable, hand-washable clothing. T-shirts and shorts are acceptable near the beach and in tourist areas; long-sleeve shirts and pants protect your skin from ferocious sun and, in some regions, mosquitoes. Leave your jeans behind—they take forever to dry. Pack a waterproof, lightweight jacket and a light sweater for cool nights, early mornings, and trips up volcanoes; you'll need even warmer clothes for trips to Chirripó National Park or Cerro de la Muerte and overnight stays in San Gerardo de Dota or on the slopes of Poás Volcano. Bring at least one good (and wrinkle-free) outfit for going out at night.

Women might have a tough time finding tampons, so bring your own. For almost all toiletries, including contact lens supplies, a pharmacy is your best bet. Don't forget sunblock, and expect to sweat it off and reapply regularly in the high humidity. Definitely bring sufficient batteries, since they're expensive here.

Snorkelers staying at budget hotels should consider bringing their own equipment; otherwise, you can rent gear at most beach resorts.

You have to get down and dirty—well, more like wet and muddy—to see many of the country's natural wonders. This following packing list is not comprehensive; it's a guide to some of the things you might not think to bring. For your main piece of luggage, a sturdy internal-frame backpack is great, but a duffel bag works, too. You can get by with a rolling suitcase, but then bring a smaller backpack as well.

▌ PASSPORTS

U.S. citizens need only a passport to enter Costa Rica for stays of up to 90 days. Make sure it's up to date—you'll be refused entry if the passport is due to expire in less than one month. To be on the safe side, make sure it is valid for at least six months. The only way to extend your stay is to spend 72 hours in Nicaragua or Panama—but don't expect to do that undetected more than a couple of times. Customs forms ask how many visits you've made to Costa Rica in the past year.

Costa Rica has one of the highest rates of passport theft in the world. Travelers in Costa Rica are not required to carry their original documents with them at all times, although you must have easy access to them. Photocopies of the data page and your entry stamp are sufficient. Although there have been reports from around the world about security problems with in-room safes, if your hotel doesn't have a safe in reception, locking a passport in a hotel-room safe is better than leaving it an unlocked hiding place or carrying it with you.

▌TIP→ For easy retrieval in the event of a lost or stolen passport, before you leave home scan your passport into a portable storage device (like an iPod) that you're carrying with you or e-mail the scanned image to yourself.

If your passport is lost or stolen, first call the police—having the police report can make replacement easier—and then call your embassy (⇨ *Emergencies, below*). You'll get a temporary Emergency Travel Document that will need to be replaced once you return home. Fees vary according

PACKING LIST FOR COSTA RICA

■ Quick-drying synthetic-fiber shirts and socks

■ Hiking boots or shoes that can get muddy and wet

■ Waterproof sport sandals (especially in the Osa Peninsula, where most transportation is by boat, and often there are no docks)

■ Knee-high socks for the rubber boots that are supplied at many lodges

■ A pair of lightweight pants (fire ants, mosquitoes, and other pests make covering yourself a necessity on deep-forest hikes)

■ Pants for horseback riding (if that's on your itinerary)

■ Waterproof, lightweight jacket, windbreaker, or poncho

■ Day pack for hikes

■ Sweater for cool nights and early mornings

■ Swimsuit

■ Insect repellent (with DEET, for forested areas and especially on the northern Caribbean coast, where there are pockets of malaria)

■ Flashlight or headlamp with spare batteries (for occasional power outages or inadequately lighted walkways at lodges)

■ Sunscreen with a minimum of SPF 30 (waterproof sunscreens are best; even if you're not swimming, you might be swimming in perspiration)

■ Large, portable water bottle

■ Hat and/or bandannas (not only do they provide shade, but they prevent perspiration from dripping down your face)

■ Binoculars (with carrying strap)

■ Camera (waterproof, or with a waterproof case or dry bag, sold in outdoor-equipment stores)

■ Film (film in Costa Rica can be expired and is expensive)

■ Imodium and Pepto-Bismol (tablet form is best)

■ Swiss Army knife (and remember to pack it in your checked luggage, never your carry-on—even on domestic flights in Costa Rica)

■ Ziplock bags (they always come in handy)

■ Travel alarm clock or watch with an alarm (don't count on wake-up calls)

■ Nonelectric shaving utensils

■ Toilet paper (rarely provided in public bathrooms)

to how fast you need the passport; in some cases the fee covers your permanent replacement as well. The new document will not have your entry stamps; ask if your embassy takes care of this, or whether it's your responsibility to get the necessary immigration authorization.

GENERAL REQUIREMENTS FOR COSTA RICA	
Passport	Must be valid for 1 month after date of arrival
Visa	Required for Americans (free upon entry)
Vaccinations	None required
Driving	International driver's license not required; CDW is optional on car rentals
Departure Tax	US$26

▮ RESTROOMS

When nature calls, look for signs that say SERVICIOS SANITARIOS or simply SANITARIOS. Toilet paper is not discarded into some toilets in Costa Rica, but rather in a trash bin beside it. Septic systems are delicate and the paper will clog the toilet. At some public restrooms you might have to pay 50¢ or so for a few sheets of toilet paper. At others, there may not be any toilet paper at all. It's always a good idea to have some tissues at the ready. Gas stations generally have facilities, but you may decide not to be a slave to your bladder once you get a look at them. On long trips, watch for parked buses; generally this indicates some sort of better-kept public facilities.

Find a Loo The Bathroom Diaries (⊕ *www. thebathroomdiaries.com*) is flush with unsanitized info on restrooms the world over—each one located, reviewed, and rated.

▮ SAFETY

Violent crime is not a serious problem in Costa Rica, but thieves can easily prey on tourists, so be alert. The government has been shamed into creating a Tourism Police unit, whose 250+ officers can be seen on bikes or motorcycles patrolling areas in Guanacaste, San José, and the Arenal area. Crimes against property are rife in San José. In rural areas theft is on the rise.

For many English-speaking tourists, standing out like a sore thumb can't be avoided. But there are some precautions you can take:

■ Don't bring anything you can't stand to lose.

■ Don't wear expensive jewelry or watches.

■ In cities, don't carry expensive cameras or lots of cash.

■ Carry backpacks on your front; thieves can slit your backpack and run away with its contents before you notice.

■ Don't wear a waist pack, because thieves can cut the strap.

■ Distribute your cash and any valuables (including credit cards and passport) between a deep front pocket, an inside jacket or vest pocket, and a hidden money belt. (If you use a money belt, carry some cash in your purse or wallet so you don't have to reach for the hidden pouch in public.)

■ Keep your hand on your wallet if you are in a crowd or on a crowded bus.

■ Don't let your purse just dangle from your shoulder; always hold on to it with your hand for added security.

■ Keep car windows rolled up and car doors locked at all times in cities.

■ Park in designated parking lots, or if that's not possible, accept the offer of the *guachimán* (a term adopted from English, pronounced "watchie man")—men or boys who watch your car while you're gone. Give them the equivalent of a dollar per hour when you return.

■ Never leave valuables visible in a car, even in an attended parking lot.

■ Padlock your luggage.

■ Talk with locals or your hotel staff about crime in the area. Never walk in a narrow space between a building and a car parked on the street close to it, a prime hiding spot for thieves. Never leave a drink unattended in a club or bar: scams involving date-rape drugs have been reported in the past few years, targeting both men and women.

■ Never leave your belongings unattended anywhere, including at the beach or in a tent.

■ If your hotel room has a safe, use it, even if there's an extra charge. If your room doesn't have one, ask the manager to put your valuables in the hotel safe and ask him or her to sign a list of what you are storing there.

■ If you are involved in an altercation with a mugger, immediately surrender your possessions and walk away quickly.

Scams are common in San José, where a drug addict may tell tales of having recently been robbed, then ask you for donations; a distraction artist might squirt you with something, or spill something on you, then try to clean you off while his partner steals your backpack; and pickpockets and bag slashers work buses and crowds. To top it all off, car theft is rampant. Beware of anyone who seems overly friendly, aggressively helpful, or disrespectful of your personal space. Be particularly vigilant around the Coca-Cola bus terminal, one of the rougher areas but a central tourism hub.

Don't believe taxi drivers when they say the hotel is closed, unless you've personally gotten out and checked it yourself. Many want to take you somewhere else to earn a commission. If a taxi driver says he does not have change and the amount is substantial, ask him to drive to a store or gas station where you can get change. This might be enough to prompt him to suddenly "find" the difference to give you. Avoid paying with large bills to prevent this.

A number of tourists have been hit with the slashed-tire scam: someone punctures the tires of your rental car (often right at the airport, when you arrive) and then comes to your "aid" when you pull off to the side of the road and robs you blind. Forget about the rims: always drive to the nearest open gas station or service center if you get a flat.

Lone women travelers will get a fair amount of attention from men; to avoid hassles, avoid wearing short shorts or skirts. On the bus, try to take a seat next to a woman. Women should not walk alone in San José at night or venture into dangerous areas of the city at all. Ask at your hotel which neighborhoods to avoid. Ignore unwanted comments. If you are being harassed on a bus, at a restaurant, or in some other public place, tell the manager. In taxis, sit in the backseat. If you want to fend off an earnest but decent admirer in a bar, you can politely say, *"Por favor, necesito un tiempo a solas"* (I'd like some time on my own, please). Stronger is *"Por favor, no me moleste"* (Please, stop bothering me), and for real pests the simple *"Váyase!"* (Go away!) is usually effective.

▍TAXES

The airport departure tax for tourists is $26, payable in cash or with Visa. All Costa Rican businesses charge a 13% sales tax. Hotels charge a 16.4% fee covering service and tax. Restaurants add 13% tax and 10% service fee to meals. Tourists are not refunded for taxes paid in Costa Rica.

▍TIME

Costa Rica does not observe daylight saving time, so from November to March it's the equivalent of Central Time in the United States (one hour behind New York). The rest of the year, it is the equivalent of Mountain Time in the United States (two hours behind New York).

Time Zones Timeanddate.com (⊕ *www.timeanddate.com/worldclock*).

▮ TIPPING

Bellhop	$1–$5 per bag, depending on the level of the hotel
Hotel Concierge	$5 or more, if he or she performs a service for you
Hotel Doorman	$1–$2 if he helps you get a cab
Hotel Maid	$1–$3 a day (either daily or at the end of your stay, in cash)
Hotel Room-Service Waiter	$1–$2 per delivery, even if a service charge has been added
Tour Guide	$10 per day
Waiter	10%–15%, with 15% being the norm at high-end restaurants; nothing additional if a service charge is added to the bill

Restroom attendants in more expensive restaurants expect some small change or $1. Tip coat-check personnel at least $1–$2 per item checked unless there is a fee, then nothing.

Costa Rica doesn't have a tipping culture, but positive reinforcement goes a long way to fostering a culture of good service, which is hit-and-miss. Tip only for good service. Taxi drivers aren't tipped, but it's common courtesy to leave an extra 200–300 colones if they've helped you navigate a complicated set of directions. ▮TIP→ Do not use U.S. coins to tip, because there is no way for locals to exchange them.

Chambermaids get 1,000 to 1,500 colones per day; for great service try to leave up to 10% of your room bill. Concierges are usually not tipped. Room-service waiters should be tipped about 500 colones, as should bellhops (more in the most expensive hotels).

Restaurant bills include a 13% tax and 10% service charge—sometimes these amounts are included in prices on the menu, and sometimes they aren't. If the menu doesn't indicate whether service is included, ask. An additional gratuity is not expected, especially in cheap restaurants, but people often leave something extra when service is good. Leave a tip of about 200 colones per drink for bartenders, too.

At some point on a trip, most visitors to Costa Rica are in the care of a naturalist guide, who can show them the sloths and special hiking trails they'd never find on their own. Give $10 (or 5,000 colones) per day per person to guides if they've transported and guided you individually or in small groups, and about 10% of the rental to a hired driver of a small car. Give less to guides or drivers on bigger tours. For tour guides, it's okay to pay with U.S. dollars.

▮ TOURS

BIKING

Costa Rica is mountainous and rough around the edges. It's a rare bird that attempts a road-biking tour here. But the payoff for the ungroomed, tire-munching terrain is uncrowded, wildly beautiful off-road routes. Most bike-tour operators want to make sure you're in moderately good shape and do some biking at home. Others, such as Coast to Coast Adventures, have easier one- and two-day jaunts. Lava Tours offers great expert- and intermediate-level riding, as well as "gravity-assisted" (cruising down the paved road from Poás Volcano, for example) trips. Bike Arenal has biking packages in the Arenal area for all skill levels, with short and long ride options for each day. Operators generally provide top-notch equipment, including bikes and helmets, but welcome serious bikers who bring their own ride. Leave the hybrids at home—this is mountain-biking territory. Operators usually meet you at the airport and take care of all logistics. All companies can design custom tours for extreme cyclists if requested.

Topographical maps (not biking maps per se) are generally provided as part of the tour, and include unpaved roads that are useful. If you're striking out on your own, these maps can usually be found at San José's Lehmann bookstore for about

$3. Some basic Spanish is highly recommended if you're going to do it yourself.

■ TIP→ Check with individual airlines about bike-packing requirements and blackouts. Cardboard bike boxes can be found at bike shops for about $15; more secure options start at $40. International travelers often can substitute a bike for a piece of checked luggage at no charge (if the box conforms to regular baggage dimensions), but U.S. and Canadian airlines will sometimes charge a $100 to $200 handling fee each way.

■ TIP→ Most airlines accommodate bikes as luggage, provided they're dismantled and boxed.

Contacts Bike Arenal (☎ 2479–7150, 866/465–4114 in North America ⊕ www.bikearenal.com). **Coast to Coast Adventures** (☎ 2280–8054 in Costa Rica ⊕ www.ctocadventures.com). **Lava Tours** (☎ 2281–2458, 888/862–2424 in North America ⊕ www.lava-tours.com).

BIRD-WATCHING

You will almost definitely get more out of your time in Costa Rica by taking a tour rather than trying to find birds on your own. Bring your own binoculars but don't worry about a spotting scope; if you go with a tour company that specializes in birding tours, your guide will have one. Expect to see about 300 species during a weeklong tour. Many U.S. travel companies that offer bird-watching tours subcontract with the Costa Rican tour operators listed below. By arranging your tour directly with the Costa Rican companies, you avoid the middleman and save money. Selva Mar, a tour agency specializing in the Southern Zone, runs comprehensive tours through Birding Escapes Costa Rica.

Contacts Birding Escapes Costa Rica (☎ 2771–4582 in Costa Rica ⊕ www.birdwatchingcostarica.com). **Costa Rica Expeditions** (☎ 2257–0766 in Costa Rica ⊕ www.costaricaexpeditions.com). **Horizontes** (☎ 2222–2022 in Costa Rica ⊕ www.horizontes.com).

DIVING

Costa Rica's Cocos Island—one of the best dive spots in the world—can be visited only on a 10-day scuba safari with *Aggressor* or *Undersea Hunter*. But Guanacaste, the South Pacific, and to a lesser extent, the Caribbean, offer some respectable underwater adventures. Bill Beard's Costa Rica in the Gulf of Papagayo, Guanacaste, is a diving-tour pioneer and has countrywide options. Diving Safaris, in Playa Hermosa, has trips to dive sites in Guanacaste. In the South Pacific, Costa Rica Adventure Divers in Drake Bay arranges five-night trips. In this same area, Caño Island is a good alternative if you can't afford the money or time for Cocos Island, particularly in the rainy season, when dive sites closer to shore are clouded by river runoff.

Contacts Aggressor (☎ 800/348–2628 in North America ⊕ www.aggressor.com). **Bill Beard's Costa Rica** (☎ 877/853–0538 in U.S. ⊕ www.billbeardcostarica.com). **Costa Rica Adventure Divers** (☎ 2231–5806, 866/553–7073 in the U.S. ⊕ www.costaricadiving.com). **Diving Safaris** (☎ 2672–1259 in Costa Rica ⊕ www.costaricadiving.net). **Undersea Hunter** (☎ 2228–6613, 800/203–2120 in North America ⊕ www.underseahunter.com).

FISHING

If fishing is your primary objective in Costa Rica, you are better off booking a package. During peak season you may not even be able to find a hotel room in the hot fishing spots, let alone one of the top boats and skippers. If you're less of a planner, some Fodor's readers say they've had good luck hanging out at "fish bars" in popular areas and asking around for recommendations. The major fish populations move along the Pacific coast through the year, and tarpon and snook fishing on the Caribbean is subject to the vagaries of seasonal wind and weather, but viable year-round. San José–based Costa Rica Outdoors has been in business since 1995, arranging fishing packages; it is one of the best bets for full service and honest advice about where to go, and works with the widest range of operators around the country. More than 100 outfits have high-quality, regionally based services. Anglers in the know recommend Kingfisher Sportfishing in Playa Carrillo, Guanacaste; Bluefin Sportfishing and J.P. Sportfishing Tours in Quepos; The Zancudo Lodge near Golfito; and Río Colorado Lodge on the northern Caribbean coast.

Contacts Bluefin Sport Fishing (☎ 2777–0000 in Costa Rica ⊕ www.bluefinsportfishing.com). **Costa Rica Outdoors** (☎ 2231–0306, 800/308–3394 in U.S. ⊕ www.costaricaoutdoors.com). **J.P. Sportfishing Tours** (☎ 2244–6361, 866/620–4188 in U.S. ⊕ www.jpsportfishing.com). **Kingfisher Deep Sea Fishing** (☎ 2656–0091 in Costa Rica ⊕ www.costaricabillfishing.com). **Río Colorado Lodge** (☎ 2232–4063, 800/243–9777 in North America ⊕ www.riocoloradolodge.com). **The Zancudo Lodge** (☎ 2776–0008, 800/854–8791 in U.S. ⊕ www.thezancudolodge.com).

GOLF

Putting on a green against a dramatic Pacific backdrop isn't the first image that springs to mind for Costa Rican vacations, but the increase in luxury resorts and upscale tourism has created a respectable, albeit small, golfing circuit in the Central Valley and along the Pacific coast. Most packages maximize links time with side excursions to explore the country's natural riches. Costa Rica Golf Adventures Ltd. organizes multiday tours at four- and five-star lodgings.

Contacts Costa Rica Golf Adventures (☎ 2239–5176, 877/258–2688 in U.S. ⊕ www.golfcr.com).

HIKING

Most nature-tour companies include hiking as part of their itineraries, but these hikes may be short and not strenuous enough for serious hikers. Let the tour operator know what you expect from a hike. Ask a lot of questions about hike lengths and difficulty levels before booking the tour or you may be disappointed with the amount of time you get to spend on the trails. The following companies cater to both moderate and serious hikers.

Contacts Gap Adventures (☎ 800/708–7761 in North America ⊕ www.gapadventures.com). **Serendipity Adventures** (☎ 888/226–5050 in North America, 2558–1000 in Costa Rica ⊕ www.serendipityadventures.com).**The Walking Connection** (☎ 800/295–9255 in North America ⊕ www.walkingconnection.com).

SURFING

Most Costa Rican travel agencies and tour companies have packages that ferry both veteran and would-be cowboys (and cowgirls) of the ocean to and between the country's famed bicoastal breaks. Local experts at Alacran Surf (which works with Surf Costa Rica) really know their stuff, and offer standard or custom packages. Del Mar Surf Camp on the Pacific specializes in women-only surf lessons and packages. Learn how to surf, camp on the beach, and delve into personal development on the Costa Rican Rainforest Outward Bound School's weeklong adult surf journeys.

Contacts Costa Rican Rainforest Outward Bound School (☎ 800/676–2018 in North America, 2278–6058 in Costa Rica ⊕ www.crrobs.org). **Del Mar Surf Camp** (☎ 2643–3197 in Costa Rica ⊕ www.costaricasurfingchicas.com). **Alacran Surf** (☎ 2280–7328 in Costa Rica, 888/751–0135 or 619/955–7171 in North America ⊕ www.surf-costarica.com).

SPANISH-LANGUAGE PROGRAMS

Thousands of people travel to Costa Rica every year to study Spanish. Dozens of schools in and around San José offer professional instruction and homestays, and there are several smaller schools outside the capital. Conversa has schools off Paseo Colón, and in Santa Ana, west of the capital, offering hourly classes as well as a "Super Intense" program (5½ hours per day). On the east side of town, ILISA provides cultural immersion in San Pedro. Mesoamérica is a low-cost language school that is part of a nonprofit organization devoted to peace and social justice. La Escuela D'Amore is in beautiful Manuel Antonio. Language programs at the Institute for Central American Development Studies include optional academic seminars in English about Central America's political, social, and economic conditions.

Contacts Conversa (☎ 2221–7649, 888/669–1664 in North America ⊕ www.conversa.net). **ILISA** (☎ 2280–0700, 800/464–7248 in U.S. ⊕ www.ilisa.com).**Institute for Central American Development Studies** (*ICADS* ☎ 2225–0508 in Costa Rica ⊕ www.icads.org). **La Escuela D'Amore** (☎ 2777–1143, 800/261–3203 in North America ⊕ www.edcostarica.com). **Mesoamérica** (☎ 2253–3195 in Costa Rica ⊕ www.mesoamericaonline.net).

VOLUNTEER PROGRAMS

In recent years more and more Costa Ricans have realized the need to preserve their country's precious biodiversity. Both Ticos and far-flung environmentalists have founded volunteer and educational concerns to this end.

Volunteer opportunities span a range of diverse interests. You can tag sea turtles as part of a research project, build trails in a national park, or volunteer at an orphanage. Many of the organizations require at least rudimentary Spanish. Most of the programs for volunteers who don't speak Spanish charge a daily fee for room and board. The Caribbean Conservation Corporation (CCC) is devoted to the preservation of sea turtles. Earthwatch Institute leads science-based trips studying monkeys, turtles, or the rain forest. The Talamancan Association of Ecotourism and Conservation (ATEC), as well as designing short group and individual outings centered on Costa Rican wildlife and indigenous culture, keeps an updated list of up to 30 local organizations that welcome volunteers. Beach cleanups, recycling, and some wildlife projects don't require proficiency in Spanish. The Costa Rican Humanitarian Foundation has volunteer opportunities with indigenous

communities, women, community-based clinics, and education centers. They also organize homestays.

The Institute for Central American Development Studies (ICADS) is a nonprofit social justice institute that runs a language school and arranges internships and field study (college credit is available); some programs are available only to college students. ICADS can also place students with local social service organizations, environmental groups, and other organizations, depending on interests. The Costa Rica Rainforest Outward Bound School offers two adult programs that combine self-exploration with a truly rural learning experience.

Contacts Costa Rica Rainforest Outward Bound School (☎ 2278–6058, 800/676–2018 in U.S. ⊕ www.crrobs.org). **Costa Rican Humanitarian Foundation** (☎ 8390–4192 or 2282–6358 in Costa Rica ⊕ www.crhf.org). **Institute for Central American Development Studies** (*ICADS* ☎ 2225–0508 in Costa Rica ⊕ www.icads.org).

Caribbean Conservation Corporation (☎ 2297–5510 in Costa Rica, 800/678–7853 or 352/373–6441 in U.S. ⊕ www.cccturtle.org). **Earthwatch Institute** (☎ 978/461–0081 or 800/776–0188 in North America ⊕ www.earthwatch.org). **Talamancan Association of Ecotourism and Conservation (ATEC)** (☎ 2750–0398 in Costa Rica ⊕ www.ateccr.org).

▌ VISITOR INFORMATION

The official tourism board, the Instituto Costarricense de Turismo (ICT), has free maps, bus schedules, and brochures. These folks could do better with the information they provide, but their Web site is comprehensive. Arrive armed with specific questions and know that they will not recommend hotels. You'll also find a small desk at Juan Santamaría airport. Visitor information is provided by the Costa Rica Tourist Board in Canada and in the United States.

Contacts **Instituto Costarricense de Turismo** (*ICT* ☎ *2299–5800, 866/267–8274 in North America* ⊕ *www.visitcostarica.com* ✉ *Aueropuerto Internacional Juan Santamaría* ☎ *2437–2400* ✉ *Plaza de la Cultura, C. 5, Avdas. Central–2* ☎ *2222–1090*).

ONLINE TRAVEL TOOLS

Info Costa Rica has a Web site with good cultural info, and chat rooms. **Horizontes** is a tour operator that offers nature vacations but also has extensive information on Costa Rica and sustainable tourism on its Web site. The **U.S. Embassy's comprehensive site** has health information, travel warnings, lists of doctors and dentists, and much more. The **REAL Costa Rica** slips in a bit of attitude with its information, and is a bit lax on updating, but scores high marks for overall accuracy. Scope out detailed maps, driving distances, and pictorial guides to the locations of hotels and businesses in some communities at **CostaRicaMap.com**. The **Association of Residents of Costa Rica** online forums are some of the region's most active and informed, with topics ranging from business and pleasure trips to the real-estate market. For current events, check out the English-language newspaper **The Tico Times**.

Contacts **All About Costa Rica Association of Residents of Costa Rica** online forums (⊕ *www.arcr.net*). The **REAL Costa Rica** (⊕ *www.therealcostarica.com*). **InfoCostaRica** (⊕ *www.infocostarica.com*). **Costa Rica.com** (⊕ *www.costarica.com*). **Horizontes** (⊕ *www.horizontes.com*). **U.S. Embassy Costa Rica** (⊕ *www.usembassy.or.cr*). **The Tico Times** (⊕ *www.ticotimes.net*).

INDEX

PHOTO CREDITS

member. **Chapter 3: San José:** 71, R1/Alamy. 72, Lindy Drew. 73 (top), R1/Alamy. 73 (bottom), Costa Rica Tourist Board (ICT). 77, Pietro Scozzari/age fotostock. 78, Choice Hotels International, Inc. 79 (top), Hotel Rincón de San José. 79 (bottom), Hotel Presidente. 80, Ronald Reyes. 91, R1/Alamy. 96, José Fuste Raga/age fotostock. 107, Neil McAllister/Alamy. 114, Liz Stuart, Fodors.com member. 120-121, Lindy Drew. 122 (top and center), Lindy Drew. 122 (bottom), David L Amsler/iStockphoto. 123-25 (all), Lindy Drew. **Chapter 4: The Central Valley:** 127, jvcostarica, Fodors.com member. 128, Pablo Arroyo and Margaret Kalacska. 129 (top and bottom), Costa Rica Tourist Board (ICT). 132, mrsviv07, Fodors.com member. 133 (top), Alvaro Leiva/age fotostock. 133 (bottom), R1/Alamy. 134, Xandari Resorts. 135 (top and bottom), Dawn Pando. 136, Brian Allen, Fodors.com member. 141, Lindy Drew. 154, travelib costa rica/Alamy. 157, Gay Bumgarner/Alamy. 161 (top), Index Stock Imagery/photolibrary.com. 161 (bottom) and 162 (top), Jordi Camí/age fotostock. 162 (center), steve bly/Alamy. 162 (bottom), North Wind Picture Archives/Alamy. 163 (top), Yadid Levy/age fotostock. 163 (bottom), steve bly/Alamy. 164 (top left), Kenneth Hong/Flickr. 164 (top right), Angela Hampton Picture Library/Alamy. 164 (center), JORDI CAMI/Alamy. 164 (bottom), Jordi Camí/age fotostock. 165 (top left), ©Marvin Dembinsky Photo Associates/Alamy. 165 (top center), Index Stock Imagery/photolibrary.com. 165 (top right), J1/Alamy. 165 (bottom), Arco Images GmbH/Alamy. 169, Ronald Reyes. 170, Lindy Drew. 172, Neil McAllister/Alamy. 177, Linda137, Fodors.com member. 179, Costa Rica Tourist Board (ICT). **Chapter 5: The Northern Plains:** 181, Msoberma, Fodors.com member. 182, Leethal33, Fodors.com member. 183 (top), Pablo Arroyo. 183 (bottom), Costa Rica Tourist Board (ICT). 186, robrick, Fodors.com member. 187 (top), imagebroker/Alamy. 187 (bottom), JORDI CAMI/Alamy. 188, owlwoman, Fodors.com member. 189 (top), vogelmutter, Fodors.com member. 189 (bottom), racegirl, Fodors.com member. 190, Jason Kremkau. 191 (top), Ginita215, Fodors.com member. 191 (bottom), Fernando Ramírez/age fotostock. 192, Chris Fredriksson/Alamy. 193 (top), Laguna del Lagarto Lodge. 193 (bottom), Danita Delimont/Alamy. 194, Lindy Drew. 199, JuanAmighetti/Costa Rica Tourist Board (ICT). 206, sportster, Fodors.com member. 211, Jan Csernoch/Alamy. 215, Sylvain Grandadam/age fotostock. 223, Jill Chapple, Fodors.com member. 224, Y.Levy/Alamy. 226, Tiffnco, Fodors.com member. 227 (top left), Kevin Schafer/Alamy. 227 (bottom left), Justine Evans/Alamy. 227 (right), Kevin Schafer/Alamy. 232, Pattie Steib/Shutterstock. 247, Lindy Drew. 251, Errol Barrantes/Costa Rica Tourist Board (ICT). **Chapter 6: North Pacific:** 255 and 256, Thornton Cohen. 257 (top), Mark Gabrenya/Shutterstock. 257 (bottom), Gpkbrand, Fodors.com member. 260, Danita Delimont/Alamy. 261 (top), Zach Holmes/Alamy. 261 (bottom), Catherine Scott/iStockphoto. 262, imagebroker/Alamy. 263 (top), Sylvia Cordaiy Photo Library Ltd/Alamy. 263 (bottom), R1/Alamy. 264, Thornton Cohen/Alamy. 265 (top), Mark Gabrenya/Shutterstock. 265 (bottom), Kevin Schafer/Alamy. 266, Tim Calver. 267 (top), The Harmony Hotel, Nosara. 267 (bottom), Borinquen Mountain Resort & Spa. 268, PDSF, Fodors.com member. 273, Luis Alberto Aldonza/age fotostock. 280, R1/Alamy. 292-93, John Coletti/age fotostock. 294, Antonio Jorge Nunes/Shutterstock. 295 (top), Mboja, Fodors.com member. 295 (bottom), Chinamom, Fodors.com member. 296 (left), Juan Amighetti/Costa Rica Tourist Board (ICT). 296 (top right), Sam Chadwick/Shutterstock. 296 (bottom right), imagebroker/Alamy. 301, Eyal Nahmias/Alamy. 308, Guillen Photography/UW/Costa Rica/Alamy. 317, Yadid Levy/Alamy. 323, Peter Arnold, Inc./Alamy. 324, Inger Hogstrom/age fotostock. 325, Krasinsky, Fodors.com member. 326 (left), Stephen Turner/wikipedia.org. 326 (top center), Jaimi DeFeo, Fodors.com member. 326 (bottom center), wikipedia.org. 326 (top right), Snowmanradio/wikipedia.org. 326 (bottom right), www.birdphotos.com/wikipedia.org. 327 (top left), JUNIORS BILDARCHIV/age fotostock. 327 (bottom left and top right), wikipedia.org. 327 (bottom center), Dario Sanches/wikipedia.org. 327 (bottom right), Jerry Oldenettel/wikipedia.org. 330, Jason Bazzano/age fotostock. 337 and 344, ImageSync Ltd/Alamy. 348, Jon Arnold Images Ltd/Alamy. 354, Costa Rica Tourist Board (ICT). **Chapter 7: Central Pacific:** 357, Gwendolyn Morris, Fodors.com member. 358 (top), TorontoJeff, Fodors.com member. 358 (bottom), Plumboy, Fodors.com member. 359, Ruthalan, Fodors.com member. 361, TorontoJeff, Fodors.com member. 362, ARCO/F Scholz/age fotostock. 363 (top), jwb5555, Fodors.com member. 363 (bottom), Stephen Saks Photography/Alamy. 364, volcanogirl, Fodors.com member. 365 (top), LynneL, Fodors.com member. 365 (bottom), Highwind1, Fodors.com member. 366, Hotel Sí Como No. 367 (top), Arenas Del Mar Beach & Nature Resort. 367 (bottom), Freank Duffy. 368, esp05, Fodors.com member. 374, Hemis /Alamy. 378, R1/Alamy. 381 and 386, Yadid Levy/Alamy. 394-95, Reinhard Dirscherl/photolibrary.com. 404, Leethal33, Fodors.com member. 408-409, Chris Cheadle/age fotostock. 410 (top), Timur Kulgarin/Shutterstock. 410 (bottom), Thornton Cohen. 411 (left), Sandra Salvadó/age fotostock. 411 (right), LOOK Die Bildagentur der Fotografen GmbH/Alamy. 412, Pablo Arroyo. 418, Colleen George, Fodors.com member. 425, Costa Rica Tourist Board (ICT). 428, Sylvain Grandadam/age fotostock. **Chapter 8: South Pacific:** 433, Chad Clark, Fodors.com member. 434 (top), Cutestcookie, Fodors.com member. 434 (bottom), Carsinio, Fodors.com member. 435 (top), Volcanogirl, Fodors.